P9-CPW-908

JUL   2001

Chicago Public Library

REFERENCE

Form 178 rev. 1-94

CHICAGO PUBLIC LIBRARY
SOUTH CHICAGO BRANCH
9055 S. HOUSTON   60617

Temperate Forests

Temperate Forests

Michael Allaby

Facts On File, Inc.

Temperate Forests

© 1999 by Michael Allaby

All rights reserved. No part of this book may be reproduced or utilized in any form or by any means, electronic or mechanical, including photocopying, recording, or by any information storage or retrieval systems, without permission in writing from the publisher. For information contact:

Facts On File, Inc.
11 Penn Plaza
New York NY 10001

Library of Congress Cataloging-in-Publication Data

Allaby, Michael.
Temperate forests / Michael Allaby.
p.   cm.—(Ecosystem)
Includes bibliographical references (p.   ) and index.
ISBN 0-8160-3678-0
1. Forest ecology. 2. Forest health. 3. Forest management. 4. Forests and forestry. 5. Forests and forestry—Economic aspects.
I. Title. II. Series.
QH541.5.F6A46 1999
557.3'0912—dc21 98-23458

Facts On File books are available at special discounts when purchased in bulk quantities for businesses, associations, institutions or sales promotions. Please call our Special Sales Department in New York at (212) 967-8800 or (800) 322-8755.

You can find Facts On File on the World Wide Web at http://www.factsonfile.com

Text design by Cathy Rincon and Sandra Watanabe
Cover design by Cathy Rincon
Illustrations by Richard Garratt

Printed in Hong Kong

Creative FOF 10 9 8 7 6 5 4 3 2

This book is printed on acid-free paper.

Contents

R01917 95576

CHICAGO PUBLIC LIBRARY
SOUTH CHICAGO BRANCH
9055 S. HOUSTON 60617

White oak at sunset, eastern North America
(Gary Braasch/ENP Images)

A long time ago, and for tens of thousands of years, northern Europe, Canada, and most of the northern United States lay buried beneath vast ice sheets, thousands of feet thick. Then, as the world warmed and the ice began to recede, plants sprouted. Seeds and spores, carried on the wind or dropped by birds, germinated and brought color to cold, barren lands. In time the first plants gave way to others, to woody shrubs, and, among the shrubs, a few trees. Little by little, the bare ground, freed by the retreat of the ice, turned to forest. This was the forest of the temperate regions—the temperate forest.

In fact, it was not one forest but many. Different forests supported different communities of trees, and the plants and animals that lived with them, but the forests comprised a number of principal types. Near the Tropics, around the Mediterranean and in some of the southern parts of North America, the trees and shrubs were broadleaved but retained their leaves through the winter. These were broad-leaved evergreen forests. Elsewhere, in regions of mist and very high rainfall, there were temperate rain forests. In other places, and more extensively, the forest trees were broad-leaved but leafless in winter. These were the broad-leaved deciduous forests. To the north of them, in a wide belt running across Canada, Europe, and Asia, grew a vast coniferous forest, the boreal forest known in Russia as the *taiga*.

Together these different types of forest constitute the temperate forests of the world, forming one of the great vegetation types, or biomes. They occur almost wholly in the Northern Hemisphere, because in the Southern Hemisphere there is much less land in temperate latitudes.

This book is about the temperate forests. It begins with a few descriptions and definitions. What do we mean by "temperate forest"? Where are they to be found? How did they come to be the way they are?

Setting the Scene

Having framed the questions, the book provides some of the answers. These will take you on an excursion through time. Before you can understand the origin of the temperate forests, you must know how the lands where they grow came to lie in the temperate regions. As you explore the way continents move, you will see how these movements explain some otherwise rather curious facts about the distribution of particular trees. Forests grow in certain types of soil. The book explains how soil forms and is classified scientifically, how water flows through it, and what forest soils are like.

Soils develop because of a process called weathering. Despite the name, not all weathering is directly caused by the weather, but much of it is. So the book tells some of the story of the climates of temperate regions, why weather happens the way it does, and how it affects the forests. Climates are changing constantly, and trees are quite sensitive to these changes. This makes it possible for scientists to use evidence of trees that grew in the distant past to trace the history of those changes.

Trees and Forest Communities

Having set the scene, as it were, with the lands in their proper places and the soils described, the book explains a little about the workings of plants in general and trees in particular. It describes how wood forms and what it is. A description of trees must explain the differences between the two main kinds of trees found in temperate forests, those with flowers and broad leaves and those bearing narrow, sometimes needlelike leaves, and cones—the conifers.

Visit a forest and you see more than just trees. There are plants of many kinds, and animals living on and among the plants. A forest is a community of living things, and the scientific study of relationships within communities and between them and the environments they inhabit is called ecology. Quite a large section of the book is devoted to an outline of ecological ideas, especially as these apply to forests. Forests support a wide variety of species of plants, fungi, animals, and single-celled organisms. In other words, they are biologically diverse: the modern contraction of "biological diversity" gives us "biodiversity." The book explains what this means.

The following pages are devoted to descriptions of individual species of trees. Obviously, they cannot hope to be complete, but they do include the most common coniferous and broad-leaved trees of North America and Eurasia. They also tell where each species originated: most are now cultivated in places thousands of miles from where they grew naturally, so it is worth remembering where they began. What is now the most common tree in Britain, for example, is a native of the coastal regions of the northwest United States and far western Canada.

Forests and People

The final section of the book, amounting to about one-third, concerns the relationship between people and the temperate forests. There has always been a relationship, of course, for as the forests expanded northward following the end of the last ice age, humans were not far behind, and they very soon began altering the forests. That was long before the earliest written record, and so the book explains a little of how scientists can reliably reconstruct what happened.

By the time of the first written records of forests, the changes wrought by human activity were well advanced, and in southeastern Europe some of the adverse consequences were being experienced. In northern Europe steps started to be taken to conserve the forests.

Clearly, forests were important, but they were not always loved. The book contrasts the efforts to conserve forests with the way forests were portrayed in folklore and literature, often as dark, dangerous, inhospitable wildernesses.

Whether or not people liked their forests, they certainly depended on them, for fuel, building timber, and wood for making furniture and a vast array of everyday articles, each tree yielding wood with characteristics that suit it to particular uses. This section of the book describes some of the products of temperate forests and the ways they have been used.

We still depend on our forests, of course—nowadays for paper as well as wood—so the condition of the temperate forests concerns us all. In the following section you will read about the effects on forests of pollution by acid rain, of the possible consequences of climatic change, and also about the effect on soils of deforestation. This is followed by accounts of the present state of each of the principal types of forest and forest conservation.

Forest Management and Plantation Forestry

Productive forests must be managed, and in Europe they have been managed for more than 1,000 years. The final section of the book describes some of the types of management that have been used over the centuries and the kinds of forest they produced. This may surprise you. The medieval forests of much of western Europe were not closed and dark, like the primeval forest, but open to the sky and more like parkland.

More recently, the growing of trees in plantations has become the most common technique for providing the forest products we need, and in years to come plantations are likely to become still more widespread as ancient and old-growth forests are protected for conservation reasons. Plantation forestry and the modern way of controlling forest weeds, pests, and diseases are described in some detail. Modern forestry is a great deal more complicated than it may seem: there is much more to it than simply planting rows of trees.

Times change and attitudes change with them. When plantation forestry began, the goal was a dependable supply of good-quality timber, mainly from straight, relatively fast-growing, coniferous trees, such as spruces, pines, hemlocks, firs, and larches. Now we realize that forests are valuable in other ways. They are intricate mosaics of natural habitats that support a wide variety of species. Forest composed of self-sown trees and other plants that have remained relatively undisturbed for a long time provides the best habitat, but plantations support a considerable amount of wildlife and, with some modification, they can support a great deal more. Plantations are now planned with wildlife conservation in mind. Forests within convenient reach of cities also have a very high amenity value. They are places where families can walk, picnic, and relax in safe, interesting surroundings. The more accessible modern plantations provide recreational opportunities as well as timber.

The task has taken us several centuries, but at last we have tamed our forests. They are no longer the wild, dark, frightening places of legend, to be cleared so we can see danger approaching from afar. Our farmers now produce as much food as we can eat, so we no longer need to clear away the forests to make fields for growing crops or raising livestock. Perhaps for the first time we are able to appreciate forests for their beauty and tranquillity, and for the plants and animals that live in them. We are learning to cherish them, by preventing the felling of the more valuable or interesting natural forests, relying on plantations to supply the forest products we need, and seeking to enhance the biological and aesthetic value of those plantations.

That journey, from the primeval forest to the plantation, from the forest as the enemy to the forest as a friend, is the subject of this book.

Temperate Forests

What Is a Temperate Forest?

As the last of the winter snow melts and water, sparkling in the spring sunshine, drips from the boughs, green shoots break through the ground surface. Soon a carpet of spring flowers will pattern the forest floor in bright colors and then disappear as the buds, first on one tree, then another, burst into leaves, intercepting the sunlight and plunging the floor into deep shade.

Summer is the green time, when the trees are in full leaf. It ends when the days grow shorter and the nights cooler, the green is transformed into the reds, oranges, and browns of fall, and the forest is revealed in what many people consider its true magnificence. That, too, is brief. Each in turn, the trees shed all their leaves into the swirling winds that heap them in careless piles through which children wade and kick their way, leaving the trees themselves bare, their twigs silhouetted as delicate traceries against the sky. Rain now gives way to snow, puddles freeze, the ground is frozen hard, and the yearly cycle is complete.

We delight in forests that change their appearance so dramatically with the seasons and, of course, it is not only the trees and herbs that change. Forests support a wide variety of animals and they, too, adjust their lives to the seasons. Spring, which fosters the brief flowering of herbs, also brings the first migrant birds. Summer produces the insects. Mammals, though rarely seen, forage and hunt while food is available.

Not all forests change in this way. The changes are adaptations to a seasonal climate and do not occur in the Tropics, where the seasons are absent or not so clearly defined. Changing forests, then, are the product of seasonal climates, and these are found in temperate regions of the world. Changing forests are also temperate forests.

Deciduous or Evergreen

Trees that shed their leaves in fall are said to be deciduous, from the Latin *de,* meaning "down," and *cadere,* "fall." Most deciduous trees, but not all of them, also have broad leaves. Oaks, maples, horn-beams, and beeches are broad-leaved deciduous trees. They are angiosperms, plants that produce seeds enclosed within an ovary (page 59). Plants producing seeds that are not enclosed in ovaries are called gymnosperms, and the most abundant examples are the coniferous trees. Their seeds are borne in the female cones and their leaves are often in the shape of needles; the botanical term describing this leaf shape is "acicular." Needles are shed, but not all at the same time, so most coniferous trees are evergreen. Larches are an exception. They are deciduous conifers. Their needles, like the leaves of broad-leaved deciduous trees, turn golden in fall, bringing patches of bright color to the otherwise dark green pine forest.

Just as some coniferous trees are deciduous, there are broad-leaved trees that are evergreen. Holly is a familiar example and some oaks, such as the holm oak, cork oak, and kermes oak of the Old World and the live oak of the New World, are also evergreen.

All of these trees grow in forests, although you will often see them growing by themselves, in parks, or in patches of woodland much too small to be considered forests. They are adapted to seasonal climates, and so they are trees of temperate forests, because it is in temperate regions that climates are seasonal, but the seasons to which they are adapted vary. Broad-leaved evergreen trees require mild, wet winters and can tolerate hot, dry summers. Broad-leaved deciduous trees are best suited to warm, wet summers but can tolerate winters cold enough for the ground surface to freeze, provided it does not remain frozen long. Coniferous deciduous trees tolerate severe winters and grow well in northern Siberia, but thrive because of their ability to grow rapidly during the short spring and summer. Coniferous evergreens also tolerate severe winters and short summers.

What Is a Forest?

Clearly, temperate forests are highly variable. Their character and composition change from one region to another. They are also by far the most extensive of all forest types. Tropical forests occur within the Tropics, as their name suggests, but beyond the tropic of Cancer in the north and tropic of Capricorn in the south, the forests are temperate. In high latitudes they extend to the limit of tree growth, their trees gradually becoming more widely spaced and more stunted until the forest gives way to tundra. Over the world as a whole, temperate forests now occupy about 8 million square miles (20.7 sq. km), but this is a much smaller area than they once covered, before the trees were felled for timber and to provide land for farming (page 138).

This great diversity of forest types is made more comprehensible by a system of classification, and the first word requiring definition is "forest" itself. The word is derived from the Latin *foris,* meaning "out of doors," and in medieval times people talked of the *forestem silvam,* the wood (*silva*) that lay outside the land enclosed by fences. Cultivated fields were enclosed, as were parks in which deer were raised, and the forest lay beyond the enclosures. In Norman England, substantial parts of this forest were set aside for hunting, much of it for the use of the king, and it was subject to special "forest" laws. The designation of the hunting forest used the word "forest" in its old sense of "outside," regardless of whether or not the area was covered with trees. Much was what we would call "forest," because that was the natural vegetation in most lowland areas, but to this day you will find the name retained for certain uplands, heaths, or bogs where trees have never grown in historical times. Dartmoor, for example, is a large area of upland moor in southwest England, and a national park. Forest plantations (page 198) occupy some areas, but most is too exposed and has soils that are too thin for trees to thrive. Nevertheless, the southern part of the moor is still shown on maps as "Dartmoor Forest." The apparently inappropriate name recalls the fact that at one time it was an area set aside for hunting, probably by the king.

Nowadays, "forest" means either a community of trees growing so closely together that in summer the leaves of one overlap those of its neighbors to form a continuous canopy, or the trees making up such a community. As a verb, "to forest" means "to plant with trees." To qualify for the name, the canopy of a forest should cover at least 60 percent of the total area. If the canopy covers less than 60 percent of the area, so the crowns of most of the trees do not touch, the plant community is called "woodland." It is more open, like parkland. Its trees are more widely spaced and they usually spread more widely than the crowded trees of a forest. Between the trees there are areas of grass or shrubs, contributing to the parklike appearance.

Types of Forests

Forests are also named according to their type. At the most general level they may be broad-leaved deciduous (also known as summer deciduous), broad-leaved evergreen, or coniferous

Fall foliage on Stevens Point Pass, Washington (Alan Kearney/ENP Images)

(also called boreal) forest. In each case at least 80 percent of the trees must be of the type giving the forest its name. A mixed forest contains both broad-leaved and coniferous trees, and there will be more of one than of the other, but the less numerous type must constitute at least 20 percent of the total. These names are of limited use, however, because they describe types of forest that may be typical of entire regions of continents, with many local variations, and it is often the variations that matter.

More specifically, and helpfully, forests are identified by the trees dominating them. Usually two species are named, but sometimes three, and the dominant is named first. In ecology, the "dominant" species is the one having the greatest influence on the composition and form of a community. This is commonly, but not invariably, the biggest or most abundant (page 98).

If you visit the oak–maple forests of Illinois or the pine–hemlock forests of Maine you will see many species of plants, but the overall impression of those forests will be provided by the trees that give them their names. Those are the plants you will remember. As a rule of thumb, the

named trees should amount to at least half of all the trees present and should give the forest its character.

Travel through a large forest and its type is quite likely to change from place to place. In the pattern of vegetation natural to the southeastern United States, for example, broad-leaved evergreen forest along the coastal plain of the Carolinas gives way to oak–pine forest on the higher ground to the west and then to oak–chestnut forest in the Blue Ridge Mountains. These names refer to the natural communities and are retained even if the communities, or species within them, have long since disappeared. American chestnuts still exist, of course, but almost all of those forming part of natural forest communities were killed in the first half of this century by an outbreak of chestnut blight (page 108).

Temperate forests, then, are the forests that occur naturally in those parts of the world where the climate is temperate. This is a vast area and within it climates vary considerably, although all are strongly seasonal and there are several quite distinct types of forest reflecting these variations.

Where Are Temperate Forests?

Bordering the Tropics in both hemispheres there is a rather vaguely defined subtropical belt. These are the latitudes in which the principal deserts of the world are found. It is in the still higher latitudes of the temperate regions that temperate forests occur, bounded on one side by the subtropical deserts and semiarid regions, such as the savannah grasslands, and on the other by tundra and the polar deserts.

As a map of the world shows, however, the distribution of temperate biomes is far from even. Excluding Antarctica, there is much more land in the Northern Hemisphere than the Southern, and the southern landmasses do not extend into such high latitudes as those in the north. The southernmost tip of Africa lies within the subtropical belt, and although South America extends much farther south, the continent tapers sharply. Even then, Cape Horn, the southernmost tip of South America, at 55°47' S, is in the same latitude as Copenhagen and Edinburgh. Dunedin, in the south of South Island, New Zealand, is at 45°52' S, in approximately the same latitude as Portland, Oregon, and Venice, Italy. In the Northern Hemisphere there is very much more land in latitudes higher than these.

It is in these higher latitudes that there are substantial areas within which temperate forest of one kind or another is the natural vegetation. As the map shows, apart from the southern tip of South America and New Zealand, temperate forest is found only in the Northern Hemisphere. There it forms a continuous belt across Canada and northern Europe and Asia (together known as Eurasia). It also occurs in the eastern United States, with southward extensions on the eastern sides of North America and Asia.

Travel through a part of the world shown on vegetation maps as "temperate forest" and you should not expect to see forest everywhere. Indeed, over large areas you will see rather few forests. Most land in France and Britain, for example, is farmed and you will see fields rather than forests. In Pennsylvania you will see large forests, covering well over half the land area of the state, but these have been planted to replace the original forest, which was cleared to provide land for agriculture and fuel for industry. Vegetation maps show the type of vegetation that existed prior to human interference and that might be expected to reestablish itself were that interference to cease.

Trees Need a Moist Climate

Forests do not occur in the interior of large continents, even in middle latitudes. The climate there is strongly continental (page 50), with hot summers, very cold winters, and low rainfall. It is not the winters that limit the extent of forests, but the summers and the overall rainfall. Where hot, dry summers last for more than about eight months of the year, and the annual rainfall is less than about 16 inches (400 mm), most trees find it difficult to survive. The vegetation becomes scrub, dominated by shrubs with isolated trees scattered among them. As the climate becomes drier the trees become rarer, eventually giving way to semidesert scrub and chaparral, then to desert. Where winter is the dry season, forests give way to grassland.

Broad-leaved deciduous trees require a minimum of about 120 days a year in which the temperature is higher than 50°F (10°C) and it is short summers that mark the high-latitude boundary of broad-leaved forests. Hardier species can tolerate rather less than 120 warm days a year, but they become increasingly interspersed with coniferous species, forming mixed forest.

Conifers need only about 30 days a year with temperatures about 50°F (10°C), so they can grow in much higher latitudes than broad-leaved

Temperate forests

- Tropic of Cancer
- Equator
- Tropic of Capricorn

□ broadleaved/mixed forest

■ coniferous (boreal) forest

trees. The most northerly forest in the world is in Siberia, at 70°50' N. It is a larch forest, dominated by dahurian larch (*Larix gmelini*), a magnificent tree that grows to a height of almost 100 feet (30 m) and confines its leaf production and growth to the very brief summer.

Taiga, Lichen Forest, and Boreal Forest

As summers grow shorter with increasing distance from the equator, only hardier tree species manage to thrive and they become more widely spaced. The forest becomes thinner, with trees occurring in isolated clumps separated by areas of heathlike vegetation and lichens. This belt of parklike vegetation separates the closed-canopy conifer forest from the tundra. Some people call it taiga, but Russian ecologists generally use the Russian word *taiga* to describe the whole of the coniferous forest that stretches from Norway eastward to the Pacific, and this use has been adopted by most ecologists and geographers of other nationalities. Those who use "taiga" as the name for the entire coniferous forest call the parklike border between it and the tundra "lichen forest."

The coniferous forest is also known as the boreal forest. This simply means "northern," from Boreas, the Greek god of the north wind. There is no paradox over using the name for Southern-Hemisphere forests, for no such forests exist in the Southern Hemisphere. No land extends into a sufficiently high southern latitude.

Within these great forest belts, there are areas where trees grow sparsely, if at all. Temperature decreases with altitude, just as it does with latitude, and beyond a certain height this restricts tree growth and eventually inhibits it altogether.

Krummholz and Timberline

On some mountains, lower temperatures resulting from increasing altitude cause trees to become more widely spaced and stunted, in a belt of what is called *Krummholz*, a German word meaning "crooked wood." Elsewhere this does not happen, and the timberline is abrupt. The timberline is the boundary below which there is forest and above which there are no trees at all.

Since temperature decreases with height, and the heights of mountains are invariably measured from sea level, the altitude of the timberline is determined by the sea-level temperature. This varies with latitude, so the lower the latitude the higher is the timberline. In the Sierra Nevada the timberline is at about 11,500 feet (3,500 m), in the Canadian Rockies it is at about 6,500 feet (1,980 m), and in the central Alps it is at about 6,800 feet (2,000 m), but in the mountains of New Guinea, where the temperature at sea level is much higher, it is at about 12,600 feet (3,800 m). Within a particular geographic region, the height of the timberline varies from place to place, depending on the amount of shelter from winds and exposure to sunlight.

Sclerophyllous Forest

Where forests have not been cleared over the centuries, there are substantial differences in type. Regions with a Mediterranean climate are found in Southern California, on a much smaller scale in parts of Chile and the southern tip of South Africa, and, of course, around the shores of the Mediterranean itself.

Here, the summers are dry and hot, the winters wet and warm, and the annual rainfall averages 20 to 40 inches (500–1,000 mm), falling mainly in winter. There are long, dry periods and the plants are xeromorphic (adapted to withstand drought). The forests comprise sclerophyllous trees, and so the forest is said to be sclerophyllous.

Sclerophyllous trees are evergreens with small leaves which are often hard, leathery, or stiff, and sometimes have prickles around the edges, like holly. The bark is thick and the buds are well protected. These are all adaptations to drought. In California and around the Mediterranean, the original forest was dominated by evergreen oaks and pines. New and Old World species differed, but the overall composition of the natural forests is similar.

Temperate Rain Forest and Giant Redwoods

Further north, winters are cooler, the annual rainfall is higher, and there are warm temperate rain forests. Most of the trees are broad-leaved evergreens, in North America including evergreen oaks and magnolias in the forests of this type along the Gulf and Atlantic coasts as far north as North Carolina.

In some places the broad-leaved species are mixed with conifers, the most famous of which are the Sierra redwoods (*Sequioa dendron giganteum*) and giant redwoods (*Sequoia sempervirens*) of California and, to the north of them, forests of western hemlock (*Tsuga heterophylla*), western red cedar (*Thuja plicata*), and Douglas fir (*Pseudotsuga menziesii*).

Temperate rain forests also occur in New Zealand, where southern beech (*Nothofagus*) is dominant, in the north together with kauri pine (*Agathis australis*). This type of forest is absent from Europe and rare in Asia, although it does occur in southern China and Japan, mainly dominated by evergreen oaks and magnolias.

Sugar maple in late fall Mt. Battle, Maine (Gary Braasch/ENP Images)

Extent of Temperate Forest

When most of us picture broad-leaved forest, however, what we have in mind is the broad-leaved deciduous type, also known as summer deciduous forest. We think of this for the simple reason that it is by far the most extensive. Originally, forests of this kind covered some 3 million square miles (7.8 million sq km), blanketing almost all of Europe and much of the eastern half of the United States.

Unfortunately for the trees, the European climate that favors them also favors farming and little of the original forest remains. Substantial areas have been allowed to survive in North America, however. Again, their detailed composition changes from place to place and in the north the broad-leaves are interspersed with conifers, to produce a belt of mixed forest between the summer deciduous forest and the boreal forest.

The boreal forest covers a total of nearly 6 million square miles (15.5 million sq km), making it the biggest forest in the world and considerably more extensive than the tropical rain forests. Were we to choose one type of forest to represent the forests of Earth, it would have to be the boreal conifer forest.

How Did Temperate Forests Develop?

Three centuries ago, much of North America was blanketed in forest. A thousand years ago, so was most of Europe. To people trying to find food in them, the primeval forests must have seemed timeless, as though they had always been there and had always been just as they were then. As the centuries passed, of course, vast areas of forest were cleared, but had they remained undisturbed we like to think we would be able to see them today in that some condition. It is tempting to think of them as essentially eternal.

The temptation must be resisted, for on our dynamic Earth nothing is eternal. Everything changes, but over timespans that are so long compared with our brief lifespan, change can be difficult to detect. Were your great-great grandmother to walk beside you through a surviving remnant of that original forest, it is unlikely that she would notice any difference from the forest she remembered from her own youth. It would look just the same. Yet, on an Earth that has supported life for close to 4 billion years, five human generations, perhaps amounting to 125 years, is the merest instant. Even 1,000 years is a very short time indeed. Forests change, but they change slowly, and it usually takes them a great deal longer than this.

At one time, much more than 1,000 years ago, many areas that now support forest lay deep beneath ice sheets (page 54), and no plants of any kind grew there, far less broad-leaved trees. Delve deeply enough into the past and you reach a time before the trees of our modern broad-leaved forests existed at all. They had not yet evolved and at a still earlier time neither had those of the coniferous forests (page 58).

There was a time, then, before the "timeless" forests existed. There was a period during which they developed. One day, far in the future, perhaps they will vanish. Forests do change.

Natural Mechanisms of Change and Human Intervention

Trees also move around, not individually, of course, but by distributing their seeds over a wide area. This allows them to colonize available sites

Dew on sugar maple leaves, Eastern hardwood forest, North America
(Alan Kearney/ENP Images)

and so extend their range as opportunity affords. They may encounter barriers they cannot cross, such as oceans, deserts, and mountain ranges, but where they can establish themselves they will.

This in itself is a mechanism for change. When seeds from an invading species germinate successfully, the young plants occupy space and take up from the soil nutrients that would otherwise have been available to other species and as they grow taller they shade smaller plants nearby. By exploiting resources more efficiently, or just differently, new arrivals can increase in number, but their increase implies a decrease in numbers of rivals for those resources. In time, the invaders may replace those rivals completely and the plant community will have changed its composition. It will still be forest, but forest of a subtly different type.

Change of this kind is happening all the time and is particularly noticeable in Britain. People have been importing trees to Britain and planting them at least since Roman times. At first they are usually difficult to grow, but eventually some become naturalized to the British soils and climate. Then they can escape from cultivation by seeding themselves and, in the case of trees, this allows them to invade forests and establish themselves there. Were land to be abandoned to the plants that established themselves naturally, inevitably the resulting community would include naturalized species. Ecologists distinguish native from naturalized species, defining native species as natural, when classifying forests by age, for example as primeval or old-growth forest (page 90).

One of the most invasive trees in Britain is *Acer pseudoplatanus,* the sycamore or great maple (note that the American sycamore is any one of several species of plane trees, *Platanus,* and quite different from the European sycamore, which is a maple). It was introduced to Britain some time before 1500, but was not widely planted until the 18th century. It now produces seed more prolifically and regularly than most native trees, colonizing disturbed ground and invading old, neglected stands of trees, and it is advancing rapidly. Most forests now contain some sycamore and many are dominated by it.

Rhododendron ponticum, known in Britain, for good reason, as the common rhododendron and closely related to the North American *R. catawbiense,* was introduced in the 18th century as an ornamental. It escaped from cultivation and naturalized itself in the last century and is now highly invasive. It spreads rapidly, shading the ground and preventing the growth of tree seedlings.

Today, the commonest tree in Britain, although it grows only where it has been planted deliberately, is Sitka spruce (*Picea sitchensis*), imported for its timber from western coastal regions of North America. People have also moved trees around, planting them in places where they do not occur naturally.

If introducing trees can alter vegetation patterns, so can their selective removal. The first use people made of the primeval European and American forests was as a source of timber, but not just any timber. Some trees have wood that is good for building houses or ships, some grew very straight and provided masts and spars for sailing ships, the wood from others makes durable railroad sleepers, strong and attractive furniture, or the handles of tools. Some provided fuel, as wood or charcoal. Individual trees were sought, as they are sought today in the tropical forests, and forest areas containing few trees of economic value were ignored. In time, the valuable forests shrank and the less valuable ones expanded. In North America, many species of oak and maple were of little value, which is why these trees are now commoner than they once were.

Environmental Limitations

Even without human intervention, forests change their composition over time. *Rhododendron ponticum,* native to southern Europe and Turkey and now an invasive introduction and troublesome weed in Britain, grew naturally in Britain around 120,000 years ago, when the average temperature was about 4°F (-15.6°C) warmer than it is today.

Like all plants, trees have particular nutrient requirements and there are limits to the range of temperature and moisture they can tolerate and much narrower limits within which they grow most vigorously. Each species has its own preferred environmental conditions, although those of many species overlap. As the example of *Rhododendron ponticum* demonstrates, small differences can have disproportionately large effects.

Nutrients and moisture are supplied by the soil, and soils develop through the combined influences of climate and biological activity (page 10). Temperature, of course, is a feature of climate. Climate, therefore, is by far the most important factor determining the type of vegetation that establishes itself, and the global distribution of vegetation types closely follows that of climate types (page 48). Our use of "temperate forest" reflects this affinity. It follows that when the climate changes, after a delay the type of vegetation also changes, by a kind of ecological opportunism.

Suppose, for example, an area of sclerophyllous forest is adjacent to broad-leaved deciduous forest and, further north, the broad-leaved forest gives way to coniferous forest. Tree seeds regularly travel across these boundaries, but the boundaries remain. Sclerophyllous trees grow slowly and if their seeds germinate in an area supporting deciduous species the seedlings are crowded out by their neighbors, which grow much faster. In the north, seedlings of broad-leaved trees germinating among the conifers are killed by the long winter to which the conifers are adapted.

Trees also determine many of the characteristics of the soils in which they grow. The needles of conifers and the leaves of broad-leaved deciduous trees decompose differently and at different rates, for example, and the soils of broad-leaved and coniferous forests are dissimilar. This difference may be enough to inhibit invaders.

Now suppose that the climate changes, becoming warmer overall and in places drier. Broad-leaved deciduous trees require moderate rainfall. If the climate becomes drier, they will suffer, but drought causes no difficulties for the sclerophyllous species. Their seedlings will now survive better than those of the deciduous species around them and the sclerophyllous forest will spread. At the boundary between broad-leaved and coniferous forest, broad-leaved species will also be able to expand into regions that have become warm enough for them. Such migrations happen slowly and many ecologists fear the response may be too slow for the rapid climatic warming some climatologists are now predicting (page 174), but in the past there have been many climatic changes with consequent changes in vegetation patterns.

Can Change Be Reversed?

The causes of change may be reversed. People may cease the selective logging of economically valuable species. Land that was turned to other uses by the clearing of forest may be abandoned. Climates that have warmed may grow cooler.

Ecological change will follow, but the emerging pattern is unlikely to reproduce that which existed prior to the first change, and may not even approximate it, because the starting point has shifted. New communities will include naturalized species, for example, and the abandonment of selective logging does not mean the logged species will return, because the resources they need were commandeered long ago by other species and winning them back may be impossible.

Clearing forest and putting the land to other uses changes the soil. There are substantial differences between forest soils and farm soils and the differences are even greater if the ground has been used for buildings or roads. Trees may colonize the area, but it is unlikely that the original forest will return.

The forests we see and enjoy today are the product of a continuing process of change. Our own activities and those of our ancestors have strongly influenced that process, but they did not introduce it into an essentially static environment. Forests have been changing since they first appeared. What we see now, in those forests humans have not disturbed, is the state they have reached thus far and from which they are already moving. They are changing even as we look, but at a rate so slow our senses cannot detect it.

Plate Tectonics and Tree Distribution

Plants travel. They migrate from one part of the world to another, much as animals do, but they move a great deal more slowly. Seeds are carried on the wind or by birds, float on rivers or the sea, cling to the coats of animals, and sooner or later they fall to the ground. If they land on soil that is moist enough for them and contains the nutrients the young plants need, and if the temperature suits them, the plants colonize the new area into which chance has carried them.

A plant species must start its journey from somewhere. There must be a region of the world in which it first appeared and from which it spread. As it spread, it must have occurred at some time in all the regions through which it passed. Even if it is not present now, there should be traces of its passage. It will have left remains, isolated individuals perhaps, or at the very least its pollen in the soil. Pollen grains are sealed within coats (called exines) so tough they can survive millions of years without decaying, especially in peaty soils. These coats bear patterns of markings, called colpi (singular *colpus*) or sulci (singular *sulcus*); the two names are synonymous. Colpi patterns vary in such a way that they can be used to identify the family, and sometimes the genus or even the species, of the plants that produced the

pollen. Palynologists, the scientists who study ancient pollen grains, provide information with which paleobotanists and paleoecologists reconstruct past vegetation patterns and communities. Plant migrations can usually be traced, but there are exceptions.

Disjunct Distribution

Magnolias are attractive trees that have been planted all over the world, wherever the climate is mild and moist enough for them. Like all plants, there are certain places where they occur naturally, where they have not been planted by humans. These are the places to which they are native. One of these is the eastern part of the United States, through Central America and the Caribbean islands, with two smaller regions in tropical South America and a larger area in southeastern South America. In the temperate regions of these places magnolias are components of natural forest, and it is not too hard to imagine them having migrated overland to the places where they are found today. But magnolias are not confined to the New World. Magnolias also occur naturally in the southern tip of India and

throughout Southeast Asia as far as New Guinea, but they are not native to Australia, just a short distance from New Guinea.

Southern beeches (*Nothofagus*) have a similarly odd distribution. They occur naturally in New Guinea, southeastern Australia, Tasmania, and New Zealand. But they are also found down the southwestern coastal strip of South America. *Araucaria,* the genus that includes the Chile pine or monkey puzzle tree (*A. araucana*), occurs naturally in South America, New Guinea and northeastern Australia, and islands of the South Pacific.

These trees are examples of what botanists call a discontinuous, or "disjunct," distribution. They turn up in widely separated places and there are no traces of the route they followed. Some animals, such as the marsupials of Australia, New Guinea, and North and South America, also have a disjunct distribution.

If this is curious, so is something else. Look at a map of the world and it seems as though the coastlines of South America and Africa ought to fit together. If you could push them toward one another they would join and if your atlas shows the edges of the continental shelves, where the land is covered by water, the fit is even better. Over the centuries many people have noted this curiosity. Francis Bacon (1561–1626) remarked on it. As time passed, scientists noted other strange coincidences. The rocks on the west coast of Africa are identical to those in eastern South America and also to rocks in Antarctica, Australia, and India. High mountains contain fossils of seashells. How did they get there? It was not until 1967 that all the pieces of the puzzle were brought together in what is now known as the theory of plate tectonics ("tectonic," an adjective from the Greek *tectonikos,* "carpenter," refers to deformations of the Earth's crust and changes caused by such deformations).

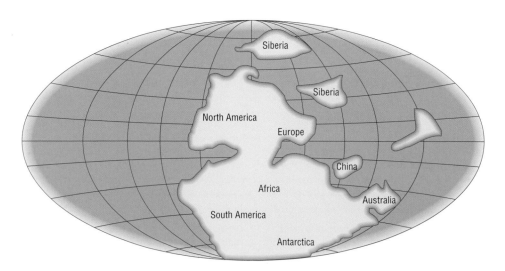

Earth, 360 million years ago

Plate Tectonics

We now know that Earth's crust and the mantle beneath are not solid and unchanging: the crust is composed of many plates of varying sizes. The Pacific Plate is about 7,500 miles (12,000 km) across, for example, and the Nazca Plate about 1,800 miles (2,900 km). Sometimes plates cease to move in relation to one another and their margins become sealed as a permanent join.

At present, the eight major plates are the African, Eurasian, Pacific, Indian, North American, South American, Antarctic, and Nazca (between the eastern edge of the Pacific Plate and the western edge of the South American Plate). The more important minor plates include the Cocos (to the north of the Nazca Plate, close to western Central America), Caribbean, Somali (in the western Indian Ocean), Arabian, Philippine, and Anatolian (beneath Turkey). Continental plates are about 75 miles (120 km) thick, but thicker beneath mountain ranges, and those beneath the oceans are about 40 miles (64 km) thick.

Their movement is continuous. At present, for example, the Atlantic is growing wider by about 0.8 inch (20 mm) a year as the North and South American Plates move westward, and the Himalayas are still being formed as a result of a collision that began 40 million years ago when the Indian Plate, moving northward, reached the Eurasian Plate and kept going. The Red Sea is a rift that is opening. Eventually, as the Eurasian Plate moves away from the African Plate, it will become a vast ocean. The bottom drawing shows the present map of the world, with the directions in which the continents are being carried.

Given this information, it is possible to calculate where the plates were at various times in the past. The middle drawing (right) shows the situation about 65 million years ago. Then, the Atlantic was much narrower than it is today, North and South America were not joined, and India had not yet reached Asia. As the top drawing shows, in the still more remote past, about 135 million years ago, North America was joined to Europe and South America to Africa. It was the shapes produced by the separation of South America and Africa which first encouraged people to suppose they might once have been joined. These time scales seem very long, but compared with the age of Earth itself, which is about 4.6 billion years, the crustal plates are moving fairly quickly. The middle drawing shows the map of the world as it was when the dinosaurs and many other groups of animals became extinct, and mammals were small and mainly nocturnal. Dinosaurs were flourishing 135 million years ago, but flowering plants had only recently evolved (page 61) and were spreading throughout tropical and middle latitudes.

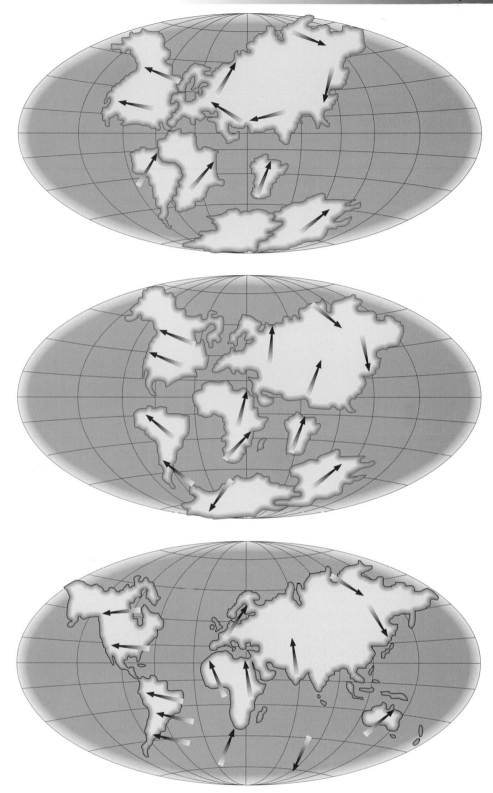

Continental drift

Scientists have been able to trace the journeys of the continents into the much more distant past. The map on page 8 shows what a map of the world might have looked like 360 million years ago, when most of the continents were joined in a single supercontinent. This was not Pangaea, which had not yet formed, but it shows that what have now become North America and Europe straddled the equator.

Reconstructing the past movements of continents allows us to solve the riddle of the disjunct distribution of plants and animals. These groups lived on a continent that split and were carried thousands of miles in opposite directions on the drifting fragments. This mechanism also shows that more than the climate is involved in determining the composition of forests. Plants spread by the scattering of their seed, but over a much longer period they are also taken wherever they are carried by the land on which they grow.

Soil Formation and Development

Walk through a forest and it is the trees that will hold your attention. A forest is its trees, after all. Away from well-trodden paths, however, you may also notice the ground beneath your feet. This may be soft, springy, and comfortable to walk on, or hard and uneven. After rain it may be muddy, or water may soak into it quickly, leaving it dry underfoot. Here and there you may see a bank where some of the roots of a tree are exposed.

What your feet feel beneath the layer of dead leaves or pine needles is the soil. Forests consist of trees; trees are plants; and plants grow in soil. Soils are not all the same and each type is best suited for a particular kind of vegetation. The soil you find in a forest will be different from the soil in a corn-field, and even forest soils vary from one type of forest to another (page 15). As any farmer will tell you, soils can vary considerably from one field to the next and even from one part of a field to another part of the same field. There are now computer-aided farming systems that take read-ings from sensors in the soil and transmit radio messages telling the farmer how much to increase or decrease the amount of fertilizer applied to dif-ferent areas, according to variations in the soil and the requirements of the crop. What is more, soils are changing constantly in response to changes in the conditions to which they are subjected. Like plant communities, soils are dynamic systems.

Life Story of the Soil

Anything that changes over time has a history, a record of past times when it was different from the way it is now, and histories usually have beginnings. If soils have histories, this suggests there was some time, perhaps long ago, before those histories began and, therefore, before the soils themselves existed. Put this way, we can think of soils being "born," passing through a period when they are "young," becoming "mature," then "aging," and eventually "dying." Pedologists, the scientists who study soils, use most of these words, although they do not usually think of soils "dying."

You and I have parents. Trees grow from seeds produced by older trees, which are their parents. Being born implies the existence of parents. It follows that if soils can be born they, too, must have parents, and so they do. A soil is born from "parent material," which is rock, and the process by which it is born and ages is called weathering.

Consider an exposed rock surface and the forces to which it is subjected. Movements within

Earth's crust bend and fracture it, so its surface bears many cracks and fissures. When it breaks, small fragments are detached. These can be blown by the wind or carried by water, which throw them against one another and against larger rocks, breaking them into still smaller fragments. Rain seeps into cracks. It is naturally acid, from the car-bon dioxide and other gases that have dissolved into it from the air, and it reacts chemically with the rock it contacts. These reactions dissolve some of the compounds from which the rock is made, which weakens the rock so more fragments are detached from it. Away from the tropics, in win-ter the water may freeze. When water freezes it expands with great force, widening the cracks and causing more tiny fractures. In spring, the ice melts and more fragments are freed. In summer, the Sun beats down on the rock, heating it. As it is heated, the rock expands, but it is only the sur-face that expands, because that is where the heat is trapped, insulating the rock below the surface. This causes yet more fractures and detaches yet more fragments.

All of this is weathering due to the weather, to rain, changes in temperature, and wind. By itself, this kind of weathering will reduce rock to fine grains. Even without the help of water, at least for hundreds of millions, or perhaps billions, of years, it has produced the desert sands of Mars and even without wind the dust of the Moon. On Earth, though, the weathering is also biological.

Birth of a Soil

Bacteria can live almost anywhere. They thrive in the hot waters that gush from volcanic vents on the deep ocean floor and they have been found living on the surface of ice sheets. Compared with these, the cracks in rocks are hospitable places, presenting them with far more opportu-nities than problems. Inside a crack, bacterial colonies are sheltered from the wind and direct sunlight and they can obtain nutrients from the substances dissolved from the rock into rain water. To protect themselves further, the colonies secrete a tough, jellylike covering and lie sealed beneath it.

They penetrate further into the rock, along microscopically tiny fissures, and their own waste products also react with ingredients of the rock. The bacteria contribute to the weathering process for lichens, the next arrivals.

A lichen is a partnership of two kinds of liv-ing organisms, a fungus and an alga or cyanobac-

terium. Fungi are not plants, but organisms that obtain mineral nutrients through a network, in some cases a very extensive network, of fine fila-ments called hyphae. An alga (plural *algae*) is a simple plant, individuals of many species consist-ing of only one cell. Cyanobacteria (which used to be known as blue-green algae) are a type of bacteria. Both algae and cyanobacteria can use sunlight to convert carbon dioxide and water into sugars. Combined in a lichen, the fungus provides secure anchorage and supplies minerals and the alga or cyanobacterium supplies sugars. Lichens can grow on apparently bare rock surfaces.

As material continues to accumulate from the wastes and dead remains of the bacteria and lichens, in time the first true plants can gain a hold. These are often mosses, and within deeper cracks, where more organic material has col-lected, there may be a blade or two of grass or a small flowering herb.

Mosses, grasses, and herbs add more organic material and slowly, as this mixes with the tiny mineral fragments from the weathered rock, soil starts to develop. On Mars and the Moon, where there is no contribution from organic material, the surface material is properly called regolith, not soil.

Pedogenesis, which is the scientific term for the formation and development of soils, is often a slow process, but not always. In Ukraine there is a fortress, called Kamenetz, which was abandoned in 1699 and fell into ruin. Its floor now lies beneath a layer of soil varying from 4 to 16 inches (10 to 40 cm) thick that has developed from the limestone slabs of which the floor was made.

Not all soil develops from solid rock and if the parent material has already been broken into small fragments it can become a true soil much more quickly than the floor of the Kamenetz fortress. Very fine mineral particles, deposited as silt on river floodplains, can be blown by the wind to places where it accumulates as "loess." Glaciers scour the rocks over which they flow, grinding stones into small grains that are left behind when the climate warms and the glaciers retreat. Some types of volcanoes eject vast amounts of ash, which is rock reduced to a pow-der. If materials like these occur in places where there is enough warmth and rain for plants to grow, they can be converted into soil in less than a century. The careful reclamation of mineral waste tips, where mining companies dump the shattered and crushed rock that is left after the useful materials have been extracted, can produce several inches of soil in just a few years.

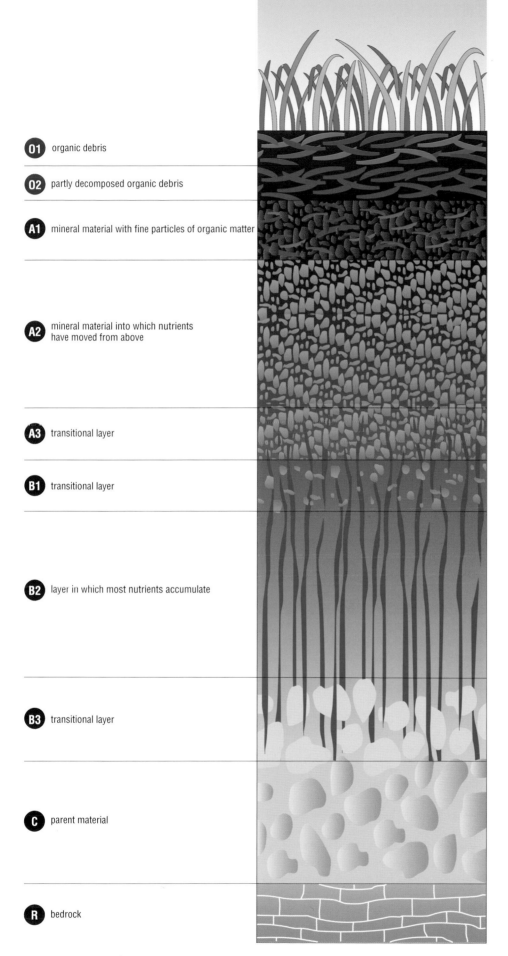

O1 — organic debris

O2 — partly decomposed organic debris

A1 — mineral material with fine particles of organic matter

A2 — mineral material into which nutrients have moved from above

A3 — transitional layer

B1 — transitional layer

B2 — layer in which most nutrients accumulate

B3 — transitional layer

C — parent material

R — bedrock

Soil profile

Soil Horizons

Once soil has started to form, bigger plants can grow in it. Their roots penetrate more deeply and when the roots die they leave channels through which air and water can move, and vegetable matter on which a variety of bacteria and small animals can feed. Under favorable conditions, little by little the maturing soil grows deeper and the community of organisms living in it becomes more complex, until the soil is a fascinating and bewilderingly complicated ecosystem in itself, while all the time the weathering processes continue.

As it matures, the soil also acquires a definite structure. It forms layers, which can be exposed by cutting a trench through the soil, deep enough to reach the underlying parent material. The exposed cross-section of the soil is called a soil profile and the layers it reveals are called horizons.

Horizons are highly variable and often incomplete, but the figure to the left shows them as they might appear in a profile through the soil of a broad-leaved deciduous forest. As the diagram shows, there are many horizons, grouped into four principal categories and labeled O, A, B, and C. Pedologists often label soil horizons in much more detail than is shown here, with subscripted abbreviations to indicate chemical composition, but this simplified diagram illustrates the general principle and the labeling scientists use.

At the surface there is a thin layer, a few inches thick at most, O1, of leaves, twigs, and other plant and animal material. Fungi and small animals are busily feeding on this. Beneath the O1 horizon, the O2 layer consists of plant and animal material that has been partly decomposed by the activities of the organisms feeding on it. The two O horizons contain more organic material than the deeper horizons. The total thickness of the O horizons varies greatly from one soil to another.

Decomposition breaks down complex organic molecules into smaller molecules. Many of these are soluble and as rain drains downward through the soil (page 16) they dissolve and are carried into lower horizons. This transport of soluble compounds is called leaching and it occurs mainly in the A horizons.

The A1 horizon consists mainly of mineral particles, but these are mixed with fine organic particles from above, which usually give the A1 horizon a dark color. Compounds leaching from A1 flow down into A2, which is much paler. This horizon is composed of mineral particles through which soluble compounds are leaching. Beneath A2, the A3 horizon is similar, but mixed with material from the underlying B horizon, so it is transitional between A and B. The A horizons are what farmers and gardeners call the topsoil.

B horizons, or "subsoil," are where the leached compounds accumulate. At the top of the layer, B1 is another transitional horizon, generally similar to B2, but mixed with some material from A3. The B2 horizon, which in many soils is the thickest, comprises mineral particles and the accumulation of dissolved compounds. Beneath it, B3 is transitional to C, and the C horizon is the partly weathered material from which the overlying soil has developed. It lies above the bedrock, which some scientists call the R horizon.

How Soils Grow Old

This level of organization and complexity represents the mature phase in the life cycle of a soil. At first, the young soil is not so strongly stratified and may consist of nothing more than a layer of organic material less than half an inch thick and missing altogether in some places overlying the main mass of undifferentiated mineral particles. A young soil may have only two horizons, A and C, and its properties are derived mainly from the parent material, with little contribution from living organisms.

Nor will mature soil remain mature. As compounds dissolve from the upper horizons and leach deeper and deeper, gradually they will be lost. Rainwater, which carries them into the lower horizons, eventually joins the groundwater (page 18) and flows with it away from the area. The lost compounds may be replaced by those leaching into the area, but this is not always the case, especially on high ground where there is little soil further up the slope to supply them.

Eventually, as leaching continues, the soil ages and its character changes. Differences between the A and B horizons become extreme, as the A horizon is depleted of substances that accumulate in the B horizon. Fertility declines in the old soil, with consequences for the vegetation it supports. This may become more diverse, as the more aggressive, dominant species start to fail. These are plants that compete vigorously for nutrients but require large amounts of them. As the supply dwindles, the dominants lose vigor and a wider range of species with more modest requirements is able to flourish.

Aging leads to "senility." Only the least soluble compounds survive in a senile soil and the vegetation comprises shallow-rooted plants exploiting nutrients released by decomposition near the surface. Finally, the soil is fully weathered. Depleted of even its relatively insoluble constituents, its fertility is extremely low.

Climate and Aging

The rate at which a soil forms and ages depends largely on the climate, proceeding fastest where rain falls reliably throughout the year and the ground is frozen for only a few weeks each year or not at all. This describes temperate climates, and it is they that produce and age soils most quickly. In a dry desert there is too little rain to support the vigorous plant growth needed to provide organic material and to supply the water that dissolves and leaches compounds. Soils may start to develop, but horizons fail to form and so the soils remain young for as long as the climate stays arid. Much the same happens in very high latitudes, where the ground remains frozen most of the year, and there are regions of permafrost, where a layer below the soil surface remains frozen all year round. Again, there is little opportunity for soils to mature. They remain young and lack clearly marked horizons.

Climates also exert a more subtle influence. Gradations of temperature and moisture that in themselves have little effect on soil development nevertheless may have a large effect on vegetation which in turn changes the character of the soil. The difference between the climatic conditions suitable for sclerophyllous, summer deciduous, and boreal forest are not great. All grow in temperate climates, but differences in vegetation are reflected in chemical differences. Nutrient requirements vary from one tree species to another—especially between coniferous evergreens and broad-leaved deciduous species—and fallen leaves decay at different rates. You need only compare the floor of a broad-leaved deciduous forest with that of a conifer forest to see this difference. Needles lie a long time on the ground, forming a mat, and decay slowly. Leaves of sclerophylls, which are tough and usually have a waxy outer coat, also decay slowly. Holly leaves remain on the ground much longer than the leaves of summer deciduous trees, which rot quickly and are mixed into the surface soil horizon.

Soil Types

Climate and vegetation may combine to produce and develop soils, but they have no influence at all over the mineral composition of the original parent material. This is rock and rocks vary widely. Granite is quite different from limestone, for example, and limestone is different from sandstone. Rock is made from minerals, crystalline substances with definite chemical compositions, but there are many minerals and countless combinations in which they can occur. As a rock weathers, its mineral composition will determine

UDDEN-WENTWORTH SCALE OF GRAIN SIZES (mm)

boulder	more than 256
cobble	64–256
pebble	4–64
granule	2–4
very coarse sand	1–2
coarse sand	0.5–1
medium sand	0.25–0.5
fine sand	0.125–0.25
very fine sand	0.062–0.125
silt	0.031–0.062
clay	less than 0.031

the kind of chemical reactions that take place and the size of the resulting particles. Soils weathered from different parent materials will differ chemically and physically and this may affect their subsequent development.

Take a handful of soil and you can learn quite a lot about its mineral composition simply by feeling it. If it is dry you should moisten it until it has the consistency of modeling clay. Pinch off a small amount and rub it between your finger and thumb. If it feels gritty the soil is mainly sand, if it feels rough but not gritty it is mainly silt, and if it feels smooth and rather greasy it is mainly clay. If the soil dries quickly and when you squeeze it with your fingers it does not stick to them, the soil is mainly silt. If it dries slowly and is sticky, it is clay. Further tests, in which you squeeze a lump of soil to see how easily it breaks apart, roll it into a thread to see how thin you can make the thread without it breaking, and press it through your finger and thumb to make a ribbon to see whether this is possible and, if it is, how long you can make the ribbon before it breaks, allow you to estimate the relative proportions of sand, silt, and clay.

These differences in feel and strength are due to the size of the mineral particles from which the soil is made and they strongly influence many of its important characteristics. To a pedologist, the words "pebble," "sand," "silt," and "clay" have quite precise meanings. There are several classification systems, but the table above gives the sizes in the Udden-Wentworth Scale, which is widely used. The measurements are in millimeters (mm); 1 mm = 0.0394 inch.

The size and shape of its particles determine the rate at which water drains through a soil (page 16). It also affects the rate at which weathering affects it. This is a matter of geometry, because weathering occurs at surfaces and the smaller the particle the bigger its surface area in relation to its volume.

Suppose the particles to be spherical (which they are not, but the argument still holds good). The volume of a sphere with a diameter of, say, 2 will be 4.2 and its surface area 12.6. Dividing the surface area by the volume gives a ratio of 3:1. Double the diameter, to 4, and the volume is 33.5, the surface area 50.3, and the ratio 1.5:1. A given volume of soil will contain more particles if they are small than if they are large, those particles will have a greater combined surface area on which weathering processes can act, and so that soil will weather faster if the two soils experience similar weathering conditions.

The fertility of the two soils will also differ for the same reason. It is weathering that releases soluble compounds into the water moving through the soil and it is from the soil solution that plant roots obtain their mineral nutrients. Clay soils, therefore, are inherently more fertile and productive than sandy soils, but because their tiny particles pack together more closely water does not drain easily through them.

Soil Classification

At one time, people believed soil was simply a mixture of mineral particles, organic matter, and air. It was pretty much the same everywhere, had always existed, and did not change over the years and centuries. To farmers it was the medium that supported plant growth, to engineers it was the base on which buildings, bridges, and roads were constructed.

Around the middle of the last century, however, scientists were starting to realize that this was a very inadequate description. Indeed, it was misleading to talk about "soil" at all. The soil in one place might be so different from the soil somewhere else that it would be more sensible to talk of "soils," in the plural, and of each individual soil as occupying a particular area to a particular depth and surrounded by other, different soils.

This concept was strengthened by the publication in 1840 of a book called *Die organische Chemie in ihrer Anwendung auf Agrikulturchemie und Physiologie* (Organic chemistry in its application to agricultural chemistry and physiology) by the German chemist Justus Liebig (1803–73). In it Liebig showed that plants take specific compounds from the air and soil—rather than being nourished by directly consuming decayed organic matter called humus, which was the prevailing idea—and that soils can be improved by the addition of fertilizers in the form of simple, inorganic, chemical compounds. Liebig was already famous for his discoveries and for having revolutionized the teaching of chemistry. In later years he was recognized as the greatest chemist in Germany and probably in the world. Not surprisingly, his findings about soil were widely read, and led to the founding of the fertilizer industry.

A Russian Beginning

Scientists set about studying soils in detail; from those studies they hoped to be able to describe each type of soil, classify them, and map their distribution. Many European and American scientists took part in this enterprise, but one of the first and most influential was a Russian geologist and geographer, Vasily Vasilievich Dokuchaev (1840–1903).

Dokuchaev originally intended to become a priest, but changed to a course in natural sciences while a student at St. Petersburg University. He was appointed curator of the geological museum at the university and in 1877 he was commissioned by a group called the True Society of Economics, which wanted to boost farm production

in the grasslands, to undertake a four-year survey of the soils of the steppes. His results were published in 1882, as a book the title of which can be translated as "Russian Chernozem." He suggested that soils evolve through the combined action of physical weathering and biological activity and have histories starting with their formation. He became director of the Kharkov Institute of Agriculture and Forestry in Ukraine and the year his work on steppe soils was published he embarked on another four-year survey, this time of soils in the province of Nizhni Novgorod (now Gor'kiy) to the east of Moscow. Later, the work he had started was continued by one of his former students, Konstantin Dimitrievich Glinka (1867–1927).

Climate was held to be the main factor in the formation of what Dokuchaev called normal soils and in the first of the 14 volumes of his report on the Nizhni Novgorod survey, he proposed a method for classifying them. His "normal" soils, typical of the climatic region in which they occurred, came to be known as zonal soils. Soils that were altered because of local circumstances, such as waterlogged soils, and soils with excessive amounts of salt were called intrazonal, and soils that had barely started to form, such as desert sands, or that had been transported by wind or water away from the region where they formed, were called azonal.

A system of classification had begun, in which each of these main soil orders (zonal, intrazonal, and azonal) was subdivided into suborders and "great soil groups." Reflecting the large volume of work done by the Russian scientists, many of the great soils groups had Russian names. The Russian for "soil" is *zemlya* and many of the names end in *zem*. *Chernozem* is the black soil of steppe grassland, *brunizems* are prairie soils, *podzols* are fairly old, weathered, ash-colored soils, *solonchaks* are saline soils, *solonetz* is a poorly drained soil, *sierozem* is a pale, desert soil, and *rendzinas* are grassland soils developed over chalk or limestone.

Russians led the field for many years. *Pochvovedeniye* ('Soil Behavior'), the world's first journal on soil science, was Russian, launched in 1899, and the first soil science textbooks were also Russian. The first American journal on the subject, *Soil Science,* began publication in 1916 at Rutgers College and the first British journal, *Journal of Soil Science* did not appear until 1949.

At first only the soil surface was examined. It was a Danish scientist, P. E. Muller (1840–1926), who showed that the lower layers of a soil need to be taken into account in the description and classification. Glinka developed this and worked

out a way to label the subsurface layers, but it took a long time for the idea to gain acceptance and it was not fully incorporated into soil classification until the Second International Congress of Soil Science, held in Russia in 1932.

American Studies

Meanwhile, American soil scientists were as active as their Russian colleagues, but less concerned with investigating the processes involved in the formation and development of soils. They were kept informed of the Russian work by C. F. Marbut (1863–1935), a geologist and geographer who did much to promote pedology in the United States and whose work achieved worldwide recognition. Russian publications were often translated into German, and Marbut translated them from German into English. The Americans conducted many soil surveys and the U.S. Soil Survey was established in 1898 with Milton Whitney as its first director. Marbut was appointed consultant scientist to the U.S. Soil Survey in 1910 and in 1913 he became director, or scientist in charge, as the director was known.

Surveying and attempts at classification continued and by the late 1940s American scientists had made much more progress than their colleagues elsewhere. Gradually the old Russian names were replaced, although not by familiar American words.

Modern Soil Taxonomy

Compiling a complete classification proved very difficult. By 1975, when the U.S. Department of Agriculture published a manual describing the scheme its soil survey staff had devised, more than 10,000 soil types had been identified in the United States alone, but the work had been thorough and what is now known as the U.S. Soil Taxonomy has been adopted as the system used by pedologists throughout the world.

It begins by dividing soils into 10 main groups, called orders. These are then divided further into 47 suborders and below these are great groups, subgroups, families, and soil series, with six "phases" in each soil series. The entire system generates tens of thousands of names, all of which look very strange when you meet them for the first time. The 10 orders (usually written with an initial capital) are: Entisols, Vertisols, Inceptisols, Aridisols, Mollisols, Spodosols, Alfisols, Ultisols, Oxisols, and Histosols.

Entisols, a made-up word, are soils found only locally and formerly known as azonal. The suborders, all ending with *ents,* are aquents, arents, fluvents, orthents, and psamments.

Vertisols, from the Latin *verto,* "turn," are soils that have been inverted, so what was once below the surface now lies on top. Vertisol suborders, all ending in *erts,* are torrerts, uderts, usterts, and xererts.

Inceptisols, from the Latin *inceptum,* "beginning," are very young soils. The suborders, all ending in *epts,* are andepts, aquedepts, ochrepts, plaggepts, tropepts, and umbrepts.

Aridisols, from the Latin *aridus,* "dry," are desert soils. There are only two suborders, both ending in "ids," the argids and orthids.

Mollisols, from the Latin *mollis,* "soft," are the soft soils of grasslands and forests, the most fertile and agriculturally productive of soils. The suborders, all ending in *olls,* are albolls, aquolls, borolls, rendolls, udolls, ustolls, and xerolls.

Spodosols, from the Greek *spodos,* "wood ash," are acid, ash colored, weathered soils from which most soluble compounds have leached. They used to be called "podzols," and the process by which iron and aluminum oxides and hydroxides leach from the upper soil horizons is called "podzolization." The suborders, all ending in *ods,* are aquods, ferrods, humods, and orthods.

Alfisols, a made-up word, are similar to Spodosols. They develop in moist, temperate climates, often over a clay parent material. The suborders, all ending in *alfs,* are aqualfs, boralfs, udalfs, ustalfs, and xeralfs.

Ultisols, from the Latin *ultimus,* "last," are red or yellow podzolized soils, more heavily weathered than Alfisols. They are ancient soils, near the end of soil development. The suborders, all ending in *ults,* are aquults, humults, udults, ustults, and xerults.

Oxisols, from the French *oxide,* "oxide," are even more weathered than Ultisols and well into soil senility. They contain lumps or layers of solid iron and aluminum oxides and hydroxides called laterite. Oxisols occur mainly, but not exclusively, in the tropics. The suborders, all ending in *ox,* are aquox, humox, orthox, torrox, and ustox.

Histosols, from the Greek *histos,* "tissue," are the soils of bogs, consisting mainly of organic material. The suborders, all ending in *ists,* are fibrists, folists, hemists, and saprists.

You can work out the meaning of the suborder names if you understand the origin of their prefixes. *Aqu-,* for example, suggests water, so "aquents" are wet surface deposits, *psamm-* means sandy, *xer-* means arid, *plagg-* is derived from "plaggen," a farmed soil produced by many years of plowing and manuring, *ud-* describes a soil that is moist for most of the summer, *ust-* one that holds a limited amount of moisture during the period of maximum plant growth, and *fluv-,* from the Latin *fluvius,* "river," refers to stream deposits.

Water Flow and Drainage

When it rains, in most places the water does not accumulate on the ground. Puddles may appear on city streets and in parking lots, but walk through a forest and, except in depressions along well-trodden paths, the rain usually disappears almost at once. The soil may be damp, but it is not waterlogged and if the weather turns fine and warm, before very long the soil will look and feel dry. It dries because water evaporates from it, but this affects only the upper layer. Dig a few inches beneath the surface and you will find moist soil. Even when it has not rained for some time, the soil will be moist below ground, although you will need to dig fairly deeply to find it during a prolonged drought.

Water moves through soil laterally, vertically downward, and vertically upward. Plants, which must absorb water at least occasionally, obtain it from the soil, not directly from the falling rain. All the precipitation that falls from clouds comes originally from the sea, of course, and all of it returns to the sea, but it moves slowly, allowing plants to capture a portion of it (page 18).

Particles, Porosity, and Permeability

Apart from the peaty soil found in bogs, or on land that was once boggy and has since been drained, soil consists mainly of mineral particles. Even in a soil rich in organic matter most of the volume comprises solid particles weathered from rock. Particles pack together, but their shapes are irregular and they do not fit closely, like bricks. There are spaces, called pores, between them and it is through these spaces that water can travel. The total amount of space between soil pores determines the porosity of the soil.

The smaller the particles are, the more of them there will be in any given volume. Surprisingly, perhaps, the size of the particles does not necessarily affect the total amount of pore space, the porosity, of the soil. The figure below shows three boxes of particles, all of them spherical in shape, but differing greatly in size. It looks as though there is more empty space in the box containing the bigger particles, but in fact the amount of pore space is the same in all three. If these were soil particles, all three soils would be equally porous. You could check this by filling a jar in turn with large, medium-sized, and small particles and seeing how much water you can add to the jar before it overflows, which will be a measure of the volume of pore space.

Porosity is an indication of the amount of water the soil will hold. In this case, all three soils will absorb the same amount, but they will not retain equal amounts. This is because water can flow more easily through some than through others. Although the total amount of pore space is the same in each, water can pass through a few large spaces more easily than through many small ones. "Permeability" is a measure of the ease with which water flows through a soil (or any other material). The soil in the box on the left, containing one very large particle, is more permeable than that in the center, with eight particles, which in turn is more permeable than the soil on the right, with many small particles. People often confuse "porosity" and "permeability," but they mean quite different things.

Porosity, Permeability, and Drainage

Rain falling on the soil on the left will drain downward very rapidly. It will not be long before the surface dries thoroughly. It will take rather longer for water to drain through the soil in the center, so its surface will remain moist for longer. When rain falls on the soil on the right, however,

Particles

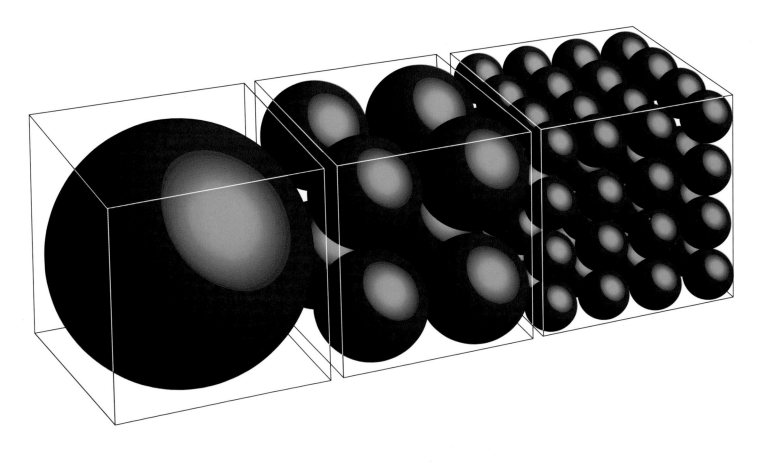

it will soak into the ground, but then drain only very slowly. The soil will remain moist much longer than the other two soils. Permeability, then, depends not on the total amount of pore space, but on the size of the pores and the tiny channels that, in a real soil, link them.

The shape of the particles also affects permeability. Sand grains, for example, are usually very angular. This increases the size of pore spaces without increasing overall porosity, and greatly increases permeability. Clay particles, on the other hand, are minute (page 121) and flat-sided, so they stack together leaving extremely small pore spaces. Clay soils are very porous, but relatively impermeable. They hold water, and after prolonged rain clay can turn into a heavy, sticky, cold, structureless mass, as anyone knows who has tried working it.

Some of the water falling to the ground and wetting the surface evaporates during its passage through the air or from the ground. Water that does not evaporate flows. If the rain is very heavy and the ground bare of vegetation, the impact of rain drops can batter fine soil particles closer together until they form a thin but impermeable cap over the surface. Water then flows horizontally across the surface of sloping ground or lies in pools on level ground. Surface flow is a major cause of soil erosion on hillslopes.

Vegetation slows the fall of water drops. Stand in the open during a heavy shower and you can feel the force with which the rain strikes you, especially if it is being driven by a strong wind. Stand in a forest during that shower, and the wind will be much lighter, because the trees slow and deflect it, and the rain will drip gently from the leaves and branches above you. Less of it will reach the ground, because of the amount that remains in small depressions on branches and the much greater amount that forms thin films over leaves and branches. This water evaporates rather than falling further.

Capillarity

Watch water soaking into the ground and you might suppose it sinks under its own weight, that it is continuing its fall. Indeed, water draining vertically is called gravitational water, but the image is misleading. Water does have weight, causing it to move downward, but it is more accurate to think of water not sinking into the ground, but being sucked into it from below, at a speed determined by the permeability of the soil. The "sucking" is caused by capillarity, or capillary attraction, and it is due to a peculiar property of water itself.

A molecule of pure water consists of two atoms of hydrogen and one of oxygen. Hydrogen atoms carry a positive electrical charge, oxygen atoms a negative charge, and they are bonded by

the attraction of opposite charges. The molecule is not symmetrical, however, both hydrogen atoms being bonded to the same side of the much larger oxygen atom and separated by an angle of 104.5°. This leaves the molecule with a very small positive charge on its hydrogen side and an equal negative charge on its oxygen side. Such molecules are said to be polar. Their polarity allows water molecules to attach to one another, when the hydrogen side of one bonds to the oxygen side of another. Hydrogen bonds are weak, but they also allow water molecules to attach to other substances.

When water is held in a container, water molecules, because they are polar, will cling to the sides (this is called adherence) as well as to one another (called coherence). This causes the water to move up the sides of the container, drawing more water behind it. Eventually the water will reach a height where the force making it rise precisely balances the weight of the water column itself. After that it can rise no farther. Consequently, the smaller the container, the less the water column inside it weighs, and the further water will travel up it. This movement, caused by the water itself, is called capillarity or capillary attraction, and it can draw water in any direction.

Soil Moisture Tension

There is another way to think of this. Picture a beaker filled with water. At the bottom, water molecules are being subjected to pressure by the weight of water above them. Obviously, this water pressure decreases with height in the beaker, because there is less water above, and at the surface the water pressure is zero.

Now imagine a narrow tube is inserted vertically into the water. Inside the tube, above the surface, the water pressure will be still lower. It will be less than zero and will decrease with increasing height up the tube. That difference in water pressure causes the water to rise. Water pressure above the column is negative (less than zero), and working with negative quantities is inconvenient, so soil scientists simply eliminate the minus sign, giving the pressure a positive value, and call it "soil moisture tension" (SMT). It then represents a pulling force (tension) rather than a pushing force (pressure).

SMT varies inversely with the size of the pore spaces. The smaller the pore spaces, the greater the SMT. Values for water pressure and SMT are given in the same units as those used to report atmospheric pressure. This can cause confusion, because these forces are due wholly to the water and not at all to atmospheric pressure.

Capillarity can exert a force in any direction, however. As water drains down through a soil, the

pore spaces beneath it are dry and there is an SMT drawing it down faster. At the same time it is also being drawn to the sides. You can see this effect by spilling a colored liquid onto a thick stack of kitchen towels or blotting paper, because they also absorb liquids by capillarity. The color soaks sideways as well as downward.

Where Permeability Changes

When water soaks downward into the soil, almost all of it does so because of capillary attraction. Some may drain directly through the larger pore spaces, but only if these are open at the surface. In the boxes of particles in the diagram on page 16, water would drain readily through the bigger pore spaces simply because they are so large; realistically, they are unreasonably so. If the large pore spaces are closed, atmospheric pressure will prevent water from flowing out of them in the same way that it prevents water flowing from a tube if you insert it into water with both ends open, then seal one end with your thumb and withdraw it. It is rare for soil pore spaces to be open. Moving water tends to wash small particles into them, thus sealing them.

Suppose, though, that the water is draining through a layer of fine-grained soil which overlies a layer of gravel or coarse sand. Common sense seems to suggest that when the water reaches the more permeable material it will drain even faster. In fact, though, this is not what happens. Its movement ceases, at least temporarily, because the more permeable material contains much bigger pore spaces and, therefore, exerts a smaller SMT. The SMT pulling the water sideways in the fine-grained soil is greater, so it will sink no further until the fine-grained layer holds so much water that almost all the pores are filled, meaning the soil is close to saturation. This reduces the SMT and when it falls to a value lower than that in the coarse-grained layer, the water will resume its downward movement.

Some of the best farm soils in the northwestern United States work like this. In the basin of the Columbia River there are fine soils overlying sand and gravel which are renowned for their capacity to retain water.

An ordinary shower following a long period of dry weather will wet the ground, but if you dig into it you find that the moisture penetrates only a certain distance and below it there is dry soil. Water soaks only so far, but the wetted soil may then remain moist for quite some time. The upper, moist soil, from which water has drained as far as it can, is said to be at field capacity, an amount of water that varies widely depending on the size of the soil particles. The water is held there by SMT. This also varies, but water will move out of this region only if it is drawn by an SMT greater than that which retains it.

Groundwater and Water Table

Finally, if enough water arrives at the surface the downward movement will continue until it is checked by a layer of impermeable material. This may be rock or tightly compacted clay. Water can drain no further vertically, so it accumulates, completely saturating the soil above the impermeable layer. It is then called groundwater and the upper boundary of the saturated soil, above which some pore spaces are still free of water, is called the water table.

The height of the water table varies from time to time, depending on the amount of water draining into it. During a drought it falls and after prolonged rain, or when a thick layer of snow melts in spring, it rises. Where rainfall is distributed fairly evenly through the year and droughts are rare, the height of the water table will change little. A well is a hole cut from the surface to a depth below the water table. Groundwater will fill the bottom of the hole to the height of the water table.

Groundwater also flows, but very slowly, because it must move through soil pore spaces. Speeds vary widely, depending on the permeability of the material through which it flows, permeability being much more important than the gradient. Commonly, groundwater moves from a few feet a day to a few feet a month, but through limestone with many underground caverns it can travel at more than one mile per hour and through clay or shale, with low permeability, it may move less than one foot in a century.

Aquifers

Flowing groundwater is called an aquifer. It is through aquifers that chemical compounds leached from the surface soil horizons are removed. Just above the water table, in the unsaturated soil, capillarity produces a layer, the capillary fringe, where groundwater is being drawn upward.

Aquifers eventually discharge their water. Where the soil is shallow or drains poorly, they bubble through the surface, as springs. Beneath deeper soil they emerge only on low ground, where the water table, as measured by its level in the higher ground to either side, is above the surface level. There the water in the aquifer flows as a river and the low ground becomes a river valley.

An aquifer into which water can drain from directly above, so there is no impermeable layer between the water table and the ground surface, is said to be unconfined. In its journey, eventually to a river, lake, or the sea, the aquifer may flow through a layer of permeable material that lies beneath an impermeable layer, often consisting of densely compacted clay forming a "lens." The acquifer is then moving between two impermeable layers, one above and below, and is said to be "confined." Water draining from the ground surface may accumulate above the upper impermeable layer. It then forms a second, "perched," aquifer with its own water table. Because the perched aquifer lies fairly close to the surface, the soil above it will be shallow and poorly drained. This may lead to the development of a catena.

Catenas

Water, and the compounds dissolved in it, play an important part in the weathering processes by which soil is produced (page 10). Variations in the way water drains through a soil and moves as groundwater can therefore lead to the development of markedly different soils all from the same parent material.

A group of neighboring and closely related soils that develop from the same parent material but differ because of drainage or some other factor is called a catena. Catenas sometimes form on hillsides. The diagram below shows how this can happen. Near the top of the hill, the ground is fairly level and the soil there is well drained. As water drains downward, however, gravity causes it also to move some distance down the slope and a few small particles tend to move with it. Where the slope is steepest, the gravitational, downslope movement accelerates and the drainage is excessive. At the bottom of the slope the soil receives the water and all the sediment from higher levels.

Consequently, there is a progressive change in the type of soil from the bottom to the top of the hill, with the soils at the bottom and top being substantially different from one another. Soil horizons are much more clearly defined in well-drained soil. In the diagram below, the area with cross-hatch shading indicates the B horizons, in which compounds leached from the A horizons accumulate. At the top of the hill, there are deep A and B horizons. Where drainage is excessive the B horizons become very thin, and at the bottom of the hill, where drainage is poor but material accumulates, the B horizons dominate the soil.

Formation of a catena

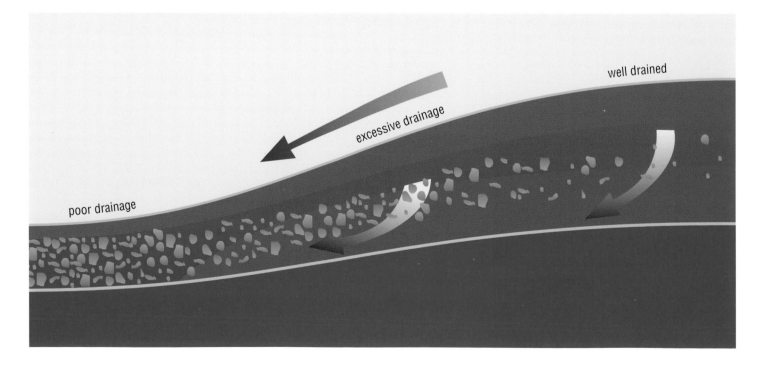

well drained

excessive drainage

poor drainage

mixed broad-leaves

mixed broad-leaves and conifers

well drained

excessive drainage

meadow

poorly drained

Drainage and Forests

Drainage and distribution

Frost action and even burrowing animals can alter drainage patterns and lead to the development of a catena. There can also be more than one water table, and a perched aquifer.

Soil drainage helps determine the character of a forest. Different tree species have different requirements and tolerances. Some root more deeply than others. Many coniferous trees have fairly shallow roots, temperate broad-leaved trees have deep ones, and most species suffer if the soil around their roots is waterlogged, because root cells need oxygen, which they can obtain only from air trapped between the particles in unsaturated soil.

Where the climate supports both broad-leaved deciduous and coniferous trees, their distribution can be affected by drainage, as the diagram above shows. Provided the ground is not too high and exposed, on the well-drained soil you will find a variety of broad-leaved species, with roots that penetrate down to the capillary fringe. As the drainage deteriorates, conifers occurs, mixed with the broad-leaved trees. Their shallower roots are not troubled by the high water table because they do not reach that far. Where the drainage is really poor, you may find few trees or none at all. If the ground is flooded from time to time, young tree saplings will be killed by the water, but sedges and some grasses will thrive, so the forest will give way to meadow.

Trees that can tolerate prolonged drought, called xerophytes, have rooting systems that do not reach all the way to the capillary fringe. In a temperate climate, the soil above the water table is at or close to its field capacity most of the time, but when it dries the trees survive. Roots of other trees, such as sycamore (*Platanus*), birch, willow, and cedar in lower latitudes, reach all the way to the capillary fringe, assuring them of a permanent water supply in all but the severest droughts. They are called phreatophytes.

Circulation of the Atmosphere

If you live between about latitude 30° and 60°, in either hemisphere, your home is in the temperate region of Earth. You will enjoy a temperate climate and the forests in your region will be temperate forests. Move into lower latitudes and the climate will become subtropical, move into higher latitudes and it will become subarctic. Near the equator, the climate is hot and humid, near the poles it is very cold and, surprisingly perhaps, dry. The arctic and antarctic regions are cold deserts, despite all their ice.

We are so used to this gradation of temperature from the equator to the poles that we take it for granted, yet the reason for it is not as obvious as it seems. No other planet in the solar system has a climate even remotely like our own. On the Moon, for example—which is a satellite, but big enough to be treated as though it were a small planet—the climate is quite unlike any climate on Earth, even though Earth and the Moon are both the same distance from the Sun. In one day the temperature on the Moon ranges from a high of about 260°F (127°C) to a low of -280°F (-173°C). The temperature is much the same at all latitudes and there are no seasons.

The Atmospheric Blanket

The difference, of course, is that Earth has a very much denser atmosphere than the Moon (it is not true that the Moon has no atmosphere; it does, but in daytime the lunar atmosphere contains only about one-ten trillionth (10^{-13}) the amount of gas as Earth's atmosphere and at night it contains only one-tenth of the daytime amount). If Earth had an atmosphere as thin as that on the Moon, temperatures here would be similar to those on the Moon.

When a body is heated, it radiates its heat. When the Moon is heated by the Sun, its surface temperature rises and it radiates its heat back into space. During daylight, the difference between the heat absorbed and the heat reradi-

ated produces the daytime temperature. At night, when there is no input of heat, the surface continues to radiate the heat it absorbed during the day and so its temperature falls to the pre-dawn minimum, after which it starts rising again.

On Earth, the surface of land and sea is also warmed by sunshine and it also radiates its absorbed heat, but not all of it. The warmed surface is in contact with the atmosphere and air at the surface is warmed by that contact. Air can and does move, but it cannot escape from the planet, so it acts like a blanket, keeping the surface warmer than it would be otherwise.

The Greenhouse Effect

If that were all, the average temperature over the surface of Earth would be about -9°F (-23°C). All the oceans would be frozen to a considerable depth and the air would be very dry indeed. There would be no forests and no people. The frozen Earth could support nothing more complex than bacteria. Simply having an atmosphere is not enough. What matters is the composition of that atmosphere and, in particular, the presence in it of very small concentrations of certain gases.

The Sun radiates at all wavelengths, but very short-wave gamma, X, and most ultraviolet radiation is absorbed at the top of the atmosphere. Radiation reaches the surface most intensely at wavelengths between 0.2 μm and 4.0 μm (1 μm = 1 micrometer = one-millionth of a meter = about 0.00004 inch). These are the wavelengths of visible and long-wave ultraviolet light and infrared radiation (heat). Nitrogen and oxygen, the gases comprising nearly all of the atmosphere (it is 78.1 percent nitrogen and 20.9 percent oxygen) are almost completely transparent to radiation at these wavelengths. It passes through them as though they were not there, and is absorbed at the surface.

ALBEDO	
Surface	**Albedo (%)**
fresh snow	75–95
dry sand	35–45
concrete	17–27
broad-leaved deciduous forest	10–20
plowed field	5–27
asphalt	5–17
coniferous forest	5–15
field crops	3–15

The warmed surface then radiates its absorbed heat, at longer infrared wavelengths between about 4.0 μm and 100 μm and some of this radiation is absorbed by minor gaseous constituents of the atmosphere. Water vapor absorbs radiation between 5 μm and 8 μm and again in certain longer wavebands. Carbon dioxide absorbs at 4 μm and between 13 μm and 17 μm. Methane, ozone, nitrous oxide, and some other gases also absorb long-wave radiation, each at particular wavelengths. This leaves an "atmospheric window," between about 8.5 μm and 13.0 μm, where radiation is not absorbed and escapes into space.

Atmospheric molecules that absorb radiation then reradiate it in all directions, some of it outward into space, some sideways, but about two-thirds of it down toward the surface. This warms the air and the surface. At night, when the surface is not being warmed by the Sun, the blanket of warmed air slows the rate at which the surface cools, but radiation continues to escape so that overall there is a balance between the amount of incoming and outgoing radiant energy.

This delayed cooling is often called the greenhouse effect. The name is misleading, because air in a greenhouse is warmed by the sunlight entering through the glass, then trapped by the glass so it cannot mix with cooler air from outside. The atmospheric mechanism is quite different, but the popular name is now so firmly established it is fruitless to try substituting a more accurate one. Increasing the thickness of the panes of a glasshouse would have no effect on the temperature inside (actually, it might lower it slightly by blocking some of the incoming sunlight) but increasing the atmospheric concentration of gases that absorb in the infrared waveband would raise the temperature. Such an induced warming is also known as the greenhouse effect, but is more correctly called the enhanced greenhouse effect (page 174).

Albedo

When light and heat from the Sun reach the ground, some is reflected without warming the surface at all. How much is reflected depends on the color of the surface. We make use of the same principle when we wear pale clothes in summer, to reflect heat, and dark clothes in winter, to absorb it.

Scientists call the reflectivity of a surface its albedo. Albedo can be measured and its value is expressed as a percentage of the incoming radiation that is reflected, either directly (e.g. 80 percent) or as a decimal fraction (e.g. 0.8). Obviously, radiation that is not reflected is absorbed, and this radiation comprises heat as well as visible light, warming the surface, and the surface warms the air in contact with it. The albedo has a direct effect on local climates.

As the table on the previous page shows, albedos vary widely. Some are self-evident. Freshly fallen snow reflects so much bright sunlight it will dazzle you, or actually hurt your eyes, unless you wear dark glasses. Others may be less clear. Broad-leaved deciduous forest reflects more light and heat than coniferous forest. Look at them, and you can see that coniferous forest is a much darker color than broad-leaved forest. This means coniferous forest, being darker, absorbs more radiant heat than does broad-leaved deciduous forest, which is appropriate since most conifers grow in cooler regions than broad-leaves.

Angle of Sunlight

Regardless of albedo, some parts of Earth are warmed by the Sun more intensely than others. Earth differs from the Moon in this respect, because it is much bigger. It is a matter of geometry and the figure below shows why. Picture a place on the surface where the Sun is directly overhead, as shown in drawing A, and suppose there is a narrow beam of sunlight. There, the Sun illuminates a relatively small area. In B, where the Sun is lower in the sky, a larger area is illuminated by a beam of similar width. The beam transmits the same amount of energy in both cases, but in A it is concentrated into a smaller area than in B, so all the energy of the beam is received by a smaller area in A than in B and, therefore, it will be warmer.

The Tropics are defined as the region within which the Sun appears directly overhead at noon on at least one day in the year. The Arctic and

Angle of sunlight

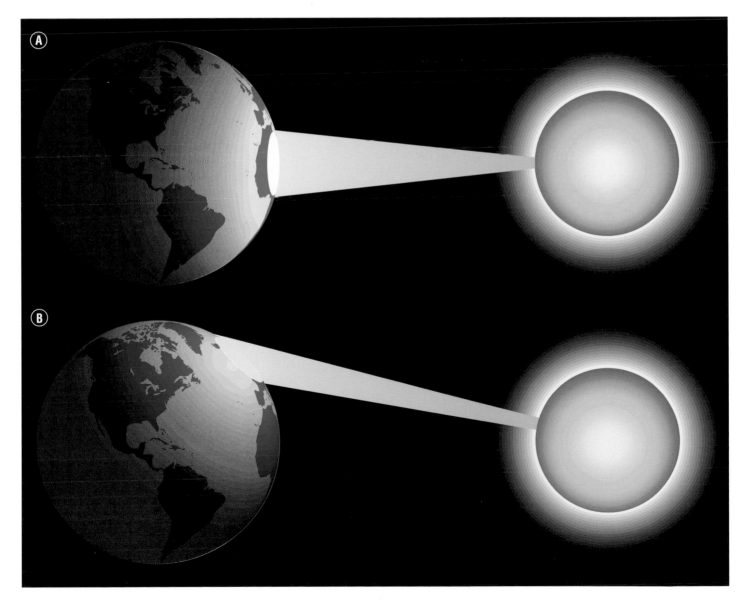

Antarctic Circles define the regions north and south of which respectively there is at least one day in the year when the Sun never sinks below the horizon and one day in the year when it never rises above the horizon.

This shows why land at the poles is colder than land at the equator, but when the general picture is considered in much more detail and actual amounts of energy calculated, a curious fact emerges. In a belt between 40° N and 35° S, the surface receives more energy than it reradiates and in latitudes higher than about 75° N and S the surface radiates more energy than it receives. Consequently, the average temperature should be about 25°F (14°C) warmer than it is at the equator and about 45°F (25°C) colder at the poles. There can be only one explanation of the more moderate temperatures that really exist. Heat is being transferred from low to high latitudes. Heat transfer of this kind requires a fluid medium, and Earth has two. The heat is carried by the atmosphere and the oceans.

Ocean Currents and the Trade Winds

Currents circulating in all the oceans form gyres, approximately circular flows of surface water. The water is warmed near the equator and as it moves

into higher latitudes it warms the air in contact with it. Then it curves back towards the equator, as the cold-current part of the system, to be warmed again. Air in high latitudes is warmed and air in low latitudes is cooled.

Air also moves, both vertically and horizontally, and it, too, transports heat away from the equator. Like many scientific discoveries, our understanding of how it does so came as a by-product of the search to explain an apparently quite different puzzle.

Centuries ago, sailors found that winds in the Tropics were very reliable. North of the equator they nearly always blew from the northeast and south of the equator from the southeast. Indeed, these winds were so dependable and so important to commerce that they were called trade winds.

Very close to the equator itself, however, there were regions where winds were often light and variable, or the air was quite still, and ships were becalmed. This is where the trade winds converge in a belt called the Intertropical Convergence (ITC) Zone. These windless areas came to be called the doldrums and they were encountered in the "horse latitudes," where sailors would sometimes throw horses overboard in an attempt to lighten the ship so such little wind as there was would move it. Being becalmed was not merely inconvenient, it was extremely dangerous. Supplies of fresh water could be exhausted. Scientists then began to wonder why the trade winds are so reliable.

Edmund Halley (1656–1742), the English astronomer for whom the famous comet is named, was the first to attempt an explanation. He suggested in 1686 that air over the equator is heated strongly. It expands, rises, and is replaced near the surface by cooler air, the trade winds. He was nearly correct, but not quite, because the circulation he described would make the trade winds blow from due north and due south. He had not explained the easterly component.

It was not until 1735 that an explanation was offered for that, by the English meteorologist George Hadley (1685–1768). Hadley accepted much of the Halley explanation. His idea was that the warm air rises to a great height, flows away from the equator in both directions, then sinks and flows back toward the equator. In fact, the air forms a vast convection cell. He also pointed out that while the air is moving, Earth is also turning in an easterly direction. It is this motion that swings the returning air so it approaches the equator from the northeast and southeast.

Like Halley before him, he was almost correct. Hadley had described the convection cell, but he was wrong about the reason for the change in direction of the flowing air. That was not explained until 1856, by the American meteorologist William Ferrel (1817–91), who said the swing is due to the tendency of moving air to turn about its own vertical axis, like water flowing down a drain.

Hadley Cells, Ferrel Cells, and the Three-Cell Model

What Hadley had identified was the convection cell driving the circulation. He believed the equatorial air travels all the way to the poles, sinks there, and returns at low level, so there is one cell covering the entire Earth. We know now that the real situation is much more complex and that the rotation of Earth prevents the formation of a single, planetwide cell. What really happens is that in several equatorial regions warm air rises to a height of about 10 miles (16 km), moves away from the equator, cools, sinks between latitudes 25° and 30° N and S, and flows back to the equator as the surface trade winds. There are several of these convection cells and they are known as Hadley cells, in recognition of the man who came so close to describing them accurately in the course of explaining the trade winds.

Air over the poles is also sinking and flowing away at low level, forming a second system of cells. The Hadley cell circulation in the Tropics and the polar circulation drive a third, midlatitude set of cells, discovered by William Ferrel and known as the Ferrel cells. This is the central feature of the general circulation of the atmosphere.

Hadley cells

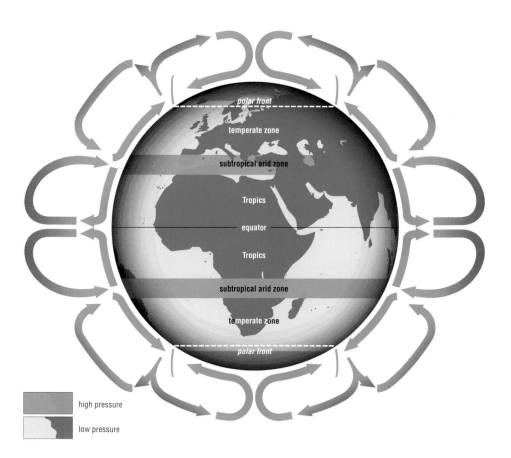

polar front
temperate zone
subtropical arid zone
Tropics
equator
Tropics
subtropical arid zone
temperate zone
polar front

high pressure

low pressure

It is called the three-cell model, and the figure on page 22 shows how the system works, the arrows indicating the direction of air flow. It is the mechanism by which air movements transport heat from the equator to the poles, although the meridional (north or south) movement of air is fairly weak, except in the Hadley cells.

Distribution of Pressure and Rainfall

The figure also indicates some of the consequences of this circulation. When air is warmed from below it expands and rises (page 24). This produces a region of low atmospheric pressure at the surface. As the air rises it cools, and as it cools its water vapor condenses, producing clouds and precipitation. In equatorial regions, where air is rising into the Hadley cell circulation, there is generally low surface pressure and a great deal of rain. That is why the Tropics are generally humid.

By the time it reaches its maximum height the air is very dry and very cold. It then sinks, on the descending side of the Hadley cells. As it descends it is compressed, and when air is compressed it grows warmer. It reaches the surface as warm, but still extremely dry air, and produces a region of generally high surface pressure in the subtropics. That is why a belt of hot, dry deserts circles Earth in the subtropics.

Not all the air on the descending side of the Hadley cells flows back toward the equator. Some spills the other way, toward the poles. In middle latitudes, this warm air flowing at low level away from the subtropics meets cold air flowing away from the poles. Where the two types of air meet there is a boundary, called the polar front. It is shown as straight line in the figure on page 22, but in fact it is wavy and moves with the seasons. It also produces the polar front jet stream (page 34), a very fast, high-level, westerly wind. Local areas of low pressure called depressions form beneath the jet stream and are dragged eastward by it.

The middle latitudes are where warm and cold air meet and complex weather systems move in a generally easterly direction in both hemispheres. Combine this with the overall weakness of the Ferrel cell circulation and the seasonal migration of the polar front and its jet stream, toward the equator in winter and toward the poles in summer, and it is easy to see why the temperate regions have such variable weather.

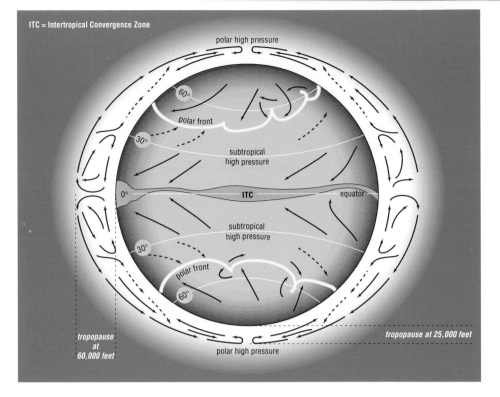

Global wind belts

In summer, the usual position for the polar front jet stream is across Washington, Montana, then slightly south across the center of Lake Michigan, and north again just to the south of the Canadian border. In winter it forms a wavy line from about Los Angeles, through northern Texas and to South Carolina. To the north of the front there is cold, polar air, and to its south there is warm, tropical air.

Wind Belts

Air moving toward the equator will be swung to the west, producing generally easterly winds, and air flowing away from the equator will be swung to the east, producing westerly winds. Over Earth as a whole, the easterly and westerly winds balance. It is as well that they do. Air moving over the surface experiences friction. This slows the wind, especially over land (which is why wind speeds are lower over land than over the sea), but it also reflects Earth in its rotation. Obviously, the effect is much greater on the winds than on solid Earth, but friction works both ways and, though small, the effect is real. If there were more westerly than easterly winds, gradually they would accelerate Earth's rotation, and if there were more easterlies than westerlies they would slow it. The

rate of rotation remains constant (or, at least, its variations can be explained in other ways), so we can be confident that the latitudinal winds balance.

They do so as wind belts, shown in the figure above with the arrows indicating the direction of prevailing winds. This diagram completes the picture. It shows the vertical circulation as actually more complex than the figure on page 22 suggests, and marks the position of the permanent areas of high pressure; low-pressure areas lie between the high-pressure areas. The ITC lies slightly north of the equator, with the easterly trade winds to either side of it. In midlatitudes, between the subtropical high-pressure region and the polar front, the prevailing winds are westerlies and in polar regions they are easterlies. The tropopause is the upper boundary to the lowest layer of the atmosphere, the "troposphere," which is where weather occurs (page 31).

The atmosphere works like a vast machine transporting heat and insulating the surface. It is this machine that produces our weather and, in the midlatitudes, the climates in which temperate forests thrive.

Evaporation, Condensation, and Precipitation

Imagine it is the middle of winter and you are standing at the edge of the forest looking across a frozen lake. Beneath the ice, the water is liquid and it will remain unfrozen all winter. Above the lake the air contains water vapor, invisible because it is a colorless gas. In the scene before you, ice, liquid water, and water vapor are all present in the same place at the same time.

We are quite used to this, of course. When you take ice out of the freezer and use it to cool a drink, water is present as solid, liquid, and gas simultaneously. Commonplace though it may be, however, this is really highly remarkable. There is no other substance that can exist in all three states at the same time at the temperatures and atmospheric pressures found at the surface of Earth. What is more, if water did not possess this unusual property our climates would be very different.

The Water Molecule and Density of Water

Water is hydrogen oxide, H_2O, its molecule comprising one atom of oxygen bonded to two atoms of hydrogen arranged at an angle of 104.5°, so there is hydrogen, carrying a positive electric charge, at one side of the molecule and negatively charged oxygen at the other. The hydrogen end of the molecule can then form a further bond with the oxygen of another molecule, as is shown in the figure on page 25. This is a hydrogen bond and it occurs only between molecules in which hydrogen is bonded to oxygen, nitrogen, or fluorine.

Heating makes water molecules move faster. Hydrogen bonds break and reform repeatedly, molecules move farther apart, and the liquid expands. Cooling makes the molecules move closer together, and the liquid contracts.

As water freezes, however, the angle between hydrogen atoms on the molecules widens, to 109.28°, and the resulting structure is rather open, causing the water to expand as it crystallizes into ice. Water reaches its maximum density at 39.2°F (4°C) and as the temperature falls to 32°F (0°C) and it freezes, its density decreases. That is why ice floats on top of water. Floating ice insulates the water below, by restricting the loss of heat into the air. Fish and other aquatic organisms are able to live in water protected by a layer of ice. If ice were denser than liquid water, so water froze at the surface and the ice sank, the lake would fill with ice from the bottom up and the plants and animals would be killed.

Latent Heat

Heat is a form of energy. When a substance is heated, its molecules absorb some of that energy and it makes them move faster. When liquid water is heated, its strings of molecules move faster and if it is heated enough the hydrogen bonds linking molecules into strings start to break. Eventually, with enough heat absorbed, some individual molecules will be moving so fast they are able to break away from the surface. This is evaporation, the change from liquid to gas, and it occurs only when water has absorbed enough energy to break the hydrogen bonds.

The absorbed energy does not alter the temperature of the water; all of it is used in breaking hydrogen bonds. It is called latent heat, and more latent heat is needed to vaporize water than to vaporize most substances. For pure water, it takes 597 calories of energy to change one gram (1 g = 0.035 ounce) from liquid to gas (2.5 x 10⁶ joules per kilogram).

Latent heat is also needed to change ice into liquid water, but less of it, because this phase change requires only some of the hydrogen bonds to break. Melting one gram of ice absorbs 80 calories (0.335 x 10⁶ joules per kilogram).

Water can also change directly from gas to solid or solid to gas, without passing through the liquid phase. This is called sublimation, and it requires 676 calories for each gram (2.83 x 10⁶ joules per kilogram), the sum of the latent heats of vaporization and melting.

A sufficient fall in temperature causes water vapor to condense into liquid, and liquid water to freeze. Hydrogen bonds reform, and exactly the same amount of latent heat is released as was absorbed in breaking them. That heat must come from somewhere, and it is taken from or transmitted to the surrounding medium. You can cool yourself on a hot day by bathing in cold water and allowing it to evaporate from your skin, because your body supplies the latent heat for its evaporation.

Vapor Pressure, Saturation, and Humidity

Whether water will evaporate or sublime depends partly on its temperature (though it will always evaporate if it is boiled) and partly on the air adjacent to it. Air is a material substance and, therefore, it has mass, and the gravitational attraction between the masses of the air and Earth gives the atmosphere weight. This weight is felt as atmospheric pressure: in effect, the weight of the air, all the way to the top of the atmosphere, pressing down on the instrument measuring it.

Air is a mixture of gases, however, each of which contributes to the overall pressure, and these can be considered separately, as the partial pressure exerted by a particular gaseous constituent of the atmosphere. Water vapor is one of the atmospheric gases. Its partial pressure is known as the vapor pressure.

At the surface of liquid water or ice, detached molecules are constantly leaving and entering the air. They exert a vapor pressure of their own, by pushing against the air, and water vapor already present in the air exerts a countervailing pressure, holding them down. The higher the temperature of the water or ice, the greater the vapor pressure from its surface, and the drier the air the lower its vapor pressure. When the vapor pressure in the layer of air immediately above the water or ice surface is higher than the vapor pressure exerted from the surface, water cannot pass through this layer to the air beyond and as many molecules return to the surface as leave it. The air above the surface is then said to be saturated, although strictly speaking it is the vapor that is saturated. If the vapor pressure from the surface is greater than the vapor pressure in the surface layer of air, that layer is unsaturated. Molecules will pass through it and the water will evaporate or, if it is frozen, sublime.

The word "surface" suggests the boundary between the air and a lake or the sea. That is a surface, of course, but the tiniest of droplets and ice crystals also have surfaces and they, too, have internal and external vapor pressures that determine whether or not they will evaporate or sublime. This becomes very important in the formation and dissolution of clouds.

How much water vapor air can hold varies according to the air temperature. Warm air can hold more than cold air, and as temperature rises the amount of water vapor the air can hold increases rapidly. Air at 104°F (40°C) can hold six times more water vapor than air at 50°F (10°C). The amount of water vapor present in the air as a percentage of the amount needed to saturate the air at that temperature is called the relative humidity (RH); the RH of saturated air is 100 percent.

Adiabatic Cooling and Heating

Chill an inflated balloon and it will shrink and the surface will wrinkle. Warm it and it will expand again. Warm it enough and it will burst.

The air inside the balloon expands and contracts as its temperature changes, but the quantity of air in the balloon—the number of molecules—remains constant. The molecules simply take up more or less space. This alters the air's density, because any given volume of air, say one cubic inch, contains more or fewer molecules.

Consider now what happens when air is warmed by contact with the surface of land or water. It expands, decreasing its density. It then weighs less than the air immediately above it and it rises.

As it expands, its molecules must push surrounding molecules out of the way and in doing so they expend some of their energy. They move more slowly, which is another way of saying the air cools. This cooling is called adiabatic, from the Greek *adiabatos,* meaning impassable, because no heat is exchanged between the cooling air and its surroundings.

Water molecule

When air is compressed, as it is when it moves into a region of denser air, it warms adiabatically, as its molecules move closer together and gain energy from the surrounding molecules that compress them.

Lapse Rates

When air is warmed at the surface, it rises and cools adiabatically by an average of 5.4°F every 1,000 feet (-14.8°C per meter). This is called the dry adiabatic lapse rate (DALR). The air will contain some water vapor, but how much it can hold depends on its temperature. There will be a height, called the condensation level, at which its temperature falls so low that it can no longer contain all the water vapor it has been carrying. This is its "dewpoint" temperature, at which water vapor will start to condense into liquid droplets and cloud will start to form. The condensation level will mark the cloud base, and above the cloud top the RH of the air will be low

enough for droplets to evaporate. If the condensation level is at the surface, the condensing water vapor will form mist or fog.

Condensation releases latent heat, warming the air, and once the relative humidity of the air reaches 100 percent, as it rises farther it cools at the saturated adiabatic lapse rate (SALR) of about 3°F per 1,000 feet (-16°C per km). These figures for the DALR and SALR are averages, and locally they can vary somewhat. The actual lapse rate, measured at a particular time in a particular place, is called the environmental lapse rate (ELR).

Condensation Nuclei

Water vapor will condense at a relative humidity as low as 78 percent if the air contains minute particles of a substance that readily dissolves in water. Salt crystals and sulfate particles are common examples. If the air contains insoluble particles, such as dust, the vapor will condense at an RH of about 100 percent. If there

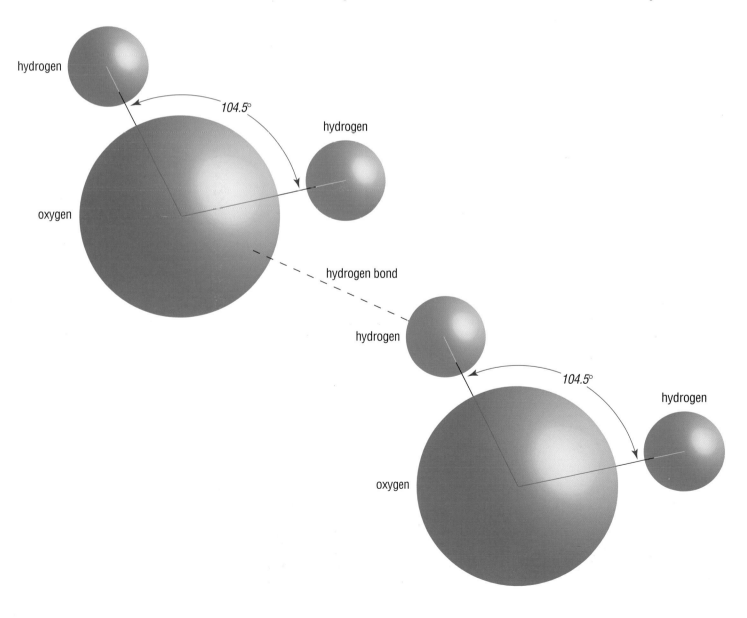

hydrogen

hydrogen

104.5°

oxygen

hydrogen bond

hydrogen

104.5°

hydrogen

oxygen

are no particles at all, the RH may exceed 100 percent and the air will be supersaturated, although the relative humidity in clouds rarely exceeds 101 percent.

The particles onto which water vapor condenses are called cloud condensation nuclei (CCN). Over land, each cubic inch of air contains an average of 82,000 to 98,000 CCN (5,000–6,000 per cubic centimeter); over the open ocean, they contain about 16,000 (1,000 per cubic centimeter). They range in size from 0.001 μm to more than 10 μm diameter, but water will condense onto the smallest particles only if the air is strongly supersaturated, and the largest particles are so heavy they do not remain airborne very long. Condensation is most efficient on CCN averaging 0.2 μm diameter.

Cloud Droplets and Raindrops

At first, water droplets vary in size according to the size of the nuclei onto which they condense, but an average cloud droplet has a diameter of about 20 μm. Inside the cloud, these start to fall. Their descent is slowed by the buoyancy of the air, updrafts, and friction, so their rate of descent, called their terminal fall velocity, is determined by subtracting the effect of retarding forces from the gravitational acceleration.

Small droplets fall so slowly that a gentle updraft will keep them airborne, and should they fall into the drier air below the cloud, they will evaporate long before they reach the ground. In order to reach the ground, the droplet must be much larger.

Drizzle consists of droplets about 300 μm in diameter, and an average raindrop has a diameter of about 2,000 μm. To become drizzle, a cloud droplet must increase its volume more than 3,000 times and to become a raindrop it must grow 10 million times bigger. In fact, they must grow even more than this, to allow for evaporation losses below the cloud. Complicating matters further, as droplets grow they also lose water by evaporation, because they are warmed by the latent heat of condensation that formed them.

What Makes It Rain

In middle and high latitudes, most clouds contain some ice crystals, even in summer. When the temperature at ground level is 60°F (15.5°C), at about 5,000 feet (1,525 m) in dry air it will be 32°F (0°C). Even when the ground-level temperature is 90°F (32°C), the air at 10,500 feet (3,200 m) will be at freezing temperature. In 1911 Alfred Wegener, who first proposed continental drift (page 9), suggested these ice crystals might play a crucial role in forming raindrops and his idea

formed part of a theory devised by the Swedish meteorologist Tor Bergeron and confirmed in 1935 by the German meteorologist Walter Findeisen. It is known as the Bergeron-Findeisen process, with no mention of the contribution made by Alfred Wegener.

Ice always melts when its temperature exceeds 32°F (0°C), but water does not always freeze at that temperature. Just as CCN are needed for water vapor to condense, ice nuclei are needed for ice crystals to form. Without them, water may remain liquid at much lower temperatures as supercooled water. In pure air it can be supercooled to -40°F (-40°C) before it freezes spontaneously.

Where both are present together, there will be many more supercooled droplets than ice crystals, because CCN are much more abundant than ice nuclei, of which there may be no more than one in every 6-0 cubic inches (1 per thousand cubic centimeters) of air at 14°F (-10°C). Over ice, the saturation vapor pressure is greater than it is over water, so water will freeze more readily onto ice than it will condense onto water droplets. Ice crystals will grow, but removing water vapor from the air lowers the relative humidity, and the supercooled water droplets will evaporate.

When an ice crystal is big enough it will fall, often gathering other crystals as it does so, to form snowflakes. Snowflakes form best at 23°–32°F (-5–0°C), because at these temperatures thin films of water coating the crystals freeze on contact, fixing the crystals together. The ice will melt if it enters warmer air lower in the cloud or below it, and fall as rain. Most of the rain falling in middle latitudes, therefore, in fact is melted snow, even in the middle of summer.

Warm Clouds

This is not the whole story, however, because there are also warm clouds, which contain no ice because their tops do not reach the height at which water freezes. In warm clouds, raindrops form by a "collision-coalescence" process.

Cloud droplets are not all the same size. They may average 20 μm in diameter, but some are smaller and others can grow by further condensation until they are up to 100 μm across. Large droplets fall faster than small ones, so a big droplet passes through a mass of small droplets and will collide with those directly in its path.

Colliding droplets may simply ricochet away from each other or, if they are about the same size, merge temporarily then break apart into smaller droplets. Where one droplet is much bigger than the other, and they collide more or less head-on, they will coalesce. Droplets must reach

a minimum diameter of 36 μm before they will coalesce. Those smaller than this are swept apart by the airflow surrounding them. Once coalescence starts, however, it accelerates and a drop can grow to a diameter of 400 μm within about 50 minutes. In most clouds, droplets grow big enough to fall as precipitation within an hour.

Between the Cloud Base and the Ground

Where the cloud base is high you often see trails or streaks extending from its underside. Called virga, this is rain or snow falling from the cloud and evaporating, because below the cloud, droplets enter unsaturated air and start to evaporate. They also enter warmer air in which ice crystals and snowflakes may start to melt. Water that survives long enough to reach the ground is called drizzle if the droplets are less than 0.02 inch (0.5 mm) in diameter and rain if they are larger.

Snow will fall only if the freezing level, the height below which the air temperature is above freezing, is lower than about 1,000 feet (300 m), and snow rarely falls when the air temperature near the ground is higher than 39°F (4°C). In warmer air the snowflakes melt before they reach the ground and at 34°–35°F (1–1.5°C) precipitation usually consists of a mixture of snowflakes and raindrops, known as sleet in Britain (in North America, sleet consists of ice pellets the size of drizzle droplets).

Any moisture passing from the air to the surface is called precipitation. Fog and mist are forms of precipitation; it is fog if it reduces horizontal visibility to less than 900 yards (1 km) and mist if the visibility is greater than this. Dew and frost are also types of precipitation, frost or rime ice forming when water vapor sublimes onto surfaces that are below freezing temperature.

Rain and drizzle are distinguished by the size of their liquid droplets. They may fall as supercooled droplets that freeze on contact with a surface. This is freezing rain or freezing drizzle and covers everything it touches with a coating of clear ice. This can cause serious damage to trees (page 47).

Snow, snow pellets, and snow grains are also distinguished by size. Snow pellets are usually spherical, bouncing and breaking when they strike hard ground, and 0.02–0.08 inch (0.5–2 mm) in diameter. If their diameter is less than 0.04 inch (1 mm), they are snow grains.

Hail comprises more or less spherical lumps of ice. They form by accretion in tall clouds, often storm clouds (page 41). Ice pellets are formed high in the cloud; they fall, and water condenses on them, which freezes as the pellets are carried upward by strong updrafts. This continues until the hailstones are too heavy to be carried aloft, so they fall from the cloud. The bigger the hailstones, the stronger the updrafts and the more violent the conditions inside the cloud. The manner of their growth gives them a layered structure, rather like the layers of an onion. Hailstones that are made partly from snow and therefore are soft, are called graupel.

Sometimes small ice crystals fall from clouds or water vapor sublimes into ice crystals in clear air outside clouds. This forms minute particles, called ice prisms or diamond dust, that hang suspended in the air and glitter as they catch the sunlight. Water vapor will sublime directly, without the presence of ice nuclei, if the temperature falls to -40°F (-40°C), and you will see ice prisms only when the air temperature is extremely low.

Transpiration

Enter a forest on a bright summer day, and the air will feel cool. There is no mystery about this. The trees cast shade, and you are no longer exposed to direct sunshine. If the sky is cloudy, however, the air will still feel cooler than the air outside the forest. The difference will be less, and will vary from one type of forest to another, but it is real. Scotch pine (*Pinus sylvestris*) forest in Italy is almost 6°F (3°C) cooler in August than the surrounding open countryside. Norway spruce (*Picea abies*) and beech (*Fagus sylvatica*) forests are almost 8°F (4°C) cooler.

It is true, of course, that even on an overcast day diffuse sunshine can deliver a considerable amount of warmth, but this cannot be the full explanation. Provided there is no wind, so shelter from the trees does not reduce wind-chill, forest air is cooler even in winter, although the difference between temperatures inside and outside the forest is only about half what it is in summer. Further-more, there are exceptions to the rule that, far from contradicting this curious phenomenon, support it. Maquis is a dense type of sclerophyllous vegeta-tion, with shrubs and forests that originally were dominated by holm oak (*Quercus ilex*), and there the summer temperature inside the forest may be as much as 4°F (2°C) higher than the temperature outside, although in winter it is about 1°F (.5°C) cooler. Maquis occurs in the Mediterranean region and there are similar vegetation types in southern California and South Africa.

Cooling by Evaporation

These marked temperature differences are due to the evaporation of water, which takes latent heat from the air. When it rains over a broad-leaved deciduous forest, the trees intercept on average nearly half the precipitation in summer, when the trees are in leaf, and nearly one-quarter of it in winter, when they are bare. Water coats leaves in the forest canopy and runs down the branches and trunks. Pine trees intercept about one-third of the precipitation, but this varies according to its intensity. When the rain is light they intercept almost all of it, but when it is heavy, four-fifths flows directly to the ground. All of the water wet-ting the trees evaporates, and this cools the air.

This explanation is less convincing than it seems. The same amount of rain falls outside the forest as inside, and it also coats the leaves of grasses and herbs. Obviously, being much smaller, they intercept less rain than trees, so more water reaches the ground, but much of it evaporates, just as it does inside the forest. In any case, rain cools the air even before it reaches the ground, because the raindrops are cool (most are melted snow, see page 26) and much evaporation occurs between the cloud base and the ground. What is more, the cooling effect in a forest persists undi-minished even when it is not raining and all sur-faces are dry.

Water Lifted by Plants

Some other factor must be at work, and it is. The plants themselves are removing water from the ground and releasing it into the air. The process is called transpiration. All green plants transpire

Sugar maple in late fall Mt. Battle, Maine (Gary Braasch/ENP Images)

water, but the amount is proportional to their size and trees transpire a great deal. An Old World silver (or common) birch tree (*Betula pendula*), bearing around 250,000 leaves, may transpire 95 gallons (360 liters) of water a day in summer. To calculate the amount transpired by a birch forest, simply multiply by the number of trees. A maple transpires about 53 gallons (200 liters) an hour. A German forest of Norway spruce has been found to return the equivalent of more than 13 inches (330 mm) of rain a year to the air through the combined effects of transpiration and evaporation from plant surfaces. The rate at which water is transpired by trees greatly exceeds the rate at which water would evaporate from an open surface, such as a lake, under similar conditions of temperature and relative humidity.

Not only do transpiration and evaporation from surfaces cool the air, they increase the relative humidity. Many years ago this effect was measured outside and inside a north Michigan forest of birch (*Betula*), beech (*Fagus*), and maple (*Acer*); the readings were taken at the same time every day over several months. From mid-June until early September, the relative humidity inside the forest was consistently higher than that outside. In European forests the average relative humidity over the year ranges, according to tree species, from about 4 percent to more than 9 percent higher than levels measured outside.

Transpiration moves water from the ground and releases it into the air, so it can occur only when water is available below ground. This explains the apparent anomaly of the maquis forest. There, the rain falls mainly in winter and the summer is very dry. Sclerophyllous plants adapt to the lack of soil moisture by greatly reducing their rate of transpiration. Consequently, air inside a sclerophyllous forest is warmer and drier than air outside, where the wind lowers the temperature.

Although evaporation from surfaces and transpiration are distinct processes, in practice it is impossible to measure them separately in the open. Measurements of transpiration are made under controlled laboratory conditions. Outdoors they must be measured together. Combined, they are called evapotranspiration.

Because of the water moving from the ground to the air by evapotranspiration, more cloud may form in the moister air above the forest than there would be otherwise, and some of the cloud will produce precipitation. If the forest is cleared over a large area, say for providing land for building or growing crops, the reduction in evapotranspiration can make the climate generally drier. Trees slow the wind by absorbing the energy from it, so forest clearance usually makes the climate windier. This will tend to dry the soil, because the rate of evaporation increases in proportion to wind speed (see page 170).

Water Transport in Plants

All living organisms need water. In plants it is used for photosynthesis (page 72), but this requires very little. More than 90 percent of the water entering a plant leaves it by transpiration. During summer, a broad-leaved tree leaf must replace all the water it contains every hour.

Water enters plants by passing into the cells of root hairs through the permeable membranes that coat them. Inside the root, mineral nutrients useful to the plant are allowed to pass through selectively permeable membranes. This movement, called osmosis, allows certain molecules to pass through the membrane from a strong to a weak solution and sets up a tension, drawing molecules through the membrane. As one moves it draws another behind it and another behind that. As molecules cross the selectively permeable membrane, the osmotic tension drawing them is transferred to the root hairs and from them to the film of water coating soil particles. Roots of some plants exert a strong force, of up to 220 pounds per square inch (15 kg/sq cm), others much less or virtually none, and the root system is able to shut down when necessary, sealing itself to prevent water flowing back into the soil.

Inside the tree, the water moves upward, against gravity, all the way to the topmost leaves. If the tree is a Sierra redwood (*Sequoiadendron giganteum*), this may be more than 300 feet (90 m) above the ground. Roots can draw water into the plant, but not to the topmost leaves. Even the most efficient mechanical vacuum pump can raise water no higher than 33 feet (10 m), so water must rise through a tall plant by some other means.

How Sap Rises

The water is not pushed as by a pump, but pulled from above, traveling through very narrow vessels that together make up the xylem. This water is the sap, which leaks when a stem is cut.

Leaves are covered with an impermeable skin, but one with microscopically small pores, called stomata (singular stoma), that can open and close by means of guard cells, which shrink or swell in response to changes in light intensity. The stomata open during the day and close at night, although a shortage of water can also make the guard cells close them during daylight. The density of stomata varies widely from one species to another, but many have about 200,000 per square inch (31,000 per sq cm) of leaf surface, most located on the underside.

Stomata open onto a network of air spaces in the mesophyll layer of the leaf, and it is through them that carbon dioxide is absorbed for photosynthesis. Oxygen, the by-product, is excreted. Photosynthesis is driven by sunlight, which is why stomata open during the day. They close at night when photosynthesis is impossible, to prevent further water loss.

The spaces in the mesophyll are coated with a film of water and the air in contact with them is saturated with water vapor. Outside the leaf, the vapor pressure is lower, so water is constantly evaporating from the mesophyll, through the stomata, and into the air.

As water evaporates through the stomata, molecules are lost from the film coating the mesophyll spaces. The remaining water is drawn by adhesion into small indentations in the cell walls, but attraction between water molecules resists any increase in the surface area of the water. This pulls the water into a bulge, or "meniscus." As the meniscus shrinks and becomes more spherical, its pull increases on molecules in the remaining film of water. These molecules are attached by hydrogen bonds to others, forming a link to the water in the xylem vessels and, through them, all the way to the roots as an unbroken chain of water molecules stretching from the leaf surfaces to the soil. Water molecules also adhere, but less strongly, to the walls of the xylem vessels.

In this way evaporation from leaf surfaces draws water through the plant at up to 30 inches (760 mm) a minute. The tension is so strong that it draws the walls of the xylem vessels inward, sometimes making a measurable difference in the thickness of a tree trunk.

Transpiration is an inevitable consequence of the need all cells have for water and the need plants have for stomata through which to exchange gases. The flow of water also transports mineral nutrients, and evaporation cools leaf surfaces. In very hot weather it can cool them by 20–30°F (6.6°–1.1°C), keeping their temperature below that at which the enzymes needed in photosynthesis are inactivated.

Air Masses and Fronts

Return for a moment to the lakeside you imagined in the last section, but suppose now that it is summer and a blazingly hot day. You can feel the Sun beating down on your body. Take off your shoes and the sandy shore of the lake will burn your feet. Plunge into the water, however, and it will feel cold, perhaps very cold. You may find this curious. After all, the lake is exposed to just as much sunshine as the dry land beside it. Somehow it just fails to warm up. If you visit the coast you will know the ocean behaves in precisely the same way, and if you live near the coast you may also know that, in early winter, the sea is warmer than the land.

Land heats up in summer much faster than the sea, and in winter it cools much faster. This greatly affects air passing over land and sea, which is warmed or cooled by contact with the surface. It is why the interiors of continents have much hotter summers and colder winters than coastal regions and islands, which receive air that has crossed an ocean and been cooled by it in summer and warmed by it in winter (page 50). The effect is due to the relatively high heat capacity of water.

Heat Capacity

The heat capacity (also known as specific heat capacity or thermal capacity) of a substance is the amount of heat required to raise the temperature of a unit mass of that substance by one kelvin (1 K = 1°C = 33.8°F). In scientific units, the unit mass is one gram (= 0.035 ounce) and the amount of heat is measured in joules (1 cal. = 4.186 J). The amount of heat required varies with temperature, so the temperature at which heat capacity is measured must always be stated. Water has a higher heat capacity than most substances, which means it absorbs a large amount of heat with only a small rise in temperature and releases all that heat as it cools.

The table above gives the heat capacity for a range of substances and shows that almost five times more heat is needed to raise the temperature of seawater by 1 K than it takes to warm rock (granite) or sand by the same amount. In some cases the figures are averages.

The amount of heat a surface absorbs is partly determined by its albedo (page 21), but when the Sun is high in the sky and its albedo is low, water absorbs more than any solid because it is transparent. About one-fifth of the solar radiation falling on the ocean penetrates to a depth of 30 feet (9 m) and turbulence in the water carries the warmed water much deeper. The oceans act as "heat sinks,"

partly because of the high heat capacity of seawater and partly because of their huge volume.

Continental and Maritime Air

Air is constantly on the move, traveling from west to east in middle latitudes. It crosses continents, oceans, and islands, but its journey takes time. Air leaving Asia takes days, or even weeks, to cross the Pacific before it reaches America. Then it takes more days to cross the American continent and several days more to cross the Atlantic before reaching Europe. During its travels, the air is in contact with the land or sea surface, and this changes it.

During World War I, Scandinavia was no longer able to receive reports from weather stations in other European countries, because information about the weather could be of use to an enemy (the broadcasting of weather forecasts also ceased in World War II, for the same reason). The difficulty for Scandinavians was solved by one of the most famous of all meteorologists, Vilhelm Frimann Koren Bjerknes (1862–1951). Born in Oslo, Bjerknes became a professor at Stockholm and Leipzig Universities, and in 1904 published *Weather Forecasting as a Problem in Mechanics and Physics.* This was one of the first scientific studies of weather forecasting. In 1917 he returned to Norway to found the Bergen Geophysical Institute. From there, he and his colleagues established a network of weather stations throughout Norway, and these fed information to the institute.

Studying these reports, from many scattered locations, led Bjerknes and his colleagues to consider in more detail how the atmosphere works to produce weather. In 1921 Bjerknes published *On the Dynamics of the Circular Vortex with Applications to the Atmosphere and to the Atmospheric Vortex and Wave Motion,* a somewhat unromantic title for his description of the conclusions they had reached.

These now form the basis of our understanding of climate and weather, and they begin with the concept of the "air mass." While it remains over a large land mass or ocean, in a high or low latitude, the air over a wide area acquires characteristics that are much the same throughout. Everywhere, the pressure, temperature, and humidity will vary little at the surface or when measured anywhere at any level above it.

Air masses are classified according to the "source regions" where they acquired their characteristics. Those forming over the ocean are called maritime (m), those forming over continents, continental (c), and the latitude in which

HEAT CAPACITY

Substance	Temp. (°F)	Heat capacity
dry air	68	1.006
ice	-6	2.000
ice	30	2.100
pure water	60	4.186
seawater	63	3.930
granite	68	0.800
granite	212	0.840
white marble	64	0.900
sand	68–212	0.800

they originate makes them tropical (T), polar (P), or arctic (A). The southwestern United States, for example, lies beneath a continental tropical (cT) air mass, but in winter the continental polar (cP) air mass that is over northern Canada in summer spreads to cover most of the land east of the Rockies as far south as Texas. Northwest Europe, ordinarily beneath maritime polar (mP) air, experiences warm weather in summer whenever maritime tropical (mT) air extends northward and bitterly cold weather in winter when cP air spreads westward from northern Siberia.

As an air mass moves away from the region where it formed, its characteristics change. Contact with the surface may warm or cool it. If it is heated from below, the warmed air rises, rapidly spreading the warming throughout the air mass and, at the same time, making the air unstable (page 38). When surface air is cooled, it sinks, becoming stable, but with a layer of warmer air some distance above the surface, which cools much more slowly by radiating its heat into space.

This affects the type of clouds that form and the weather they bring. Sheets of cloud (called stratiform cloud), bringing steady drizzle or rain, form in stable air and heaped clouds (called cumuliform cloud), bringing showers and storms, form in unstable air.

When air is warmed, it is able to hold more water vapor and if the warmed air crosses the ocean, water will evaporate into it. Warm, moist air will lose much of its water if it is cooled, and by the time it has crossed a continent it will be dry.

Fronts

Since an air mass occupies a defined area, it must have boundaries where it is adjacent to another air mass with quite different characteristics. You might suppose that where two air masses border one another, they will mix until there is a wide belt of air intermediate in character between the two. There is some mixing, but this is not really what happens. The border is up to 120 miles (190 km) wide, but compared with the size of an air mass this is narrow and it is quite clearly defined.

That is how it would remain, were it not for the fact that air masses move at different speeds. Cold air generally travels at up to twice the speed of warm air, so a cold air mass advances by pushing warm air ahead of it. There is conflict between the two. When Bjerknes and his colleagues were considering this, the stories in the newspapers were dominated by accounts of World War I battles, conflicts of a different kind. This is what led them to call the boundary between two air masses a front.

Air masses extend from the surface all the way to the tropopause. This is another boundary, between two layers of the atmosphere—the troposphere and the stratosphere. In the lower layer, the troposphere, temperature decreases with height. The rate of decrease, called the lapse rate, is fairly constant and averages about 3.5°F per 1,000 feet (6.5°C per kilometer). At the tropopause, the temperature reaches a minimum. This varies with the season, but usually averages about -60°F (-51°C) in summer and -90°F (-68°C) in winter.

Above the tropopause, in the lower stratosphere, the temperature either remains constant with height or, more usually, increases. This is a temperature inversion, where warm, less dense air overlies cooler, denser air. It prevents air from rising further by convection, so there is little exchange of air across the boundary, although huge storm clouds may penetrate it.

Surface temperatures are higher at the equator than at the poles, and there is more convection. Given the constant lapse rate, this means the height of the tropopause varies from an average of 10 miles (16 km) at the equator to 5 miles (8 km) at the poles, with local variations raising the tropopause higher above warm air and lowering it over cold air.

As air rises and cools adiabatically, its capacity for holding water vapor decreases and at the tropopause the air is very dry. Almost no water vapor enters the stratosphere.

Highs, Lows, and the Coriolis Effect

Cyclones and anticyclones are regions in which the atmospheric pressure changes over a horizontal distance to reach a minimum or maximum at the center. Where the pressure is low, air will tend to flow towards the center to equalize it, and where it is high air will tend to flow outward.

These are fairly large areas, up to 1,200 miles (2,000 km) across, and when air flows for a long distance north or south over the surface of Earth it does not move in a straight line, but follows a curved path. Places on the surface where the atmospheric pressure is the same are joined on weather maps by lines called isobars, and the wind flows approximately parallel to the isobars rather than across them, with a strength proportional to the distance between isobars. "Cyclone" is from the Greek *kuklos,* meaning "wheel" (from which we also get "cycle" and "bicycle").

The reason for the curved path was discovered in 1835 by the French engineer and mathematician Gaspard Gustave de Coriolis (1792–1843) and it is known as the Coriolis effect, abbreviated to CorF because the effect used to be called a force, although no force is involved. It is due to the rotation of Earth.

Because Earth is a sphere, its circumference is greater at low latitudes than at high latitudes. As the entire planet rotates, from west to east, a point on the equator travels faster than a point on, say, the Arctic Circle, because it must cover a greater distance in the same time. At the equator, a point on the surface is moving eastward at about 1,036 mph (1,668 km/h) and a point at latitude 50° is moving at about 666 mph (1,072 km/h).

A body of air moving away from the equator will be traveling at the speed of the equator, but the further it travels, the slower the surface beneath it will be traveling. This will cause it to "overtake" the surface in an easterly direction. Consequently, when air, water, or anything else not attached to the surface moves away from the equator, its path is deflected to the east. Bodies approaching the equator are deflected to the west for the same reason. The magnitude of the effect is proportional to distance from the equator, reaching a maximum at the poles, and also to speed of movement.

Pressure-Gradient Force and the Geostrophic Wind

Air is drawn toward a center of low pressure by the difference in pressure and with a force proportional to the rate of pressure change, or pressure gradient. This is called the pressure-gradient force (PGF). As it moves, however, the air is deflected by the Coriolis effect and a point is reached where the PGF and CorF balance and the air flows parallel to the isobars, in the Northern Hemisphere counterclockwise around centers of low pressure and clockwise around centers of high pressure. In the Southern Hemisphere these directions are reversed.

Any increase in either the PGF or CorF causes a balancing increase in the other. The resulting movement is called the geostrophic wind (from the Greek *geo,* "earth," and *strepho,* "to turn"). The geostrophic wind occurs only well above the ground, however, because near the ground the air movement is slowed by friction, and this causes it to flow slightly across the isobars.

On either side of a front between cold (high pressure) and warm (low pressure) air, therefore, air will be flowing in opposite directions and the advancing cold air will be moving beneath the less dense warm air. "Cold" and "warm" are relative terms, meaning only that one air mass is colder or warmer than the other. In summer, cold air with its associated high pressure can bring very hot weather. A front is named according to the air mass behind it. If cold air is advancing it is a cold front and if warm air is advancing it is a warm front.

Frontal Depressions

In middle latitudes, where weather systems are strongly influenced by the polar front jet stream (page 34), fronts tend to develop into frontal systems centering on a cyclone, or depression, and the diagram on page 32 illustrates the steps in this event. This is the sequence that produces the weather typical of middle latitudes, in which temperate forests thrive.

At first the front is straight, with air flowing in opposite directions on either side. Then (1) a tongue of warm air at the surface pushes into the cold air, forming a small wave in the front. Cold air moves around the crest of the wave (2) making it more pronounced and trapping a wedge of warm air. At the same time warm air rides up the slope of the cold front. Advancing cold air, on the left in the diagram, produces a cold front and warm air still pushing into the cold air, on the right in the diagram, produces a warm front.

It is now a frontal system. At the crest of the wave, where warm air is being lifted most strongly, a center of low pressure forms. This is the depression. Cold air continues to undercut and lift warm air until a substantial part of the warm air has been lofted clear of the ground (3). Once this happens, the fronts are said to be occluding.

On weather maps, representing the situation at surface level, a cold front is conventionally depicted as a line with triangles along it and a warm front as a line with semicircles along it. Where the fronts are occluding the triangles and semicircles alternate along the line marking the front. Finally (4) all the trapped warm air has been lifted well clear of the surface, above the cold air. The depression dissipates as the lofted air cools and reaches heights where its density is equal to that of the surrounding air, the frontal wave shrinks, and the front is more or less straight again.

From the first appearance of the frontal wave to the final dissipation of the occluded front, the process usually takes from four to seven days.

Weather Associated with Frontal Systems

Frontal systems are three-dimensional, and the drawing does not describe what you experience as one passes overhead. As the system approaches, you are in a region of (relatively) cold air. First the warm front arrives, with the region of warm air behind it, then the cold front, with cold air behind it.

Weather maps depict fronts as lines across the surface. These mark the surface position of the front and may give the impression that fronts are either confined to the surface or rise vertically from it. In fact, fronts slope, so the weather a front brings starts to arrive some time before the front itself crosses a point on the surface.

The diagram on page 33 shows a vertical cross section through the entire system, which is traveling from left to right (from west to east). The drawing distorts the true situation, because it grossly exaggerates the slope of both fronts, although it does show the cold front sloping more steeply than the warm front. This distortion

is unavoidable, because a diagram of the system that portrayed the frontal slopes to scale, with the tropopause three inches above ground level, would be about 40 feet (12 m) long.

Warm fronts slope very gently indeed, at an angle of $\frac{1}{2}$ –1°. Cold fronts have a steeper slope, of about 2°. When the point is directly overhead where the upper edge of a warm front meets the tropopause, its lower edge is meeting the surface more than 600 miles (950 km) away, and it will be many hours before it arrives. Similarly, when the

Development of frontal systems

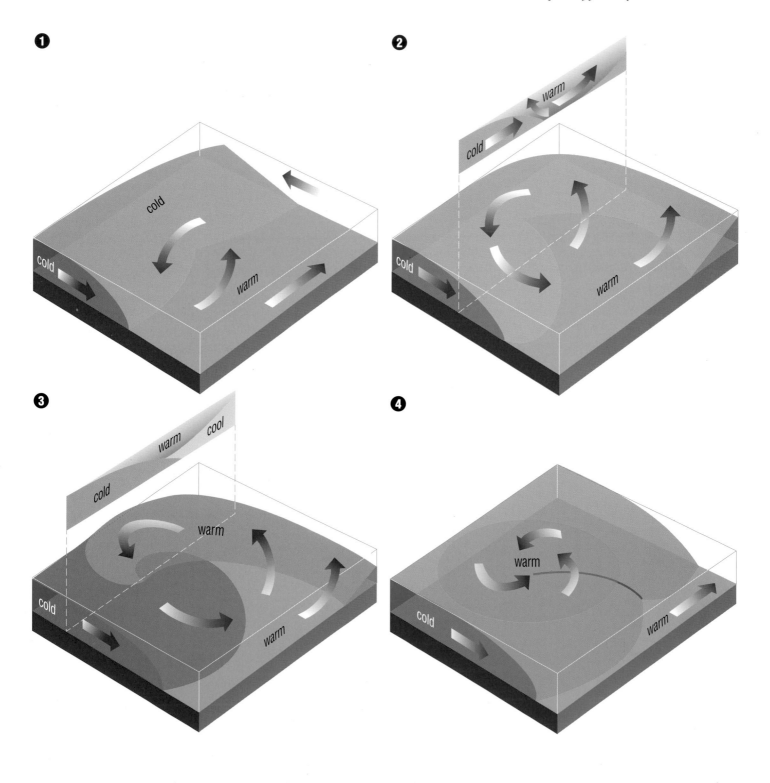

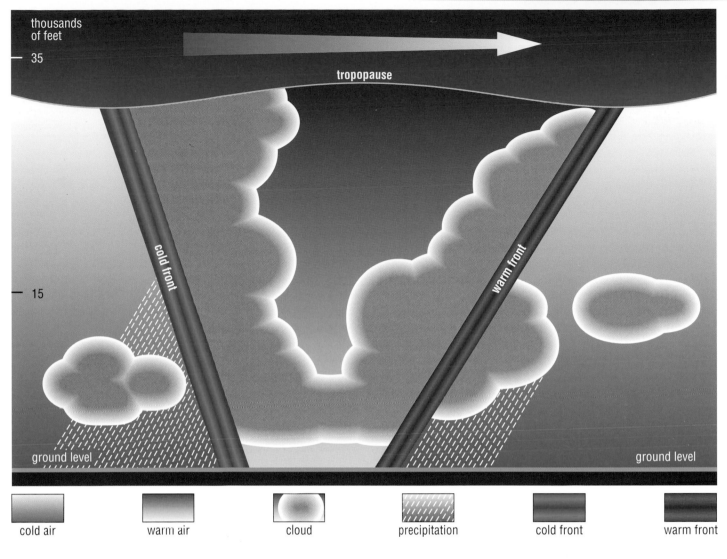

cold air	warm air	cloud	precipitation	cold front	warm front

Frontal system

cold front passes at ground level, it will be several hours before its upper edge, probably 200 miles (320 km) away, passes overhead and the front clears completely. Since a cloud forms as warm air is squeezed between the two fronts, if the warm-sector air is moist, the cloud may persist for quite a long time.

Depending on conditions in the warm sector behind the warm front (page 39), the first indication of its approach may be wispy, high-level cloud. This thickens steadily to cover more and more of the sky, and its base becomes lower. Precipitation begins when the warm front is quite near. A low cloud usually persists throughout the warm sector, but its type changes with the approach of the cold front, which passes more quickly.

Red Sky at Night

Water vapor condenses onto cloud condensation nuclei (page 25), minute particles that float in the air. In dry air, the particles float freely, most densely in the lower atmosphere, and behind a cold front the air is usually dry.

Gas molecules and these particles scatter sunlight in all directions, but short wavelengths are scattered more than longer wavelengths. When the Sun is low in the sky, so radiation passes at a shallow angle through a great depth of air holding many particles, the shorter wavelengths are scattered and absorbed, leaving only the longer orange and red wavelengths. This is why the sky is often red around dawn and sunset and it is also why a red sunset often heralds a fine day. It means the air to the west is dry. This is the direction of the sunset—and also the direction from which weather is approaching—and by the following morning the dry air will usually have arrived. It is one of the few items of weather folklore that is reasonably reliable. A red sky at dawn, on the other hand, is a less dependable sign. It means the dry air is to the east, but tells you nothing about conditions to the west, from where a frontal system may or may not be advancing.

The Polar Front and Jet Streams

During World War II, aircraft began routinely flying at high altitudes for the first time. There were flights in both directions across the Atlantic and, in particular, there were many American flights over the Pacific.

It was not long before aircrews flying near Japan started reporting something very strange. Crews found that some journeys took much less time than the navigator had calculated before take-off, some took much longer, and sometimes navigators had to make major inflight corrections in the direction they were flying to avoid having their aircraft carried miles out of their way. Similar peculiarities were reported in transatlantic flights, but it was near Japan that the effect was strongest.

It was the Norwegian meteorologist Jakob Bjerknes, son of the famous Vilhelm (page 30), who solved the puzzle. Close to the tropopause in certain places there is often a narrow belt of wind blowing at great speed from west to east. This wind came to be known as the jet stream. The map below shows how the jet stream affected airplanes flying near Japan, where the jet stream blows in both summer and winter and is especially strong, and how it sometimes affected flights across the North Atlantic, but had no effect on airplanes flying anywhere else.

It made a big difference to flight times. The jet stream often reaches speeds of up to 150 miles per hour (240 km/h) and in winter, when it is stronger, it sometimes blows at double that speed. A headwind with that force not only slows the aircraft, it may cause it to run short of fuel. Aircrews cannot rely on it always being there or be sure it will carry them in the direction they wish to fly. Also, there is more than one jet stream. Apart from the one shown in the map, known as the subtropical jet stream, there is a more variable polar front jet stream, and in summer an easterly jet stream blows over southern India. There are also others that appear locally from time to time and then disappear. Modern civil airliners try to avoid the jet stream altogether, by flying above it, in the stratosphere.

The Polar Front

You may notice that the track of the jet stream lies close to where equatorial air, on the descending side of the Hadley cells (page 22), meets cooler air, along a line that moves northward in summer and southward in winter. It is also close to the polar front. In fact, the polar front jet stream produces the strongest winds, but the subtropical jet stream is more constant, so the average position of the jet stream, which is what the map shows, is close to the position of the subtropical jet stream.

In summer the temperature difference between high and low latitudes decreases. This allows the front between polar and tropical air to move northward. In winter, as the polar regions cool, the front migrates towards the equator. Clearly, the jet stream is related to differences in air temperature.

Thermal Wind

The direction and strength of wind is determined by the balance between the PGF and CorF (page 31)—the steeper the pressure gradient, the stronger the wind. On a weather map the distance between isobars indicates wind speed; the closer together the isobars are, the stronger the wind. Well clear of the surface, where friction has no effect, wind speed increases and flows parallel to the isobars as the geostrophic wind.

Isobars indicate atmospheric pressure across a horizontal surface, but there is another way to think of them. On an ordinary map, contour lines are also drawn on a horizontal surface (the map itself) but they represent heights above the surface. You can use contour lines to map the landscape,

Jet stream

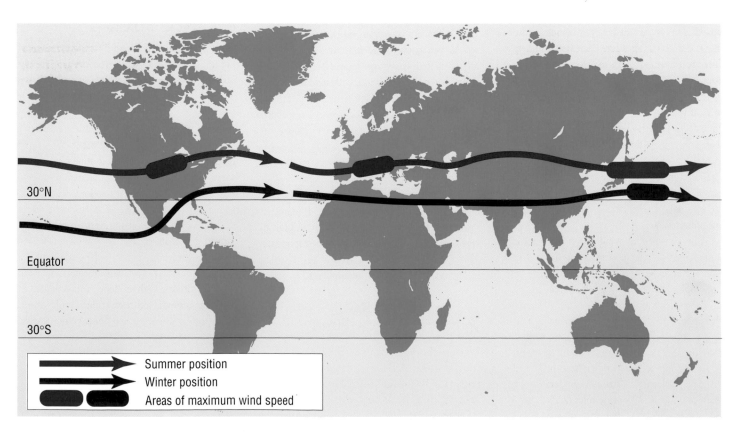

30°N

Equator

30°S

Summer position
Winter position
Areas of maximum wind speed

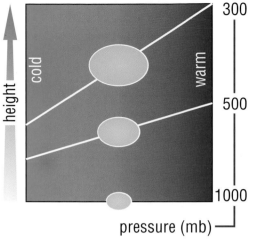

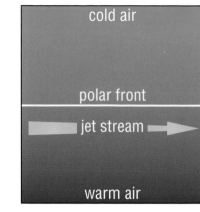

Pressure gradient

showing the hills and valleys. Isobars can be used in the same way. You cannot see the resulting hills and valleys in the sky, but it is possible to draw them. This makes it easier to see that pressure changes across gradients and that some gradients are steeper than others.

It is also possible to draw a vertical cross section that relates pressure to altitude. This reveals that above one place on the surface the pressure may be, say, 500 millibars at a certain height and nearby it is 500 millibars at a different height. Again, gradients appear, because the cross section cuts through an imaginary surface (called an isobaric surface) across which the pressure is the same everywhere.

Diagrams of this type reveal something that would not be immediately obvious without them: atmospheric pressure decreases with height faster in an area of high surface pressure than it does in an area of low surface pressure. In other words, the 500-millibar level is at a lower altitude in cold than in warm air. This happens because cold, dense air presses down with greater weight than warm, less dense air, and it compresses the lower air more, so that a larger proportion of the total amount of air is held at a low level. With increasing height, therefore, pressure decreases more rapidly than it does in warm air, which is less compressed.

The geostrophic wind blows with a force proportional to the pressure gradient, so if that gradient changes with height, so must the geostrophic wind. A cross-sectional diagram showing isobaric surfaces at various heights clearly reveals such changes in gradient. As the figure above illustrates, this gradient increases most across a front, where cold air lies to one side and warm air to the other. At some altitudes this can produce a horizontal temperature gradient of up to 1.5°F over 5 miles (2.7°C over 10 km), leading to a marked difference in the rate

at which pressure decreases with height. In the figure, the 500-millibar surface slopes less steeply than the 300-millibar surface and at still higher levels the gradient would be even steeper. The circles on each surface indicate the wind, their size increasing as wind speed increases.

What the diagram cannot do is identify air on one side as high-pressure and on the other as low pressure, because the lines are cross sections through isobaric surfaces, across which the pressure remains constant. Instead, one side is marked "cold" and the other "warm." The thickness of each layer of air is proportional to the mean temperature within it, and wind blows at right angles to the pressure gradient associated with changing temperature. For this reason it is called the thermal wind and in the Northern Hemisphere it blows with the cold air on the left; in the diagram the wind is blowing away from you, into the paper.

As you move away from the Tropics into higher latitudes, average temperatures decrease and it is the thermal wind, with cold air on the left in the Northern Hemisphere and on the right in the Southern Hemisphere, that generates high-level westerly winds in both hemispheres. It is at the subtropical and polar fronts, however, that the temperature gradient is most pronounced. The polar front, especially, marks a sharp boundary between polar and tropical air. Not surprisingly, that is where the thermal wind is strongest—its strength increases with altitude to reach a maximum just below the tropopause. These are the polar front jet streams, blowing from west to east in both hemispheres.

Vorticity and Rossby Waves

Except at the equator, air flowing over the surface tends to rotate about a vertical axis, due to the rotation of Earth. This is called its planetary vorticity and is equal in magnitude to the Coriolis effect (page 31). The air may also have "relative

vorticity" due to its motion. The sum of the two vorticities is called the absolute vorticity and, because of the conservation of angular momentum, it remains constant.

Major topographic features, such as the Rockies and the Tibetan plateau, deflect the flow of high-level air. If the air is deflected poleward its planetary vorticity increases, but its relative vorticity decreases to maintain a constant absolute vorticity. The decrease in relative vorticity swings the air toward the equator, but this increases its relative vorticity, decreases its planetary vorticity, and swings it back again. This sets up a series of very long waves along the jet stream. Between three and six complete waves (crest to crest) encircle Earth, each of them up to 3,700 miles (6,000 km) long.

In 1940 the Swedish-born American meteorologist Carl-Gustaf Arvid Rossby (1898–1957) showed that, when there is a certain relationship between their wavelength and the wind speed within them, the waves become stationary. They are then "standing waves," like the waves you can make in a rope when it is fastened at one end: when you move the other end up and down, the waves produced stay in the same places along the rope. They are called Rossby waves (and also occur in ocean currents). By convention, where the wave swings poleward it is said to form a ridge, and where it swings toward the equator it forms a trough.

Convergence, Divergence, and Weather Systems

As the jet stream flows toward a trough, it is turning in a counterclockwise direction, just like the wind around a cyclone, causing air to be drawn into it. This is called convergence. Pressure increases where air converges, and high-level convergence produces higher pressure at the surface. Approaching a ridge, the jet starts turning clockwise, and this causes air to flow out of it, or diverge. Divergence produces a region of low pressure, air is drawn up from below to replace it, and a region of low pressure is produced at the surface. As the figure at the bottom of page 36 shows, this leads to the formation of frontal weather systems. In fact, it is the main cause of the formation and movement of such systems in middle latitudes, with cyclones (or depressions) forming beneath jetstream ridges, cold fronts ahead of troughs, and warm fronts behind ridges. In the figure, the thick, wavy line represents the jet stream, flowing from left to right, and cold and warm fronts are marked with triangles and semicircles respectively.

There are exceptions to this pattern, but it is often accurate. The figure at the top of page 36

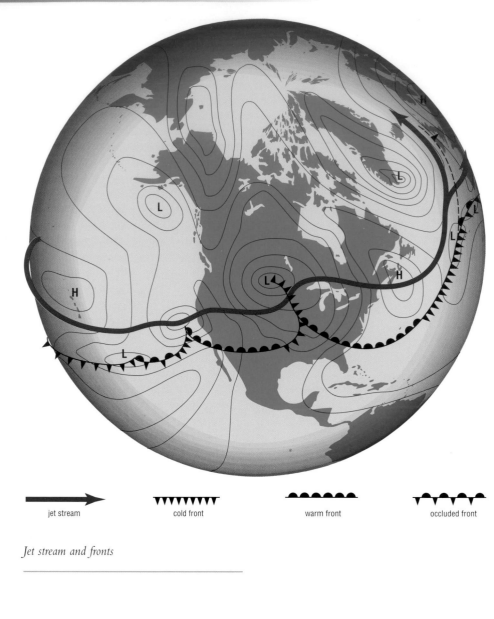

Jet stream and fronts

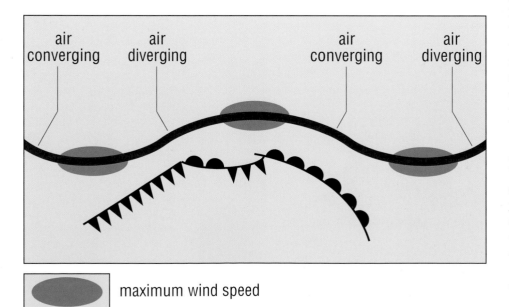

maximum wind speed

Divergence

shows how it affects conditions at the surface. The figure is a typical weather map, but with the jet stream added (and dividing into two in the east). There are cyclones (marked *L*) close to the jet-stream ridges and anticyclones (marked *H*) close to the troughs. The map, with the jet stream in its summer position, suggests that the Canadian prairie provinces and the central northern states are experiencing wet, windy weather, but there is fine weather over eastern coastal regions and fine, warm, settled weather is approaching from the Pacific.

Weather systems move, which is how we can be sure that within a day or two the bad weather over central North America will have given way to the cloudy, but probably dry and calm weather approaching as a weak trough, and it will not be long before the arrival of fine weather presently over the Pacific. It is this constant movement of weather systems that makes midlatitude weather so changeable and difficult to forecast. Frequent change also ensures that precipitation is distributed fairly equally through the year. It is what produces the climate in which temperate broad-leaved deciduous and coniferous forests flourish.

When Weather Systems Stand Still

That movement is also driven by the jet stream, which produces the systems, at a speed roughly equal to 70 percent of the speed of the geostrophic wind in the warm air (behind the warm fronts). Commonly, weather systems travel eastward at about 20 miles per hour (30 km/h) in summer. In winter, when the north-south temperature gradient is stronger, they move at about 30 miles per hour (50 km/h).

There are times, however, when the weather seems to stick. Warm, dry conditions may persist long enough in summer to produce drought, which can cause severe damage to trees (page 47). Clear, cold, windless days can follow one another for weeks in winter. Alternatively, rain in summer and snow in winter can continue day after day and seem endless. When this happens, and a particular type of weather is prolonged, it is often because of changes in the jet stream.

Inefficient heat transfer allows warm air to accumulate in the Tropics. High-latitude air becomes relatively cooler, and steadily the north-south temperature gradient grows steeper and the jet stream stronger. Eddies then start to develop along the polar front, some cyclonic, with wind circulating counterclockwise around cyclones, others anticyclonic, with wind circulating clockwise around anticyclones. This leads to major changes in the jet stream, culminating in its temporary breakdown.

West-to-east airflow is called zonal flow, and the state of the upper-level westerly winds is measured by an "index cycle" related to an index of zonal flow, called the zonal index. The figure below shows, in a very simplified form, the main stages in the index cycle.

At first (1) the flow is strongly zonal, with Rossby waves of small amplitude (distance between trough and crest at right angles to the direction of flow). The amplitude of the waves increases (2) and eventually becomes extreme (3). At this stage, the overall airflow is still from west to east, but along a wavy path that in places flows from the northwest and in others from the southwest. Finally (4) the flow breaks down into isolated cyclones (the two lower circular patterns, where the wind flows counterclockwise) and anticyclones (the upper pattern, with a clockwise flow). After that, the energy of motion (kinetic energy) of the eddies is transferred to the overall flow, and the strongly zonal flow reestablishes itself.

The cycle usually starts in a particular place, then moves westward (in the opposite direction to the zonal flow) at about 60° of longitude a week, the entire cycle taking from three to eight weeks to complete. Its effects are less marked in summer than in winter, because in winter the temperature gradient and jet stream wind speed are at their highest.

Remember that the polar front separates cold, arctic air from warm, tropical air and this separation produces typical weather. Across North America, the weather is colder north of the front than it is to the south. Air reaching America across the Pacific loses most of its moisture as it crosses the Rockies, bringing dry conditions to the continental interior. As the index cycle develops, however, cold air is drawn southward and warm air northward.

This compensates for the deficiency in heat transfer of the Hadley cell circulation, but it can cause dramatic changes in weather. Bitterly cold, arctic air can be carried far to the south and mild, tropical air far to the north. It is not unknown for temperatures to change from record lows to record highs in the space of a week and the sudden arrival of arctic air can produce a cold wave. That is a sudden drop in temperature over 24 hours that may necessitate emergency measures to protect people and farm animals. It can also cause great distress to wildlife.

Blocking Anticyclones

Stage 4 of the index cycle isolates huge eddies of air, usually about 900 miles (1,450 km) in diameter, which can remain motionless and persist for days or even weeks. Deep, cold cyclones form to the south, producing wet, windy conditions. To the north, anticyclones bring generally dry weather.

As the zonal flow resumes, these eddies survive for a time and the anticyclones, because they are stationary with respect to the surface, block the passage of weather systems, which are diverted around them. This produces prolonged spells of anticyclonic weather and can contribute to the development of drought, while at the same time exposing areas north or south of the block to frontal systems that might otherwise miss them. Each individual blocking anticyclone may last for only a short time, but repetitions of the index cycle can occupy a substantial part of a summer or winter; their cumulative effect is considerable.

At present it is impossible to forecast the index cycle. It may be that the zonal flow becomes unstable as its speed increases and this triggers the breakdown, but no one really knows. Nor do climatologists understand what drives weather cycles that operate over longer periods, of years and decades.

What is clear is that the climates of temperate zones, marked by the eastward progress of frontal systems and a westerly air flow, are largely produced by the jet stream and that the jet stream is a consequence of the large-scale convective mechanism by which heat is transferred from low to high latitudes. This explains the great changeability of mid-latitude weather, one result of which is the distribution of precipitation fairly evenly through the year. It also explains some of the prolonged spells of weather that occur periodically when the westerly flow temporarily breaks down, due to a weakness in the convective mechanism. It is the jet stream that causes the conditions to which temperate forests are adapted, and the index cycle that can radically alter those conditions.

Index cycle

Weather Systems

When air is warmed it expands, its density decreases, and it exerts less pressure at the surface. When it is cooled it contracts, becomes denser, and exerts a greater pressure. The difference in densities prevents air masses from mixing. Warm air rides above cold air, and cold air undercuts warm air and lifts it clear of the ground. This is how the battle of the air masses is fought at fronts between them.

The battle usually produces clouds and precipitation along fronts and around a depression or, more technically, a cyclone. "Cyclone" is the meteorological name for an area of low pressure. The fierce storms that are also called cyclones are an extreme version occurring only in the Tropics, so they are known as "tropical cyclones" (page 40). There are also "extratropical cyclones." These, too, are ferocious storms that form around areas of low pressure, but in the Arctic, along the edge of the sea ice. An area of high pressure is known as an anticyclone.

Clouds form when air is cooled below its dew point temperature (page 25) and they are cooled by being made to rise. Cold fronts force warm air to rise. Air also rises as it crosses high ground, often producing a dry region in the "rain shadow" on the downwind side of a mountain range. In North America, the climate east of the Rockies is drier than that to the west for this reason.

Sometimes the flow of air across a north-south mountain range produces a "lee depression," as air moving down from the ridge diverges and starts turning counterclockwise (cycloni-cally). Strong heating of the surface in summer also causes air to rise and clouds to form, and if the rising air starts turning cyclonically it will produce a "thermal depression." Intense heating is needed to produce a thermal depression, however; they form in Arizona, but rarely in forested regions.

Temperate forests are sometimes affected by polar depressions. These develop in the North Pacific or North Atlantic when unstable maritime air moves south from polar regions along the eastern side of a long north-south ridge of high pressure. No more than about 600 miles (1,000 km) across, they are much smaller than frontal depressions, but can be very intense and bring severe weather.

Stable and Unstable Air

Clouds are of different types, classified by their appearance, and also as "high," "medium," and "low" by the height of their bases. The height at which clouds start to form depends on the humidity of the air. Relatively dry air must be lifted higher than relatively moist air before its water vapor starts to condense. Which type develops depends on the stability of the moist air.

Suppose air is forced to rise, for whatever reason. As it rises it will cool adiabatically (page 25). The temperature of the air surrounding it also decreases with height, but not necessarily at the same rate. Measure the air temperature at the surface (for example 50°F, 10°C) and at any height above the surface (call it 15°F at 10,000 feet, -9°C at 33 km) and the rate of cooling is 3.5°F per 1,000 feet (50 - 15 = 35; 35 ÷ 10 = 3.5), or -15.8°C per kilometer. This is the environmental lapse rate (ELR).

Air moving across the ground may start warmer, however, say at 60°F (15.5°C), and as it rises it will cool at the dry adiabatic lapse rate (DALR) of 5.5°F per 1,000 feet (9.8°C per kilometer). At 5,000 feet it will be at 32.5°F (5.75°C at 1 km), which is the same temperature as the surrounding air and it will rise no further. If water vapor is condensing in moist air, it will cool more slowly, at the saturated adiabatic lapse rate (SALR) of 3°F per 1,000 feet (6°C per kilometer) and, as the graph below shows, it will still be warmer than the surrounding air by the time it reaches the tropopause.

In the graph showing the ELR, DALR, and SALR, lines above the ELR line represent air that is warmer than surrounding air at that height and lines below the ELR represent air that is cooler. In the real world, of course, rising warmed air will start to cool at the DALR, then water vapor will start to condense and its rate of cooling will slow to the SALR.

Rising air that cools more slowly than the ELR is said to be unstable. At any given height it will be warmer than its surroundings and will continue to rise. Stable air cools at the same rate as, or faster than the ELR, so it reaches a height

Air temperature

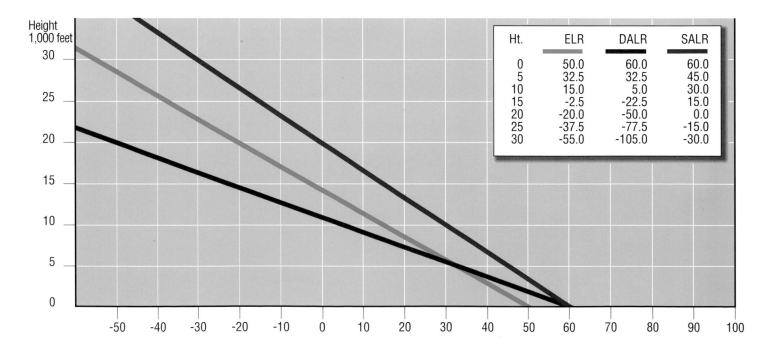

Ht.	ELR	DALR	SALR
0	50.0	60.0	60.0
5	32.5	32.5	45.0
10	15.0	5.0	30.0
15	-2.5	-22.5	15.0
20	-20.0	-50.0	0.0
25	-37.5	-77.5	-15.0
30	-55.0	-105.0	-30.0

Height 1,000 feet

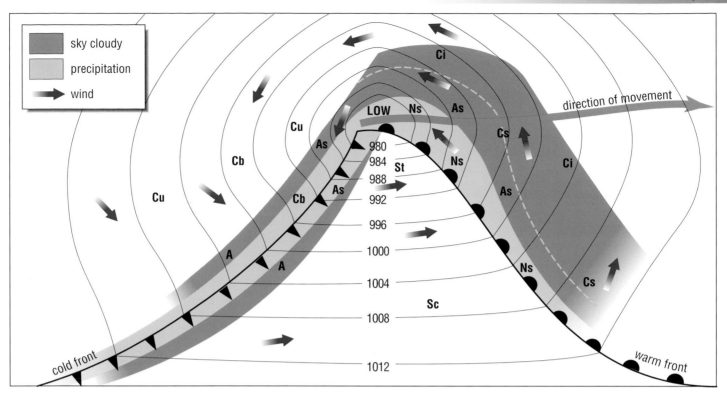

Frontal depression

at which it can rise no farther and it may start to sink. This affects the type of cloud that forms and the weather associated with it.

Frontal Cloud

In a frontal depression, of the kind that produces most midlatitude weather, a wedge of warm air is trapped inside colder air. This air may be stable or unstable. If it is stable, it will rise ahead of a cold front to only a limited extent, then sink again to its former level behind the front. A front of this type, called a kata-front, produces very little weather, although clouds may form along it. Unstable warm air will rise vigorously along a cold front, in this case called an ana-front (the Greek *ana* means "up," *kata* means "down"), and the frontal system will produce a great deal of precipitation.

As the cold front advances, warm air is lifted. This reduces the surface atmospheric pressure in the warm-air sector. Air converges to fill it, starts turning cyclonically (page 31) and a cyclone, or depression, forms. The system is now a frontal depression, comprising a warm front, a warm sector, and a cold front. The figure above shows such a depression as it is represented on weather charts. The shape is familiar from newspaper and television weather forecasts, but here the isobars are labeled with their pressures and the direction of movement and areas of cloud and precipitation

are shown. These indicate that both fronts are ana-fronts. If either was a kata-front, it would produce less high cloud, and cloud would not extend so far ahead of the warm front.

A warm front has a very gentle slope, of about $\frac{1}{2}$ –1°, which is between approximately 1:130 and 1:60. Air is forced to rise up it by the advancing cold front, but the rise is very gentle. The first air to rise along a warm ana-front is raised all the way to the tropopause. Its water vapor forms minute ice crystals spread by the wind into thin wispy cloud called cirrus (Ci in the figure). The appearance of cirrus is often the first indication of an approaching warm front.

Behind it, the cloud spreads to cover most of the sky, but still as a thin sheet of ice crystals through which the Sun remains clearly visible if slightly pale. This is cirrostratus (Cs). "Stratus" is cloud that forms a level, featureless sheet; "cirro-" means it is at high level. The advancing front brings the cloud base lower, but the type of cloud remains the same.

Cirrostratus gives way to medium-level alto-stratus (As), through which the Sun is barely visible as a pale disk with indistinct edges, and this is followed by nimbostratus (Ns), obscuring the Sun and with a base at a still lower level. Precipitation begins as the nimbostratus arrives.

Along a warm kata-front, the cloud is of a more heaped, cumulus type, but the cloud top is much lower, often reaching no higher than 10,000 feet (3 km). By the time stratocumulus (Sc) appears, blanking out the Sun completely, the front is already quite close, and precipitation usually begins at once.

Behind the warm front lies the warm sector, containing the wedge of warm air. There the sky is completely covered by low stratocumulus and stratus (St) cloud, but the layer of cloud is not deep, and it produces little or no precipitation.

The cold front moves at about double the speed of the warm front and is about twice as steep. It "shovels" warm air upward, and if it is an ana-front, this produces heaped (cumulus-type) cloud mixed with the layered cloud. The cloud extends all the way to the tropopause and it can include cumulonimbus (Cb), which produces very heavy showers, often with thunder and lightning.

As the front passes, which it does fairly quickly because of its speed, breaks start appearing in the clouds. These grow bigger, until what had been fairly continuous precipitation gives way to increasingly isolated showers interspersed with fine intervals.

A cold kata-front produces stratocumulus, which is dense but not deep, and there is no cumulonimbus, a cloud that can form only in unstable air. The precipitation is continuous for a short time, but not unduly heavy and there are no thunderstorms.

When the depression has passed, there is usually a spell of fine weather associated with the cold air mass, but it does not last. Except when blocking breaks the pattern, midlatitude frontal depressions tend to occur in "families" of three or four along the ridges in the jet stream (page 36), each cold front extending to the southwest and joined at its end to the next warm front, all of them being carried eastward by the general westerly airflow.

Extreme Weather: Hurricanes, Tornadoes, Drought

Hurricanes

Not all depressions are associated with fronts—one type of nonfrontal depression brings the most savage weather known. Technically it is known as a tropical cyclone. More familiarly, tropical cyclones that form in the North Atlantic are called hurricanes, those that form in the Pacific are typhoons, and those that form in the Bay of Bengal are cyclones. They also go by other local names: in Australia, for example, a storm of this type, arriving from the Pacific, is sometimes called a willy-nilly.

Tropical cyclones can be several hundred miles in diameter, with a central "eye" up to 40 miles (65 km) across, and they pack the energy of thousands of atomic bombs. All of them form in the same way and bring the same kind of devastation. We usually think of the damage they do in terms of buildings destroyed and people injured by flying debris, of wind and floods caused by torrential rain and storm surges, but they cause just as much destruction in the countryside. Hurricanes can demolish large areas of forests, and sometimes they do.

As their name suggests, tropical cyclones occur only in the Tropics, but once formed they often move out of the Tropics. In North America they can travel as far as New England and, occasionally, even to eastern Canada, and from time to time one will cross the Atlantic as far as northwest Europe. Outside the Tropics, these cyclones weaken, but their original energy is so great that even when weakened they remain capable of causing severe damage, and they can regain some of their lost strength in their passage across the ocean if they meet and combine with frontal depressions.

In the Tropics, the prevailing winds are easterlies. These carry the storms westward. As they move, they accelerate, and swing away from the equator, to the right in the Northern Hemisphere and left in the Southern, along a curved path around the subtropical region of permanent high pressure and into the westerly airflow of middle latitudes. This produces the typical Atlantic hurricane track, carrying hurricanes across the Caribbean, northward up the east coast of the United States, then out into the Atlantic again. Some remain over the sea, out of harm's way, but others move further west, through the Gulf and northward overland through the Carolinas.

They travel at 10–15 miles per hour (16–25 km/h) and, because they are moving, wind speeds around them vary. As the figure below shows, to the right of the eye, facing in the direction the storm is moving, the speed of the storm adds to that of the wind and to the left of the eye it reduces it. If the average wind speed is 130 miles per hour (210 km/h) and the storm is moving at 12 miles per hour (20 km/h), the actual wind will blow at 142 miles per hour (230 km/h) to the right of the eye and 118 miles per hour (190 km/h) to the left.

Structure of a Tropical Cyclone

A fully developed tropical cyclone covers an area of up to 20,000 square miles (52,000 sq km) and its clouds tower to more than 40,000 feet (12 km). Above the center, pressure is high and air sinks from there into the eye, warming adiabatically as it descends, adding to the warming by the release of latent heat from clouds surrounding the eye.

In the eye, winds are light and there are few clouds. Surrounding the eye there is a wall of towering cumulonimbus cloud producing torrential rain, usually accompanied by thunder and lightning. Air is rising rapidly inside the cloud and being swept out and away at the top. It is here, in the wall surrounding the eye, that wind speeds reach their maximum. Beyond this wall of cloud there is a region free from precipitation, where the cloud base is high, often at around 20,000 feet (6 km). Still farther from the eye, the cloud base descends again and the rain resumes.

Seen in cross section, as in the figure on the next page, the storm appears as distinct towers of cloud on either side of the eye. From above, these can be seen as spiral bands. Air rises by convection in the clouds and some sinks from the high-level anticyclone in the regions between bands. At the edges of the tropical cyclone, the upper cloud is predominantly cirrostratus and the lower cloud cumulus, but there may be up to 200 towering cumulonimbus storm clouds closer to the center.

A tropical cyclone can survive only while it has access to an unlimited supply of warm, moist air at the surface. Once it crosses a coast, the air

Hurricane

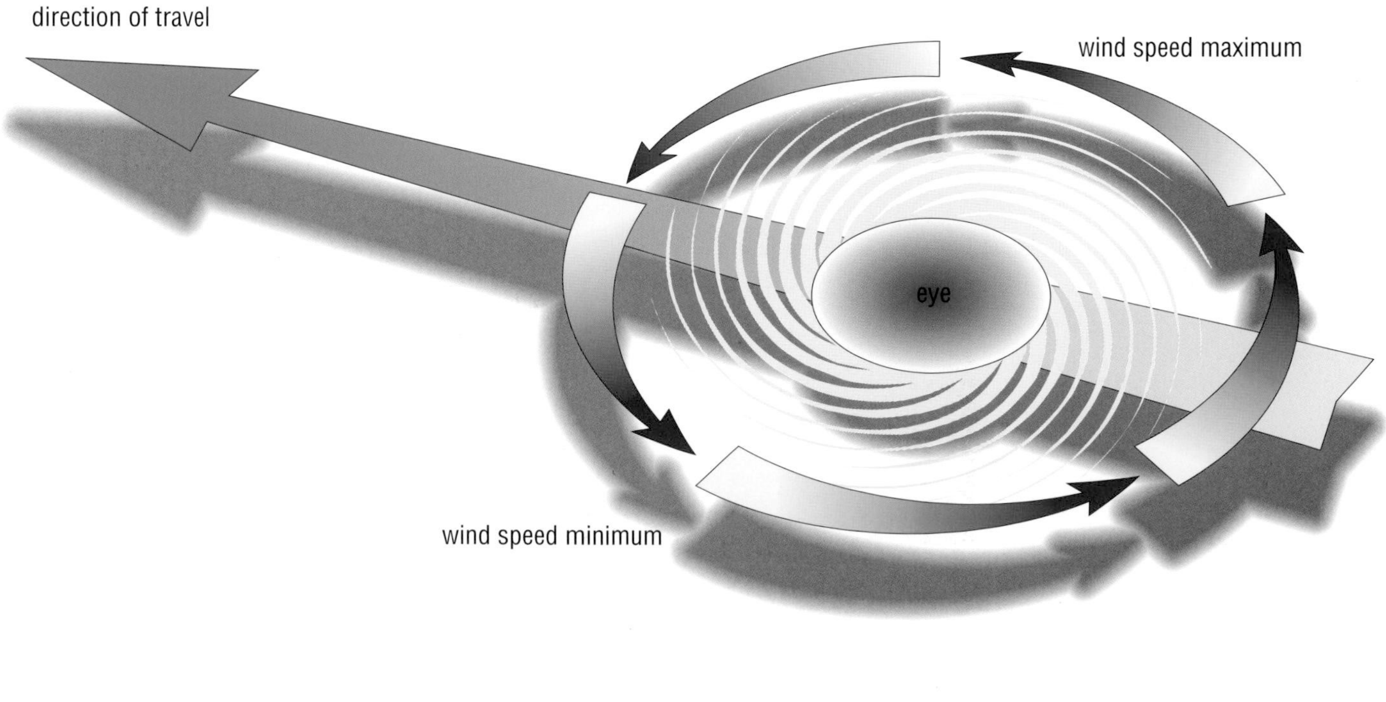

direction of travel

wind speed maximum

eye

wind speed minimum

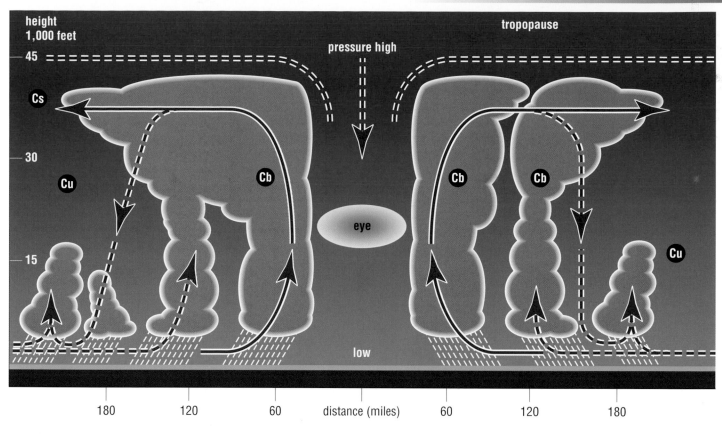

height
1,000 feet

tropopause

pressure high

45

Cs

30

Cu

Cb

Cb

Cb

eye

15

Cu

low

180   120   60   distance (miles)   60   120   180

Tropical cyclone

feeding it is much drier. If it remains at sea, as it moves out of the Tropics it crosses colder water. Dry air and a cool sea both weaken it, and few tropical cyclones last more than a few days. This does not mean they cease to be dangerous, because they weaken from tropical cyclones to tropical storms. The air in the core is then cool rather than warm and wind speeds decrease, but a tropical storm is still extremely large and severe. They produce large amounts of rain and winds of gale force that can do considerable damage.

Extratropical Cyclones

As well as tropical cyclones, there are also extratropical cyclones. These are also circular systems, with bands of cloud containing cumulonimbus and a more or less cloud-free eye. Only a few hundred miles in diameter, they are smaller than tropical cyclones and their winds usually reach no more than about 45 miles per hour (72 km/h), with gusts to 70 miles per hour (112 km/h).

They form near Antarctica and in the North Pacific and Atlantic, at fronts between very cold and much warmer air. These can form where continental polar air from North America meets maritime tropical air warmed by the Gulf Stream and extending unusually far north, or where a low over the sea draws in extremely cold air,

often at -40°F (-40°C), from above adjacent sea ice, producing a temperature difference that can reach 70°F (21°C).

Extratropical cyclones develop rapidly and travel at up to 35 miles per hour (55 km/h). Like tropical cyclones, they dissipate rapidly when they cross land, but they last long enough to bring heavy falls of snow driven by fierce winds, and they are quite strong enough to bring down trees.

Tornadoes

Tornadoes also consist of rapidly rotating air, but "twisters" are produced by a mechanism quite different from that which generates tropical cyclones. Most, but not all, are associated with violent thunderstorms. They occur in all parts of the world, but the Great Plains of North America experience far more of them than any other region.

When a tornado sweeps through a town it leaves a trail of destruction. When one sweeps through a forest there may be no one to observe it, but a winding swathe of dead and injured trees, some uprooted or snapped in two, others stripped of their branches and leaves, marks its passing, and the storm that spawned the tornado often harms trees over a wider area.

Thunderstorms and Squall Lines

Thunderstorms develop in very unstable air. The condensation of water vapor in air rising convec-

tively releases latent heat to drive further lofting and the resulting cumulonimbus cloud towers to a great height. Within it, ice crystals near the top acquire a positive electric charge and hailstones and larger water droplets at a lower level acquire a negative charge. The low-level negative charge can then induce a positive charge at the ground surface. Lightning occurs, with the sudden and violent heating of air that causes the explosive expansion we hear as thunder, when sparks flash between these separated charges.

Inside the cloud, the vertical air currents are violent, moving at 20–70 miles per hour (30–112 km/h), and in both directions. An airplane flying through such a storm is alternately lifted and dropped with enough force to cause structural damage.

The internal circulation forms a convection cell. Warm air rises, cools, and descends. When precipitation starts, snow, hail, or rain close to freezing temperature falls from the cloud base. This drags air with it, cooling it at the same time, causing a strong downdraft of cold air beneath the cloud. As this strikes the ground it spreads and interferes with the inflow of air feeding the updrafts. The downdrafts come to dominate and precipitation deprives the cloud of moisture. Then the convection cell breaks down, the storm dies away, and the cloud dissipates. Ordinarily this takes no more than an hour or two, which is the lifetime of a typical storm cloud.

Storms can become much more extensive, however, when they form a little way ahead of a cold kata-front. The front, advancing into warmer air, causes sufficient lifting to trigger instability and produce a line of thunderstorms. This is called a squall line. It can extend for hundreds of miles and, driven by a strong high-level wind, it moves across the ground at up to 45 miles per hour (70 km/h).

The life of an individual storm cloud is brief, but along a squall line as one dies the cold downdraft that spreads beneath it and chokes the inflow of air also lifts warm air nearby. This air also becomes highly unstable and forms a new storm cloud by stealing the warm air from its parent, so that the death of one cloud causes the birth of another beside it.

Supercells

Ordinarily, a storm cloud chokes to death when its downdrafts overpower its updrafts, depriving it of the warm, moist air it needs. Sometimes, though, a cloud escapes this fate. Then it can last for several hours, rather than two hours at most, and it can grow into a truly immense, terrifying storm.

In most clouds, the updrafts and downdrafts form several convective cells, but in the giant cloud they merge into a single "supercell." Updrafts and downdrafts separate, so they flow in different parts of the cloud and the downdraft is unable to choke the updraft. These vertical currents move at up to 100 miles per hour (160 km/h) and at the rear of the cloud, the cold downdraft leaves the base as a wind that can gust almost to hurricane force. Ahead of the cloud, warm air is drawn in so strongly that it, too, produces a wind that can gust to hurricane force, defined as 75 miles per hour (120 km/h) or more.

Mesocyclones

Inflowing air is converging strongly and this sets it rotating counterclockwise (in the Northern Hemisphere) and accelerates it, because of the conservation of angular momentum. This can start an entire section of the cloud rotating, especially if the wind above the cloud blows at an angle to the air leaving the cloud, giving it an extra twist. The high-level wind sweeps out the top of the cloud, at that height made entirely from ice crystals, into a characteristic shape resembling a blacksmith's anvil.

The rotating section, up to 6 miles (10 km) across, is called a mesocyclone. It begins in the middle of the cloud and extends downward. The storm is now "tornadic," which means it is capable of triggering tornadoes. The cross section through a tornadic storm, shown in the diagram on page 43, gives an idea of its structure. The cloud top may be at a height of 50,000 feet (15 km) or more, inside the lower stratosphere.

Below the cloud, at the center of the vortex of inflowing air, the atmospheric pressure is extremely low, because of the rate at which air is rising. At ground level inside the vortex the pressure may be equal to that outside the cloud at a height of several thousand feet. This draws down the base of the cloud. The first warning of a tornado is usually this extension below the main cloud, turning fairly quickly and with fragments of cloud moving vertically up and down its exterior. This is the wall cloud.

It is then that the vortex is likely to become visible, as a funnel, narrower at the bottom than at the top, snaking this way and that below the cloud. It is dangerous only when it touches the ground. This is a tornado.

A storm that can produce one tornado will often produce several, so tornadoes can occur as families. When the tornadic storm is one of many similar storms, strung out along a squall line, tornadoes can appear almost simultaneously in places many miles apart.

The Tornado Funnel

In a tornado, all the air is moving upward. You can see it because the extreme low pressure near the core makes inflowing air expand, and its water vapor condenses. The funnel cloud forms in the vortex itself, and is not drawn down from the cloud above. Dust and loose debris are swept up by the inflow and carried into the vortex. They darken it, and when it touches the ground there is a small cloud of flying debris around its base. Over snow, however, a tornado can be blazingly white.

Most tornadoes are no more than half a mile (800 m) across at the base of the funnel, but a vigorous one can produce several other tornadoes wandering erratically around its edge, smaller but often even more violent than their parent.

Modern radar can measure the wind speed around the funnel vortex. In a really fierce tornado this can reach around 300 miles per hour (480 km/h). No other weather system on Earth can generate winds of this speed.

There is a scale for categorizing tornadoes, as "weak," "strong," or "violent," by their wind speeds and the damage they do. In most cases it is the damage that is examined after the tornado has passed, and the force is estimated from that. There are two classes in each category, so the scale runs from 0 to 5. A weak tornado, with winds of 40 to 112 miles per hour (65–180 km/h), can break branches from trees or snap entire trees. Strong tornadoes, with winds of 113 to 206 miles per hour (181–330 km/h), will uproot whole trees and leave them flattened. A violent tornado generates winds from 206 to more than 300 miles per hour (331 to more than 480 km/h) and will toss mature trees around as though they were small sticks.

Drought

Trees grow where soil and climate supply the resources they need. Water is one of those resources, but unlike mineral nutrients in the soil, in temperate regions water is not always available. Ordinarily, this causes no difficulties, because trees are well adapted to seasonal variations produced by the climates in which they grow (page 88). Sometimes, however, the usual distribution can break down, leading to prolonged drought. This can cause great harm (page 47).

A drought is a period of low rainfall, or no rain at all, at a time of year when rain is usually expected, leading to a shortage of water serious enough to cause harm to plants and animals and inconvenience to humans. No place is immune from drought, not even the humid tropics.

Blocking

Droughts affecting the forests that grow in middle latitudes are caused by blocking. A large anticyclone, or a ridge of high pressure extending from one, becomes stationary and remains so for weeks, or even months, blocking the west-to-east path of the frontal depressions that bring rain. The rain does not vanish, it is simply diverted somewhere else, leading to the apparent paradox that a drought in one place can mean floods in another.

If you could look down on Earth from a point in space directly above the North or South Pole, and spend some time watching the drifting clouds, you would see that air moves around the poles. This movement is called the circumpolar vortex and it is dominated by the jet streams, which are the strongest winds (page 34).

From your space station you would not be able to see the jet streams directly, but you might notice that although the weather moves around the pole beneath you, it does not always follow a straight path. From time to time it meanders, sometimes in big loops that carry weather systems closer to the pole or farther away from it. These are due to meanders in the jet stream and they can end with the flow breaking down into a series of isolated cells (see the diagram of the index cycle on page 37). After that, the usual west-east (zonal) flow establishes itself once more.

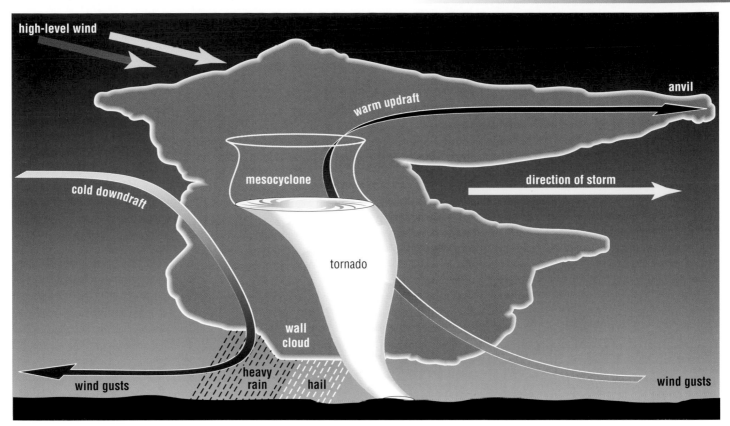

Tornadic storm

Big loops in the flow can reach almost to the Arctic Circle at the top and to the Mediterranean at the bottom; undulations of similar size in the Southern Hemisphere are mainly over ocean, extending only to southern South America and South Island, New Zealand. When the zonal flow resumes it may do so far from some of the isolated cells, and they may be left behind.

These are cyclones (low pressure) in about the latitude of Spain and New York, and anticyclones (high pressure) in the latitude of Britain and Newfoundland. Both cyclones and anticyclones are slow-moving or stationary, so in areas affected by them the weather seems to "stick" and remains so until the blocking cell moves away or disappears. They obstruct the passage of weather systems and may reverse the wind direction, bringing easterly winds where ordinarily the winds are mainly from the west. In Europe, this can bring dry, continental air westward over regions usually exposed to moist westerly winds from the Atlantic.

Summer and Winter Drought

It is in summer that blocking anticyclones cause drought in middle latitudes, usually accompanied by high temperatures, which make the soil dry out even faster. From May 1975 until August 1976, a blocking anticyclone in the North Atlantic shifted the tracks of depressions between 5° and 10° to the north, reducing rainfall over southern England by half and producing the severest drought since 1698 and temperatures above 90°F (32°C), which is extremely high for Britain.

Winter blocking also brings dry weather, but by itself that causes fewer problems in winter than in summer. Temperate forest trees require little water in winter and drought then does not harm them. Low temperatures also reduce greatly the rate of evaporation, so soil dries much more slowly. Trees may be damaged by the cold, however, especially in Europe where the anticyclonic circulation draws air westward from Siberia. In February 1979, it was so cold that thin ice formed in the North Sea, near the Danish coast.

In middle latitudes, blocking due to meanders in the jet stream is the principal cause of unusually hot, dry summers and cold, dry winters. Spells of extreme weather may be occurring more frequently now than they did in the past, although it is difficult to be certain, because there are few reliable records extending far enough into the past and determining what constitutes "extreme" weather is somewhat subjective.

What is certain is that forests, like all plant communities, are well able to tolerate the climates in which they grow, with a margin of tolerance for extremes. Fierce winds or drought may cause serious damage, but it is damage from which forests can recover, provided it is inflicted only occasionally (see the next section). It is the too-frequent repetition of such assaults that causes real, lasting harm.

Effect of Severe Weather on Forests

Most tree diseases are caused by fungi. The word "fungus" suggests the visible mushrooms, toadstools, and brackets you can find in forests, especially in the fall, but these are just the fruiting bodies from which fungi release their spores. Most disease-causing fungi produce fruiting bodies that are far too small to see. The main part of the fungus lies below ground or inside the tissues of trees. A fungus consists of a mycelium, which is a network of very fine filaments, called hyphae, often extending over a large area. It is the mycelium that weakens the tree.

Before a fungus can attack, however, there must be a point through which it can enter the tree, and this is usually a wound, left when a branch falls or is broken, caused by a blow from another tree as it falls or by a glancing blow from a stone as it rolls down a hillside, or, very often, by an animal. Deer and squirrels strip bark from tree trunks, which can allow fungi to enter. Certain insects bore through tree bark and they can carry fungal spores with them, transmitting disease in the same way that some mosquitoes transmit malaria to humans. This is how Dutch elm disease is spread (page 108). A tree that is weakened in this way, mechanically, is less able to withstand the wind than a healthy tree, so often it is the diseased trees that fall first.

Root Depth and Crown Height

Even among healthy trees, some are more likely than others to be brought down by a strong wind. As well as obtaining nutrients and water, roots anchor trees, but some trees root more deeply than others. Oaks, for example, have deep roots that are slightly flexible, so they can sway to some degree in a strong wind. Other broad-leaved trees and many conifers have shallow, weaker roots. Beeches and spruces are particularly vulnerable to wind, because their main roots snap.

Trees that stand taller than those around them are also vulnerable, because their height increases their exposure to the wind. Look at a forest from above and you will see that most trees of a particular species grow to very much the same height. This is because the wind has a powerful drying effect. It evaporates water vapor faster than the tree can replace it (page 28), desiccating and killing the leaves, and preventing any tree from growing taller than its neighbors.

On exposed sites you will see trees "sculpted" by the wind, so most of their branches and leaves are on the more sheltered side. The entire tree may lean away from the prevailing wind. This is also due to wind desiccation, and is very common along coasts, where the wind blowing off the sea carries salt spray, which increases the drying effect. The sculpted shape also protects the tree from being blown down by the wind. Branches, twigs, and leaves that might be caught by the wind are on the downwind side and largely sheltered by the trunk.

Flat, open leaves catch the wind and during the growing season, before the tree detaches them in the fall, they are firmly attached. The wind on a single leaf has only a small effect, of course, but a full-sized broad-leaved tree has hundreds of thousands of leaves. This makes broad-leaved trees more vulnerable to the wind in late spring and summer than in fall and winter. Leaves of coniferous trees, reduced to needles, offer little resistance to the wind, but this advantage is offset by the fact that many conifers grow taller than broad-leaved trees. Where the two occur together in a mixed forest, the crowns of the

Effect of rotating wind

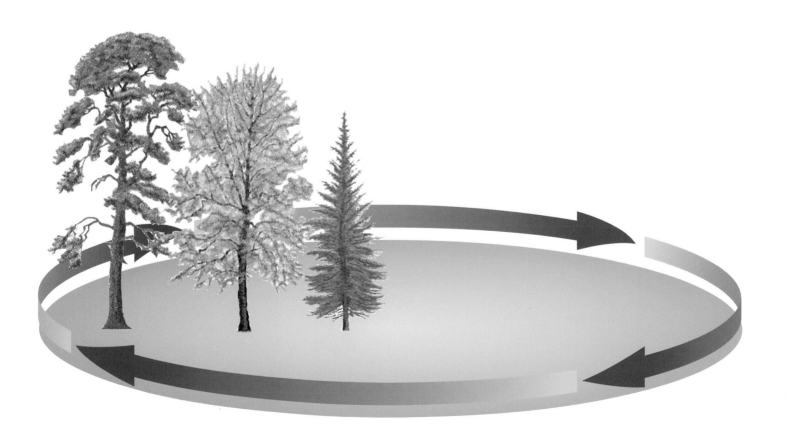

Area in Britain where forests were devastated by the October 1987 wind storm

it is less than 10 percent of the speed outside. For broad-leaved deciduous forests, the extent of wind reduction depends on the season. At a point inside a mixed forest in Tennessee, the wind speed was reduced to 12 percent of that outside the forest in January, when the trees were bare, but to 2 percent in summer, when they were in full leaf.

Below the level of the canopy, the force is borne by trees near the forest edge. You might expect, therefore, that trees near the edge are most at risk of being blown down, but this is not necessarily the case. Perhaps because they are more exposed, they are also strong. It can even happen that trees inside the forest fall, but those at the edge remain standing.

In the boreal forest, however, wind storms are not the most serious cause of harm. There, fire is much more destructive. Broad-leaved forests usually grow in moister habitats, where it is more difficult to start and sustain a fire, and the trees themselves are not especially flammable. Conifers, on the other hand, grow on drier sites, often with a thick layer of dead, dry needles carpeting the forest floor, and the trees themselves contain resin, which burns readily and fiercely. Fires that start naturally, rather than being accidentally ignited by people, are due to lightning. Although forest fires are often spectacular, frightening, and, of course, very dangerous to homes, they are not necessarily harmful to the forest, despite destroying so many mature trees (page 94).

Wind, even strong wind, is normal, of course. It can break branches and blow down trees, but although these are events that change the forest locally, they have no effect on the forest as a whole. Occasionally, however, the change may be more drastic.

Tornadoes and Hurricanes

Tornadoes demolish everything they touch and can cut a swathe of total devastation through a forest. Most do not travel far, but they have been known to leave tracks several miles long. While tornadoes can happen anywhere, forests are especially vulnerable across that part of the Great Plains known as Tornado Alley, which experiences more of them than any other region in the world (page 41).

The aftermath of a tornado is easily recognized. Apart from its narrow width, the tornado track is filled and lined with trees lying in all directions, felled by a twisting wind that hit them from several sides. On level ground, windblown trees usually fall in the direction of the wind; on

conifers often stand clear of the main canopy. Increased exposure, combined with their generally shallower root system, means that in a mixed forest the conifers are more likely to be blown down than the broad-leaved trees. Conifers are also more likely to suffer because their shallow roots allow them to grow on thinner soils than broad-leaved trees, and these soils are often found in high, windy places.

Wind Force

A strong wind exerts considerable force, and when it blows across a forest, almost all the force is absorbed by the trees. The wind strength 100 feet (30 m) inside a temperate forest is less than 80 percent of that outside. Move 200 feet (60 m) inside and the wind speed is halved, and at 400 feet (120 m),

steeply sloping ground fallen trees tend to lie with their tops pointing downhill. The diagram on page 44 illustrates the effect of a rotating wind, loosening and weakening roots by exerting pressure on trees from different directions in succession.

Tropical cyclones (page 40) are also rotating winds, but on a very much larger scale. In the southeastern United States, where hurricanes moving in from the Caribbean cross the coast, conifer forests have been repeatedly devastated.

Windstorm damage can occur outside regions usually prone to tropical cyclones, and it has done so throughout history. On December 21, 1694, for example, a gale uprooted entire forests in Scotland. A few years later, in 1703, one of the worst storms in British history, lasting from November 24 to 27 and bringing winds of up to 80 miles per hour (129 km/hr), blew down more than 17,000 trees in the southeastern county of Kent.

Much more recently, the storm of 1987 caused even more damage in southeastern and eastern England. It struck on October 15 and destroyed 19 million trees. The map on page 45 shows the area within which the trees felled amounted to about one-sixth of the total volume of timber standing at the time.

That storm began as a fairly mild Atlantic hurricane, which crossed the ocean and moved up the English Channel. Weak by hurricane standards, its winds were still strong enough to wreak havoc. Hurricanes that reach New England have already weakened, but still retain a substantial proportion of their original force. In 1938, for example, a storm struck with winds of more than 100 miles per hour. It killed 600 people, and in

Massachusetts it also destroyed a large area of forest that was growing on level ground and on slopes directly exposed to the wind.

Predicting wind damage can be difficult. Obviously, trees growing on thin or soft soil are at risk, because they are insecurely anchored, and trees growing on high ground are at risk because they are very exposed. Beyond that, the wind is almost whimsical in its effects. The trees most severely affected by the 1938 New England storm were those growing on level ground and wind-facing slopes, but the 1987 English storm was most severe on slopes sheltered from the wind. Deep valleys usually afford shelter to trees, but if the wind direction is approximately aligned with the valley, it will be funneled and accelerated by the shape of the land surface. Tornadoes travel farthest on level ground, but over short distances their tracks are little influenced by the lie of the land. Indeed, a high ridge that tends to trigger severe and sometimes tornadic thunderstorms in warm, moist air crossing it may increase the likelihood of tornadoes on what is otherwise the more sheltered side.

Rotating winds strike trees from first one direction and then another, but to a lesser degree and more erratically, so do all winds, especially inside a forest. Wind moving near ground level is deflected by obstructions, producing eddies. Trees produce countless eddies in a wind blowing through a forest. Again, trees are being pushed this way and that. Those able to swing on deep, vertical roots can withstand this treatment, but it may bring down those with shallow, weak roots.

Silhouettes of two conifers and two broad-leaved trees: from left to right, Scotch pine, Sitka spruce, pignut hickory, and pin oak

Wind Damage

Wind rips branches from trees and hurls them to the ground. This does not kill trees directly. They can survive the loss of a few branches. It does leave a wound, however, and wounds can become infected, in trees just as in animals. Fungal disease spreads slowly into the main body of the tree, weakening and sometimes hollowing it, and after some years it may be toppled by another strong wind. Meanwhile, the disease afflicting it may spread to its neighbors, also weakening them.

Not all trees that fall are uprooted. Weakened ones, especially, may simply snap in the wind, leaving behind a very jagged stump, called a snag, several feet tall. Breaking the trunk does not kill a tree immediately, but in time it will die, leaving an upright skeleton that will probably fall later.

Falling trees, parts of trees, and branches injure other trees. Forest trees grow close together. When one falls it is more than likely to knock over one or two others and these may topple still more. Those that do not fall may be injured by falling neighbors. Branches may be torn from them and bark stripped from their trunks. Smaller saplings and seedlings, along with woody shrubs growing on the forest floor, are crushed by falling trees. Indirect wind damage of this kind can be extensive and, of course, it increases the likelihood of fungal infection.

Snow and Ice

Winter snow can turn a conifer forest into a scene of fairy-tale beauty. Conifers are adapted to cold, snowy winters, of course, but snow can also damage them. Only loose, wet snow will cling to tree branches, but it is heavy. One cubic foot of wet snow weighs about 6 pounds (100 kg per cubic meter), and over the length of a main branch the weight can be considerable. Coniferous trees have somewhat flexible branches and in some species the branches incline downward, helping them to shed snow, but as the diagram on page 46 shows, this is not true for all species. Scotch pine has branches that extend almost horizontally and those of Sitka spruce are horizontal or incline upwards. A heavy load of snow may break them, although it is usually only small branches or those already weakened by disease that break. The diagram also shows that the greater number of small branches and twigs makes broad-leaved trees much more vulnerable. They can be severely damaged if snow breaks their branches in spring, after leaves have started to open.

Avalanches move with enough force to uproot trees and will sweep away whole areas of forest. Where avalanches are common events, they tend to flow along certain tracks, identifiable by the gaps they leave in forests.

Freezing rain can also break branches. It occurs when super cooled rain (droplets below freezing temperature) strikes a cold surface and freezes instantly. An "ice storm," caused by heavy, freezing rain, can quickly coat surfaces with a thick layer of clear ice—ice is about 10 times heavier than snow. Ice storms tend to break the smaller branches, stripping trees of their crowns, sometimes over a wide area. Ice storms are fairly common. There was a severe one in late November of 1996, for example, affecting Texas, Oklahoma, Arkansas, and Missouri. The crowns grow again, but in areas especially prone to ice storms, repeated loss of crowns may stunt the trees.

Drought

Drought is more insidious. Trees are affected when the rate of evapotranspiration (page 28) is high and a prolonged period of low rainfall has lowered the water table (page 18), or when water below ground is frozen. Forests growing in Mediterranean climates, where summers are ordinarily dry, and in high latitudes—where winters are cold enough to freeze water all the way from ground level to the top of the water table—are adapted to periods when water is not available, although even there summer drought and winter cold can persist long enough to cause harm. Damage occurs much sooner, however, in regions where rainfall is usually distributed evenly through the year.

Some tree species are more tolerant of drought than others. Conifers tend to survive better than broad-leaved species. Birch and beech are especially sensitive, but many species of oak, ash, and chestnut are fairly resistant.

Water Stress

While its roots remain within reach of soil moisture, a tree (or any plant) will take in water and transport it, as sap, through its stem and branches, and it will evaporate through the stomata (pores) in its leaves. Water fills the vessels through which it moves and this maintains the rigidity of soft tissues and the shape of leaves.

If insufficient water is available in the soil, or the rate of evaporation from stomata exceeds the rate at which water can replenish leaves, the tree will experience water stress. Its cells will lose their rigidity; the first obvious sign of water stress is the wilting of leaves on broad-leaved trees. Conifers show no immediate sign, but unless the water supply is restored quickly, both broad leaves and needles will die, turn brown, and be shed.

Water stress also causes leaf stomata to close. This reduces the loss of water, but it also prevents the exchange of gases, slowing and eventually halting photosynthesis. Wilting therefore halts the growth of the tree. Water stress also reduces the rate at which proteins are synthesized, so the entire metabolism of the tree slows. Continued drought may then affect twigs and later branches. As they are deprived of water, they start to die. Eventually the condition may spread to the entire tree.

Forest Damage

Regardless of species, the first trees to be affected are the young seedlings. They are not old enough to have put down deep roots. After them, the taller saplings and immature trees suffer. Then it is the old trees. They are fully grown and already approaching the end of their lives. When the old trees die and fall they create gaps in the forest canopy, but gaps that may take a long time to fill, because of the shortage of young recruits. This can alter the composition of the forest by eliminating a substantial part of an entire generation of certain species.

Severe drought in a broad-leaved deciduous forest produces an effect resembling the fall season. Trees shed their leaves and stand bare and dormant, as they do in winter. In subsequent years many recover, but by no means all of them, and those that do are likely to grow more slowly than they did prior to the drought. Of those that appear to recover, some will have suffered damage so severe that they die back slowly. They continue to produce leaves year after year, but fungi invade them and little by little they die. Eventually there will come a year when they remain leafless. Then they will slowly disintegrate, losing a branch or two now and then and eventually falling.

During a summer drought, all forests become increasingly vulnerable to fire. This adds to the damage, but is rarely as harmful as it looks.

Wind, snow, ice, and drought are natural phenomena. If a particular forest experiences one of them repeatedly it will act as an agent of natural selection. Those trees most severely affected by it will gradually disappear from the community, leaving the most tolerant species to predominate.

Climatic Regions

Most school atlases include a map of the world showing the distribution of types of vegetation. It shows tropical rain forest in the Tropics, desert in the subtropics, and indicates those parts of the world where you might expect to find grasslands and temperate forests. Compare this map with one showing climatic regions, and you will see the regions are almost identical.

This will come as no surprise. It is mainly the climate that determines the type of vegetation that will grow in a particular place, so the two maps are bound to be very similar. What is more, the first attempts to classify climates did so on the basis of the vegetation characteristic of them. In other words, the climate determines the vegetation type and the vegetation type defines the climate. Since the reasoning is circular, it is no wonder that vegetation and climate maps agree.

Throughout the 18th and 19th centuries, botanists were traveling to what were then the most inaccessible corners of the world in search of previously unknown plants. Thousands of specimens were shipped to Europe and America, and many were eventually bred to produce commercial crop plants and popular ornamentals. All botanists knew that certain types of plants grow in certain parts of the world, and some began to speculate about why this should be so.

By the middle of the 19th century, finding answers to this question involved taking account of new ideas about plant classification and evolutionary mechanisms. Improved classification allowed relationships among plants to be identified and new ideas about the way evolution works improved understanding about how those relationships arose. Together, these helped to explain the geographical location of particular plants in a very general way, although the disjunct distribution of some plants remained a mystery (page 8). Exploration, combined with studies of classification, or taxonomy, and evolutionary theories contributed to the emerging scientific discipline of what is now called biogeography. The scientists asking the questions were plant geographers, working in a field now known as phytogeography or geobotany.

The Köppen Plan

Two of the leading plant geographers at that time were the Swiss botanists Augustin Pyramus de Candolle (1777–1841) and his son, Alphonse Louis Pierre Pyramus de Candolle (1806–93). Both were professors at the University of Geneva,

Augustin of natural history and, later, Alphonse of botany. After Augustin died Alphonse continued his work. In 1885 Alphonse showed how plants are adapted to the environments in which they occur naturally. This work was taken further by the German botanist Andreas Franz Wilhelm Schimper (1856–1901), who proposed that climate is the key to plant distribution. It was from this idea that climate classification developed.

It culminated in the system for classifying climates devised by Wladimir Peter Köppen (1846–1940), who was born in St. Petersburg, Russia, of German parents, and worked mainly in Germany. He became a meteorologist, but started as a botanist and was very influenced by the ideas of the botanists of his day. Today there are several systems in use for classifying climates, but that of Köppen is the most popular with geographers and biologists. It is based on the classification he first described in a series of publications starting in 1900 and outlined fully in 1918, although he continued revising it until his death.

Everyone recognized that temperature and rainfall determine the type of vegetation that can grow. Temperate forests grow in temperate climates, with warm or at least mild summers, cool or cold winters that do not last too long, and moisture available for most of the year. This much is obvious. What Köppen did was to relate vegetation types more precisely to mean monthly temperatures and precipitation, and to mean annual temperature.

What matters to plants is not the amount of precipitation, but the availability of moisture in the soil, and this is related to temperature. The higher the temperature, the greater the rate of evaporation and, therefore, the higher the proportion of precipitation reaching the ground that vanishes before plants can derive any benefit from it. This is called the effective precipitation, measured as precipitation minus evaporation, and the relationship is expressed as the ratio r/t, where r is the mean annual rainfall in centimeters and t is the mean annual temperature in degrees Celsius.

Köppen began by dividing the world into six sets of climatic regions, all but one of them based on temperature. This broad division is then refined by taking account of effective precipitation, generating a set of subdivisions. These allowed Köppen to set boundaries to the climatic regions. There are many subdivisions, some defined by precipitation and some, in warmer regions, by additional features of temperature.

Geographers can use the Köppen climate classification in two ways. If they have details of the

climate of a region, they can predict the type of vegetation that should grow there, and if they know the type of vegetation, they can deduce what the climate is like. Going further, they can summarize the system by drawing a map that shows the distribution of vegetation in an imaginary continent. On a map of this kind, the high-latitude limit of boreal forests is located at about 60°, where summer temperatures do not rise above 50°F (10°C). Broad-leaved deciduous forests lie to the south of the boreal forest, and there is desert surrounded by a margin of steppe grassland covering much of the center of the continent.

To do this, however, the map has to be based on certain assumptions. The imaginary continent must be low-lying, because temperature decreases with increasing altitude. It must also be flat, because when weather systems cross hill or mountain ranges they lose moisture as air rises, making the climate on the windward side wet and producing a dry rain shadow on the lee side, often extending for a considerable distance.

Köppen made the further assumption that climate is the sole determining factor for vegetation. Certainly it is the most important one, but differences in soils also influence the distribution of plants. Nor are the boundaries of vegetation types, defined by minimum temperatures, entirely accurate or entirely constant. Those Köppen used were based on botanical surveys undertaken in the last century. These were only approximate then and most will have shifted since.

Figures for the mean temperature and precipitation at a particular place are calculated over as long a period as the records permit, and temperature means are calculated separately for daytime and nighttime. A sequence of years in which weather conditions deviate from the mean may be enough to shift the boundaries of the vegetation. The use of averages is unavoidable, because of the wide variation possible in individual years, but averages can conceal gradual changes. In other words, the Köppen boundaries are too rigidly defined.

Despite these criticisms, the classification remains useful as a general description of the relationship between vegetation and climate. The vegetation and climate maps in your atlas are most likely based on the Köppen system.

The Thornthwaite Plan

The most widely used alternative to the Köppen classification is the one devised by the American climatologist Charles Warren Thornthwaite (1889–1963).

The Thornthwaite classification, which he first proposed in 1931, was based on the relationship between precipitation and evaporation. He abandoned entirely the use of vegetation boundaries to define climatic boundaries. Instead, he measured precipitation, temperature, and evaporation. Thornthwaite classification identified five principal types of climate: humid, moist subhumid, dry subhumid, semiarid, and arid. As with the Köppen scheme, this broad classification is then refined by adding further details about variations in the availability of moisture through the year to allow for climates that have a seasonal distribution of precipitation.

The Thornthwaite system corresponds reasonably well with the vegetation types found in temperate climates, although it is less reliable for tropical and semiarid areas. It and the Köppen scheme are the two classifications most widely used, but there are many others. Between 1909 and 1970, there have been nearly 30, some more completely worked out than others. In 1969, for example, A. N. Strahler produced one based on air-mass source regions (page 30), fronts, and general climatic conditions that identified 14 types of climate. Another is based on the major global wind belts.

Botanists Yield to Climatologists

As they have developed, the systems for classifying climates have increasingly tended to move away from the botanical origin of all such systems and have become essentially climatological. This change is entirely natural. When the first attempts were made much more was known about the global distribution of vegetation than about climates and how they work. Early systems had little alternative but to be primarily botanical.

The reason for this has little to do with the introduction of more sensitive instruments for measuring temperature, humidity, and pressure, and nothing at all to do with advances in mathematics. It is due to improvements in communication.

When botanists were exploring the world, identifying and collecting plants and mapping their distribution, they could take as much time as they needed and could afford (this was usually limited, because most of them financed their expeditions from the sale of the specimens they shipped back to their home countries). They traveled by sea and moved overland by whatever means were available, often on horseback or foot, or by boat.

This was fine for collecting specimens and recording the general weather conditions they encountered, but useless for developing a broad understanding of how climates are produced. To do that it is necessary to map weather systems on a scale large enough to cover entire continents and oceans, which is impossible unless conditions can be recorded by many observing stations at the same time and transmitted to a central point. Until the middle of the last century, reports could travel no faster than a messenger could carry them on horseback, but in 1844 the first telegraph line opened, between Baltimore and Washington. Within a few years the telegraph network had expanded widely and the American physicist Joseph Henry (1797–1878) used the resources of the Smithsonian Institution, of which he was elected secretary in 1846, to gather weather reports from all over the United States. The system he devised formed the basis of the one developed later by the U.S. Weather Bureau, and in 1851 the first weather map was shown in public, at the Great Exhibition in London.

Once the telegraph network covered North America, Europe, and parts of the other continents, it became possible to start issuing weather reports and then forecasts. Regular daily bulletins were first issued in 1869, from the Cincinnati Observatory, and in Britain the Meteorological Office published its first regular weekly report in 1878. Weather reports and forecasts were useful and funding was provided for the work needed to compile them and for the scientific research needed to improve them. The scientific study of climates (climatology) developed alongside the study of weather (meteorology) and as understanding of atmospheric processes advanced, it became possible to define climatic regions and to classify them. This project, initiated by botanists, passed to climatologists.

All systems for classifying climates aim to provide a very general description. It is important to bear this in mind. The weakness of the Köppen scheme arises from its imposition of boundaries that are too rigid and too sharply defined. There are many places where you will often see a marked change in the weather if you travel no more than 20 miles, and if such an alteration is usual it will amount to a climatological difference that will be reflected in the natural vegetation. The difference may be slight, but it is real, and it could alter the boundary between two major types of climate and vegetation. Atmospheric conditions vary, sometimes greatly, on a scale of just a few square miles, and generalizations about climates can never be more than approximate.

Approximations are sufficient for the classification of climates, provided we bear in mind that they are approximations, but nowadays attempts are being made to increase their precision. The primary aim now is to improve predictions of the regional consequences of possible climate change (page 174) by taking account of the small scale on which such important events as cloud formation occur. If this proves possible, it may lead to ways of classifying climates in more detail, which means on a more local scale.

Continental and Maritime Climates

Try to name the place in the Northern Hemisphere that has the coldest winters and (unless you already know the answer) the chances are you will suggest the North Pole, or perhaps northern Greenland. At all events, it will be somewhere uninhabited. Your guess is entirely reasonable, but it is wrong. The coldest place in the Northern Hemisphere is Verkhoyansk, in eastern Siberia, and, although it lies in a sparsely populated region, it is far from uninhabited. It is a small town, with a population of about 2,000, and in February, the coldest month, its citizens shiver in temperatures that have been known to fall to -90.4°F (-68°C).

For comparison, and just to convince you that Verkhoyansk really is colder than Greenland, the lowest winter temperature recorded at Thule, Greenland, also in February, is -41°F (-40.5°C), which is cold enough for anyone, but still warmer than Verkhoyansk. Thule, also called Qaanaaq, is the most northerly town in the world, with a population of around 600. Nor is the difference due to altitude. Lying 328 feet (100 m) above sea level, Verkhoyansk is somewhat higher than Thule, at 121 feet (37 m), but the 207 feet (63 m) separating them should make Verkhoyansk the colder by only 0.7°F (-17.4°C).

In summer, however, the people of Verkhoyansk win hands down. Their warmest month is July, when the highest temperature recorded was 98°F (37°C). In Thule, the highest temperature recorded (admittedly from data covering only three years) is 59°F (15°C).

Mean Temperatures and Temperature Ranges

These are extremes, of course, but Verkhoyansk is also colder on average. The mean annual temperature there is 1.1°F (-17.1°C) and at Thule it is 12°F (-11°C), and Verkhoyansk has a much wider range of mean temperature. There is a difference of 129°F (54°C) between the maximum and minimum mean temperatures, compared with a difference of 67°F (19.4°C) at Thule.

It is the range of temperature that is significant. Despite being further south, Verkhoyansk has much hotter summers and colder winters than Thule. This is because Thule lies on the coast, albeit of a frozen sea, and Verkhoyansk lies in the middle of a vast continent. Thule enjoys a maritime climate, and Verkhoyansk a continental climate. All climates become cooler with increasing distance from the equator, but maritime climates are less extreme than continental climates.

Indeed, the most extreme continental climate in the world does not produce a desert, though nothing much grows around Thule: Verkhoyansk lies in the heart of the boreal forest, or taiga, that extends for 6,000 miles (10,000 km) from the Baltic to the Sea of Okhotsk.

Continents, Maritime Regions, and Temperature Ranges

The difference is no less marked in lower latitudes. Compare, for example, San Francisco, at latitude 37°47' N and 52 feet (16 m) above sea level, with Kansas City, at 39°07' N and 741 feet (226 m) above sea level. The difference in altitude should make Kansas City about 2.4°F (-16.4°C) cooler than San Francisco and, indeed, the mean annual temperature at Kansas City is 55°F (13°C) and at San Francisco it is 57°F (14°C). The range of mean temperature, however, distinguishes the continental from the maritime climate. At Kansas City the difference between the highest and lowest mean temperatures is 67°F (19.4°C) and at San Francisco it is only 24°F (-4.4°C).

Old World comparisons yield similar results. Ekaterinburg (which used to be called Sverdlovsk) in Siberia and Oban, on the west coast of Scotland, both lie slightly north of 56° N. In Oban, with a maritime climate, the mean temperature is 48°F (9°C) with a range of 28°F (-2.2°C). Ekaterinburg has a continental climate, with a mean temperature of 32°F (0°C) and a range of 75°F (23.8°C).

Ocean Currents

Maritime climates are produced by air that traveled a long distance over an ocean. This moderates its temperature, but by an amount that depends on the temperature at the sea surface and this is affected by ocean currents. Air reaching western Europe crosses the warm Gulf Stream or its northeasterly extension, the North Atlantic Drift. In winter this can raise the temperature of the air by as much as 17°F (-8.3°C) between Iceland and northern Scotland and it ensures that the Norwegian coast is free from ice throughout the winter.

California receives air that has been cooled by crossing the California Current, flowing south from the Arctic. As a consequence, Lisbon has a climate several degrees warmer than that of San Francisco, in about the same latitude, but a wider temperature range, of 36°F (2.2°C). The mean

Taiga vegetation, Alaska Ranges
(Gerry Ellis/ENP Images)

TEMPERATURE		
	mean °F/°C	range °F/°C
Continental		
Verkhoyansk	1.1/-17.1	129/72
Ekaterinburg	32/0	75/42
Kansas City	55/13	67/37
Maritime		
Thule	12/-11	67/37
Atka	40/5	28/16
San Francisco	57/14	24/13
Oban	48/9	28/16
Lisbon	62/17	36/20

where A is the annual temperature range in degrees Celsius, B is the angle of latitude, and K is an index of continentality ranging from -12 for extreme maritime conditions to 100 for extreme continental conditions (although these values are not limits and can be exceeded). Applying this equation makes it possible to rank places by their degree of continentality as: Verkhoyansk, 112; Kansas City, 79; Ekaterinburg, 65; Thule, 44; Lisbon, 34; San Francisco, 16; Atka, 14; and Oban, 12.

Calculating the degree of continentality shows clearly the effect of the Rockies. Los Angeles has an index value of 40 and Phoenix of 91. In Europe, Bordeaux has a value of 37, Munich and Warsaw, far inland, each have a value of 44, and it is not until Moscow that the index rises to 59.

temperature in Lisbon, at 38°43' N, is 62°F (17°C). Similarly, Atka, in the Aleutian Islands, at 52° N, has a cooler climate than Oban, although it is a few degrees further south. At Atka the mean temperature is 40°F (4.4°C), but the range of temperatures is exactly the same as that in Oban. The table above sets out the mean temperatures and ranges for the places named.

Thule has a wider temperature range than other maritime regions because the sea around it is frozen. This reduces the moderating influence of the ocean. Elsewhere, it is the much higher heat capacity of the oceans compared with dry land that results in maritime climates experiencing a smaller temperature range than continental climates (page 30).

Moisture

Air masses that acquire their essential characteristics over the interior of a continent are drier than those that form over oceans. Obviously, this makes continental climates drier than maritime climates, but in temperate and high latitudes the difference

is sometimes small or even nonexistent. In the examples mentioned here and summarized in the table, Kansas City has a wetter climate than San Francisco and Thule is drier than Verkhoyansk.

Mountain ranges running approximately north-to-south affect the characteristics of air masses crossing them. This effect is large in North America, where the western coastal belt has a maritime climate, but air is dried by its passage over the Rockies. To the east of the mountains the continental climate begins abruptly and still not very far inland. In Europe, there is no comparable mountain range, while the Mediterranean extends far into the continent. Consequently, the oceanic influence extends far inland and the change from a maritime to a continental climate is fairly gradual.

Measuring Continentality

A gradual change from one type of climate to another implies degrees of continentality. There are several ways this can be calculated, usually from the annual temperature range. One widely used method is based on the equation: $K = 1.7(A/\sin B) - 20.4$,

Climates and Forests

Continental climates, because of their extremes of temperature and generally low precipitation, tend to favor coniferous forests. Ekaterinburg, on the eastern slopes of the Ural Mountains, and Verkhoyansk much farther to the east and north, both lie in the taiga, where the predominant trees are pines (*Pinus*), spruces (*Picea*), firs (*Abies*), and larches (*Larix*), each species being dominant in certain areas. Maritime climates, with less variation in temperature and generally higher precipitation, usually favor broad-leaved deciduous forest. Latitude affects the distribution, because broad-leaved species are less tolerant than conifers of long, cold winters, which even maritime climates experience in high latitudes. Around Oban, for example, the forests are mainly of broad-leaved species, but inland, where the increasing altitude of the Highlands reduces temperatures, these give way to forests that include the only native British conifer, Scotch pine (*Pinus sylvestris*).

Both continental and maritime climates can support temperate forest, provided there is sufficient moisture. Where precipitation is very low, forests give way to steppe grassland in lower latitudes and to tundra in higher latitudes. Across Eurasia, it is the availability of water that determines these boundaries, but the transition is gradual. To the north and south of the taiga there is a fairly broad belt in which the trees are more widely spaced, with other vegetation between them, forming forest-steppe and forest-tundra (called taiga by some western scientists).

AVERAGE ANNUAL RAINFALL			
	inches	mm	distribution
Continental			
Verkhoyansk	5.3	135	wet summer
Ekaterinburg	16.7	426	wet summer
Kansas City	37.3	947	dry winter
Maritime			
Thule	2.5	67	wet summer
Atka	69.3	1,761	even
San Francisco	22.1	563	dry summer
Oban	57.3	1,451	even
Lisbon	27.7	708	dry summer

Trees as Climatic Indicators

Visit a European forest and you will probably see many trees coated with ivy (*Hedera helix*). Ivy may also cover parts of the forest floor and you can also find it growing on walls. It is an Old World plant, not related to the American poison ivy, but it has been introduced and is now grown widely in North America. It is a woody climber, and a broad-leaved evergreen, cloaking trees with dark foliage that is clearly visible in winter, when the trees themselves are bare, and when the ivy dies, its stems often hang from the trees like the lianes that are so common in tropical forests.

Its resemblance to a tropical liane is no coincidence, because that is really what ivy is. It belongs to a family (Araliaceae) of several hundred tropical species. They are especially common in Southeast Asia, but a very few species of ivy occur naturally in parts of Europe and now, as introductions, in North America.

Ivy has never quite lost all its tropical preferences, however, and although vigorous enough in some places to be considered a weed, it remains very sensitive to temperature. It will not produce fruit and seed where the mean temperature in the coldest month of winter falls below 35°F (1.6°C) and a prolonged hard winter will kill it. Nor will it thrive where summer mean temperatures fall below about 55°F (13°C).

This explains why it is so clearly visible in winter. It rarely occurs in evergreen coniferous forests, because they grow naturally in regions with long, very cold winters. You find it in broad-leaved deciduous forests. As befits so close a relative of tropical plants, it is also intolerant of drought. In the northern United States and southern Canada it is not the hard winters that kill it, but the hot, dry summers.

The Holly and the Ivy

Holly (*Ilex aquifolium*) is another plant that grows far from the tropical habitats favored by its many relatives in the family Aquifoliaceae. Like ivy, it is a broad-leaved evergreen and rarely produces seed where mean winter temperatures fall below about 31°F (-0.5°C) and summer temperatures below about 55°F (13°C). Today, European holly grows naturally from North Africa and western Turkey to the north of Scotland, and along the coast of Sweden and Norway. Northern Europe marks the limit of its range. Between 1939 and

Pacific yew tree, Pacific Coast, North America (Gerry Ellis/ENP Images)

1942 there were several hard winters that killed most holly trees as far south as northern Germany. Where it thrives, it can form quite an extensive stand of trees, a "hollywood."

European holly has several North American relatives, the one most like it in appearance being *Ilex opaca,* which grows in southern Texas, around the Atlantic coast as far north as Massachusetts, and inland along the valleys of the Mississippi and Missouri Rivers to Indiana. Tropical American hollies are found in Central and South America.

Like ivy, it is a tree associated with Christmas. The name "holly" is from the Anglo-Saxon *holegn,* a "holy" tree used to decorate houses in winter. Probably the Romans used it in their Saturnalia rituals and Christians continued the tradition. By retaining their leaves through the winter, when the deciduous trees around them are bare, ivy and holly symbolize renewal and eternal life, reminding people that spring will return. Mistletoe (*Viscum album*), a parasite of forest trees that is also associated with Christmas, is also limited by climate. Unlike holly and ivy, it can tolerate winter temperatures as low as 19°F (-7°C), but must have warm summers, with mean temperatures no lower than about 63°F (17°C).

Holly cannot tolerate a continental climate. It is widespread in western Europe and in North America along coasts and major river valleys where a large body of water moderates the continental conditions, but absent from the interior of continents, where the climate is too dry and temperatures are too extreme.

Plants such as ivy and holly have fairly precise climatic requirements. This means they can be used as indicators of climate. Wherever you find ivy and holly, you will know that the region has a mild, maritime climate. Holly can grow as far north as 62° along the Scandinavian coast, only because that coast is washed by the North Atlantic Drift extension of the warm Gulf Stream. Mistletoe implies warm summers.

Yew (*Taxus baccata*) also demands a maritime climate and cannot tolerate hard winters. Like holly, it grows as far north as 63° along the Norwegian coast, where the ocean current produces a moderate climate, but it is more widespread further south and occurs only in the western, maritime region of Europe.

Pollen and Climate

This, you may think, is not a very useful contribution to our understanding of either botany or climatology. After all, we hardly need the presence of particular plants to tell us whether a climate is maritime or continental. We can measure it for ourselves. The holly and the ivy produce pollen, however, and pollen grains can remain in the soil long after the plants which produced them have vanished (page 140). If you find pollen grains from ivy or holly in a region that now has a strongly continental climate, you can be certain that at some time in the past its climate was maritime. You can make an educated guess about the type of forest that once occupied the site.

Ivy, holly, and mistletoe are not the only climatic indicators. Lime trees (*Tilia* species) need warmth, and are often planted in towns to provide shade in summer (where aphids feeding on them can secrete surplus sugars, as "honeydew," dropping up to two pounds on every square yard [one kg per square meter] of sidewalk and parked cars beneath the tree). They grow in Britain, but it is warm enough for them produce seed only in the south. *T. americana,* the American lime or basswood grows as far north as southern Canada.

Indicators of Cold Climates

Other trees are typical of cold climates. Dwarf birch (*Betula nana*) and juniper (*Juniperus* species) grow where the climate is too cold for other trees. Should the climate become warmer, so forests colonize the land, bigger trees shade the dwarf birch and juniper, which disappear. Today these trees grow only in the far north, but their pollen is found much farther south, left from a time when the climate was much colder.

Alder (*Alnus* species) and willow (*Salix* species) grow on wet ground and along riverbanks. Over the centuries since people began cultivating what had once been forest, much of what was wet land has been drained and now grows crops. The pollen survives, however, and alder produces unusually large amounts of it. Where alder and willow pollen are found, the land was once waterlogged and, therefore, the climate was moist.

This can also indicate a change in climate. After a forest became established, if the rainfall increased, water would drain toward the lower ground. In time this would produce areas where the ground was waterlogged. The dominant trees would be killed by the high water table and their place would be taken by alder and willow. The forest would come to include glades of alder and willow growing on the wet ground: the presence of their pollen in an area dominated by the pollen of other tree species would be evidence of a climate change of this kind. To this day there are mixed forests with glades of alder and willow in parts of Europe and the eastern United States.

Forests are their trees, of course, but herbs growing on the forest floor also produce pollen, and the herbs are characteristic of the types of forest in which they occur. Their pollen can also be used to reconstruct past climates and the vegetation associated with them.

Many flowering herbs that are now cultivated grew originally on the forest floor. They flower in spring, during the brief period of warming before the trees have had time to open their leaves and shade them. This is an event that takes place only in deciduous forests, so the presence of these herbs where no one has planted them implies that the area was once broad-leaved deciduous forest. Where a road is bordered on both sides by cultivated fields, the profusion of spring flowers along its shoulders tells you a forest once stood in that place.

The Two Dryas Episodes

Pollen gathered from soils that can be dated is used to reconstruct the changing climates of the past. Perhaps the best known pollen comes from a plant that indicated a sharp, rapid, and long-lasting deterioration in climate.

As the last ice age was ending and the glaciers retreated, trees typical of cold climates, such as birch (*Betula* species) began to appear. Then their pollen was overlaid by that of the mountain avens (*Dryas octopetala*), a flowering herb of mountainsides and the far north. The trees had died, and the ground was carpeted with mountain avens, showing that the climate had suddenly grown much colder. The pollen is found all over the Northern Hemisphere, indicating a widespread change.

Because it was the discovery of its pollen that led to the realization of what had happened, the period is called the Dryas. In fact, it happened twice, so there is an Older Dryas, lasting from about 12,200 to 11,800 years ago, and a Younger Dryas, from about 11,000 to 10,000 years ago. During each Dryas, the glacial retreat halted and in places was reversed. Temperatures fell almost to their ice-age levels.

Today mountain avens is a popular ornamental plant. It is widely grown in rockeries, by gardeners who are perhaps unaware of it's great historical importance.

Holocene Recolonization

The world of 18,000 years ago was very different from the one we see today. Ice sheets covered almost half of Europe, northern Asia, and North America as far south as Seattle in the west and New York in the east, with a broad extension as far south as Cincinnati and Kansas City. The thickness of the ice varied from place to place, but on average it lay 5,000 to 10,000 feet (1.5 – 3 km) deep on all the northern continents, completely burying entire ranges of hills.

Over North America the Cordilleran ice sheet covered the northwest, and most of the northern part of the continent lay beneath the Laurentide ice sheet. Further east, the Greenland ice sheet covered Greenland and the Fennoscandian ice sheet lay over Europe and Asia, with a smaller Siberian ice sheet to its east. Over most of Siberia the climate was very dry, and the amount of snowfall was too small for large ice sheets to form, although there were several small ones. The map on page 59 shows the approximate area covered by ice at its greatest extent. The northern North Atlantic and Arctic Oceans and the North Sea were covered in thick ice all year round, of course, so it was possible to walk between Asia and North America and between Britain and the European mainland. In the Southern Hemisphere there was an ice sheet on each side of the Andes.

Ice Ages and Glaciers

Over the last 2 million years, during the Pleistocene epoch, the ice sheets have advanced three or four times and then retreated again for interludes, called interglacials, lasting between 10,000 and 20,000 years. At present we are living in an interglacial called the Holocene (in Britain it is often called the Flandrian).

Ice ages, or glacials, have different names in different places. The most recent is known in North America as the Wisconsinian, in Britain as the Devensian, in northern mainland Europe as the Weichselian, and in the Alps as the Würm. These names all refer to the same glacial, although there are local variations in the dates of its onset and end. It was at its height about 18,000 years ago, when average temperatures over land were about 36°F (2.2°C) lower than they are today. Because the ice sheets contained so much water, sea levels were as much as 525 feet (160 m) lower than they are now and in latitudes low enough to be free from ice there were large areas of dry land that were inundated when the ice sheets melted and sea levels rose again.

Ice sheets flow. As more and more snow falls over the center, its weight compacts the snow beneath until it forms ice, and then squeezes it outward, so the base of the sheet moves, very slowly, downhill. (There is no real difference between an ice sheet and a glacier, and scientists use the words interchangeably.) The "river of ice" many people think of as a glacier is known technically as a valley glacier, because it flows along a defined valley. A glacier flows into the sea or into a region where temperatures are above freezing and the ice melts, releasing meltwater to form rivers.

Obviously, no plants can survive beneath the ice sheet, and for some distance beyond its edges the ground is permanently frozen below the surface. This is "permafrost." Its surface thaws briefly in summer and it supports tundra plants, but large trees cannot grow in it. Tundra vegetation covered most of Europe south of the ice sheets. South of the Laurentide ice sheet, there was a belt of tundra 60 to 125 miles (100–200 km) wide, but pine and spruce forests grew over much of the eastern United States as far south as Florida. Scientists believe Japan remained forested throughout the glaciation.

Temperate forests do not disappear. The expansion of the arctic region pushes the vegetational belts in lower latitudes closer to the equator.

The Glacial Retreat

Then, starting about 14,000 years ago, the climate gradually grew warmer and as the temperature rose above freezing around the edges of the glaciers, the ice commenced its long retreat. The warming was not a steady process. There were times when it halted, or reversed, and there were the two major Dryas reversals (page 53), but by about 8,000 to 10,000 years ago the edge of the permanent ice lay close to its present position.

Meltwater moistened the ground south of the retreating glaciers and the first plants appeared. At first, these were sedges and grasses. They helped soil to form (page 10) and when there was a sufficient depth of soil the first trees arrived.

All the plants colonizing these bare landscapes arrived as seeds carried from the south. In North America and eastern Asia, there was no major geographical barrier between the newly exposed lands and the established grasslands and forests. In Europe, however, the migration of plants was restricted by the Alps and, to their south, by the Sahara. Redwoods (*Sequoia* species) and tulip trees (*Liriodendron* species) grew in

Europe before the glaciation, but became extinct as the expansion of European glaciers trapped them; they survived in the south of Asia and North America. Following the glacial retreat, these and many other species were able to recolonize North America and Asia, but not Europe. That is why to this day Asian and American temperate forests contain far more tree species than do European forests.

Glacier Bay

The sequence in which plants colonized is known mainly from pollen, but there is one place where it has been observed directly. In southeastern Alaska, the edge of the glacier flowing into Glacier Bay has retreated about 330 feet (100 m) over the last two centuries, and recolonization can be dated either by counting the rings on older trees or from recorded observations. The first arrivals were mosses and herbs, including mountain avens (*Dryas octopetala*), a plant that enriches the soil with nitrogen, by means of bacteria around its roots, and so encourages other colonizers. Then came willows (*Salix* species), followed by American green alder (*Alnus crispa*) and cottonwood (*Populus* species). Sitka spruce (*Picea sitchensis*) then entered, forming dense forest. Finally, the spruce forest developed into forest dominated by western hemlock (*Tsuga heterophylla*) and mountain hemlock (*T. mertensiana*).

This sequence seems to have been broadly typical of the way much of North America was recolonized. At first, scattered mosses and herbs established themselves on the bare ground. As sedges, grasses, and a few shrubs arrived a tundra vegetation developed, interspersed with patches of grassland. By around 15,000 years ago, spruces arrived. They were scattered at first, but the gaps soon filled to produce forest dominated by spruce and tamarack (*Larix laricina*), a species of larch. The forest must have looked much like the present-day taiga of Siberia. In the warmer regions to the south, the spruce-tamarack forest was replaced by one of oak (*Quercus* species) and balsam fir (*Abies balsamea*), the traditional American Christmas tree. Then pines (*Pinus* species) appeared, including jack pine (*P. banksiana*). They require warmer conditions than most conifers, and they were joined by maples (*Acer* species) and hickory (*Carya* species). The forest was changing from a boreal to a mixed conifer and broad-leaved deciduous type, and by about 8,000 years ago it was dominated by hemlocks (*Tsuga* species) and beech (*Fagus* species).

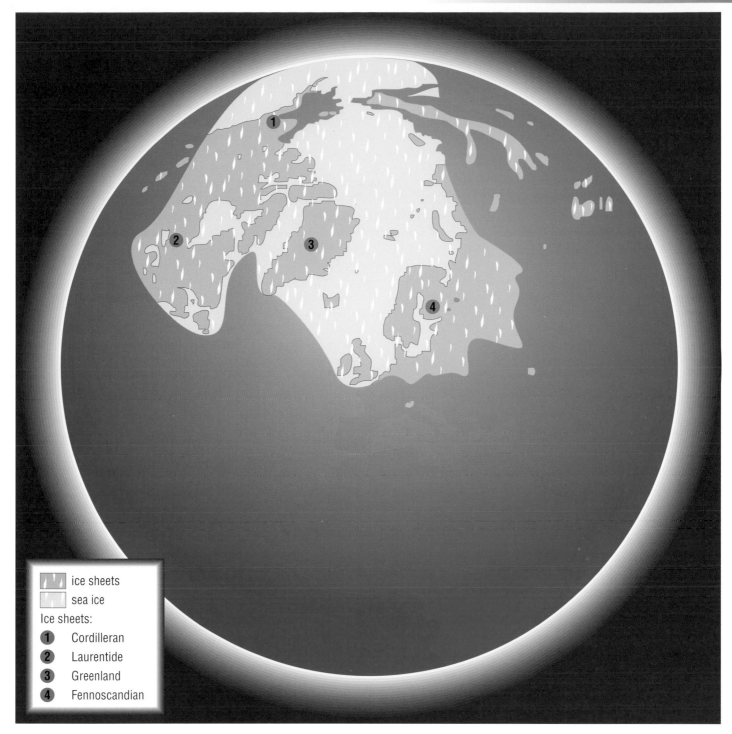

Ice age at greatest extent

ice sheets
sea ice
Ice sheets:
① Cordilleran
② Laurentide
③ Greenland
④ Fennoscandian

European Recolonization

In Europe, recolonizing plants began moving northward around 13,000 years ago. After the sedges and grasses, the next to arrive were the juniper (*Juniperus communis*) and the arctic willow (*Salix herbacea*) and dwarf birch (*Betula nana*), plants that grow close to the edge of the tundra. By about 12,000 years ago these had been joined by downy birch (*B. pubescens*), silver birch (*B. pendula*), and aspen (*Populus tremula*), which need warmer conditions. At this stage the trees grew in the north as scattered patches of woodland (copses) separated by tundra vegetation, and the landscape was quite open, like parkland. In the south, trees grew closer together, as forest dominated by downy birch.

The northward migration was then interrupted by the Younger Dryas (or Loch Lomond) stadial. A stadial is a cold period that is shorter and milder than a full glaciation (and a mild interlude shorter and less warm than an interglacial is an interstadial). During the Dryas, the West Highlands of Scotland were buried once more by an ice sheet hundreds of feet thick and the birch copses survived only in isolated, sheltered places.

Around 10,000 years ago, as temperatures started rising again, colonization resumed and this time it was fairly rapid. Hazel (*Corylus avellana*) was abundant by 9,000 years ago and over most of northern Europe it was soon followed by birch and Scotch pine (*Pinus sylvestris*), producing birch-pine-hazel forest. This forest remained in northern England and Scotland, but further south it gave way to forests of elm (*Ulmus* species) and oak.

Relicts and Refugia

Major climate changes never happen smoothly, and the Younger Dryas stadial (page 53) was only the most dramatic of the fluctuations associated with the end of the last ice age. Throughout the Northern Hemisphere, during what is known as the subarctic period, land exposed by the retreat of glaciers was colonized by tundra vegetation. This gave way to cool, moist conditions in the preboreal period, when spruce (*Picea* species) and fir (*Abies* species) advanced in eastern North America and pines (*Pinus* species) and birch (*Betula* species) appeared in Europe. The preboreal was followed, about 9,000 years ago, by the boreal period, when climates became warmer, drier, and more continental (page 50), favoring pines and oak (*Quercus* species) in North America and pines and hazel (*Corylus avellana*) in Europe. The boreal period, marking the beginning of a long, warm interlude called the Hypsithermal, was followed around 7,000 years ago by moister, more maritime conditions in the Atlantic period, which encouraged oak and beech (*Fagus* species). The sub-Atlantic period, starting around 3,000 years ago and marking the end of the Hypsithermal, was still moist, but cooler.

Rates of Colonization

Such changes affect vegetation patterns, but at different rates, and there is always a delay before plants and animals respond to change. When the climate warmed vigorously at the start of the boreal period, birch (*Betula* species) and aspen (*Populus* species) advanced into new ground at a rate of about half a mile (1 km) a year. Oak (*Quercus* species) and elm (*Ulmus* species) followed in the Atlantic period, but rather more slowly, and beech (*Fagus* species) and spruce (*Picea* species) moved north at less than 550 yards (500 m) a year. Cooling has a much more immediate effect, because established trees fail to survive and may disappear from an area within a very few years.

Often, though, the changes are less than total, leaving places where plant communities—and the animals associated with them—survive from earlier times. Climatic warming allows new species to invade, but in mountainous regions, for example, the older species may migrate up the mountainsides and survive at a higher altitude. There are "sky islands" of this kind high in the mountains of Arizona and New Mexico and at several places in the southern United States and in Nova Scotia,

Canada, there are populations of eastern four-toed salamanders isolated from the main range of this population, which lies to the north. The map of North America below shows the approximate location of these groups. Probably they lived in the boreal forest that covered the south during the Wisconsinian glaciation and remained when warmer conditions caused the forest itself to migrate farther north.

More surprisingly, perhaps, there are also places where plants have survived a deterioration in climate. Even an advance of the ice sheets leaves some areas ice-free, and scattered plant and animal communities may survive in sheltered spots, close to the sea, perhaps, where the proximity of water moderates the climate. Isolated areas where the ground is moist may remain and retain their vegetation pattern, as the surrounding land dries into desert. A local area where the type of vegetation is typical of an earlier climatic period, and markedly different from the pattern surrounding it, is called a refugium (plural, *refugia*) and a plant species that survives from an earlier time is called a relict, or relic.

Location of four-toed salamanders

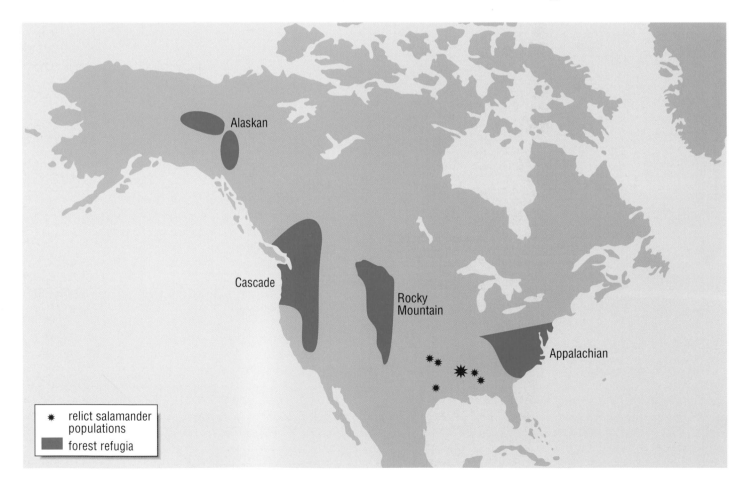

* relict salamander
  populations
◼ forest refugia

Two refugia in the United Kingdom: Upper Teesdale in the north and the Lizard Peninsula in the South

Surviving Extinction

It can even happen that one species survives the extinction of all other members of its genus. The maidenhair tree (*Gingko biloba*) survived in the gardens of Chinese monasteries and is the only remaining representative of a very ancient group of trees. The dawn redwood (*Metasequoia glyptostroboides*) is another relict species, the only member of its genus and, in the view of some botanists, sufficiently different from all other redwoods (for one thing it is deciduous) to warrant classification in a family of its own. It was first identified as a fossil in 1941 and believed to have been extinct for the last 26 million years. Then, in 1945, it was found growing in southern China. It is an attractive tree, now grown widely in parks and gardens, but it is still called a relict, even though it is no longer rare.

Lusitanian Flora

The most southerly point in mainland Britain is the Lizard Peninsula, at the far tip of Cornwall (see map above). It is not forested, but its vegetation is unusual, containing many plants that are rare elsewhere, even in the rest of Cornwall, such as Cornish heath (*Erica vagans*). This type of vegetation, called Lusitanian, also occurs in southwest Ireland,

where it includes the strawberry tree (*Arbutus unedo*), a plant otherwise found in the much warmer coastal regions of Portugal. The Lizard and southwest Ireland are refugia of a plant community that is believed to have survived the most recent glaciation in another refugium somewhere in southwest Europe, then migrated northward in the very earliest stages of the glacial retreat along European coasts that were later submerged. The Lusitanian vegetation may once have been fairly widespread, but it survived subsequent cool episodes only in places with an especially mild climate.

Upper Teesdale

The most famous British refugium occupies about 80 square miles (207 sq. km.) in Upper Teesdale, a wild, remote part of the north of England (see map, left). Far from being forested, Upper Teesdale is remarkable because although some of the advancing trees probably reached it, they disappeared again before they could displace the vegetation that was already established. As a result, this upper part of the valley of the river Tees, at a height rising to about 1,500 feet (460 m), bears a cover of plants scientists believe to be typical of those that covered a much larger area just as the last of the glaciers were retreating. There are many grasses and flowering herbs, some of them rare, and dwarf birch (*Betula nana*) grows in Upper Teesdale. This tree also occurs on Lüneberg Heath, Germany, where it is also a relict species.

American Forest Refugia

In North America, there are four refugia—in Alaska, the Appalachians, the Cascades, and the Rockies—shown in the map on page 56—where coniferous forest survived throughout the Wisconsinian glaciation, some of them covering a much larger area than they do now. Surrounded by tundra and steppe grassland, the Alaskan refugium occupied two separate ice-free areas, and possibly included some offshore islands. The Pacific refugium, on the western slopes of the Cascade Range in Washington and Oregon, then extended south into California. The Rocky Mountain refugium covered a large area in Montana and Idaho, and the Appalachian refugium, centered on the middle of the Appalachian range, extended westward, south of the Great Lakes. During the glaciation, coniferous forest grew at a much lower altitude on mountainsides than it does now.

Widespread Refugia

Upper Teesdale, the four North American areas of boreal forest, and to a lesser degree the Lusitanian

flora of the Lizard and southwest Ireland, are major refugia, and easily recognized, but changing climates also leave more numerous, if subtler, clues. Plant seeds are dispersed in various ways (page 68) and if they fall on ground that suits them, they will germinate and grow. As a glaciation draws to an end and the climate warms, conditions at a high altitude will remain glacial for much longer.

Temperature decreases with height, but the decrease is counted from its sea-level value, so if the temperature rises at sea level it will also rise high in the mountains. During a postglacial warming, this may change a mountain climate from one too cold to support plants at all to one capable of supporting plants of the type that grew at a lower level during the ice age. Even if the overall climate becomes temperate, at a higher level, in exposed places, the climate may remain glacial and occupied by vegetation that was once more widespread. These are refugia. Small, scattered, and not easily recognized, such late-glacial survivals are found in many upland and mountain areas of Europe and North America.

Later, as the forests rapidly migrated northward, habitats unsuitable for the colonizing trees, perhaps because their soils were too acid, alkaline, or wet, would be surrounded and isolated. These, too, would become refugia.

Rising sea level and the inundation of low-lying ground forms offshore islands. If colonizing species are unable to cross the stretch of open water to reach an island, its colonization may be halted, and it, too, may become a refugium. Many river estuaries in temperate latitudes are river valleys that were inundated when the sea rose following the glacial retreat. There are remains of forests, now on the seabed and partly exposed at very low tides. Ireland is not a refugium, but if the sea level were to fall by 300 feet (90 m) it would be joined by land bridges to Wales and Scotland. Since the end of the last ice age, the sea has risen by much more than this, separating mainland Britain from Ireland, and Ireland has only about 70 percent of the plant species found in Britain. Britain is much larger than Ireland and has a more varied and somewhat less strongly maritime climate, which accounts for some of the disparity, but it is also partly due to the separation of the two islands before post-glacial colonization was complete.

Relict species and refugia are of considerable scientific interest and, therefore, they are allotted a high priority when sites are selected for conservation. Much can be learned from relicts about the evolutionary history of plants, and refugia provide information about the individual components of vegetation that was once widespread. This may be especially important if, as many climatologists suppose, the climate is now changing (page 174).

Evolution of Trees

Trees look very different from all other plants. You may not be able to name the many species of trees, shrubs, herbs, and grasses you see on a visit to the countryside, but you do not need a botany course to be able to recognize a tree when you see one or, for that matter, a shrub, herb, or grass. These are easily distinguished from one another, and a tree is the most recognizable of them all.

A tree towers above the plants around it and, unlike herbs and grasses, its stem and branches are hard to the touch. It is tempting to suppose that trees are profoundly different from all other types of plant, that they represent some sort of pinnacle of plant development, an ultimate form to which the entire history of plants has led.

The truth is less dramatic. It is only its size that differentiates a tree from other plants and the trees we see around us today are not the only plants to have grown tall. Technically, a tree is defined as a plant that is capable of growing to a height of 33 feet (10 m) or more, often with the lowest branch 4 feet (1.2 m) above the ground, that typically has only one main stem—although there are exceptions to this—and that does not die back at the end of each growing season, although it may shed its leaves. This definition is based on the appearance of the plant, especially on its size, and it tells us nothing directly about the structure of the plant or how it works. We could call any plant a tree if it conformed to this description, regardless of its relationship to other plants we also call trees. Indeed, broad-leaved trees are more closely related to the flowering herbs growing beneath them than they are to coniferous trees.

The Emergence of Plants

Plants are distinguished from animals and fungi by the way they obtain food. Plants (and some bacteria) "manufacture" sugars from carbon dioxide and water by the process of photosynthesis (page 72). Animals obtain their food by eating plants or other animals. The earliest plants, single-celled green algae, first emerged in water. These are still widespread; they are what make stagnant water and some seawater green. In some algal species, cells join together into filaments. You often find these in shallow water, attached to a solid surface. Other algae grew much bigger, into seaweeds. Then, about 425 million years ago, plants began to grow on land. Probably these were filamentous algae growing around coasts and lake shores, where they were frequently immersed by tides or floods.

Some descendants of these algae then acquired a "cuticle," an outer coating like a skin, that covered them entirely and prevented them from drying out. They also developed protective coats for their reproductive cells. These adaptations helped plants to survive out of water. Plants of this type have flourished ever since: they are the mosses, liverworts, and hornworts, of which there are about 17,000 species living today.

In other plants certain cells joined together to form "vascular tissue," bundles of tubes through which water and nutrients could pass. You can see this vascular tissue in the veins of leaves. Plants could then grow much bigger and more complex, because the plant itself could transport nutrients to tissues needing them and, therefore, each individual cell was no longer required to provide for itself. Not all the cells of a plant had to engage in photosynthesis, so some cells could live in permanent darkness, below ground or inside the plant.

Specialization was necessary. Carbon dioxide and mineral nutrients are dispersed throughout water, so every part of an aquatic plant is bathed in them while also being exposed to sunlight. On land, however, water and mineral nutrients are located below ground. One part of the plant has to be responsible for obtaining them, and also for anchoring the plant, and a different part of the plant has to perform photosynthesis. So roots came to be differentiated from the parts of the plant that grow above ground.

Wood and Trees

Gravity then had to be overcome. Walk along a sheltered beach at low tide and you will see untidy heaps of flattened seaweed. As the tide rises, the seaweed floats up to stand erect, like a submarine forest. This is possible because the plant is buoyant, but buoyancy is no help out of water. Land plants had to stand erect by some other means in order to maximize their exposure to light.

For small plants, the rigidity of their water-filled cells, called turgor pressure, was sufficient, but it would not support the weight of a large plant. Greater rigidity was attained when some plants began to produce lignin inside the walls of their cells. Lignin is a hard material that remains after the death of the cell that produces it: dead cells collapse, but the lignin remains. The process is called lignification, and the resulting material is wood.

With wood to provide rigidity and vascular tissue to transport water and nutrients, driven by transpiration (page 28), plants could grow tall, and some began to do so at once. Growing taller raised them higher than the plants around them, which increased their exposure to light. They also developed leaves that presented large surfaces to the sun, thus maximizing their photosynthetic activity.

The First Forests

Since a tree is defined principally by its size, that development allowed the first trees to appear and, with them, the first forests. Once established, the forests covered vast areas and remained the dominant form of vegetation for more than 200 million years.

They were not at all like modern forests, however, because the early trees were very different from the trees that grow today. They included *Calamites,* which grew with its roots in water and reached a height of about 50 feet (15 m). Their only modern relatives are about 15 species of horsetails (*Equisetum*), small plants of wet places. There was *Lepidodendron*, an even more impressive tree, with a very straight trunk up to 6.5 feet (2 m) in diameter, that grew more than 130 feet (40 m) tall. Its surviving relatives are the clubmosses, such as *Lycopodium* and *Selaginella*. (Despite their name, they are not true mosses.) The forests also contained tree-ferns. Their descendants still exist—you can often see them growing in botanic gardens, the commonest species being *Dicksonia antarctica*. The forests comprised many species, of which these are only examples, and around 300 million years ago they grew close to the equator on flat, low-lying, swampy ground. When they and the plants around them died, they decomposed only partially in the airless swamp mud. Later, compression and heating turned them into the vast coal deposits that supply a great deal of our fuel.

Most of these swamp species of the Carboniferous period became extinct around 280 million years ago, when the climate became drier and the swamps turned into dry land. Among them, though, there were less impressive plants that could tolerate drier conditions: with the disappearance of the swamp giants, their moment had arrived.

Gymnosperms

These plants were different because they produced seeds. During its life cycle, every plant passes through two distinct forms, each of which gives rise to the other. The process is called the alternation of generations (page 64) and the two forms are called gametophytes and sporophytes. In early plants, such as mosses, the gametophyte generation was the bigger of the two, but in later plants, including all present-day clubmosses, ferns, trees, and herbs, the plant you see is the sporophyte generation. The new plants had gametophytes that were even smaller than those of other plants, and instead of being jettisoned to develop in the soil independently, the sporophyte retained them within its own, moist tissues. There, the embryo of what would grow into a new plant was surrounded with a store of food and enclosed in a covering. This was a seed, but at first it was not held in a chamber specialized for the purpose. The seed was naked. The Greek word for naked is *gymnos* and for seed *sperma,* so these plants are known as gymnosperms.

As the old forest trees disappeared, the gymnosperms took their place. Gymnosperms were better adapted for life on land, because their reproduction was safer and more efficient (page 64). As they continued to evolve, the gymnosperms diverged to form four groups. All of these survive to the present day (page 61), although only one has really prospered. The group that has flourished, and is seen everywhere, is that of the conifers. *Konos* is the Greek word for cone, *phero* means carry, so the conifers are "conebearers."

Flowering Plants

Despite the success of the gymnosperms, most of the plants we see around us today do not belong to this group. Palms, broad-leaved trees and shrubs, flowering herbs, and grasses are all angiosperms. The name refers to a container (Greek *angion*), the ovary, in which the seeds (*sperma*) are borne. The ovary develops from a flower, and so angiosperms are also known as flowering plants.

The group first appeared about 130 million years ago and expanded to occupy all but the driest and coldest regions. Today about 235,000 species of angiosperms are known, compared with 721 species of gymnosperms. The deciduous forests, from the Tropics to middle latitudes, are composed mainly or entirely of angiosperms.

Seed Plants, Conifers, Flowering Plants

In all, there are more than 12,000 species of ferns, including the tree ferns. Around 300 million years ago other species of much bigger tree ferns formed an important component of vast forests. Today, you will see ferns growing in many temperate forests, some on the ground and others on the branches of broad-leaved trees. They are commoner now than they used to be. In the last century ferns were fashionable as houseplants, and those that ornamented homes, hotels, and restaurants were collected from the wild, seriously depleting their natural populations. They are still popular—though less so than they were then—but now they can be cultivated, so ferns you buy in pots to take home have been grown in nurseries. Cultivation, combined with laws forbidding people from collecting wild plants, has allowed their numbers to recover.

Examine a fern leaf, often called a frond, and you will see it has veins, the vessels that carry water and nutrients, showing that ferns are vascular plants, like the trees and herbs that grow in modern forests. The veins are branched, an arrangement that probably evolved through the development of small veins linking closely spaced larger ones. The botanical name for a leaf of this kind, found in ferns and all seed-producing plants, is "megaphyll." Many ferns have compound leaves, in which each main frond is divided into many small leaflets, as shown in the diagram (right).

Producing Spores

Turn the fronds (megaphylls) over to examine their undersides and you will see rows of what look like dark spots along the leaflets of just some of them. Often there are two parallel rows of spots. Leaflets bearing these spots are known as sporophylls; the spots are called sori (singular, *sorus*).

Sporophylls are reproductive leaflets, specialized to form part of the reproductive mechanism of the plant. Each sorus is a cluster of tiny structures called sporangia (singular, *sporangium*) and each sporangium is a container filled with spores. All ferns produce sporangia, but not all of them bear their sporangia in clusters, so not all of them have sori. When conditions are right, a sporangium springs open and throws its spores into the air.

Spores form inside the sporangia from "spore mother cells." Each spore mother cell divides meiotically (by reduction division), producing four haploid cells (each with one set of chromosomes,

Fern

rather than the two sets in most [diploid] cells). These haploid cells, with toughened outer walls, are the spores. They are extremely small and all of them are identical. They do not contain the embryo of a new plant, so they are quite different from seeds. Since they are so small and light, the wind can carry them long distances. Those that land in a favorable spot grow into the structure forming the next stage in the life cycle of the plant.

Ferns, then, are vascular plants that do not produce seeds. They are classified in the plant division Pterophyta, by far the largest of the four divisions of seedless vascular plants surviving to the present day. Whiskferns, which are not really ferns, comprise the division Psilophyta. Club-mosses, or groundpines, which are neither mosses nor pines, form the division Lycophyta, and horsetails form the division Sphenophyta.

The Cost of Relying on Spores

Spores work well enough. All the simpler plants, such as mosses and liverworts, reproduce by means of them, as do fungi and some bacteria. They evolved early in the history of life on our planet, and since they are still used, clearly they have stood the test of time.

Unfortunately, the organisms that produce them pay a price for their simplicity. The new plant that develops directly from a spore must start at once to obtain its own food. All the spore provides is a set of genetic instructions: it contains no store of food to see the young plant through its first few days of life. Spores themselves can remain viable for long periods and develop only when they are moist, but if the new plant had even a small amount of protection, it would have a much better chance of surviving should a brief spell of cold or dry weather occur while it was trying to establish itself. Not surprisingly, the mortality rate among young plants is very high. To compensate for this, a fern produces hundreds of millions of spores every season. Each spore is so small the plant needs to invest very little material or energy to produce it, but it loses much of this advantage by having to produce spores in such large quantities.

What Is a Seed?

By about 360 million years ago, one group of plants, the gymnosperms (page 59), had evolved a means of improving the survival chances of their young. Instead of releasing spores, they retained them until the new plant had grown the structures from which roots and leaves could develop quickly; this rudimentary plant is called an embryo. It is surrounded by a store of food sufficient to keep it nourished until its leaves are big enough for it to produce its own food by photosynthesis (page 72), all enclosed by a coat tough enough to protect the embryo from harsh conditions. Together, the embryo, its food store, and the outer coating comprise a seed. Gymnosperms were the first seed plants.

Today there are four groups, or divisions, of gymnosperms. Cycads form one group, the division Cycadophyta. They are sometimes called sago palms and are rather like palms in appearance, but botanically they are very different. The ginkgos, forming the division Ginkgophyta, are reduced to only one species, the maidenhair tree (*Ginkgo biloba*), which is grown quite widely as an ornamental. The gnetae, division Gnetophyta, comprise a number of species, including trees, that are quite different from each other. The division does include one of the most remarkable of all plants, *Welwitschia mirabilis* (or *W. bainesii*), which grows only in the deserts of southwest Africa. It produces the biggest of all plant leaves—huge, straplike structures that grow more than five inches (12.7 cm) a year and wear away at their tips—obtains all its moisture from dew and fog, and is said to live for more than 1,000 years.

Conifers and Their Cones

Conifers, comprising the division Coniferophyta, are by far the most abundant and familiar of all gymnosperms. The pines, spruces, firs, larches, hemlocks, and redwoods of our coniferous forests all belong to this division.

As their name suggests, all of them produce cones. In fact, they produce two types of cone. Pollen cones consist of very small sporophylls (reproductive leaves) with large numbers of sporangia. Haploid cells produced in the sporangia develop into pollen grains that are dispersed by the wind. Ovulate cones are composed of scales, each containing two ovules, and each ovule contains a sporangium, called the nucellus, enclosed by walls, called integuments, with a single opening, the micropyle. A pollen grain falling on an ovulate cone enters the ovule through the micropyle, fertilizes eggs formed in the ovule, and this leads to the development of the seed (see page 65 for a fuller description).

The Emergence of Flowers

No one knows just how angiosperms appeared. Their fossils have been found in rocks about 120 million years old, but their ancestry is uncertain. What is certain is that by about 65 million years ago they had become far more numerous than any other type of plant, and they remain so still. There are less than 1,000 species of gymnosperms living today, but well over 200,000 species of angiosperms. All of them are classified in one division, the Anthophyta, comprising two classes—the Monocotyledonae or monocots and Dicotyledonae or dicots. Grasses, cereals, sugarcane, lilies, bamboos, and palm trees are monocots. The broad-leaved trees of temperate forests are dicots, as are most of the herbs growing in association with them. All of them share the production of flowers. A flower is a reproductive structure in which ovules are contained inside an ovary. The ovary protects the ovules and the seeds that develop from them.

Many flowers have brightly colored petals and many mature ovaries become fruits, with the seeds hidden inside them. Bright colors attract insects and other animals to a store of nectar, which is a sugary liquid. As they move about inside the flower, consuming the nectar, they also transfer pollen, thus allowing fertilization to take place. Edible fruits also attract visitors, including humans, who help distribute the seeds they contain (page 68). There are other differences between angiosperms and gymnosperms (page 63), and not all angiosperms produce colored flowers or edible fruits. For example, grasses, which are pollinated by the wind, have drab, inconspicuous flowers. Many trees produce inedible seeds. The important distinguishing feature of angiosperms is their protection of ovules inside an ovary.

All three groups of vascular plants continue to live side by side. Ferns, producing and releasing spores, are common and widespread. Gymnosperms, pollinated by wind and producing "naked" ovules, dominate the forests of high latitudes. It is the angiosperms that have proved most successful, however, and it is they that provide us with the great majority of our ornamental plants and our food, as well as with the trees of our most beautiful forests.

How a Tree Works

In spring a deciduous forest is an enchanted place. In that brief interval between the thawing of the ground and the bursting of the leaf buds on the trees, sunlight dapples the forest floor. There is enough light for the small herbs to flower and produce their seeds and, in the larger clearings, the grasses are in the bright green flush of their first growth of the year. As you gaze at the grasses, the flowers, the small shrubs and tree saplings, and the trees towering above your head, you may well imagine you are seeing plants that function in many, quite different ways. Yet it is only its size that distinguishes a tree from any other plant. The oaks, beeches, hornbeams, redwoods, and all the rest work in exactly the same way as the smallest of the herbs growing around their bases.

Every land plant grows and repairs its tissues by absorbing nutrients from the ground. Sunlight, harnessed by photosynthesis (page 72) in its green leaves and released by respiration supplies the energy it needs to grow, repair itself, and reproduce. It uses water to transport nutrients, in a constant stream from the roots to the leaves, where it evaporates (page 28).

When a seed germinates, the emerging plant forms two structures. One will become the stem, and eventually the main trunk of a tree, the other, called a radicle, becomes the root system. Almost from the start, the plant divides itself into two distinct parts, the shoot system above ground and the root system below. These two main parts of the plant, illustrated in the diagram at right depend on one another. The roots, being below ground and therefore in perpetual darkness, cannot perform photosynthesis to synthesize sugars. These must be supplied from the leaves, above ground. The shoot system cannot obtain mineral nutrients, which are found only in the soil, so these must be supplied by the roots.

Roots

A tree root is woody, like the trunk and branches, but roots and shoots differ in their structure and the way they grow. Most dicots (page 61) produce a large taproot, often penetrating to a considerable depth. In some plants, but not trees, this also doubles as a food-storage organ. Carrots, sweet potatoes, and parsnips are taproots of this kind. Monocots and gymnosperms produce roots that grow to the sides

Principal parts of a flowering plant

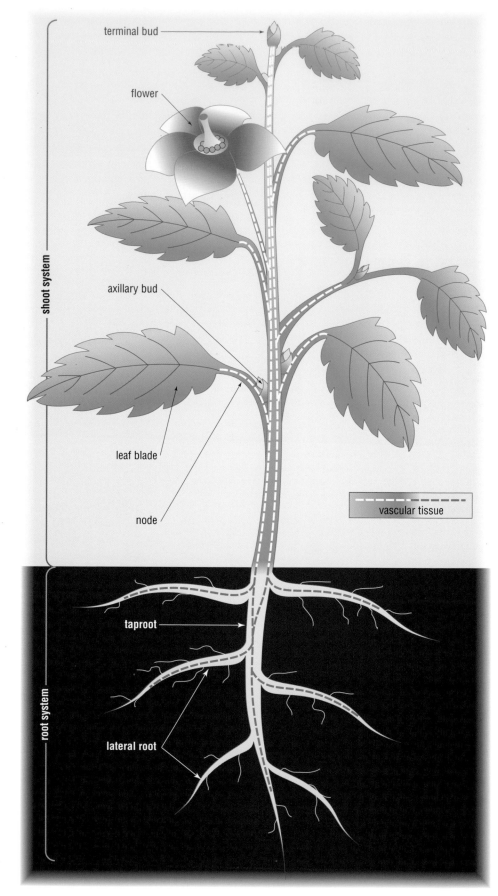

terminal bud

flower

shoot system

axillary bud

leaf blade

node

vascular tissue

root system

taproot

lateral root

and are shallower. Taproots branch to produce lateral roots and, whether they grow from a taproot or directly from the base of the main stem, lateral roots branch into smaller and smaller side roots, and eventually into a mass of fine fibers. The volume of soil occupied by the root system may be greater than the volume of air occupied by the parts of the tree that are above the ground.

As the growing root pushes its way through the soil, its tip is protected from damage by a tough cap that is constantly renewed as it wears away. Behind the tip, the root surface consists of a layer of cells, each of which is capable of growing an extension rather less than one-fifth of an inch (4 mm) long. These extensions are the root hairs: it is through them that water and nutrients are absorbed. Root hairs occur just behind the growing tip of each of the smallest root fibers. As the root continues to grow, the older hairs are shed, along with the outer layer of cells of which they are a part.

Obtaining Nitrogen

Dig up a pea or bean plant complete with its roots, carefully brush away some of the soil, and you will see masses of white or gray nodules, each about as big as the head of a map pin, clinging to the roots. These are colonies of bacteria that are able to convert gaseous nitrogen, present in the air between soil particles, into nitrate (NO_3), some of which passes into the plant root. In return, the bacteria obtain carbohydrates from the plant. Peas, beans, lupins, and a large number of related plants are called legumes, and their relationship with "nitrogen-fixing" bacteria has been known for a long time (page 76).

Nitrogen is a key ingredient of amino acids, from which proteins are made. This makes it an essential nutrient element for all living organisms. Plants are unable to absorb nitrogen in its gaseous form; it must be combined with another element. In the soil, nitrogen is present in the amino acids in dead organic matter and, when these dissolve, as dissolved organic nitrogen (DON). As the amino acids break down, the nitrogen occurs as ammonium (NH_4), which is then converted to nitrate. Most plants can use nitrogen as DON, NH_4, or NO_3, but some have clear preferences. White spruce (*Picea glauca*), for example, absorbs NH_4, but has difficulty utilizing NO_3. This tree is grown extensively for pulp production, to make paper, but when it is planted on ground that has been disturbed by clear-felling a previous tree crop, it often grows weakly and may even be displaced by other species, probably because disturbing the soil stimulates the reactions that convert NH_4 to NO_3.

The Soil Community

Relationships between plants and other organisms are not confined to legumes. Alder trees (*Alnus* species), which are not legumes, have similar nodules on their roots, and most plants depend on soil microorganisms to process nutrients into forms their roots can absorb. About 95 percent of all vascular plants form associations between their roots and fungi called mycorrhizae, meaning "fungus roots," in which root cells link with fungal hyphae. This arrangement unites the plant roots with the fungal mycelium and greatly increases the surface area through which nutrients can be absorbed. The fungus supplies the plant with nitrogen, which it obtains as compounds the plant cannot use directly, and the plant passes carbon directly to the fungus.

Soil organisms also require nutrients, of course, so plant roots must compete to obtain those they need, and plant roots exude chemical compounds as well as absorbing them. The rhizosphere, which is the soil around the roots of a plant, is like a chemical factory with a vast array of fungi, bacteria, and other microorganisms, as well as the roots themselves, all engaged in processes so complex that scientists have not yet been able to describe fully how it all works.

Xylem

Once inside the root, nutrients dissolved in water enter the xylem, which transports them to every other part of the plant. In gymnosperms, the xylem consists of specialized cells called tracheids. These are long, approximately cylindrical cells with tapered ends lying end to end, so they overlap, as shown in the diagram above. Their walls are strengthened with rings or spirals of lignin, the tough material that gives wood its strength. Lignin does not cover the entire exterior of the cells. Gaps remain, as pits where the wall is thin enough for the nutrient solution to pass through, and it moves along from one tracheid to the next through the pits in the overlapping sections. Angiosperms also have tracheids, but in addition they possess a more efficient type of cell, called a vessel element. These are generally rather wider and shorter than tracheids. They have pits, but their end walls are perforated, forming a lumen or opening, so the cells provide an open tube, called a vessel, through which the solution flows freely.

Xylem tracheids and vessels run from the tips of the roots to every part of the plant and form the channels through which water and mineral nutrients are distributed. Carbohydrates, produced in the leaves by photosynthesis, are transported by another set of tubes, called the phloem. Xylem cells are dead, but phloem cells are alive, although they lack nuclei and other components found in most cells.

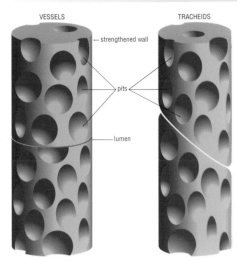

Vessels and tracheids

Phloem

Each phloem cell, called a sieve element, is cylindrical in shape and its ends, called sieve plates, are perforated. The sieve elements are joined at their sieve plates to form sieve tubes. Although they lack nuclei, in angiosperms each sieve element is closely linked to one or more companion cells to either side of it. These possess nuclei and ribosomes and are the sites of intense metabolic activity. Botanists believe they may provide the sieve elements with the energy and nutrients they need. In gymnosperms, the sieve elements are not associated with companion cells, but they are surrounded by parenchyma cells, which may serve the same purpose. Parenchyma cells are unspecialized plant cells that manufacture and store a range of products. In leaves, photosynthesis takes place in parenchyma cells, and elsewhere in the plant they store starches and sugars. When you eat root vegetables and fruit, it is mostly parenchyma cells you are eating.

Together, sieve tubes, tracheids, and, in angiosperms, vessels form the vascular system of the plant, transporting water and materials from where they are produced or obtained to where they are needed. When you cut a stem, the plant exudes sap. This is material being transported by the vascular system and it is of two kinds. Phloem sap is rich in sugars and often tastes sweet. Xylem sap is mostly water, in which mineral nutrients and some amino acids are dissolved. The two systems, xylem and phloem, lie side by side in vascular bundles; there are many vascular bundles in the trunk and main branches of a tree. As the vascular system extends into the smaller twigs, then leaf stalks, and finally the veins of the leaves, the number of vascular bundles decreases.

Reproduction

All trees reproduce sexually, but for many that is not the only method available. When you see a clump of trees all of the same species and growing close together surrounded by trees of a different species, there is a good chance that the clump has arisen asexually. Genetically, all the trees are identical and form a clone. Some trees reproduce in this way more readily than others. Elms (*Ulmus* species) and limes (or basswoods, *Tilia* species) are especially prone to this type of vegetative reproduction. Near the climatic boundary of their range, where the summer is not always warm and sunny enough for them to produce viable seed, it is this strategy that allows them to survive in what would otherwise be an inhospitable region.

Plants are able to reproduce in this way because they grow by the repeated division of unspecialized cells in tissues called meristem. Meristem cells can continue dividing indefinitely, provided they have the nutrients and warmth they need, and the tissues they produce may specialize later. That is why cutting a branch from a tree, or cutting the whole tree almost at ground level, often produces a mass of new twigs, a fact

that has been exploited for centuries as a way to produce thin poles (page 195). Similarly, a healthy, cut twig will produce a mass of undifferentiated cells, called a callus, at the cut end from which new roots will grow, producing a new plant.

Many trees can be "layered." A young, pliable branch is bent over until it touches the ground, then held there by a peg. In a little while it will produce roots and shoots and can then be cut free from its parent.

Apart from meristem tissue, much of the bulk of a plant consists of parenchyma cells. These are also undifferentiated and can be induced to develop into whole new plants. Valuable tree species, mainly ornamentals or orchard trees, are usually propagated vegetatively, nowadays often by culturing a batch of cells until there is a young plant big enough to be planted. Because all such progeny are identical, the technique ensures that they possess all the desirable characteristics of the parent plant, and clones can be produced cheaply in large numbers.

Basswoods and limes are often propagated by layering, but this is not the method used naturally

Douglas fir cone, Pacific Coast, North America (Gerry Ellis/ENP Images)

by elm trees. They produce new shoots at intervals along their lateral roots, so a clump of elms is not simply a clone: the trees are often literally a single plant, all sharing the same root system. Several dicot species spread in this way, and because they can continue to do so for much longer than the lifetime of any individual tree, it allows them to achieve something approaching immortality. In the Mojave Desert, California, there is a clone of creosote bushes that is believed to be 12,000 years old.

Alternation of Generations

Most trees reproduce sexually, however, and to do so their life cycle takes them through two distinct forms, a progress known as the alternation of generations. One generation is called the gametophyte, the other the sporophyte, and each gives rise to the other. The two generations differ in structure and appearance and one is much bigger and more prominent than the other. In mosses, liverworts, and hornworts, the plant you see is the gametophyte generation. In all larger plants, including trees, it is the sporophyte and the gametophyte is tiny and retained within specialized organs of the sporophyte.

The dominance of the sporophyte generation and the protection of the gametophyte within the body of the sporophyte is one of the ways plants have evolved for life out of water. On land, organisms are exposed to more intense solar radiation, including radiation at ultraviolet (UV) wavelengths, than they are in water, which absorbs UV radiation. This can damage chromosomes, so possession of two copies of each gene may mean that losing one copy is not disastrous. It makes sense, therefore, to expose only diploid cells (with two copies of each gene) and to protect haploid cells (with one). Also, in earlier plants fertilization involved sperm swimming toward eggs through water. Mosses can manage this if there is just a film of water covering the plant, but it would present serious difficulties for larger plants and, of course, it would make the colonization of dry habitats impossible. Instead, gymnosperms and angiosperms use pollen to deliver their sperm, making water unnecessary, and the fertilized egg then develops into a seed (page 66), rather than the spore produced by simpler plants. Seeds are protected against drought, cold, and other harsh conditions, and they can be dispersed over land more or less efficiently (page 68).

Mitosis and Meiosis

The essential difference between the generations lies in their chromosomes, the threadlike structures carrying the genes that are found in the nucleus of every cell. Most cells carry two copies of each chromosome and are called diploid. Sporophytes are diploid. Cells carrying a single copy of each chromosome are said to be haploid. In animals, including humans, spermatozoa and ova (egg cells) are haploid and all other body cells are diploid. In plants, the gametophyte is haploid. Gametophytes cannot develop into sporophytes directly but produce sperm and egg cells. These reproductive cells are known as gametes (in animals as well as in plants) and it is from the union of gametes to form a fertilized female gamete, called a zygote, that the diploid sporophyte develops.

All living cells increase their number by dividing. Diploid cells do so by mitosis, in which each chromosome replicates itself, producing a pair of "sister chromatids." As the nucleus divides in two, the chromatids separate, one going to each emerging nucleus, so the process results in two daughter cells, each with a full diploid complement of chromosomes. Haploid cells are produced from diploid cells by meiosis, a different process. The chromosomes replicate once, but the cell divides twice, producing four daughter cells, each with a single set of chromosomes. When haploid cells unite at fertilization, their chromosomes join and the resulting cell is diploid.

Pollen grains, produced by the male part of the plant and containing sperm, are male gametophytes. Eggs, produced by the female part of the plant, are female gametophytes. In some species, male and female gametophytes are produced on the same plant, in others on separate male and female plants. Some angiosperms produce male and female gametophytes in the same flower, others in separate male and female flowers. A species is said to be monoecious if it bears male and female organs in separate structures but both on the same individual plant. This arrangement reduces the risk of the plant pollinating itself that might arise if both were in the same structure and is often found in plants, such as grasses, that are pollinated by wind. If male and female organs are borne on separate plants the species is said to be dioecious. The terms are derived from the Greek *oikos*, meaning "house," so monoecious means "single-house" and *dioecious* "double-house."

The Cones of Conifers

The alternation of generations can be traced fairly easily through the life cycle of gymnosperms, illustrated in the diagram (left). Gymnosperms produce both male and female cones. In some species, such as European larch (*Larix decidua*) and Norway spruce (*Picea abies*), these occur on different branches of the same tree, but in others, such as Scotch pine (*Pinus sylvestris*), they form on the same branch. Male cones are small and insignificant, although in some species they are a different color from the leaves and look a little like flowers (although they are not true flowers). The big, handsome cones people collect to decorate their homes or predict the weather, and that foresters collect when they need seeds, are female cones. (Cones collected for their seeds should be gathered while they are still green.) Female cones form at the tips of branches. It takes several years for them to mature, during which time the branch continues to grow, so you find mature cones some distance from the tip.

The mature tree is the sporophyte generation. Its male cones comprise very small sporophylls, or reproductive leaves (page 60), each of which contains a large number of sporangia. A sporangium is a protective capsule containing diploid cells. These divide by meiosis, each cell producing four haploid cells. These develop into pollen grains, and the pollen grains are male gametophytes, although they are immature until they start to grow.

Gymnosperm life cycle

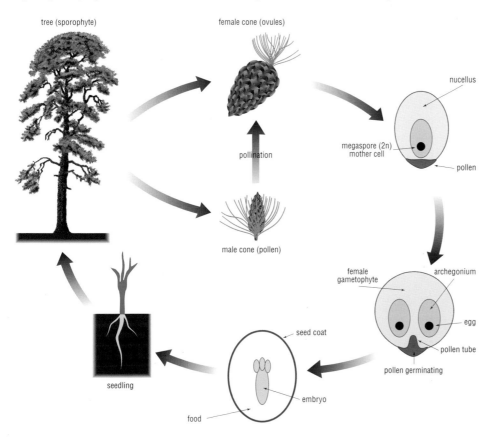

tree (sporophyte)

female cone (ovules)

pollination

male cone (pollen)

nucellus

megaspore (2n) mother cell

pollen

female gametophyte

archegonium

egg

pollen tube

pollen germinating

seed coat

embryo

food

seedling

Female cones are made of tough, woody scales and each scale contains two ovules surrounded by protective tissues, called integuments. An ovule comprises a sporangium, called the nucellus, and a (diploid) megaspore mother cell. There is a single opening to the nucellus, called the micropyle.

The Gymnosperm Reproductive Cycle

When the pollen is ready, the male sporangia split open. At this stage, each pollen grain consists of a single cell attached to two air-filled sacs, which make it very light. Pollen leaves the sporangia and some of it falls onto female cones, where a single pollen grain is drawn into each ovule through the micropyle. The pollen grain germinates and starts to grow a pollen tube that advances into the nucellus. Pollination is then complete.

Meanwhile, the megaspore mother cell divides by meiosis to produce four haploid cells, only one of which survives. It is called a megaspore and it divides repeatedly, forming the immature female gametophyte. Inside the female gametophyte, two or three archegonia develop; these are very simple structures, each containing an egg.

Pollination usually occurs in spring. Some trees produce seeds in the fall of the same year, but in many species more than a year elapses between pollination and fertilization. During this time the archegonia develop and the pollen grain matures. The pollen tube continues to grow into the nucellus until it reaches the megaspore. While it is growing, two sperm cells are produced inside the pollen grain, making it a mature male gametophyte. When the pollen tube reaches the megaspore, the sperm travel along it and unite with the eggs. This is fertilization. The female gametophyte contains two or three eggs. All of them may be fertilized, but only one is likely to develop further.

Fertilization unites the haploid sperm and egg cells to form a diploid zygote, a cell that divides repeatedly by mitosis, eventually becoming an embryo. The embryo is destined to become the new sporophyte generation. It has a whorl of two, three, or many rudimentary leaves, called cotyledons or seed leaves, the number varying according to species, and a radicle, which will become the root. The embryo is surrounded by a store of nutrients derived from tissues of the female gametophyte and both the embryo and its food store are enclosed in a seed coat produced by the parent plant, the seed coat and its contents comprising the seed. Although the seed coat pro-

tects the embryo, the seed as a whole is still located on the scale of the cone, and is not enclosed by any other structure.

In due course, the seed will be released and dispersed (page 68), usually by the wind. Those seeds that reach a favorable spot will germinate into seedlings, which grow into mature trees, thus completing the cycle.

The Flowers of Flowering Plants

Angiosperms produce flowers. Like all plants, their complete life cycle involves an alternation of generations, but the gametophyte generation is contained within the flower. The plant you see is the sporophyte.

Flowers come in an almost infinite variety of sizes, shapes, and colors. *Rafflesia arnoldii*, a parasite of the roots of tropical trees, has flowers up to 32 inches (80 cm) in diameter. These are the biggest of all flowers (and they smell of rotting meat, to attract the flies that pollinate them). At the other extreme, there are many plants with flowers no more than about one-10th of an inch

Parts of a flower

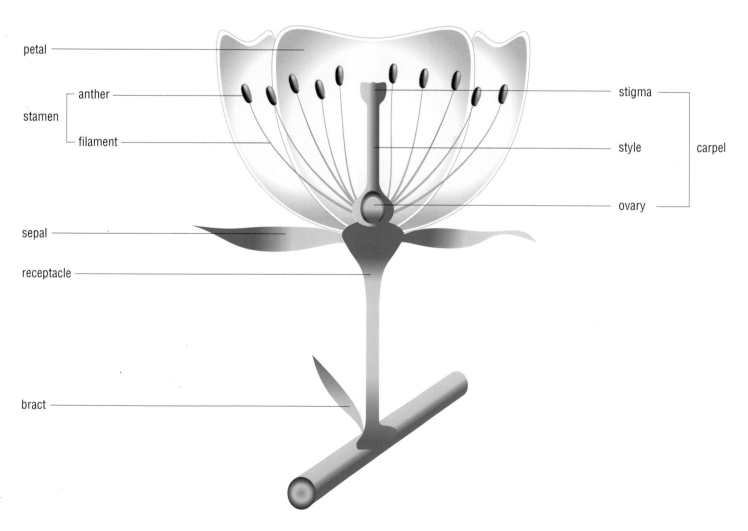

(3 mm) across, though such tiny flowers (florets) usually occur in large clusters (inflorescences), so they look bigger. A sunflower, for example, is actually a composite of hundreds of small florets.

Despite their huge variety, all flowers can be described in relation to a generalized type, shown in the diagram on page 66. Working from the outside of the plant inward, this comprises sepals, petals, stamens, and carpel. Bracts are small leaves, often modified, that grow where the flower is attached to the plant stem. Stamens, each consisting of a long filament topped by a clublike anther, are the male part of the flower. The stigma, style, and ovary, together forming the carpel, are the female part. The enlarged end of the peduncle (flower stalk), to which the carpel and stamens are attached, is the receptacle. If the ovary is attached to the receptacle above the point of attachment of the filaments (as in the diagram), it is said to be superior. An inferior ovary is attached below the filaments.

The flower shown here possesses both stamens and carpel. Such a flower is said to be perfect. Not all flowers are perfect. Some lack stamens; these are female flowers, and described as carpellate because they have only a carpel. Others lack carpels. Having only stamens and, therefore, being male, they are called staminate. Carpellate and staminate flowers are imperfect.

The flower in the diagram on page 66 is also complete, in that it possesses sepals and petals, as well as stamens and carpel. Some flowers are incomplete. Grasses, for example, produce flowers lacking petals. Sepals, which are usually green, are the leaflike structures that contain the flower bud, collectively the sepals comprise the calyx. Petals evolved to attract pollinating insects or, less commonly, birds. Pollinators recognize the shape and color of their preferred flowers, inside which they can feed on nectar, which is secreted by the nectary, an organ at the base of the flower. Flower scents evolved for the same reason: many insects are acutely sensitive to odors and can locate flowers by following a gradient of increasing odor intensity.

The Angiosperm Reproductive Cycle

The angiosperm reproductive cycle follows the same general course as that of gymnosperms, but with a few important differences. Inside each of the anthers there are several sporangia, called pollen sacs, each sporangium containing many diploid cells called microsporocytes. These divide by meiosis, each microsporocyte producing four haploid microspores, which divide by mitosis to produce pollen grains, enclosed in very tough, almost indestructible coats. These are the immature male gametophytes.

In the carpel, the ovary contains one or more ovules, the number varying according to species, and each ovule contains a diploid cell called a megasporocyte. This divides by meiosis, producing four haploid cells, only one of which survives, as the megaspore. This is the female gametophyte.

Pollination occurs when pollen grains are deposited on the stigma, which is sticky, to hold them once they arrive. Plants that are pollinated by animals are arranged in such a way that pollen grains adhere to the pollinator when it enters the flower, and stick to the stigmas of flowers it visits later. This is an economical method, and the plant can achieve pollination by producing pollen in only modest amounts. Wind pollination is much less reliable: wind-pollinated plants must produce truly vast quantities of pollen to have any real hope of success. If you are unfortunate enough to suffer from hay fever, you will know only too well that when the grasses are flowering, the air is filled with microscopically small pollen grains.

With both male and female gametophytes in a perfect flower there is a risk that the flower might pollinate itself. Over many generations this would be genetically disadvantageous. The advantages of sexual reproduction arise from the mixing of genes from separate parents, and without such mixing harmful recessive genes will be expressed more frequently in the offspring. Some plants allow self-pollination, but most do not and they have three ways of avoiding it: within an individual flower, the male and female gametophytes may be produced at different times; the structure of the flower may make it almost impossible for a pollinating animal to collect pollen from the anthers and transfer it to the stigma of the same flower; and finally, the plant may produce a chemical block that inactivates any of its own pollen grains that happen to reach its stigma.

Once it has stuck to the stigma, a pollen grain develops two sperm, the male gametes, thus becoming the mature gametophyte, and starts extending a pollen tube down between the cells of the style and into the ovary. When it reaches an ovule the pollen grain discharges sperm. In all gymnosperms except for *Ephedra,* a shrub that grows in the American desert, only one sperm cell is involved in fertilization, but an angiosperm uses two, for double fertilization. One sperm fertilizes the egg, which develops into the diploid zygote. The other fertilizes two nuclei inside the ovule, forming a cell with three sets of chromosomes. This divides to form endosperm, the nutritive substance that will sustain the embryo.

Seeds and Fruit

Most monocots produce enough endosperm to nourish the young seedling after the seed has germinated. In many dicots, all the endosperm is absorbed into the cotyledons (seed leaves).

The zygote, developing into a embryo, the endosperm, and the seed coat surrounding them together comprise the seed. In angiosperms this still remains inside the ovary, which develops into the fruit.

Not all fruits are edible, and not all edible fruits are really fruits at all. Apples, for example, are the swollen receptacle, with the true fruit, containing the seeds, at its center, forming the core. They are known as "false fruits." As the fruit develops at the base of the flower, the other flower parts die and are shed.

Think of fruit and what springs to mind is probably an orange, pear, or plum, but fruits come in many kinds. Peas and beans are seeds, and the pods that contain them are fruits. Nuts are fruits, usually with a single seed and a woody outer coat, with the exception, among nuts that are widely eaten, of Brazil nuts. Those are the seeds, and as their shape suggests they develop as groups of between 12 and 24, arranged in a circle. They are held inside a hard, woody container. Botanically, the inedible container is the fruit, but it is discarded. Cereal grains, from which we obtain flour and other types of meal, are also fruits, in this case of a type botanists call a caryopsis: a caryopsis is a dry fruit that contains a single seed and does not break open of its own accord.

Seeds are dry, but with most plants water can pass through their protective coats. When it does so, the absorbed water makes the seed swell, bursting the coat, and the water also activates enzymes that start digesting the endosperm or contents of the cotyledons. Nutrients move to the growing part of the embryo and before long the radicle emerges and starts growing downward, followed by the shoot, which grows upward, breaks through the ground surface, and spreads its cotyledons to commence photosynthesis. A new plant has appeared and the reproductive cycle is complete.

How Trees Disperse

Once seeds are ripe, they are released, but this presents a difficulty. Trees could simply detach their seeds, allowing them to fall to the ground, but then the vast majority would land around the base of the parent. Some might germinate, but the emerging seedlings would find themselves competing for light, water, and nutrients with their overwhelmingly bigger parent. One or two might manage to become established, but even they would be unable to grow very tall until the parent tree died and fell.

As they fall, however, seeds are affected by the wind. This will carry at least some of them away from their parent. In addition, tree seeds are produced on branches, not on the main trunk, so they are released a little way from their parent. Where seeds fall to the ground in this way, a few land very close to their parent, most a short distance away, and a few are carried farther—the seed density decreases rapidly with distance.

Big Seeds and Small Seeds

The seeds of most trees need to germinate fairly quickly. When scientists examined part of a forest that had been standing in the White Mountains, New Hampshire, for 95 years, they found 1,150 seeds of yellow birch (*Betula lutea*), 530 of paper birch (*P. papyrifera*), and more than 90 of other tree species to every square yard (961, 445, and 78 per sq m respectively), all waiting in the ground for an opportunity to germinate and grow, but in many cases their wait will have been in vain. Of seeds released within the previous year, few will still be capable of germinating by the following year. Seeds of most broad-leaved trees remain dormant for six to 18 months, but few can survive much longer. While they remain viable they comprise a valuable store, called a seed bank, with seeds ready in position to provide a new tree to fill the smallest space that appears in the forest.

There are exceptions, however, and some trees produce long-lived seeds. Often they do not release them until the parent tree falls or is destroyed by fire (page 95). Many pine trees (*Pinus* species) produce seeds of this kind, dispersing them when the surrounding ground is clear and they have the best possible chance of germinating. Until then they are stored, still in their cones, on branches high up in the tree crown. This storage of seeds in a forest canopy is called serotiny (from the Latin *serotinus,* meaning "late").

Obviously, the smaller and lighter the seed the farther the wind will carry it. This might seem to favor small seeds, but it is not quite so simple. Seeds carry a store of food with them, and the larger the store the better the start in life it gives them. If they discard some of this baggage in order to travel light, they will go farther, but arrive relatively ill-equipped, and many will die. The tree can compensate by producing much larger numbers of small seeds, or it can produce well-endowed seeds, carrying heavy loads of food. These may not travel far, but may germinate better on their arrival.

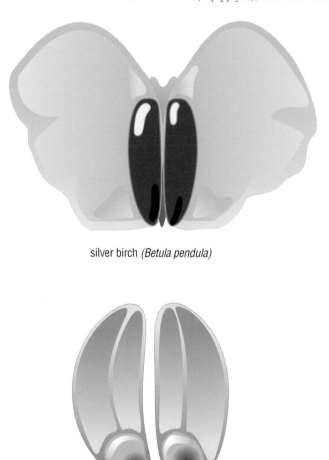

silver birch *(Betula pendula)*

Sitka spruce *(Picea sitchensis)*

field maple *(Acer campestre)*

Winged Seeds

In both cases the parent has to supply the material from which its seeds are made and this involves an expenditure of energy. Everything in nature has to be paid for, and in the case of reproduction the bill is paid by the mother, in terms of the material from which the seed and structures surrounding it are made. Since there is an unavoidable cost, many trees have evolved a different way of allocating resources. They produce medium-sized seeds, in fairly large quantities, and equip them with "wings." Winged seeds are very common.

Most gymnosperm trees, although not all of them, produce winged seeds. These vary consider-

Winged seeds

ably in size, but that of Sitka spruce (*Picea sitchensis*), shown in the diagram on page 68, is typical. All are single-winged. Winged seeds evolved first in gymnosperms, but many angiosperms have retained them. Again they vary greatly in size, but in angiosperms the seeds usually have two wings, like those of silver birch (*Betula pendula*) and field maple (*Acer campestre*) shown in the illustration.

Wings, made from material supplied by the parent tree, slow the rate at which the seed falls to the ground. In still air, the seed will fall approximately vertically, but if there is even the slightest wind, slowing its descent increases the length of time during which the seed is available to be carried by it; the wing acts like a sail. The seed travels farther than it would if it lacked wings. Even so, most winged seeds land within a short distance of the tree that released them.

Air transport is a form of passive dispersal that involves only the tree itself and, because all tree seeds are fairly large and, therefore, heavy, its efficacy is rather limited. Flowing water might offer an alternative means of passive dispersal that would carry seeds much farther, but very few plants of any kind make use of it. Even most aquatic plants produce their seeds out of the water. Obviously, some seeds from riverside trees fall into the water, but since they have no sure way of returning to dry land, they are doomed to fail.

Food Hoarders

Trees can and do exploit certain mammals and birds as dispersal agents, however, by offering them a reward. As you know, tree squirrels bury acorns and other tree seeds. In North America, the eastern gray squirrel (*Sciurus carolinensis*) prefers to feed on the seeds of hickory, beech, and oak, but will take other food if these are scarce. In Britain, where this animal is known as the gray squirrel, its preferred foods are seeds of oak, beech, sweet chestnut, and hazel. The Eurasian red squirrel (*Sciurus vulgaris*), which is the native British squirrel (the gray was introduced in the late 19th and early 20th centuries) prefers conifer seeds and cones.

Squirrels take tree seeds in order to eat them. Clearly, this does not benefit the tree, but in years when the weather is favorable, trees are able to produce vast quantities of seeds, presenting squirrels with far more food than they can eat. They continue collecting food, but hoard the surplus in their nests, in holes and cracks in trees, and in the ground, where they bury seeds, several at a time, an inch or two (2–5 cm) below the surface. The eastern gray is much more apt to store food than the Eurasian red is in Britain, but the red is also a great hoarder in eastern Europe, where the winters are harder. Their food hoards keep them supplied through the winter (they do not hibernate), but they do not remember where they have hidden food and have to locate it by scent, which is possible only when the ground is moist. Inevitably, many of the seeds they store remain undisturbed and germinate.

Some birds also hoard seeds. One of the most remarkable is the jay (*Garrulus glandarius*), a member of the crow family that is found throughout most of temperate Eurasia, but not in North America. It also buries acorns, carrying up to five at a time, the biggest one in its bill and the others in its throat and esophagus. The more acorns it carries the farther it flies with them, taking some more than a mile from the tree where they were collected. Then it buries them individually, unlike squirrels, which bury them in groups. In the course of a season a jay may bury well over 4,000 acorns. What is remarkable is that when the bird needs to eat them, it does not search by scent (most birds have at best a very poor sense of smell) but remembers where it buried each acorn. It rarely needs all of its stored acorns, so some of them are allowed to germinate.

In these cases, both the animals and the trees benefit. The animals find food and in doing so disperse the tree seeds. Edible seeds and the habit of hoarding food have evolved together for the mutual benefit of the participants. This is an example of coevolution.

Hoarding behavior does not always benefit the trees, however, and squirrels and jays may be exceptional. A North American bird, the acorn woodpecker (*Melanerpes formicovorus*), also hoards acorns, but it hides them in holes it drills in dead wood, such as fence posts, where they have no chance to germinate.

Fruit Eaters

Hoarding behavior by animals is an unreliable way to disperse seeds, not least because the seeds themselves are the bait. Angiosperms have evolved a much better method. They produce fruit that is edible, often rich in sugar to provide food energy for any animal that eats it, with the seeds concealed inside. Generally, the seeds have tough coats that make them not only unpalatable but indigestible. Just to help matters along, fruits are often brightly colored, making them easy to find, and their color changes as they (and the seeds inside them) ripen, so fruit-eaters need not waste time with unripe fruit, and trees need not risk losing seeds before they are ready to germinate.

You need only watch birds feeding in late summer and fall, or talk to any fruit grower, to see just how effective this strategy is. If the seed is large, like the stone in a cherry or plum, the bird or mammal eating the flesh of the fruit will simply discard it. If they are small, like those of an apple or rowan (*Sorbus aucuparia*), they will be swallowed, travel through the gut unaltered, and be deposited with the feces. This will also provide nutrient for the young plant, and it explains why trees with small seeds can spring up in the most unlikely places.

Fruits can achieve a wide seed dispersal. Those that are swallowed may be carried several miles before being deposited on the ground. Even those that are discarded as the fruit is eaten may be carried well clear of the parent tree, because fruit is often taken away to be eaten out of range of competitors who might try to steal it.

How Wood Forms

Trees and shrubs have stems and branches that are woody. Other plants do not produce wood, and so plants are often described as being woody or nonwoody. It is wood that gives woody plants their rigidity and mechanical strength and, of course, wood is the most useful material we obtain from trees.

Coniferous trees, and all gymnosperms, produce softwood. Broad-leaved trees produce hardwoods. These names refer to the working properties of the wood, and give an idea of such matters as how easy the wood is to cut and how quickly it blunts saws, planes, and chisels. The information is generally reliable, but there are exceptions. Balsa, the softest of all wood, comes from *Ochroma lagopus.* This is a broad-leaved tree, so balsa is classified as a hardwood. Wood from most larches (*Larix* species) is fairly hard, on the other hand, but since larches are gymnosperms their wood is automatically listed among the softwoods. In gymnosperms, the vascular system consists only of tracheids and in angiosperms it also includes vessel elements (page 68), but this is the only essential difference in the cellular structure of softwoods and hardwoods.

Primary and Secondary Growth

Look at the exposed base of a felled tree and you will see that the trunk, or stem, is made entirely of wood. You may notice, however, that the wood is not quite the same color throughout. In some parts it is darker than in others. You will also notice the many concentric dark and light rings—probably you know that the number of rings indicates the age of the tree, because one pair of light and dark rings forms each year. Around the outside, the woody trunk is enclosed in a layer of bark. This is darker than the wood, and has a very rough, uneven, exterior surface.

At the tips of its twigs, a tree produces a terminal bud, a dome-shaped mass of cells which divide to form new tissue. This lengthens the twigs and, therefore, makes the tree bigger. This is known as primary growth, but if it were all that happened the tree would quickly turn into a rather curious plant. Its branches would grow longer, and the tree as a whole would grow taller, but neither its trunk nor its branches would grow any thicker. It would be so spindly it could not support its own weight and would sprawl across the ground more like a bramble or wild rose than the spruce or oak it was supposed to be. In fact, of course, the trunks and branches of trees also grow thicker—their thickening is known as secondary growth.

The figure below shows a cross section through the trunk of a tree. It is clear from this that there are two types of wood: heartwood and sapwood. Between them these account for all but the outermost layer of material, the bark. As the drawing shows, the structure is not quite so simple, mainly because the bark is a much more complex substance than it may seem.

Vascular Cambium

The key to secondary growth and the production of wood is the layer of vascular cambium. Cambium is a layer of tissue in a woody plant compris-

Cross section of a tree trunk

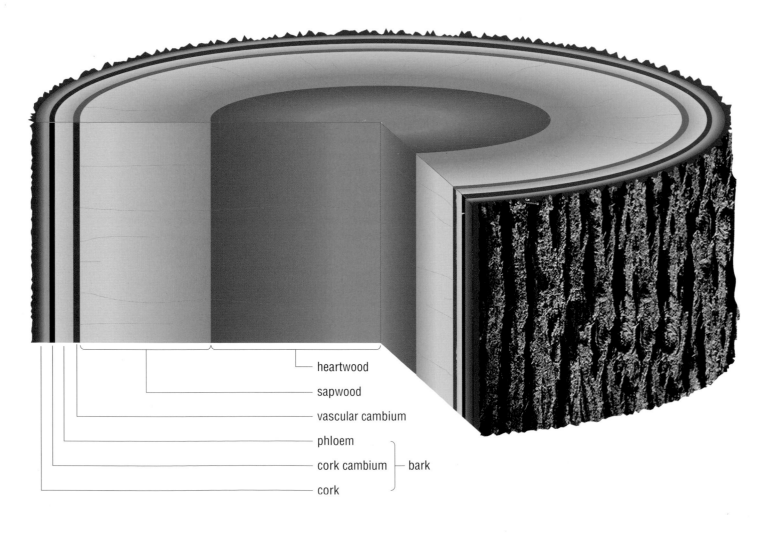

- heartwood
- sapwood
- vascular cambium
- phloem
- cork cambium ⎤ bark
- cork ⎦

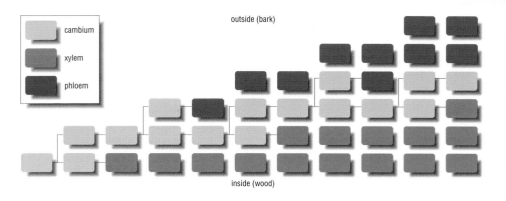

outside (bark)

cambium
xylem
phloem

inside (wood)

Secondary growth

ing cells that give rise to other tissue on one or both sides. In most trees this layer is no more than one cell thick, but the cells forming it are parenchyma cells (unspecialized, "all-purpose" plant cells) that have acquired the capacity to divide in such a way as to produce specialized cells. In botanical terms they have become meristem tissue.

The cambium cells occur inside the vascular bundles (page 63) and in the pith rays. These are layers, each comprising a few vertically stacked parenchyma cells, usually acting as starch stores, that run radially, from near the center of the stem to the bark. In the xylem, rays also provide channels for the lateral transport of water and nutrients.

A meristem cell is sometimes called an initial and any cell derived from it a derivative. In the case of the vascular cambium, each initial first divides to produce two cells like itself (two initials). Then one of the two initials becomes a different kind of cell. The diagram above shows how this works. Starting on the left of the diagram, one cambium (initial) cell divides. There are then two cambium cells. The one on the inside (nearest the center of the tree) turns into a xylem cell and the other cambium cell divides to produce two more cells like itself. The outer one (nearest the outside of the tree) turns into a phloem cell and the other divides. The inside cambium cell turns into another xylem cell, the other divides, the outer turns into a phloem cell, and so it continues. A central layer of cambium, never more than two cells thick, generates phloem on the outside and xylem on the inside. These are the two types of vascular tissue, which is why this is known as the vascular cambium. Cambium cells in the pith rays divide in a similar fashion to extend the rays.

The diagram of the tree trunk on page 70 shows the layer of phloem. The inner layer, of xylem, to its right in the drawing, is what is called the sapwood. Phloem and xylem that result from cell division in the vascular cambium form part of the secondary growth, which thickens the trunk and branches of a tree, and they are known as secondary phloem and xylem. Phloem comprises the tissues through which nutrients are transported from the leaves to other parts of the plant and, therefore, it is essential to the survival of the tree. If it is cut through all the way around the trunk, so its nutrient transport ceases, the tree will die. This is "ring barking," and the phloem forms the innermost layer of the bark.

Cork Cambium

Beyond the phloem there is a second region of cambium, the cork cambium. It gives rise not to vascular tissue, but to epidermis, the skin of the plant, which is made from cork cells. A meristem initial in the cambium changes into a derivative. The derivative lays down a layer of suberin, a waxy material, in its walls and then the cell dies. It has become a cork cell, dead and with a waxy coating. The layer of cork cells protects the interior of the trunk or branch from losing water, and from damage or invasion by insects. Usually the layer of cork cells is quite thin, but there is one famous exception, the cork oak (*Quercus suber*) of southern Europe and North Africa. It produces a very thick cork layer and the cork can be stripped every eight or 10 years for a century or so without harming the tree. *Q. suber* is the source of all commercial cork.

Unlike the vascular cambium, the cork cambium is not a permanent feature. It does not form a layer surrounding the trunk or branch, but occurs as a cylinder of cells. After a few weeks these cells lose their meristemic ability, turn into cork cells, die, and the cork cambium disappears. As the trunk or branch grows thicker, however, more "skin" is needed to contain it. The existing skin splits, producing the characteristic rugged appearance of the outside of a tree, and new cork cambium forms to produce cells to fill the gaps, but eventually no meristemic cells are left and parenchyma cells in the secondary phloem become meristemic and turn into a cylinder of cork cambium.

Sapwood and Heartwood

Inside the vascular cambium, the secondary xylem transports water from the roots to the rest of the tree, and each year a new layer of xylem is added. As the tree grows, more xylem vessels are needed to keep it supplied with water, but since each new layer forms as a cylinder laid outside the cylinders of previous years, the xylem circumference grows continually and the xylem contains an annually increasing number of vessels. The growth of new secondary xylem keeps pace with the increasing demand for water.

As new layers of xylem are added around the outside, layers on the inside die. Tracheids and (in angiosperms) vessel elements produce lignins in their cell walls. This strengthens the cells and when the cells die the lignins remain, forming a central core of strongly lignified dead cells. Often, these cells fill with various waste products, altering their color and making this wood easily distinguishable from the sapwood. The central core of dead xylem, no longer transporting water, comprises the heartwood, a column of tough material that adds greatly to the overall strength of the tree.

How Growth Rings Form

In temperate regions, plant growth ceases for a time in winter. This is obvious in the case of primary growth, which you can see, but it also applies to secondary growth. It is this annual cessation and resumption of secondary growth that produces the annual growth rings you can see in any cross section of a tree trunk or branch.

When growth begins, in spring, the vascular cambium starts producing tracheids and vessel elements that have large diameters and thin walls. They appear pale and, because of their size, they form a fairly wide band around the secondary xylem. By later summer, the cambium is producing cells of smaller diameter with thicker, darker walls. They pack more densely into a narrower band. When growth ceases for the winter, the year's accumulation comprises a wide, pale band on the inside and a narrow, dark band on the outside. The two together represent the growth for that year—the following spring a new band of big, pale cells will be deposited outside the dark band from the previous year.

Counting annual growth rings reveals the age of the tree, but the rings can reveal much more information than that. If the weather was good during the growing season, the tree will have grown well and the growth ring will be wide. If the weather was poor, there will have been less growth, and the ring will be narrow. A knowledge of the precise climatic preferences for a particular tree species, combined with a careful study of its annual growth rings, can be made to reveal climatic changes over the years.

Photosynthesis

Spring is the green time. In a broad-leaved deciduous forest it is the season when buds burst open and the trees hide their branches beneath young, bright green leaves. Even in the evergreen coniferous forest, there is some intensification of the green. Broad-leaved shrubs and herbs, the undergrowth that borders paths and fills the open spaces, produces its fresh leaves and the conifers, too, resume their growth, producing new needles, brighter than their older neighbors.

In fall, the colors change. Before leaves are shed, sugars, minerals, and other nutrients move out and into the tree branch. They are stored until the following spring, when they will be supplied to new leaves. As summer gives way to fall, leaves cease making chlorophyll. Its green color fades and the colors of other compounds become visible. Leaves turn yellow, red, or brown before they

wither with the loss of their water supply, are detached from the tree, and discarded.

Green is the color of the most important type of chlorophyll; chlorophyll is the compound that allows plants to manufacture sugars from carbon dioxide and water. The process is called photosynthesis, literally the assembly, or synthesis, of a complex substance using the energy of light. It is the process on which most life depends.

Light, Shade, and Solarization

Obviously, it requires light, but not too much. If the light is too intense, photosynthesis slows down. The effect is called solarization and is probably due to reactions that destroy chlorophyll or stop certain essential reactions. Some plants are

more sensitive to this than others. Those adapted to life in the shade, where they can photosynthesize at relatively low light levels, suffer badly if they find themselves exposed to full sunlight. Such shade-loving plants grow on the floor of a temperate forest. If trees fall, exposing areas of ground to bright sunlight, the shade-lovers disappear and opportunistic light-lovers take their place until young trees have grown up to shade the ground once more and allow the shade-lovers to return. Plants that grow in open habitats, on the other hand, tolerate quite high light levels.

Photosynthesis also requires warmth. It ceases altogether when the temperature falls below 21°F (-6°C) and proceeds very slowly at temperatures close to freezing, but between 32°F (0°C) and 95°F (35°C) its rate doubles with every 18°F (-7.7°C) temperature rise. Above 95°F (35°C) the rate decreases rapidly and when the temperature exceeds about 113°F (45°C) photosynthesis ceases and, within a fairly short time, the plant dies.

Photosynthetic Pigments

Chlorophyll absorbs light at quite precise wavelengths, and slight variations in chlorophyll molecules allow them to absorb at different wavelengths. Other compounds also absorb light energy and can pass it on to chlorophyll molecules. Substances that absorb light are called pigments and the color of a pigment is that of the light it reflects, not of the light it absorbs.

One type of chlorophyll, known as chlorophyll a, is also called P700, because it absorbs most strongly at a wavelength of 700 nanometers (nm), in the far red part of the spectrum. Another type of chlorophyll a, known as P680, also absorbs red light, but most strongly at 680 nm. Chlorophyll a is blue-green, because this is the color of the light it reflects, and both P700 and P680 versions play important parts in photosynthesis, in what are called photosystem I (PSI) and photosystem II (PSII) respectively. Chlorophyll b, which is chemically slightly different from chlorophyll a, is yellow-green.

The most important of the other pigments are the xanthophylls, which are yellow, and the carotenoids, which are various shades of red through orange. Each absorbing at a different wavelength, these pigments expand the waveband of light plants can use. Both PSI and PSII contain

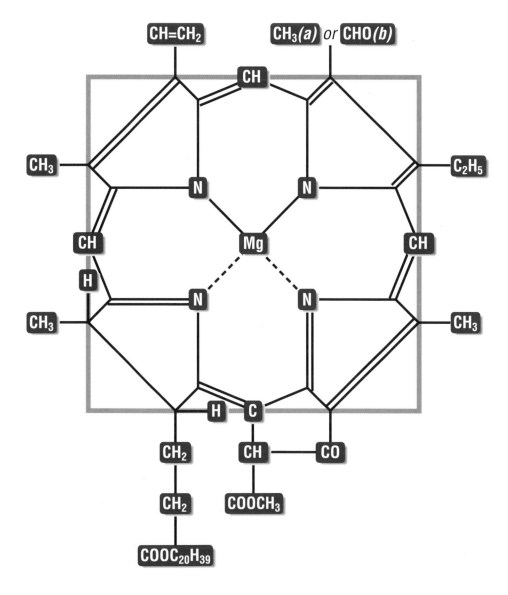

Chlorophyll

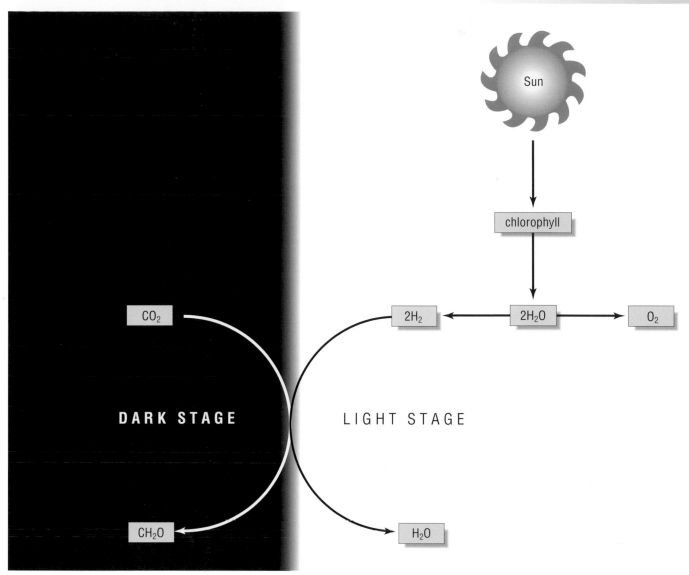

Light stage

---

these non-chlorophyll pigments. PSI also contains P700 and PSII contains P680.

Chloroplasts and Chlorophyll

Chlorophyll occurs within plant cells inside structures called chloroplasts. Chloroplasts can reproduce by dividing, independently of the cell containing them, and they have their own DNA. This, the manner in which they divide, and the structure and chemistry of their inner membranes resemble features of simple organisms that live independently, and most biologists believe that the chloroplasts in plant cells are the descendants of organisms that once lived independently, but that entered and became incorporated into bigger cells. This merger probably happened more than 2 billion years ago, after chloroplasts had been powering themselves by photosynthesis for some hundreds of millions of years. The story began, obviously, with the development of chlorophyll, and as a side effect of photosynthesis the atmosphere gradually accumulated its by-product, oxygen.

A chlorophyll molecule is very large and complex. The diagram on page 72 shows its general structure. The pigment comprises the "head" of the molecule, shown enclosed inside a gray border. Chemically, it is a porphyrin ring centered on an atom of magnesium (Mg). Chlorophylls a and b differ in the group shown in the upper right corner; chlorophyll a has a CH_3 group at this position, while chlorophyll b has CHO. At its base, abbreviated in the figure as $COOC_{20}H_{39}$, there is a long "tail" of carbon and hydrogen. This tail is water-repellent and attaches the chlorophyll molecule to the membrane in the chloroplast.

A chloroplast is lens-shaped, about 2–4 μm by 4–7 μm, and comprises a double outer membrane containing a dense liquid called the stroma and stacks, called grana, of membranes, called thylakoid membranes, that form disk-shaped capsules each enclosing a thylakoid space and keeping it separate from the stroma. The chlorophyll molecules, of types a and b, and xanthophyll and carotenoid molecules are in the thylakoid membranes. The stroma also contains starch grains and fat molecules. Chloroplasts are concentrated in the cells, called mesophyll cells, that form the interior of leaves and each mesophyll cell contains between 30 and 40 chloroplasts.

The Light Stage

When chlorophyll, held in the thylakoid membranes of chloroplasts, is exposed to light, it is "excited." The chlorophyll molecule absorbs a photon of light with energy precisely equal to the amount needed to raise one electron from its usual orbital, called its ground state, to a higher-energy orbital, called its excited state. The excited electron escapes from the molecule, but is captured by a neighboring molecule, known as a primary electron acceptor. This acceptor molecule passes (donates) an electron (not necessarily the same one) to another acceptor molecule and so on along an electron-transport chain.

The overall result, shown in the diagram on page 73, is that the energy supplied by the photon is used to split a water molecule into hydrogen and oxygen. The oxygen is released into the air, and the hydrogen passes on to the next stage in the process. The splitting of water molecules to provide hydrogen comprises the light stage, or light reactions, of photosynthesis. It is the dark stage, or dark reactions, in which the hydrogen is combined with carbon dioxide to produce sugars. The entire sequence can be summarized by a very simple equation:

$$6CO_2 + 6H_2O \xrightarrow[\text{chlorophyll}]{\text{light energy}} C_6H_{12}O_6 + 6O_2$$

In the presence of light energy and chlorophyll, carbon dioxide reacts with water to yield sugar and gaseous oxygen.

In reality, of course, the process is more complicated. The diagram on page 73 shows that the light stage involves the splitting of water to provide hydrogen. This is true, but it is not all that happens.

Water molecules sometimes split of their own accord into hydrogen (H+) and hydroxyl (OH-) ions, so there are always a few of these ions inside a cell. When the absorption of photons causes chlorophyll molecules to release electrons, some of these electrons combine with hydrogen ions to form hydrogen atoms. Free hydrogen atoms can attach themselves to a hydrogen acceptor, nicotinamide adenine dinucleotide (NADP), so NADP becomes NADPH (sometimes called NADP.H2). Thus the NADP is reduced and in this form it enters the dark stage, in the course of which it is oxidized by losing its hydrogen and can be used again in the light stage. The chlorophyll molecule has lost an electron in this reaction, however, leaving it with a positive charge. The hydroxyl ion (OH-) has an extra electron, which it donates to the chlorophyll. This returns both the chlorophyll and hydroxyl to their neutral state and hydroxyls can then combine to produce water with the release of oxygen: $4OH \rightarrow 2H_2O + O_2\uparrow$. That is how the oxygen comes to be released.

Cyclic and Non-Cyclic Photophosphorylation

At the same time, other electrons released by the chlorophyll are accepted by ferredoxin (one of a group of proteins containing iron) and then pass along a series of carriers, all of them at slightly different energy levels. Energy removed from the electrons is transferred to molecules of adenosine diphosphate (ADP), allowing the ADP to take up an additional phosphate group and become adeno-

sine triphosphate (ATP). The reversible change between ADP and ATP absorbs energy as the third phosphate bond is formed (ADP becomes ATP) and releases it again as the bond is relinquished (ATP becomes ADP). This is the principal mechanism by which energy is transported around every living organism and released where it is needed.

So the light energy striking the chlorophyll molecule provides chemical energy as well as hydrogen. Eventually, the last of the electron carriers passes the electron back to the chlorophyll molecule, completing the cycle. Because it uses light energy to establish high-energy phosphate bonds, the process is known as cyclic photophosphorylation.

The electron from the hydroxyl (from water) also travels along an electron transport chain, in this case one involving both photosystems (I and II). Photosystem I (PSI) is at a higher energy level than photosystem II (PSII). Light striking PSI releases an electron that is passed to NADP, and it is replaced in PSI by an electron passed from PSII to plastoquinone (one of a group of complex organic molecules) and then to PSI. As it passes along the chain, its energy is increased and this allows the formation of more ATP. This is also photophosphorylation, in this case known as noncyclic photophosphorylation to distinguish it from the other, cyclic, form of photophosphorylation.

The Dark Stage and the Calvin Cycle

The action then moves from the thylakoid membranes to the stroma, which is where the dark reactions occur. The light reactions release energy, but the dark reactions absorb it, and the energy is supplied as ATP. Carbon is reduced, the hydrogen for

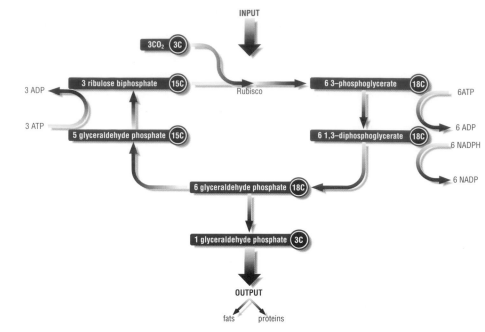

The Calvin cycle

the purpose being provided from the splitting of water in the light stage and carried by NADPH. Carbon and hydrogen are then used to construct sugars in a series of steps discovered by a team at the University of California at Berkeley, led by the American biochemist Melvin Calvin (1911–97), for which he received the 1961 Nobel Prize for Chemistry. The process is known as the Calvin cycle. It is a cycle because one of its key materials, ribulose biphosphate (RuBP), is broken down and then reconstituted so the process can begin again.

A molecule of carbon dioxide is attached to RuBP with the assistance of an enzyme, RuBP carboxylase (rubisco). Because photosynthesis is so widespread and rubisco is so abundant inside the stroma of chloroplasts, this enzyme may be the most plentiful protein on Earth. RuBP has five carbon atoms, so the addition of carbon dioxide produces a 6-carbon compound. This is very unstable, and it immediately divides into two molecules of a 3-carbon compound, phosphoglyceric acid, or 3-phosphoglycerate (PGA).

An enzyme then transfers an additional phosphate group from ATP to each PGA, producing 1,3-diphosphoglycerate. NADPH donates two electrons. These reduce the carboxyl group (COOH) on 1,3-diphosphoglycerate to a carbonyl group (CO), an arrangement that stores more energy, and the product is six molecules of glyceraldehyde phosphate, a 3-carbon sugar. In a series of steps, one of these molecules is built into a 6-carbon sugar that can be converted to starch for storage. The remaining five molecules are used to reconstruct ribulose biphosphate (RuBP), allowing the cycle to be repeated, and energy for the reactions is supplied by the conversion of ATP to ADP.

The cycle is rather complicated, but it is easier to understand if you follow the way carbon atoms are assembled. The figure on page 74 names the intermediate compounds, with the number of molecules, and beside each name indicates the number of carbon atoms present at that stage. The input to the cycle, at the top of the diagram, consists of carbon dioxide, with one carbon atom, and the output, at the bottom of the diagram, is a 3-carbon sugar that is then processed further to make starch, fats, and proteins. The cycle must be repeated three times in order to incorporate the three carbon atoms from three carbon dioxide molecules. The energy driving the cycle is supplied by the ATP-to-ADP mechanism, using nine ATP units. Six NADPH molecules supply the high-energy electrons needed to bond together the atoms comprising the sugar.

Three molecules of carbon dioxide join three molecules of the 5-carbon ribulose biphosphate, forming unstable 6-carbon molecules that divide. There are now 18 carbons (three 6-carbon molecules, which become six 3-carbon molecules). Three of these leave the cycle as its output, in the form of one molecule of glyceraldehyde phosphate, leaving 15 carbons to be reconstituted as the three molecules of ribulose biphosphate, which complete the cycle.

C3 , C4, and CAM Pathways

The first product in the cycle is 3-phosphoglycerate, a compound with three carbon atoms, and for this reason plants that use this version of the dark stage of photosynthesis are known as C3 plants. There are also C4 plants, in which the first product is a 4-carbon molecule, phosphoenol pyruvic acid (PEP). This leads to a much more efficient version of photosynthesis—C4 plants evolved more recently than C3 plants. The C4 pathway requires more ATP and more water than the C3 pathway, but it yields more sugar for a given leaf area, so C4 plants grow faster than C3 plants. They can also tolerate higher light intensities and lower atmospheric carbon dioxide concentrations. There are many C4 plants, but most are grasses, including sugarcane and corn (maize), or desert plants. All trees, including those of temperate forests, are C3 plants.

Another group of plants of dry climates, including cacti and the pineapple, close their stomata during the day, which conserves water, and open them at night. This is the opposite of the pattern followed by most plants, and it requires a different mechanism, called the crassulacean acid metabolism (CAM) after the plant family in which it was first recognized, the Crassulaceae. CAM plants absorb carbon dioxide at night, store it in the form of organic acids until daylight, then close their stomata, use sunlight as a source of energy for producing ATP and NADPH, and release the stored carbon dioxide into the Calvin cycle.

Photorespiration

Photosynthesis is a complex process, but it is not very efficient. Only a very small proportion of the sunlight falling on plants is captured by chlorophyll and once carbon dioxide has been fixed, a considerable amount is lost again by a process called photorespiration. C4 plants minimize photorespiration, but in some C3 plants it can rob the plant of as much as half of the carbon entering the Calvin cycle.

The trouble arises because rubisco, the enzyme that facilitates the union of ribulose biphosphate and carbon dioxide, is able to accept oxygen instead of carbon dioxide, and has no particular preference for one rather than the other. During daylight, the light stage of photosynthesis releases oxygen as a by-product, so leaf cells contain oxygen. They also contain carbon dioxide, which enters through the stomata and is incorporated in the Calvin cycle, or dark stage. How much of each gas the leaf cells contain depends largely on the light intensity. The brighter the light, the more photons chlorophyll molecules capture, the more water molecules are split, and the more oxygen is produced. Its dependence on light intensity is why this form of respiration is called photorespiration and it is most extreme on bright, sunny days in summer.

If the cells contain more oxygen than carbon dioxide, rubisco will gather it and combine it with RuBP. Instead of the two 3-carbon molecules of the Calvin cycle, this produces one 3-carbon molecule, which continues in the cycle, and one molecule of glycolate, a 2-carbon compound. This leaves the Calvin cycle and is broken down elsewhere in the cell, in a series of stages, releasing carbon dioxide. Respiration is the oxidation of carbon to carbon dioxide, but in this case it confers no known benefit on the plant. Photorespiration produces no ATP, so it consumes energy rather than releasing it, and it robs the Calvin cycle of carbon, thereby reducing the amount of sugar produced by photosynthesis.

Photosynthesis and Productivity

Inefficient and wasteful as it may be, photosynthesis is nevertheless the process on which almost all life depends (there are some ecosystems, around volcanic vents in the deep oceans and in sulfur springs and boiling muds, where light never penetrates and no organisms practice photosynthesis). Its overall output is impressive; biologists have calculated that each year green plants synthesize around 180 billion tons (160 billion tonnes) of carbohydrates.

When the young leaves burst forth in spring, and even the conifers resume their growth and produce pale, new needles, it is a sign that the frozen ground has thawed, the temperature has risen, and photosynthesis is beginning once again. Photosynthesis makes plant growth possible. It does so partly by assembling carbohydrate to be used structurally, but mainly by providing energy. Sugars, converted to starch, store energy that is released by the process of respiration (not photorespiration). That energy, used to convert ADP into ATP, transported as ATP, and released to cells by converting ATP back into ADP, drives the plant metabolism by which mineral nutrients from the soil are combined with carbon, oxygen, and hydrogen obtained by photosynthesis to form the complex organic (carbon-based) compounds from which cells and tissues are constructed. Photosynthesis is the suite of processes by which light energy is captured and held in order for the necessary materials to be assembled for growth and reproduction.

Nitrogen Fixation and Denitrification

Life on our planet is based on proteins. Sugars and fats supply our bodies with fuel, but proteins are the building blocks from which tissues are constructed. Enzymes and hormones, which control chemical reactions, are also proteins.

Proteins are arrangements of amino acids. About 80 amino acids occur naturally, and about 20 of these commonly occur in proteins. All amino acids comprise an amino group (NH_2) and a carboxyl group (COOH), both attached to the same carbon atom, to which a side chain is also attached. The side chain is different for each amino acid.

Amino acids are synthesized by plants, in which they are assembled to form plant proteins. Herbivorous animals obtain their amino acids by eating plants and carnivores by eating herbivores. Animals can alter many of the amino acids they obtain from plants to construct proteins that suit their own requirements, but ultimately it is plants that supply the raw materials. Those raw materials include carbon, oxygen, and hydrogen, and also nitrogen. Carbon, oxygen, and hydrogen, the ingredients of carbohydrates, are obtained in the first instance by photosynthesis (page 72) from atmospheric carbon dioxide and water. Nitrogen is also obtained from the air, but by a different route. Essential though it is, plants cannot obtain their own nitrogen. They need help.

Persuading Nitrogen to Form Compounds

It is not that nitrogen is scarce. We breathe air that is about 78 percent nitrogen. We inhale it and we exhale it again unaltered. Nitrogen gas (N_2) is very reluctant to engage in chemical reactions, which means plants cannot assimilate it. Once it has been induced to combine with oxygen or hydrogen, however, its character changes. Then it will participate in reactions and can be used in the synthesis of amino acids. The trick is to persuade it to join another element in the first place.

Enough energy will do it. Nitrogen fertilizer is made in factories by heating air to 750–930°F (400–500°C) under about 200 times atmospheric pressure in the presence of a catalyst. Lightning supplies enough natural energy to oxidize nitrogen in a series of steps that produce nitric acid (HNO_3) that is washed to the ground in rain (contributing to the natural acidity of all rain) where it forms nitrates (NO_3) that can be used directly by plants. Lightning "fixes" a considerable amount of atmospheric nitrogen, but soil microorganisms fix very much more, and it is their activities that make available most of the nitrogen entering plant roots.

Colonies of *Rhizobium* bacteria in nodules attached to the roots of leguminous and some nonleguminous plants (page 63) fix large amounts of gaseous nitrogen, but they are not alone. There are also free-living bacteria that fix nitrogen, those of the genera *Azotobacter* and *Clostridium* being the most closely studied. Certain sulfur bacteria, including members of the genera *Chromatium, Rhodospirillum,* and *Chlorobium* also fix nitrogen in the soil and in aquatic systems there are cyanobacteria, including *Nostoc* and *Anabaena* species, that also do so.

Some of these organisms require oxygen (are aerobic), others cannot tolerate it (are anaerobic), some perform photosynthesis, others do not. The nitrogen-fixing talent is distributed among a disparate group of microorganisms. What they are all believed to have in common is nitrogenase, an enzyme that makes nitrogen react with hydrogen at ordinary environmental temperatures and pressures, to produce ammonia: $N_2 + 3H_2$ energy $\rightarrow 2NH_3$.

Nitrification

Plants can use ammonia, but most of it is seized by aerobic bacteria. As a group, they are known as nitrifying bacteria, because of the way they process nitrogen. In the soil, free ammonia, dissolved in water, combines with carbon dioxide to form ammonium (NH_4) carbonate ($(NH_4)_2CO_3$). Certain bacteria then oxidize the ammonium carbonate, a chemical reaction that releases energy the bacteria can use:

$$(NH_4)_2CO_3 + 3O_2 \rightarrow$$
$$2NHO_2 + CO_2 + 3H_2O + energy.$$

This is how *Nitrosomonas* and *Nitrococcus* bacteria live. The somewhat unstable nitrous acid (HNO_2) they produce combines with magnesium or calcium to form a nitrite (Mg or $Ca(NO_2)_2$) and this is the wherewithal for another group, *Nitrobacter*, which obtains its energy by oxidizing the nitrite into nitrate (Mg may take the place of Ca):

$$2Ca(NO_2)_2 + 2O_2 \rightarrow$$
$$2Ca(NO_3)_2 + energy$$

These are not the only bacterial species involved. There are several others that oxidize ammonia to nitrate. All of these processes are known as nitrification.

Nitrogen Recycling

Nitrogen fixation is the original source of all soil nitrogen, but once fixed it is recycled repeatedly and returns to ammonia in the course of its cycle. Bacteria and other soil organisms die. So do plants and animals that live on the surface. All living organisms produce waste. Wastes and the remains of once-living organisms are deposited on or in the soil. All this dead organic matter contains nitrogen, as proteins or as nitrogen compounds that are the end product of protein metabolism. Some of this nitrogen returns to the soil as ammonia. Fungi and bacteria that obtain their nutrients from dead organic matter convert the remaining nitrogen compounds into ammonia or ammonium (NH_4). From there the nitrogen is taken up by nitrifying bacteria, converted to nitrate, and in that form taken up again by plants.

Plants have preferences. Most coniferous trees take up ammonium more readily than nitrate, for example, although, like most plants and microorganisms, they are able to utilize ammonium, nitrate, or amino acids dissolved from dead organic matter. At Hubbard Brook Experimental Forest, a broad-leaved deciduous forest in New Hampshire, scientists have measured the fixation of nitrogen by soil microorganisms as 12.5 pounds of nitrogen per acre per year (14 kg ha^{-1} yr^{-1}). In addition, they found 5.8 pounds per acre per year (6.5 kg ha^{-1} yr^{-1}) was deposited by rain. Of the total, about 85 percent of the nitrogen available to trees was bound in nitrate and the remainder in ammonium.

Once nitrogen enters the cycle, living organisms hold onto it tenaciously. When it is returned to the soil, as dead organic matter, it does not remain there long before plant roots absorb it again, and in a forest a large amount of nitrogen is held by the trees themselves.

At Hubbard Brook, part of the study involved measuring the effect of felling all the trees in a particular area. This greatly reduced transpiration, of course (page 28), so much more of the rain drained directly into the groundwater, which increased the rate at which nutrients were leached from the soil. The effect on the loss of nitrogen was the most dramatic, however. The rate at which it left the area, as nitrate dissolved in water, increased 60-fold. This indicates the amount that is constantly being cycled in a temperate forest and should serve as a warning of the pollution that may result from widespread forest clearance.

Evergreen plants use nutrients, including nitrogen, more efficiently than deciduous plants.

This is due partly to their more efficient mechanisms for withdrawing and storing nutrients from leaves before they are shed, and partly to the fact that evergreen leaves live much longer than do deciduous leaves.

Denitrification

Suppose you were a visitor from another galaxy, sitting in your spaceship somewhere out in the asteroid belt where you could remain undetected, and that you were studying the planets of the solar system for signs of life. You would conclude that this star system was dead, except for the third planet. There you would notice some very curious features, one of which is the large amount of nitrogen in the atmosphere.

On Mars and Venus, the two neighboring planets, the atmosphere contains almost no nitrogen and that is how it should be on Earth. Lightning oxidizes nitrogen into compounds that are both soluble in water and stable. Rain washes them to the surface and there they should remain. Even if the atmosphere started with a large amount of nitrogen, it would take no more than a few million years for all of it to disappear into the oceans. It was this type of reasoning that led the British chemist James Lovelock to conclude that the chemical composition of its atmosphere can reveal whether or not a planet supports life and that, if it does, it is the living organisms that create and maintain living conditions they find tolerable. This is the idea he developed as the Gaia hypothesis.

Clearly, therefore, not only is atmospheric nitrogen being brought to the surface, sufficient nitrogen is also being returned to the atmosphere to maintain a constant concentration. In other words, as much nitrogen returns to the air as is taken from it. The organisms responsible for this part of the cycle are known as denitrifying bacteria, and the process is called denitrification.

The bacteria concerned, and there are several species, have no interest in the welfare of the planet, of course, or in the neat balancing of the nitrogen budget. They reduce nitrogen compounds in order to obtain their oxygen, which they use to oxidize sugars or, in the case of *Thiobacillus denitrificans,* sulfur. This reaction releases energy the bacteria use to synthesize the organic compounds they need for their own maintenance and reproduction.

Thiobacillus denitrificans releases gaseous nitrogen (N_2). Other bacteria, including species of *Pseudomonas, Micrococcus,* and *Clostridium,* produce ammonia. Ammonia is very soluble in water, but it boils at -29°F (-34°C), so it vaporizes at once if it comes out of solution. This returns a little to the air, where some of it may be oxidized, but most is captured by nitrifying bacteria and remains in the soil until *T. denitrificans* succeeds in converting it to unreactive pure nitrogen.

The amount of nitrogen fixed and returned to the atmosphere each year is very small compared with the amount held firmly by living organisms and cycled from one to another within ecosystems. Nevertheless, nitrogen fixation, nitrification, and denitrification all depend on bacteria and, to a lesser extent, on fungi, which use these processes to obtain energy for themselves. Without them, no plants could grow, because they would have no access to nitrogen in a form they could absorb and nitrogen is an essential ingredient of proteins. Forests, and all the plants and animals that inhabit them, are able to exist only because of the activities of bacteria—single-celled organisms so small they can be seen only with the help of a powerful microscope and so ancient they have been the only form of life throughout most of the history of our planet.

History of Ecological Ideas

A forest is an extensive group of trees, but it is also much more. In the first place, even a plantation forest usually contains more than one species of tree and a natural forest will contain several. Pisgah Forest, in New Hampshire, is fairly typical of a mixed, old-growth forest; it comprises five principal tree species and several less common ones. In Europe, the Białowieża Forest, in Poland, contains oak, hornbeam, lime, and spruce in some areas, and alder, ash, willow, elm, and pine in others. It is a large forest, occupying 482.5 square miles (1,250 sq km) of a plain, most of it inside the boundaries of a national park, and its composition varies from place to place.

It is the trees that define the forest, but there are other plants as well. You will see shrubs and herbs growing in the shade of the trees, climbers, such as ivy, using the trees for support, ferns, mosses, and liverworts in moister places, and lichens growing on exposed rocks and on the branches of some trees. All the plants depend on soil organisms, including fungi. Fungi are everywhere, below ground and out of sight, but at the right time of year you may find the large fruiting bodies produced by some of them—mushrooms, toadstools, puffballs, and chanterelles, and stinkhorns are just a few of the many species. Then there are the insects, birds, mammals, and reptiles that inhabit the forest; many of the mammals and reptiles live secretively, so you will be lucky to see any sign of them.

The forest, then, is a living community of plants, animals, fungi, and microorganisms, all of them interacting with one another, and all of them ultimately reliant on the energy and nutrient elements captured by the photosynthesizing green plants. Since all these organisms, living side by side within a clearly marked boundary separating the area from adjacent ones with distinctly different characters, interact with one another, it is possible to study them as a community, rather than as isolated individuals.

The Economy of Nature

This possibility grew out of ideas about evolution that were being discussed in the 18th and 19th centuries. These ideas branched in several directions, but one line pursued the concept of the "economy of nature." According to this, organisms all live together in harmony, endowed by God with the means to satisfy their biological needs, and are thus able to supply human needs. It was closely linked to the idea of "natural theology," a theory with a long history which held that plants and animals had been designed by God to coexist harmoniously, each performing its ordained function, and that through the study of nature the divine purpose might be revealed.

Natural theology led to the romantic, and very misleading, idea of a "balance of nature," (page 90), but it also led to more rigorous studies of communities. These were first proposed by the eminent German zoologist Ernst Heinrich Haeckel (1834–1919), who sought to work out all the implications of the Darwinian theory of the evolution of species by natural selection. In 1866, Haeckel published a two-volume work called *Generelle Morphologie der Organismen* (General Morphology of Organisms), in which he coined the word "Oecologie," deriving it from the Greek *oikos,* meaning household. He intended the new word to describe the study of a kind of large-scale economy of nature, in which all species are engaged. In effect, the new science (for that is what it amounted to) would concern itself with the details of how organisms reacted among themselves to manage the "household" in which they lived. The modern spelling, "ecology," was adopted at the International Botanical Congress in 1893.

Ecology and the Ecosystem Concept

One of the earliest British ecologists, and to this day one of the most eminent, was Professor Sir Arthur George Tansley (1871–1955). He began the introduction to his book *Practical Plant Ecology* (published in 1923) with a definition.

> The word ECOLOGY, as is well known, is derived, like the common word economy, from the Greek oikos, *house, abode, dwelling.* In its widest meaning ecology is the study of plants and animals *as they exist in their natural homes*; or better, perhaps, the study of their household affairs, which is actually a secondary meaning of the Greek word. (The italics are his.)

In 1935, in an article in the journal *Ecology,* Tansley coined another word that has become no less familiar, and introduced it to a wider readership in *Introduction to Plant Ecology,* a revised second edition of his *Practical Plant Ecology* that was published in 1946. He grouped all the living organisms together with the physical and chemical aspects of the climate and soil that affect them and described them as component parts of a single system, which he called an "ecosystem."

The Zurich-Montpellier and Uppsala Schools

Nowadays you can study ecology as a subject in its own right, and so start your professional life as an ecologist. This is a very recent development, however—most ecologists started out as botanists. In Europe, one of the leading early figures was a Swiss botanist, Josias Braun-Blanquet (1884–1980). He worked first at Zurich, then became the first director of the Station Internationale de Géobotanique Méditerranéenne et Alpine, at Montpellier, France. From about 1913, he and his colleagues became known as the Zurich-Montpellier (or ZM) School. They set about classifying plant communities, based on the smallest area a particular association of plants could occupy. For oak woodland, for example, this minimal area was about 240 square yards

(200 sq m) and a minimal area was calculated for every type of vegetation. An area is then marked out inside a stand that occupies not less than the minimal area for its type. All the plants inside the marked area, known as a relevé or *Aufnahme,* are recorded, together with the area each covers and the way it grows. This defines their "sociability." Relevés are then grouped into classes, called phytocoena, which can be compared. The ZM approach led to the foundation of an entire scientific discipline, called phytosociology, or the sociology of plants.

At about the time the ZM School was developing its approach, ecologists at Uppsala, Sweden, were devising a somewhat similar scheme, though (confusingly for students) with their own terminology. The Uppsala School was led by J. Rutger Sernander (1866–1944) and Gustaf Einar Du Rietz (1895–1967).

Frederic Clements and Climax Theory

In the United States, ecologists were moving in a rather different direction. For a time they were strongly influenced by Eugenius Warming (1841–1924), a Danish botanist who maintained that plants have particular physical qualities that allow them to grow in some places but not in others. He also recognized that the development of a community of plants is strongly affected by other organisms, such as parasites.

Then a group of botanists broke away from the Warming school, not so much because they thought it mistaken as because they could not apply it in their own work. Led by Frederic E. Clements (1874–1945), they were studying the prairie, a task made urgent by the expansion of farming into natural grassland. The classification of types of vegetation works well enough when an experienced botanist looks at the trees in a forest, or even the shrubs comprising heathland or tundra, and can quickly identify the most important components of the ecosystem. Prairie grassland is composed of plants all of fairly similar size, forming an exceedingly complex mixture. It cannot be characterized simply by looking at it.

Instead, Clements devised a method in which measured areas, called quadrats, were marked off and then catalogued by listing every plant species and the number of individuals of each species growing inside the quadrat. This technique is still widely used by ecologists.

Clements did more. He cleared all the vegetation from some quadrats, then recorded the order in which plants recolonized the bare ground. This led him to propose that plants colonize an area in a predictable sequence, which he called a succession, also known as a sere and composed of seral stages. Eventually, he maintained, the succession reaches a climax. This is the final stage in its development—provided it is not severely perturbed from outside, for example by a substantial change in climate, it will undergo no further modification. This image, of groups of plants of different types succeeding one another

until a stable condition is established, proved attractive. As originally proposed it was rather too simple, and later modifications allowed for different types of climax arising from a similar starting point. But the theory of climaxes became firmly established in Europe as well as in North America. In temperate regions, for example, it came to be widely believed that forest is the natural climax and that when humans abandon an area of land, eventually forest will appear and remain until some outside factor alters or destroys it.

Not all ecologists accepted this theory. Soon after Clements proposed it, Henry Allan Gleason (1882–1973), another American ecologist, cast doubt upon the whole idea. Gleason pointed out that plants scatter seed all over the place and will grow wherever they can. If similar plant communities appear in two places, it is because conditions in those places are similar. He rejected utterly the idea that successions proceed in anything like an orderly fashion or that the outcome can be predicted.

Ecology is a young science. It is barely more than a century since its name was coined, and all the research on which its accumulated knowledge is based has been conducted in this century. Ecologists still have much to learn and many of their ideas are somewhat fluid, constantly under review, and liable to be altered in the light of new findings. In some ways this is unfortunate, because ecologists are now called on to advise on a wide variety of environmental matters and there are many questions to which the answers are still unknown.

Food Chains and Food Webs

A forest, any forest, can be described as an ecosystem. This means that a line can be drawn around the forest: on one side of the line there is forest and on the other side of the line there is some other kind of vegetation, such as farmland. This other type of vegetation may also constitute an ecosystem.

In the real world, it is not usually quite so simple, except on seacoasts, the banks of large rivers and lakes, or where humans have defined the boundaries by erecting a fence around the forest, then building or plowing right up the edge of the fence. Left to itself, the forest does not so much end as fade away. The trees become more widely spaced. More shrubs and undergrowth grow in partly shaded clearings. In open spaces there are grasses and herbs. Eventually, the forest gives way to parkland, which is mainly grassy, but with isolated trees, or groups of trees (called copses).

Natural ecosystems grade into one another, with an area of overlap, which in some cases is quite wide. This overlap is called an ecotone and it often supports a larger variety of plant and animal species than the main ecosystems to either side of it (page 100).

Systems and Feedback

"Ecosystem," the word coined by Sir Arthur Tansley, sounds as though it is short for "ecological system," although Sir Arthur did not say so straight out. We know what "ecological" means, and its derivation (page 78). "System" is a word that means different things to different people. A geologist knows what a system is, but it is not at all the same thing as the system a chemist understands, and a chemical system is not in the least like a biological system. In this case, since ecology is one of the biological, or life, sciences, you might suppose that "system" would be used in its biological sense, but you would be wrong. The concept of an ecosystem is most closely related to engineering. To an engineer, a system is an assemblage of components that interact in such a way as to form a coherent whole and that regulates its own performance. In other words, it is a kind of engine.

Think of an engine, in a factory perhaps. It has many parts, all of them essential, assembled so the engine as a whole forms a discrete unit. You can see it, on the factory floor, and people can

walk around it. Many engines are designed to run at a constant speed. If the engine runs faster, a device called a governor partly closes a valve, restricting the fuel supply and slowing the engine. If it runs too slowly, the governor makes the valve open. This is what engineers call a feedback mechanism. In this case the feedback is negative, because when the engine speed changes the change is corrected. Positive feedback can also occur. Then, when the engine runs faster the valve opens, making it run faster still, and when it runs slowly the valve closes, slowing it further.

This is the sense in which an ecosystem, such as a forest, is a system. It has inbuilt mechanisms for self-regulation and, therefore, it is fairly stable. Those mechanisms arise from the relationships among the species comprising the forest. The dominant species are trees, of course, but they are not alone. Animals feed on the trees and are hunted by other animals, and dead organic matter feeds soil animals, fungi, and bacteria, which return nutrients to the trees. Finally, there are parasites, which feed on all the organisms in the ecosystem, including the bacteria and one another. The relationships on which feedback mechanisms are based are feeding relationships.

Food Chains

You can see how this works. Trees produce leaves and there are caterpillars that feed on those leaves. If there are so many caterpillars that they eat all the leaves, the caterpillars will starve. Few of them will grow into butterflies and moths, so fewer eggs will be laid and next year there will be fewer caterpillars. The trees will produce new leaves and fewer of them will be attacked. Caterpillar numbers rarely increase to this extent, however, because there are small birds that feed on caterpillars. The more caterpillars there are the more food there will be for hatchling birds and, when the young leave their nests, there will be more birds to eat up the caterpillars. Sadly for them, small birds also have enemies, of course. There are hawks, watching them from above and waiting for a chance to swoop and grab them. Once again, the more small birds there are, the more food there will be for baby hawks, but if the hawks eat too many small birds they will reduce their own food supply and some of them may starve.

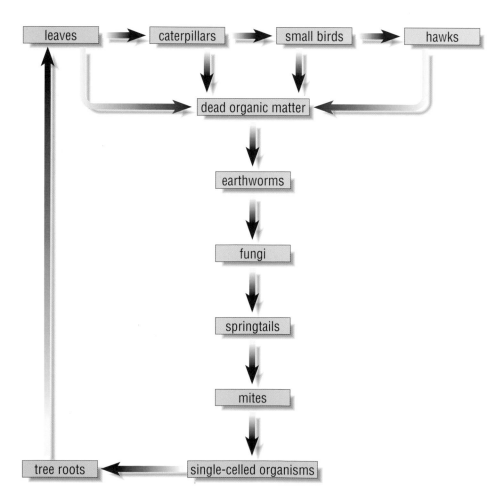

Food chain

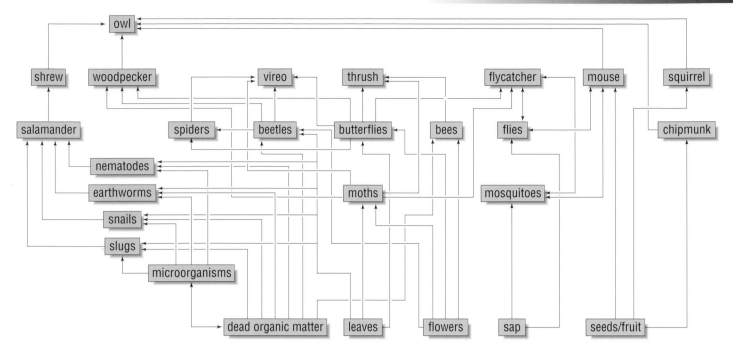

Food web

It is all feedback—the leaves, caterpillars, small birds, and hawks form a chain, called a food chain. Each link in the chain affects the links to either side. If there are more leaves there can be more food for the leaf-eating animals, so their numbers will increase and, in the end, there can be more hawks. In this example the chain has four links: leaves–caterpillars–small birds–hawks. The trees are called primary producers, because they convert carbon dioxide, water, and mineral nutrients into leaves. The herbivorous caterpillars are primary consumers, the insectivorous small birds are secondary consumers, and the carnivorous hawks are tertiary consumers.

Go into a forest in summer and if you search you will find caterpillars feeding on leaves and, if you stay still and quiet, you will see small birds feeding on the caterpillars. You may even see a hawk hunting small birds, but this is a much rarer sight, because there are far more small birds than there are hawks (page 83).

Limitations of the Food Chain Concept

Wait and watch for long enough, however, and you may come to realize that life in the forest is not quite so simple. Caterpillars are around for only a short time, so how do the small birds manage for the rest of the year? Some of them eat buds or seeds, others rummage among the dead leaves on the forest floor for the invertebrate animals that live there. So not all the insectivorous

birds feed on insects all the time. Nor do the hawks feed exclusively on insectivorous birds. They also eat seed-eating birds and, when times are hard, they will eat insects themselves.

Perhaps, while you are waiting, you notice some berries that look delicious, so you eat a few. This makes you part of the forest ecosystem, but where do you fit? Humans eat berries, fruit, and nuts, but they also eat meat. If you try to fit yourself into a food chain you are likely to turn up in several different places.

There is another way in which this food chain is incomplete. It runs only in one direction—from leaves to hawks—but there is also another chain that begins with dead leaves and other organic waste and ends with simple inorganic compounds that can be absorbed by tree roots. Add this part of the chain and what began as leaves → caterpillars → small birds → hawks is transformed into the rather more complicated pattern shown in the diagram on page 80. Even this is an oversimplification. It shows that all the members of the upper part of the chain contribute dead organic matter for recycling, but, of course, the organisms engaged in decomposition (called saprobes or saprotrophs) also produce dead organic matter, so what is shown as a neat straight chain is really a confusing tangle of loops.

The concept of the food chain is useful. It shows that a forest, or any other ecosystem, is regulated by feeding relationships, and it illustrates how nutrients are recycled. It can also be used to demonstrate how certain poisons, such as chemically stable insecticides, can be concentrated as they are passed along it. This is called biological magnification. Using the diagram as an example, if each caterpillar absorbs a dose of insecticide that is too small to kill it, the bird feeding on

caterpillars absorbs that small dose with every caterpillar it eats. Being chemically stable, the insecticide may accumulate in the body of the bird. Hawks then absorb the accumulated dose from each of the small birds they eat. At each stage in the food chain the insecticide concentration increases, possibly reaching levels high enough to harm animals at the top of the chain, in this case hawks.

Food Web

You cannot take the food chain idea any further than this, and a careful look at what goes on in any ecosystem shows why. Examine the leaves or pine needles in a forest and it is soon obvious that they provide food for more than just caterpillars. Beetles, aphids, and other insects also eat them, several species of birds feed on the insects, and in addition to the insects and birds the forest contains mammals and, probably, reptiles and amphibians.

Try to represent this and the picture ceases to be of a food chain, and becomes one of a food web. The diagram above shows a food web for a broad-leaved deciduous forest in eastern North America. It is quite difficult to trace all the relationships in it, yet despite looking complicated, the diagram in fact is greatly oversimplified. Thrushes as well as salamanders eat snails, for example, and a hungry mouse will not turn up its nose at the chance of a snack comprising a beetle. Nor is the owl likely to be the only predatory bird. There will probably be hawks, and almost certainly there will be snakes, weasels, badgers, martens, and cats. Despite its limitations, however, the food web gives a much better impression than a food chain of the relationships within an ecosystem.

Ecological Pyramids

Try to figure out how a forest works by tracing what everything eats and you will soon be hopelessly confused. There are hundreds of species, their numbers fluctuate, and everything is busily eating everything else. Spend an hour or two at it and you will have a splitting headache and a firm conviction that your forest is an incomprehensible mess.

Fortunately, there is another way to approach the task. First you must identify the organisms at each level. That is to say, identify the plants, which are the primary producers, then identify the animals that feed on the plants (primary consumers), the carnivores that feed on the herbivores (secondary consumers), and the carnivores that feed on other carnivores (tertiary consumers). You have now divided all the members of the ecosystem into groups according to the way they feed. These are called the trophic levels, from the Greek *trophe,* meaning "nourishment." If there are omnivores, such as humans, you will need to measure or estimate the proportion of the food they obtain from plants and how much from herbivorous and carnivorous animals, and allocate some of the omnivores to each trophic level accordingly.

Counting and Sampling

The next step is to count the number of individual organisms at each trophic level. Working your way through the entire forest, counting absolutely everything, would take a very long time. Instead, you take samples, using a sampling technique that makes your sample statistically reliable. This means your samples must be taken randomly.

It sounds much more difficult than it is. One way is to use a large-scale map. Over the map you superimpose a grid, then you use a set of random number tables to select points within the grid, which you mark on the map, marking as many points as you will need samples.

Map, and possibly compass, in hand, you march confidently into the forest and find each of the sample sites marked on your map. At each site you mark out an area, called a quadrat, using string and pegs. The quadrat can be any size, but in sampling a forest it usually has an area of 12 square yards (10 sq m) or 24 square yards (20 sq m). It can be rectangular or circular. Then you count every plant and animal inside each quadrat. It is still a slow job, but it is better than counting the entire forest!

Alternatively, you can take a random walk, which saves using a map and grid. Walk into the forest and pick a place from which to start. This can be anywhere. Then use random numbers, from random number tables, to find out how many steps to walk in a straight line. Where that walk ends you mark the spot, then turn 90°, tossing a coin to decide whether to turn left or right and always using the same rule, such as heads for left, tails for right. Take the next random number, walk that number of steps in a straight line, mark the spot to which that takes you, turn left or right, and keep repeating the process until you have as many sample sites as you need. Then you place a quadrat on each site and count the contents.

Counting Animals

Quadrats are all very well for counting plants, but animals are mobile and other methods are needed. Mammals can be trapped, marked, and released. Total numbers are calculated by comparing the number of marked and unmarked individuals trapped subsequently, using a standard algebraic equation. This does not harm the animals, but the technique must be used with care. Some individuals hate the traps, become "trap shy," and having been caught once will always avoid being trapped again. Others enjoy the food and nest provided in the trap and keep returning. Such individuals can distort the findings, because the traps are no longer taking a random sample of the population.

Insects can be brushed from low vegetation and pupae can be collected and counted. Birds can be observed from the ground and identified

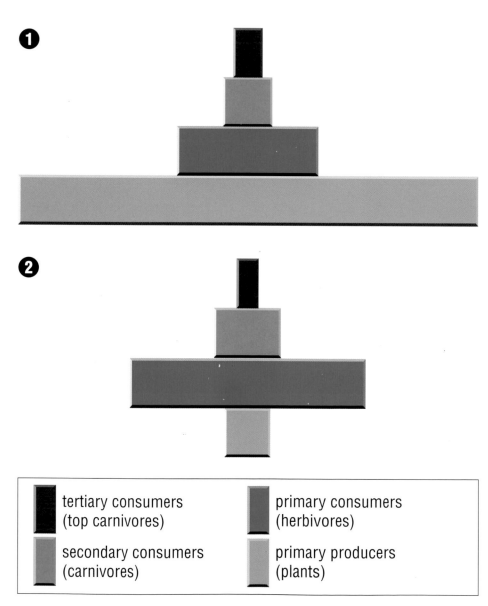

①

②

	tertiary consumers (top carnivores)		primary consumers (herbivores)
	secondary consumers (carnivores)		primary producers (plants)

Ecological pyramid

by their songs. Sampling soil organisms requires special equipment, but the techniques are standardized and not too difficult.

Pyramid of Numbers

At the end of the project you have data from which to compile a table of species, grouped according to the way they feed, and the number of individuals in each. You may decide to represent your results in the form of a graph and there is a type of graph devised especially for the purpose. It is rather like a histogram laid on its side, with bars, all of similar width, set one above another.

The lowest bar represents the primary producers, its length proportional to the number of individual plants. Centered on top of it is the second bar, its length being proportional to the number of primary consumers (herbivores). A bar for secondary consumers (carnivores) is laid above that, and one for the tertiary consumers (top carnivores) above that. The result is often something like the top diagram on page 82 (1), in the shape of a stepped pyramid. Because of this it is usually called an ecological pyramid. It was invented by a very distinguished British zoologist and ecologist, Charles Sutherland Elton (1900–91), so it is sometimes known as an Eltonian pyramid.

When you think about it, the shape is fairly obvious. If you imagine sheep eating grass, there must be more grass plants than there are sheep or some of the sheep will go hungry. Similarly, if hawks hunt small birds, there must be more small birds than there are hawks.

In the case of a forest, however, a pyramid that counts the number of individual organisms at each level may not have this apparently obvious form. It is more likely to resemble the lower diagram (2). This is because trees are big, so there are not many of them. One tree can provide food for many small herbivores, so the pyramid may be much narrower at the base than it is at higher levels. If this were a subtropical forest, on the other hand, and the primary consumers were elephants, the pyramid would change shape again.

Pyramid of Biomass

Using the number of individuals to characterize ecosystems is not very satisfactory, because there is no way to allow for large numbers of small organisms and small numbers of big ones. For this reason, the pyramid of numbers, as this pyramid is known, is little used.

One alternative is the pyramid of biomass. Biomass is the weight, or mass, of living matter in a given area. That area can be any size; it is possible to talk of the biomass of the planet Earth. It can also refer to all the living organisms present or just some of them. To construct a pyramid of biomass for an ecosystem it is necessary to calculate the biomass at each trophic level.

This solves the problem of size. Instead of counting the number of individuals in each quadrat or sampling area, they are collected and sorted according to their feeding type, dried in an oven, and then weighed. It is necessary to dry them, because organisms vary greatly in the amount of water they contain and this can also vary over time. Drying removes the water, so only solids are weighed. In the case of large animals, it is enough to estimate the number present. There are then standard formulae you can use to convert the number of individuals to a weight of dry matter.

A pyramid of biomass makes no distinction between mice and deer. Size does not matter, only total mass. The resulting pyramid is shaped like the upper one in the diagram (page 82) and conveys much more information than a pyramid of numbers, because it compares like with like. It begins, at the base, with the primary production, a figure representing all the leaves, stems, branches, roots, fruits, seeds, and so forth produced by green plants and measured as dry matter. Above this bar, the second level shows the total amount of dry matter in all the primary consumers. Higher levels also represent total dry matter. This makes it possible to measure how much of the dry matter at each level becomes incorporated into the organisms at the level above. As the pyramid shows, rather little of the matter produced by plants forms the bodies of herbivores, and rather little "herbivore stuff" forms the bodies of carnivores. The amount varies, but on average no more than 10 percent of biomass is transferred from each level to the one above.

This explains why an ecological pyramid seldom has more than four trophic levels. A fifth level would contain very few individuals indeed, and a sixth layer would probably contain too few to comprise a viable breeding population. This is why top predators, such as hawks (page 81), are always fairly uncommon. If predators are individually large, like tigers, a huge area of land is needed to supply them with food. Big predators have always been rare and always will be. (Food is more plentiful in some places than in others, but a tiger needs a territory of 25 to 250 square miles (65–650 sq km) to provide it with enough to eat.)

Pyramid of Energy

Despite being a great improvement on the pyramid of numbers, the pyramid of biomass does not illustrate the most fundamental basis of the relationship between trophic levels. Primary productivity begins with photosynthesis (page 72). This is powered by sunlight, and so you can think of it as plants capturing energy. A proportion of this energy passes to animals which eat plants, a proportion of their energy to the carnivores which eat them, and so on.

The energy involved at each level can be measured (page 104) and when it is represented graphically the result is a pyramid of energy, which looks very much like the pyramid of biomass, and like the upper pyramid in the diagram. Ecologists consider the pyramid of energy the most fundamental of the ecological pyramids, and the most informative.

Decomposers

Pyramids of numbers, biomass, and energy portray trophic relationships that begin with living matter. Plants produce food for herbivores, which are eaten by carnivores. It all happens above ground, because that is where plants conduct photosynthesis.

Below ground there is another community and it, too, consists of groups of organisms that pass food from one trophic level to another. The species comprising the soil community are very different from those living above ground, but the community is no less complex. It includes herbivores and carnivores, and it can be described by food webs and ecological pyramids.

Since the above-ground pyramids are right side up, with the widest band at the bottom, it is tempting to draw the pyramid for below-ground communities the other way, with the broadest band at the top. This would indicate that one pyramid describes relationships above ground and the other those below ground. If it is a pyramid of numbers, this is the way it may form, because as nutrients pass from one trophic level to the next the organisms feeding on them become smaller and, therefore, more numerous. Contriving to turn the pyramids upside down is misleading, however. It should be shown like any other pyramid, with the first band at the bottom, whether or not it is the widest. The difference between the above- and below-ground pyramids arises only from the material comprising the lowest band. Instead of fresh, living, primary produce, below ground it is dead organic matter.

Dead Organic Matter

A forest floor is covered with dead leaves and conifer needles, twigs, branches, and, here and there, whole trees that have fallen. These are the most obvious and by far the most abundant forms of dead organic matter, but they are not the only ones. Insects molt, discarding their old exoskeletons, and snakes shed their skins. Mammals drop hairs, birds discard worn out feathers and eggshells, deer shed their antlers, and, of course, all animals produce urine and feces. This is all dead organic matter, and the primary resource for the soil community.

Fungi and bacteria are often the first to arrive. This is because they are everywhere, as spores in the air and on the dead material itself even before it falls to the ground. They feed on sugars and starches. Removing these weakens the structure of the material so it tends to break apart.

What remains is more resistant to attack by fungi and bacteria, but the fungi themselves are food to some animals, including certain species of ants, termites, beetles, and nematodes.

The Soil Community

Look among and beneath the dead leaves on the ground and you will find woodlice, snails, slugs, earthworms, millipedes, and various insect larvae. These all feed on the leaves and similar plant material, shredding it into tiny pieces. They drag it below the ground surface and move it from the place where it fell, spreading it throughout the uppermost soil layer, where smaller animals can reach it.

These include worms smaller than the earthworms, as well as mites and springtails. None is more than 0.08 inch (2 mm) long, so you need a good magnifying glass to see them.

They are far from being the smallest animals. When they have eaten their fill, what remains passes to nematode worms, rotifers, and single-celled protozoans, all of them less than 0.004 inch (100 μm) long and visible only with the help of a microscope. Then the material returns to the bacteria.

Large soil animals, called the megafauna, are fairly mobile. If you rummage among the dead leaves, or dig a few inches into the soil, you will come across a few of them, such as earthworms and woodlice, but others sense your approach and burrow out of your reach. Smaller animals, of the mesofauna, such as springtails, mites, and curious animals called tardigrades, are barely visible to the naked eye, and the smallest of all, the single-celled protozoans comprising the microfauna, cannot be seen at all. This makes the soil and even the top layer of litter seem sparsely inhabited. Nothing could be further from the truth. In a temperate forest, beneath every square yard of the soil surface there may be close to 850 species of animals (1,000 per m²), never mind the fungi, bacteria, and others, and those animals are present in vast numbers. Each square yard of forest floor may conceal more than 8 million nematode worms, 80,000 springtails, and 80,000 mites, as well as around 40,000 animals of assorted other species (10 million, 100,000, and 50,000 per sq m, respectively). In broad-leaved deciduous forest, if the soil is not too acid, there may be several hundred earthworms, but their numbers can vary greatly over quite short distances. These larger animals are sometimes called detritivores, because they feed on waste material, or detritus.

Megafauna, Mesofauna, and the Forest Floor

The megafauna and mesofauna play a more important part in the decomposition of material in a forest than they do in other ecosystems. Grasses and herbs are softer than the leaves and wood of trees, so they are broken down more easily by the microfauna. On a forest floor, however, as the megafauna and mesofauna chew plant fragments into ever smaller pieces, they increase vastly the total surface area of those fragments. As they eat they also drop feces, and their fecal pellets keep the material on which they fall moist, which facilitates fungal and bacterial attack, and also makes it easier for material to be washed below the surface by rain or dragged there by animals. Worm casts, which you often find lying on the surface early in the morning, are the most familiar example of feces produced by the megafauna: they have usually disappeared, back below ground, within a few hours. Charles Darwin calculated that every year the earthworms in grassland near his home brought about 20 tons of their feces to the surface of each acre (50 tonnes per hectare). Their casts are what remains of material they have dragged below the surface and passed through their bodies.

Plant material is very tough. Plant cell walls contain cellulose, and woody material contains lignin, which is the principal component of wood. There are also some very complex proteins, as well as suberin, from which cork is made. These substances are broken down chemically, in reactions assisted by enzymes. Cellulases—enzymes that catalyze the breakdown of cellulose—are produced by certain species of bacteria and protozoa. Most other enzymes are secreted by fungi. In order to work, enzymes must come into direct contact with the compounds that will react. Different fungi produce different enzymes, so many species contribute to the breaking down of all the resistant compound. It is the soil animals that break material into smaller pieces, so increasing the surface area on which the chemical reactions take place.

Mutualism and Predation

A few animals, including some species of earthworms, snails, and insect larvae, can produce their own cellulases. Those unable to do so recruit assistants, leading to mutualism, which is a mutually beneficial partnership. Termites carry communities of bacteria and protozoa in their guts. These organisms produce the enzymes needed to break down cellulose and lignin, allowing the termites to feed on dead wood, which is plentiful. Woodlice also harbor gut microorganisms that produce cellulases. Other animals, including certain species of springtails, ants, and termites, wait for microorganisms to break down tough material, then feed on the microorganisms. There are even ants and termites that cultivate fungal "gardens." They gather leaf fragments, chew them, assemble them in special places, sow them with fungal spores, then feed on the fungi.

While these animals are grazing, others are hunting them. The soil community includes carnivores. There are small spiders, harvest spiders (Opiliones, also known as harvestmen and daddy longlegs), and centipedes, all of them formidable predators of animals smaller than themselves.

Sequence of Decomposition

Since some of the chemical compounds in dead organic matter are more difficult to digest than others, there is an order in which they are broken down and disappear. Sugars are the first to go. These are easy to digest, and some are soluble, so they are washed away by the rain.

Starches are next to go, and then hemicelluloses. This is a group of sugars that occur in the cell walls of plants in association with cellulose. They are easily hydrolyzed; hydrolysis is a reaction between a substance and the hydrogen and hydroxyl ions in water that splits molecules of the substance in two. Pectins, carbohydrates that also occur in plant cell walls, disappear at about the same time as hemicelluloses, and so do proteins.

After that, the really tough compounds start to decompose. Cellulose is first, followed by lignins and then suberins, the fatty compounds that make cork water resistant. Finally cutin is digested. This is another fatty substance. It occurs in cell walls and helps waterproof them.

Rate of Decomposition

All plants are made from these ingredients, and this is the order in which they are consumed, but the proportions vary. After all, not all plants are the same. Humans eat plants, and we have no trouble distinguishing the taste and texture of one vegetable from those of another. Not surprisingly, therefore, some plant remains vanish more quickly than others. Fruits do not last long. Mammals and birds enjoy them, but even while they are nibbling and pecking the fungi and bacteria are busily at work stripping out the sugars and starches. In most cases, when those have gone not much of a fruit remains. Where oak and beech trees grow together, fallen oak leaves disappear faster than those of beech. Conifer needles are eaten only slowly.

Decomposition continues through the year, but it proceeds more vigorously in summer, when the ground is warm. This alters the contents of the larder on the forest floor as the year progresses, a change that is much more marked in a deciduous forest, where leaves fall all together, than in an evergreen one, where leaves are shed at a constant rate that does not vary with the seasons.

Mostly small and hidden below ground, the decomposers are easily overlooked. Like all organisms, they feed, reproduce, and die, but in doing so they make life possible for others. At the end of the processes of decomposition, dead organic matter has been taken apart completely and transformed into simple chemical compounds. Dissolved in water, these compounds can pass through the walls of root cells and so sustain living plants. The forest is defined by its trees, but the trees appear by arrangement with the soil community.

Habitats and Niches

Perhaps you live in the city. At night, streetlights illuminate the street outside your home, making it safer for people walking after dark. There are shops not too far away where you can buy groceries, clothes, and everything else you need. A fire engine will arrive in minutes should your home catch fire, and a police force and courts uphold the rule of law. The city has schools, museums, libraries, theaters, art galleries, and concert halls, as well as swimming pools, parks, gymnasiums, and sports fields.

Life in a real city is not quite so stress-free as this makes it sound, of course. Things go wrong, services break down, some people are unemployed, there is bad housing and poverty. All the same, for the whole of human history people have thought that cities are good places to live. If you were an ecologist, you might say that the city is a good habitat. Temperate forest is also a good habitat, as is the soil beneath the forest floor. The word "habitat" has the same meaning in all three cases, but clearly there are differences: humans have always found forests extremely difficult places to live (page 146) and although domestic cats fare well enough in cities, the lynx (*Felis lynx* in Europe and Asia, *F. canadensis* in North America) would find our streets, shopping malls, and even our parks very inhospitable.

Whose Habitat?

Habitats must be defined in relation to the species they accommodate. It is meaningless to describe an area simply as "good habitat" without naming some organism that might find it so. Golden eagles, woodchucks, giant redwoods, seaweeds, whales, and walruses all have quite different requirements and what is good habitat for one would be intolerable for another.

Animals and plants do not live in isolation, of course. What is good habitat for one species will be just as hospitable for several more, but each will experience it differently. Cities provide good habitat for humans. When we think of a city we imagine its buildings, streets, transportation systems, services, and amenities, the ability of the city to satisfy our needs. Cities also support a surprising amount of wildlife, however, comprising many other species. Try imagining the city as it appears to the feral pigeons that roost on its high buildings and feed on its squares, to the rats that inhabit the dark, secret places, to the house mice, the sparrows, or the cockroaches. Similarly, a forest provides habitat

for a wide variety of species, but it does so by satisfying their quite distinct needs. The insect larvae feeding on leaves in the canopy provide food for insectivorous birds, which are hunted by birds of prey, as are the small rodents rummaging in the litter on the forest floor. To each of these and to countless others above and below ground, the forest represents something different. The only thing on which all these species would agree is that they find whatever it is they need within this specified area.

Stable, Unstable, and Ephemeral Habitats

This may seem to leave "habitat" as a word that is impossible to define; like beauty, it is in the eye of the beholder. Ecologists are not left entirely helpless, however, because it is possible to describe a habitat as stable, unstable, or ephemeral. If it is stable, conditions for those species at home in it will remain hospitable all the time. If it is unstable, conditions will change, so the habitat is more hospitable at some times than at others. If it is ephemeral, hospitable conditions will occur only occasionally and then disappear quickly. From this point of view, you might think of a city as a stable habitat, because the shelter, protection, food, services, and amenities it provides are available at all times. A temperate forest, on the other hand, is unstable; conditions in it vary widely between summer and winter.

Closer inspection reveals that matters are not quite so simple. The city may be stable as far as humans are concerned, but its nonhuman inhabitants are affected by the seasons, just like forest-dwellers, and for some organisms the part of the city or forest they occupy appears and vanishes rapidly and unpredictably. The half-eaten burger thrown in a trash can or dead mouse on the forest floor is a valuable resource to a host of flies and bacteria, but before long the trash can is emptied, the corpse gone.

We humans are adapted to life in a stable habitat and the cities we have been building for thousands of years reflect that adaptation. It makes us think less stable habitats are necessarily inferior and so they are for us, but not for species adapted to them. Adaptation to unstable or ephemeral circumstances requires an organism to grab as much as it can of the briefly abundant resources before they disappear, and the best way to do that is by adopting a particular reproductive strategy.

Reproductive Strategies

Where the habitat is stable, it is best for a species to maximize its competitive advantages. It can do this by producing few offspring and caring for them over a fairly long period so by the time they must fend for themselves they are nearly fully grown and well equipped to do so. This is known as K-selection. Humans reproduce in this way; ours is a K-species.

In unstable conditions, this would not work; a better strategy is to maximize reproductive efficiency. The best way to do this is to produce a large number of offspring quickly, the moment the habitat becomes favorable. The young enter the world small and vulnerable, but are able to feed rapidly and grow fast, so they seize the resources while they are available. This is called r-selection and it ensures that by the time the resources vanish enough offspring will have matured to guarantee there will be another generation as soon as the good times return. Rats, house mice, and locusts reproduce in this way; many r-species are pests exploiting food we provide in vast amounts but only briefly, such as farm crops and full granaries.

Reproductive strategy is one way in which a species adapts to its habitat, but what matters is the stability or instability of its own portion of the habitat, not of the habitat as a whole. You see evidence of this whenever a piece of meat is left for a few days in warm weather. It becomes infested with fly larvae, which mature rapidly into a swarm of flies. The meat is an unstable portion of the larger habitat of house and city, which is stable. Forests last for many years. They are stable, but within a forest there are many parts of the overall habitat that are unstable or ephemeral. Fruits, seeds, mature pine cones, and the fruiting bodies of forest fungi are available only in certain months, for example, and a puddle of water may evaporate in a matter of hours.

This type of adaptation can also determine how often members of a species breed, a choice of conditions known as semelparity and iteroparity. Which strategy works best depends on several factors, including the size of individuals and whether or not large size confers an advantage in a particular habitat. Many annual plants reproduce only once in their lifetime. Species using this one-shot reproductive strategy are said to be semelparous. Other plants—including forest trees and almost all animals—are iteroparous, meaning that they reproduce more than once in their lifetime.

Ecological Niches

The statement that Caroline and Harry live in the city, or that the gray squirrel (*Sciurus carolinensis*) lives in the forest, tells you nothing about how Caroline, Harry, and the squirrel make their livings. You know where they live, but not how they live. Where they live, or their habitat, is their address. Admittedly, the mailman would need more detail than "G. Squirrel, The Forest," but at least he would not go looking for the squirrel in the middle of a lake or on the seashore.

If its habitat is the address of a species, what it does to make a living at that address is its ecological niche. Caroline drives a bus. That is her job,

so you could say it is her niche in her city habitat. It pays her wages that enable her to buy food and pay the rent. The gray squirrel feeds mainly on seeds, leaves of trees, and fungi. In spring and summer its diet is more varied and it spends most of its time high in the forest canopy. In fall, when the leaves are less nutritious but seeds are appearing, it spends more time on the ground, storing food in caches, and in winter it is on the ground a good deal, feeding on its stores. That is how Caroline earns her living and how "G. Squirrel" earns his.

You can think of an ecological niche as the presence of a range of factors. These might include, for example, the daily and annual range of temperature, annual precipitation and its distri-

bution through the year, the pattern of light and shade, the availability of shelter and nesting sites, and the existing population of plants, fungi, and animals. Taken together they amount to an opportunity. If a particular species is able to travel to the place where the opportunity exists and then to take advantage of it, it will have occupied its ecological niche.

Which species is first on the scene is a matter of chance, but the one that arrives will define the niche. There are many ways resources can be exploited, but no two species will exploit them in precisely the same way. In other words, a niche does not exist until it is occupied and the species occupying it also creates it. Each ecological niche is unique.

Tree Adaptations to Climate

It is easy to take our familiar surroundings for granted, to assume that plants and animals we see often are just as common everywhere.

Perhaps hickory trees (*Carya* species) grow near your home. *Carya illinoensis* produces the pecan nut, which is believed to have played a very important part in American history. Highly nutritious, they were eaten by Native Americans, and European settlers were growing them in plantations by 1775; now, of course, they are grown on a very large scale. If hickory trees are common in your neighborhood you may be tempted to think they are common all over the world, at least in temperate regions. As the map below shows, this is far from the truth. About 20 species of *Carya* are native to North America, two more are native to China, and that is all the hickories there are. They may be common where you live, but in the world at large they are rare.

What is true for hickories is also true for most other tree species, though to a lesser degree. Elms (*Ulmus* species), for example, occur widely in temperate regions, and in Asia extend almost to the equator, but there are large gaps in their distribution (which may be widening because of disease; page 108). Birch (*Betula* species) is much more widespread. It grows naturally as a component of broad-leaved deciduous and coniferous forests, and dwarf birch (*B. nana*), which reaches a height of only 20–40 inches (50–100 cm), grows in the tundra, inside the Arctic Circle. Among the gymnosperms (page 59), the spruces (*Picea* species) are probably the most widespread.

Pecans are grown commercially on a large scale, so you may well find hickory trees growing outside the area shown in the figure. Probably you will not find birches growing outside the range shown on the map, but this is only because the area is already so large. Many birches are attractive

trees, grown for ornament. Numerically, Sitka spruce is now the commonest tree in Britain, but spruces do not occur naturally in western Europe. They are grown for their timber. It is possible to cultivate trees outside the area in which they occur naturally, and throughout history people have been taking their favorite trees with them whenever they moved and planting them around their new homes. Ecologists distinguish between species that are native to a region and those introduced by humans, some of which have become naturalized (page 90).

Climatic Limits

Climate is the most important factor allowing some species to thrive but not others, and this limitation is very evident in Britain. Lying between latitudes 49°58' N (Lizard Point) and 58°37' N (Dunnet Head), the mainland of Great Britain (the Orkney and Shetland Islands lie farther to the north) is at the climatic limit for many tree species. The map of the United Kingdom (page 89) uses three widely grown native species to illustrate the point. Field (or common) maple (*Acer campestre*) grows naturally only in the southern half of England and in east Wales, hornbeam (*Carpinus betulus*) in the southeast quarter of England, and small-leaved lime (*Tilia cordata*) in central and eastern England and east Wales.

Trees, like all green plants, photosynthesize carbohydrates to obtain the energy they need; photosynthesis is a process limited by temperature (page 72). It ceases altogether when the temperature falls below 21°F (-6°C) and works most efficiently at temperatures higher than 41°F (5°C). Throughout the temperate region winter tem-

peratures regularly fall below 41°F (5°C) and often below 21°F (-6°C), so there is a period during which photosynthesis is so restricted that trees cannot grow. Increasing distance from the equator produces lower winter temperatures, but these are not important in themselves. When it is already too cold for photosynthesis, a still lower temperature makes no difference. What matters is the length of the cold period—the higher the latitude, the longer that period will be.

Flowering plants produce flowers and, from fertilized female flowers, they develop seeds (page 66). It is an effective method of reproduction, but it has one disadvantage: it takes time. A tree cannot produce flowers until its own metabolism becomes active, although it does not have to wait for its leaves to commence photosynthesis. The hornbeam produces flowers in April, before its leaves open. The field maple and small-leaved lime flower after their leaves open, the field maple in May or June, the small-leaved lime in June or July. In all three, seeds ripen by September or October. The birch flowers in April, the male flowers (catkins) having developed the previous fall and hung waiting through the winter, and the seeds are ripe by July or August. For all broad-leaved trees the entire reproductive process takes place between spring and late summer or early fall. An unusually long winter, late frosts that damage early-flowering species (such as hornbeam), or a cold, dull summer that slows growth, can severely reduce seed production. Trees native to northern Europe, including Britain, are not able to produce seed every year and, when they do, the seed is often sterile. Limes (*Tilia* species) require warmth during the growing season. They, as well as elms, reproduce mainly by vegetative means (page 64). Even then, when abundant seed is produced, it must wait in the ground at least until the following spring, and often for more than a year, before it can germinate. During that time it represents a food source for many animals and much of the seed is eaten.

Birch has such a wide range, extending so far north, because its season is very short and its seeds, produced in copious amounts, are usually viable and germinate quickly. On bare ground in high latitudes, birch is often the first tree to appear.

Flowering plants reproduce more efficiently than conifers, provided they have the length of growing season they need. They are adapted to short winters and warm summers.

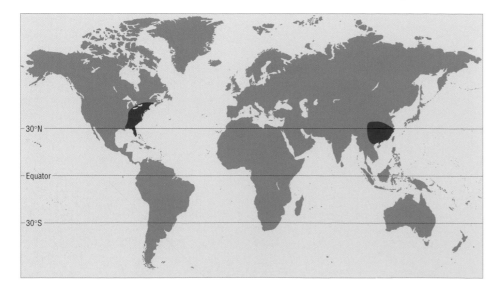

World distribution of hickory

The Conifer Advantage

Where the growing season is short, conifers have the advantage. They take much longer to produce seeds, but unlike flowers their cones are tough and not damaged by cold. They are adapted to long winters and can tolerate cool summers. Except for the larches (*Larix* species), they bear leaves (as needles or scales) throughout the year. Even during winter, they photosynthesize on sunny days and the first hint of spring finds them ready and waiting. They do not have to produce fresh foliage before they can begin growing.

Cool winters present trees with a further problem. Water freezes and precipitation falls as snow, remaining on the ground surface. Roots can absorb water only in liquid form, so prolonged freezing temperatures are equivalent to drought. Drought also occurs in lower latitudes, of course, as a dry season that is the equivalent of the high-latitude winter.

Trees have adapted to seasonal water shortage in two ways. The first involves severely restricting water loss. Leaves are covered with a thick, tough cuticle, and the stomata are reduced in number and sheltered in pits or crevices in the leaf surface. In conifers, the leaves are also reduced in size. They have the form of long, narrow needles, as in pines (*Pinus* species) and larches (*Larix* species) or are like tiny, overlapping scales, as in cypresses (*Cupressus* species) and the western red cedar (*Thuja plicata*). These principal forms are illustrated in the diagram.

Broad-Leaved Evergreens

It is not only gymnosperms that have adapted to drought by evolving leaves protected by a thick,

Leaves of conifers

often waxy cuticle through which water loss is much reduced. So have the broad-leaved evergreen trees of lower latitudes. Many of these leaves also have sharp prickles around their edges to discourage browsing animals. Holly (*Ilex aquifolium*) is a familiar example that grows well in higher latitudes. Many ornamental varieties are cultivated for their attractive foliage, but holly is the dominant tree in some woods. These are trees of the sclerophyllous forests. Most have been cleared, but this was the type of vegetation natural to the Mediterranean region, central and southern California, parts of Chile and South Africa, and southern and western Australia, where the summers are long, hot, and dry.

Deciduous Trees

The alternative is to grow leaves rapidly, early in spring, and shed them in fall. This seems wasteful, but it works well. Deciduous forests occur where temperatures range from about -22°F to 86°F (-30°C in winter to 30°C) in summer and precipitation is spread fairly evenly through the year. The growing season lasts five or six months. This is as long as the tree needs leaves so they can be thinner and flimsier than the leaves of evergreen trees.

As summer draws to a close, the days grow shorter and the temperature starts to fall. Leaves respond to these changes by progressively reducing their production of auxins, which are chemical substances that stimulate plant growth, and increasing their production of ethylene, which inhibits cell growth. No more chlorophyll is produced and many of the nutrient elements in the leaves are transported back into the branch or trunk of the tree and stored there until they are needed the following spring. There is a layer of parenchyma cells near the base of the leaf stalk (the petiole). This layer weakens until a gust of wind is enough to

Climatic limits of trees in the United Kingdom

detach the leaf. The process by which a deciduous tree loses its leaves is called abscission.

Abscission incurs some cost, in energy and materials, but this is minimized. The withdrawal of nutrients before leaves are discarded helps, and once the leaves are on the forest floor, decomposition is fairly swift. Deciduous leaves disappear much more quickly than conifer needles or the leaves of broad-leaved evergreen trees, and the nutrients they contain are recycled. It is a highly sophisticated adaptation to climate that works well over a large part of the temperate regions.

pine (*Pinus*)

western red cedar (*Thuja plicata*)

larch (*Larix*)

Primeval Forest, Ancient Woodland, Old-Growth Forest, Plantations

Forests are dynamic communities of plants and animals, changing constantly in countless small ways in response to changing circumstances. Over long periods, these small changes can accumulate, making a forest today substantially different from the forest that occupied the same site in earlier times.

People used to believe in the "balance of nature" and some environmentalists still do. It is an essentially religious concept, holding that God created natural systems in such a way that their internal checks and balances maintain them in a stable condition. The difficulty with the concept is its implication of stasis. It suggests that a naturally balanced system never changes, which is not only mistaken, it is impossible. There is an "economy of nature," based on the way plants and animals use resources and recycle materials, but this is a dynamic concept, suggesting adaptability, and quite different from the static idea of "balance." Unless systems are able to adjust to changes in the conditions around them, those changes may destroy them. Any climatic change, for example, will cause difficulties for certain species and their populations will decrease in number. This will allow other species, better suited to the changed conditions, to flourish and, perhaps, eventually to replace the disadvantaged species. If the system is a forest, it will remain forest, but it will become a different kind of forest. Were the "balance of nature" to be static, so the disadvantaged species could not be replaced, the forest would disappear. There is a balance, in the sense that all complex systems regulate themselves, but it is not one that precludes change.

What Does "Natural" Mean?

Change is natural, but recognizing the fact presents a further problem. Looking at an area of forest, how can you tell whether its development has been affected by human activities and, if so, to what extent? Did its trees grow with no help from humans, from seed produced by neighboring trees, or were they planted? Perhaps the whole forest was planted long ago and there is no record of the planting. Did the trees arrive of their own accord, advancing as the climate grew warmer after the ice sheets had retreated, or did people bring them? Sweet chestnut (*Castanea sativa*) grows in many English forests, but it was brought to Britain by the Romans. *Acer pseudo-platanus,* the tree known in Britain as the sycamore, was introduced around the 15th century or a little later. It has invaded many forests and is now very common.

What, then, does "natural" forest mean? In practice, forests (and other ecosystems) are classified according to their naturalness, but the classification is difficult and rather vague, although its underlying concept is simple enough. This is that while deer, beavers, and many other animals live in and affect the development of forests, only humans deliberately manage forests, thereby altering them in planned ways, so the degree of naturalness is inversely proportional to the amount of human intervention.

It can be argued, of course, that humans are as much a part of nature as any other animals and it is entirely natural for us to live the way we do. After all, ants, termites, and prairie dogs build elaborate shelters for themselves, prairie dogs deliberately kill woody plants around their colonies, and grazing animals, such as deer and cattle, kill tree saplings, thereby encouraging the growth of grasses and herbs. Why should we consider ourselves superior (or inferior)? This view renders the word "natural" at best relative: a backyard, growing flowers and vegetables, can be said to be more natural than the street and the farmed countryside more natural than the city.

Value of Undisturbed Habitat

Naturalists, however, attach importance to the idea of naturalness, mainly because they believe a habitat undisturbed by humans and allowed to develop in its own way is likely to support a wider range of species than a managed habitat. This is often the case. Ecologists also regard a natural habitat as being of greater scientific importance than one modified by human activity, because it affords them greater opportunity for learning how natural systems function. The understanding they acquire is of practical use in evaluating the likely consequences of different types of land management in areas adjacent or similar to the forested area.

Inevitably, efforts to protect areas designated as "natural" often lead to conflict. It most commonly arises over competing uses for land, but there are also disputes over the desirability of managing established forests. In October 1996, environmentalists managed to halt an operation in the Headwaters Forest, California, in which the Pacific Lumber Company planned to remove dead, diseased, and dying trees from groves of redwoods and Douglas firs in an area of old-growth forest. The protest was triggered by a worker who accidentally knocked down a healthy hemlock tree. Here, the conflict was between those who sought to manage the forest and those who wished it to be left undisturbed.

Primeval Forest and Wilderness

Conflicts cannot be resolved unless there is an agreed definition of "natural forest." At one level, this is not too difficult. Until the first humans reached it, the development of a forest must have been guided entirely by nonhuman events. Clearly, that primeval forest was natural. In 1981, in the first edition of his book *Woodland Conservation and Management,* George F. Peterken proposed that this forest be called "original-natural."

Had the forest, or some part of it, never been invaded by humans, even though they lived not far away, it would have remained undisturbed. By now it would be substantially different from the original-natural forest, however, because over the thousands of years since humans arrived the climate has changed several times and soils have also developed. Nevertheless, the changes have not been wrought by humans. Peterken suggests calling this kind of forest "present-natural."

In areas remote from human habitation, such forests still survive as wilderness. By definition, a "wilderness" area is one in which humans have never lived permanently, or only as isolated individuals or families, and that has never been managed or exploited economically. It is not a formerly occupied area that has been abandoned. Defined this way, there are areas of true wilderness in North America and Europe, but whether they comprise truly primeval forest is more doubtful. Prehistoric peoples almost certainly exerted some influence and in the United States ecologists prefer to classify forests that have remained unchanged since the arrival of Europeans as "pre-settlement." Europeans are more generous with their use of the word. The Germans, for example, consider some of their forests to be primeval (*Urwälder*).

Despite the changes over the centuries, a present-natural forest may still retain similarities to the original-natural forest and it may be possible to tell, for example by studying pollen found below ground, that the forest has descended directly from the primeval forest. Peterken calls this kind of forest, containing clues to its own past, "past-natural."

Colonization of Abandoned Land

Abandoned land can never become true wilderness, but plants and animals will colonize it in an entirely natural way: no one would deny that a forest established under these circumstances is more natural than one in which all the trees were

Old-growth canopy, Cascade Range, Oregon (Gerry Ellis/ENP Images)

planted by foresters. Take any area of land, suppose that all the people left, their buildings and roads were demolished, and the debris removed, and that the area transformed itself instantly into a mature forest. This forest would be what Peterken calls "potential-natural." The idea sounds fanciful, but it is extremely important. Obviously (and fortunately), no one has the power to remove all the people in this way, and to clear away every last bit of evidence of their presence. Even if that were to happen, plants would return a few at a time and it might take centuries for a mature forest to develop. Nevertheless, it is valuable to be able to predict what that forest would be like, assuming the climate and soils remained unaltered. This knowledge tells us what those homes, roads, and so forth are replacing. When a change in land use is proposed any-

where, a calculation of the potential-natural state of the area helps in evaluating the ecological effects of that change.

Plants are quick to start colonizing bare ground. Left undisturbed, the first arrivals will soon be replaced and slowly the plant community will come to be dominated by woody plants, and in many places eventually by trees (page 92). If the abandoned area is large enough, it may become forested. This forest, which Peterken calls "future-natural," will not contain those trees of the original-natural forest that have become extinct and it will contain introduced species that have become naturalized and invasive. It will be forest, but one quite unlike the original-natural forest.

Forests That Were Planted

Most forests fail to qualify in any of these categories, because they have been deliberately managed by humans, but since all forests support some wildlife, all of them are somewhat natural. This has led to alternative ways for classifying forests.

Forestry, which is the deliberate planting of entire forests for commercial exploitation, began in the 17th century and that is also when woods and forests were first shown on British maps. In Britain, therefore, a forest or woodland that is known from records to have been in existence continuously since 1600 or earlier is called "ancient." Woodland younger than this is "recent." If an ancient forest or woodland is known to have been in existence prior to the clearance of the surrounding primeval forest, it is classed as "primary." If it came into existence later than that, it is "secondary."

Old-Growth Forest

North American ecologists are reluctant to describe their forests as "virgin." Instead, they use the classification "old-growth." Unfortunately, "old-growth" is no more easily defined than any of the other terms. Designation of an old-growth forest is based on assessments of the sizes of the trees and fallen wood, and the number of tree species present. While forests conforming to these criteria could develop on abandoned farmland or from forests that were once managed, in fact most are pre-settlement forests and probably primeval. Indeed, many old-growth forests are likely to be older than the German *Urwälder.*

"Naturalness" is a difficult concept and no one would attempt to use it in classifying forests were it not for the usefulness of the resulting classification. It allows ecologists to identify those forests likely to be of greatest scientific value and it helps in assessing the environmental consequences of proposed developments.

Succession and Climax

When an old building is demolished, sometimes the rubble is cleared away and then the site is left undisturbed for a few weeks or months. Except in the depths of winter, within days a few plants will start to appear. At first they will be small and hard to see, but before long they will cover the whole area and then they will flower. One of the most poignant sights in a city devastated by bombing is the gaudy mass of flowers that quickly arrive, seemingly from nowhere, to brighten the ruins of what once were homes. In Britain, November 11 is called "Poppy Day," when people wear artificial common (or field) poppies (*Papaver rhoes*), sold to raise funds to care for veterans, and decorate wreaths with them to commemorate the lives lost in the two world wars. This red poppy is used because during World War I it carpeted the battlefields of Flanders.

Bare ground seldom remains bare for long. The plants do not come from nowhere, of course. Some arise from tiny, light seeds that ride the wind in their billions and occasionally fall on fertile ground. Others, including the common poppy, have seeds that remain viable for decades and germinate when some disturbance removes competing plants, allowing them access to light and moisture. They are opportunists, those first plants with their cheerful flowers, and they do not last. Other plants arrive to displace them. Leave the demolition site longer, and grasses will appear, then brambles. It is as though one group of plants prepares the way for the next in a fairly orderly sequence.

Cowles and Postglacial Chicago

One of the first studies on this process came from the American botanist Henry Chandler Cowles (1869–1939). In 1899 and 1901 Cowles published two papers in the *Botanical Gazette* (which he edited from 1925 until 1934) describing the vegetation around Lake Michigan and Chicago. His major statement on long-term succession appeared in 1901, as "The plant societies of Chicago and vicinity," published by the University of Chicago Press in the *Bulletin of The Geographic Society of Chicago.* He described the plant communities that had succeeded one another since the final retreat of the ice sheets in Illinois, as water drained from the huge, glacial Lake Chicago, leaving the present much smaller Lake Michigan and the Chicago plain.

Cowles reported in his *Botanical Gazette* papers that stable sand dunes around Lake Michigan were colonized by basswood (*Tilia americana*).

As the climate became increasingly moderate, the community dominated by basswood gave way to others adapted to these conditions, until there was a mesophytic community (one comprising plants that thrive where there are no extremes of temperature and moisture is available through the year) dominated by maple (*Acer* species) and beech (*Fagus grandifolia*). As Cowles saw it, the vegetation pattern changed constantly, but it reached a kind of optimum, or climax, state with the mesophytic community.

Attaining this state was not the end of the process, because the pattern could change further, away from the climax, and then return to it. His study of the draining of Lake Chicago and the emergence of the Chicago plain described the way a landscape had developed over many thousands of years. Vegetation patterns were related to landscape changes, which in turn were related to climatic changes, and so the ecological succession of plants was unending. It could never reach a final state in which it would remain for ever, because as it approached a kind of mesophytic ideal, the climate or landscape would change. If you picture a succession as a path toward a target, the target keeps moving, so it can never be reached.

Clements and the Superorganism

Frederic Edward Clements (1874–1945), a botanist and ecologist initially at the University of Nebraska and from 1907 at the University of Minnesota, took the theory of succession further. His monograph "Plant succession: analysis of the development of vegetation" appeared in 1916 in the *Publications of the Carnegie Institution,* Washington, and was so well received that Clements was appointed to a post at the Carnegie Institution and moved from Minnesota to Washington, D.C., where he remained for the rest of his life. In the years that followed he wrote or coauthored close to one thousand papers describing successions in various sites all over the country. It was a remarkable achievement for anyone, and especially for a man who was unwell much of the time during his later years. Assisted by his wife, Edith, Frederic Clements worked so hard and wrote so much that his ideas became very influential and his textbook, *Plant Ecology,* first published in 1929, brought his views to generations of students.

Anyone who sets out as Clements did to describe a plant succession has to devise some means of classification. Without this, it is impossible to show any change at all. At one time there must be a community of one kind and later one

of a different kind, but those kinds must be defined and named, then allotted a position within a classificatory system.

This need arises only because we must attach names to things in order to discuss them. Our discussion may then deal accurately enough with the overall process, but the named stages of the process sound fixed, as though one morning you might arrive and discover that the "stage 1" you noted a week ago had gone and now the site was occupied by a "stage 2" community. In reality, the change is seamless. You can observe it at all only by visiting the site at quite widely spaced intervals to take "snapshots" that freeze the process at particular points and allow the community present at one time to be compared with that present at a later time. It is helpful to think of these communities, separated by intervals of time, as distinct stages, but there is a danger in the approach Clements recommended that they may come to resemble organisms in their own right, or "superorganisms."

Up to a point, the idea of a superorganism is quite persuasive. In the northeastern United States, for example, most of the broad-leaved deciduous forests are composed of various combinations of a limited number of species of beech, birch, maple, and oak, with their associated shrubs and climbers. Over much of Britain, the original, primeval forest was dominated by oak (*Quercus robur*) and hazel (*Corylus avellana*). Large tracts of boreal forest contain just one or two species of trees. Certain species do seem often to occur together and it is convenient, and not wholly misleading, to think of them as though they were a superorganism.

Climax Theory

Clements worked initially on the ecology of prairie grassland. His first major publication, written in collaboration with his Nebraska colleague Roscoe Pound (1870–1964), was *The Phytogeography of Nebraska,* published in 1898, which became a standard botany textbook (phytogeography is the scientific study of the spatial distribution of plants). He believed the grassland community really was a superorganism, an assembly of plants and animals locked together in a network of inevitable relationships among themselves and with the nonliving factors in their environment in such a way that the assembly behaved as though it were a single organism. It reached its final state, the climax, by passing through a succession of previous states, called a sere, each seral stage of which was also like a single organism, but one that matured, died, and was replaced. If the sere begins on bare ground it is known as a primary sere or prisere. Prior to the climax no seral stage could endure, because its component species competed with one another while at the same time altering the physical and chemical conditions around them in ways that were eventually detrimental to them.

The climax was reached when the dominant mesophytic plants prevented the establishment of invading species that might later become dominant. This was a stable condition. The climax composition was very predictable, because Clements believed the succession was a process of reproduction and, as he explained in *Plant Succession and Plant Indicators* (1928), this must inevitably lead to the adult form, in a community of plants as much as in an individual plant. According to Clements, only one climax is possible, so this is sometimes known as the monoclimax theory.

Clements's account of a sere is sometimes called the interactive theory of climax, because it advances through the interactions of all the species in the succession. Clements seems to have pictured the succession as something like a single organism which is born, grows, and matures when it reaches its climax condition. Clear away the vegetation from an area and in time it will reform with exactly the same species in exactly the same proportions.

This can be seen in many parts of Massachusetts, New Hampshire, and Maine, where much, but not all, of the pre-settlement forest was cleared to provide farmland between about 1700 and 1850. Farming subsequently declined, and land was abandoned. The trees returned, now as secondary forest very similar to the original type, with remains of the old field walls running here and there through it.

Clements and his colleagues wanted to help farmers by showing them the effect they had on natural assemblages of vegetation. Understanding the natural succession and climax would allow ecologists to advise farmers on ways to improve their methods, so farming became less disruptive and crop yields more dependable. At the same time it taught farmers that the natural vegetation is very resilient. It can be cleared away, but, given the opportunity, it will return of its own accord. Clements had good news for both farmers and conservationists.

Can a Superorganism Die?

If it is true that a sere resembles the growth of a single organism, you may have noticed something odd about it. This organism appears or is born, grows, and matures, but that is as far as it goes. Real organisms do not stop there. They grow old and feeble, and die. The monoclimax theory makes no allowance for this. Cowles did not believe that a final equilibrium could ever be reached, but Clements disagreed. His monoclimax could not evolve. Once attained it was changeless—his optimistic message was based on that idea of changelessness.

Natural changes in climate can modify a succession or its climax. A climate that is hotter or drier than that of the region as a whole, or that becomes hotter or drier than it used to be, produces a "preclimax." A cooler or wetter climate produces a "postclimax."

Walk through most forests and you will find their composition varies from one place to another. This is not surprising. Some places are relatively low-lying and wet, others high and exposed. Soils wash down hillsides, so those at the bottom of a slope are often a little different from those at the top. Humans have interfered with most forests, but have been more active in some places than in others. All these very local variations are reflected in differences in the succession and climax. The area as a whole may be occupied by a forest climax, but within that overall climax there will be many local climaxes, all a little different and all equally stable. Sir Arthur Tansley called this a polyclimax, meaning a climax composed of many smaller climaxes, and it is an alternative to the monoclimax theory.

Gleason and the Individualistic Hypothesis

Frederic Clements was very influential, but his monoclimax theory was challenged, most strongly by Henry Allan Gleason (1882–1973), who developed what is known as the individualistic hypothesis. This says that a climax plant community comprises species that have come together largely by chance; it is an assembly of individuals. They just happened to be the ones that arrived at a site where the soil, illumination, temperature, and moisture suited them and, because they found the habitat hospitable, they thrived, coming to dominate the site to the exclusion of would-be invaders. Clear all the plants away and, of course, the site will be recolonized, but there is no guarantee that the climax community that develops there will be identical to, or even closely resemble, the original community.

The individualistic hypothesis predicts that species will be distributed according to gradients in the resources they need, such as light, warmth, moisture, and nutrients. The more abundant the resources, the more members there will be of the species needing them, and assemblages of species will comprise those which just happen to be in that area. If Clements was right, the community of plants found in a particular area will comprise species that are dependent on one another and are almost always found together.

Are There Such Things as Successions and Climaxes?

Ecologists still talk of successions and climaxes, and the terms are used widely in textbooks and even more in the writings of environmental campaigners, but in recent years they have become unfashionable among scientists. In damaging the interactive hypothesis, the individualistic hypothesis also weakened itself—now the whole idea of climaxes and seres leading to them appears to generate more difficulties than it solves.

Gleason showed that a vegetation pattern changes smoothly along a gradient. This means it cannot be regarded as a superorganism, because it cannot be clearly defined. You cannot draw a boundary around it, because it is much too variable, both spatially and over time. Nor is it always true that each stage in a succession prepares the way for the next. Sometimes this is what happens, but at other times it does not and there seems to be no way of predicting whether it will be so in a particular instance.

Even the central idea, of the stability of the climax, turns out to be illusory. In the case of a forest, which develops slowly and lives a very long time, stability can be measured only in a forest that has remained completely undisturbed for centuries. It is doubtful whether such a forest exists anywhere in the world. Disturbance is entirely natural, and in some cases essential for the continuation of the forest (page 94), so the forest climax cannot be stable in the sense intended by Clements, Tansley, and Gleason.

Relationships within communities of plants are much more complex than the early ecologists imagined and their development is affected by many more factors than climate, soil, and the plants themselves. Nevertheless it remains true that starting from bare or disturbed ground plants will appear and disappear until a community develops that is capable of enduring much longer than any of those preceding it. Ecologists may prefer not to call this a climax, but so far they have found no other name, and the idea of the sere leading to it also remains useful, provided it is understood as a very general description, rather than a detailed account of what really happens.

Fire Climax

Smokey the Bear used to warn people of the danger of forest fires, and *Bambi,* the Disney movie enjoyed by millions of people, underlined the danger. It depicted forest animals fleeing in terror from a fire advancing almost as fast as they could run. This was the popular view of forest fires and until quite recently many foresters and wildlife conservationists shared it. A forest fire is a terrifying sight, after all, and extremely dangerous for people living in its path. It makes obvious sense to take care not to start a fire accidentally, and if one does start, to extinguish it as quickly as possible, before it can do much harm.

For many years the management policy for natural forests was to prevent fires and, if that failed, to extinguish them rapidly. Then, in 1988, a fire started in Yellowstone National Park and despite the heroic efforts made to check it the fire raged out of control until the first winter snows extinguished it. By that time it had burned about almost 1 million acres (400,000 ha). That amounted to 45 percent of the total area of the park.

The fire seemed like a major disaster, but by spring of the following year new plants were emerging and it was clear that a new succession had begun. After a few years not only had the forest recovered, it had been invigorated.

Meanwhile, management policy was being altered. Since 1992, it has called for fires to be suppressed in some parts of the park, but if surface litter accumulates to more than a certain extent, fires will be started to remove it. Elsewhere in the park naturally occurring fires are controlled, but not prevented. It is now recognized that, in certain types of forest, fires are a natural phenomenon to which the plant and animal communities have adapted. Fire serves a useful purpose, in fact, and sometimes it is used as a management tool.

Lightning and Litter

In the dry climate of Yellowstone, decomposition is a slow process. Litter accumulates on the forest floor, and from time to time a fire removes it. While it is important not to start forest fires, most are sparked by lightning, not people. Dry electrical storms, with lightning but no rain, are common in the western United States. Year after year lightning ignited the litter on the floor of the Yellowstone forests, but the fire was dowsed before much of the fuel could be destroyed. As a consequence, the layer of needles, leaves, twigs, and other dead material grew steadily thicker, and all of it was tinder-dry. By 1988 so much dry material had accumulated that when the fire began it could not be dowsed.

Not all forests suffer equally from fires. They are uncommon in broad-leaved deciduous forests. This is partly because such forests occur in fairly wet climates, where litter on the forest floor is usually too wet to burn and decomposes quickly. Nor are the trees themselves very combustible. Their leaves contain enough water to make them slow-burning and difficult to ignite; their wood also burns slowly.

Coniferous forests are much more vulnerable. Their wood contains resins, which are highly

Forest burn scar, Yellowstone National Park, Wyoming
(Gerry Ellis/ENP Images)

flammable, their needles contain much less water than broad-leaves, and the forests tend to grow in climates that are drier than those of broad-leaved forests. Studies of forests in northern Sweden found that prior to 1900, when it became official policy to prevent and fight fires, around 1 percent of the forest area burned each year and the same areas would catch fire at intervals of about 80 years. Not all the fires started naturally; for centuries local people had been periodically setting fires to remove trees and provide pasture for their livestock. Once a fire is blazing, of course, how it started makes no difference to its progress. In the United States, a huge forest fire at Yacholt, Washington, destroyed some 250,000 acres (nearly 100,000 ha) of forest in 1902 and in 1933 one in Tillamook, Oregon, burned a similar area. Some forests in Minnesota have burned repeatedly and prior to European settlement about 80 percent of the total area burned every century.

Types of Forest Fire

Not all forest fires turn into raging infernos. Most burn only a small area before dying of their own accord. Those that spread do so across or beneath the surface or through the canopy. Surface fires burn through the litter, spreading rapidly and destroying herbs and some shrubs. They scorch the trunks of large trees, but usually without causing them serious harm, although they can kill seedlings and small trees. Ground fires produce no flames, burning below ground and spreading quite slowly.

The spectacular forest fires featured in movies are usually crown fires. These are driven by the wind and can spread very rapidly through the forest canopy, leaping from tree to tree. Blazing cinders are carried upward by convection, blown ahead of the fire by the wind, then fall back into the canopy, sparking new fires. The heat may be so intense as to cause firestorms. The rapid, convective rise of hot air causes air to converge strongly near ground level. As it converges, the air starts turning cyclonically (counterclockwise) and is accelerated, producing a twisting wind, like a tornado. After it has passed the forest is reduced to charred sticks rising from a thick layer of ash. The 1988 Yellowstone fire was of this type.

Adaptation to Fire

You might wonder how any living thing could survive a conflagration of this kind, yet clearly many do. North American forests have burned repeatedly throughout their history, but after each fire they have established themselves once more.

Trees growing in fire-prone areas have adapted to fire in various ways. Opportunist species, which are quick to colonize open or disturbed ground, are killed by fire, but their seeds are not. These species produce seeds in prodigious amounts. The seeds disperse widely and germinate rapidly. This strategy allows species such as quaking aspen (*Populus tremuloides*), balsam poplar (*P. balsamifera*), and paper birch (*Betula papyrifera*) to occupy sites cleared by fire in the northern and western United States and to mature and produce seed before the conifers grow taller and shade them. The early colonizers are intolerant of shade, so they disappear as the conifers grow.

The coast redwood (*Sequoia sempervirens*) and Sierra redwood (*Sequoiadendron giganteum*) have spongy bark that is very difficult to ignite and thick enough to insulate the sensitive tissue beneath. Provided its temperature remains below about 149°F (65°C), the vascular cambium (page 70) will not be destroyed. You can punch the trunk of one of these trees without hurting your fist, and the tree can remain unscathed by most fires. A redwood that is burned so badly that it falls often sprouts vigorous new growth from the stump.

Other trees regenerate rapidly from snags (standing dead trees). Pitch pine (*Pinus rigida*) is one. Other pines not only survive fires, but positively depend on them. These are the species that produce serotinous cones, such as longleaf pine (*P. palustris*), also called pitch pine and jack pine (*P. banksiana*). These cones remain tightly closed on the tree until they are heated by a fire. Then they open to release their seeds into the ash. Fire-prone forests also harbor seeds of certain shrubs and herbaceous plants that are similarly adapted, germinating only when a fire has heated them.

Most animals, but not all of them, can also survive fire. In the 1988 Yellowstone fire, about 250 elk or wapiti (*Cervus elaphus,* known in Britain as red deer) died from smoke inhalation, out of a population of around 31,000 present in the park at the time. Birds and many mammals simply move out of the way of the fire. Others shelter in burrows or beneath logs. Those that leave do face danger, because predators patrol just ahead of the fire front on the lookout for fleeing prey. But in general, *Bambi* painted a very misleading picture, because forest fires appear to cause few animal casualties.

Fire and the Soil

After a forest fire the ground is covered with ash. This is rich in certain nutrient elements, especially potassium, phosphorus, calcium, magnesium, and sodium, which are washed down into the soil by the first rain, temporarily increasing soil fertility. Below the surface, microbial activity in the soil often increases after a fire.

During a fire in the surface litter, temperatures are commonly around 194°F to 248°F (90°C to 120°C), but they fall sharply below the surface, and at a depth of a few centimeters they are tolerable for most organisms. Some plants produce chemical compounds that remain in the soil and that inhibit bacteria. These include phenols, found in such substances as tannins, and the fire will burn off a proportion of them. The fire also produces charcoal and scientists now believe charcoal absorbs the phenolic compounds. This removes the inhibiting factor, allowing bacterial activity to increase, and the activity includes nitrification (page 76). Together, the mineral nutrients washed down from the layer of ash and the additional nitrate produced by the invigorated soil bacteria strongly boost soil fertility.

At the same time, fire clears away plants that shaded the soil and in places blackens the surface, which increases its capacity for absorbing heat. Since more sunlight can penetrate to the surface where more of it is absorbed, the soil is warmer after a fire than it was before. This, too, stimulates microbial activity, the germination of seeds, and plant growth.

Fire Climax

Where forest fires occur repeatedly, at fairly regular intervals, they come to determine the type of climax vegetation, which is known as a fire climax or pyroclimax (from the Greek *pur* meaning "fire"). This comprises species tolerant of fire or even dependent on it, and the opportunist species capable of waiting for a chance to occupy temporarily vacant sites. Within the forest, repeated burning tends to produce stands of trees all of similar age, although in a large forest this pattern is quite complex, because different areas within the forest may burn at different intervals.

In regions that are not subject to regular burning, fires are much more harmful. Where species are not adapted to fire, they are less likely to survive or regenerate. Nevertheless, in regions where they are common, forest fires cause good as well as harm and the forests soon recover.

Arrested Climax

Farmers and gardeners spend a great deal of time fighting weeds. Once you start growing crops, rival plants appear and if they are not removed, the best you can hope for is a drastically reduced yield. If you really do nothing at all about the weeds, you are quite likely to lose your entire crop. Nowadays there are herbicides to help in the fight, but for most of history weeding has been a slow, tedious, and often back-breaking task. No wonder that a break from weeding with a hoe was an occasion for a party, or "hoedown." In parts of Africa, the tradition of hospitality calls for a visiting stranger to be given a meal and a bed and the following morning to be handed a hoe.

A "weed" is simply a plant that grows in the wrong place and competes for nutrients, water, and sunlight with the plants sown by people. Ecologically there is not the slightest mystery about what weeds are or why they make so much hard work for us, but to understand what is happening you need to imagine the land as it might have been before humans started to cultivate it.

At that time what is now the farm or garden would have been covered with plants, forming a community that changed little over the years. It was a climax community, of temperate forest, perhaps. In order to grow crops, the trees and undergrowth had to be cleared. This left bare ground, but bare ground that held countless seeds, just waiting for an opportunity to germinate. Bare ground will soon be colonized by pioneer plants, growing from that stored seed or from seed carried there on the wind, and a new succession will have begun (page 92).

Pioneer plants are usually annuals. They complete their life cycles, from germination to seed production, within a single season, which means they must germinate and grow fast. This gives them a clear advantage on a bare site. Perennial species grow more slowly, so they appear later, but once they have appeared they put down permanent roots from which they produce new growth every year. This allows them to crowd out most of the annuals and so the perennials dominate the site until they are crowded out in their turn by larger perennials that shade them.

Ecology of Crop Growing

A prisere, which is a succession starting on bare ground, begins with annual species and during a succession the total amount (the biomass) of plant material steadily increases; when a climax is reached the total biomass remains constant. Most crop plants are also annuals. There are exceptions, such as fruit trees and bushes, but cereals and vegetables are grown from seed sown into bare ground for each crop. As annuals, they grow fast and on bare ground they have no competition for light, water, and nutrients. That is how agriculture and horticulture work.

Ecologically, therefore, annual crop plants are equivalent to the pioneer species that begin the prisere. Not surprisingly, they are soon joined by other annuals. These are not too difficult to control provided they can be killed or removed before they produce seed, but among them, and growing more slowly, there are the perennials. These are much more difficult to control, because most of them can propagate vegetatively (page 64), and will grow a new plant from just a fragment of root.

The perennials represent the next seral stage in the progress toward a new climax. Their appearance is unavoidable: unless they are controlled, they will spread to replace most of the annuals, and the crop will vanish. Weeds are a fact of life with which farmers and gardeners must live.

Season after season, the ground is tilled, the prisere commences, and by suppressing weeds the succession is prevented from advancing. The sere, or succession, is held in check; it is an arrested climax.

Arable fields and garden plots are ecologically unstable, because without human intervention their floristic character would change radically. This does not mean farming and gardening are unsustainable, of course, but only that annual crops will not grow of their own accord.

Grassland Plagioclimax

It is not only annual crops that farmers grow. They also tend livestock, and traditionally sheep and cattle have always been fed on grass (although today many are fed other diets). Grass is also a crop; fields of pasture occupy a seral stage in which the dominant plants are perennial herbs. The fields remain in this state indefinitely, because grass tolerates constant grazing by livestock, but woody plants are destroyed by being bitten off close to ground level. Sheep and cattle, and rabbits in parts of Britain and most of Australia, hold the ecological succession in check.

Provided grazing is sustained, grasslands remain unchanged. They are stable enough to constitute an ecological climax, but this is not the climax that would exist in the absence of grazing.

This was demonstrated during the 1970s on the English Downs. These are chalk and limestone hills from which the forests were cleared thousands of years ago and which are now maintained as grassland by the grazing of sheep and rabbits. During the 1970s, sheep farming declined and the rabbit population was drastically reduced by myxomatosis. Grazing ceased over large areas of downland and within a few years scrub invaded. Had events been left to take their course (and conservationists not controlled the scrub to protect the rare downland herbs), the Down grasslands would have reverted to forest. Instead, sheep farming became profitable again, the rabbit population recovered, grazing was resumed, and the grassland returned.

Permanent grassland of this kind represents an arrested climax, which is a type of plagioclimax (from the Greek *plagios,* meaning "oblique"). A plagioclimax is a climax resulting from human intervention. It may be stable, and may comprise only native species, but it results from a sere that has been deflected from the path it would otherwise have followed. If the succession has been arrested at one of its stages, removing the inhibiting factor will allow it to resume, but it will not necessarily proceed to the climax that would have existed had the sere not been interrupted.

Effects of Land Management

Plantation forest is also a plagioclimax (page 112). Usually trees are grown commercially on land that was formerly covered by natural forest, although where agricultural land is scarce, forestry may be pushed into marginal lands that were formerly low quality pasture, because agricultural land commands a higher price than forested land. Forests that are planted on formerly forested land are substantially different from the original forests. Fast-growing conifers are often preferred to the broad-leaved deciduous trees that once grew naturally on the site. Were the plantation to disappear, a new succession might lead to some kind of broad-leaved climax.

Managing the land can change it irreversibly, leading to plagioclimaxes as stable as true climaxes. This is a major fear in some areas of tropical forest, and there are temperate examples illustrating what can happen. Most European heathlands have resulted from the repeated burning of the original forest. This accelerated the leaching of nutrients from the upper soil horizon, a process called podzolization, producing an infertile, acid soil unsuitable for trees.

Farming also alters soils. If it is good farming, of course, returning nutrients removed from the soil by the crop, the soil fertility improves, and whether it is good or poor, regular tillage will produce a soil substantially different from one that remains uncultivated. Should farming cease, the succession will resume, but the changed soil is one of the factors that may prevent the replication of the original climax.

Old Field Recolonization

In northern Vermont, most of the original forest was cleared either for arable farming or for use as pasture, and boreal forest, growing in the area but at a higher altitude, was logged for timber. Later, farming ceased and forest returned. The new forest comprises the same tree species as the original forest, but in very different proportions. Beech (*Fagus grandifolia*) is much rarer now, because it grows mainly from old roots and is slow to regenerate, so it suffered badly from clearance. Maple (*Acer* species), birch (*Betula* species), pine (*Pinus* species), and poplar (*Populus* species) are more abundant than they were. Even the boreal forest changed as a result of logging, with spruce (*Picea* species) becoming rarer and fir (*Abies* species) and hemlock (*Tsuga* species) more abundant. The forest has returned, but it is not the same forest.

In North Carolina, on high ground near the foothills of the mountains, cultivated fields were abandoned twice, some toward the end of the 19th century and others after 1930. All the old fields have reverted to pine forest, but they have been recolonized differently. On the first fields to be abandoned, shortleaf pine (*Pinus echinata*) is more common than loblolly pine (*P. taeda*); on those abandoned in this century the positions are reversed. No one knows why this should be so. It may be that at the time of the first colonization the nearest forest was some distance away, and seeds of shortleaf pine were better able to make the journey. Shortleaf pine seeds are small and disperse widely. Later, there were plantation forests nearby, and loblolly pine is extensively cultivated, so its seeds were available. Shortleaf pine grows on poor soil, but loblolly pine grows faster. Perhaps the poorest fields were abandoned first, favoring shortleaf pine, or the use of manures and fertilizers in this century favored the loblolly pines on the fields abandoned later.

So many explanations are possible that it is pointless to speculate. What matters is the clear example this story provides of the way successions can diverge. They appear to be highly sensitive to small variations in the conditions affecting them. This means that a plagioclimax will always differ from the climax that would develop in the absence of human intervention and that, while the cessation of intervention will allow a succession to resume, it is very unlikely to continue on the course it was following prior to its interruption. This does not mean that a plagioclimax or arrested climax is necessarily inferior to the climax that would have developed otherwise. It may support as many species and be no less resilient, but it will be different and over large areas of the world human activity over the centuries has undoubtedly had a profound effect.

Forest Structure

Some plants are more tolerant of shade than others, and this extends to trees. Tolerant species, such as field maple (*Acer campestre*), sugar maple (*A. saccharum*), hornbeam (*Carpinus betulus*), and eastern hemlock (*Tsuga canadensis*), can survive in the shade. Depending on their species, they may continue to grow slowly but steadily whether or not they are exposed to direct sunlight, or grow to the size of seedlings or small saplings and remain at that size until the light intensity increases, when they grow rapidly. Eastern hemlock falls into the former category, sugar maple into the latter.

Tolerant species can grow beneath a closed forest canopy, even if they are present only as seedlings. Most maximize their light absorption by having many layers of leaves. They grow slowly, but are long-lived. Their strategy is to wait, if necessary for many years, until one or more of the surrounding trees fall, creating a hole in the canopy. Then they grow rapidly to their full size, filling the gap, and flower and produce seed.

Seeds of many tolerant species are not dispersed very widely, so these species appear fairly late in a succession and are typical of climax forest, but there are exceptions. Holly (*Ilex aquifolium*), for example, is a tolerant species, but it sometimes appears on open ground as a pioneer, because birds find its berries attractive and distribute its seeds over a wide area.

Intolerant species, such as downy birch (*Betula pubescens*) and silver birch (*B. pendula*), are often pioneers, arriving early in a succession, growing rapidly, and dispersing seeds widely, before other species grow up to shade them, but there are also slow-growing intolerant trees. These thrive by establishing themselves in situations that in some respect are too harsh for their competitors, so they run no risk of being shaded.

There are also tolerant species that produce widely dispersed seed and intolerant species that grow very slowly, so they can take advantage of gaps when these appear. Whether or not a species is tolerant depends on its sensitivity to solarization (page 72) and its compensation point. Green plants absorb carbon dioxide and use it in photosynthesis. They also respire, which involves the oxidation of carbohydrates and the excretion of carbon dioxide as a waste product. There is an intensity of light, which varies from one plant species to another, at which the amount of carbon dioxide absorbed is exactly equal to the amount excreted. This is the compensation point. At light levels above the compensation point plants can grow, because they gain more carbon than they lose, but growth is impossible at levels below the compensation point, because there is a net loss of carbon. Tolerant plants have a low compensation point, but are often very sensitive to solarization. Intolerant plants can continue to photosynthesize in very bright light, but have a high compensation point.

Shade and the Canopy

In a mature forest, the foliage of each fully grown tree touches that of its neighbors, so together the tree crowns form a closed canopy, completely covering the sky and shading the ground. The cover is complete throughout the year in an evergreen forest, but absent in winter in a deciduous forest. This absence allows more light to reach the forest floor in winter, when the temperature is too low for plant growth, but also in early spring, when temperatures are rising. Many plants exploit this fairly brief exposure to light and so a deciduous forest usually supports a richer variety of smaller plants than does a coniferous forest.

There are gaps in all forests, however, where trees have fallen, and in those gaps, or clearings, light can penetrate to the surface. As the diagram (left) shows, how much light reaches the forest floor is a matter of simple geometry. In the upper drawing on the left, there is a large gap between trees. As the Sun crosses the sky the whole of the floor between them

is lit and, although nowhere is lit all the time, the total period of illumination for some part of the clearing, indicated by the distance between the two "suns," is fairly long. The gap (bottom illustration) is much smaller, so the Sun takes a much shorter time to cross it. The two gaps each end with a single tree, but a wider area is also illuminated, less intensely because of partial shading, and the size of that area is also greater around the large gap than around the small one. An area that is illuminated more brightly or for longer than another will also be warmer. This, too, affects the rate of tree growth.

Rain falls in much the same way as light, because usually the wind causes it to descend diagonally. Trees shelter the ground as well as shade it. Where water is often scarce, a large gap will receive more rain than a small gap and, again, tree growth will be accelerated.

Suppose the sapling of a tolerant species were growing at the center of each gap in the diagram. It would grow much faster in the gap on the top, where it was fully illuminated for longer each day, than it would in the gap at the bottom. This means the bigger the gap, the faster it will vanish.

Forest Stories

As trees fall and are replaced, gaps come and go and conditions in the forest slowly change. Seeds germinate, plants grow, and each time the conditions around them temporarily improve, they grow a little bigger. By the time the largest trees have grown to their full size, the forest has acquired a distinct vertical structure, with plants growing to several different heights. These heights form recognizable strata, or stories.

Botanists usually describe the commonest plant species in an area, or the species which gives the area its distinctive character, as the dominant. Foresters use the word differently, applying it to trees that are taller than their neighbors. The tallest trees in the forests, or dominants, are all more or less of the same height. Between them, not reaching quite the same height, but still forming part of the canopy, there are smaller, codominant trees. These belong to the same species as the dominants and should an adjacent dominant fall a codominant will grow just a little larger and take its place. Smaller and lower than the codominants, there are subdominant trees, also of the same species. Together, the dominants, codominants, and subdominants comprise the main story of the forest and their crowns touch, forming the forest canopy, as illustrated in the diagram on page 99.

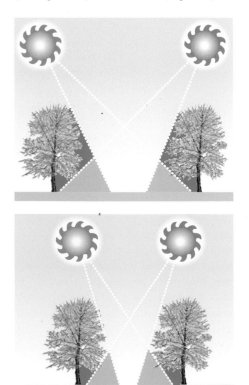

Shade and gap size

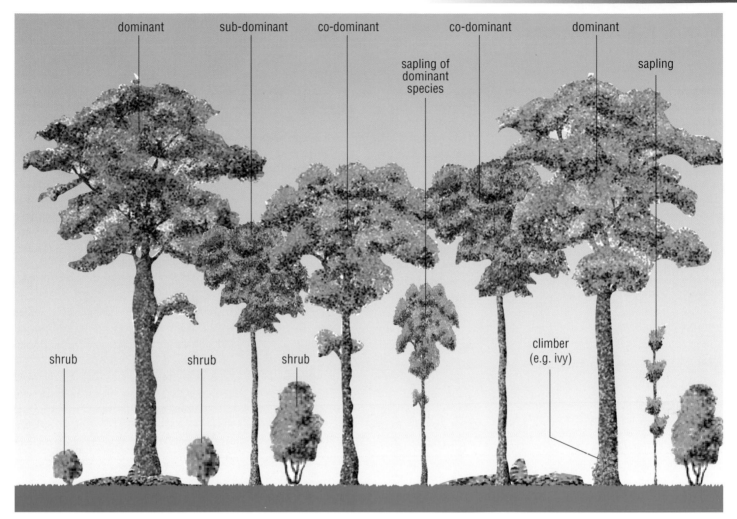

dominant   sub-dominant   co-dominant   co-dominant   dominant

sapling of dominant species

sapling

shrub   shrub   shrub

climber (e.g. ivy)

Forest structure

Shaded by the branches of the trees comprising the main story, there are young trees of the same species as the dominants, which cannot penetrate all the way into the canopy until the tree above them falls (although it may bring down the smaller tree with it). These are said to be suppressed. They, along with smaller trees that are more than 33 feet (10 m) tall but not tall enough to reach the canopy, comprise the understory.

Technically, a tree is a woody plant more than 33 feet tall when fully grown. Plants shorter than this (and usually bushier) are shrubs. Below the understory of trees, therefore, is the shrub layer. Shrubs can be up to 33 feet tall, but some are very much smaller, so the shrub layer comprises plants taller than 3 feet (1 m). Woody plants (shrubs) smaller than this, such as bramble (*Rubus fructicosus*), form a dwarf shrub layer.

Beneath all the trees and shrubs there are the nonwoody plants. The tallest of these, which may stand more than 1 m high, comprise the tall herb layer. Some grasses grow taller than this, but they are not usually counted as members of this layer. To make the distinction, the tall herb layer is sometimes known as the forb layer, a "forb" being a broad-leaved (i.e., not a grass), herbaceous plant. Herbs less than 3 feet tall comprise the herb, or field layer and below them there is the ground layer, of very low-growing plants, such as mosses. In addition to these there are the lianes, or climbers, such as ivy (*Hedera helix*), which cannot be placed in any layer, and the epiphytes (plants that grow on the surface of bigger plants, such as some ferns that grow on the branches of trees).

Not all forests possess all these layers and the number of layers often varies from one part to another of the same forest. There is rarely an understory in temperate forests, for example, unless one has been planted (page 112), and the development of the lower layers is critically dependent on the amount of light penetrating the canopy. Although a mature forest has a closed canopy, some trees produce a denser canopy than others. Sometimes, especially in coniferous forest, the ground is too deeply shaded for most plants, even tolerant ones.

Animal Distribution

Animals are also distributed throughout the vertical structure. Each layer has its own microclimate, with small variations in temperature and humidity that attract some animals and repel others. A study of a European forest dominated by oak (*Quercus* species) and hornbeam, for example, found that of all the bird species present, 15 percent nested on the ground, 25 percent nested in the herb and shrub layers, 31 percent on or in the trunks of canopy trees, and 29 percent in the canopy itself. The same study found that 52 percent of the birds foraged for food on the ground and 23 percent foraged in the foliage of the trees.

Squirrels spend part of their time on the ground and part in the canopy, but most mammals are confined to the ground or to the surface and to burrows beneath the surface, a habitat they share with many invertebrates, although some invertebrates, such as snails and millipedes, will climb into the herbs or up the trunks of trees. Most insects are quite particular about the conditions they demand and so the species distribute themselves among the forest layers, although there are exceptions, such as ants and some beetles, which climb readily and are active at all levels.

Its complex vertical structure makes a mature forest one of the richest of temperate habitats.

Forest Communities

Forests look much the same wherever you go within them. Indeed, historically their reputation has been partly based on the ease with which people can become severely disoriented. You can walk among the trees for hours without seeing any recognizable change and, unless there are well-made paths and signposts to guide you, there is a real risk of becoming lost. You might suppose, therefore, that since there is often so little obvious change throughout a vast forest, when the forest changes as a whole it does so evenly, with every part being affected at more or less the same rate and in the same way.

Lumpiness

It turns out that no ecosystem is that simple, including the temperate forests. C. S. Holling, an ecologist at the University of Florida, has discovered that the factors controlling change in ecosystems vary in scale and timing in big jumps, with nothing between the jumps. This makes ecosystems lumpy, rather than even.

In a spruce forest, for example, the population size of insects that eat needles varies seasonally, so there is a seasonal variation in damage to the trees from this cause. Variations in the canopy take place on a scale of tens of years, and competition between spruce trees and broad-leaved species produces changes measured over about a century. If it is true, this lumpiness should accumulate to produce cycles—some long, some short—in seed output, populations of birds and mammals, the body size of animals, and the prevalence of fires. Scientists have not yet verified the idea, and not all of them accept it, but there is some evidence to support it. Within a particular ecosystem (in fact, the Everglades, but the same should be true for temperate forest) vertebrate land animals (amphibians, reptiles, birds, and mammals) fall into groups of certain body weights, with very few of intermediate size, and species invading the habitat make their first appearance at the edge of an area occupied by a particular body-size group.

Partitioning

This suggests that a forest, or any other ecosystem, is made up of compartments, each with its own occupants. In effect, the animals partition the forest among themselves and, because of the vertical structure of the forest (page 98), the partitioning is repeated in each story. This can often reduce competition between species, because

although two or more closely related species may feed on very similar food, they may not compete for it if they obtain it in different ways.

In North American deciduous forest that has developed in a moderately moist climate (known as a mesic environment), for example, black-capped or Carolina chickadees (*Parus atricapillus* or *P. carolinensis*) feed on insects in the shrub layers and tufted titmice (*P. bicolor*), close relatives of the chickadees, feed on the same diet in the understory and main story. There are two species of vireos which feed on insects in the canopy, but the red-eyed (*Vireo olivaceous*) searches for them on leaves and the yellow-throated (*V. flavifrons*) on twigs.

Seasonal migration causes substantial changes in the size and composition of the bird population. A study of a broad-leaved deciduous forest in Ohio found there were about 1–2 permanent bird residents to each acre (2.5 to 5.0 per ha), a number that changed little from season to season, although it was closer to the lower value in summer and to the higher value in fall, winter, and spring. Winter visitors started arriving in September and departing in April. Their population reached a maximum of about 3 per acre (7.5 per hectare) in November and December. In April the summer visitors began arriving. Their population reached a maximum of about 7 per acre (17.5 per hectare) in May and June, but then started declining. In late April and early May and again from September to early November migrants were breaking their journeys by stopping over in the forest for a time to rest and feed. Their numbers peaked twice, in spring and fall, each time at around 15 per acre (37.5 birds per hectare).

Birds are highly mobile, but they are not the only partitioners of the habitat. Among the mammals, white-footed deer mice (*Peromyscus leucopus*) and flying squirrels (*Glaucomys sabrinus*) nest and feed 33 feet (10 m) or more above the ground, although flying squirrels often descend to the floor to see what food they can find among the litter and around decaying logs. "Flying" squirrels are not capable of powered flight like bats, of course, but they glide from a high location on one tree to a lower one on another or to the ground. Eastern chipmunks (*Tamias striatus*) also forage for food above ground and on the forest floor, but they cannot glide and do not climb so high as flying squirrels. Deer mice (*Peromyscus maniculatus*) live and feed in the shrub layer, on the ground, and in burrows below ground. Red-backed mice (in fact they are voles, genus *Clethri-*

onomys) and shrews (*Sorex* species) dig more permanent tunnels, and hairy-tailed moles (*Parascalops breweri*) spend most of their time below ground.

Mosaic Ecosystem

Animals partition the resources available to them; these resources are provided in the first instance by the vegetation, which varies from place to place within the forest, depending on such factors as local differences in the soil, moisture, and exposure to wind and light. Local habitat differences affecting plants and partitioning by the animals feeding on the plants and on each other combine to compartmentalize the forest in many ways. The resulting structure is often extremely complex.

In fact, the ecosystem of a forest can also be regarded as a mosaic of smaller ecosystems. These adjoin one another, as every ecosystem must adjoin another, and there is some overlap. A boundary where two large, adjacent ecosystems overlap slightly is called an ecotone; it often supports a markedly wider variety of plant and animal species than the ecosystems on either side of it.

Edge Effect

This richness results from what is known as the edge effect, illustrated in the figure on page 101. It shows two overlapping ecosystems, drawn as circles. For simplicity, each is shown as supporting only three species, illustrated as squares in one ecosystem and circles in the other, the squares and circles being shaded in three different ways. One ecosystem contains only squares, the other only circles, but the area where they overlap contains both squares and circles. That area also provides conditions peculiar to itself. At the natural boundary between a forest and grassland, for example, the forest does not end sharply. The trees become more widely spaced, more shrubs grow between them, and the forest thins gradually: the thin forest provides conditions quite different from those of either the full-canopy forest to one side or the open grassland to the other. The area of overlap thus supports species that find its conditions congenial. In the diagram three of these are shown, as triangles shaded in three ways. The final tally is that the two main ecosystems each support three species, but where they overlap there are nine species.

Extending this image to the three-dimensional mosaic of habitats in a forest will give you an idea of its ecological complexity. It also reveals the fact that the richest habitat is often to be found at the forest edge, in the ecotone between an area that is forested and an adjacent area that is not.

Harmful Edge Effects

This seems to imply that clearing part of a forest can increase the number of plant and animal species by increasing the length of forest edge—for many years this was the prevailing view among conservationists. Like many rules of thumb it is only partly true, and if applied too enthusiastically it can be highly disruptive. Nowadays, when forest ecologists speak of edge effects they do so disapprovingly.

What the concept ignores is that the habitat mosaic includes regions deep inside the forest, inhabited by species which benefit from the protection afforded by the forest surrounding them. There are many species that cannot thrive close to the edge, so as the forest is carved into ever smaller blocks, their habitat is reduced. Eventually they may disappear altogether.

The edge effect

Around the edge of the forest, more light penetrates and the climate is warmer and drier than that of the interior. Plants intolerant of shade find it congenial, so they flourish at the expense of shade-loving plants. The edge climate is also windier, because inside the forest trees shelter one another. This means trees at the forest edge are at greater risk of being blown down by the wind. When windblown trees fall they may bring down others with them directly, or indirectly by falling against them, causing fatal damage. Each time this happens the edge area, with its attendant species, is extended a little further into the forest.

The vulnerability of deep-forest species is also partly due to the fact that grazing herbivores, predators, and parasites can enter the forest from the edge. White-tailed deer (*Odocoileus hemionus*), for example, browse on low-growing vegetation, but are uncommon deep inside a large forest. Where the forest has been fragmented, by local clearances or the building of roads, the deer have access to more of it and their overbrowsing can kill some plant species and prevent others from regenerating. Canada yew (*Taxus canadensis*) has been greatly reduced by white-tailed deer in some forests in Canada and the northern United States. Other species of deer have caused similar harm elsewhere in North America and in Europe. Ground-nesting birds may be particularly at risk and the danger to them increased still fur-

ther if they find the forest-edge habitat attractive; foxes and domestic cats and dogs also find the area attractive, not least for the opportunities it affords for dining on eggs, fledglings, or even adult birds.

A Vast Forest, Consisting Only of Edge

Most of us see only as much of a forest as is visible from the road. We may stop the car and walk in among the trees a little way, but few people venture as much as a half-mile (1 km) into the forest. We see only the forest edge, and the plants and animals we see are those of the edge. If the forest is big enough to possess an interior far away from the edge, there you will find a different range of plants and animals. But if there are so many clearings and roads that no part of the forest is far from the edge, and walking a half-mile into the trees will bring you to farmland or another road, the interior may have been lost. In that case, the entire forest may consist of edge, and the familiar roadside species will be the ones occurring throughout it. This may be so even though the forest looks big on the map and driving through it takes a long time. The habitat loss results not from wholesale destruction, but from increasing the area of edge at the expense of inte-

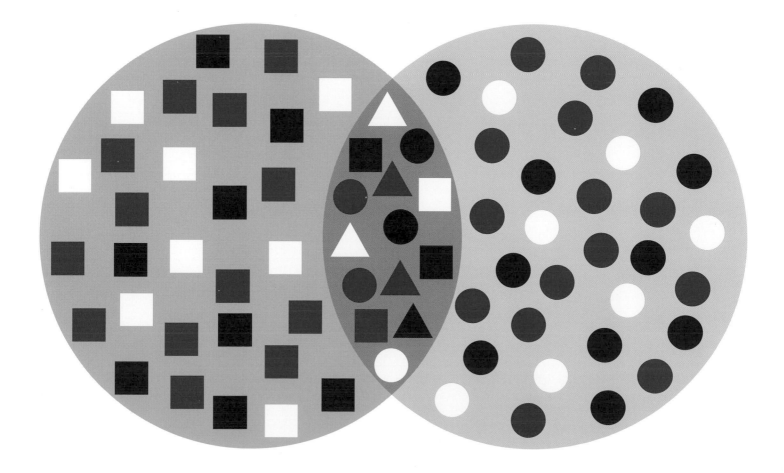

rior, and in this way reducing the richness of the mosaic.

An undisturbed forest has edges and, therefore, an ecotone border supporting more species than the interior, but the rate at which clearance and road building can alter the relative proportions of forest interior and edge is dramatic. It is a matter of simple geometry. Suppose there is a circular forest with an area of 100 (the units are unimportant). Its circumference (the edge) will be 35.45. Two forests, each with an area of 50, will amount to the same total area (100), but a circle with an area of 50 has a circumference of 25, so two such circles have a circumference of 50. Halve the area again, to 25, and the edge length is 17.7, so for four such circles with a combined area of 100 it is 70.8. It is not difficult to see how injudicious clearance can produce a forest that is nothing but edge, despite occupying a large total area. When this happens, the benefits of increased diversity at the edge are lost, because the interior habitat is lost.

Edges formed by clearance can also allow a secondary succession to commence. In temperate regions these pass through a stage where they are all but impenetrable scrub. This reduces the value of the habitat for many species, as well as destroying its amenity value for people. When the succession reaches its climax (page 92) the result will be an area of woodland that is different from the main forest and ecologically rather isolated from it. Interestingly, the impenetrable thicket resulting from secondary growth that follows forest clearance in India, and is often seen there along roadsides, is known as "jungle" (and this is the correct meaning of the word). "Jungle" is from the Hindi *jangal*, and the Hindi word comes from the Sanskrit *jangala*, which can mean desert as well as forest.

European Broad-Leaved Deciduous Forest Types

Temperate forests are usually described by up to about three of their dominant tree species, the most important being named first. Over much of northern and part of central Europe, beech (*Fagus sylvatica*) is by far the commonest forest tree. In England, however, except for the southeast, beech gives way to small-leaved lime (*Tilia cordata*), or hornbeam (*Carpinus betulus*) in a small area of East Anglia, and in northern England and Scotland to wych elm (*Ulmus glabra*), although this species has largely succumbed to Dutch elm disease (page 108) and disappeared.

In the mountainous regions of Europe, beech grows with silver fir (*Abies alba*), producing beech–silver fir forests. There are also birch-oak forests (*Betula pendula, Quercus robur,* and *Q. petraea*) on the poorer, acid soils in the lowlands. On moister soils the forests are more often hornbeam-oak.

On sunny sites in the warmer climate of southern Europe the forests are of sessile, pubescent, and pedunculate oak (*Quercus petraea, Q. pubescens,* and *Q. robur,* respectively) mixed with field maple (*Acer campestre*), small-leaved lime, and ash (*Fraxinus excelsior*). Broad-leaved evergreens, such as holm oak (*Quercus ilex*), form forests with several species of pines on lowland sites bordering the Mediterranean.

Further north, the European boreal forests are composed of various combinations of Norway spruce (*Picea abies*), Scotch pine (*Pinus sylvestris*), birch, aspen (*Populus tremula*), and rowan (*Sorbus aucuparia*), often with juniper (*Juniperus communis*) in the understory.

White-tailed deer feeding, North America (Steve Gettle/ENP Images)

North American Broad-leaved Deciduous Forest Types

Broad-leaved deciduous forest in North America occurs naturally in the eastern United States and southeastern Canada from southern Ontario and Quebec to New Brunswick, Prince Edward Island, and Nova Scotia. In New England, most of the original forest was cleared in the past for farming, but when farming proved unprofitable the forest was allowed to regenerate, but with a somewhat different composition.

The original Canadian forest—and in the United States the forest around the Great Lakes extending eastward from Minnesota—is known as the northern hardwood forest. It consists of white pine (*Pinus strobus*), together with sugar maple (*Acer saccharum*), beech (*Fagus grandifolia*), and yellow birch (*Betula alleghaniensis*), as well as varying amounts of hemlock (*Tsuga canadensis*). This forest forms an ecotone boundary between the fully broad-leaved forests to the south and the coniferous, boreal forest to the north. Moving north through the ecotone, the maple, beech, and birch become more scattered, their places taken by white spruce (*Picea glauca*) and balsam fir (*Abies balsamea*).

South of the northern hardwood forest, in Wisconsin and Illinois, the natural forest is of sugar maple and basswood (*Tilia americana*), sometimes with red oak (*Quercus rubra*). To the south of that, through Wisconsin and Indiana as far as Texas, the forest is dominated by black oak (*Quercus velutina*), white oak (*Q. alba*), pignut hickory (*Carya glabra*), and shagbark hickory (*C. ovata*), with flowering dogwood (*Cornus florida*) forming the understory in many places. Further south again, into the Gulf states, there is oak–pine forest, dominated by white oak and loblolly and shortleaf pine (*Pinus taeda* and *P. echinata*). In the east, this type of forest extends northward in a broad band as far as the southern tip of Massachusetts. To its east, as far north as Massachusetts and from the Great Smoky Mountains, on the border between Tennessee and North Carolina, to the coastal plain, the original forest was oak–chestnut, with red oak, chestnut oak (*Quercus prinus*), and tulip tree (*Liriodendron tulipifera*). The chestnut has now all but disappeared, due to chestnut blight (page 108), and oak has replaced it.

West of the oak–chestnut forest there is mixed forest, varying in composition from place to place. To its north, around the southern borders of the Great Lakes, but extending south into Illinois, Indiana, and Ohio, there is beech–maple forest, dominated by beech and sugar maple, with basswood also occurring in the canopy.

Temperate Rain Forest

On the Pacific Coast, from California to Alaska, the climate is mild and moist and in some places fog is frequent. In Vancouver, British Columbia, for example, the average daytime temperature in January is 41°F (5°C) and in July and August, which are the warmest months, 74°F (23°C). Rain falls throughout the year, but is rather heavier in winter than in summer, with an annual average of 57.4 inches (1,458 mm). In this climate, the natural vegetation is temperate rain forest.

This is forest dominated by huge conifers, such as Douglas fir (*Pseudotsuga menziesii*), western hemlock (*Tsuga heterophylla*), western red cedar (*Thuja plicata*), and the redwoods. The forest canopy is between 197–230 feet (60–70 m) tall in many places, but some of the redwoods are taller. *Sequoiadendron giganteum,* the tree known as the Sierra redwood, big tree, giant sequoia, mammoth tree, and wellingtonia, grows to 330 feet (100 m) and the coast redwood (*Sequoia sempervirens*) to 394 feet (120 m). In Washington, Sitka spruce (*Picea sitchensis*) also forms part of the forest.

There is also temperate rain forest in southern Chile. The Valdivian Rain Forest, to the west of the Andes, is dominated by broad-leaved evergreens, such as Chilean laurel (*Laurelia serrata*) and Winter's bark (*Drimys winteri,* named after a Captain Winter who sailed with Sir Francis Drake and used the bark from this tree to treat scurvy among the ship's crew), mixed with the monkey-puzzle tree, or Chilean pine (*Araucaria araucana*) and Patagonian cypress (*Fitzroya cupressoides*).

Temperate rain forest also occurs in southern Japan and southern China, where it is dominated by evergreen oaks and magnolias, with some pines. Around the Black Sea and as far south as the Caspian, in Transcaucasia, the Colchic Forest is a relict of a type of vegetation that existed more than 2 million years ago, before the Pleistocene ice ages. It is also temperate rain forest, and rich in tree species, although much of it has been cleared to provide land for growing tea.

Parts of eastern Australia and Tasmania and much of New Zealand, where the climate is mild and moist, also support temperate rain forest. The dominant trees are the southern beeches (various species of *Nothofagus*) and coachwood (*Ceratopetalum apetalum*). In Australia these grow alongside conifers such as bunya bunya (*Araucaria bidwilli*), Moreton Bay pine, or hoop pine (*A. cunninghamii*), and various species of kauri pine (*Agathis*). In New Zealand the forests are dominated by *Nothofagus*, growing with red pines (*Dacrydium* species) and podocarps (*Podocarpus* species) as well as the kauri pine, or cowdie pine (*Agathis australis*).

It is important to remember that these forest types are the ones that occur naturally. Visit a particular region and it does not follow that you will see the forest said to be native to that region or, indeed, any forest at all. People have been clearing and altering forests for thousands of years.

Energy Flow

According to some engineers, the bicycle is the most efficient means of mechanical transport ever invented. It is efficient because it greatly augments the power your leg muscles can deliver, so you travel farther and faster on the same amount of fuel. The fuel, of course, is the food you eat, and you need eat no more food to prepare for a bike ride lasting an hour than you would for a walk lasting an hour.

We use food partly as fuel, to provide our bodies with energy. The energy is released by the oxidation of carbon contained in the sugars, starches, and fats we eat. Carbon oxidation is a chemical reaction that releases energy. It is the reaction that warms our homes and powers our cars. In our bodies, the bringing together of oxygen and a source of carbon, the oxidation itself, and the excretion of the reaction product, carbon dioxide, together comprise respiration.

All living organisms need energy and they all obtain it by respiration, although anaerobic bacteria do not use oxygen (but carbon loses electrons and so the reaction is oxidation, nevertheless). Oxygen is easily obtained from the air and, since oxygen is slightly soluble in water, aquatic organisms use dissolved oxygen. Carbon is also present in the air, as carbon dioxide, but photosynthesis (page 72) is the only biological process for reducing it (adding electrons and separating its carbon and oxygen) and storing the carbon in a form that allows it to be oxidized once more. Only green plants can store carbon in a useful

form, so animals, fungi, and protozoans must obtain the carbon they need from plants or from one another.

Relationships within an ecosystem are based on feeding. Those linking species can be represented as food chains or webs (page 80) and those between entire trophic levels as ecological pyramids (page 82). These representations were never wholly satisfactory, because they dealt with the structure of an ecosystem, but tended to overlook what happened in decomposition and said very little about the ecosystem as a whole.

Ecological Energetics

In 1942, the American ecologist Raymond L. Lindemann proposed a more comprehensive way of studying ecosystems. His paper, "The trophic–dynamic aspect of ecology," published in the journal *Ecology,* became a classic and a new field of scientific study developed from his idea. The field is called ecological energetics; what Lindemann proposed was the study of the flow of energy through an ecosystem.

Energy, after all, is needed to "drive" any ecosystem and so relationships within the system are based on the flow of energy. When we eat, most of our food is used to provide our bodies with energy. It is the energy that matters and, according to the first law of thermodynamics, energy can change its form (from chemical to

kinetic, for example) but it can be neither created nor destroyed. Within any ecosystem there must be an original energy source, a route by which it passes from organism to organism, and a "sink" into which ultimately it is poured. In a forest ecosystem the Sun is the original source of energy and eventually all of the energy captured by photosynthesis is expended in respiration and, in conformation with the second law of thermodynamics, converted into heat, warming the air. Clearly, Lindemann was proposing something very sensible; it was also helpful, because the flow of energy is surprisingly easy to measure, at least in principle.

Solar energy is captured by photosynthesis and used to manufacture carbohydrates, proteins, and the other compounds from which living tissues are composed. The tissues, therefore, are where the captured energy is stored. Weigh those and the result will be proportional to the amount of energy stored in them. Alternatively, their stored energy can be measured directly, by burning the material in an oven equipped with a calorimeter, which is a device for measuring the amount of energy released. The material is dried before being burned, because the water content of biological material is highly variable and would make it impossible to compare one sample with another accurately. On average, 1 gram

Pyramid of energy

(0.035 ounce) of oven-dried plant material releases 4–4.5 kcal (16.7–18.8 kJ) and of animal tissue 5–5.5 kcal (20.9–23.0 kJ).

All ecosystems can be studied in this way and, because the techniques and energy units are standard, ecosystems and parts of them can be compared directly. The total quantity of living organisms, in an entire ecosystem or some part of it, is known as the biomass, or standing crop, and it can be reported in units either of mass or of energy, because they both come to the same thing.

Entire systems do not have to be dried and burned, of course, but only samples from which the biomass can be calculated. Biomass samples taken at different trophic levels allow the flow of energy to be traced through the system. Lindemann proposed in his paper that the efficiency of transfer can be calculated by comparing the amount of energy assimilated at one trophic level with that assimilated at the preceding level; this is known as Lindemann's efficiency. Measuring it in the field is difficult. Consumer organisms seldom occupy only one trophic level. Sheep, which are herbivores and, therefore, primary consumers, also eat significant amounts of insects and other invertebrate animals clinging to the herbage. This makes them tertiary consumers (consuming primary consumers) when they swallow herbivorous insects, but places them at a much higher trophic level when they consume predators such as spiders and centipedes. There are other techniques for comparing trophic levels, but they all encounter this difficulty. Nevertheless, comparisons can be made under laboratory conditions and, with care, from field samples.

Efficiency of Ecosystems

These comparisons show that most of the energy assimilated at each trophic level is used for respiration at that level and is not available to the level above. On average, between 10 percent and 20 percent of the energy assimilated at one level is passed to the level above, so that is the ecological efficiency of ecosystems. Respiration (the reaction by which energy is released) accounts for much more of the energy assimilated by homeotherms (animals such as mammals and

birds, which use some of their food to maintain a constant body temperature) than of poikilotherms (animals such as fish and invertebrates, which have no metabolic means for regulating body temperature). Herbivorous homeotherms have an efficiency of 0.3 percent to 1.5 percent and poikilotherms of 9 percent to 25 percent. The efficiency of carnivorous homeotherms is 0.6 percent to 1.8 percent and of poikilotherms 12 percent to 25 percent. Most of the animal biomass in any ecosystem consists of poikilotherms, so they strongly affect the overall efficiency of the ecosystem.

Animals eat primarily to obtain fuel for their bodies. If only 10 percent of the energy at one trophic level is available to the level above, the amount being transferred soon dwindles to insignificance, as the diagram on page 104 shows. The pyramid of energy is the third of the ecological pyramids devised by Sir Charles Elton (page 84), and the majority of ecologists consider it the most useful. It demonstrates that biomass at the third trophic level, of carnivores (secondary consumers), is so small it is uncertain whether the system could support a fourth level, although some do support higher levels. Big carnivores, such as tigers, must always be rare.

Productivity

Once biomass of any kind can be measured as the energy it represents, it becomes possible to study ecosystems in much greater detail. The amount of new biomass synthesized in a given period (usually a year) by the plants of an ecosystem is known as the primary productivity (or production) of that system. The total amount is called the gross primary productivity (GPP) and is adjusted to the net primary productivity (NPP) by deducting the amount of energy used by the producers in respiration. When the amount consumed is also allowed for, the rate at which biomass accumulates is the net community productivity (NCP).

NCP is related to production (P) divided by respiration (R). If P/R = 1, NCP = 0, and the ecosystem is in a steady state. If P/R > 1 (NCP > 0) it is growing (accumulating biomass), and if P/R < 1

(NCP < 0) it is deteriorating (losing biomass). Measuring the NCP and P/R ratio makes it possible to determine the state of an ecosystem. During a sere, both will have positive values, but when a climax is reached NCP will be at or close to 0 and P/R = 1.

NPP provides the best measurement for comparing ecosystems, and combined with the biomass (standing crop) per unit area it can be used to calculate the ratio of annual production to biomass (P/B). Regardless of its size or type, this reveals the productivity of the ecosystem in a way that permits direct comparisons, because the greater the P/B, the more productive the system is. In a New York oak–pine forest, for example, the annual NPP of the trees was measured as 1,060 grams per square meter and the tree biomass as 9,700 grams per square meter, giving a P/B of 0.11. This ratio varies according to the type of forest and climate. Forests in the Great Smoky Mountains have ratios of 0.02 to 0.03.

Everyone knows that tropical forests are the richest of all ecosystems on land and, because they are so lush and their plants grow so vigorously, we tend to assume they are also the most productive. Indeed, in a tropical rain forest, the mean annual NPP is 2,200 grams per square meter, which is the highest of any ecosystem on land. The biomass is also high, however, and P/B = 0.05, about half that of the oak–pine forest in New York. Temperate forests of all types (broad-leaved evergreen, broad-leaved deciduous, and boreal) average P/B = 0.04, which is not much lower than the value for tropical rain forest. Not surprisingly, perhaps, the highest P/B for any land system is 0.65 for cultivated farmland.

These ratios do not alter the fact that the tropical forests contain considerably more biomass than temperate forests and that their NPP is higher in total. Over the world as a whole, the annual NPP for tropical rain forests and seasonal forests is 54.3 billion tons (49.4 billion t) and for temperate forests 27 billion tons (24.5 billion t). Both types occupy about the same total area, tropical forests covering 9.5 million square miles (24.5 million sq m) and temperate forests 9.3 million square miles (24 million sq km), so tropical forests are cycling carbon and mineral nutrients much faster than temperate forests.

Nutrient Cycling

There is a classic school demonstration you may still remember from one of your earliest science classes. The teacher lights a candle, covers it with a bell-jar, and everyone watches to see what happens. After a little while, the candle flame falters and dies. The demonstration shows that, when the candle burns, carbon in the wax from which it is made is oxidized, using oxygen from the air inside the jar. Oxygen goes on being replaced by carbon dioxide until insufficient oxygen remains in the jar to sustain the oxidation, which slows and then stops. Flames will burn only so long as there is enough oxygen to feed the oxidation; the way to extinguish flames is to smother them with blankets, water, foam, or a nonflammable gas such as carbon dioxide or nitrogen, and so cut off their oxygen supply.

The bell-jar demonstration is extreme, but outside, in the natural world, the composition of the air really does change from time to time, on a very local scale. We are aware of it ourselves, when the air feels stuffy or stifling. Usually it feels this way because its humidity and temperature both increase. The remedy is to open a window, or step outdoors, into the fresh air.

Deep inside a forest, the trees sometimes have a similar problem. Photosynthesis absorbs carbon dioxide, transpiration releases water vapor, and up in the canopy this happens on a very large scale. That is where most of the leaves are, because it is where the sunlight is brightest, so the canopy is rather like a factory, manufacturing carbohydrates to sustain the trees. Not surprisingly, the "tree factory" affects the air. It removes carbon dioxide, adds water vapor, and the air in the canopy grows quite warm, because it is held there, moving little, and is warmed by contact with the sunlit trees.

Above the canopy the wind blows freely, but the air is fairly still where it is held among the leaves of the tree crowns and between crowns, in the canopy, so there is a marked wind shear due to the difference in wind speed inside the canopy and in the air immediately above it. This shear causes gusts and eddies that bring air from above down into the canopy. Air from outside, which is relatively cool, dry, and rich in carbon dioxide, replaces the warm, moist canopy air that is depleted in carbon dioxide.

The Carbon Cycle

Photosynthesizing leaves "grab" carbon dioxide molecules. This removes them from the air, but the moving air brings more. There is a constant supply. Eventually, of course, photosynthesis would strip the air of all carbon dioxide were there no route by which it could return, but it does return, or at least most of it does. Its carbon is incorporated into every cell of the plant that captured it and every cell of every animal that eats it, but some is lost again rapidly. It is used in respiration, to supply energy, and respiration oxidizes the carbon again, to carbon dioxide that is returned to the air. Carbon that is used to make structural materials, such as proteins and celluloses, is held for longer, but eventually cells and organisms die and decompose. Decomposition (page 84) is performed by organisms which consume those structural materials, break them down, and oxidize their carbon to provide energy. Photosynthesis captures carbon dioxide molecules and respiration releases them once more.

There is some loss. Carbon dioxide dissolves in water to form carbonic acid (H_2CO_3). Aquatic plants also photosynthesize, using carbon dioxide obtained from the water, and are eaten by aquatic animals. There are also plants and animals that combine calcium with bicarbonates (HCO_3) to make shells and plates of calcium carbonate ($CaCO_3$). In water, too, the carbon is oxidized by respiration, but a small proportion of shells, plates, and dead organic matter accumulates in seabed sediments before it can be fully decomposed. These sediments are compressed into rocks. Crustal movements return some to the surface, millions of years later, allowing chemical weathering to return them to living cells, and some are subducted down into the mantle. This loss is made good by volcanoes, which release into the air carbon dioxide from rocks carried upward from below Earth's crust.

Like all the chemical elements used to make and sustain living organisms, carbon is constantly recycled.

Nitrogen

Nitrogen is also an atmospheric gas. It is an essential ingredient of proteins, compounds that are used in the construction of living tissues, which perform a wide variety of other functions. Hormones and enzymes are proteins, for example. Atmospheric nitrogen is oxidized by lightning and converted into nitrate (NO_3), ammonia (NH_3), and ammonium (NH_4) compounds by nitrogen-fixing bacteria in the soil, some of them living in close association with plant roots.

When dead organic matter is decomposed, most of the nitrogen from large, complex molecules is converted into simple compounds that dissolve in the soil water and once more enter plant roots, but denitrifying bacteria convert some of it into gaseous nitrogen, returning it to the air (page 77).

For part of the time, a nitrogen atom is in the air, for a time it is a component of living tissue, for a time it is dissolved in flowing water. Like carbon, it is engaged in an endless cycle, called a biogeochemical cycle or a nutrient cycle, because it is an essential nutrient element that is being cycled. The cycles are chemical, because they involve chemical elements, compounds, and reactions. They are also geological, because the cycles also, on a longer timescale, involve the rocks from which mineral elements are taken, and the sediments in which they are deposited and from which they are returned to living organisms; the cycles also remove elements by the subduction of crustal plates and return them by volcanism. The cycles are also biological, because for part of the time the elements are incorporated in living tissues. Rock, water, air, and living cells are like compartments into which biogeochemical cycles can be divided.

Every year, lightning and bacteria between them fix about 165 million tons (150 million tonnes) of nitrogen by combining it with oxygen or hydrogen. This is the rate at which nitrogen moves naturally from the air (geological) to the living (biological) compartment of the biogeochemical cycle and, therefore, the rate at which the element is made available for new plant growth.

Farmers need nutrients in addition to those that are supplied naturally, because agriculture alters the cycle. Plant and animal agricultural products, made partly from mineral compounds obtained from the soil, are removed from farms. Unless the nutrients they contain can be replaced, in time the stock of them in soil will be depleted, the soil will become infertile, and crop yields will fall. This is why farmers grow legumes such as beans and alfalfa, plants with their own nitrogen-fixing bacteria. When the legumes die or are removed as crops their roots remain in the soil, enriching its nitrogen content for the crop that follows. More important, farmers add fertilizer, manufactured in factories where nitrogen is made to combine with hydrogen.

Human activities, especially the use of fertilizers containing nitrogen, are now fixing nitrogen at about the same rate as lightning and naturally occurring bacteria. In addition, by draining wetland and plowing grasslands to provide more land for cropping, we are accelerating the natural cycle. In other words, we have approximately doubled the rate at which nitrogen is entering the biological compartment of the cycle. No one knows what effect this will have in the long term, although scientists suspect it may be making forests grow faster in Europe and North America.

Phosphorus

Within living organisms, energy is used to attach a phosphate group (the process is called phosphorylation) to adenosine diphosphate (ADP), making it into adenosine triphosphate (ATP), the form in which it is transported. The phosphate contains phosphorus (P), making this another essential nutrient element, and one that also forms part of nucleic acids and animal bone. It is needed only in small amounts. Plants consist of no more than about 3 percent of phosphorus by weight. It is often the limiting element, however, because most soils contain even less in a form that can enter plant roots. When fertilizer runoff from farmland causes algal blooms in lakes and reservoirs, almost invariably it is phosphorus that causes the problem, not nitrogen.

Phosphorus enters the cycle from phosphate rock, which as the name suggests is a rock composed of phosphate minerals such as apatite $(CA_5(PO_4)_3(F, Cl, OH))$, in which calcium (Ca), phosphorus (P), and oxygen (O) are combined with fluorine (F), chlorine (Cl), or hydroxyl (OH). Chemical weathering (page 10) releases phosphorus from this insoluble rock as orthophosphate $(H_2PO_4, HPO_4,$ and if conditions are very alkaline, $PO_4)$. Orthophosphate is soluble and is the form in which phosphorus enters plants, but the soil water around plant roots contains only about 0.000003 percent orthophosphate, and orthophosphate that is not taken up by plants may be lost to them. If the pH of the soil is below 5.5 it will form insoluble compounds with iron and aluminum and if the pH is above 7.0 orthophosphate will form insoluble compounds with calcium and other elements.

The phosphorus that does enter the biological compartment of the cycle tends to remain there for some time. It is so valuable to living organisms that they recycle it rapidly. In a fairly remote part of New Hampshire there is an area of broad-leaved forest drained by the Hubbard Brook; the chemical composition of the brook water has been monitored for many years, so there is a reliable inventory of the rate at which substances leach out of the forest soil. Combined with analyses of the soil, this shows that each year weathering adds 1.34–1.60 pounds of phosphorus to each acre of soil (1.5–1.8 kg per ha), and the decomposition of organic material releases 8.9 pounds per acre (10 kg per ha), but Hubbard Brook carries away only 0.006 pounds per acre (0.007 kg per ha). In southern Ontario, forests on soils derived from igneous rocks were found to be losing an average of 0.04 pound of phosphorus from each acre (0.05 kg per ha) through streams draining the area, and those growing on soils derived from sedimentary rocks an average of 0.09 lb per acre (0.1 kg/ha). Where the area was partly forest and partly pasture, the comparable figures were 0.1 lb per acre (0.1 kg/ha) and 0.3 lb per acre (0.3 kg/ha) respectively.

As with nitrogen, the amount of phosphorus available naturally is sufficient for the needs of intact ecosystems, but not for farm crops, and farmers have been adding phosphate fertilizers since the 1840s. These are made by grinding phosphate rock to a powder and subjecting it to treatments that convert some of the phosphate to soluble forms. Treatment with sulfuric acid (H_2SO_4), for example, yields a product containing 18–22 percent of the phosphoric acid P_2O_5, which is soluble. Further treatment can more than double the P_2O_5 content, and reacting P_2O_5 with ammonia (NH_3) produces a range of ammonium phosphates, which are completely soluble in water and provide nitrogen as well as phosphorus.

Eventually, phosphorus reaches the ocean, but as the Hubbard Brook and Ontario studies show, ecosystems release it only very slowly, and forests release it at about half the rate at which it moves out of pastureland. Once it does reach the ocean it is virtually trapped, because it readily forms insoluble compounds that collect in the seabed sediment. Marine animals, which incorporate phosphorus in their bones and excrete the surplus, return some of it to the land, most notably as the droppings of seabirds which collect in some places as guano. A small amount returns from the air, as dry particles or in rain. Measured as orthophosphate (PO_4), sites in the southeastern United States receive annually an average of about 0.1 lb per acre (0.1 kg/ha) in rain and 0.2 lb per acre (0.3 kg/ha) as dry particles. The main route by which phosphorus moves from the sea to the land is geological. Changing sea levels sometimes isolate arms of the sea, which then dry out, leaving the mineral constituents of the original seawater as evaporite deposits, often rich in phosphate. Alternatively, seabed sediments are compressed and heated to form sedimentary rock and crustal movements raise those rocks above the surface, where chemical weathering can release their phosphates once more.

Potassium and Sulfur

Potassium, another nutrient plants need in relatively large amounts, is widely distributed in rocks and is released by chemical weathering. In plants it is involved in the synthesis of proteins, in the maintenance of a water balance, and in the opening and closing of stomata. In animals it is also involved in the functioning of nerve cells. It is recycled by plants and very little moves out of the soil. Hubbard Brook carries away about 1.5 lb per acre (1.7 kg/ha) each year, but the net loss is much smaller, because precipitation and the deposition of dry particles supply about 1.0 lb per acre (1.1 kg/ha).

Sulfur is an essential component of some amino acids and therefore of proteins. Volcanoes release it into the air, as sulfur dioxide (SO_2), and it also occurs in many rocks and, in a few places, as the element itself. Some plants can absorb it in gaseous form, as SO_2 taken directly from the air, but most absorb it through their roots, as sulfate (SO_4) dissolved in soil water. In recent times our practice of burning fossil fuels (especially some coals) that contain relatively large amounts of sulfur compounds has increased the amount of SO_4 present in the air, where it is oxidized and dissolves in water to form sulfuric acid (H_2SO_4). This is carried to the land in precipitation or is deposited directly onto surfaces from dry air. It contributes to acid rain (page 164), but also supplies soils with valuable plant nutrient. Now that steps are being taken to reduce the amount of SO_2 in smokestack gases, a few years from now farmers may find it necessary to use sulfur-based fertilizers.

Sulfur leaches from soils fairly readily, accumulating, mainly as calcium sulfate $(CaSO_4)$, only where the climate is very dry.

Sulfur in seawater is absorbed by certain species of plankton, and especially by a particular single-celled alga, *Emiliania huxleyii*, which may use it in its own internal chemistry controlling the amount of salt it contains. As a product of this chemistry it produces and releases dimethyl sulfide $((CH_3)_2S)$, or DMS. Some of the DMS is oxidized in the water, but some escapes into the air. In very dilute form it gives the sea its characteristic smell. In the air, the sulfur in DMS is oxidized in a series of steps to sulfate (SO_4). Water vapor readily condenses onto sulfate particles. Over the open ocean, thousands of miles from land where the air is almost completely free from dust, DMS is by far the main source of the condensation nuclei that lead to the formation of cloud. Some of the cloud, containing the sulfur that came originally from DMS released by *Emiliania huxleyii*, is carried over land and the sulfur is returned in precipitation that is acid, but naturally so.

Tree Predators and Parasites

At one time, the chestnut was an important component of deciduous forests in eastern North America. *Castanea dentata,* the American chestnut, is a handsome tree, on favorable sites growing rapidly to a height of about 100 feet (30 m), and its timber had many uses. Then, in about 1904, some chestnut trees were imported from China and they brought with them a fungus, *Endothia parasitica.*

In Asia, trees infected with *Endothia parasitica* suffer only mild symptoms, hardly qualifying as those of a disease. In America, however, it was different. On Long Island, New York, the fungus infected American chestnuts and killed them. The sickness was fatal and spread fast, also killing European sweet chestnuts (*C. sativa*), which were being grown in orchards (this species provides the best chestnuts, or marrons). The disease was called chestnut blight. Not only was the infection invariably lethal, its spread was uncontrollable. Desperate attempts were made to halt its advance, but by around 1940 the American chestnut had been almost eliminated, leaving thousands upon thousands of dead trees. Some individuals did prove resistant to chestnut blight and so the tree has not vanished completely, and European sweet chestnuts are still cultivated, mainly in California and the Pacific northwest, but chestnut trees ceased to form an important part of American forests.

There are stretches of RNA, rather like viruses but lacking the protein coat all viruses have, which cause disease in *Endothia parasitica.* Known as h-factors, they have been isolated and used to infect the fungus experimentally. If the tests succeed, scientists hope they may have found a way to treat chestnut blight.

Chestnut blight was certainly among the worst of all forest disasters, but it was neither the most widespread nor the most devastating. Europe as well as North America has suffered severely and repeatedly from a fatal disease of elm trees and, like chestnut blight, it is caused by a fungus that may have originated in Asia.

Dutch Elm Disease

Dutch elm disease was noticed in France in 1918 and the fungus responsible was identified in the Netherlands in 1919. This was unlikely to have been the first outbreak of the disease; John Claudius Loudon, the 19th-century authority on gardening, referred to it in 1838. It was because the first accurate identification of the fungus was made by Dutch scientists that the disease came to be called "Dutch" elm disease. Confusingly, this led some people to suppose it a disease of Dutch elms, of which there are several, all hybrids, or that it originated in the Netherlands. Neither is true.

An outbreak of the disease in the 1920s reached North America and caused a great deal of harm. By about 1940 it had died down in Europe, although not in the United States, where the native elms (*Ulmus americana*) are more susceptible and more insect species were involved in transmitting the infection. In the 1960s the disease returned to Europe, with increased virulence. There were then about 30 million elm trees in Britain. That epidemic killed some 25 million of them. Their loss profoundly altered the appearance of the landscape, because as well as growing in forests, elms grew in many of the hedges bordering fields, so they formed a visually prominent component of the countryside. In fact, the disease spread more slowly in forests than it did along hedgerows and among elms planted in city parks, because the wych elm (*Ulmus glabra*), which is the species most often found growing in forests, is rather more resistant to the disease than the hedgerow and field elms (*U. procera* and *U. minor* respectively).

Elms propagate mainly vegetatively, from shoots that grow from the roots, and although Dutch elm disease killed the trees, in many cases their roots survived and, gradually, elms began to reappear. Then, in the 1990s, Europe began to suffer a new outbreak.

Dutch elm disease now occurs almost everywhere that elm trees grow. It has spread across Europe and Asia as far as the Chinese border. In North America it began in the Great Lakes region and spread both east and west, all the way to both coasts.

The first culprit was a fungus, *Ophiostoma* (formerly *Ceratocystis*) *ulmi,* that blocks the xylem vessels. It is spread by small beetles that burrow into the bark of elms to make nuptial chambers in which adults mate. The larvae feed on the sapwood, emerging as adults, which then feed on elm sap. Several beetle species behave in this way. In Europe, the fungus is carried mainly by *Scolytus scolytus,* a beetle about 0.2 inch (5 mm) long and *S. multistriatus,* about 0.1 inch (3 mm) long. When they attack a tree they do so in vast numbers; in fact their larvae are capable of killing a tree without any help from the fungus.

It was *S. multistriatus* that was carried, along with the fungus, from Europe to America in logs to be made into veneer for furniture. Being smaller than *S. scolytus,* it can carry fewer fungal spores and so is less efficient at transmitting the infection, but in North America another bark beetle, *Hylurgopinus rufipes,* is also a vector for the infection, so between them they sustained the epidemic.

Ophiostoma ulmi is vulnerable to diseases of its own, caused by agents known as d-factors, similar to the h-factors that attack *Endothia parasitica.* It may have been the spread of d-factors that checked the first outbreak. The second outbreak, in the 1960s, was caused by *Ophiostoma novo-ulmi,* a much more virulent species. Scientists have isolated about 40 d-factors and hope to be able to use the more effective of them to combat the disease. At the same time they are hoping to modify elm trees genetically so they produce substances that kill either the bark beetles or the fungus.

Ambrosia Beetles

There is more to the elm bark beetles than the appalling damage they cause. These members of the family Scolytidae, together with the families Platypodidae and Lymexylonidae, are known as "ambrosia beetles." They cannot survive without ambrosia fungi. There are several genera of ambrosia fungi and each species of beetle ordinarily uses only one species of fungus. Depending on the medium on which they are growing, the fungi can change their form; under certain conditions they are fluffy, like the mold that grows on stale bread, and under other conditions they are much denser, like yeast.

On its front legs, every ambrosia beetle has a small pocket, called a mycangium, which always contains spores of the preferred fungus. That is why it was inevitable that the *Scolytus* beetles that crossed from Europe to America would also carry Dutch elm disease. When it bores into a tree, the beetle spreads spores from its mycangia along the sides of its tunnel. The spores germinate rapidly and soon the tunnel is lined with a velvety, yeast-like, fungal coating, the fungus feeding on nutrients it obtains from the wood. The beetle larvae then feed on the fungus. Ambrosia was the food of the gods in Greek mythology, so that is what the fungus is called and why the beetles are known as ambrosia beetles. The beetles tend their ambrosia. Look inside one of their tunnels and you will find no fragments of wood from their tunneling or beetle droppings. All such material is removed: the beetles leave it outside the tunnel entrance, where it sometimes accumulates. They rarely eat wood (unlike termites). The fungus itself stains the wood a dark color, and a discoloration around a tiny hole is an indication of an attack by ambrosia beetles.

Clearings in natural European coniferous forests are often caused by more limited attacks from bark beetles. First the insects kill one or two trees, then move to a few more adjacent to them. This creates an opening that wind damage may widen. Bark beetles also extend gaps made when wind storms have blown down trees, by feeding on the fallen timber and moving from there into standing trees nearby.

Tramp Species

Chestnut blight and Dutch elm disease illustrate the devastation that can be caused when species are introduced to parts of the world where they find new opportunities. The North American epidemic of Dutch elm disease is milder than that in Europe, because *Scolytus multistriatus* is a much less effective vector than *S. scolytus*. Should *S. scolytus* cross the Atlantic, however, the disease might become much more severe. Similarly, a North American disease that causes oak trees to wilt, caused by the fungus *Ceratocystis fagacearum,* is not serious, but should the fungus cross to Europe its character might change. In Europe there is an oak bark (ambrosia) beetle, *Scolytus intricatus,* which could disseminate the fungal spores very efficiently, causing a serious epidemic.

Harmful species are not introduced deliberately, of course. They are carried, unobserved, in cargoes transported by sea or air, in ballast carried by ships, and in some cases even on the soles of the shoes worn by passengers. Humans have unwittingly spread many species around the world in this way. The black rat (*Rattus rattus*) and brown rat (*Rattus norvegicus*) are famous examples, and the familiar house mouse (*Mus musculus*) has traveled all over the world in the same way. Its ancestors lived in the Middle East and may have accompanied humans westward in pre-Roman times. Animals, plants, and fungi that hitch rides in this way are known as tramp species, and they are hitching rides still.

Great Spruce Bark Beetle

Great spruce bark beetles (*Dendroctonus micans*) apparently originated in Asia and over the course of a century or so they spread westward from Siberia to France. Then, in August 1982, they were found in a spruce plantation in Shropshire, England. The species is now well established throughout Europe, including the British Isles.

Many insect pests prefer to feed on dead or dying trees, which limits the harm they do, but others, including the great spruce bark beetle, attack healthy trees. Streams of resin flowing from the trunk are usually the first sign of an infestation. All species of spruce (*Picea*) are susceptible, and the beetle is sometimes found on other conifers.

Adults bore into and through the bark, where the females lay 250 or more eggs in one or more brood chambers. The larvae feed beneath the bark, breaking and blocking xylem vessels as they do so. On a large enough scale this damage reduces the vigor of the tree and may eventually kill it by breaking all the vessels. When the larvae mature into adults, they disperse. They have functional wings, but are unable to fly in temperatures below 73°F (23°C). They do not allow cool weather to confine them to the place where they emerge, however, and usually move by crawling.

The beetle arrived in Britain without its principal enemy, a predatory beetle, *Rhizophagus grandis,* which controls the pest population very effectively in Russia, Belgium, and probably elsewhere, so British scientists imported a stock of this species from Belgium. *R. grandis* beetles locate the places where great spruce bark beetle larvae are feeding. They wound the larvae, then lay their own eggs nearby. When the *R. grandis* larvae hatch they feed on the *D. micans* larvae, mature into adults, then go off in search of more *D. micans.* The predators are now reared and released into great spruce bark beetle infestations. It is an example of biological pest control, but one that is often used in conjunction with other methods. Bark may have to be stripped from infested parts of trees and the exposed area sprayed with insecticide, and if the attack is extensive a whole area of forest may have to be clearfelled and the timber treated and then removed.

Aphids and Adelgids

Like Dutch elm disease, but less severe, beech bark disease is caused by a fungus carried by an insect vector. As the name suggests, it attacks beech trees, and both the European (*Fagus sylvatica*) and American (*F. grandifolia*) species are vulnerable. The insect is the felted beech coccus (*Cryptococcus fagisuga*). There is no mistaking its presence, because it covers large areas of the trunk and branches with a kind of waxy wool. This can allow the fungus, *Nectria coccinea,* to establish itself. Small, black spots appear on the bark and start exuding a dark liquid, then the fungus produces fruiting bodies on the bark. These are tiny, bright red, and roughly spherical. The disease retards the growth of trees and can kill them.

The felted beech coccus is one of many species of woolly aphids. There are many species

of aphids. They feed on sap; most specialize in one or just a few plant species. *Elatobium abietinum,* for example, feeds on the needles of Sitka spruce (*Picea sitchensis*) and can defoliate a tree completely, although the tree usually recovers.

The Adelgidae is a family of insects with a way of life very similar to that of the aphids (Aphididae), but its members occur only on conifers. They always reveal their presence by covering themselves with a white, woolly coating and, like aphids, some produce honeydew.

Adelgids are serious pests of forest trees. When you see a stand of larch (*Larix* species) in which the canopy is obviously discolored, the culprit may well be *Adelges laricis,* an adelgid that causes dieback, in which the tips of branches die first and the disease spreads back into the main body of the plant. Some adelgids cause the formation of galls. *A. abietis,* for example, causes pineapple gall on Norway spruce (*Picea abies*), the species most often grown in Europe as a Christmas tree.

Adelges piceae is a European species. In Europe it attacks the stems of fir trees, especially the giant fir (*Abies grandis*). This is a North American species that is grown extensively in Europe for its timber. Ironically, it was introduced to British plantations partly because it was no longer practicable to grow its European equivalent, the silver fir (*Abies alba*) commercially. Silver fir occurs naturally in the mountains of central and southern Europe and was planted widely in Britain in the last century. Then *Adelges nordmannianae* (or *nuesslini*) was accidentally introduced from eastern Europe and, in the relatively mild British climate, caused so much damage to young trees that the growing of silver fir had to be abandoned. For a long time the giant fir remained virtually immune to insect attack, but a tree represents a vast store of food and where there is food, sooner or later something will come along to eat it.

Adelges piceae then found its way to the United States and Canada. Its attacks first became noticeable in 1962, high in the Great Smoky Mountains, where it has killed vast numbers of trees. There the insect is known as the balsam woolly adelgid; it feeds on the trunks and branches of balsam fir (*Abies balsamea*), red spruce (*Picea rubens*), Fraser fir (*Abies fraseri*), and yellow birch (*Betula lutea*). The noble fir (*Abies procera*) is also subject to severe attacks by species of *Adelges*. These attacks can kill the tree. Other stem-feeding insects do little harm directly, but may open the way to a much more serious fungal attack. Weymouth or white pine (*Pinus strobus*), for example, can become infested with *Pineus strobi,* which may be accompanied or followed by *Cronartium ribicola,* a rust fungus that causes much more harm than the insect alone.

There are some insects that attack the roots of trees as well as the bark. Pine weevils (*Hylobius abietis*) breed in the roots of coniferous trees and in the stumps of trees that have been felled. Their larvae, which are white, legless grubs up to 0.8 inch (2 cm) long, feed in the root or stump for between one and two years. They then turn into adults, climb into a young tree, and feed on its bark. In extreme cases they can girdle the tree and kill it. Weevils comprise the superfamily Cuculionoidea, with around 50,000 species of beetles, sometimes known as snout beetles, in which, to a greater or lesser extent, the head is extended into a kind of beak, called a rostrum, with the mouthparts at its tip. Many are pests of crop plants or stored food.

Moths and Sawflies

Caterpillars, the larvae of moths and butterflies, feed on leaves and some specialize on conifer needles. Budworms are especially harmful. *Choristoneura pinus* is the pine budworm, feeding mainly on jack pine (*Pinus banksiana*), and its close relative *C. fumiferana* is the spruce budworm. Despite its name, the spruce budworm does not confine itself exclusively to spruce. Indeed, its outbreaks seem to begin where balsam fir (*Abies balsamea*) is abundant and summers are often warm and dry. Eastern Canada and Maine have suffered several large outbreaks, each lasting several years, for example from 1807 to 1818, 1870 to 1880, and 1904 to 1914.

Moths that attack trees are sometimes very attractive. The pine beauty moth (*Panolis flammea*) is well named, with intricately patterned chestnut and white wings and long "fur" over the back of its head and "shoulders." Even its larva is pretty, with a chestnut-colored head and dark blue body with longitudinal chestnut and pale blue markings. Altogether it is the kind of insect you might want to protect until you learn that in northern Scotland it has destroyed entire forests of lodgepole pine (*Pinus contorta* var. *latifolia*).

It is another immigrant to Britain, possibly a tramp species. Long known for its destructiveness in continental Europe, its entry to Britain was spectacular. In 1976 it completely defoliated and killed 445 acres (180 ha) of lodgepole pine in Sutherland, in the far northwest of Scotland. There have been several outbreaks since then covering hundreds of acres. These occur when the population of moths increases. They spend from August to the following March in the soil as pupae and emerge as adults in April. In April and May the females lay their eggs on pine needles and from June to August the caterpillars devour the needles. Lodgepole pine is a native of northwestern North America that grows well on poor soils of the Scottish moors. Before lodgepole pine was imported, the pine beauty moth fed on Scotch pine (*Pinus sylvestris*), but Scotch pine is little harmed by it. Perhaps the tree has adapted to deal with the caterpillars, or maybe Scotch pine harbors predators that feed on them. Perhaps the severity of pine beauty moth outbreaks illustrates what can happen when two introduced species meet for the first time. It provides a clear warning to North American foresters of what they might expect should the moth find its way across the Atlantic, although fortunately that is unlikely.

Pine beauty moth is not the only moth with larvae that feed on lodgepole pine. There are also the pine looper moth (*Bupalus piniaria*) and larch bud moth (*Zeiraphera diniana*). Despite its name, the larch bud moth is not especially fond of larch, much preferring pine or spruce. The caterpillar that defoliates larch is the larch casebearer (*Coleophora laricella*).

Broad-leaved trees also attract moths, of course. *Operophthera brumata* is the winter moth, so called because the adult females emerge from their pupae in the soil between October and February. They have only vestiges of wings and crawl up trees to lay their eggs. These hatch as green caterpillars that feed on many broad-leaved trees, especially oak, and also spruce. Adults of the northern winter moth (*Operophthera fagata*) emerge in October and November and its caterpillars feed, in May and June, mainly on birch leaves. It is called northern because it was first recorded in Britain, in 1848, in Cheshire, in the northwest of England. It is now known to have a much wider distribution, and both these winter moths occur throughout Europe and over most of Russia.

Caterpillars of leaf-roller moths live in little compartments they construct with silk between leaves or flowers, or in leaves they roll up. The oak leaf-roller moth (*Tortrix viridana*), a small, pale green moth, lays its eggs on oak trees (*Quercus* species), sometimes in such vast numbers that its larvae can defoliate the tree. Sawflies can also cause considerable harm. Their larvae look like caterpillars, but unlike most true caterpillars they have a pair of legs on each segment of their abdomens, and sawflies are closely related to bees, wasps, and ants (Hymenoptera), not to moths and butterflies (Lepidoptera). Female sawflies have an ovipositor, the organ through which eggs are laid, with sharp teeth along its edges, like a saw. Using its ovipositor like a saw, the female cuts a hole in a leaf or twig into which she lays her eggs. When the caterpillars hatch they feed on the leaves and, just like true caterpillars, they have prodigious appetites. *Diprion pini* and *Neodiprion sertifer* are both pine sawflies that attack forest trees throughout Europe. *D. pini* causes only minor damage, but *N. sertifer* attacks lodgepole pine and can defoliate it in outbreaks that last several years and usually end when the insects succumb to a viral disease. The larch sawfly (*Lygaeonematus erichsonii*) is a European species that found its way to North America, where it became a highly destructive pest.

Just like insects that bite humans, many of the insect pests of forests are harmful more for the infections they transmit than for the amount they eat. Many of these infections are fungal, but certain fungi need no help from insects to destroy the trees they parasitize.

Fungi

In fall, temperate forests are good places to hunt for fungi, visible then as the fruiting bodies from which they release their spores. Many are colorful, some are strangely shaped, some grow on the ground in forest clearings, and some grow on the trunks of trees. These include the bracket fungi and fungi that produce curious, reddish-brown sheets with a white border, all curled and twisted, at or close to ground level.

One of these, *Heterobasidion annosum*, accounts for around 90 percent of all the decay in conifers grown in Britain and is an extremely serious enemy of coniferous trees throughout the temperate regions of the world. Once airborne fungal spores have entered the cut surface of the stump of a felled tree, the infection spreads through the stump, into the roots, and from there to the roots of neighboring trees, crossing where roots touch below ground. The disease it causes is known as Fomes root rot (because the fungus used to be classified in the genus *Fomes*). Firs are not always killed by it, but pines are very susceptible. Curiously for so devastating a fungus, unless *H. annosum* establishes itself quickly it fails, because it competes poorly with other fungi. One of these, *Peniophora gigantea*, is harmless, so the stumps of cut pines can be protected by painting them with spores of this species suspended in water.

True Fomes is *F. fomentarius*. It attacks the sapwood of broad-leaved trees and kills them; it is quite common throughout Europe and North America, although in Britain it is confined to the Highlands of Scotland, where it grows only on birch trees. In the forests of central Europe, *F. fomentarius* prevents most beech trees (*Fagus sylvatica*) from reaching a very old age: it attacks them when they have grown to almost their full height. The fungus hollows out their trunks, then its fruiting bodies appear as projecting brackets all the way up the trunks. Branches fall and then the trunk splits.

Apart from the damage it does, its principal claim to fame is that it is the original tinder fungus, and people are believed to have been using it for this purpose 10,000 years ago. After suitable processing it becomes highly flammable, and is easily ignited by the spark made by striking flint. Since Roman times it has also been used to cauterize wounds, and more recently by dentists, to clean and dry teeth cavities before filling them. Its suede-like texture has led to its being used to make pouches and items of clothing.

Artist's (or false tinder) fungus (*Ganoderma applanatum*) is a similar bracket fungus, with which *F. fomentarius* used to be confused. Fairly common in the forests of Europe and North America and also found in parts of South America and islands of the Caribbean, it also grows on beech trees, causing them to rot and eventually killing them. It is called "artist's" fungus not because artists have any use for it, but because patterns drawn with a sharp point on the white surface where spores are produced turn brown and are fairly permanent. The related *G. lucidum* also causes trees to rot. It attacks most broad-leaved species, but is found only in Europe.

Honey Fungus

Serious though these are, the most destructive of all fungi, and probably of all tree parasites, is *Armillaria,* the honey fungus. It is common throughout the temperate regions, and different species of *Armillaria* attack different tree species with varying degrees of severity. Infection begins in the stump of a fallen or felled tree and spreads outward through the soil as black rhizomorphs, strands that look like bootlaces and give the fungus its other common name, bootlace fungus. The rhizomorphs usually infect young trees, entering near ground level, and broad-leaved species are more vulnerable than conifers. The rhizomorphs can penetrate healthy bark or enter through the tiniest crack in a root, and then the fungus spreads to rot the entire tree. It is a serious parasite of all woody plants, and it also attacks pit props in mines, possibly causing mining accidents. Its fruiting bodies are toadstools and some species are edible.

Honey fungus possesses the property of bioluminescence. That is to say, it glows in the dark with a green light, produced in specialized cells when a compound called luciferin is oxidized in the presence of the enzyme luciferase. Because the fungus can permeate apparently healthy wood, it makes the wood seem to glow. At one time, a piece of glowing root was believed to have magical powers. This may be the origin of the sorcerer's wand.

Mammals

Fungi that cause disease are described as parasites, but the distinction between a parasite and a predator is rather fuzzy. Both are species that feed on other species, often killing them in the process. This is what fungi do. Predators move from one prey individual to another, which seems to imply they are animals, but in their own way so do fungi. Think of the "bootlaces" spreading out in search of targets for honey fungus. Predators are usually bigger than their prey—cats are bigger than mice, for example—but it is hard to apply this rule when the prey is the size of a tree. Are defoliating insects parasites or predators? Perhaps it is a distinction without a difference, since the result is the same no matter what we call it.

The question arises because there are also mammals that feed on and seriously harm trees. These are herbivores, so it sounds strange to call them predators, but it sounds even stranger to call them parasites.

Deer, rabbits, hares, sheep, and goats eat leaves and the tender young growing shoots of trees. This is browsing. It rarely kills the tree and, of course, browsers can feed only to the height they can reach. It is harmful only in plantations, where it can alter the shape and rate of growth of trees.

Attacks on bark are more serious, because this can allow fungal infection to enter and may weaken the tree, and if the bark is stripped all the way around the trunk, the tree will die, because the phloem tubes will be broken; this is called "girdling." Several species of deer strip bark from trees and so do tree squirrels and voles. Deer also rub their antlers against trees to remove the velvet from them, or as part of their territorial or mating behavior. This causes fraying, leaving the bark hanging in shreds. This can kill the tree, although in a forest only a small number of trees are attacked.

An ecosystem is a community of plants and animals that feed on one another. Temperate forests are no exception and what we may think of as the damage insects, fungi, and mammals do to trees is rarely damage to the forest itself. That survives—even if one species of trees is reduced in number or even eliminated, others take its place and what was forest remains forest. No member of the community of organisms inhabiting a natural forest can be regarded as a pest or weed. It is only in plantations, where trees are a crop, that fungi and animals feeding on them are seen as pests competing with the forester.

Natural Forest and Plantation Forest

When a tree dies and eventually falls to the ground, it provides food for a hierarchy of animals, fungi, and bacteria. Together, these organisms break down the structure of the fallen tree, then its cells, and finally the large, organic molecules from which its cells are made, converting them into smaller, simpler, inorganic compounds that can dissolve in water present in the soil and enter the root systems of living plants (page 84). In other words, the chemical substances from which the forest plants are made are constantly recycled.

Suppose, though, that a farmer, who owns the forest, calculates it is more profitable to grow corn than trees, so he has all the trees felled and removed, the old roots ripped from the ground, the land plowed, and a crop sown. What had been forest will have become arable fields and when the corn crop ripens it will be harvested. This breaks the nutrient cycle by removing most of the plants from the area, rather than allowing them to decompose on the spot.

A different landowner might make a different decision. Although it is true that corn is more profitable than trees, she might feel that since the forest supports many attractive animals and plants, as well as providing a popular amenity for local people, it should not be cleared. All the same, she might decide it could be managed in such a way as to bring in an income. As trees matured they could be felled and their timber sold, and young trees planted to replace them.

Breaking the Cycle

So the forest remains, but the cycle has been broken, nevertheless. Removing the felled trees prevents them from decomposing in exactly the same way that the harvesting and removal of the corn crop prevents its decomposition, and in both cases the removal of the crop removes from the soil the nutrients that would otherwise have been returned to it in the course of the cycle. In time, this must lead to the depletion of the soil and a decline in yields. The remedy is to apply plant nutrients, usually in the form of fertilizer. Like arable crops, managed forests need "feeding" (page 106).

Applying fertilizers can replace the plant nutrients removed by cropping, but the nutrient cycle remains broken at the point where dead plant material is converted into simple nutrient compounds. This conversion is accomplished by organisms that feed on the material and on one another. Reducing the amount of dead matter

available to the decomposers also reduces the size and possibly the complexity of their population. Ecologically, therefore, the repeated removal of timber alters the character of a forest.

Timber can be a crop just as much as corn or potatoes, but there are differences in the way it can be obtained. Removing selected mature trees while leaving the others untouched has little effect on the overall composition and appearance of the forest. Its ecological effects are local, confined to the area around each of the felled trees. Plantation forestry, on the other hand, is much more like arable farming. When the trees mature, the crop is harvested and a new crop is then sown on the same land.

Natural Forests and Plantations

The difference between a natural forest and a plantation is very much like that between a field of wheat and a natural meadow. Both types of forest begin on bare ground. Left to be colonized naturally, what will become the natural forest progresses slowly through a series of vegetation types (page 92) and it will be a century or more before the forest matures. During this time, species continually arrive and those that can find the resources they need remain. Once established, this diverse climax community of plants, animals, fungi, and microbes remains in existence for a long time, constantly adjusting to minor changes.

A plantation is very different. In most cases, the bare ground on which it begins will have been plowed and possibly drained. Early seral stages will be omitted, and the ecosystem will jump directly to the planting of tree seedlings belonging to the climax species. These will grow in the absence of the other species of herbs and shrubs that would accompany the colonizing trees of a natural forest. Indeed, invading plants that might inhibit the growth of the desired trees will be regarded as weeds and suppressed.

Since the aim of a plantation is to produce a crop of timber for sale, the forester will grow those tree species most likely to achieve this. In practice this favors coniferous species, which grow faster than broad-leaved species. It also means each area within the plantation will contain the species that grows best on that site and, almost invariably in the case of conifers, this will be just one species. An area growing only one species is called a monoculture. A plantation of broad-leaves may contain two or three species. In Britain, however, many natural broad-leaved forests, but by no means all, contain six or more tree species.

The best trees from a commercial point of view are not necessarily those that occur naturally in the area chosen for a plantation. This is especially true in Britain, where for many years the principal need was for softwood timber, from coniferous trees. The only coniferous trees native to Britain are Scotch pine (*Pinus sylvestris*), yew (*Taxus baccata*), and juniper (*Juniperus communis*), none of which grows well on the poor, upland soils where forestry was encouraged because agriculture was impossible or unprofitable. Species imported in the last century were planted. These came mainly from North America and had been grown successfully as ornamentals, thus proving they could thrive under British conditions. Consequently, British plantation forests are dominated by Sitka spruce (*Picea sitchensis*), Douglas (or Oregon) fir (*Pseudotsuga menziesii*), and lodgepole pine (*Pinus contorta*), together with Norway spruce (*Picea abies*), Corsican pine (*Pinus nigra*), and Japanese larch (*Larix kaempferi*).

More recently, increasing demand for hardwoods has led to the establishment of more broad-leaved plantations and these do grow predominantly native species. In North America, with a wider range of suitable species, plantations are stocked with species native to the continent, if not to the area in which they are being grown.

Even-Aged Monocultural Stands

Obviously, seedlings that are all planted at the same time will grow to form a block of trees all of the same age. In a natural forest, a similar area will often contain trees of all ages, although this is not always the case. Scientists have been able to plot the distribution of tree species in parts of the original forest that grew over much of Europe before people started managing or clearing parts of it and have discovered it consisted of a mosaic of patches, each composed of even-aged stands. This pattern is not surprising, given the events that affect forests. Fires, floods, and similar disturbances are usually limited in scale, each time leaving an area cleared of all vegetation. This bare ground is then recolonized from the surrounding forest, producing an even-aged stand. Few areas of a forest are immune from disturbance, so the eventual result is likely to be the patchwork of even-aged stands that seems to have developed in the original, primeval forest.

Large blocks of coniferous trees, all of the same species and all the same size, often growing in straight rows, are monotonous and unpopular with conservationists. Foresters have responded to the criticism and nowadays plantations are designed to be more diverse. Areas adjoining roads, wet ground, and more difficult terrain are left unplanted, so they can be colonized naturally. Forest blocks are less rigidly geometrical in shape, and in some places trees have been cleared to make glades and to improve access to riversides.

Change cannot be rapid. Trees, even fast-growing conifers, take around 50 years to reach a size at which a whole stand is clear-felled. This means the shape and pattern of plantations can be changed only gradually. Desirable changes are now being made in areas that were planted half a century ago and have now completed their rotation.

There is considerable difference between a plantation and a natural forest, but this should not be exaggerated. It is true that within a plantation blocks are clear-felled and replanted, producing even-aged stands. Undisturbed forest also tends to form such stands, however, so in this respect the plantation is not quite so unnatural as it may seem. Nor is monoculture necessarily unnatural. In temperate forests, there are areas in which only one or two tree species grow naturally.

Conservationists sometimes point out that plantation forest supports less wildlife than natural forest. This may be true in some cases, but a large, mature plantation comprises many blocks at different stages of development, each supporting a range of species that together amount to a fairly rich community. If the plantation is established on land that was previously unforested and is a long way from other forests, it may take a long time, centuries perhaps, for forest species to colonize it. This may be the basis for much of the ecological criticism of plantations. Eventually, though, those species will arrive provided the plantation remains in being.

Meanwhile, the vast majority of forests in Europe and the United States are either plantations or, at the very least, managed. There are very few areas, and in Britain none, that have not been managed by humans in some way, even though they may have been forested continually for centuries. The distinction between natural and plantation forests is sharply defined only at the extremes. An unmanaged (or poorly managed) forest of native species, complete with dying, dead, and fallen trees in varying stages of decomposition bears little resemblance to the neat rows of an exotic species in an even-aged plantation stand. The difference is less stark between an area that is natural forest, but managed by the removal of certain trees, their replacement by planted seedlings, and the control of unwanted species of plants and animals, and a similarly managed area of plantation.

What Is Biodiversity and Why Does It Matter?

Plantation forestry is a type of farming. Trees take much longer to grow than other farm crops, but, just like a farmer, the forester prepares the ground, plants seedlings raised from seed in a nursery (called an orchard), applies fertilizer, removes weeds, controls pests, thins the crop as necessary and, some decades later, gathers in the harvest.

All the same, a plantation is different from a natural forest. Ecologically, an area in which trees are felled when they reach about 50 years of age is not at all the same as one in which trees of the same species have grown, died, fallen, and regenerated from their own seed or roots for several centuries. The natural forest ecosystem will support a wider range of species than the plantation ecosystem and when natural forest is cleared to make way for a plantation some of that diversity of species is lost. The area is still forest, but the biodiversity of the area has been reduced.

"Biodiversity" has become fashionable in recent years and the importance of the concept it describes was recognized internationally in June 1992, at the United Nations Conference on Environment and Development, held in Rio de Janeiro. It was there, at the so-called "Rio Summit" or "Earth Summit," that representatives from more than 150 nations signed the Convention on Protecting Species and Habitats, better known as the "Biodiversity Convention." The convention came into force (and became a treaty) at the end of 1992, by which time the number of signatories had risen to 167. These nations—and those like the United States, which accepts the principles of the treaty but is not certain of its details or implications and therefore unwilling to sign—have committed themselves to taking whatever steps they can to preserve biodiversity.

Defining Biodiversity

No one would urge us to reduce biodiversity. It is a self-evident good everyone can support, but

there is a difficulty. Biodiversity is a contraction of "biological diversity" and most people instinctively think it means the number of different living organisms there are in a given area. Unfortunately, it is rather more complicated when you try to define it more precisely. Then, the expression seems to mean something like the "variety of life," but if that is what biodiversity means, the only way to protect it is probably to protect all living things. Many people would support that, but scientists faced with the task of applying the concept have to make choices, and they find that when biodiversity is defined in this way it is so broad as to encompass just about everything.

The United Nations Environment Program (UNEP) defines biological diversity as: "the variability among living organisms from all sources, including, inter alia, terrestrial, marine and other aquatic ecosystems and the ecological complexes of which they are part. This includes diversity within species, between species, and of ecosystems." U.N. support for conserving biodiversity is not new. The World Charter for Nature, which the U.N. adopted in 1984, states that all species warrant respect regardless of their usefulness to humanity.

Taking the U.N. definition as a starting point leads to the idea of biodiversity at three levels: "within species" implies genetic diversity, the variation from one individual to another; "between species" refers to the difference between one species and another; and the diversity of ecosystems refers to the features that make each community of organisms unique. The second definition, of the diversity of species, is the one to which the World Charter for Nature refers and that most people would prefer, but as the UNEP statement shows, it is not the only one. There is a hierarchy, and it is possible to divide its three levels into five: genes, populations, species, associations and communities (see, for example, page 78), and ecosystems or landscapes. Having gone this far, it is quite easy to subdivide the hierarchy further, into any number of levels.

All the members of this hierarchy, from genes to landscapes, are individual things, but some scientists prefer to look at biodiversity from a different perspective. They emphasize the importance of processes. Individual living things are dynamic. Genes are constantly being divided, reassembled, and shuffled in the course of cell division and are altered randomly. These altered (mutated) genes disseminate among populations, where some vanish and others become fixed. Cell division, mutation, and dissemination are processes. Individual organisms require food, so the cycling of nutrient elements is important to them, and that is another process. You cannot protect a species, a gene, or an ecosystem without safeguarding the processes on which it depends and its own function, which is also a process, so the two approaches are complementary.

Measuring Biodiversity

Despite the difficulties over definition, there are now ways biodiversity can be measured. This is vital, because if biodiversity is being lost and we wish to reduce the rate of loss, we must know how much is being lost and how fast. Measurements of biodiversity are based on comparing chromosomes, proteins, other biochemical compounds, and DNA from cell nuclei, mitochondria, and chloroplasts. One consequence of these studies has been to cast doubt on what used to be the conventional idea of "species." Boundaries between one species and another are now much harder to draw than they were. The old definition was based on the idea of a group whose members either do not mate with members of other groups or, if they do mate, produce hybrid offspring that are infertile. This is now considered unsatisfactory, because there are too many exceptions to it. Scientists now rely more on differences among genotypes; genotype is the complete genetic constitution of an individual.

Once it can be measured, the distribution of biodiversity can be plotted on maps. This leads to the identification of hot spots, where there is a great deal of biodiversity under threat, usually because the entire area is likely to be developed or put to another use.

A widely used technique for identifying these hot spots is called "gap analysis." It was devised in 1978 by Michael Scott, an American ecologist who now works for the Biological Resources Division of the U.S. Geological Service. First a number of important or endangered species are identified. Then the range of each of these is plotted separately on a map and all the maps are assembled as overlays above a map showing wildlife reserves and other protected areas. The result shows whether the protected areas coincide with the species ranges and also exposes gaps, where biodiversity is high but there is little protection. The gap analysis technique is only as accurate as the maps it uses, so these are being improved and updated.

Why Preserve Biodiversity?

Most people take it for granted that biodiversity should be preserved, but from time to time the reasons for preserving it have to be stated. Clearing an area of forest might provide land for farming, housing, mining, or any number of alternative uses that would bring obvious material benefit to people locally or even nationally, so anyone urging that the forest remain as it is must produce cogent reasons.

Usually, the answer given is a practical one. Essentially it amounts to saying that it would be more useful to leave the forest untouched than to clear it. This is the reason most likely to be accepted, because it compares one kind of utility with another.

Forests provide timber and wood pulp for making paper, but in temperate regions most of this is supplied from plantations, growing just a few species. A natural forest contains different tree species, and probably more of them, and their wood may be of considerable commercial value—if not now, then at some time in the future. Wild trees may also possess heritable qualities, such as resistance to particular pests or diseases, that could be transferred to cultivated species by genetic modification.

It is not only the wild trees that would be lost when the forest was cleared. So would most or all of the smaller organisms and, with them, species and substances of possibly immense value. These may well exist in familiar, temperate forests, unknown because until now no one has bothered to look for them.

On a 270-acre (109-hectare) tract of land at West Danby, New York, that was scheduled to be sold (presumably for development) in 1996, a graduate student from Cornell University, doing fieldwork on fungi, identified the sexual form of a tiny mold fungus from which the drug cyclosporin is obtained. The discovery made it possible to identify and propagate the fungus and increased interest in species closely related to it that may also produce compounds of pharmaceutical value.

It is not only fungi that may prove useful. Very little is known about the bacterial populations of forest soils, and bacteria are now being genetically modified to break down industrial pollutants, recover valuable metals and other substances, and perform a wide range of other valuable tasks. Plants themselves may produce substances with therapeutic properties. Taxol, found in the bark of the Pacific or western yew (*Taxus brevifolia*), inhibits ovarian, breast, and lung cancer. That tree grows along the Pacific coast of North America, from California to British Columbia.

Pharmaceutical prospecting in temperate forests has barely begun and it seems foolish to destroy what might turn out to be the source of treatments for many human ailments. In purely commercial terms, the U.N. Environment Program has estimated that throughout the industrialized countries, in 1985 the retail value of drugs derived from plants was about $43 billion and rising. Most of these drugs are from tropical plants, but the size of the market should be a consideration for anyone thinking of ways to turn a profit from land supporting nothing but a few square miles of "useless" unmanaged forest.

Domestication and the Selective Breeding of Trees

Natural biodiversity provides a reservoir of genetic information that is important in other ways, because using plants (and animals) alters them. Trees that provide us with food or some other useful product, like citrus fruits, olives, or rubber, have changed over the thousands of years they have been cultivated. Forest trees, grown in plantations for their timber, have not been altered to the same extent, but this is merely a consequence of the relatively short time during which they have been grown in this way. Domestication brings change, and forest trees have not yet been fully domesticated.

Historically, the change begins as soon as people gather seed from wild plants and sow it. They select seed from the plants that yield the biggest or best crop. When it is time to gather seeds from these, again the biggest or best are chosen. This is artificial selection and, like natural selection, it can produce major modifications.

The domestication of forest trees has started with the selection of species to satisfy certain demands. Apart from the quality of their timber, these include their suitability for the soils and climates in which they are to be grown. Sitka spruce (*Picea sitchensis*) grows well in Britain, for example, but it is not just any Sitka spruce, grown from seeds gathered at random. In North America, this species grows from Alaska to Oregon, over a 1,500-mile (2,400 km) north-to-south range, and although all the trees belong to the same species, those growing in the north and south have adapted to rather different conditions—another example of biodiversity. Trees from the middle of the geographic range are best suited to the north and west of Britain and those from Washington to the southwest.

Improved breeds of many commercially important species, some of them hybrids, result from crossbreeding between related species to transfer desirable characteristics from one to the other. American and European poplars have been crossed in this way to produce varieties that are resistant to certain diseases and European and Japanese larch hybrids are beginning to enter commercial cultivation.

Genetic Modification and Micropropagation

Traditionally, plant breeders selected plants on the basis of their physical appearance, known as their phenotype. Today breeders are also geneticists and work from genotypes. As this approach develops it will allow them to identify the genes responsible for particular characteristics and transfer these to other species. This will greatly accelerate the process, but it will be helped if the natural biodiversity is preserved in the wild, to provide a reference against which change can be measured.

It is now fairly routine to produce trees by micropropagation. This is a technique for producing vast numbers of identical copies, or clones, of an especially desirable tree. Tissue samples, usually comprising meristem cells (page 71), are grown in cultures and develop into whole plants. In this way it is possible to copy a plant more than 100,000 times in a year.

Increasingly, trees grown in plantations are likely to differ genetically from their wild relatives and ancestors. This is also what happened to our agricultural crop plants, but today it is happening very much faster. The cultivated varieties will be greatly superior for the purpose for which they are grown, but they may also resemble one another much more closely than would a stand of wild trees. From time to time it may be necessary to improve them further by crossing them with, or incorporating genes from, a wild relative. This will then be seen as yet another reason for preserving the wild forests and their biodiversity.

Gymnosperm Trees

Common Gymnosperm Trees of the New World

The gymnosperm trees of New World forests can be grouped as incense cedars, cedars, cypresses, swamp cypresses, firs, hemlocks, larches, pines, redwoods, and spruces. They are best known by their common names, but some trees have several common names, so the same species may go by different names in different places. Common names are unreliable guides to botanical relationships. "Cedars" and "cypresses," for example, may or may not belong to the main genera *Cedrus* (cedars) and *Cupressus* (cypresses), and may or may not be closely related to one another. For this reason the botanical name is more useful, and although these names are revised from time to time, until everyone is used to a new name the old name is usually given as well.

INCENSE CEDARS

Incense cedars are a case in point. There are eight species of them, and none are true cedars (*Cedrus*). Of the eight species, five occur in New Zealand and New Caledonia, in the Pacific, one on the Pacific coast of North America, one in China, and one in Taiwan. At one time all eight were classified in the same genus (*Libocedrus*), but the North American, Chinese, and Taiwanese trees have now been placed in the genus *Calocedrus*. As though to confuse matters further, there is also a Chilean incense cedar, the only species in the genus *Austrocedrus*.

North American incense cedar (*Calocedrus decurrens*) can grow to a height of 148 feet (45 m) and is shaped like a narrow cone. Cultivated varieties, grown as ornamentals throughout temperate regions, are often almost cylindrical. The name "decurrens" refers to the tiny, scalelike leaves. These are markedly decurrent, which means their bases extend down the stem, below the points where they join it, so they cover the stem completely. Beneath the leaves, the bark is reddish brown and deeply furrowed. Wood from the incense cedar is light, resistant to decay, and fragrant. It is used to make a range of products, including pencils, boxes, and fence posts.

ARBORVITAE

Western red cedar (*Thuja plicata*) belongs to the group of trees known as arborvitae, which means "tree of life," and is sometimes called the giant arborvitae. It grows to a height of 100–200 feet (30–60 m). Its glossy, scale leaves have a fruity smell, which is very strong when they are bruised, and the cones are tiny, no more than a half inch (1.2 cm) long. The tree is native to western North America, where it is an important source of timber (and also occurs in China and Japan and at the tip of South America). Its wood is used to make weatherboarding and roof shingles and it is also the tree most often used by Native Americans to make totem poles.

In the east, the American or white cedar (*T. occidentalis*) is a smaller tree, up to 65 feet (20 m) tall, with cones 0.3–0.5 inch (0.8–1.2 cm) long.

FALSE CYPRESSES

American cypresses belong to the genus *Chamaecyparis* or false cypresses. Both *Chamaecyparis* and *Thuja* have scale leaves that hug the twigs so closely you can see no bark or leaf buds beneath them. Feel the tip of a leaf-covered twig, however, and if it is soft and fleshy the tree is a *Thuja* and if it is thin and hard it belongs to a *Chamaecyparis*.

Lawson cypress, or Port Orford cedar (*C. lawsoniana*), grows naturally in the far west of the United States, in California and Oregon, but it is a hardy, very attractive, spire-shaped tree and widely cultivated, with more than 200 named varieties. It can grow 80–165 feet (25–50 m) tall and its timber, which has a spicy, fragrant odor, is of high quality, with many uses in building, furniture, and boatbuilding.

SWAMP CYPRESSES

Swamp cypresses comprise three closely related species in the genus *Taxodium*, all of them growing naturally in the southern and southeastern United States and Mexico. Related to the redwoods (family Taxodiaceae), they are deciduous or evergreen in part of their range, with pale green leaves growing either in one plane to either side of their shoots or all around them. As the name suggests, they often grow in swamps or shallow rivers, but they will also grow in well-drained soil. One specimen of Mexican (or Montezuma) cypress (*T. mucronatum*), called El Gigante, is said to be still growing in the village of Santa Maria del Tule, where it was seen by Hernán Cortés, who wrote about it more than 450 years ago. This species grows to about 165 feet (50 m). It is evergreen in Mexico, but deciduous in cooler regions.

Pond cypress (*T. ascendens*), also known as upland cypress, grows to about 80 feet (25 m) and occurs in the southeastern United States as far west as Alabama. The commonest of the three is the swamp cypress *T. distichum,* with pale green, feathery leaves. Both the pond and swamp cypresses are also known as bald cypresses.

FIRS

Firs belong to the genus *Abies* and their leaves are needles, in most species flat, rather than the scales borne by the cedars and cypresses.

Perhaps the best known and most widespread North American fir is *A. balsamea,* the balsam fir or balm of Gilead, which grows over much of the continent as far north as the Arctic Circle. It, and Fraser's balsam fir (*A. fraseri*), are the species most often used as Christmas trees.

These are small compared with other North American firs. The red fir (*A. magnifica*), for example, grows as a very symmetrical tree 230 feet (70 m) or more tall. It is native to Oregon and California. Red silver fir (*A. amabilis*) grows to a height of 260 feet (80 m) in natural forest, although to less than half that size in cultivation. It occurs naturally in the mountains of British Columbia, Alberta, Washington, and Oregon. In natural forest, the grand fir (*A. grandis*) or giant fir can grow to 330 feet (100 m). This species is widely grown in plantations, because it tolerates a wide range of soil conditions and grows fast, but rarely to more than half the height of which it is capable. Its timber is used to make furniture, boxes, and in building, and is also pulped for paper.

DOUGLAS FIRS

Douglas firs were formerly placed in the genus *Abies,* but are now recognized as a genus of their own, *Pseudotsuga,* although they are not closely related to the hemlocks (*Tsuga*). There are two North American species. The large-coned Douglas fir (*P. macrocarpa*) is a tree up to 80 feet (25 m) tall, with cones 4–7 inches (10–18 cm) long, that is native to southwest California.

Oregon (or gray) Douglas fir (*P. menziesii*) is the most commercially important timber tree in North America, although its quality is somewhat variable. It grows naturally in British Columbia and throughout the western United States, as far

Opposite: Bald cypress tree with buttress and knee, Okefenokee Swamp, Georgia (Michael Durham/ENP Images)

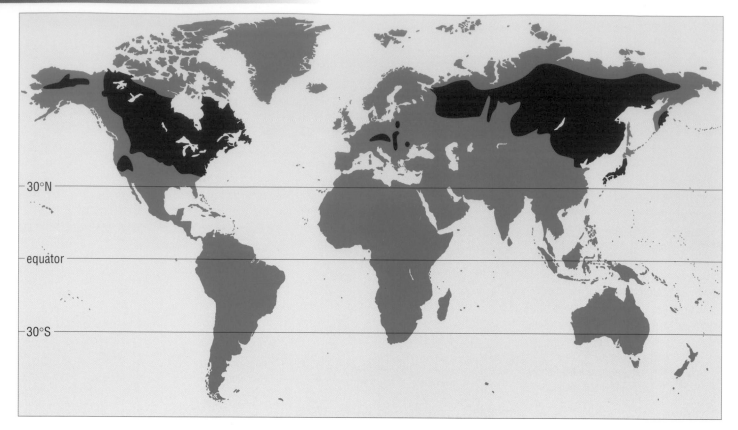

south as Mexico. Around half of all the forest trees in this region are Oregon Douglas firs. It can grow to 330 feet (100 m) and its timber is used for just about everything that can be made from wood, from houses, boats, and railroad freight cars to furniture and flagpoles.

HEMLOCKS

Hemlocks (*Tsuga* species) have a rather disjunct distribution. They occur naturally in eastern and western North America, in the Himalayas, and in eastern China, Taiwan, and Japan. They are handsome trees, roughly pyramid-shaped and with horizontal or slightly drooping branches.

In the western United States, mountain hemlock (*T. mertensiana*) is a tree 100 feet (30 m) tall, with some individuals in natural forest growing to 165 feet (50 m), that is native to the mountains from Alaska to California. Both it and western hemlock (*T. heterophylla*) are often grown as ornamentals, but western hemlock is also widely grown in plantations for its timber. The tree occurs naturally near the Pacific coast, where it grows to a height of 100–200 feet (30–60 m). You can recognize western hemlock by its needles, which are of uneven lengths and crowd along the twigs in a very haphazard fashion.

LARCHES

Larches (*Larix* species) are among the most attractive of all trees. They are tall with a graceful pyramid shape, but their beauty lies in their deciduous foliage. This takes the form of bunches of needles that change color in the fall, shortly before they are shed, producing patches of gold amid the otherwise dark green forest.

Two species are native to North America. Tamarack (*L. laricina*), also known as hackmatack, eastern larch, and American larch, grows naturally in Alaska, Canada, and in the eastern United States as far south as Pennsylvania. It grows up to 65 feet (20 m) tall. Western larch (*L. occidentalis*), or West American larch, is taller, reaching a height of 148–180 feet (45–55 m). Larch timber is tough and durable and both species provide wood with many uses, including construction, telegraph poles, and railroad sleepers.

PINES

True pines belong to the genus *Pinus,* which comprises nearly 100 species distributed throughout temperate regions of the Northern Hemisphere. A number of unrelated trees, some from the Southern Hemisphere, also have the common name "pine," but North American pines are true pines. One species of bristlecone pine (*P. longaeva*) is famous for living so long that scientists have developed from it a chronology against which other dates, including radiocarbon dates, can be calibrated. The tree grows in California and some individuals are more than 4,600 years old. Correlating their growth rings with those of dead pines has produced a chronology extending more than 8,000 years into the past. Related bristlecone or hickory pines (*P. aristata*) grow in the mountains

World distribution of larch trees

of Colorado, Arizona, and New Mexico, but are not so long-lived.

Pines form important components of North American forests. Shore pine (*P. contorta*) is native to western coastal areas. The lodgepole pine is *P. contorta* variety *latifolia*. It grows in inland forests and was the tree preferred by Native Americans for making the frames of their lodges, hence its common name. It is a slender tree, often no more than 33 feet (10 m) tall, and is widely cultivated for timber because of its tolerance for poor soils. Its cones are said to be serotinous, meaning that they are stimulated to open and release their seeds only after they have been heated by fire, a feature lodgepole pine shares with several other species (page 94). It grows in the west, from Alaska to California. In Canada, almost to the Arctic Circle, and in the northeastern United States its place is taken by jack pine (*P. banksiana*), a tree about 65 feet (20 m) tall that also produces serotinous cones.

Jack pine is one of the "hard" pines. Although all coniferous trees produce "soft" wood, compared with the hard wood of broadleaved trees, pines are subdivided commercially into two groups, as soft or hard, depending on the ease with which they can be worked with carpentry tools. The soft and hard designation refers to the amount of resin in the wood. Soft pine has little resin, hard pine has much more.

Surprisingly, perhaps, given its longevity, bristlecone pine is of the soft variety. Monterey and lodgepole pines are hard.

Longleaf, or pitch pine (*P. palustris*), another hard pine, also withstands fire well. Its terminal buds, from which new growth develops, are protected by a thick layer of leaves. These prevent the temperature rising high enough to kill the buds, so the tree survives while the surrounding vegetation is destroyed. On the coastal plain of the southeastern United States, the first European colonists found large areas covered by pure stands of longleaf pine. These probably developed because of fires that for thousands of years had been occurring naturally at intervals of three to 10 years, producing conditions only this species could tolerate. It is a big tree, growing to 130 feet (40 m), and where it is grown for timber or pulping to make paper foresters sometimes use fire to remove competing trees. The name "longleaf" refers to its bright green needles, which are up to 17.75 inches (45 cm) long.

Loblolly pine (*P. taeda*) is another fire-resistant species. It is a hard pine with abundant resin and a fragrance which gives it an alternative common name of frankincense pine, but the resin is of too poor a quality to be of commercial value. It is a tall tree, up to 100 feet (30 m) and occasionally to 165 feet (50 m), and its needles, up to 10 inches (25 cm) long, are bluegreen. It covers large areas of poor, sandy, or marshy land, called pine barrens, of the eastern and southeastern United States and often colonizes abandoned arable land where the soil is depleted of nutrients due to bad farming. There it is known as the old-field pine.

The American pine with the most extensive range is the ponderosa pine (*P. ponderosa*), also known as the western yellow pine and the bull pine. It occurs naturally in mountainous areas from British Columbia south to the Black Hills of South Dakota and from there south to Texas and Mexico, and also down the northern part of the Pacific coast, where commercially it is second in importance only to the Douglas fir.

Coulter pine (*P. coulteri*) also grows in southern California and Mexico. It grows to about 80 feet (25 m) tall, but its most remarkable feature is the size of its cones, which give the tree its alternative common name, of big-cone pine. These are 10–14 inches (25–35 cm) long, about 6 inches (15 cm) in diameter, can weigh 4 pounds (1.8 kg) or more, and their hard scales end in long, sharp, curved spines, like claws. The digger pine (*P. sabiniana*), of California, is closely related and very similar. Its cones also have scales with long,

curved, spines, and the cones are often 6 inches (15 cm) across, although they are only up to 9 inches (23 cm) long. The seeds of both types are large and resemble nuts. Native Americans used to gather them for food.

Timber from soft pines can also be valuable. American soft pines are further divided into four groups: white pines produce very pale wood; stone pines grow mainly near the timber line and are important mainly as protectors of watersheds; foxtail pines have needles that live for 15 years or more, so as more and more accumulate, branches acquire a bushy appearance, like a fox's tail; nut pines produce the seeds sold as pine nuts or pine

kernels. Most of the "nuts" come from from the nut pine (*P. edulis*).

One of the most valuable of all North American timber trees is a soft pine, the eastern white pine (*P. strobus*), also known as the Weymouth pine. It grows to a height of 80–165 feet (25–50 m) and its wood is white, with a very even grain. At one time it dominated forests that stretched from the Atlantic coast westward to Minnesota and Manitoba and south to Georgia, but so many trees have been felled that today few mature specimens remain. It is the only soft pine to occur naturally east of the Great Plains. There is an equivalent species, no less valuable, on the other

Coastal redwood, Pacific Coast, North America (Gerry Ellis/ENP Images)

side of the continent. The western white pine (*P. monticola*) occurs in the northwestern United States and British Columbia. It is much the same size as the eastern white pine, but its wood is slightly darker. Its young shoots are covered in down, a feature that distinguishes it from *P. strobus*.

A third North American soft pine—one that has also been extensively harvested for its timber and commands one of the highest prices of all United States timbers—has the distinction of being probably the biggest pine in the world. The sugar pine (*P. lambertiana*), also a white pine, grows to a height of 165–330 feet (50–100 m), with a trunk that can be 12 feet (3.7 m) across. It grows in California, which is where almost all the timber from this species is produced, the small remainder (about 5 percent) coming from Oregon. Its seeds are edible, but it is called the "sugar" pine because, when damaged, its heartwood exudes a sweet sap.

REDWOODS

Redwoods are the most famous of all American trees. They have been planted in many parts of the world, but are native only to the Pacific Coast. There are only two living species, nowadays classified in separate genera in the same family (Taxodiaceae) as the swamp cypresses. The dawn redwood (*Metasequoia glyptostroboides*), native to southern China, is probably related, although some scientists believe it should be placed in a family of its own.

The coast redwood (*Sequoia sempervirens*) grows naturally in the fog belt, along the coast from southern Oregon to Monterey, California. It is rarely found growing naturally more than 25 miles (40 km) from the coast or at an altitude higher than 3,500 feet (1,000 m). It produces seeds prolifically, but barely 25 percent of them germinate and trees reproduce mainly vegetatively, by producing suckers. New trees grow readily from the stumps of fallen or felled trees.

The Sierra redwood (*Sequoiadendron giganteum*) grows on the slopes of the Sierra Nevada at altitudes of 3,000–8,500 feet (900–2,600 m). This is the tree with several common names. As well as Sierra redwood, it is known as the big tree, giant sequoia, mammoth tree, and wellingtonia and is so impressive that some individuals have names of their own. The General Sherman tree, for example, stands in the Sequoia National Park. It has been measured in every dimension: it is 272.4 feet (83 m) tall, 27 feet (8 m) in diameter measured 8 feet (2 m) above ground level, and the circumference of its base measures 101.5 feet (31 m). It is estimated to weigh about 6,167 tons (5,595 t).

It is a huge tree, but both redwoods are huge. Coast redwoods can grow to a height of 400 feet (120 m) and Sierra redwoods to 330 feet (100 m). They are also long-lived: coast redwoods commonly live between 400 and 800 years or even

longer. Sierra redwoods were thought to be the most long-lived of all trees until the age of bristlecone pines was measured. One that was cut was found to be 3,200 years old.

Both redwoods have a thick, spongy bark you can punch hard without hurting your fist. The bark is almost impossible to ignite and protects the tree against fire.

Timber from the coast redwood is soft, fine-grained, easy to work, and the size of mature trees means it can be produced as long planks up to 6 feet (2 m) wide. Its popularity led to extensive cutting after about 1860, but through the efforts of conservationists the rate of felling declined from the 1940s and large forests remain, some of primary stands, others from regrowth. Sierra redwoods have survived better, because their timber is more brittle and so less in demand.

The name "sequoia" honors Sequoya, a Native American who died in 1843. Believing the settlers derived their power from being able to write down information, Sequoya devised an alphabet of 86 characters, representing every syllable in the Cherokee language. His alphabet was easy to learn and proved popular. Eventually it allowed books and newspapers to be published in Cherokee.

SPRUCES

Spruces (*Picea* species) are tall, mainly conical trees, with horizontal or hanging branches at irregular intervals along the stem. When their needles fall (or are pulled away gently) a small peg is left behind on the stem. This distinguishes spruces from firs, which have round, flat scars where needles have been detached. Spruce needles grow singly, unlike pines, in which the needles grow in bunches. Spruce cones hang down, fir cones are upright or at right angles to the stem, and pine cones are hanging, upright, or at right angles to the stem, depending on the species.

Spruces in which the branches hang and the smaller branches bearing the needles hang down below them have a distinctly weeping habit. Brewer's spruce (*P. breweriana*), also known as weeping spruce and siskiyou spruce, is a striking example, with branches that often touch the ground. A tree up to 130 feet (40 m) tall, it grows in the mountains of Oregon and northwestern California.

At lower altitudes and along the coast from Alaska to California, Sitka (*P. sitchensis*) is the commonest spruce, named after the town of Sitka, in southern Alaska. It grows to 200 feet (60 m) tall and sometimes more, making it the largest North American spruce, and commercially important but probably less so than Engelmann spruce (*P. engelmannii*), a smaller tree, growing to a height of 63–165 feet (20–50 m).

The Colorado spruce (*P. pungens*) has distinctly blue needles. The blue varieties are called glauca (the Latin *glaucus* means "bluish-green" or

"gray"). There is also a variety of blue spruce with pendulous branches, called Kosteriana spruce. Colorado spruce grows up to 165 feet (50 m) tall, at altitudes rather lower than those preferred by Engelmann spruce, from the Yellowstone National Park to Idaho, Utah, and Arizona.

The eastern spruces are the red, white, and black, and all three are of great commercial importance. Red spruce (*P. rubens*) occurs from Nova Scotia south to the Appalachians and Georgia. It grows to a height of 60–100 feet (18–30 m) or more, with trunks 24 inches (60 cm) in diameter, and is grown in plantations for its timber. As its botanical name suggests, white, or Canadian spruce (*P. glauca*) has bluish needles. Growing to a height of 60–70 feet (18–21 m) and sometimes to 120 feet (37 m) it forms pure stands over large areas and elsewhere forms forests with other coniferous trees, birch, aspen, or balsam poplar. It grows naturally in Alaska and across Canada, up to the northern limit for tree growth, and in the east in Labrador, New York, and around the Great Lakes. It shares this range with black spruce (*P. mariana*), a rather larger tree, 65–165 feet (20–30 m) tall, which also has rather bluish needles. Spruce gum is obtained from black spruce.

All the North American spruces produce soft, light-colored, straight-grained, rather lustrous wood, containing very little resin and having no taste or odor. Spruce wood has many uses and, because sounds make it resonate, sounding boards in pianos and the bodies of violins, guitars, and other stringed instruments are often made from it. It is also used to make chipboard, hardboard, and other types of board, and it is the best wood for making rayon and cellophane. Most spruce, however, is pulped to make paper.

Common Gymnosperm Trees of the Old World

Stretching from the shores of the Baltic Sea in the west to the Sea of Okhotsk in the east, from the northern climatic limit for tree growth to the edge of the steppe, the southern shore of Lake Baikal, and the Chinese border in the south, there lies what is by far the biggest forest in the world. This is the taiga, the mainly coniferous forest that forms a great swathe across northern Europe and Siberia, effectively from the Atlantic to the Pacific. It measures more than 10,000 miles (6,200 km) from west to east and covers approximately 2.7 million square miles (6.9 million sq km).

Its composition varies greatly with latitude. In the north it becomes very open, like parkland, as it grades into tundra. In the south, for example to the south of Irkutsk, there are places where it becomes swamp forest, and on mountain slopes it extends into regions covered with mixed or broad-leaved forest at lower altitudes.

Around the Mediterranean, the natural vegetation is sclerophyllous forest (page 5). This comprises broad-leaved evergreen trees as well as conifers. The gymnosperms in this region also include species belonging to the groups found elsewhere.

FIRS

The northern forest is dominated by fir, pine, larch, and spruce, often with juniper. Firs occur in the forests of western and central Siberia, throughout China as far south as the Himalayas, in east Asia and Japan, in Turkey and Syria, in central and southern Europe, and around the Mediterranean. The true firs, all of which belong to the genus *Abies,* are often called silver firs to distinguish them from species that have fir in their common names despite belonging to other genera.

The three most important firs native to Japan are the momi and nikko species and Veitch's fir. The momi, or Japanese fir (*A. firma*) is a conical tree occurring in southern Japan that grows to 100 feet (30 m). The nikko fir (*A. homolepis*) grows to a similar height and is found in the mountain forests of central Japan. Several species of firs are widely cultivated as ornamentals. Nikko fir grows in cities better than most firs, because it is fairly tolerant of air pollution. Like the nikko fir, Veitch's fir (*A. veitchii*) occurs in the mountains of central Japan. It is rather smaller than the nikko fir, reaching about 80 feet (25 m), and although it shares its tolerance for airborne pollutants, it tends not to live for so long.

Korea, to the south of Manchuria and in the same latitude as Japan, is mountainous and the Korean fir (*A. koreana*) is native to the mountains of the south. It is a conical tree and fairly small, growing to no more than 60 feet (18 m) and often less, especially in cultivation.

Further west, the Siberian fir (*A. sibirica*) is the dominant fir over much of the taiga, in central Asia together with the Turkestan fir (*A. semenovi*). The Siberian fir is similar to, and the Old World equivalent of, the North American balsam fir (page 116). These give way in the northern part of the Caucasus to the Caucasian, or Nordmann fir (*A. nordmanniana*), a column-shaped tree that grows to a height of 165 feet (50 m) or more. Continuing westward, the Cilician fir (*A. cilicica*) is native to the mountains of northern Syria and southeastern Turkey, part of the region known in ancient times as Cilicia. The tree grows to about 100 feet (30 m).

The common fir of the mountains of central and southern Europe is the silver fir (*A. alba*), sometimes called the common or European silver fir to distinguish it from other firs that are also called silver. The (common) silver fir grows to about 165 feet (50 m) and occurs naturally at altitudes between 2,600 and 6,000 feet (800–1,800 m). In many parts of Europe this is the species most often used as a Christmas tree.

The sclerophyllous vegetation of the Mediterranean includes three species of fir, their common names identifying the countries in which they occur. In each case they grow naturally only in the mountains. Algerian fir (*A. numidica*) is rather rare in the wild, being confined to just a few areas of the coastal mountains. It is a handsome, almost columnar tree, growing to a height of 80 feet (25 m). It is closely related to the Spanish fir (*A. pinsapo*), which occurs naturally in the mountains of southern Spain. This tree is also known as the hedgehog fir, because its short, rigid needles, about 0.8 inch (2 cm) long, grow all around the stems and stand out almost at right angles, like the prickles on a hedgehog.

HEMLOCKS

Hemlocks (*Tsuga* species) have a much more restricted distribution. In the Old World they occur naturally only in southern China and Japan. Chinese hemlock (*T. chinensis*) is a tall tree, growing to 165 feet (50 m) in its natural habitat, but specimens grown for ornament in other parts of the world are usually very much smaller.

Two species of hemlock are found in Japan, one mainly in the center and north of the country, the other in the south. Like Chinese hemlock, both are much bigger where they grow in natural Japanese forests than they are when cultivated. Northern Japanese hemlock (*T. diversifolia*) reaches a height of about 80 feet (25 m) in Japanese forests, and the southern species, called Japanese, or southern Japanese hemlock (*T. sieboldii*) grows to about 100 feet (30 m), but cultivated specimens of both species reach barely half these heights and are often no bigger than shrubs.

JUNIPERS

Junipers are distributed throughout temperate regions of the northern hemisphere, with some species extending into the Tropics. There are about 60 species of them, all belonging to the genus *Juniperus*. Junipers have two kinds of leaves, although some species, including the common juniper (*J. communis*), bear only the young type. Young leaves are needles, sharply pointed and growing in groups of three or in opposite pairs. Adult leaves are scalelike, pressed closely to the stem and overlapping.

Most juniper species are small trees or shrubs and some alpine and subarctic varieties of the common juniper are no more than 12 inches (30 cm) tall, but there are also quite tall juniper trees and just below the treeline on the mountains of Europe and Asia there are forests dominated by juniper. Where it is obtainable, juniper wood is used in building, for fences and roof shingles, and for making furniture. Juniper also yields aromatic oils and tars with many pharmaceutical, perfumery, and other uses. It is also used as a flavoring for some meats, especially venison, and in gin. The word gin is a corruption of "geneva," which has nothing to do with the Swiss city, but is from *genévrier*, the French for "juniper tree."

Chinese juniper (*J. chinensis*) can be a low shrub, but it also occurs as a tree shaped like a narrow cone and 65 feet (20 m) tall that occurs in Mongolia, China, the Himalayas, and in Japan. It is often cultivated in gardens and parks, and there are many varieties. The needle, or temple, juniper (*J. rigida*) is one of the species that produces only juvenile, needlelike leaves, the feature which gives it its common name of needle juniper. It grows naturally in Japan, Korea, and Manchuria, where it is sometimes a small tree, about 43 feet (13 m) tall with branches that hang down, and sometimes a shrub. In cultivation it is usually a shrub. Drooping juniper (*J. recurva*) also produces only needlelike leaves, growing in threes, but in this species they are crowded together, overlapping, and pressed close to the stem, and the plant itself is a shrub or small tree about 33 feet (10 m) tall, with spreading, hanging branches. It grows in southwestern China, the Himalayas, and in Burma, where the variety *coxii* is called the coffin juniper, because its wood is used to make coffins.

Junipers also form part of the vegetation of the Mediterranean region and Near East. Syrian juniper (*J. drupacea*) is a narrow, conical tree 33–40 feet (10–12 m) tall, bearing only juvenile needle leaves, that grows in Syria and other parts of Asia Minor, as well as in Greece. Prickly juniper (*J. oxycedrus*) also occurs in Syria and east as far as the Caucasus, as well as in Spain and North Africa. It has only needle leaves and is a small tree about 33 feet (10 m) tall.

Despite its name, Spanish juniper (*J. thurifera*) has a range extending from the Caucasus through Asia Minor, across North Africa and into southwestern Europe. It bears adult, scale leaves and is a tree about 40 feet (12 m) tall. Phoenician juniper (*J. phoenicia*), also bearing scale leaves, grows all around the Mediterranean and in the Canary Islands.

LARCHES

Larch (*Larix* species) occurs in the Alps and the mountains of eastern Europe and then throughout most of the Asian taiga and into Japan (see map, page 118). They are one of the commonest trees in the taiga and also occur further south, in the mixed forests. Over most of the taiga the Siberian larch (*L. sibirica*) is predominant, a tall tree, reaching a height of 100 feet (30 m). East of the Yenisei River, the Siberian larch first mixes and hybridizes with, then gives way to the Daurian or

Dahurian larch (*L. gmelinii* or *dahurica*). The Daurian or Dahurian region is a large area of plains and low hills, with an extreme continental climate and areas of permafrost. It takes its name from the Dagur (*Dahur* is the Latinized form), a people living in northern Manchuria. The Daurian larch tolerates a wide variety of soils and has very shallow roots, which allows the tree to find water very efficiently in the upper soil. This enables Daurian larches to grow in permafrost areas and their range extends further north than that of any other larch.

Japanese larch (*L. kaempferi*) is a much bigger tree, reaching a height of 100 feet (30 m). It occurs naturally in the mountains of Japan. In 1861 it was introduced in Britain and around 1910 foresters became interested in it because it grows faster than the native European larch (*L. decidua*) and seemed to thrive better in the British climate. Consequently it began to be grown widely in commercial plantations. About 1904, larches of both species were growing on the estate of the Duke of Atholl, at Dunkeld in Scotland, and female flowers of *L. kaempferi* were pollinated by male flowers of *L. decidua*. The resulting hybrid, known as Dunkeld larch (*L. x eurolepis*) or hybrid larch, exhibits heterosis, or hybrid vigor. This means the first-cross hybrids grow faster than either parent, are more resistant to pests and diseases, and are more tolerant of poor soils. They are now grown widely in plantations, from seed produced in nurseries where the two parent species are grown in alternate rows to increase the likelihood of cross-fertilization.

PINES

Pines (*Pinus* species) are probably the most widespread coniferous trees in temperate regions of the Old World. Except for the far north and the steppelands and deserts of the continental interior, they occur throughout Europe and Asia north of the Himalayas. Pines grow over such a vast area because they tolerate a wide variety of soil and climatic conditions. In the taiga, forests of Scotch pine (*P. sylvestris*), stone pine (*P. cembra* or *sibirica*), and larch occupy more than half the total area.

Scotch pine, the only conifer native to Britain (and the subspecies *scotica* grows naturally only in Scotland), has needles growing in pairs. The tree reaches a height of 65–130 feet (20–40 m), with a straight trunk up to 4 feet (1.2 m) in diameter. It is one of the hard pines, with a range extending from the Atlantic to Kamchatka. The Norsemen of old knew it as the *fur*, and it is often called fir in Britain, Germany, and Scandinavia, although it is a true pine (*Pinus*), not a fir (*Abies*). It forms an important component of the forests of Germany and Poland as well as the taiga proper.

Swiss and German woodcarvings, which are famous, are best made with the wood of the stone pine, a soft pine also known as the Swiss stone pine, Siberian stone pine, arolla pine, and, in Russia, the cedar. It grows to about 80 feet (25 m), sometimes more. As its names suggest, its range is wide. It occurs in the Alps at altitudes of 4,000–6,000 feet (1,200–1,800 m), over the whole of the west Siberian plain and basin of the Yenisei River, and it also occurs in America. Its seeds yield an oil used locally for cooking and formerly for lamps.

In the Far East, the Scotch and stone pines are joined by several species with a very local distribution, including the mourning pine (*P. funebris*), an endangered species, the Korean cedar pine (*P. koraiensis*), and the Japanese dwarf pine (*P. mugo* or *pumilia*), a stunted tree that occurs on mountain ridges. The same hard pine also grows in the mountains of central Europe, where it is known as the mountain pine. It closely resembles Scotch pine, but seldom grows larger than a bush, with long stems that sometimes take root where they touch the ground. In German-speaking regions it is called *Krummholz* (literally, "crooked wood") or *Knieholz* ("knee-(high)-wood"). Another tree is also known as the mountain pine. This is *P. uncinata,* a much bigger tree, up to 80 feet (25 m) tall, which grows in the mountains of southern Europe from the Pyrenees to the Alps.

A little to the east, the Austrian pine (*P. nigra*) grows in Austria and the Balkans. A fine tree, often planted elsewhere for ornament, it grows to a height of 130 feet (40 m) or more. Its straight, fairly rigid needles grow in pairs and are 3.5–6.3 inches (9–16 cm) long. It has no value as a timber tree, but is sometimes used in shelter belts and, because it is very bushy when young, as a "nurse" tree that protects seedlings of a more valuable species and is removed once thay have grown big enough to fend for themselves. The subspecies *P. n. maritima* is the Corsican pine, in which the needles are 4.7–7.0 inches (12–18 cm) long and immediately recognizable because they are twisted. Corsican pine is an important timber tree.

At altitudes of 7,000–12,000 feet (2,100–3,700 m) in Bhutan, parts of Nepal, and Afghanistan, the Himalayan, Bhutan, or blue pine (*P. wallichiana,* a soft pine also known as *P. griffithii* and *P. excelsa*) usually grows about 115 feet (35 m) tall, but can reach 165 feet (50 m). The "blue" in its name refers to the bloom on its needles. These grow in bunches of five and are 4.7–8.0 inches (12–20 cm) long. The Chinese pine (*P. tabuliformis*), a tree about 80 feet (25 m) tall, grows in southern China and Korea, and in northwestern China there is the lace-bark pine (*P. bungeana*), a tree of similar size. Its common name refers to the way patches of its bark fall away, exposing the brightly colored wood beneath.

Aleppo pine (*P. halepensis*) is a fairly small tree, up to 50 feet (15 m) tall, that grows around the shores of the Mediterranean and in parts of the Near East including, of course, the area around the town of Aleppo, in Syria. In Italy and elsewhere in the Mediterranean region, the Italian stone pine (*P. pinea*) is also known as the umbrella pine, because of its shape. Since the days of ancient Rome and still today, it has been grown for its edible seeds, called pignons (the name means "pine-nut," those sold in America as "pignoli" are probably from *P. edulis*, the nut pine). These ripen when they are nearly four years old and are kept in their cones until needed, to prevent the oils they contain from oxidizing and becoming rancid. At the western end of the Mediterranean and in North Africa, the cluster or maritime pine (*P. pinaster*) is a tree about 100 feet (30 m) tall that grows vigorously in coastal sand. It has been used extensively to stabilize sand dunes on the coasts of the Bay of Biscay and, to a lesser extent, in many other parts of the region and even in southern England, where it has become naturalized. On some sandy soils in France cluster pines have provided protection for other trees, so whole forests have developed.

ARBORVITAE

Arborvitae (*Thuja* species) are trees usually associated with America, where they include cedars of commercial importance, but several species occur in China and Japan. Most are fairly small, the Korean arborvitae (*T. koraiensis*) often being no more than a shrub, but sometimes growing into a conical tree about 30 feet (9 m) high. Chinese arborvitae (*T. orientalis*), of northern and western China, is of similar size, while the Japanese arborvitae (*T. standishii*) is bigger, growing into a handsome, conical tree about 65 feet (20 m) tall.

Hiba arborvitae differs from the others in having much broader branchlets (twigs) bearing larger scale leaves and much more rounded cones with thicker scales. It also grows much more densely near its base than other arborvitae. These differences have persuaded scientists to classify it in a genus of its own, *Thujopsis dolobrata*. It is a handsome tree, shaped like a pyramid and growing to a height of about 50 feet (15 m) and there are many cultivated ornamental varieties. In Japan, where it occurs naturally, its wood is used for building.

SPRUCES

Spruce (*Picea* species) occurs throughout temperate regions of the Northern Hemisphere and on mountainsides in lower latitudes. Like firs, these trees have dense foliage and they cast a deep shade, making natural spruce and fir forests dark, gloomy places. Often they are eerily quiet, for their shelter means there is little air movement near ground level.

Over much of the western part of the taiga Norway spruce (*P. abies*) is the commonest species, recognizable by its thick, blunt needles, red-brown shoots, and long cones. This is the tree most widely used in northern Europe as a Christmas tree, especially for the big trees erected in public open places, although in Germany the common silver fir (*Tannenbaum* in German) is preferred. The Christmas tree that stands every year in Trafalgar Square, London, is a Norway spruce donated by the people of Norway to the people of London. Norway spruce is a slender, conical tree that grows to a height of 165 feet (50 m). It yields timber that is widely used as "white wood" or "white deal." Purified, its resin is known as Burgundy tar, used in high quality varnishes, and its leaves and shoots are processed to make Swiss turpentine or, processed in a different way, to make a spicy alcoholic drink known as spruce beer. Its bark is used in tanning leather.

As its name suggests, Serbian spruce (*P. omorika*) occurs naturally in Serbia and Bosnia-Herzegovina, especially on limestone soils near the River Drina, and less commonly in other parts of southern Europe. It is a narrow, almost columnar tree that reaches a height of about 100 feet (30 m). It is cultivated for ornament and in northern Europe grown for timber. Its branches are more or less horizontal and its leaves are flattened with pointed ends, distinguishing the tree from most spruces, which have needles that are diamond-shaped in cross section. The needles are 0.5–0.7 inch (1.2–1.8 cm) long and in two rows on either side of the stem and almost at right angles to it, like the teeth of a comb (the technical term for this arrangement is pectinate).

South of the Kirghiz Steppe of central Asia, the Tien Shan mountain range runs about 1,520 miles (2,450 km) from west to east. Its lower slopes are covered with broad-leaved forest, but above about 5,600 feet (1,700 m) this gives way to spruce forest, dominated by dense pure stands of Tien Shan spruce (*P. tianshanica*).

To the south of the Tien Shan range, Himalayan spruce (*P. smithiana*) grows in the western Himalayas. Also known as west Himalayan spruce, morinda spruce, and khutrow, the Smith of its botanical name is Sir James Edward Smith (1759–1828). Carolus Linnaeus (Carl von Linné, 1707–78) was the Swedish botanist who introduced the system of using two names to classify plants and animals. After he died, Sir James Smith bought his manuscripts and natural history collection and took them to London. When the Linnean Society was founded, in 1788, Smith became its first president and after his death the material from Linnaeus was bought by the society, which still owns it. Himalayan spruce is a large tree, usually growing to a height of 100–165 feet (30–50 m) but some grow much taller, and it is an important timber tree in forests at around 10,000 feet (3,000 m). It has a weeping shape, much like that of Brewer's spruce (page 120). An even taller tree grows at the opposite end of the Himalayas. Sikkim, or east Himalayan spruce (*P. spinulosa*) can grow to a height of 200 feet (60 m).

To the east of the mountains, several spruces occur in western China. Chinese, or dragon spruce (*P. asperata*) is an attractive tree, with rather blue foliage, that is often grown as an ornamental. In natural forests it can be 100 feet (30 m) tall, but most cultivated specimens are smaller. Likiany, or Likiang spruce (*P. likiangensis*) was first discovered near the town of Lichiang in Yunnan Province of western China, which gives it its name, and the tree also occurs in Tibet. It grows to a height of about 100 feet (30 m) and the outermost two rows of needles on each stem overlap like tiles (the technical term for this arrangement is imbricate) and point forward.

Several species of spruce are native to Japan. Alcock spruce (*P. bicolor*) is similar to Sakhalin spruce, although smaller, reaching only about 80 feet (25 m). Both species, and also Likiany spruce, have needles that are diamond-shaped in cross section, but somewhat flattened, so the diamonds are wider than they are high. Tiger-tail spruce (*P. polita*) can grow to 130 feet (40 m) and is grown for ornament in Europe and America. Its shiny, deep green, four-sided needles are 0.6–0.8 inch (1.5–2.0 cm) long, curved, stiff, and with a very sharp point, rather like the claws of a cat. Yeddo spruce (*P. jezoensis*) grows to 165 feet (50 m) and occurs over much of northeast Asia as well as Japan. Its needles, 0.4–0.8 inch (1–2 cm) long, are pointed but not sharp like those of the tiger-tail spruce. Hondo spruce is a variety (*hondoensis*) of this species with shorter needles that thrives better in cultivation.

YEWS

Yews (*Taxus* species) differ from coniferous trees in not producing seeds in cones and in lacking resin canals in their wood and leaves. Instead of cones, their seeds are contained in a fleshy, scarlet covering. This is the only part of the plant that is not extremely poisonous to all mammals. Fallen leaves and twigs remain poisonous, even when they are brown and withered. Because they are so dangerous, farmers clear yews from their land, but they are dangerous only if eaten; yews are perfectly safe to touch. They are most often found in graveyards, where they are not disturbed and can reach a great age (1,000 years or more), and in gardens, where they are grown for ornament. Cultivated varieties are often cut and trained into exotic shapes and they make excellent tall, dense hedges. In places, however, they survive in forests. Their hard, durable wood is valuable but not easily obtained, and used for floor blocks, panels, and veneers in cabinet-making. Traditionally it was the preferred material for making longbows.

The common, or English yew (*T. baccata*) occurs naturally throughout Europe, North Africa, and the Near and Middle East. It grows to a height of 40–65 feet (12–20 m) and has flat leaves, narrow but not quite needles, up to 1 inch (2.5 cm) long and usually in two rows, one on either side of the stem.

Japanese yew (*T. cuspidata*) occurs in the forests of eastern Siberia and China as well as Japan. Its leaves are similar to those of the common yew but are not arranged in two rows. Chinese yew (*T. celebica*) reaches no more than about 40 feet (12 m), often less, and is barely more than a shrub. It occurs widely in China and Taiwan and its range extends almost to the equator in the Philippines and Sulawesi, Indonesia.

Angiosperm Trees

Common Angiosperms of the New World

The broad-leaved forests of temperate regions occur in latitudes immediately below those of the boreal forest, or taiga, with which they merge across wide belts of forest comprising both broad-leaved and coniferous trees. In higher latitudes, the broad-leaved trees are deciduous, as an adaptation to the low temperature and aridity of winter, when water is likely to be frozen. In lower latitudes many broad-leaved trees are evergreen, and in Mediterranean climates often sclerophyllous. Many of the broad-leaved tree genera found in temperate forests continue into the Tropics and equatorial regions.

ALDER

Alders (*Alnus* species) not only tolerate cool weather and wet ground, they positively prefer them. This allows them to grow beside rivers and lakes, where the soil is wet but their roots can remain above the water table. In some places they form pure stands, as alderwoods, either isolated from other types of forest or enclosed by it to form distinct regions beside rivers and lakes and in low-lying areas within the main forest.

They are small trees and shrubs, with simple, alternate leaves. Their flowers are catkins and their fruits are woody and look very like small pine cones.

Alders occur in America from the northern limit for tree growth, in Alaska and across Canada, throughout North America except for desert regions, through Central America, and down the western side of South America.

Probably the most widespread species are the American green alder and Sitka alder. The American green alder (*A. crispa*), growing to about 10 feet (3 m), grows in the mountains of the east, from Labrador to North Carolina. Sitka alder (*A. sinuata*) grows in the west, from Alaska (Sitka is an Alaskan town) to Northern California. It is slightly taller, reaching about 43 feet (13 m).

Alder bark is sometimes used in tanning leather, and Native Americans used to hollow out the main stems of the red, or Oregon alder (*A. rubra*) to make canoes. Today the wood is still used to make furniture and paper. It also occurs naturally in the west, from Alaska to California, Idaho, and Oregon, as a tree up to 80 feet (25 m) tall. The name "red" refers to its shoots, which are bright red.

ASH

Ashes (*Fraxinus* species) are small trees and shrubs occurring from the Great Lakes south as far as Mexico. Their leaves are opposite and their flowers usually have no petals. The fruit is a samara, a seed with a single wing, produced in bunches.

White ash (*F. americana*) is a tree up to 130 feet (40 m) tall that grows in eastern North America. It is cultivated as an ornamental and, like most ashes, its wood is valuable for furniture and interior carpentry. Other species occurring naturally in the east are also known by colors. Red ash, or green ash (*F. pennsylvanica*) is a smaller tree, reaching no more than 65 feet (20 m). Blue ash (*F. quadrangulata*) is much the same size and black ash (*F. nigra*) grows to about 100 feet (30 m). All four species are commercial sources of timber. Small

Alder catkins (male), temperate North America

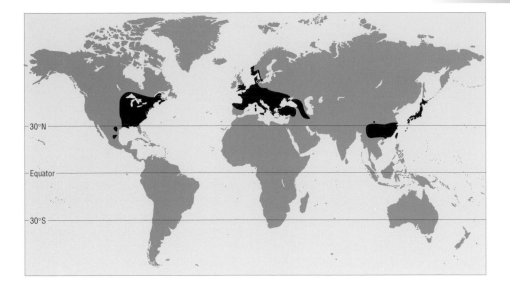

World distribution of beeches

amounts of wood are also obtained from the pumpkin ash (*F. profunda*), a small tree that grows in the coastal swamps of the southeastern states.

ASPEN, COTTONWOOD, BALSAM POPLAR, POPLAR

Aspens, cottonwoods, balsam poplars, and poplars all belong to the genus *Populus* and occur throughout the temperate regions of the Northern Hemisphere. They grow quickly into medium-sized or large trees. Their flowers are catkins that appear before the leaves, and the fruits are capsules with long silky hairs at their bases. These look rather like cotton bolls, which is why some species are known in America as cottonwoods.

Populus trees are divided botanically into four types of which one occurs naturally only in China. Those found in North America are the white and gray poplars and aspens; the balsam poplars; and the black poplars and cottonwoods. Trees hybridize readily within their own groups, but less commonly with members of other groups. Wood from poplars is light, strong, odorless, and fairly nonflammable. It is used to make food containers, brake blocks for railroad cars, matches, and long ago it was the best wood for making arrows.

Quaking aspen, or American aspen (*P. tremuloides*) has the largest range of any North American tree, occurring from Alaska in the west and Labrador and Newfoundland in the east, south to Pennsylvania, Missouri, and Nebraska, and extending into the Sierra Nevada and Mexico. Its leaves grow on flat stems, which makes them tremble in the slightest breeze. It is a large tree, growing to a height of 100 feet (30 m).

In the second group, the balsam poplar or tacamahac (*P. balsamifera*) occurs naturally in the north, from Labrador to Alaska and south across the northern United States. It is a big tree, up to 100 feet (30 m) tall. Balsam is a resinous gum, sometimes used as an ointment, that has a strong fragrance. The balsam poplars exude it from their leaf buds, releasing a pleasant odor in spring. The balm of Gilead, which grows wild in the northeastern United States and southeastern Canada and was once very popular as an ornamental, is a natural hybrid (*P. X candicans*) of uncertain origin, but possibly between the balsam poplar and the eastern cottonwood. On the western side of the continent, from Alaska south to California, the western balsam poplar or black cottonwood (*P. trichocarpa*), is a quick-growing tree, up to 120 feet (37 m) tall or sometimes to 200 feet (60 m), with timber that is used for veneering and pulping.

Cottonwoods proper—comprising the third group, of trees with more or less triangular leaves—include the eastern cottonwood or necklace poplar (*P. deltoides*), a large, broad tree, growing to a height of 150 feet (45 m). Although native to the east, its range extends from Quebec to Montana and south to Texas and Florida. It is an important source of timber and is planted extensively along city streets. Many ornamental varieties and hybrids are cultivated.

BASSWOOD, LIME, LINDEN

Basswoods, limes, and lindens all belong to the genus *Tilia*, which occurs naturally over the eastern half of the United States. These are all moderate-sized trees with broad, toothed leaves borne on long stalks. They thrive on moist soil that is neither very acid nor alkaline. *Tilia* wood has many uses and is especially popular for making piano keys.

Basswood, or American basswood, American lime, or American linden (*T. americana*) occurs naturally in the northeastern United States and southeastern Canada, but has been planted in the streets and squares of cities over most of America. It grows as a conical tree, to a height of about 70 feet (21 m), then broadens to produce a dome-shaped crown with big leaves, about 4.7 x 4.0 inches (12 x 10 cm). White basswood (*T. heterophylla*) also grows in the east. It may be a variety of *T. americana*, but its leaves are somewhat smaller.

BEECH

Like *Tilia*, beeches (*Fagus* species) occur naturally in the eastern United States and part of southeastern Canada. There is only one native species and its distribution is shown in the figure (left). American beech (*F. grandifolia*) grows to about 80 feet (25 m). Where it grows near cultivated beeches from other parts of the world it can be identified by its leaves. These are larger than those of most species and have clearly marked serrations around the edges.

SOUTHERN BEECH

Southern beeches (*Nothofagus species*) are close relatives of beeches and interesting because of their discontinuous distribution (page 8). They occur only in the Southern Hemisphere and, in the New World, only in Chile and southern Argentina, but there are several species.

Some are large. Coigue, or Dombey's southern beech (*N. dombeyi*), of central and southern Chile, can grow to a height of 165 feet (50 m). It is a broad-leaved evergreen, as are the coigue de Magallanes (*N. betuloides*) and roble de Chiloe (*N. nitida*). Both occur in Chile and Argentina, coigue de Magallanes in the south of the region and roble de Chiloe to its north, and both are trees up to 100 feet (30 m) tall. *Roble* is the Spanish word for oak. Southern beeches are not oaks, of course, but their timber is very similar, which is how some of the commercially important species have earned this name.

BIRCH

Birches (*Betula* species) grow naturally throughout the Northern Hemisphere, the ranges of some of them extending into the Arctic, including southern Greenland. They are deciduous, broad-leaved, wind-pollinated trees or shrubs with flowers as catkins that emerge at the same time as the leaves. Many have very attractive bark, especially the paper birch or canoe birch (*B. papyrifera*), which has bark that peels off in layers, like sheets of paper. It is the most widespread of all North American birches, occurring over the northern parts of the continent from Labrador to Alaska and to New England, Nebraska, and Washington. Its height varies from about 50–100 feet (15–30 m) and it is widely planted for ornament, in the Old World as well as the New. Its bark is waterproof and was used by Native Americans for covering canoes. The wood is also used for roofing and fuel.

Sweet birch, also called black birch and cherry birch (*B. lenta*) occurs in eastern North America and is a source of timber, used mainly for flooring and furniture, in Pennsylvania and West Virginia. The name "sweet birch" refers to the sweet-smelling oil that is obtained from its bark and wood. Its bark is very dark, which is why it is called the black birch, and reminiscent of the bark of a cherry tree. It grows to about 80 feet (25 m).

As a timber tree, yellow birch (*B. alleghaniensis,* formerly known as *B. lutea*) is much more important. Its wood has many uses, for flooring, furniture, and boxes. In World War II, the frames of the wings and fuselage of the Mosquito fighter bomber were made from it. The tree grows to 100 feet (30 m) from Newfoundland to western Minnesota and south to Georgia.

BUCKEYE, HORSE CHESTNUT

Buckeyes or horse chestnuts (*Aesculus* species) are deciduous trees and shrubs that occur naturally throughout the United States. The "buckeye" of the name is the seed, which is large, shiny, and known in Britain as a "conker."

Red buckeye (*A. pavia*) grows to about 13 feet (4 m). Native to the southeastern United States, it is cultivated widely as an ornamental, partly for its flowers and partly for its foliage, which turns a brilliant red at the end of the summer. Sweet buckeye or yellow buckeye (*A. flava* or *A. octandra*) grows in the same region, but is a substantial tree, growing to 100 feet (30 m). Ohio buckeye (*A. glabra*) is a tree up to 26 feet (8 m) tall that grows naturally in the central and southeastern United States. In the west, the California buckeye (*A. californica*) is a tree up to 40 feet (12 m) tall.

CHERRY

Cherries belong to the genus *Prunus,* along with plums, apricots, peaches, and almonds, and there are about 200 species in the world as a whole. The pin cherry or wild red cherry (*P. pennsylvanica*) grows naturally in North American forests. Despite its name it has a range extending from the Atlantic to the Rockies. It is a tree up to 40 feet (12 m) tall.

CHESTNUT AND ELM

Chestnuts (*Castanea* species) occur naturally in the eastern and southeastern United States, but American chestnut (*C. dentata*), once an important component of many forests, is now uncommon, having been almost destroyed by chestnut blight (page 108).

Elms (*Ulmus* species) have also suffered, although Dutch elm disease may have affected

Pacific dogwood leaves, temperate west North America (Michael Durham)

North America less severely than it did Britain. Nevertheless, American elm, or white elm (*U. americana*) is no longer so familiar a shade tree on American streets, squares, and campuses. It is a big, handsome tree, reaching a height of 130 feet (40 m), native in southeastern Canada and throughout the United States east of the Rockies. Many individual trees have been named for famous people. The American elm is an important source of timber, used for many purposes.

Slippery elm (*U. rubra*) is about half the size of American elm. It occurs naturally within an area defined by a line drawn from Quebec to North Dakota and from there to Texas. The "slippery" of its name refers to a fragrant, mucilaginous substance with therapeutic properties obtained from its inner bark. Branches and twigs of the cork elm, or rock elm (*U. thomasii*) have flanges, or "wings," of cork. This tree grows to about 100 feet (30 m) and occurs naturally in the northeastern United States and eastern Canada. It yields hard, dense wood.

DOGWOOD

Dogwoods (*Cornus* species) occur over the eastern half of North America south of the Great Lakes and in the west from northern California to British Columbia. Flowering dogwood (*C. florida*) grows up to 23 feet (7 m) tall in the understory of forests in the east. Nuttall's dogwood or Pacific dogwood (*C. nuttalli*) grows in the west. Most specimens are up to 50 feet (16 m) tall, but some reach 100 feet (30 m).

GUM

Gums are deciduous trees which form an important component of forests in the southern United States and Central America. There are two distinct types. Sweet gum (*Liquidambar styraciflua*), found in the southeastern United States, Mexico, and Guatemala, is a deciduous tree growing to about 150 feet (45 m) in the wild, but barely one-third that size when cultivated, which it often is for its magnificent fall colors. Its valuable timber is sometimes called satin walnut.

The other gums, or tupelos, belong to the genus *Nyssa*. The best known is the black gum, tupelo, or pepperidge (*N. sylvatica*), a tree somewhat similar to an oak. It grows to about 100 feet (30 m) in swamps or moist soil on hillsides, and is much cultivated for its fall foliage. Water gum, twin-flowered nyssa, or tupelo (*N. biflora*) is similar, but only about half the size, and *N. ursina*, the third member of the group in which the flowers are borne in groups of two or more, is a shrub.

The second group, in which flowers are borne singly, contains three species. The cotton gum, or water tupelo (*N. aquatica*) grows to about 100 feet (30 m) and the sour tupelo, ogeche lime, or ogeche plum (*N. ogeche*) grows to about 30 feet (9 m) on riverbanks. As its common names suggest, its fruits are edible. *N. acuminata* is a shrub, about 16 feet (5 m) tall, occurring in pine swamps. All the tupelos yield a valuable wood.

HICKORY

Hickories (*Carya* species) are deciduous trees, belonging to the same family (Juglandaceae) as walnuts, that occur naturally throughout North America east of the Great Lakes. They grow fast, yield valuable timber, and their fruits are nuts, which are edible in some species. The trees are often cultivated for their nuts and also for ornament.

The most important edible nut is the pecan, obtained from the tree of the same name (*C. illinoensis*). It grows in the Mississippi Basin (its fruits were once known as Mississippi nuts), rapidly reaching a height of 150 feet (45 m). Bitternut hickory, or swamp hickory (*C. cordiformis*) is

smaller, growing to about 90 feet (27 m). The coating to its nuts contains so much tannin the nuts are inedible. The nuts of water hickory, or bitter pecan (*C. aquatica*) are also inedible for the same reason. It is a small tree, about 50 feet (15 m) tall, that grows in swamps and rice fields.

In addition to the pecan, shagbark (*C. ovata*), big shellbark (*C. laciniosa*), and Carolina (*C. carolinae-septentrionalis*) hickories are the most important sources of edible nuts. Shagbark hickory, or little shellbark hickory, yielding hickory nuts, is a tree up to 118 feet (36 m) tall that sheds its bark in narrow strips. The big shellbark hickory, or kingnut, is very similar, but its kingnuts are yellow-brown, rather than white, like hickory nuts. All the hickories produce useful wood, used traditionally for making the handles of tools.

HOLLY

Holly (*Ilex* species) often form part of the understory in broad-leaved forests and about 15 species occur naturally in the New World. Most species are evergreen, but not all, and they grow naturally in the southeastern United States and Central America. The most widespread is American holly (*I. opaca*), which is a small tree, up to 50 feet (15 m) tall. It produces red berries. The inkberry (*I. glabra*) produces black ones. It is a shrub no more than 6.5 feet (2 m) tall. Another bearer of red berries is emetic holly (*I. vomitoria*), also known as Carolina tea, cassena, Indian black drink, and yaupon, a tree up to 26 feet (8 m) tall. It was used medicinally by Native Americans in the Southeast and some Caribbean islands, where it occurs naturally.

Red holly berries are used for Christmas decoration, usually with their leaves, but not in the case of the winterberry, or dogberry, or black alder (*I. verticillata*) a shrub up to 10 feet (3 m) tall that grows in swamps. It is deciduous, its leaves turning black before they fall, but the berries

remaining. Smooth winterberry, or hoopwood (*I. laevigata*) is very similar and also grows in swamps, as is the possum haw (*I. decidua*), a shrub or small tree, up to 33 feet (10 m) tall.

HORNBEAM

Only one species of hornbeams (*Carpinus* species) occurs naturally in North America. This is the American hornbeam, or American muscle tree, or blue beech (*C. caroliniana*) and, as the map below shows, it is distributed over much of the western part of the United States and Central America. It is a small tree, growing slowly to about 40 feet (12 m). It is often planted for ornament, because of the splendid fall colors of its leaves, and its wood is used mainly to make tool handles.

MAGNOLIA

Magnolias (*Magnolia* species) are famous for their large, showy flowers and are cultivated widely. Some are evergreen and some deciduous. They occur naturally in the southeastern United States, extending into Central America, and in southern and eastern Asia. The genus is named for Pierre Magnol (1638–1715), a French professor of botany and medicine.

The most important American forest species are the Fraser and southern magnolias. Fraser magnolia, or ear-leaved umbrella tree (*M. fraseri*) is deciduous, grows to about 40 feet (12 m), and produces big, fragrant flowers. It occurs in the southern Appalachians. Southern magnolia, or evergreen magnolia, or laurel magnolia, or bull bay (*M. grandiflora*) is a pyramid-shaped, evergreen tree up to 100 feet (30 m) tall, with fragrant, cream-colored flowers up to 12 inches (30 cm) across, that grows on the southeastern coastal plain. The umbrella tree (*M. tripetala*), up to 40 feet (12 m) tall, produces flowers with a strong and unpleasant smell. It is closely related to the southern magnolia, and so is bigleaf magnolia

World distribution of hornbeam

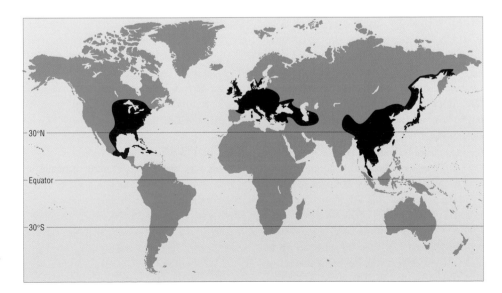

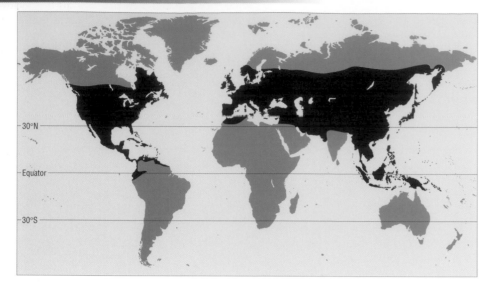

World distribution of oaks

(*M. macrophylla*), a rather larger tree that produces leaves 12–40 inches (30–100 cm) long and flowers up to 14 inches (35 cm) across.

MAPLE

Maples, comprising more than 100 species of *Acer*, are distributed throughout the temperate regions of the Northern Hemisphere and in places extending into the Tropics. As a commercial source of timber, the Oregon maple, or bigleaf maple (*A. macrophyllum*) is probably the most important native species. It occurs from Alaska to California and is a tall tree, growing to 100 feet (30 m). The vine maple (*A. circinatum*), up to 40 feet (12 m) tall, is the only other maple native to the Pacific Coast. It grows on riverbanks from British Columbia to California. Further inland, rock maple, or dwarf maple (*A. glabrum*) and bigtooth maple (*A. grandidentatum*) grow near mountain streams. Both are small trees, up to 40 feet (12 m) tall.

Apart from timber, the best known maple product is the syrup, obtained from the sap by a process devised by Native Americans living around the Great Lakes and near the St. Lawrence River. Syrup is produced mainly from the sugar maple (*A. saccharum*), a tree up to 80 feet (25 m) tall and, to a lesser extent, from the very similar black maple (*A. nigrum*). The leaf of the sugar maple, in its red, fall color, is the national emblem of Canada.

Red maple (*A. rubrum*) grows to about 100 feet (30 m) and is found in most natural woods on low-lying sites in the East. It is often cultivated for its spectacular fall colors, as is the silver maple (*A. saccharinum*), which grows naturally from Quebec to Florida. Striped maple, or moosebark, or moosewood (*A. pennsylvanicum*), a tree up to 40 feet (12 m) tall, often occurs in the understory of eastern maple forests. As its name indicates, its smooth bark is striped green and white. It also has large leaves that turn bright red in the fall. On higher ground its place may be taken by mountain maple (*A. spicatum*), which grows to about 25 feet (7.5 m).

OAK

Oaks (*Quercus* species) belong to the same family (Fagaceae) as beeches and southern beeches. Most are trees, but some are shrubs, some are deciduous and others are evergreen.

There are about 600 species of oaks and, as the figure above shows, they occur naturally throughout most of the temperate Northern Hemisphere, extending through Central America and the Caribbean islands into the northern Andes and in Asia reaching through the Malayan Peninsula and Indonesia. Outside the temperate regions oaks are found only in mountain ranges, where temperatures are cool. They grow from sea level to an altitude of 13,000 feet (4,000 m). The widest variety is found in North America, with more than 85 native species, where oaks form an important component of many forests, the greatest concentration of species occurring in the Sierra Madre highlands of Mexico.

Commercially, oaks are of great importance. Their timber is one of the strongest, most durable of hardwoods. Timbers from different species are often classified as red or white oak. White oak is the harder and more durable, but both types are used for the same purposes.

Most of the oaks native to North America are large trees and many provide valuable timber. Those occurring in the eastern United States yield some of the finest timber in the world for structural use and cabinetmaking, but oaks have other uses. Some supply fuel, others acorns that are edible for humans or farm livestock, tannins used in tanning leather and formerly for making blue-black ink, from oak marble galls induced by the gall wasp *Andricus kollari*. Bark from the black oak is the source of quercitrin, which is processed to make yellow flavine and red flavine, the basis of dyes used to color wool. Many species are grown for ornament, some of them producing spectacular colors in fall. Oaks also feature strongly in folklore and literature (page 146).

Evergreen oaks are often known as live oaks. Most North American oaks are deciduous, but some species are evergreen. The live oak (*Q. virginiana*) is said to produce the most durable of all oak timbers. It used to have many uses, including shipbuilding, but is now scarce. It grows to about 65 feet (20 m) and occurs in the southern states and Mexico. Californian live oak, or encina (*Q. agrifolia*), found in California, is somewhat larger, reaching 80 feet (25 m). Along the coastal ranges of California and southern Oregon, on mountainsides up to about 9,000 feet (2,800 m), there is the canyon live oak, or maul oak (*Q. chrysolepis*). It is only about 60 feet (18 m) tall, but more than twice as wide as it is high, with strong wood that was formerly used to make farm tools. The interior live oak (*Q. wislizenii*) has leaves resembling those of holly.

Laurel oak (*Q. laurifolia*), found along the Gulf Coast and in Florida, is semievergreen, which means it retains some of its leaves through the year. It is a tall tree, growing to 100 feet (30 m). The laurel oak growing in the uplands is *Q. haemispherica*. Willow oak (*Q. phellos*), native to the coastal plains of the southeastern United States, is semievergreen in the southern part of its range and deciduous further north. It is a tall tree, growing to 65–100 feet (20–30 m) with leaves resembling those of a willow, which give it its name. These are yellow when they first open, then turn green, and in fall turn yellow again. Willow oak is grown as a shade tree along streets and is also an important source of red oak timber.

Other oaks are deciduous. The white oak (*Q. alba*) is the source of some of the most valuable timber, used for shipbuilding, to make railroad sleepers, furniture, and barrels. It is a huge tree, growing to a height of 150–165 feet (45–50 m), with a trunk up to 5 feet (1.5 m) across, that occurs on the eastern side of the continent. Burr oak, or mossy cup oak (*Q. macrocarpa*), another eastern species, is even bigger, sometimes reaching 180 feet (55 m), with a trunk as much as 7 feet (2 m) in diameter. The name mossy cup refers to a fringe of scales, resembling hairs, around the rim of the acorn cup.

Chestnut oak, or basket oak, or rock oak (*Q. prinus*), with edible acorns, and swamp chestnut oak (*Q. michauxii*) have leaves resembling those of chestnuts. They are big trees, up to 100 feet (30 m) tall, occurring naturally in the eastern United States. Chestnut oak grows on dry ground, mainly on upland sites, and swamp chestnut oak is confined to permanently wet ground on the coastal plain. Overcup oak (*Q. lyrata*) is also a tree of the coastal wetlands. Its common name refers to its acorn cups, which are thin, scaly, and completely enclose the nut. Swamp white oak (*Q. bicolor*), another tree of wet ground in the southeast, grows to about 80 feet (30 m) and yields dense, hard wood that has been used in construction and to make railroad sleepers, but also for cabinetmaking. The same area is also the habitat of the water oak (*Q. nigra*), a tree of similar size.

The most valuable oak of the Mississippi valley is the Shumard oak (*Q. shumardii*). It grows to 100 feet (30 m), sometimes more, and its leaves turn a magnificent red in the fall. The leaves bear tufts or pale hairs on their undersides, which distinguishes them from those of the scarlet and red oaks.

Black oak, or quercitron oak (*Q. velutina*), found in forests on the eastern side of the continent, is also a tall tree, growing to a height of 100–165 feet (30–50 m). It is one of the red oaks, as are the northern and southern red oaks. The northern red oak (*Q. rubra*) grows faster than other oaks native to the region, sometimes at a rate of 8 feet (2.5 m) a year, to reach a height of about 80 feet (25 m). It occurs in forests from Canada to Florida and Texas. The southern red oak, or cherrybark oak (*Q. falcata*), growing to a similar size, occurs on dry land in the southeastern United States. It has dark, gray-brown bark with narrow ridges, somewhat reminiscent of the bark of a cherry.

Shingle oak (*Q. imbricaria*) has leaves resembling those of a willow, like the willow oak, although in this case the tree is deciduous. It is fairly small, reaching no more than about 50 feet (15 m) in natural woods, but often growing taller when cultivated, and occurs widely in the central and eastern United States in forests on rich, moist soil on hillsides and river banks. Its common name refers to the fact that early settlers used its wood to make roof shingles and clapboard.

The most important western timber tree is the Oregon white oak (*Q. garryana*), used for flooring and making furniture. It occurs from British Columbia to California. California white oak (*Q. lobata*) and California black oak (*Q. kelloggii*), trees about 80 feet (25 m) tall that occur in California and Oregon, are less important commercially. However, acorns from the California black oak were once the staple food of Native Americans living in the area, and wood from this tree was their principal fuel.

RHODODENDRON

Rhododendron (*Rhododendron* species) occur naturally over most of North America, except for the Great Plains. They are shrubs, but in some places they are important components of the understory in broad-leaved forest and can form dense thickets. The commonest species are *R. catawbiense,* which grows to a height of about 10 feet (3 m), and rosebay rhododendron (*R. maximum*), which reaches more than 12 m (40 feet). Both are evergreen.

PLANE, SYCAMORE

Plane trees (*Platanus* species) have a very discontinuous distribution. In all, there are six or seven species. One occurs in southeastern Europe and eastward as far as Iran, one in Southeast Asia, and all the others in North America. The sycamore (*P. occidentalis*), also known as the American plane, buttonwood, and buttonball, may well be the largest broad-leaved tree in North America. It grows to a height of 165 feet (50 m), with a diameter (always measured at chest height) of as much as 11.5 feet (3.5 m). It grows on rich, alluvial (deposited by a river on what was once a floodplain), lowland soils in the eastern and southeastern United States, sometimes in pure stands, but more often in association with a number of other broad-leaved species.

White oak tree, Colleton River, South Carolina (Gary Braasch/ENP Images)

Its western equivalent is the California sycamore, or California plane (*P. racemosa*), which grows in the Californian coastal ranges and Sierra Nevada. Not quite so large as the eastern species, it reaches a height of about 130 feet (40 m). The Arizona sycamore (*P. wrightii*), which occurs in the southern states and Mexico, is smaller, growing to about 80 feet (25 m). American sycamores are not closely related to the European sycamore (which is a maple).

TULIP TREE

If plane trees have a discontinuous distribution, tulip trees (*Liriodendron species*) have an even more extreme one. They are deciduous trees related to the magnolias (family Magnoliaceae) and today there are only two species. One occurs naturally in North America, the other in a few locations in central China.

The American species is the tulip tree (*L. tulipifera*), also known as the tulip poplar, yellow poplar, and whitewood. It grows naturally from Nova Scotia to Florida and as far west as Michigan and is cultivated widely elsewhere. It forms an important component of broad-leaved forests, where it grows rapidly on moist, fertile soils to fill gaps caused by the death of other species, and it can live for 500 years. Apart from its large, tulip-like flowers, which open in summer, its unusual, four-lobed leaves turn a splendid orange and yellow in the fall. The tree itself is tall and stately, with dense foliage for most of its height. It grows to 200 feet (60 m). Its timber, called whitewood, is valuable and used for house interiors.

Walnut

Walnut trees (*Juglans species*), related to hickories, occur throughout North America south of the Great Lakes, their range extending through Central America and into tropical South America. All walnuts produce nuts, but not all of them are edible, and some walnuts are better known for their timber. Because of its beauty, it is used to make valuable items, such as furniture, pianos, and gunstocks. Some nuts that are not eaten provide oils used in soaps and paints, and some yield dyes.

Most are big trees that often live for several centuries. The black walnut (*J. nigra*) grows to a height of 115 feet (35 m) or more. It occurs naturally from southern Ontario, New England, and Michigan to Georgia and Texas and this is the species most famed for its timber. Oils from its nuts are used in food. The range of the butternut, or white walnut (*J. cinerea*) extends farther north than that of the black walnut. It grows to about 65 feet (20 m) and its wood is also used to make furniture.

There are several western species. The Texas walnut (*J. microcarpa*) grows naturally in the Southwestern United States and Mexico. It is a small tree, growing to only about 33 feet (10 m). The Arizona walnut (*J. major*), growing on alluvial soils on upland plains and mountain valleys at altitudes of 1,500–6,000 feet (450–1,800 m) from Arizona into New Mexico and Mexico, is slightly bigger. It reaches a height of about 50 feet (15 m).

WILLOW

Willows (*Salix species*) occur throughout the world, except for New Guinea and Australasia, although they are rare in the Tropics and commoner in the Northern than the Southern Hemisphere. There are about 400 species in all, some small shrubs, but others large trees. They are pollinated by insects; their flowers are catkins, with male and female flowers borne on separate plants. The black willow (*S. nigra*) is the largest North American species. Growing to the east of the Rockies, it is a tree up to 100 feet (30 m) tall, sometimes taller, and its wood is used mainly to make boxes. Peach-leaved willow (*S. amygdaloides*), another eastern species, grows to 65 feet (20 m). In the Pacific states, red willow (*S. laevigata*) can reach 50 feet (15 m) and western black willow (*S. lasiandra*) 45 feet (14 m).

Common Angiosperms of the Old World

As in the New World, temperate broad-leaved forests occur in Europe and Asia to the south of the taiga. The transition from boreal to broad-leaved forest is not abrupt. Many forests are mixed, containing both coniferous and broad-leaved species; a mixed forest is defined as one in which the majority of trees are of one type but at least 20 percent are of the other type. Such forests are extensive, especially in Russia, where they occupy a much larger area than those of the purely broad-leaved type.

In the north, where winter temperatures usually remain below freezing for some time, most broad-leaved trees are deciduous. In the south, where summers are hot and dry, they tend to be evergreen, often sclerophyllous, and sometimes with leaves reduced in size, in both cases to minimize water loss.

ALDER

Alders (*Alnus species*) occur throughout the Northern Hemisphere, as far north as northern Norway and throughout all but the extreme north of the taiga, and as far south as the Himalayas. They are trees and shrubs of damp places, growing on lake shores and riverbanks, or on wet, peaty soils, where they can form forests, sometimes known as carrs. The most widespread is the black alder or common alder (*A. glutinosa*), a tree that grows to a height of up to 115 feet (35 m), although it is usually smaller. It has rather rounded leaves, which makes it easy to distinguish from the gray alder or speckled alder or European alder (*A. incana*), in which the leaves are pointed and, as one of the common names suggests, rather gray in color. It is a smaller tree, reaching only about 65 feet (20 m).

ASH

Ashes (*Fraxinus species*) occur throughout Europe and Asia, including the Indian subcontinent and Vietnam, as far north as southern Scandinavia and the southern edge of the taiga, and also in North Africa. They are one of the most important trees in European folklore (page 146), some myths holding that humans are made from ash wood. Its cultural significance may be due, at least partly, to its usefulness. Its wood is light, but hard and springy, warps very little, and is durable. Spears, tool handles, and wagons are made from it, and it also burns well. The traditional yule log is of ash.

Common ash or European ash (*F. excelsior*) is probably the most famous representative of the genus. It is a big, handsome tree, up to 150 feet (45 m) tall, that occurs naturally throughout Europe, including Britain. In winter it is recognizable by its black leaf buds, which stand out clearly against the pale gray bark. Later in the year, like all ashes, it produces bunches of winged seeds, called "keys." The Mediterranean and North African species is the narrow-leaved ash (*F. angustifolia*). This is smaller than the common ash, growing to about 80 feet (25 m), and it has darker, rougher bark.

Manna is the yellow, sweet-tasting sap of the flowering ash or manna ash (*F. ornus*), a tree up to about 65 feet (20 m) tall that grows around the Mediterranean, including North Africa. In Italy and Sicily it has traditionally been used as a mild laxative, given to children. Himalayan manna ash (*F. floribunda*) is a tree twice the size of the Mediterranean species that also yields manna. This is only one medicinal use of ash. At one time the bark of the common ash was steeped in hot water and the liquor used to treat liver complaints such as jaundice, and the ashes from the fire were used for scalp infections.

BEECH

Julius Caesar wrote that beech trees (*Fagus species*) did not grow in Britain. In fact they do, and their pollen has been found in soils dated to pre-Roman times, so scientists believe Caesar was referring not to beech, but to the sweet chestnut, which the Romans introduced, and which they may have called *Fagus* rather than *Castanea*, the name by which botanists know it now.

Beeches occur naturally in the Old World only in Europe and the Near East and in China and Japan (see the map on page 125). Where they do occur they are often the dominant or co-dominant species in forests. The most widespread species is the common beech or European beech (*F. sylvatica*). It is a handsome tree, up to 100 feet (30 m) tall, that yields a valuable timber, as well as nuts that can be fed to pigs and from which oil can be extracted. In the Balkans and eastward to the Caucasus and Asia Minor, the common beech gives way to the oriental beech (*F. orientalis*). The two are very similar, but the oriental beech grows only on sites that are more sheltered than those the common beech will tolerate.

BIRCH

Birches (*Betula* species) grow naturally throughout the temperate regions of the Northern Hemisphere and southern part of the Arctic. There are about 50 species and all of them have pale, almost white bark that becomes rough and develops dark patches in older trees. The flowers are wind-pollinated catkins (sometimes called "lambs' tails"), and the seed is a little nutlet with two wings. Birches grow readily from seed and are often the first trees to colonize disturbed ground. In northern parts of its range, birch forms extensive stands; it is an important component of many forests.

Over most of the range, the trees you are most likely to see are the silver birch and downy birch. Silver birch, or European birch, common birch, or warty birch (*B. pendula*) grows throughout Europe, northern Asia, and North Africa. The "pendula" of its name refers to way the tips of its branches hang down, unlike those of downy birch (*B. pubescens*), and this is the easiest way to distinguish between the two species at a distance. "Silver" refers to the color of the bark and "warty" to the small, pale, wartlike bumps on its branches. They provide one of the two other ways to tell one species from another, because the branches of the downy birch have no "warts." In addition, the young twigs of silver birch are smooth, and those of downy birch (sometimes called the hairy birch) are covered in the hairs that give the species its common name. Both are handsome trees. Silver birch is the larger of the two, growing to about 80 feet (25 m); downy birch is about 65 feet (20 m) tall. An oil from the bark of downy birch is used in Russia in the tanning of leather and gives Russian leather a characteristic smell.

BOX

There are about 30 species of boxes (*Buxus* species) distributed around the Northern Hemisphere in regions with a Mediterranean climate and in the southern fringes of the broad-leaved deciduous forest. Boxes grow naturally across central and southern Europe, and on dry soils as far north as southern England, most famously as a grove on Box Hill, in Surrey, a place named for it. Boxes also grow on hills in eastern France and on limestone soils in the Jura region, on the border between France and Switzerland.

Box is interesting, because it is a broad-leaved evergreen, with small, shiny, leathery leaves adapted to dry conditions. Left to grow, the common box (*B. sempervirens*) is a small tree 20–30 feet (6–9 m) tall. More usually, however, it is found in the form of a hedge or a small tree cut to an ornamental shape. Its tolerance of close clipping has allowed it to be used for the dense, square-edged hedges, sometimes less than 40 inches (1 m) high used to produce the geometrical shapes of formal gardens. There are many cultivated species and varieties to provide a range of leaf shapes and colors. Further south, Balearic box (*B. balearica*) takes the place of common box. It is very similar to common box, but a little taller and has bigger, less shiny leaves.

Box produces a very heavy, hard wood with many uses that can be polished to give a fine finish. Traditionally, it was used to make woodblocks for printing finely detailed engravings; the technique was introduced around 1800 by the artist and naturalist Thomas Bewick.

Early printers had used wood blocks both for type and for illustrations, but as the industry developed, metal type replaced wooden, and illustrations were printed from finely engraved metal plates. Thomas Bewick (1753–1828) was trained as an engraver of metal, not mainly for printing, but for decorating silverware for silversmiths, and he continued with this even after his wood engraving made him famous. He rediscovered and developed the old craft.

His work is still popular. He specialized in small drawings, called vignettes, showing rural scenes, sometimes humorous and always charming, as well as drawings of animals that were used as book illustrations. He became deservedly famous and highly successful.

He preferred boxwood because it is so hard. His work contained much small detail, which required him to carve very fine lines that would not be distorted in the press. To do that he had to use very hard wood.

Its hardness probably results from the slow rate at which box grows. It adds no more than 2 inches (5 cm) to its diameter in 20 years, and often less. This produces a dense wood, in which the annual growth rings are so small as to be barely visible, and the grain is fine and uniform. The wood itself is an attractive yellow color.

Since Roman times box has been used to make woodwind musical instruments, carvings, and other fine objects. It is also the wood traditionally used to make rulers and other mathematical instruments.

CHESTNUT

Chestnuts (*Castanea* species) occur naturally in southeastern Europe and western Asia, and in eastern China, Korea, and Japan. They are deciduous trees that grow quickly, often to a large size, and live for a very long time.

The sweet chestnut or Spanish chestnut (*C. sativa*) comes from the eastern Mediterranean and was introduced to northern Europe, including Britain, by the Romans. "Spanish" may refer to the chestnuts that were being imported to Britain from Spain at about the time the tree was being introduced, but the true origin of the name is lost. The tree itself grows up to 130 feet (40 m) tall, with a trunk that can be 40 feet (12 m) in circumference.

Several species occur in China, the most important being the Chinese chestnut (*C. molissima*). It is a tree up to 65 feet (20 m) tall, found on high ground at altitudes up to 8,200 feet (2,500 m). The Japanese chestnut (*C. crenata*), also found on high ground, but not usually above about 3,000 feet (900 m), is a tree up to 33 feet (10 m) tall. Both these produce edible nuts, although they are smaller than those of *C. sativa*.

CRAB APPLE

Apple trees (*Malus* species) also occur naturally in temperate forests of the Northern Hemisphere, and cultivated apples are grown to either side of this geographic belt and in the Southern Hemisphere. There are probably less than 30 species in all, but they have been hybridized and selected for cultivation for so long that those few species have given rise to around 1,000 cultivated varieties. Some of these have escaped, established themselves in the wild, and then crossbred among themselves and with wild apples, so the position now is somewhat confused. Wild apples and escaped cultivars are both commonly known as "crab" apples.

The wild crab apple (*M. sylvestris*), a tree up to about 30 feet (9 m) in height, occurs throughout Europe and is common in Britain. Its fruits are very acid, but are used to make conserves and the wild crab provides the rootstock for most cultivated apples. In Siberia, northern China, and eastern Asia the wild apple that occurs naturally is the Siberian crab (*M. baccata*). It is taller than the European apple, sometimes reaching about 50 feet (15 m). There are many varieties of both these species and both of them are ancestors of domesticated apples.

DOGWOOD

Dogwoods (*Cornus* species) occur naturally in the Old World in western Europe and central and

eastern Asia. Common dogwood (*C. sanguinea*) is a shrub or small tree, up to about 13 feet (4 m) tall, that occurs in the understory or shrub layer of broad-leaved forests throughout Europe, including southern England. The "sanguinea" in its name refers to the blood-red color of its leaves in the fall. Cornelian cherry (*C. mas*) bears attractive yellow flowers, which appear in early spring, before the leaves, and scarlet, oval-shaped fruits, resembling cherries, that can be made into jam and syrup. It is a small tree, up to about 25 feet (8 m) tall, that grows in central and southern Europe but is cultivated more widely for ornament.

Bentham's cornel (*C. capitata*) also produces attractive fruits, in this case resembling strawberries rather than cherries. It is a tree up to 45 feet (14 m) tall found in the Himalayas and in China. Over much the same range, but extending into Japan, the table dogwood (*C. controversa*) is a little bigger. It produces attractive foliage, sometimes purple, in the fall. *C. kousa*, growing about 20 feet (6 m) tall, produces attractive flowers as well as strawberry-like fruits. It occurs in China, Korea, and Japan.

ELDER

Elders (*Sambucus* species) are small trees or shrubs that occur naturally over Europe south of Scandinavia, in North Africa, and in a belt running from the eastern Mediterranean roughly northwest across Asia, north of the Himalayas, to eastern Siberia north of Kamchatka. They grow as understory species in floodplain forests and pine forests. The most widespread European species is the common elder (*S. nigra*), which grows to about 25 feet (8 m). A white country wine is made from the flowers and a red wine from the berries. Made well, both can be of high quality; the red wine was once used to dilute imported red wines. The wood is soft and easily hollowed to make a flute, and it was being used in this way thousands of years ago.

ELM

Until they were devastated by Dutch elm disease (page 108), the elms (*Ulmus* species) were among the most common of European trees, largely because they grew in hedgerows as well as in

Koala feeding, Eastern temperate Australia (Gerry Ellis/ENP Images)

forests, so they were visually prominent in the countryside. You can identify a tree as an elm by its leaves. These are lopsided, so either the stalk, the tip, or both seems bigger on one side than the other. The edges of the leaves have "teeth," like saw teeth. This is a common feature, but the teeth of elm leaves are double (the technical term is bidentate).

Elms have occurred naturally throughout the temperate regions of the Northern Hemisphere for at least the last 65 million years and during that time they have changed very little. The last of the dinosaurs may have gazed upon them. One way to tell whether a tree grows naturally in an area is to look for it among place names, and to do that you must first find its name in the local language. The wych elm or Scotch elm or mountain elm (*U. glabra*) is a true native of Britain. In Gaelic (the native language of the Scottish Highlands) it is *leamhan* (pronounced "leven"). There is a Loch Leven, with Kinlockleven beside it, two towns called Leven (one of them in northern England), as well as Levencorroch on the Isle of Arran in the Hebrides. In fact, wych elm grows across Europe and Asia, as far as Korea and on mountainsides farther south. It is a big, spreading tree, up to 130 feet (40 m) tall. The name "wych" means "supple" or "pliant" (and is used in this sense in the name of witch [*wych*] hazel).

The elm most often seen in hedgerows or standing alone in a field is the English elm (*U. procera*), a tree about the same size as the wych elm. Elms are very variable; the best way to distinguish one species from another is by the overall shape of the full-grown tree. The English elm produces foliage on branches growing almost all the way down its trunk, so the shape is rather cylindrical. Wych elm is more spreading and shaped a little like a mushroom. The European field elm or smooth-leaved elm (*U. minor*) is shorter, reaching about 100 feet (30 m), and difficult to identify because there are very many local varieties. These occur naturally from England to central and southern Europe, North Africa, and the Near East. Where they occur they are often the commonest elm, so there are few others with which to compare them. There is also a very common elm hybrid, a cross between wych elm and European field elm, that has many varieties. The Dutch elms belong to this group.

Elms may have appeared first in China and spread to Japan, Korea, and westward from there. More species occur naturally in China and the Himalayas than elsewhere. Most have no English common names, although there is a Chinese elm (*U. parvifolia*). It grows in Southeast Asia, Korea, and Japan as well as China. It differs from most elms by flowering in the fall. In the south of its range it is almost evergreen, keeping its leaves through the winter and losing them in the spring.

Caucasian elms (*Zelkova* species) belong to the same plant family as the elms (Ulmaceae) and, like the *Ulmus* elms, the bigger ones are important timber trees, producing very hard wood. They occur naturally in two areas, from the eastern Mediterranean eastward to the south of the Caspian Sea, and in eastern Asia, from Kamchatka and eastern Siberia, through Japan and eastern China, but they are grown for ornament in parks in many other parts of the world. The Caucasian elm or Siberian elm (*Z. carpinifolia*) itself, a native of the Caucasus mountains, is rather cylindrical in shape, with a very dense mass of branches, and reaches a height of 80 feet (25 m). Cretan zelkova (*Z. abelicea*), native to Crete, is smaller, growing no more than about 50 feet (15 m) tall, and the cut-leaf zelkova (*Z. verschaffeltii*), also from the Caucasus, is also barely taller than a shrub.

EUCALYPTUS

Eucalyptus or gum trees (*Eucalyptus* species) are native to Australia, New Guinea, Indonesia, and the Philippines. This makes them predominantly tropical and subtropical, but the genus comprises about 500 species and some are grown in temperate regions for ornament or timber. They are the principal timber trees of Australia.

Jarrah, messmate, and blackbutt are especially important as sources of timber in Australia, and they are big trees. Jarrah (*E. marginata*), from southwestern Australia, grows to about 115 feet (35 m), and both messmate (*E. obliqua*), from southeastern Australia, and blackbutt (*E. pilularis*), from eastern Australia, to about 200 feet (60 m).

There are other less important timber species, some of which are even bigger. Alpine ash (*E. delegatensis*) grows to 165 feet (50 m) or more, karri (*E. diversicolor*), from western Australia, can reach 245 feet (75 m), and mountain ash (*E. regnans*) can reach an astounding 325 feet (100 m). This is the tallest hardwood tree in the world.

HAWTHORN

In all, there are probably about 280 species of hawthorn (*Crataegus* species). Most are North American, but around 35 to 55 occur in the Old World, distributed throughout the temperate regions of the Northern Hemisphere. The common hawthorn (*C. monogyna*) is a shrub or small tree, about 10 m (33 feet) tall, that grows throughout Europe and western Asia. This is the species linked to May Day traditions and the variety "biflora" is the Glastonbury thorn. In mild winters it flowers a second time in December. According to legend, the thorn arose from the staff that Joseph of Arimathea drove into the ground when he visited Glastonbury as a trader, accompanied by Jesus. May is the name given to the blossom of the Midland hawthorn (*C. laevigata*), occurring throughout Europe and North Africa. It is smaller than the common hawthorn, with smaller leaves, and, as its name indicates, it flowers in May.

Chinese hawthorn (*C. pentagyna*), up to about 20 feet (6 m) tall, is either native to a region extending from southeastern Europe to Iran and the Caucasus or has been introduced from China, its real home, and has become naturalized. Oriental thorn (*C. laciniata*), a tree of similar size, has also been introduced from China and now grows naturally in Spain and southeastern Europe.

HAZEL

Hazels (*Corylus* species) are shrubs and small trees that are very common in the understory of European broad-leaved forests. Their range covers Europe south of Scandinavia and eastward to the Black Sea, and they also grow in eastern China and Japan. They were once grown extensively for their wood (page 195) and nuts, called cobnuts, filberts, or hazelnuts.

European hazel or cobnut (*C. avellana*) is a shrub or tree up to 23 feet (7 m) tall that can form dense thickets. It was valued for its wood, but the more reliable source of nuts was the filbert (*C. maxima*), a tree of similar size that is native to southern Europe.

Turkish hazel (*C. colurna*), from eastern Europe and Asia Minor, is also cultivated for its nuts. It is a much bigger tree, reaching 80 feet (25 m) in height. Chinese hazel (*C. chinensis*) is somewhat larger, growing up to 100 feet (30 m) tall, but otherwise so similar to Turkish hazel that they used to be regarded as two varieties of the same species. It occurs in China. Tibetan hazel (*C. tibetica*), up to about 23 feet (7 m) tall, grows in Tibet and Japanese hazel (*C. sieboldiana*) is a shrub, about 16 feet (5 m) tall, that grows in Japan.

HOLLY

Holly (*Ilex* species) provides the foliage and berries we have been using to decorate our homes in midwinter at least since Roman times, and Celtic peoples also used it in much the same way. European hollies are evergreen, but some Chinese and Japanese species are deciduous.

There are about 400 species, occurring naturally in warm-temperate, subtropical, and tropical regions of both hemispheres, and their popularity as ornamentals has produced innumerable cultivated varieties. A broad-leaved evergreen, holly prefers a moist, mild climate. Under suitable conditions it forms part of the understory of broad-leaved deciduous forests and can form stands by itself, called hollywoods.

The most widespread Old World species is the common holly or European holly (*I. aquifolium*), a bushy tree up to 80 feet (25 m) tall, that grows throughout western Europe, North Africa, and western Asia. Further east, its place is taken by species native to the Himalayas, China, and Japan. Most are shrubs, but Himalayan holly (*I. dipyrena*) is a tree up to 50 feet (15 m) tall that grows in the eastern part of the mountain range.

HORNBEAM

Hornbeams (*Carpinus* species) produce very hard, dense wood, once used to make the yokes with which oxen were harnessed to plows and wagons. They are deciduous trees of Europe, the Near East, and to the east of the Himalayas, in China and Japan, but Britain is at the very edge of their range and they occur naturally only in southeast England.

The most widespread Old World species is the common hornbeam (*C. betulus*), occurring throughout Europe and Asia. It grows about 80 feet (25 m) tall and can be mistaken for beech (a fact reflected in its Latin name): it can be distinguished in late spring by its catkins, which are longer than those of beech; in winter by its leaf buds, which resemble those of beech but hug the twigs rather than pointing outwards; and in spring and summer by its leaves, which are more markedly toothed and veined than those of beech.

HORSE CHESTNUT

Horse chestnuts (*Aesculus* species) occur mainly in North America, but they also grow naturally in southeastern Europe and parts of southern Asia and Japan.

The European horse chestnut or conker tree (*A. hippocastanum*), a handsome tree up to 115 feet (35 m) or more tall, is recognizable by its large leaves composed of seven, or less commonly five, leaflets. These lack individual stalks, but the leaf as a whole has a single, long one. A native of Albania and Greece, it has been planted widely elsewhere. It was introduced to Britain in 1616 and is now naturalized. The name "horse chestnut" is believed to refer to the fact that in Turkey the seeds, closely resembling those of the sweet chestnut, were used to treat ailments in horses; other livestock will not eat them. All species of horse chestnuts are grown for ornament, but their wood is of little commercial value.

LIME (LINDEN)

Limes or lindens are a genus (*Tilia*) of about 30 species of fairly tall trees distributed throughout the temperate regions of the Northern Hemisphere, except for the drier parts of central Asia. They are recognizable by their leaf buds and flowers. Each bud is protected by two scales, one much bigger than the other, like a finger and thumb, and each flower grows on a long stalk that is attached to its bract for about half the length of both bract and stalk.

Small-leaved lime (*T. cordata*), a tree up to 115 feet (35 m) tall, occurs throughout Europe as far east as the Caucasus and, as its name suggests, its leaves are smaller than those of the broad-leaved or large-leaved lime (*T. platyphyllos*), a slightly smaller tree occurring over a similar range. In Britain, the two have hybridized to produce the common lime or linden (*T. x europea*). This is a very big tree, growing to 145 feet (45 m) or more, with a roughly conical shape and rather open, domed crown.

Caucasian linden or Caucasian lime or Crimean lime (*T. euchlora*) is smaller, reaching about 65 feet (20 m). It is closely related to *T. cordata,* but has bigger leaves; some botanists suspect it may be a hybrid between *T. cordata* and another Caucasian species. Silver pendent lime or weeping silver lime or weeping white linden (*T. petiolaris*) is often grown in parks and gardens and may come originally from the Caucasus, although no one can be sure. It grows to more than 100 feet (30 m).

MAPLE

There are well over 100 species of maples (genus *Acer*) distributed throughout the temperate regions of the Northern Hemisphere and extending into the Asian Tropics. More species occur in Asia than in Europe. The most widespread European species is the field maple or hedge maple or common maple (*A. campestre*), a tree up to 80 feet (25 m) tall and recognizable by its small, dark, deeply lobed leaves, which turn yellow or red in the fall. It occurs throughout Europe, North Africa, and western Asia. In eastern Europe its identification can be more difficult, because it sometimes hybridizes with the Cretan maple (*A. sempervirens*), a smaller tree, up to 33 feet (10 m) tall, and with the Montpellier maple (*A. monspessulanum*). Both have leaves with wavy edges rather than lobes. Cappadocian maple (*A. cappadocicum*) occurs naturally from the Caucasus to China, but is widely cultivated elsewhere. It grows quickly, reaching a height of about 80 feet (25 m). Norway maple (*A. platanoides*), occurring naturally over most of Europe, grows to about 25 m (80 feet) or more and is grown extensively for ornament.

The Old World sycamore (*A. pseudoplatanus*) is a maple, sometimes called the great maple. An attractive tree growing to 80 feet (25 m) or more, it is native to central and southern Europe. It was introduced to Britain in the Middle Ages, and mistaken by some people for the mulberry-fig or sycamorus, of Palestine, and by others for the plane tree, which is how it acquired its names. It is now fully naturalized and readily invades woodland. Trautvetter's maple (*A. trautvetteri*), of the Caucasus, is generally similar, but somewhat smaller.

Oriental maples are generally smaller than those of Europe. Many species are popular garden and park trees; perhaps the best known, with countless varieties, is the Japanese maple (*A. palmatum*). In the wild it can grow to 50 feet (15 m), but reaches barely half that in cultivation. It is grown for the red of its leaves in the fall.

OAK

Oaks (*Quercus* species) grow naturally throughout the temperate regions of the Old World and extend into the Tropics of Asia (see the map on page 128). The genus comprises around 600 species, most of them trees. Some are deciduous, some evergreen, and some half evergreen, keeping their leaves through the winter and losing them in the spring. Many are important sources of timber, but the cork oak (*Q. suber*), a native of southern Europe and North Africa, is the tree that supplies most of the world's cork.

It is one of the evergreen oaks and occurs over much the same range as another evergreen, the holm oak or holly oak (*Q. ilex*), named for its holly-like leaves (*ilex* is holly). Macedonian oak (*Q. trojana*), which grows in southern Italy and the Balkans, is also evergreen. All three grow to about 65 feet (20 m). A Chinese evergreen oak, the bamboo-leaved oak (*Q. myrsinifolia*) is smaller; its smooth-edged, narrow leaves are only faintly reminiscent of bamboo leaves.

Deciduous oaks extend into higher latitudes, but also thrive in southern Europe and Asia Minor. Perhaps the most famous is the pedunculate oak or English oak (*Q. robur*), a magnificent, spreading tree up to 150 feet (45 m) tall. It shares this range with the durmast oak or sessile oak (*Q. petraea*). The two species are very similar, but can be distinguished by their acorns. Those of pedunculate oak are attached by long stalks, while those of sessile oak have almost no stalks and sit pressed against the twig. Both oaks are important sources of timber.

OLIVE

There are about 20 species of olives (genus *Olea*), centered in Africa and distributed through much of the warm-temperate and tropical regions of the Old World, but only one of major importance. The olive (*O. europaea*) has been cultivated in southern Europe since ancient times. There is evidence that it was being grown in Asia Minor around 3700 B.C.E. and it is of great importance in all Mediterranean cultures. The tree itself is an evergreen 10–40 feet (4–16 m) tall, that can live for 1,500 years. It will not grow where winter temperatures average less than 37°F (3°C) and dies if the temperature falls to 16°F (-9°C).

PEAR

Pears (*Pyrus* species) occur naturally throughout the temperate regions of the Northern Hemisphere and there are about 20 species. The common pear or European pear (*P. communis*) is a tree up to about 50 feet (15 m) tall found throughout Europe and western Asia. This is the species from which many cultivated varieties have been bred, but others have made important contributions; the wild pear (*P. pyraster*) of central Europe is one. Fruit of the snow pear (*P. nivalis*) of Switzerland and southern Europe is sometimes used to make the fermented drink, perry. Caucasian pear (*P. caucasia*) trees are vigorous colonizers of open ground and grow in forests. They have also been used in developing cultivated varieties.

In China and Japan the oriental pear or sand pear or Chinese pear or Japanese pear (*P. pyrifolia*) is widely cultivated, the "sand" referring to the stone cells which give most pears their "gritty" texture.

POPLAR

Poplars and aspens (*Populus* species) occur throughout the Northern Hemisphere from the Mediterranean and Himalayas to the Arctic Circle. Lombardy poplar (*P. nigra* var. *Italica*), a tree that can reach a height of 100 feet (30 m), but looks taller because its branches all point upward, is instantly recognizable by its shape, which makes it possibly the most famous of poplars. This growth habit, called "fastigiate," occurs as a freak in many trees, but is difficult to propagate. In the case of the Lombardy poplar, propagation is easy because it grows well from cuttings and that, in fact, is how Lombardy poplars are grown; almost all of them are male. The tree originated in northern Italy and the first cuttings were brought to England in 1758 by Lord Rochford. The tree is now grown widely, but only for ornament or screening, for the timber is of little value.

Black poplar (*P. nigra*), from which the Lombardy poplar is derived, grows naturally throughout Europe, including Britain, and Southwest Asia. It is a big, rather cylindrical tree up to 115 feet (35 m) tall. Its bark is brown and rather rough, but the tree is called "black" to contrast it with the white poplar or abele (*P. alba*), a tree up to 65 feet

Olive trees, Europe
(Konrad Wothe/ENP Images)

(20 m) tall, which has pale, silvery bark with darker diamond-shaped marks. Gray poplar (*P. canescens*) has ridged, dark gray bark and grayish white leaves. It grows vigorously, reaching nearly 130 feet (40 m), and is found over most of Europe.

Some botanists believe the gray poplar to be a hybrid between the white poplar and the aspen (*P. tremula*), also a European species. Aspens reach a height of about 65 feet (20 m) and grow readily from suckers, so they often form dense stands. Their oval or almost round leaves with wavy edges are attached by long, slender, flattened stalks that allow the leaves to move in the slightest breeze, making the entire tree look as though it is trembling; this is how it earns the name "tremula."

Most poplars bear male and female flowers on separate trees, but there is at least one exception in the Chinese necklace poplar (*P. lasiocarpa*), a native of central and western China that is cultivated elsewhere as a curiosity. The flowers are in catkins, the males red, the females yellowish-green, and sometimes both are on the same catkin, the male at the base and the female, or a bisexual flower, at the top. The tree itself grows to a height of about 65 feet (20 m), with rather widely spaced branches that give it a sparsely covered appearance.

ROWAN

Rowans and whitebeams belong to a genus (*Sorbus*) of about 85 species of small trees and shrubs found throughout the temperate regions of the Northern Hemisphere. Rowan (*S. aucuparia*), also known as mountain ash and quickbeam, grows naturally throughout Europe and western Asia. In Scotland it grows at altitudes up to 2,000 feet (600 m), where it often stands alone. At lower levels it forms part of the understory of natural forest. A tree up to about 50 feet (15 m) tall, it is the subject of many ancient beliefs. It was believed to give protection against witches and to this day there are people who will not injure a rowan, far less fell one, for fear of the bad luck this would bring. It appears as though by magic, germinating readily from seeds dropped by birds, then growing rapidly. Its bright red berries are used to make a jelly to accompany meats such as mutton and venison, and its hard wood is used to make tool handles and other small items.

It is not the only Old World rowan. Japanese rowan (*S. commixta*) is a very similar tree, also bearing tight clusters of white flowers and red berries. It is found in Sakhalin and Korea as well as Japan. Sargent's rowan (*S. sargentiana*) is a shrub, about 16 feet (5 m) tall, that grows throughout China, and Vilmorin's rowan (*S. vilmorinii*), with rather paler berries, is a smaller shrub native to western China. Also in western China there is the Hupeh rowan (*S. hupehensis*), a tree about 50 feet (15 m) tall with berries that ripen to pale pink or white. It is grown for ornament in some European parks and gardens.

The common whitebeam (*S. aria*) grows naturally on chalk and limestone soils throughout Europe and as one or other of its many cultivated varieties it is also grown in parks, gardens, and streets. It is a small tree, up to about 50 feet (15 m) tall, with berries that are sometimes used to flavor drinks if they can be collected before the birds take them. In parts of northern England, the tree is known as the sea owler, "owler" probably being a corruption of alder, and the fruits are known as "chess apples"; eaten fresh they are unpleasant, but once they start to decay (or "blet") they are quite edible.

The service tree (*S. domestica*) grows throughout southern Europe, North Africa, and western Asia. It can reach a height of more than 50 feet (15 m), and its fruits look rather like small apples or pears, about 1 inch (2.5 cm) long. They are edible, more so when "bletted," and are used to flavor certain kinds of beer. The tree is cultivated in parts of Europe for ornament, but also for its fruit. "Service" comes from the Latin *cerevisia,* which means "beer."

The wild service (*S. torminalis*) is a larger tree, growing to more than 65 feet (20 m), although it is often smaller. Unlike most *Sorbus* species, its leaves are lobed like those of a maple, for which it is easily mistaken. The bark cracks to produce shapes that give the tree its other name, checkers, and the fruits are sometimes called checkers berries. Its range is similar to that of the service tree, but extends into southern England and Wales. Its fruits have been eaten and used medicinally, but the tree is not cultivated. It can develop from seed, but more often spreads from suckers, establishing itself very slowly. In several parts of Britain its presence is taken to indicate that woodland in which it occurs is ancient, meaning the area has been continuously forested at least since 1600, or that what is now open ground was once forested.

SOUTHERN BEECH

Southern beeches (*Nothofagus* species) occur in South America and Australasia. The more valuable timber species are South American, but some of those native to temperate Australasia are big, impressive trees, all of them evergreens. Native to southeastern Australia, the myrtle beech (*N. cunninghamii*) reaches a height of 165 feet (50 m), as does the Australian beech (*N. moorei*) of eastern Australia.

Species native to New Zealand include the silver beech (*N. menziesii*), red beech (*N. fusca*), and hard beech (*N. truncata*), all of which grow to 100 feet (30 m), and the smaller mountain beech (*N. cliffortioides*), reaching 50 feet (15 m), and black beech (*N. solandri*), growing to 80 feet (25 m).

English walnut orchard
(Gerry Ellis/ENP Images)

SPINDLE

Spindle trees are a genus (*Euonymus*) of around 175 species of shrubs and small trees, some deciduous and some evergreen, that are centered on the Himalayan region and Asia, but they also occur naturally throughout temperate regions.

The common spindle tree (*E. europaeus*) can reach a height of about 30 feet (9 m) in cultivation. In the wild it is usually smaller. Its young shoots are square in cross section and its bright red fruits have three to five lobes, making them very distinctive. The wood is very hard and was once used to make such items as skewers and spindles for spinning, which explains its name. Its charcoal

is excellent for drawing and has also been used in making gunpowder. The fruits are poisonous to sheep and the tree harbors the eggs of an aphid that attacks bean crops, so arable farmers destroy spindle trees when they find them. Despite this, the tree is grown in some parks and gardens, as are several Asian *Euonymus* species.

STRAWBERRY TREE

Strawberry trees (*Arbutus* species) are named for their edible fruits, which resemble strawberries in appearance, but not in flavor (which not everyone enjoys). There are 12 species, all of them evergreen shrubs or trees. Most are American, but some occur around the Mediterranean region, and one has an interesting extension of its range into southwestern Ireland, where it forms part of what is known as the Lusitanian flora, a relict of a former interglacial period (page 57).

This strawberry tree (*A. unedo*) grows to about 30 feet (9 m) in height and is a popular garden and park ornamental, cultivated for its foliage, clusters of delicately colored white, pink, or pale green flowers, and fruits. The Cyprus strawberry tree or eastern strawberry tree (*A. andrachne*), from the eastern Mediterranean, is up to 33 feet (10 m) tall, and has serrated leaves.

WALNUT

Walnuts (*Juglans* species) occur in the Old World in warm temperate regions from the eastern Mediterranean to southern Asia, and in eastern China, Korea, and Japan. They were introduced throughout Europe, including Britain, in Roman times and the most widespread species, the common walnut (*J. regia*), which grows naturally from southeastern Europe to China, is also known as the English walnut and Persian walnut. "Walnut" is from the Anglo-Saxon and means "foreign nut," so in England, where the tree is not a native, it is the "English foreign nut," a name not quite so peculiar as it may sound. Its crushed leaves release a dark brown pigment some people once used to darken their complexions. The tree itself grows to about 100 feet (30 m), and its timber is used to make high-quality furniture and for veneers.

Somewhat smaller trees, up to about 65 feet (20 m) tall, occur in eastern Siberia, China, and Japan. All produce edible nuts and Siebold's walnut (*J. sieboldiana*), from China and Japan, is valued for its timber.

WAYFARING TREE

Viburnums comprise about 150 species in the genus *Viburnum,* some evergreen and some deciduous, distributed in the Old World throughout temperate regions of the Northern Hemisphere, with some species in the Asian Tropics. They are shrubs or small trees. One of the best known is the wayfaring tree (*V. lantana*), which occurs throughout Europe and western Asia as a small tree, up to about 16 feet (5 m) tall, with attractive flowers and splendidly colored foliage in the fall. No one really knows how it acquired its name, but in the 16th century, writers were drawing attention to the frequency with which it was found in roadside hedges, where it cheered wayfarers.

Another attractive species is the guelder rose (*V. opulus*). It grows no more than about 13 feet (4 m) tall. Its name derives from a cultivated variety, in which all the flowers are sterile, that was first grown in a Dutch province called Gelderland, or Guelders.

WILD CHERRY

A wide range of important fruits, including plums, peaches, apricots, nectarines, almonds, and cherries are produced from trees or shrubs of the genus *Prunus,* of which there are about 400 species distributed throughout temperate regions of the Northern Hemisphere. Most of our cultivated cherries are descended from the wild cherry, or gean, or mazzard (*P. avium).* This is a tree up to 65 feet (20 m) tall or more, found in Europe, parts of Russia, and North Africa in broad-leaved forests. It is also grown for its valuable timber, as is the bird cherry (*P. padus*), though to a lesser extent.

WILLOW

The willows are another large genus (*Salix*) of deciduous trees and shrubs, in this case found everywhere in the world, except for the polar icecaps. Most prefer damp conditions and grow best along riverbanks and in marshes and swamps. Many produce valuable wood.

White willow (*S. alba*), occurring in lowland areas from Europe to central Asia, is a large tree, growing to 80 feet (25 m). It is called "white" because of the way its leaves reflect light. The only willow grown commercially in Britain for its wood is the one used to make cricket bats. The cricket-bat willow is a variety of the white willow (*S. alba* var. *coerulea*) that is grown from cuttings, often in rows along riverbanks.

Weeping willow (*S. babylonica*), a tree up to about 50 feet (15 m) tall, probably originated in Iran. Although much cultivated for its "weeping" habit, it is not very hardy in northern climates, where most willows of this form are a variety of the white willow (*S. alba* var. *tristis*).

Sallow or goat willow or pussy willow (*S. caprea*) and gray sallow (*S. cinerea*) are very similar, grow in similar places, and hybridize readily. The tree, found throughout Europe and western Asia, is about 33 feet (10 m) tall but the plant is often no taller than a shrub. Its male flowers (catkins) are collected for decoration, especially on Palm Sunday. Bayleaved willow or laurel-leaved willow (*S. pentandra*), a tree up to about 65 feet (20 m) tall, shares this range. Its dark, shiny leaves are broader than those of most willows, and resemble laurel or bay leaves.

Forest Clearance in Prehistory

As the last ice age drew to a close and climates grew warmer, little by little the edges of the glaciers and ice sheets retreated to higher latitudes and higher altitudes. Meltwater flowed, as rivers and seeds, dropped by the wind and birds, began to germinate. Plants colonized the newly exposed land and in time what had once been barren ice or sparse tundra became forest. Forests covered most of what are now the temperate regions.

Origin of the Prairie

Not everywhere was forested. By the time the first European explorers and settlers arrived, grasses and herbs were the dominant vegetation over large areas of the continental interior of North America. French explorers called the grasslands "meadow," for which the French word is *prairie*. Trees can and do grow in the prairie, not only in the tall-grass prairie but even in the mixed- and short-grass prairie where the climate is semiarid. Trees grow naturally on the sides of ridges and valleys, where the ground is not level, and tree plantations and tree belts planted to provide shelter survive for many years. Studies of pollen found in lake sediments (page 140) show that what is now a prairie landscape was—as recently as 5,000 years ago—more like open forest or parkland, with grasses and scattered groves of trees, often dominated by pines.

No one is quite sure why the trees disappeared, but the most likely sequence of events began between 5,000 and 6,000 years ago. At that time the climate became markedly drier, which favors grasses rather than trees. Trees became more widely scattered and tall grasses became dominant. This established the tall-grass prairie from eastern Iowa to western Michigan, with shorter grasses in the even drier regions to the west and south. After about 4,000 years ago the climate changed again, this time becoming cooler and moister. Trees grew well under these conditions. In the north, the boundary between the

boreal and mixed forests moved south in response to the cooler conditions, and the boundary between forest and prairie moved west, in response to increased precipitation. This did not lead to the recreation of open forest, however, because humans now began to influence events.

Prairie Fires

In those days, Native Americans living in the interior of the continent gathered plant foods and hunted game. Game was plentiful, with large herds of grazing animals, especially bison. A good way to hunt them was by lighting a fire to drive a herd into an ambush. Both natural and human-made prairie fires were common. There were huge storms then as now, and lightning readily ignited dry grass. After the fires died, fresh grass and herbs would grow vigorously from the ashes. The overall effect was not only to drive game in a way that made it easier to kill, but also to improve the pasture: thanks to the grass and herbs, there was more food for more animals. The people ate well and the herds increased in size.

This was not the only effect. On the plains, where the ground is open, fires are driven by strong winds and there is nothing to halt their spread. They travel fast, and as they do so, the flames catch those plants standing above ground level first. Trees and shrubs burn. So, too, does the grass, of course, but grass grows from a point at or just below ground level, where it is protected from all but the most intense heat. The fire does much more damage to woody plants than it does to prairie grasses. Indeed, the fire burns off a layer of dead, dry grass that would otherwise suppress the growth of fresh, new grass.

As the new flush of grass emerged, the grazing herds would return. Some tree seedlings would have survived the fire, and tree seeds would germinate in the soil. As they grazed, the bison and other large animals would bite off the growing tips of some of these emerging plants

and trample others. In time and with repeated fires, fewer and fewer trees would mature to produce seeds, so the soil would store fewer and fewer viable tree seeds, and the grassland would become permanent.

Much later, hunting with fires to drive game was replaced by farming. The natural grasses were cleared, the land plowed, and cereals, which are domesticated grasses, were grown instead. Cultivation also prevented trees from colonizing the land and the farmers produced the landscape we see today.

Scientists strongly suspect that not only large parts of the North American prairie, but also of the South American pampas and the steppe grasslands of Europe and Asia were formed in this way. In Africa, the savannah grassland is still maintained by being deliberately fired by the people who live there. Long before our ancestors began recording their history, they were drastically altering the environment in which they lived. They were clearing forests.

The First European Farmers

In northwestern Europe, forest is still the commonest natural vegetation type. When farmland is abandoned, usually scrub and then trees colonize it. Here, it was not hunters who removed the forest, but farmers. In Britain the forest clearance began around 5,500 years ago and accelerated about 2,000 years ago, during the Roman occupation (page 144).

In temperate Europe, early farmers kept pigs and cattle and possibly sheep and goats as well. Although aurochs (*Bos primigenius*), the ancestor of domesticated cattle, lived in Britain, it is believed that migrants brought cattle with them rather than attempting to domesticate the wild ones already present, and cattle were certainly taken in small boats to Ireland, where there were no aurochs.

Pigs are forest animals, feeding on the forest floor, and they would have had no effect on the forest. Cattle, on the other hand, would have eaten grass in clearings, but probably they fed mainly by browsing, eating those tree leaves and shoots they could reach. Their herders would have augmented this by climbing into the trees to cut down browse from higher levels. As they fed, the cattle would have trampled tree seedlings and damaged tree bark, sometimes badly enough to kill the tree. Cattle thus enlarged the clearings in which they lived. Sheep are not browsers. If farmers wanted to keep sheep they had to find pasture for them, and this meant clearing forest. Goats are adaptable, but around the Mediterranean they caused serious harm by eating growing shoots from vegetation that was already becoming sparse.

The Elm and Lime Decline

Browsing cattle may have been responsible for what paleobotanists call the "elm decline." Around 5,000 years ago over most of northwestern Europe, but not in North America, there was a sharp reduction in the amount of elm pollen in the soil. This is unlikely to have been due to a change in the climate, because such a change would have affected elm in some places more than others and, almost certainly, would also have occurred in North America. It may have been caused by a severe disease epidemic, Dutch elm disease (page 108) being the most likely culprit.

Alternatively, a new farming technique may have been responsible. Farmers at that time may have started to keep their cattle in pens. This would protect them from wild predators, such as wolves, and make them easier to control, but they would no longer have been able to find their own food. People would have had to bring it to them and would have gathered browse, probably preferring elm leaves and twigs to those of other species, because elm is especially nutritious. If plant material was removed each year before the trees flowered, less pollen would have been produced. In this case, the elm decline would have been a reduction in the amount of pollen, but not necessarily of elm trees.

One might have led to the other. Pollarding (removing the growing shoots) increases the vulnerability of elms to Dutch elm disease. By cutting the trees for browse, farmers may have exposed them to disease, and that may have killed them.

There was also a lime deline. This, however, was associated with climatic change. Around 2,500 years ago the climate became cooler and that is when the warmth-loving lime (*Tilia*) declined. At the same time beech (*Fagus*) expanded northward to fill the gap.

Swidden Farming

Crops were also being grown and trees had to be removed to make room for them. Early farmers practiced "swidden" farming. This is a form of shifting cultivation in which an area of land is cleared and crops are grown in it for several seasons. Then yields start to decrease, because nutrients have been removed from the soil, and weeds start overtaking and smothering crop plants. At this stage the plot is abandoned and the process repeated elsewhere, the system working as a cycle in which each plot is revisited every so many years. It is a farming system that requires a large area to feed each person.

Clearing forest is less difficult than it seems. Early European farmers used axes with blades made from chert, the stone that is called flint when it is found surrounded by chalk, and handles of ashwood. Some years ago, Danish scientists fitted a handle to a genuine chert ax blade, 4,000 years old, and found they could fell 100 trees with it before it needed sharpening. Using axes of this type, with blades of polished stone, it took three men just four hours to clear about 718 square yards (600 sq m) of birch forest. Falling trees bring down others, especially on sloping ground, speeding the process. Clearance ends with a fire to burn off shrubs and wood for which there is no use. Clearing the forest presented those early farmers with no serious difficulty.

The First Mines

Chert and flint were important industrial materials in those days, and they were mined by workers using picks made from antlers and the bones of aurochs. In Norfolk, England, there is an area of deep pits and underground galleries, called Grimes Graves, from where flint was mined around 4,000 years ago and made into tools that were traded. The mines are surrounded by spoil heaps and sites where a substantial community lived and grew food. It is possibly the earliest industrial site and it's very large: the mined area alone covers about 209,300 square yards (175,000 sq m).

Using Pollen to Study the Past

Seed plants reproduce by releasing pollen from the male organs. This is transported to the female organs, where it releases sperm for fertilization. Pollen grains themselves are extremely small and light. In some species they are transported by the wind, in others by animals such as insects and birds, and they are produced in vast quantities to allow for considerable wastage.

Inevitably, most pollen grains are lost. Of these, some fall into lakes or bogs and become incorporated into mud that accumulates as sediments. Many years later, those sediments can be examined. By then, the environment will probably have changed greatly—what was once a lake or wet ground may be dry and hard. Nevertheless, if it has not been disturbed the soil can be identified as a former sediment and the date it formed can be calculated, either by comparison with other material nearby, the date of which is known, or by measuring the decay of radioactive carbon-14 in once-living material trapped in it.

Often, scientists are able to recover pollen from the former sediment. This is possible because each pollen grain is encased in an outer coat, called an exine, so tough as to be virtually indestructible if it becomes trapped in acidic, airless conditions, such as those in the wet mud of a bog, or on the bed of a stagnant lake. It can survive unaltered in such places for many thousands of years.

Pollen Analysis

In the early years of this century, a Swedish geologist, Lennart von Post, realized that preserved pollen might be used to reconstruct past patterns of vegetation. His work, first published in 1916, mainly dealt with forests. Other pollen studies were already being made, but for a quite different purpose. Many people suffer from hay fever, a distressing complaint caused by an allergy, commonly to pollen, and medical researchers were studying airborne pollen to identify the plants releasing it. Von Post was among the first scientists to study pollen preserved from the fairly distant past.

Pollen grains evolved along with the rest of the plant that produces them. Just as plants can be differentiated into families, genera, and species, so can their pollen grains, at least up to a point. Pollen grains from different plants have different shapes and their exines are marked with grooves and pits that form characteristic patterns. Grasses and herbs can usually be identified from their pollen down to the taxonomic level of the family. Trees and shrubs can be identified to the level of genus. A very few plants can be identified at the species level. Spores from plants that do not produce seeds are sometimes preserved in the same way and can also be used for identification.

The study of such ancient pollen and spores is called "pollen analysis" and it has also led to another scientific discipline, palynology (although some people use the two names interchangeably). This involves classifying and plotting the distribution of pollen, spores, and other microfossils.

Material for pollen analysis is obtained by drilling cores, then removing samples from carefully measured depths. The pollen grains must be separated, and mounted on a microscope slide. Pollen grains are very small and can be studied only under a microscope with a magnification of about x400 or higher.

Grains are identified by comparing them with already labeled grains. This can be done from published pictures of pollen grains or by reference to a library of actual grains mounted on slides. Scientists who specialize in pollen analysis accumulate libraries of their own slides for this kind of reference use.

Interpretation

Look through a microscope and identify a pollen grain and you may think this proves that a particular plant once grew at the place from which the pollen sample came. Unfortunately, it is not so simple: pollen has to be interpreted with great care.

In the first place, some plants produce much more pollen than others. Alder (*Alnus*) and birch (*Betula*), for example, produce twice as much pollen as elm (*Ulmus*) and spruce (*Picea*), and eight times more pollen than lime (*Tilia*) and maple (*Acer*). When the grains on the slide are counted, allowance must be made for this difference in output.

The method by which the grains were transported also affects their distribution. Pollen grains from coniferous trees have small sacs that help keep them airborne, so if the pollen was carried high into the air and for a long distance, conifer pollen would travel farthest before falling. If the pollen was carried by wind at a low level, this would make less difference. Pollen can also be carried by water and this, too, will tend to sort one type of pollen from another.

The pollen retrieved from a sample of sediment represents a "death assemblage." That is to say, the pollen has been transported, possibly over a long distance, and sorted at the same time. The proportions of the plant species present as pollen may be very different from those you would have seen had you been able to visit the site when they were alive. Suppose, for example, the sediment containing the pollen came from what had been a lake bed and that the forest on one side of the lake was mainly elm, propagating itself vegetatively, and on the other side oak. What you have no way of knowing is that in those days, but not now, the prevailing wind blew from the elm towards the oak, so elm pollen would have been carried across the lake, with some falling into it, but much of the oak pollen would have been carried away from the lake. In your sample, elm would be greatly overrepresented. The aim of pollen analysis is to translate the death assemblage revealed by the sample into a life assemblage, of the plants which really grew at that place.

Relative and Absolute Pollen Frequency

There are two ways in which pollen abundance is reported. Often, the amount of pollen from each family or genus is counted as a proportion of the total amount of pollen present, and reported as a percentage. This is called the "relative pollen frequency" (RPF). It might state that the sample contained 50 percent pine, 30 percent oak, and 20 percent alder. Some scientists find this less satisfactory than reporting the "absolute pollen frequency" (APF), which is the total number of pollen grains for each plant type.

It was Lennart von Post who pointed out that unless the relative pollen productivity of each plant is known, as well as the way the pollen is dispersed and the effect of the form of dispersal on the distribution, the RPF is misleading. It suggests the proportions of the trees in the original forest, which it is not entitled to do. That is why many scientists prefer to use the APF, although the difficulties von Post mentioned are much less severe than they were then, because to a large extent this information now exists.

Obviously, once the pollen grains have been mounted on slides, they must be counted, one type at a time. Each sample must contain at least 200 identifiable grains, and preferably more, because numbers smaller than this cannot be interpreted reliably. After all, a few grains could have been blown for hundreds of miles and bear no relation whatever to the vegetation among which they fall; it is much less likely that hundreds of grains will arrive in that way. Since the purpose of the study is often not simply to determine the original vegetation pattern, but to

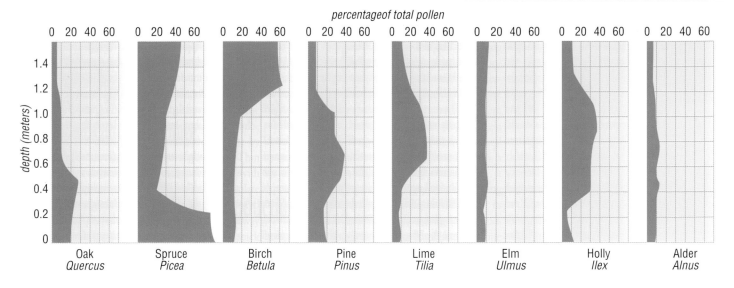

percentage of total pollen

depth (meters)

Oak — *Quercus* · Spruce — *Picea* · Birch — *Betula* · Pine — *Pinus* · Lime — *Tilia* · Elm — *Ulmus* · Holly — *Ilex* · Alder — *Alnus*

Specimen pollen diagram

observe changes in it over a period of time, there will be several samples to examine, collected from different levels. Once the grains have been counted, the resulting numbers, the raw data, are subjected to various statistical procedures to standardize the way they are interpreted.

Finally, the results are often presented as a "pollen diagram." This shows a vertical cross section through the site, with the depth marked. Each plant then occupies its own column as a block varying in width according to the percentage of the total pollen it represents at each level (the RPF). The figure above shows an imaginary pollen diagram showing what the result looks like; a real diagram would be headed with the name of the site from which the samples were taken.

History Revealed

Dates can often be assigned to depths in a sedimentary profile, so a pollen diagram shows the history of the vegetation at a particular site. Data from a number of sites can then be combined to give a vegetation history for a wide area. These have shown, for example, that in England and Wales, 10,250 years ago the forest was dominated by birch (*Betula*), pine (*Pinus*), and juniper (*Juniperus*). At 9,798 years ago + 200 years (there is always a margin of error in dating) the forest was of birch, pine, and hazel (*Corylus*). At 8,880 + 170 years ago birch had disappeared, leaving a hazel and pine forest. At 8,196 +150 years ago the forest was of pine, hazel, and elm (*Ulmus*). At 7,107 + 120 years ago it had changed to oak (*Quercus*), elm, and alder (*Alnus*). Finally, at 5,010 + 80 years ago the forest was of oak and alder.

A history of this kind is interesting, but from it we can learn something even more interesting. Tree species have climatic preferences; if one species is replaced by another over a wide area, it is probably because the climate changed. Birch, pine, and juniper suggest a cold climate, like that of the taiga or Canadian conifer forest. The arrival of hazel indicates warmer conditions. The warming seems to have continued, until the climate was mild and wet, the conditions that suit oak and alder.

Over the 80 or so years since they were introduced, the techniques of pollen analysis have been greatly refined and have been applied at many sites. They have allowed scientists to compile a history of vegetation for many areas and, from that, a history of the climate and of the environment in which animals and humans lived.

Forests in Classical Times

Ancient Greece

Dionysus was the god of the vine. Sometimes he is known as Bacchus and the drunken rituals performed by his worshippers were called "bacchanalian," a word still used to describe drunken revelries. As with most Greek gods, there was much more to Dionysus than that. For one thing, Dionysian festivals gradually developed into theatrical performances for which plays were written to be performed on a platform, called a skene, and accompanied by a commentary and dances performed by a khoros. When you go to the theater or a movie you are attending an event that can be traced all the way back to the worship of Dionysus. "Scene" and "chorus" are Greek words from those days that we still use.

He was often accompanied by pans, satyrs (the Romans called them fauns), and similar spirits. These were partly human goats and Dionysus himself was sometimes represented as a goat. Throughout Europe, spirits in the shape of goats were woodland deities, perhaps because goats like to wander in the forests, where they browse on the leaves and nibble the bark. All of them, and Dionysus himself, were associated with the cultivated crops, which they could encourage, but especially with the forests.

People would not have worshipped woodland gods and spirits unless they were familiar with forests. At one time, therefore, a substantial part of Greece must have been forested. In Homer there are references to "wooded Samothrace," "wooded Zacynthos," and trees and forests

The heavily armed hoplites, or infantry, were the foundation of the Greek military.

were often used in metaphor, for example when describing a battle as a forest fire: "Through deep glens the fierce fire rages on some parched mountainside, and the deep forest burns, and the driving wind whirls the flame every way."

Deforestation began early, however, mainly to free land for farming. In *Works and Days,* the Greek poet Hesiod (c. 800 B.C.E.), who lived in Boeotia, in southern Greece, describes the simple life and work of a farmer and extols its virtues to his brother, Perses, who apparently had made off with the bulk of the family inheritance and opted for a life of luxury and ease. Unlike the first people to settle in Greece, whose tools were of stone, these farmers had metal tools with which they could clear woodland much more quickly. The mountains were deforested first and then, as immigration and natural increase led to a rise in the size of the population, the lowlands were cleared. Thucydides (c. 465–400 B.C.E.), the greatest of all ancient Greek historians, reported that "the productiveness of the land increased the power of individuals; and in turn was a source of quarrels by which communities were ruined, whilst at the same time they were exposed to attacks from without." Strife forced people to migrate and many sought asylum in Athens, but the poor soils of southern Greece were unable to feed the burgeoning population and eventually Athenians were compelled to establish colonies elsewhere.

When Athens found itself at war with neighboring states, it needed a navy. The age of the Greek wars, leading to the establishment of the Greek Empire, reached their climax during the lifetime of Pericles (c. 495–429 B.C.E.). By then timber for shipbuilding had to be imported. Athenian expansion led to the greatness of Athenian civilization, but the loss of most of the Greek forests.

Eventually the rate of deforestation slowed. The historian Polybius (c. 200–c. 118 B.C.E.) wrote of forests in the mountains of his home country of Arcadia, in the Peloponnese. The clearance was most thorough in Attica, the southernmost part of mainland Greece. Plato (428 or 427–348 or 347 B.C.E.) stated in the *Critias* that the trees of Attica had been felled to provide building materials for Athens, leaving the uplands bare.

Other Mediterranean lands fared better. In his *Geography,* the geographer Strabo (born about 63 B.C.E.; it is not known when he died)

reported that the mountains of Spain were densely forested and there were large forests in many other parts of the Mediterranean region, although he also reported that the lowland forests of Cyprus had been cleared long ago to provide timber for shipbuilding and fuel for smelting copper and silver.

Today, more than half the land area of Greece supports scrub vegetation that has replaced the original forest. There are four distinct types of scrub, called maquis, pseudomaquis, phrygana, and shiblyak. Maquis, found in the south, includes such trees as strawberry tree (*Arbutus unedo*), holm oak (*Quercus ilex*), Judas tree (*Cercis siliquastrum*), and Aleppo pine (*Pinus halepensis*). Pseudomaquis includes some oak, box (*Buxus*), and juniper (*Juniperus*). The other types of scrub consist of shrubs. Forests do survive in the hills. There are oak and chestnut forests on the lower slopes and coniferous forests on higher ground.

The Roman Empire

Polybius worked for the Romans at a time when they, too, were expanding their empire. Eventually, this became by far the largest empire of the ancient world. In 400 C.E. it extended from Jordan in the east to the Atlantic and from North Africa, including Egypt, in the south to Britain in the north.

Many Romans became extremely wealthy, from war or trade, and took to investing their money in land, producing an agricultural system very much like our own. Land was bought and sold by speculators hoping to make a fast profit and farms became very large. Most landowners did not farm their estates themselves, but entrusted the management to bailiffs; slaves did the actual work. Small farmers found life difficult. The empire thrived on trade. This included trade in food, and the demand for food was huge. Roman Britain, comprising what are now England and Wales, but not Scotland or Ireland, became one of the most important food-producing regions of the empire and a major food exporter.

When the Romans invaded in 43 C.E., with a well-equipped army of 40,000 soldiers, they found a land that had been inhabited and much of it managed for a very long time. It is impossible to know for certain what Britain was like then, but some archaeologists believe clearance of the original-natural forest began in about 1400 B.C.E. during the Bronze Age, and that by 1000 B.C.E. there was less forest in Britain than there is today. Other scientists think about half the original forest had disappeared by 500 B.C.E. and further clearance came later, during Iron Age and Roman times.

British Farming and Industry in Roman Times

There is no doubt that the Romans, with their large estates and superior technologies, greatly intensified British farming. Agriculture expanded over most of the lowlands, large quantities of wheat and wool were exported and landowners became very prosperous. The conquest also necessitated a great deal of building. It proceeded by a series of military advances and the establishments of forts, each garrisoned by up to 1,000 soldiers. These forts, with accommodation for the troops and the civilians supporting them, were made from wood. Once an area had been subdued, colonists followed and built houses, also from wood. There was a great demand for timber.

At the same time, Britain was also industrialized. It possessed valuable ores and fuel was needed to smelt them. Iron and lead were exported, and some tin and silver. Fuel was also needed to make pottery, bricks, and tiles, and to refine salt. Before the Romans arrived, the British obtained their salt by heating stones in a fire, then throwing them into the water of a saline spring and scraping off the crust of salt that formed on the stone. The Romans taught them to produce salt by boiling brine slowly in a shallow pan. In the British climate, grain often needs drying after harvest to prevent germination. This is especially important if the grain is to be exported, because germination during transport will greatly reduce its value on arrival. Exporting farms needed grain driers. Romans liked their homes centrally heated and they enjoyed hot baths. It all needed fuel.

Wood was the only fuel, used directly or in the form of charcoal, but huge trees are not ideal. With no power tools to help, felling and then cutting them into small pieces is hard, slow work. It is more likely that each furnace, villa, and town obtained its fuel from areas nearby where small trees were coppiced (page 195) on a permanent basis.

Over much of the country, it is likely that when an opening appeared naturally in the forest, livestock were allowed in to graze. They destroyed young seedlings and prevented the clearing from closing again. Little by little, what had been closed-canopy forest gave way to a more open countryside, with large areas of pasture. Trees that survived grew to a much larger size, because they were no longer surrounded and shaded by other trees. Then, as grain crops became more important, the grasslands were plowed.

In the fifth century, Gaul (France) was conquered by the Teutons and Britain was isolated from the rest of the empire. Many troops had already been withdrawn, but the administration continued for many years independently of Rome itself. There was no time when the Roman occupation of Britain can be said to have ended. It simply decayed and Celtic influences became much stronger. By this time, most of the British original-natural forest had disappeared and with no plantation forests to take its place, Britain was no more forested than it is now.

European Forests of the Middle Ages

The Roman occupation of Britain lasted from the year 43—when an army of about 40,000 men led by Aulus Plautius landed in Kent—until early in the fifth century, when the Teutons conquered Gaul, leaving Britain cut off from the main part of the empire. After that the central government in Rome ceased to send senior officers and governors, and the rulers of Roman Britain were increasingly left to their own devices. Many troops were withdrawn before the route south was closed, but not all of them; there was no sudden end to the occupation. The empire did not depart, authority was not passed from one government to another, no flags were lowered or raised. Rome simply became irrelevant. By the sixth century, the remaining Romano-British forces and government were retreating as Saxons invaded from the east.

During the four centuries of direct Roman rule, Britain was made highly productive. Its agriculture and industries served Rome and, to provide the land and fuel they needed, forests were cleared. What happened in Britain was similar to the way many parts of Roman-occupied Europe were developed. Where land was to be settled and farmed on behalf of the Imperial Government, the area was laid out according to a careful plan, with field and estate boundaries and roads usually arranged in a grid pattern. It was not Roman organization and planning that made the agricultural expansion possible, however, but Roman technology.

Agricultural Expansion and Technology

Before the Romans arrived, only the lighter soils could be cultivated, because farmers had only a simple plow that scratched a shallow rut in the ground, throwing the soil to either side. To plow their land thoroughly they had to do the job twice, with the second set of furrows at right angles to the first. Even then the plows were useless on heavy, clay soils. Nor were the farmers able to drain low-lying, wet ground.

The Romans knew how to remove surplus water by digging ditches. This greatly increased the area suitable for cultivation, often bringing into production fine-textured, silty soils that were highly fertile once they ceased to be waterlogged. They also brought with them a variety of plows, each suitable for a different type of land. The *romanicum* was used on heavy soils, for example, the *companicum* on rather lighter soils, and the *ard*

on the lightest soils. Some plows had a coulter, which is a knife fixed to the front of the share that cuts through the soil, and some had moldboards, wing-like attachments that turned over the soil to one side, burying seeds sown before plowing.

These technological improvements—and the Romans also introduced a range of other agricultural tools—made it possible to expand farming onto the more difficult soils. To do so, it was first necessary to clear the land, and that meant removing the forest. As new land was brought into cultivation, the farmers needed housing, of course, so some timber was felled for immediate use. Wood was also needed as fuel, for providing the hot water and central heating wealthy Romans expected in their homes and for the public bathhouses used by soldiers and poorer citizens, as well as for heating grain-dryers, kilns for making bricks, mortars, and pottery, and furnaces for working metals. It was agricultural expansion that drove the forest clearance, however, rather than the demand for timber.

What we know about land use during this period is based mainly on archaeological detective work. No one at the time bothered to record what was happening, but much later a detailed record was compiled. In 1066, the most famous date in English history, William of Normandy defeated the army of the Saxon King Harold at Hastings and Britain came under Norman rule.

Domesday

William wished to know what he now possessed, so in 1085 he ordered a survey of his realm. Commissioners were sent to every corner of England (although some counties were not included because they were not then part of England) and took evidence, on oath, concerning every community. They noted the size of the population as well as detailing such matters as how much land the community had and who owned it, how the land was used, and numbers of livestock. A second team of commissioners followed behind to verify their findings. The task was completed in 1086, having taken less than one year, and the resulting documents copied into two volumes. It was exceedingly thorough, so much so that the people compared it to the interrogation they expected to receive on the Day of Judgment: they called the completed survey the "Domesday Book."

Along with much else, Domesday records the area of forest or woodland available to each com-

munity, and the result is startling. Many settlements had no woodland at all, others had very little. A place called Polroad, in Cornwall, for example, had a population of eight (including one slave), 17 acres (7 ha) of pasture, but only 3 acres (1 ha) of woodland. Some villages had 100 acres (40 ha) of woodland or more, but when the total area is added together it becomes evident that England was no longer the forested country it had once been. Some parts of the country had more forest than others, but elsewhere the landscape was one of cultivated fields and widely scattered, small woods. On average, it seems that about 7 percent of the land area was forest. This figure refers only to England (Wales and Scotland were separate countries then). Today about 10 percent of the land area of the United Kingdom (England, Wales, Scotland, and Northern Ireland) is forested. This comparison is slightly misleading, because forests cover a much higher proportion of the land area in Scotland than in England, so the proportion of forested land in England is likely to be about the same now as it was 900 years ago.

By the time of Domesday, the original forest had largely been cleared. What forest remained would have comprised mainly native species, but there may also have been some of those introduced during Roman times, such as the sweet chestnut (*Castanea sativa*).

Elsewhere in Europe, forests at that time were more extensive. To this day, a little over 28 percent of the land area of Poland is forested and the Białowieża Forest, covering 482.5 square miles (1,250 sq km), is largely virgin forest, unaffected by human intervention. In medieval times, no doubt European forests covered a larger area than they do today, but probably not a much larger area.

Medieval European Landscapes

Lowland England has been fairly densely populated for much of its history and even without the clearance in Roman times much forest would have been lost to agriculture. The effect of this can be seen when the English countryside is compared with that in much more sparsely populated Scotland. In the 16th century most of Highland Scotland below the treeline was covered with forest of pine, birch, and oak. In 1618 a poet called John Taylor walked from London to Edinburgh and then continued northwards. On his way to Braemar he walked for 12 days without seeing a single sign of human habitation of any kind, nor a single cultivated field, and he began to fear he would never again set eyes on a human dwelling. Braemar is still surrounded by forest.

The picture that emerges over the lowland regions of Europe as a whole is of a generally forested landscape, but with areas cleared for farming around cities, towns, and villages. The size and number of such cleared areas obviously depended on the size of the human population farmers had to support, so in densely populated regions—such as England, Flanders, and the Netherlands—the countryside was one of cultivated fields, open pastureland, and isolated, usually small, woods. This is the kind of landscape shown in paintings by European masters from the late medieval period and a little later, for example in "The Harvesters," by Pieter Brueghel the Elder, painted in about 1565.

Forests as a Resource

Vast tracts of forest were set aside for hunting. This was a sport for the wealthy, of course, but it was also a means of procuring food. The game that was killed was eaten, and to ensure a plentiful supply hunting forests were carefully protected. That still left large areas, remote from towns and farms, where the forest was what today we would call "wilderness."

In inhabited areas, however, what remained of the forest was an important resource. It was often called "waste" or "wasteland," suggesting it was land for which no one had any use, but that is not what "waste" meant. The waste was simply the uncultivated land beyond the better pasture and the fields where crops were grown. Although some forest areas were privately owned, usually it was land used by the community as a whole, rather than being reserved for the exclusive use of its owner.

Not only were the forests used, they were used fairly intensively. Except on the moors, where peat was obtainable, and in those places where coal could be dug from shallow mines, wood was the only fuel for cooking and heating (page 154). Ordinary homes, sheds, and barns were built wholly or partly from wood. Wood was needed for making tools, boats, wheeled vehicles, boxes, furniture, fences, and a vast array of everyday items. People used metals, of course, but the fuel used to smelt and forge them was charcoal, made from wood.

These different needs called for different kinds of wood, and this led to the development of different kinds of forest. Big machines and power tools had not been invented. There was no way people could take just any kind of wood, chop it into chips, then reassemble the chips in any shape they chose. Nor could they easily cut large timber into particular shapes. Instead, they had to choose the tree to fit the purpose. Timber was felled as the local carpenters and builders needed it and it was used at once, without being seasoned. The bent and warped timbers that can still be seen in surviving medieval buildings show clearly that these were installed while the wood was still green.

Needs varied. One village might be expanding, increasing the demand for structural timber, or it might be decided to build a new bridge over a river, while another village changed little from one generation to the next. Sometimes it might be necessary to buy timber from outside the community if no local tree was large enough. The post around which a windmill is built is immense, and might have to be bought somewhere else and carried to the building site. Its weight made that difficult, of course, so it would be bought as close to the site as possible.

Over the years this led to specialization in types of forest, and forests came to vary greatly. A forest from which people cut small wood (page 158), consisting of poles to make tool handles, fences, and other small articles, was not the same as one supplying large timber for building, and both of these were different from wood-pasture. This is open woodland, where the trees are too far apart for their crowns to form a closed canopy, allowing grasses to grow between them. Wood-pasture supplies wood and also sheltered grazing for cattle and sheep.

Preventing Overexploitation

Exploitation of the forests had to be regulated in order to ensure a continuity of supply. It was that regulation, and the techniques associated with it, that led to the emergence of different categories of forest. Powerful landowners jealously guarded their forests against overexploitation and dealt harshly with those who took more than the permitted amount of wood. Concern to conserve the forest resource seems to have been widespread: in Germany for example, the amount of wood people were allowed to take was strictly rationed. A letter has survived, written in the middle of the 12th century by a bishop of Norwich, England, rebuking his woodward (the official in charge of the forest) for giving away wood. "I appointed you the custodian of the Wood," he wrote, "not the rooter up of it . . . Guard the Wood of the Holy Trinity, as you wish to be guarded by the Holy Trinity, and to continue in my favor."

Ensuring a continuing supply of wood and timber meant no tree should be felled unless another tree would grow up to replace it. Young saplings had to be fenced to protect them from grazing animals and when trees were felled the damage they caused to others had to be minimized. Small wood could be obtained without killing the trees supplying it. Coppicing (page 195) was a common practice by the middle of the 13th century. Careful assessments were made of the amount of wood and timber particular areas of forest could yield and permitted harvests calculated accordingly. Those who broke the rules were fined.

Medieval forests in populated areas were managed, but they were not planted. They were what remained of the original, primeval forest and although their composition may have changed, such change was not planned. Unlike plantations, they were permanent features of the landscape where trees did not grow in rows, or in blocks all of similar age. They were scattered irregularly, with clearings here and there, and paths and rivers winding through them. Commercial forestry, based on orderly plantations, came later.

Forests in Folklore and Literature

Little Red Riding Hood, you will remember, was a little girl who succeeded in outwitting a wolf. Red Riding Hood (also known as Little Red-Cap: her original German name was Rotkäppchen) met the wolf soon after she had set out to deliver meat and wine to her grandmother, who lived half an hour's walk away, deep in the forest. Like all such tales, this one has several meanings, and it is not really about genuine wolves and forests. Nevertheless, stories must be set somewhere, and to the German country people from whom the Brothers Grimm collected their stories, the word "forest" would immediately evoke images of darkness and danger. Wolves lived in the forest and, although most of the time they kept away from people and were harmless, they could not be trusted. Occasionally they attacked, for no obvious reason.

Wolves were but one of many hazards facing those who wandered in the forest, and they were far from the worst. In Hansel and Gretel the two children became lost in the forest and fell into the hands of a witch, who waylaid children, then cooked and ate them.

Poor Woodcutters and Abandoned Children

Unlike the woodland immediately surrounding farms and villages, the forest was of little material value to ordinary people. Kings and nobles might hunt game in it, but it was no place to try to earn a living. Hansel and his sister Gretel were the children of a woodcutter so poor he could barely feed the family when times were good, and when famine afflicted the whole country, they faced starvation. Again, the story has deeper meanings. It was the woodcutter's second wife, the children's stepmother, who was determined to save her husband and herself by allowing Hansel and Gretel to perish from hunger, lost in the forest, and it was the children's own cleverness, courage, and loyalty to each other that saved them. People respond to images subconsciously and it is as though "dwelling in the forest" was synonymous with "living in dire poverty." Another story, "The Woodcutter's Child," tells of a woodcutter so poor it was all the family could do to place food on the table every day of the week. Snow White, another child abandoned by a wicked stepmother, finds refuge with a party of dwarfs, who protect her. They live, of course, deep in the forest.

Poverty was very real, of course, and it is only in the last hundred years or so, and then only in North America, Europe, and a few other regions that famines have ceased to be periodic in which poor people died from hunger. Desperate people really did abandon infants in the forest because they were unable to feed them. "Babes in the Wood" is a children's story based on "The Children in the Wood," a ballad believed to have been written in 1595, and several similar tales were written in England at about that time. These tell of a man who dies, leaving his property to his infant son and daughter and the children to the care of his brother. The brother hires two men to carry the children into the forest and kill them, so he can gain their inheritance. One of the assassins relents, kills his companion, and leaves the babes in the wood, where they die and are buried in leaves by a bird (a robin redbreast). The assassin is later arrested and confesses.

Universal Tales

French folk tales view forests in much the same way. "Beauty and the Beast" (*La Belle et la Bête*) teaches us that beauty is only skin-deep, and that a fearsome exterior may conceal a noble heart. Probably every culture in the world has its own version of this story. The beast, as you would expect, dwells in a palace surrounded by barely penetrable briars and brambles and set deep inside a forest. A merchant, on his way home, loses his way in the forest, comes across the apparently unoccupied palace, and plucks a rose as a gift for his daughter (La Belle), but is caught by the beast, who allows him to leave with the rose on condition that the daughter visit him. She does; eventually falls in love, and the beast is revealed as a handsome prince.

Like "Beauty and the Beast," most cultures have their own versions of all the classic fairy and folk tales. We learn many of them from those compiled by Jacob and Wilhelm Grimm (1785–1863 and 1786–1859 respectively) in Germany, Charles Perrault (1628–1703) in France, and Andrew Lang (1844–1912) in Britain. Names and minor details change, but the story remains the same, and so does its location. Forests are almost inevitably mysterious and full of concealed hazards, a metaphor for life and the ease with which people may lose their way and fall into spiritual danger. There is always hope, of course. Woodcutters, most of whom seem to have beautiful daughters, are decent, hardworking folk living in poverty, but a poverty that can be ended by a stroke of good fortune, which must always be earned.

There are exceptions, however. Russian fairy and folk tales seem to ignore the forest that covers such a vast area of their country. They set stories in countries far away, on the far side of a huge forest, as a literary device to show that what follows will be remote from events that happen in the everyday, familiar world—the equivalent of the "Once upon a time, in a far distant land. . ." opening. The forest is an obstacle, but no more. Nor are Russian stories peopled with fairies or other spirits. There are benign forces and evil monsters, the direct descendants of pre-Christian gods and demons, but they do not lurk in the darkness among the trees, waiting to leap out at travelers. The stories have their share of magic, but it is the magic of nature, involving birds and mammals that talk and involve themselves in human affairs.

Shakespeare's Wilderness

Fear and dislike of the forest were not confined to folk tales. They were part of the way most people saw the world around them. To Shakespeare, the forest was a wilderness, mysterious, secret, and dangerous. It was land that was unused and unusable, an environment inherently hostile to humans. Like other poets and playwrights, Shakespeare thought of forests in much the same way that many authors nowadays think of deserts.

As You Like It is a comedy that takes place in the Forest of Arden, where the Duke, who has been usurped by his brother, lives in exile with his supporters. The Forest of Arden was real—many Elizabethan authors referred to it—and Shakespeare described it as "this desert inaccessible, Under the shade of melancholy boughs" (*As You Like It,* Act II, Scene 7). Clearly, it was a place where a large number of people could hide. In *A Midsummer Night's Dream,* the forest, this time located somewhere not far from Athens, is inhabited by fairies and other spirits. They may be charming, and their accidental involvement with humans leads to great confusion and much merriment, but no serious harm, yet that involvement arises from the quarrel between Oberon and Titania, the king and queen of the fairies, over a changeling Titania has taken and refuses to give to Oberon, who wants the stolen human child as a page.

Dangers in the Forest

Metaphors succeed by using what is familiar to illuminate what is not. If the general idea of a journey through a forest could stand so easily for the journey through life, with the difficulty of finding a "true way" among many paths, through territory with terrifying wild beasts, witches, mischievous sprites, and malevolent demons lying in wait in every dark corner, it must be that this is something like what people really believed about forests. Had it not been part of their received wisdom that forests were best avoided, the stories could not have communicated their messages.

Forests really were dangerous places. Even today, it is surprisingly easy to become lost in one, even when there are paths. Without a compass or some other means of determining direction, there are no reference points, no landmarks to show the way, and for most of us, being lost in a large forest still means serious trouble. We are not trained to find food, drink, and shelter in a forest, far less to deal with any medical emergency that might arise.

Outlaws and Brigands

In earlier times people could come to more serious harm. Robin Hood is a folk hero, who may or may not be based on a real person, but forests did harbor bands of outlaws, and few if any of them gave to the poor what they took from the rich. The Robin Hood stories probably date from the 13th century, and originally he was not a contemporary of Richard I. He personified the discontent of the poor in the north of England with the way they were being governed, a discontent that spread to the whole country and culminated in the Peasant's Revolt in 1381.

Robin Hood was a political rebel and he was not the only one. Eadric the wild, or Eadric of the Woodland, was a Saxon rebel fighting a guerrilla war against the Normans from forests in the west of England, near the Welsh border. In 1069, Eadric and his followers led an assault on a Norman castle and burned it to the ground, and then overcame the garrison in Shrewsbury castle and for a time occupied the castle himself.

Other forest outlaws were brigands. They operated in bands and were violent. Malcolm Musard, for example, who lived in the early 14th century, seems to have started as leader of a gang of poachers in the forests of Worcestershire and Gloucestershire. After a time, he commanded about 300 followers, and took to extortion from local landowners. When one landowner, Thomas of Lench, refused to pay up, the Musard gang felled about 200 of his trees and grazed cattle on his land. Others paid up—the rector of the village of Martley is known to have paid in wheat. Eventually Musard was captured, but was acquitted of all charges and appointed Chief Forester, protecting the royal forests mainly by

the means he had always used and profiting handsomely.

There were gangs of this kind in most forests, led by men who gave themselves fancy titles. Near York there was one who called himself Lionell, King of the Rout of Raveners. There were outlaw bands that set up their own forms of government and legal systems and some of these were formidably large. William Beckwith, whose band formed a parliament and appointed local officials near Knaresborough, Yorkshire, commanded 500 or more followers in about 1390. There were times when large tracts of the forested English countryside would be under the complete control of a gang and remain so for several years. When gang leaders were caught, often they were allowed to buy a pardon, which also involved their appointment to some official position. A brigand was thus transformed into a loyal servant of the crown, the peace was restored, but the resulting officials could not shake off their background quite so easily. Local people sometimes paid a heavy price for having a former criminal as a government official.

Not all those who found refuge in the forest were especially dangerous. Some, probably petty offenders and those whose political or religious beliefs rendered them unpopular with the authorities, lived as best they could and as inconspicuously as possible. They might trap game and take some wood. Both activities were unlawful, but they took only what they needed for their own use. Some worked for the charcoal makers, who asked no questions. Any traveler encountering them would find some of these ragged, filthy, folk sullen and probably verbally aggressive. Others, though, would simply be evasive. They were not dangerous robbers, although meeting them may well have been an alarming experience.

People had some reason to fear the forest and sometimes parts of forests were cleared for reasons of security. In 1712, Viscount Weymouth cleared part of Selwood Forest, in Somerset, and built a church on the land, in order to drive out the bandits and forgers who had been operating there. Many forests harbored criminal bands, not all of them engaging in robbery. Even trees growing beside roads could conceal highwaymen.

The actual number of robbers may have been exaggerated, but the stories about them and the others who hid in the forests accorded with the general opinion—held right up until the last century—that our ancestors, as people who once lived in the forest, were necessarily barbarous, uncivilized, and rough. Our word "savage," comes from the Old French *sauvage,* from *salvaticus,* which is from the Latin *silvaticus,* a wood dweller (*silva* means "wood").

Wild Beasts

Forests also harbored wolves and, rightly or wrongly, these were much feared. When royal lands were granted to tenants in medieval times, it was often a condition that the occupant keep dogs to hunt wolves and attempt to destroy all wolves on those lands. In April 1644, the English writer John Evelyn saw the heads of wolves nailed to the gates of the castle at Blois, on the banks of the River Loire, France.

Still earlier, during the reign of the Saxon English king Athelstan (reigned 924–939) there were so many wolves in Yorkshire that near Filey someone called Acehorn built a retreat where travelers could shelter if they were being attacked. Athelstan intervened in a quarrel between two Welsh princes, then imposed an annual fine on Constantine, the Welsh king, that was remitted by his successor Edgar, on condition that Ludwall, Constantine's successor as king of Wales, pay him in annual tribute the carcasses of 300 wolves. The tribute was paid for two or three years, but then ceased because no more wolves could be found. At one time historians believed the penalty imposed by King Edgar may have brought about the extinction of the wolf in Wales; it is now thought that the wolf finally disappeared from the country about half a century later. The wolf became extinct in England some time in the late 15th or early 16th century and in Scotland, which was much more extensively forested, in the 18th century. The last one was killed in Ireland in the late 18th century.

Nowadays we try to preserve natural forest, but until about the middle of the last century, the "wild wood" was a fearful place and its clearance was to be encouraged. Drive back the forest, and many benefits follow. Land is freed for farming, reducing the risk of famine. Visibility is improved, so approaching dangers can be seen well in advance of their arrival. Travel, and trade associated with it, becomes easier and safer. Wild animals live further away from farms and habitations, so they pose less risk to people and livestock, and outlawed criminals can no longer hide in the forest and prey on communities near the forest edge. The rule of law can be extended and people can live in peace. Throughout most of history, civilization expanded by clearing the forest.

The first European settlers in North America took these attitudes with them. Behind the coastal strip, and in places reaching all the way to the coast, they faced the American Forest, in their eyes vast, desolate, and haunted by wild beasts and wild men. They set about clearing the forest, not simply to win ground for cultivation, but to make the land fit for civilized people and as settlements expanded bounties were paid for killing wolves.

As recently as 1868, the state of Minnesota paid $10 apiece for the scalps of wolves and in that year paid wolf hunters a total of $11,300.

Tree Worship

There was a great difference between the untamed forest and those parts of the forest from which people obtained wood and fuel and where their pigs were allowed to roam. This was safe and useful forest, and within it people recognized trees as individuals. Trees were once worshiped, not only in Europe and North America, but everywhere in the world. Like all natural objects, trees possessed spirits, but theirs were big, important spirits, reflecting the stature of trees themselves. Consequently, trees had to be treated with respect. In some places, only certain trees had spirits. In parts of Dalmatia, a province of Croatia, for example, trees without spirits could be cut down with impunity, but a woodman who felled one that had a spirit would either die quickly or be crippled for life—unless he used the same ax with which he cut down the tree to behead a chicken on the stump of the felled tree. Everywhere, trees were thought to be sensitive and had to be treated with great care.

The major religions displaced most of these old beliefs, but never quite banished them completely. May Day celebrations are the most widespread surviving relics of tree worship. Either on May 1 or Midsummer Day people used to cut down a tree in the nearest wood and set it up, garlanded with flowers, in the center of the village, and to decorate houses with branches. Details of the customs vary from place to place, but in one way or another May Day is celebrated with trees, branches, flowers, and a great feast throughout all of Europe and Russia.

Ash and Oak

Each species of tree has its own particular qualities and these were believed to derive from the characters of the spirits inhabiting them. Ash was one of the most important. In one of the Norse creation myths, in the beginning there was Yggdrasill, the great ash tree. One of its three roots reached to the domain of the god Ódin, one to the land of the Frost Giants, and the third to the kingdom of the goddess Hel, the land of the dead. One day, the gods Ódin, Hoenir, and Lodurr were walking along the seashore when they came across two trees. From the ash tree (Askr) they made the first man and from the elm tree (Embla) they made the first woman. The gods then brought the humans to life.

Further south, the oak was the most revered of trees. Both the Greeks and Romans associated it with Zeus, or Jupiter, the highest of the gods and directly responsible for the sky, rain, and thunder. Zeus dwelt in the Greek mountains, where the oak trees grow, and in Italy every oak was sacred to Jupiter. Among Celtic peoples, the mistletoe was sacred as well as the oak on which it grows, and the ancient Germans held the oak to be the most sacred of all trees and linked to the thunder-god Thunar, or Donar, whom we remember still every Donnerstag, Thunar's Day, or Thursday. Oaks were also sacred to the Slav thunder-god, known in Russian as Pyerun and to the Lithuanians as Perkunas. Perpetual fires, kindled with oak wood, burned in his honor and to ensure good crops men made sacrifices to oak trees and women to lime trees.

Elder and Rowan

Lesser trees also had personality. Elder would keep away evil spirits and a sprig of elder leaves worn in the hair or on the coat would give protection outdoors. Elders were grown near homes for protection, and the spirits were paid with offerings of cakes and milk. Rowan linked this world with the next and was inhabited by fairies, believed by some to be the spirits of the dead, who will fend off supernatural harm. It is lucky to have rowan growing near your home. In one Scottish legend it even saved the life of a fox. It was chased to the edge of a cliff by men and dogs and escaped by dropping from rowan to rowan.

It is not surprising that so many beliefs should be associated with forests and with the trees that grow in them. Until very recently the wild wood really was wild and dangerous, a place to be feared. At the same time, trees supplied so many needs that they became very familiar, as sensitive, spiritual beings each with its own individual characteristics.

Opposite: Gray wolf, temperate North America (Gerry Ellis/ENP Images)

The History of Forestry

On November 5, 1662, John Evelyn recorded in his diary that the council of the Royal Society met at Gresham College, "where was a discourse suggested by me, concerning planting His Majesty's Forest of Dean with oak, now so much exhausted of the choicest ship-timber in the world." This "discourse" led in 1668 to a program of planting in the Forest of Dean, today covering 27,000 acres (almost 11,000 ha) in western Gloucestershire, England.

John Evelyn (1620–1706) was a man of letters, the author of about 30 books, and he kept a diary from the age of 11. In 1661 he joined the scientific society that the following year became the Royal Society of London. He was appointed to its council and remained active in its affairs for the rest of his life.

It was in 1662 that the commissioners of the navy asked the newly formed society to comment on the depletion of timber suitable for shipbuilding, and the matter was passed over to John Evelyn. As part of his broad education, he had studied the cultivation and uses of plants in Paris and he loved trees. His reply to the navy came in the form of a book, published in 1664, called *Sylva, or a Discourse of Forest-Trees, and the Propagation of Timber in His Majesties Dominions.* The book was meant for estate owners and was in three parts. One gave instructions for growing apples for cider and a second was a general gardening manual, but the main part of it described the cultivation of different species of trees and the uses of their timber, all written in plain, but excellent English.

The book was a huge success. An enlarged second edition was published in 1670, a third, with an added section about soils, in 1679, and a fourth, enlarged still further, this time by the addition of a section on salad crops, in 1706, soon after his death. More editions appeared in subsequent years, some consisting of the forestry section by itself, the last edition appearing in 1825.

Conserving Forests

For about 150 years *Sylva* was the standard work on forestry, and its publication is often taken to mark the beginning of the deliberate planting of trees as a crop. Obviously, it was not quite that simple: Evelyn did not invent the idea of organized tree-planting. Indeed, he included in *Sylva* examples of landowners who had already established timber plantations. He was not even the first propagandist for tree-growing, but he was certainly the most famous and, perhaps, the most persuasive.

Penalties for the unlawful felling of trees were being exacted as early as the seventh century, and forest management had been practiced since Norman times. When trees were felled in the royal forests, the area was fenced to allow young trees to grow up and replace them. During the 15th and 16th centuries a number of laws were enacted to prevent overexploitation of forests.

Areas of land were not being deliberately planted with trees, however. Farm leases often required trees to be planted to replace those that were felled or died. Farmers were expected to gather seeds for this purpose and some writers of the time gave instructions for transplanting, but the policy was mainly to control felling and allow natural regeneration, rather than to plant. Plantation planting began during the 16th century, but patchily and on a small scale. Often it involved planting a mixture of seeds collected locally, then managing the resulting trees as coppice (page 195). This method imitated natural woodland.

The first recorded instance in England of planting a block of trees all of one species was in 1580, when Lord Burghley had 13 acres (5.26 ha) of oaks planted in Windsor Park (they are still there). It was not until the reign of Charles II that forestry became more widespread, starting with the planting scheme in the Forest of Dean that John Evelyn had recommended.

Shipbuilding and Profit

From about 1600, both the Royal Navy and the British merchant fleet started to increase in size. Those wooden ships were built almost entirely from British timber, apart from the masts, for which tall, straight, conifer trunks were imported. This expansion led to a widespread fear that the demands of shipbuilding would deplete the forests, the fear John Evelyn examined on behalf of the commissioners of the navy. It is very doubtful that there was a material shortage of timber. Despite their rapid expansion, the military and merchant fleets were quite small and so were the vessels comprising them. The major expansion came in the late 18th and early 19th centuries, and since suitable timber was available then it must have been available earlier, because of the rate at which oak trees grow. What is more likely is that the commissioners of the navy were offering much too low a price for timber, landowners were refusing to sell to them, and so there appeared to be a shortage.

The purpose of forestry was to make a profit. The propagandists for tree-planting, including Evelyn, made much of the amount by which tree plantations could increase the value of estates. One estimate was that after 18 years, white poplars which cost £30 ($48 at the 1997 exchange rate, although it is difficult to compare 17th-century monetary values with those of today) to plant would be worth £10,000 ($16,000). Adam Smith (1723–90), the famous author of *The Wealth of Nations,* believed timber was as profitable a crop as wheat or pasture.

Popularity of Forest Clearance

Even so, the English tradition of clearing forests persisted for a surprisingly long time. There were many landowners who believed the removal of trees improved the land. Early in the 19th century, the Board of Agriculture, a government agency, commissioned its secretary, the agricultural writer Arthur Young (1741–1820) to assess the benefits that might accrue from enclosing and cultivating open land. In his *General Report on Enclosures,* published in 1808, Young included forests as wasteland suitable for improvement. "When it is considered that some of the Royal Forests are situated upon soils which would be productive in all the usual crops raised by the common agriculture of the kingdom," he wrote, "they will, without question, appear to be an object which merits no slight attention."

Felling trees contributed to progress and there was Biblical authority for it. Psalm 74 tells us (verse 5) that "A man was famous according as he had lifted up axes upon the thick trees." William Ewart Gladstone (1809–98), a major landowner as well as British prime minister four times, certainly believed this, and his passion for tree-felling was much publicized.

This is why, when, in 1895, he visited the German chancellor, Bismarck presented him with an oak sapling to plant back home in Britain. Germans had been cultivating coniferous forest plantations for a very long time. The earliest record of one, at Nuremberg, dates from 1368. The Black Forest, covering about 2,300 square miles (almost 6,000 sq km) in Baden-Württemberg, consists mainly of Norway spruce, but only because beech and oak are kept confined to the valleys and not allowed to colonize the higher ground. The Black Forest is plantation forest.

Meanwhile, aristocratic owners of large estates were planting trees for ornamental as much as commercial reasons. Landscape designers encouraged them to create parks, with trees scattered informally. This was a highly ostentatious display of wealth, because the scale of planting was huge. Historians have calculated that between 1760 and 1835 private landowners planted at least 50 million timber trees in Britain. Many of these were imported, exotic trees, the taste for which grew to such an extent that by around 1840 it was only exotic trees or greatly improved native ones that were considered fashionable. Attitudes toward trees became thoroughly sentimentalized and in England individual trees and groves came to be cherished. In France, on the other hand, mature trees were harvested and it was rare to see an old tree.

The inadequacy of the British approach became evident during World War I, when timber had to be imported through a partial sea blockade. After the war, in 1919, the Forestry Commission was established. A government agency, its task was to acquire land and develop a state-owned forest large enough to provide a strategic reserve of timber. By 1983 the total area of national forest amounted to more than 5 million acres (2 million ha), distributed throughout England, Wales, and Scotland, most of it growing conifers.

North American Forestry

This area is about the same as that of the public forests in the United States apart from Alaska, but the area of privately owned forest is much greater than in Britain. Public forests are managed by the U.S. Forest Service, an agency within the Department of Agriculture.

As North American settlers moved westward during the last century, they cleared large areas of the apparently endless forest. Trees were so abundant there seemed no need to cultivate them and it was not until 1877 that Carl Schurz, Secretary of the Interior, persuaded Congress to take seriously the risk that if felling continued the entire American Forest might disappear. In 1891 and 1897 there was legislation authorizing the president to take land into public ownership in order to protect it from exploitation, and in 1921 and 1924 Congress authorized the federal government to buy forested land. At first, protection of the American forests was intended to safeguard watersheds, and only secondarily to produce timber. In both the United States and Canada, plantation forestry of the kind practiced in Europe is probably less important than management of the natural forest, with controls on the amounts of timber to be taken and the time allowed for regeneration.

Russian Forestry

Russian forestry is also a mixture of management and planting. Interest in protecting the forests began in the 17th century. Areas were set aside inside which felling was strictly controlled or forbidden, partly to protect watersheds. Then, in 1888, all forests, both private and state-owned, were made subject to conservation laws. Following the revolution, private ownership of forests ceased. Cutting continued according to the demand for timber, but management improved and large areas were planted, including about 15 million acres (6 million ha) of shelter belts around farmed land.

At one time, forests covered much of temperate Europe and North America, but people came to realize that if they went on taking timber as they needed it, in time the forest would disappear. They had to find a way to produce timber on a sustainable basis, so the resource would remain available indefinitely. The method they developed led to modern forestry.

Renewable and Nonrenewable Resources

Trees grow. This means that felling a tree to use its timber does not necessarily reduce the amount of timber available for future use. A new tree may grow to replace the one that was felled. If you liken trees to money in a bank account, the forester is living on the interest while the capital, which is the total number of trees, remains unchanged.

Watch a house being built in a residential part of town and you may be surprised at the amount of timber the builders use. Some houses are made entirely from wood, of course, but even if you will see walls of only bricks or stone and roofs of slates or tiles, inside it is timber that provides the framework for the roof. The whole house may be supported by a timber frame.

Perhaps, at the same time as this house is being built, not far away other builders are hard at work erecting an office block or shopping mall. These larger buildings also have frames, in this case made from steel. Steel and timber both perform the same function, steel in large buildings and timber in smaller ones. Both are materials on which we depend and to some extent they are interchangeable. It would be unusual, but you could build a house with a steel frame and a larger building with a wooden frame. For example, the medieval cathedrals of Europe are huge buildings, made from stone and timber.

We need buildings, both large and small, and therefore we must have the materials from which to construct them. These materials must be kept available so we can take what we need when we need it, like withdrawing money from a bank account. Money, stored in a bank until it is needed, is sometimes called an "asset" or "resource." When someone wants to start a business, an adviser may ask her whether she has "the resources" to do so, meaning the money it will cost. In the same way, timber and steel are resources. Without them, planning a building would be a waste of time.

Renewable and Nonrenewable

They are both resources, but there is an important difference between them. Steel consists mainly of iron, with added carbon and small, measured amounts of other metals to strengthen it and give it particular qualities. The iron itself, and also the other metals, are obtained from ores, which are minerals separated from rocks taken from the ground. Timber comes from trees and different qualities of timber are obtained by growing different species of trees. Take a ton of mineral ore from the ground and it is gone. There is a hole where it used to be. You can fill in the hole, but you cannot fill it with newly made ore similar to the ore you removed. Cut down a tree and it will leave a gap in the forest, but in this case not only can you fill the gap, you can fill it with a new tree just like the one that was felled. The metal ore is a resource that cannot be replaced once it has been used. It is what is often called a "nonrenewable" resource. Timber, on the other hand, is a "renewable" resource. Like a farm crop, it can be replaced.

Explained like this, the distinction between renewable and nonrenewable resources is very clear. At one time there were fears that one day the world would face shortages of some nonrenewable resources. Obviously, if we continue using them, eventually they will be gone. That is what "nonrenewable" means. Renewable resources were seen as much less of a problem, simply because they are easily replaced. In fact, the difference between the two kinds of resources is much less clear than it seems.

The first qualification concerns timescales. It is not literally true that certain resources are nonrenewable. Eventually, metals return to the ground as junk, the part of Earth's crust on which they lie is subducted into the mantle, and that mantle rock reemerges somewhere else to form new crust. The process takes millions of years, but

metals do not leave the planet. They are called "nonrenewable" because we use them much faster than they can be replaced naturally. Timber is replaced more rapidly, in tens of years rather than millions, but it is still possible for it to be used faster than it can regrow. Modern forestry was developed in part to avoid this risk (page 198), but it is not practiced everywhere in the world.

Resources and Reserves

A more serious complication arises from the very idea of a "resource." This is a substance for which we have a practical use—where people have a use for something other people will do their best to provide it. If we have a demand for timber, foresters will fell more trees and, if they believe the demand will be sustained, they will plant more forests. If there is a demand for a particular metal, mining companies will extract more of the ore.

These companies know how much ore their mines contain, so they can calculate how long it will be before the mine is worked out and their operations must move elsewhere. Preparing for that day, they conduct surveys to locate the places where the next mines must be opened, and they identify the most likely sources of ore to move to after that. Ores they have identified are known as "reserves." If the amount of ore has actually been measured, it is called a "proven reserve." If geologists have taken samples and calculated the amount for a mine that has not yet opened, it is an "indicated reserve." If the amount is calculated on the basis of the rock structures and past experience, but without making measurements, it is an "inferred reserve." If the presence of ore is suspected because of the types of rock, it is a "potential reserve."

Making measurements and using the word "reserve" makes it sound as though the quantities involved are precise and fixed, but it is not like that. Eventually, the highest-quality ore will have been taken from a mine. There will be plenty of ore left, but of lower quality, which means it will be more expensive to extract metal from it. Other companies may be able to produce the metal more cheaply, so the mine becomes uneconomic and must close. It can happen, however, that a new technology is developed which makes it practicable to mine poorer ores. It can also happen that demand for the metal increases rapidly and prices rise. In both cases it becomes worthwhile to work the poorer ore and the mine stays in business. At the same time, increasing demand compels companies to search more vigorously for new sources and identify new reserves. The resource may be nonrenewable, but if the demand for it increases the size of the reserves also increases. Between 1950 and 1970, because of increased demand, reserves of the principal ore for tin increased 10 percent, for copper 179 percent, for aluminum 279 percent, and for chromium 675 percent.

Technological Change

Changes in the way materials are used can also be dramatic, and rising prices can produce major savings. Most small family cars will now travel at least 35 miles per gallon (15 km per l) of gasoline, for example. About 30 years ago, most European family cars achieved no more than 25 miles per gallon (11 km per l). The improvement was the result of better car and engine design driven by higher fuel prices.

Technological change also affects the way we use resources. Copper is used mainly for electrical wiring and until recently huge amounts were needed for the cables carrying telephone lines. Today, copper telephone wires are being replaced with optic fibers, made from a special kind of glass. An increasing amount of long-distance communication travels as radio waves to and from orbiting satellites, rather than by submarine cable. Copper is much less important than it was.

Optic fibers and satellites are replacing copper wires because they are more efficient, not because there is a shortage of copper. If there were a shortage, of copper or anything else, we would find alternatives.

This does not mean we can afford to be careless in our use of resources. For one thing, any use of materials affects the environment, and the less we use, the less environmental damage we are likely to cause. It does mean, however, that hoarding a "nonrenewable" resource for the benefit of future generations is not necessarily wise. The resource may be more abundant than we suppose and in years to come technological advances may render it obsolete.

Caring for Renewables

Substitutes can also be found for most renewable resources, but it is more difficult. We have been using timber for building ever since people started making shelters for themselves, and we are still using it. Wood is still the most widely used material for making tables and chairs, cupboards and shelves, tool handles, and a vast range of other household items. There are substitutes: metals and plastics are just as good. Many people prefer wood, but the real reason its rivals have so far failed to supplant it has nothing to do with sentiment. It is simply that planting more trees is easy and cheap—at least in temperate regions—and wood requires little processing. It does not have to be smelted, refined, or synthesized in a factory, but merely stored while it matures and then cut to the desired shape. Some commodities may be as good as wood, but wood is always likely to be cheaper.

Its renewability is what gives wood its main economic advantage, but this conceals a danger. Planting more trees is easy and cheap, but only provided there is suitable land on which to plant them. In many parts of the temperate regions there are competing demands for land and most forms of land use are more profitable than forestry. A field of corn is worth less than a field of houses, but a field of trees, especially young ones that will not be ready to harvest for some years, is worth less than either. Consequently, we should take special care that our forests continue to occupy an area large enough to supply timber and wood (see pages 156 and 158 for an explanation of the difference) at a sufficient rate to match our use of them.

Forests as Sources of Fuel

Around 10,000 years ago people in southwest Asia started cultivating wheat and barley and tending domesticated livestock. In parts of China they had already been growing rice and millet for a long time. Until they domesticated crop plants and animals, people lived by gathering wild plants, hunting animals, and scavenging—stealing what meat they could from the bodies of large animals killed by more powerful predators.

When they obtained these foods, what did they do with them? Did they eat everything raw? At first they did, but then they learned how to use fire to cook their food. This greatly extended the range of foods they could eat, because many plant and animal parts are inedible or unpleasant to eat raw, but delicious cooked. The possession of fire also meant, of course, that people could move into higher latitudes, where the climate was cooler but food was abundant.

Many generations must have passed before the users of fire became makers of fire. Fires occur naturally. After a spell of dry weather lightning readily ignites withered vegetation and once a fire starts it is not difficult to keep it burning. Brands would be taken to the campsite and the fire there kept fueled. When people left on hunting or food-gathering expeditions, they would leave behind a fire damped down so it would still be alight when they returned, and a little gentle blowing would be enough to fan it into flame. Scientists believe this way of life began some hundreds of thousands of years ago and that the first people to use fire were not modern humans, just like ourselves, but our more remote ancestors. The use of fire, in other words, is older than our species.

Wood as Fuel

The fuel, of course, was wood, and for many people in developing countries today that is still the only fuel available. In 1992, for example, 13.3 percent of all the energy used in Brazil came from the burning of wood. It amounted to 301 cubic yards (230 million cubic meters) a year. In Asia and the Pacific islands, fuel-wood provides up to 80 percent of the energy used, in Bhutan accounting for 80 percent, and in Nepal for 75 percent. Even in the industrialized countries of Europe and North America, wood is widely used as fuel, especially in rural areas. It accounts for about 10 percent of all the energy used to heat homes in Norway, Sweden, and the United States; in most cases this is from choice rather than necessity, and few if any European or American families have to walk miles through the forest to gather it, as some people do in Asia and Africa.

Those who depend on fuel-wood may have to make do with whatever is available, but not all trees produce wood that burns equally well. Elder, for example, spits hot cinders, and people will not use it on their fires. Softwoods, such as pine and spruce, contain resin. They are easier to ignite and burn hotter than hardwoods, such as oak and elm.

An open log fire is a cheerful sight and wood is the most obvious of all fuels, because in most places it is so abundant and because it burns so readily. Size for size, a log fire does not warm a room so well as an open coal fire, however, and the ordinary coal fire gives out less heat than an anthracite fire. Coal, including anthracite, is a form of fossilized wood, of course, and both wood and coal are made mainly from carbon and hydrogen, but coal has been compressed and that explains why it burns more hotly: its carbon and hydrogen, the combustible ingredients, are packed more tightly together than they are in wood. One tonne of wood, dried to 20 percent moisture content, has a volume of about 3.2 cubic meters (about 100 cubic feet per ton); one tonne of coal occupies about 0.25 cubic meters (about 8 cubic feet per ton).

Coal has lost most of its water. Freshly cut green wood can contain as much as two parts of water to every part of combustible fiber by weight, and most of the smoke from a wood fire is water that has been vaporized by the heat and then condensed again into minute droplets. Wood can be dried, but unless it is dried in kilns, the dry wood still holds around 15 percent to 20 percent of water.

Composition of Fuels

Combustion is the oxidation of carbon to carbon dioxide and of hydrogen to hydrogen oxide (water). Both reactions release energy. Burning 1 kg of carbon fully to carbon dioxide releases about 33.7 megajoules (MJ) of heat (14,500 BTU per pound) and 1 kg of hydrogen releases about 164 MJ (62,000 BTU per pound). Clearly, the higher the proportion of carbon and hydrogen the fuel contains the more energy it will deliver. The table on page 155 shows how wood that has been dried completely compares with coal. It contains an average 48.5 percent of carbon by weight compared with 77 percent in the kind of shiny, black coal people burn in domestic fires and 90 percent in anthracite. Brown coal (lignite) is a low-grade fuel, rather like peat.

Early fire-users and fire-makers would have preferred the driest wood they could find. It gives a hotter flame and it weighs less, which is an important consideration if you have to carry it to the village on your back. It was perfectly adequate for providing light on dark evenings for security and a flame to drive away hungry predators. Its heat was sufficient to keep everyone warm in winter and to cook food.

Smelting

Then a difficulty arose when people began to use metals. Copper melts at 1,982°F (1,083°C). The heat from a wood fire, well made and managed, is enough to melt copper from its ore. Tin melts at only 449°F (232°C), so it was perfectly feasible to alloy copper and tin to make bronze. Iron was more difficult, however. It melts at 2,795°F (1,535°C). The problem was not that wood cannot produce enough heat, but that it is too bulky, so its heat is insufficiently concentrated.

The solution people devised was ingenious, and not at all obvious. They found a way to heat a mass of wood under airless conditions. This dries the wood and drives off its oxygen, but without allowing the wood to catch fire. As the table shows, the higher the quality of the fuel, the greater its content of carbon and the lower its content of oxygen. Anthracite contains only 2.5 percent oxygen, compared with 43.5 percent in dry wood. Drive off the oxygen and the volume of the remaining wood will be greatly reduced and the proportion that is carbon will increase.

They had invented charcoal, the substance artists use (in a purified form) for drawing and that is still used in industrialized countries as a fuel for barbecues (it also has uses in the chemical industries). Its carbon content is similar to that of anthracite, so charcoal can be described as an impure form of carbon.

Charcoal is much less dense than anthracite, but burning it produces at least 50 percent more heat than burning the same volume of wood. It is hot enough for smelting iron, and it is the fuel that was used in the metal industries until coal replaced it in the early years of the Industrial Revolution. Until well into this century, it was being made in Europe by the traditional method and small amounts still are, although mainly out of historical interest.

COMPOSITION OF FUELS
(percentage of total)

Fuel	Carbon	Hydrogen	Oxygen	Nitrogen	Sulfur	Noncombustible solids
Wood	48.5	6.0	43.5	0.5		1.5
Brown coal (lignite)	67.0	5.1	19.5	1.1	1.0	6.3
Bituminous coal	77.0	5.0	7.0	1.5	1.5	8.0
Anthracite	90.0	2.5	2.5	0.5	0.5	4.0

Charcoal Making

Small sticks and branches were used, often coppice poles grown for the purpose (page 195), and oak was the preferred tree. All the bark was removed—partly because it was used in the tanning of leather and partly because burning oak bark releases large amounts of choking, sulfurous gases.

Charcoal was made in a shallow, circular pit, about 14.75 feet (4.5 m) in diameter. The floor was of earth or ash, and there was a wooden pole, about 6.5 feet (2 m) tall at the center. Short lengths of wood were stacked around the pole, with longer sticks outside them, sloping inward, and stacking continued until a dome-shaped heap had been made, reaching almost to the top of the central pole. The stack was then covered with bracken, leaves, and turf, all packed down tightly and sealed with a coat of mud, made from a mixture of earth and ash. The central pole was withdrawn, leaving a hole, down which a small amount of charcoal was dropped. Then some burning charcoal was dropped into the hole. This ignited the charcoal and wood at the center and as soon as flames were seen, the top of the hole was sealed.

Smoke would emerge from the stack. At first it was white but later, after a day or sometimes several days, it would turn blue. Blue smoke meant the process was completed. The stack was allowed to cool and the charcoal was then ready for use.

Charcoal-making was hard and very dirty work. While a stack was smoldering it had to be checked at regular intervals. Holes in the coating had to be sealed, and the top of the central hole had to be opened to make sure the wood inside had not caught fire. If it had, water was used to extinguish the fire. Meanwhile, as one stack burned another was being prepared, and charcoal was being removed and bagged from a stack that had cooled.

Today, very few people practice the craft of the charcoalmaker. We have other fuels, other technologies, for producing the metals we use, but these are quite recent innovations. For most of history, charcoal was the most widely used industrial fuel, and wood was the fuel with which most people warmed their homes and cooked their food.

Forest Timber

"Timber" is a word with a long history that has been traced back to Indo-European, the language ancestral to almost all modern European and western Asian languages. More recently, it is closely related to the Latin word *domus,* a dwelling, so "timber" means something connected with building and, from that, a building material. At one time it meant any kind of building material. Then it came to mean wood as a building material, for ships as well as buildings, and from there the meaning broadened to include any kind of wood. Today, we often use "timber" and "wood" as though they were synonyms, but strictly speaking they are not. "Wood" is the material from which small articles are made (page 158). Timber is used to make large objects.

Apart from this general sense, "timber" can also be used specifically. Timbers support roofs and floors and provide the main structural components of ships, as "ships' timbers." In an American sawmill,

if you ask for "timber" you will be shown wood not less than 5 x 5 inches (12.7 cm wide and 12.7 cm thick), although this is a rather vague designation.

Timber and Lumber

Felled trees are stripped of their branches, then cut into logs of a length that can be transported conveniently. In North America, at this stage it is often called "lumber," a term that is not much used in Britain. Then it is measured and sold to the sawmills by solid volume, calculated by measuring the length and the diameter at mid-length, then using $V = (\pi d^2 L) - 40,000$, where V is the volume in cubic meters, d is the diameter in centimeters, π is 3.14, and L is the length in meters (to convert cubic meters to cubic feet, multiply by 35.31). Sawmills then cut the logs to popular sizes and customers specify the sizes they need.

There are exceptions. If uncommonly large sizes are needed, special arrangements must be made. Masts for a ship, for example, may be bought as logs longer than those usually sent to the sawmills, and the buyer may select in advance the individual trees that will supply them.

Seasoning

Water accounts for a substantial part of the weight of wood (page 154). Timber is not sold by weight, so customers are not paying for water, but its presence greatly affects the behavior of the wood. All timber starts wet, because of the water being transported through it. In this condition it is known as "green" timber. As it dries, its volume

Logged Douglas fir, Pacific Coast, North America (Gerry Ellis / ENP Images)

decreases. It shrinks and may do so unevenly. There may be irregular twisting and bending, called "warping," and splits may appear, flaws that are inconvenient at best and can be catastrophic in construction timbers.

To avoid this, timber is dried, or "seasoned," before it is sold. Seasoning takes place at the sawmill, after the logs have been cut into planks, boards, and timbers. Traditionally, it was done by stacking the timber in layers outdoors. Thin boards are laid crosswise across each layer, with spaces between them to allow air to circulate freely through the stack, and the stack is covered with a roof, to allow rainwater to drain away without wetting the timber. How long the stack must be left like this varies from one tree species to another and with the climate. Generally, the process takes between six and 18 months.

In practice, most timber is kiln-dried, a technique that reduces to about one week a process that otherwise takes about a year. Kilning also improves the quality of the seasoned timber. Often, outdoor air-drying and kiln-drying are combined, with the green timber starting to season in an outdoor stack and being finished in a kiln. The timber is stacked in a building resembling a large shed; heat is supplied by steam flowing through pipes; fans ensure a full and even circulation of air; and the temperature and humidity are controlled within fine limits. Timber can also be seasoned by placing it in a chamber from which the air is evacuated, then heating it strongly. This causes the water to vaporize rapidly and can season timber in 12 hours or less. Precisely how long it takes by either process, and the temperature at which the timber must be held, vary according to the tree species.

Grading and Sorting

Timber is graded while it is still green. Once its bark has been removed, knots become visible. They can determine the maximum length into which the timber can be cut, because sections with too many knots must be removed. A standard calculation based on the number of knots and other imperfections is what determines the grade.

After seasoning the timber is sorted. This time each piece is marked according to its tree species, dimensions, and grade. Then it is ready for finishing, in which two sets of sharp, rapidly revolving blades shave both sides, smoothing and slightly polishing them.

Hardness

Wood is classified as "softwood" and "hardwood." These names refer to the types of trees producing the wood, softwoods coming from gymnosperms (coniferous trees), hardwoods from angiosperms (page 61), which are trees that are flowering plants rather than cone-bearing or spore-producing ones. The "soft" and "hard" refer to differences in structure of the wood, but the names are unfortunate, because they tell us nothing about how hard the wood is. They will not warn you which woods blunt tools fastest. Balsa, the wood used mainly for model-making, is technically a hardwood, because the tree producing it (*Ochroma* species, mainly *O. lagopus*) is a flowering plant (angiosperm), but a cubic meter of its weighs no more than about 150 kg (10 pounds per cubic foot). It will not blunt tools: despite being a hardwood it is so soft that unless very sharp tools are used it tends to crumble. It is easy to hammer nails through it, but it will not hold them firmly—gluing is the best way to fix together two piece of balsa. Wood from the kauri pine (*Agathis australis*) of North Island, New Zealand, on the other hand, has a density of about 610 kg per cubic meter (38 pounds per cubic foot), yet it is classed as a softwood.

Suitability for a particular use depends on much more than the size of material, of course. Hardness is important, but this is not a matter of whether the wood is from a gymnosperm or angiosperm tree. The timber must survive the treatment for which it is intended.

Testing

When the Forestry Commission was established in Britain, in 1919, the principal need was for pit props, the timbers that support the roofs of the galleries in coal mines. Timber was preferred to steel because it is slightly elastic and, no less important, it makes loud creaking and groaning noises before it breaks, often providing enough warning for miners to escape a roof fall. Props, in coal mines or anywhere else, must withstand pressure applied on their ends, acting parallel to the grain. This is called the "compressive strength" of the timber.

Timbers may also be loaded at right angles to the grain, like a shelf held at both ends and loaded with books. This loading will cause the timber to bend; it is important to know by how much and to know the point at which it will bend no further, and break. The maximum bending strength is the stress a timber can bear when loaded slowly and continuously. This test also measures the stiffness of the timber or its "modulus of elasticity." The stiffer the timber the less it will bend under a given load. Loading is not always at the center of timber supported at its ends. Rail ties (in Britain called sleepers) carry the rails—and the weight of trains—at their ends.

Loads are not always applied slowly. Picture the floor of a dance studio, for example, where a class of dancers all jump into the air and land simultaneously. Resistance to sudden loads is measured by dropping a standard weight onto the timber repeatedly, increasing the height of the drop each time until the timber breaks.

For some purposes, wood has to be bent. This is achieved by steaming it while applying pressure, and the bending property is measured by continuing this until the timber snaps. The result is given as an S/R ratio, where S is the thickness of the timber and R is the maximum radius to which it can be bent without breaking. Beech, for example, has an S/R ratio of about 1/2, which means a piece 1 centimeter thick can be bent to a radius of 2 cm, or a piece 2 cm thick to a radius of 4 cm.

Timbers must often be fastened to one another, by joints or bolts. Fastenings will tend to depress the surface, eventually making hollows. These will loosen the fastening, with a risk that eventually the structure will fail. It is important, therefore, to measure the resistance of timber to indentation of this kind, and it is done by striking the timber with a steel ball, which exerts a known amount of force, and measuring the indentation caused. This test is accompanied by a test that assesses how easily the timber may shear, or break parallel to the grain.

It is also important to know how easy it is to work with the timber. How many hours of working are possible before saws, planes, and other edge tools need resharpening affects the cost of using a particular timber. Sharpening tools takes time, during which they cannot be used. People planning to work with a species unfamiliar to them also need to be warned of the ease with which the material splits, especially if they plan to nail or bolt it.

Most timber is exposed to attack by beetles and other insects, but some species are more resistant than others to insect attack. Again, this is a quality that must be known, and it must include the insect species to which it is vulnerable. If timber is to be used outdoors, its weather-resistance is important as a measure of its durability. Preservatives are commonly used to protect timber, but species vary in their permeability to preservatives and this must also be known.

These properties are measured on samples of timber by standard tests performed in standard ways. The results are published, so those working with timber can easily learn the species most suited to their particular requirements.

Appearance is also important. Especially attractive—and expensive—timber is often cut into very thin sheets that are glued, as veneers, to the outside of articles made from cheaper, more ordinary wood. A softwood cabinet with a walnut veneer will look like walnut but cost far less.

Small Wood

Almost all paper is now made from wood. In the world as a whole, a total of 310 million tons (282 million tonnes) of paper and cardboard was made from wood in 1996. As with any industry, the totals vary somewhat from one year to another—in 1996 production was 1.3 percent higher than it had been in 1995—but the changes are not large globally, although within a region sometimes they are. In 1995, for example, Russian output increased by 22.5 percent (although it fell by 21.1 percent in 1996).

Paper consists of fibers lying across and adhering to one another. Until the last century, the fibers were obtained from straw, various grasses, and the bark of certain trees, but the best paper was made from cloth fibers, mainly in the form of rags that were shredded. Paper was made one sheet at a time, and a really good worker could produce around 750 sheets in a day. Not surprisingly, paper was expensive.

In 1863, however, a pulpmill in Maine owned by I. Augustus Stanwood and William Tower started using wood as a source of fiber and pulping it mechanically. Within a few years several other mills were pulping wood. Prices began to fall, because once machines were available to pulp it, the temperate forests of America, Europe, and Asia were able to supply good quality fibers in vast quantities. At the same time, paper manufacture became a continuous process. Some paper of the highest quality and with special uses, such as the paper used for printing bank notes, is still made from rags. Some straw is still used and some high-quality writing and printing paper is made from esparto grass. Paper for water-color painting is often made by hand, and synthetic fibers and even asbestos are used in some papers. But more than 90 percent of all the paper we use is made by huge machines from wood pulp.

Wood for Pulping and Chipboard

Wood destined for pulping is grown for the purpose in plantation forests (page 198). You may hear people talk of economizing in our use of paper to save the tropical forests, or even the temperate forests, but although there may be good reasons for saving paper, its use threatens no forests. In Europe and North America the wood is all grown specially and felled trees are replaced. This is not the case everywhere—in Russia, for example, natural forests are felled to produce paper—but in time it will become so, because this is the most economical way to produce pulping lumber.

Most pulp is made from softwoods, but not all. Ash (*Fraxinus excelsior*), beech (*Fagus sylvatica*), and poplar (*Populus* species) make excellent pulp. Coniferous species supply most pulp, however, because these are the trees that grow fastest. Sitka spruce (*Picea sitchensis*) is the most extensively grown tree in Britain and is also the principal source of wood for pulping. It is particularly suitable, because its wood contains little resin. Norway spruce (*P. abies*) and Douglas fir (*Pseudotsuga menziesii*) are among the other conifers used for pulping. Poplars are also among the species with wood that can be cut into soft shavings and used for stuffing, called "excelsior."

Chipboard manufacture also consumes a large amount of forest wood. Chipboard has many uses in the construction industry, where panels made from it screen work sites and are made into internal partition walls. Packing cases, furniture, and a range of other articles are also made from it. Because it is made from wood chips, pressed and sealed together with resin, it is strong, does not warp, and is more durable than the plywood it has largely replaced. Plywood is made from several thin sheets of board glued together and tends to separate when it becomes wet and the glue dissolves. Attractive hardwoods are also used as veneers.

Except for veneers, these uses destroy the individual character of the wood. You cannot tell which tree species were used to make the pages of the book you are reading, nor easily identify the trees from which the chips in a piece of chipboard came. Yet although these account for a very large proportion of the output from both natural and plantation temperate forests, there are also many items made from wood for which the type of wood matters and can be recognized.

ALDER AND ELM

Clogs, for example, are the wooden shoes traditionally and now fashionably worn in parts of Europe and the United States. People wearing them live in a region with a moist climate and if their feet are to remain dry the clogs must have waterproof soles. Alder (*Alnus glutinosa*) is the tree from which they were usually made. It is very waterproof, extremely durable whether it is wet or dry, and it is easy to carve, so an entire shoe made from it can be decorated with a carved pattern. The bark, stripped before the wood is sold, can be used for tanning, and any waste chippings or ends of wood can be made into excellent charcoal.

Elm (*Ulmus* species) wood is also very resistant to water. Many years ago water pipes were

made from it and survived intact for more than two centuries. It was also used to make clogs, wheelbarrows, farm carts, and weatherboarding, but it is especially durable if it remains permanently immersed in water; where it is alternately wet and dry it does not last so well. For this reason it was used to make waterwheels, for the piles on which jetties were supported, for sea defenses, and for various structures at sea ports.

OAK AND CHERRY

Oak (*Quercus* species) also yields very durable wood that withstands prolonged immersion in fresh- or saltwater. It is the wood from which ships were made and it has also been used for sea defenses. Wood from live oak (*Q. virginiana*) is greatly prized in North America, as are the red oak (*Q. rubra*) and white oak (*Q. alba*). In Europe, most widely used species are the pedunculate oak (*Q. robur*) and durmast (or sessile) oak (*Q. petraea*). Turkey oak (*Q. cerris*) is the exception. Although the tree is attractive, its wood is not durable.

Many articles can be made from oak, and it is used for veneering. Small poles make excellent stakes for outdoor fences, gates can be made from it, and indoors it was once used to make wall paneling that was sometimes carved. Oak bends well, which means it can be used to make chairs, and it also makes other fine furniture. With a slight bend, oak staves make the best barrels for storing and maturing wine, beers, and ciders.

Wall paneling and veneers can also be made from the wood of the wild cherry (*Prunus avium*), also known as the gean and mazzard, a species that is nowadays grown commercially for its wood. The tree itself grows to about 60 feet (18 m) and its heartwood is a rich, reddish brown and rarely cracked (the technical term is "shaken"), with a very straight grain. Quality furniture and ornamental items are also made from it, and cherry wood is especially useful where its straight grain is needed. Pipes for smoking and wood-wind instruments are sometimes made from cherry.

BEECH AND BIRCH

Beech (*Fagus* species) produces wood that is hard and strongly resists compression, so the European (*F. sylvatica*) and American beeches (*F. grandifolia*) are both very valuable, but the wood deteriorates rapidly out of doors. The wood makes excellent

Opposite: Ketchikan Pulp Company, Alaska (Gerry Ellis/ENP Images)

blocks for flooring, the wedges that support ships while they are being built, high heels for shoes, and furniture. Stocks for rifles and shotguns are often made from beech, as were the wooden blocks of old-fashioned carpentry planes. Beech also bends well when steamed, so it is used to make bentwood chairs. Kitchen utensils, such as wooden spoons and bread boards, are often of beech.

Birch (*Betula* species) also perishes rapidly if it remains wet, so it is useless for outdoor applications. Kept dry, though, it has many indoor uses. In Britain, the silver (*B. pendula*) and downy birches (*B. pubescens*) seldom grow tall and straight enough to yield timber, but their wood is made into the backs of brushes, bowls, toys, and similar small items, and it is also used to make chipboard. In the past it was also used to make barrels, especially those in which herring were stored. Further north, in Scandinavia, large, thin sheets are peeled off the trunks of the same species to make plywood. In North America, the cherry (*B. lenta*) and yellow birches (*B. lutea*) yield valuable wood, used to make furniture, as does the paper birch (*B. papyrifera*). This is the tree also known as the canoe birch, because its waterproof bark used to be peeled off and used to cover the frames of canoes.

Birch twigs are used to make besoms, yard brooms made from long twigs fastened around the end of a handle. Identical besoms are also used to beat out fires in forestry plantations, which is odd, because birch twigs are the best you can find for kindling a fire.

BASSWOOD, LIME, AND WILLOW

American basswood (*Tilia americana*) also provides wood for making small items, but it is especially prized for its long, straight grain. Before it was replaced by plastic, it is what the slats of venetian blinds were made from and, covered nowadays with plastic but at one time with ivory, obtained from elephant tusks, it is the wood from which piano keys are made.

Many beautiful European carvings are made from the soft, firm wood of the large-leaved lime (*T. platyphyllos*). Lime (also called linden) wood is also used to make boxes and matches, but the wood most often used to make matches comes from poplars (*Populus* species), various groups of which are known as cottonwoods or aspens. The European aspens (*P. tremula*) and the quaking aspen (*P. tremuloides*) of North America have light, soft, yet tough wood with a straight grain, making it easy to cut into straight sticks. Arrows were made from it in medieval times.

This quality apart, it may seem a curious choice for making matches, because it is non-flammable. That is why it was formerly used to make brake blocks (for horse-drawn vehicles) that

refused to even smolder, much less burst into flames, when they were jammed hard against a fast-turning wheel. Nor does it splinter, which makes it valuable for boxes. Pallets on which goods are stacked so they can be moved around by forklift trucks are usually made from poplar. The nonflammability of poplar is a drawback to its use in matches, but is countered by impregnating the wood with paraffin wax, and the straight grain makes the matches less likely to brake when struck.

Brake blocks also used to be made from willow. Willows belong to the genus *Salix* and there are many species, not all of them large enough to supply wood that can be worked. The most important of those that grow to the size of trees in Europe are the white willow (*S. alba*) and crack willow (*S. fragilis*). White willow is used for pulp. The black willow (*S. nigra*) of North America is also tree-sized and its wood is used to make boxes. Willow wood is light, pale, strong, and does not splinter readily, which is why the *caerulea* variety of white willow is the traditional wood for making cricket bats and is known as cricket bat willow. (Baseball bats are made from any of several hardwoods, but especially ash, and nowadays often from aluminum.) Willow is also used to make the sides of the sieves gardeners use and it is cut into thin strips that are woven to make garden baskets, sometimes called "trugs," for carrying cut flowers and other produce. Smaller willows, called osiers, are woven to make baskets of all shapes and sizes.

ASH, HORNBEAM, AND HICKORY

European ash (*Fraxinus excelsior*) yields a tough, pliable wood that resists shock, so it is used for anything requiring a material that will absorb shocks without breaking. The list includes a range of sports equipment, such as hockey sticks and oars, and the handles of tools. The American white ash (*F. americana*) and Oregon ash (*F. latifolia*) are valuable for their timber, which is used to make furniture and for other indoor purposes. Ash is not durable, however, and is unsuitable for fencing or other articles that are in permanent contact with the ground, but it does make excellent firewood.

Hornbeam (*Carpinus betulus*) derives its name from its hard, tough wood and at one time it was called "hard-beam." It is the toughest of all British wood. This, combined with often being cross-grained, also means it is difficult to work, which restricts its use. Mallet heads are made from it, as well as cogwheels and pulley-blocks. Nowadays these are usually made from metal, but wooden ones were used in old windmills and watermills where grain was ground into flour.

American hornbeam, or blue beech (*C. caroliniana*), is just as hard and is also used to make

tool handles. But the most popular North American trees for this purpose are hickories (*Carya* species). Many hickories are grown for their nuts (page 127), but the wood is tough and absorbs shock well. Shagbark (*C. ovata*), shellbark (*C. laciniosa*), Carolina (*C. carolinae-septentrionalis*), mockernut (*C. tomentosa*), pignut (*C. glabra*), and sweet, or red hickory (*C. ovalis*) are the trees most often used.

SPRUCE

Conifers are usually thought of as sources of large timber or pulp, but smaller items are also made from them. Thin sheets of pine, bent to the proper shape, are used for the belly of violins and string instruments related to it; the back and sides (called ribs) of the instruments are made of hardwood.

Wood from the spruces (*Picea* species) is known as whitewood or white deal. It, too, can be used to make sounding boards for string instruments. To be suitable for work of this quality, and indeed for all high-quality work, the wood is taken from trees that have grown slowly, because of being shaded by larger trees. Slow growth results in many annual growth rings and, therefore, a fine grain. The wood must also be free from knots, a fault to which spruce is very prone. Knots are dark in color, hard and resinous, and if the wood is cut into thin sheets the knots tend to fall out, leaving holes. Removing the lower branches (called brashing) and pruning the higher ones reduces the number of knots. Sitka spruce (*P. sitchensis*) usually yields fairly coarse wood, but it can be of a quality good enough to be cut very precisely and used for high-quality furniture.

More commonly, spruce wood is used to make kitchen furniture, boxes, and packing cases. Matchboxes are usually made from cardboard nowadays, but years ago they used to be made from spruce wood, sliced very thin. Thicker slices are a major ingredient of plywood, provided they are free from knots. Until scaffolding came to be made from metal tubing and ladders from lightweight metals, these were usually made from Norway spruce (*P. abies*). Norway spruce also supplies the wood to make flagpoles and the masts of small boats, although metal masts have largely replaced wooden ones.

MAPLE, BOX, AND PEAR

The hardwood used in string instruments is often European sycamore (*Acer pseudoplatanus*) or some other species of maple. In North America, the wood of the sugar maple (*A. saccharum*) is often used. Pale pink in color, this wood is also used to make sports equipment and, if it has an attractive grain, for high-quality furniture. Kitchen utensils, bowls, and chopping boards can be made from sycamore. It is also used to make rollers for machinery and, in the days before clothes dryers, for the mangles that squeezed water out of the laundry by passing it between two rollers.

Obviously, boxes can be made from almost any kind of wood, but there *is* one genus of trees (*Buxus*) called "box." (page 131) They are grown mainly as ornamental hedges in formal gardens, where one of their advantages is that they grow very slowly. Slow growth also means the annual growth rings are very narrow and consequently that the grain is very fine. The wood is an attractive yellow color, and the boxes made from it are of the finest quality. The wood can be sculpted and carved with very delicate designs, is one of the best woods for marquetry, and can be polished to a high gloss; boxwood boxes are certainly not packing cases. Originally the common box (*B. sempervirens*) was used, an Old World species native to Britain, although the wood was more often imported from Turkey.

Boxwood is harder and heavier than wood from any other tree native to Britain and it is used for articles where hardness matters. Drawing instruments used to be made from it, before plastic replaced wood, and some school rulers still are. Musical instruments have been made from it since Roman times. It is the wood from which Thomas Bewick (1753–1828) engraved the woodblocks that made him famous. Modern woodblock engravers use a different wood, however, from *Casearia praecox*, the Venezuelan box.

If Bewick preferred boxwood, the woodcarver Grinling Gibbons (1648–1721) worked with pearwood, from the common pear (*Pyrus communis*), a tree up to above 40 feet (12 m) tall that grows naturally throughout most of Europe. In the past it has been used for a variety of ornamental work, and drawing instruments, such as set-squares and protractors, the handles for cutlery, and colored piano keys were sometimes made from it.

CEDAR, SWEET CHESTNUT, AND HAZEL

Western red cedar (*Thuja plicata*) is light and durable. It can be used outdoors, for the frames of greenhouses, gates, roof shingles, and cladding on buildings. Small boats can be made from it, and in North America trees used to be hollowed out to make light, robust canoes.

Sweet chestnut (*Castanea sativa*) wood is very durable outdoors. Fences and the posts to which they are fastened are often made from chestnut. The tree itself grows to a large size, but the wood usually contains deep cracks (shakes), which limits its value as timber. Smaller pieces of chestnut wood are used to make furniture and coffins.

Not all fences are meant to stand permanently in the same place. Farmers use temporary fences, called hurdles, to contain livestock; by moving the hurdles, the animals can be made to graze one section of pasture at a time. Gardeners also use temporary fences to provide shelter. Traditionally, hurdles were made from sticks of hazel (*Corylus avellana*) in Europe and the very similar American hazel (*C. americana*) in North America. As with so many everyday articles, farm hurdles are now more often made from metal, but weaving them from hazel was once a highly skilled job.

Even today, in this age of metal and plastic, our homes, schools, and workplaces contain countless small articles made from wood. Each article is made from the wood of those plants best suited for the purpose, and there are few plants for which no use has been found. For small items it is the quality of the material which matters, rather than the quantity, and even those trees and shrubs that produce only thin stems and branches can be used. Wood from some species of spindle trees, for example, including the common European *Euonymus europaea*, was once used to make skewers and, as its name suggests, spindles for spinning.

Modern Forests

As the glaciers retreated at the ending of the last ice age, the land they had covered was left bare. Gradually, plants colonized a belt along the southern margin of the newly exposed land. The vegetated belt expanded northward and all the time the composition of its plant communities was changing. Eventually, after thousands of years of ecological succession (page 92), the temperate regions were blanketed by forests.

It is wrong to suppose that the first modern humans to explore and hunt in the ice-free landscape roamed through a vast, primeval forest. This forest did develop, but slowly, and the first human hunters stalked their prey in a countryside that was mainly tundra, a land of bare rock interspersed with patches of grasses and sedges and scattered shrubs and small, stunted trees. Landscapes are constantly changing and they would change even without our intervention.

Humans did intervene, of course, by using fire to drive game and by clearing forests to provide land for farming (page 38). The original forest once covered about 95 percent of western and central Europe, but by the 16th century 80 percent of that forest had been cleared. "Domesday" records show that most of the English forest had disappeared by the 11th century (page 144). What happened to European forests was repeated in temperate forests throughout the world. North America was affected later, of course, as the area colonized and farmed by European settlers expanded. In the United States, nearly one-third of the total deforestation had been completed by 1850 and the remaining two-thirds by 1920. Overall, however, probably no more than about one-tenth of the original temperate forests remain in the world as a whole.

Forested Area

This makes it sound as though temperate forests have almost vanished. Combine this with the widespread concern about the rate of which tropical forests are being cleared, and it is easy to assume that, if present trends continue, before long no forests will remain, temperate or tropical. All types of forest tend to be lumped together. During attempts in April 1997 to win agreement at the United Nations for an international convention to control logging, the Canadian Natural Resources Minister, Anne McLellan, warned that the world was losing its forests at an alarming rate. She seemed to make no distinction between one type of forest or geographical region and another. If she really did believe all types of forest to be under threat, she was not alone. Many environmentalists fear that the temperate forests are disappearing, due mainly to logging.

Despite the past clearances, at present temperate forests cover about 7.7 million square miles (20 million sq km). Of this, 41 percent, or 3.2 million square miles (8.2 million sq km) lies in the Commonwealth of Independent States and 32 percent, or 2.5 million square miles (6.4 million sq km), in North America. The remaining 27 percent, or 2.1 million square miles (5.4 million sq km), is in western Europe, North Africa, Asia, southern South America, South Africa, Australia, and New Zealand.

Logging and Farming

It is very unlikely that so large an area will be cleared. Indeed, it is doubtful whether it could be cleared without a major international effort. Certainly, commercial logging is an improbable cause. Forests are cleared when land is deliberately put to a different use. It is not logging that intentionally alters the use of the land, but farming, and the main purpose of clearing forests has always been the provision of land for pasture and cropping. This is still the principal cause of forest clearance in the Tropics, but in temperate latitudes the process was completed long ago. Agricultural surpluses, and the high cost of supporting their production and then storing or disposing of them, are causing most countries in the temperate regions to take land out of agricultural production, not to increase the area of farmed land. This frees land that had been farmed for other uses, one of which is the planting of new forests (called *afforestation*). In other words, the change in land use between forests and farms that worked against the forests throughout most of history has now been reversed.

Even so, individual forests might disappear if the demand for timber were so high that for a long enough period the rate of logging exceeded the rate at which forests are able to regenerate. In British Columbia, for example, large quantities of aspen (*Populus*) are used to make disposable chopsticks for the Japanese market, and some environmentalists fear this will lead to the progressive deforestation of a large area. After all, if the chopsticks are disposable the demand should be ceaseless and the market unlimited. Logging concessions apply to defined areas, however, not to the whole forested area, and once its trees are gone the loggers must move on, eventually obtaining their supplies from plantations. In fact, the area involved is a very small proportion of the total forested area, and the forest is either replanted or allowed to regenerate naturally. Forests disappear only if the land on which they grow is converted to another use.

Temperate forests are nowadays recognized as economic and environmental assets, and most governments enforce policies that at least maintain the total forested area and more often seek to increase it. New forests are being planted and although almost 75 percent of the timber produced commercially throughout the world is taken from the temperate forests of the Northern Hemisphere, the area of most of those forests is increasing.

Replanting and Regeneration

After the period of deforestation in the United States, which ended around 1920, there was a period of about 40 years during which the total area of forest increased. Then it began decreasing again; it is predicted by the Food and Agriculture Organization of the United Nations (FAO) that for the next few decades the U.S. forest area will continue to decrease by about 740,000 acres (300,000 ha) a year. Since about 1945, the United States has been one of the world's principal timber producers, so the decrease is not surprising. European forests are expected to continue increasing in size by about 494,000 acres (200,000 ha) a year, and those in Russia by about 4.9 million acres (2 million ha) a year. Increases are due mainly to planting, of course, but the situation in temperate regions differs from that in the Tropics because it involves no loss of natural forest. The reduction in forest area in the United States affects areas of plantation or natural regrowth, not primary or old-growth forest. In the United States and Europe, including the densely forested countries of Scandinavia, almost all the timber produced is from plantation or secondary growth forest.

Cleared blocks of forest are almost always replanted, but land that was originally forested will often revert to forest if it is allowed to do so. When European settlers arrived to colonize New England, they converted much of the natural forest into a countryside of fields and pasture with scattered woods from which they obtained the timber they needed for building and wood for smaller articles and fuel. Now, some 350 years later, the remains of those fields and settlements can still be found in the form of broken walls, holes that once were cellars, and old dirt tracks. Farming was abandoned and the forest has regenerated. As the forest returned, so did the plants that naturally accompany the trees and the animals associated with them. Ecologically and floristically, the regenerated New England forest is very similar to the original forest that was cleared.

Results of a study by the U.S. Forest Service published in August 1998 revealed the rate at which forests have been expanding this century in the northeastern United States. Between 1630 and 1907, about 300 million acres (121 million ha) of forest were cleared, but since then 23 million acres (9.3 million ha) have regenerated—a 46 percent increase in the forested area in 10 states.

Disease

Appearances can deceive, however. Diseases, such as chestnut blight and Dutch elm disease, have altered the composition of the forests, and these were introduced by humans. Elsewhere in the world, there are economic pressures to weaken the protection of large forests by allowing uncontrolled logging. This will not destroy the forests, but it may alter them and some species of plants and animals may become rarer as a result.

Timber is traded internationally on a large scale, and the transport of logs from one continent to another greatly increases the risk of transmitting organisms that cause disease. It can also transport insect pests, traveling without the predators that keep their populations in check in the regions where they originate.

It is important to remember, therefore, that although the temperate forests occupy a vast area and there is no realistic possibility that they might be entirely cleared, there are risks to them that should be taken seriously. The forests will remain, but they consist of trees, other plants, and animals that can be harmed.

Forests and the World Around Them

The temperate forests, and especially the boreal forests, are so large we are inclined to think of them as complete in themselves, as though they had no close links to the world beyond their boundaries. This is an illusion, of course, and a dangerous one.

Plants and animals need water, for example, and they need air. Should the water flowing into them be contaminated, forest plants may be poisoned. The air may deposit harmful substances on leaves and the by-products of industry and transport may wash down in the rain (page 164).

Still more serious, perhaps, the climate itself may change. All plants have distinct climatic preferences and do not thrive if temperatures and precipitation amounts remain for too long outside certain limits. Average temperatures over the world as a whole have risen slightly over the past century or so and many scientists fear that climates may continue to grow warmer (page 174). Were this to happen—and there are many uncertainties surrounding the idea—the composition of forests would change, and it is not certain that all species could adapt quickly enough.

Agriculture arrived in the temperate regions long ago. As the farms expanded, forests were cleared to make fields. That process reached its peak long ago, however, and the area of land devoted to temperate agriculture is no longer expanding. Forest clearance stabilized and in most countries has now been reversed. New forests are being planted and the total forested area is increasing. This is a situation very different from that in the Tropics, where agriculture is a much more recent innovation and is still contending strongly for fertile land. But although temperate forests are much more secure than tropical forests, there are threats facing them.

Dogwood and Cottonwood forest, Ridgefield Wildlife Refuge, Washington (Alan Kearney/ENP Images)

Acid Rain

At a meeting of the Manchester Literary and Philosophical Society in 1852, a chemist called R. A. Smith read a paper that subsequently became a classic. Called "On the air and rain of Manchester," the paper described how rain falling downwind from Manchester was very acid, the acidity decreasing with distance from the city. The cause of this acidity, Smith reported, was a mixture of hydrochloric acid and sulfur compounds from the factories of Manchester. This was the first report of "acid rain." As for Smith, he was Britain's first Alkali Inspector, the head of the government agency, called the Alkali Inspectorate, responsible for regulating industrial air pollution. He did much to reduce emissions of hydrochloric acid from the alkali works producing soda for the soap and other industries.

Routine monitoring of the acidity of rainfall began the following year at Rothamsted, in southern England, but did not cover the whole of western Europe until the 1950s. In the United States, scientific studies of the toxicity to plants of sulfur dioxide were made in 1938. In 1944 damage to plants was reported in two areas along the Delaware River. Scientists from Rutgers College of Agriculture investigated and discovered that a wide range of wild and cultivated plants showed signs of injury. Air pollution was found to be the cause.

Then, in the 1960s, "acid rain" emerged as an environmental and political issue and now it was taking a different form. The problem Smith had identified was fairly simple. Pollutants emitted from sources that could be identified were falling close to those sources. A century later, however, the acidity was caused not by the pollutants themselves, but by the compounds into which complex chains of chemical reactions had altered them, and damage was occurring far from any identifiable source.

Forest Damage and Factory Emissions

Acid rain reported since the 1960s has affected temperate forests—first in Scandinavia, then in Germany, central and eastern Europe, and North America. At first, many environmentalists believed the culprit to be sulfur dioxide emitted from power plants burning oil or, more commonly, coal with a high sulfur content. The idea was that in the air, sulfur dioxide (SO_2) is oxidized by hydroxyl radicals (OH) to particles onto which water vapor condenses, to form sulfuric acid (H_2SO_4). The reactions are:

$$(1)\ SO_2 + 2OH \rightarrow SO_3 + H_2O \ ;$$
$$(2)\ SO_3 + H_2O \rightarrow H_2SO_4$$

The measures taken to deal with the original problem—localized pollution—were responsible for a new form of pollution. Poisoning is a matter of the dose to which a victim is exposed. A minute dose may cause no injury at all, a rather larger dose may cause illness, and a still larger one may be fatal. In the same way, the amount of harm caused by air pollution depends on the dose of pollutants received and this depends in turn on

Conifer trees killed by air pollution, South Wales, U.K.
(David Woodfall/ENP Images)

the concentration of pollutants in the air. That is why pollution levels are always reported as concentrations, for example in parts per million, or as an amount of a substance per unit volume of the air or water containing it, such as micrograms per cubic meter.

Pollution damage can be reduced, therefore, by diluting the pollutant; until the acid rain reports of the 1960s, it was believed that if sulfur dioxide were diluted to around 0.025 ounce per cubic foot (25 micrograms per cubic meter) of air plants would not be damaged at all. Factory emissions were diluted by redesigning smokestacks. These were made very much taller than they had been previously and they were no longer simple chimneys, which are basically vertical tubes, but more sophisticated devices that drew the fumes upward very efficiently. Gases left the stacks at a considerable speed, rising through the overlying air and rapidly mixing with it. The diluted mixture then moved away from the source and air quality at ground level improved greatly.

All was not well, however, for two reasons. The first is that the pollutants that accumulate to high concentrations near to their source form only a small proportion of the total amount of those pollutants. Regardless of the chimney height, most sulfur dioxide is diluted and carried away by the air: altering the height of factory chimneys has no effect at all on pollution levels more than about 100 miles (160 km) downwind from the source. The second problem was that dilution did not always happen. It is possible for a cloud of gas from a factory chimney to remain concentrated long enough for it to travel a considerable distance. Air quality improved greatly in industrial regions, but damage further away continued, caused by substances that were the end products of chains of chemical reactions. It came to be recognized that the only satisfactory way to reduce air pollution, and damage from acid rain, was to reduce the amounts of pollutants emitted. Emission controls were the result.

Sulfur Damage

High concentrations of sulfuric acid certainly harm trees. At one time, it was sulfur dioxide from industrial Lancashire, in northwestern England, that made it impossible to grow trees in the Pennine hills to the east. A similar case in Canada was documented in detail. In 1896, a copper smelter opened at Trail, British Columbia, located in the gorge of the Columbia River close to the U.S. border. From then until 1930 it emitted sulfur dioxide, eventually at a rate of almost 10,000 tons (9,100 tonnes) a month. At the peak of the emissions, 30 percent of the trees were dead or dying for 52 miles (84 km) southward along the gorge

and 60 percent were dead or severely damaged for 33 miles (53 km). Sulfur dioxide from a copper smelter at Anaconda, Montana, also caused serious harm in the first decade of this century.

In some parts of Europe, sulfur is still a problem, but not everywhere. Most lichens, especially the shrubby species, are very sensitive to sulfur and quite small concentrations kill them. A scale has been devised linking lichen species present at a site with the atmospheric concentration of sulfur dioxide, and the presence of tar spot, a fungal infection producing circular black marks on leaves, is also related to sulfur dioxide concentration. Sulfur dioxide kills the tar spot fungus, so the more tar spot there is, the cleaner the air. In Germany, where tree damage came to be called *Waldsterben,* "forest death," lichens grew in abundance and analyses of needles from coniferous trees confirmed that sulfur levels were very low. Something was harming the trees, but it was not sulfur.

Scientists now recognize that the phenomenon is much more complex than was once supposed. In the first place, rain is naturally acid. Acidity and alkalinity are measured on a pH scale, where pH 7.0 is neutral, values below 7.0 are acid, and values higher than 7.0 are alkaline. Carbon dioxide (CO_2) dissolves in rain droplets in a sufficient amount to give ordinary rain falling from clean air a pH of 5.6. Nitrogen oxides, from the oxidation of nitrogen gas around lightning sparks and from forest fires, and sulfur dioxide from natural fires and volcanoes, make rain still more acid, so the average pH for clean rain is about 5.0. What we call "acid rain" is precipitation with a pH below 5.0.

Airborne sulfur is not an obvious suspect. At low concentrations, sulfur dioxide is either harmless or even beneficial. Sulfur is an essential plant nutrient, so plants benefit from a modest airborne supply. The reaction by which airborne sulfur dioxide becomes sulfate takes place fairly slowly, and sulfate is less harmful to plants than sulfur dioxide. When sulfate dissolves in cloud droplets, the resulting sulfuric acid is often too dilute to harm plants directly.

Cation Exchange and Buffering

What happens when very dilute acid reaches the ground depends on the soil. The "pH" of the scale by which acidity is measured means "percentage hydrogen ions" and it is the positively charged hydrogen in acids (sulfuric H_2SO_4, nitric HNO_3, hydrochloric HCl, for example) that gives acids their chemical properties. Dissolved in water, sulfate becomes sulfuric acid, but with the sulfate and hydrogen as separate ions. With values and signs of their charges shown, the components of the acid can be written as $SO_4^- + H^+ + H^+$.

Particles of clay and decomposed organic material carry a negative charge and as an acid solution flows through the soil, the hydrogen ions are adsorbed onto them by the electrostatic attraction of positive-to-negative charge. Gradually, the soil becomes more acid, as does the water flowing through it with a load of free hydrogen ions. This is the case only where the soil lies above an igneous rock, such as granite, however, and there a high rainfall, even from the cleanest air, will produce an acid soil and water, because of the acidity of ordinary rain. Nor is rain the only source of hydrogen ions in soils. Natural decomposition processes produce organic acids, and the uptake of nutrients with a positive charge can leave an excess of hydrogen.

If the underlying bedrock is sedimentary, there is a good chance the soil will be fairly rich in calcium and magnesium. If the parent material (page 10) is chalk or limestone, the rock will be made from calcium and magnesium carbonates; the soil will have an abundance of the two metals. Calcium and magnesium atoms also carry a positive charge, so they are readily adsorbed onto clay and humus particles. A charged particle is called an ion, and one with a positive charge is a cation.

Hydrogen cations will compete for adsorption sites, and if there are enough of them they will overwhelm and displace other cations by a process called mass action. The resulting cation exchange leaves the acid molecules adsorbed onto soil particles and releases the calcium and magnesium cations to be carried away in the water. The water leaving the soil, into groundwater, rivers, or lakes, remains neutral, because when these cations dissolve, they bond to hydroxyl (OH) ions carrying a negative charge. In this neutral form they are sometimes known as base cations. The soil will not become acid for as long as most of its negative adsorption sites are occupied by calcium or magnesium, and in soils derived from such rocks as chalk and limestone, the supply is limitless. The process by which a medium neutralizes an acid in this way is called buffering.

Much depends, therefore, on the rock from which soils are derived. In southern Scandinavia, where acid rain damage to forests was first noted, the underlying rocks are granitic. The soils there are poorly buffered and both soil and soil water were fairly easily acidified. Acid water flowed into lakes and aquatic organisms were harmed as well as trees. On chalk and limestone soils, with much stronger buffering, the risks are much lower.

Other Causes

As the German forests demonstrated, sulfur is not the only cause of tree damage. Ozone came under suspicion. This is an extremely reactive gas that forms in a series of steps driven by the energy of intense sunlight in air containing fairly high concentrations of nitrogen oxides, mainly from vehicle exhausts. In the 1950s experiments were conducted to discover whether ozone from the Los Angeles basin was causing needle damage to the ponderosa pines growing in the San Bernardino Mountains of Southern California; they found that ozone can injure plants. It enters stomata and damages the membranes of cells containing chloroplasts, thus reducing the rate of photosynthesis. Experiments in Germany found Norway spruce trees were also damaged when exposed to ozone at 100–300 parts per billion mixed with acid droplets to give a pH lower than 3.0. Although the experiments seemed convincing, the damage observed experimentally did not entirely match what was seen in the forests, and the contribution of ozone remains uncertain.

Excessive nitrogen seems a more likely cause, at least for some of the damage. Gaseous nitrogen is chemically inert (page 76), but ammonia (NH_3) is an available form of nitrogen that can enter the air, dissolve in rainwater, and be washed to the ground miles from its original source. That source is most likely to be the urine of farm animals. Many forests grow on relatively poor land, where at least some plant nutrients are scarce, and it is often the availability of nitrogen that limits tree growth. If nitrogen is added in large quantities, tree growth is vigorously stimulated, but it is unbalanced, because plant tissues are short of other mineral nutrients. This nutrient imbalance inhibits the hardening processes that prepare trees for winter, increasing the likelihood that they will be damaged by cold or desiccation.

Contaminants do not always act in isolation from one another. It is possible for the effects of two or more to combine in such a way that the damage they cause together exceeds the sum of the damage each would cause separately. The phenomenon is called synergism; it is well known in several forms of pollution. No one knows whether synergistic interactions are involved in the injuries we attribute to acid rain, but it is possible.

Acid air pollution does not travel only as rain. Indeed, taking the term literally, acid rain is but a minor risk to foliage. This is because rain strikes only the upper surface of leaves and branches, then quickly runs off them and falls to the ground. Fine mist, on the other hand, consists of minutely small droplets that adhere to surfaces. They cling to both upper and lower surfaces of leaves and stay there while their water evaporates, concentrating the acid. As you know from walking through a mist, these droplets, so small they hang almost motionless in the air, can make you wetter than a shower of rain delivering the same amount of water. Acid can also be deposited on surfaces directly from dry air; water droplets are not always needed. Acid mist and dry acid deposition cause more serious damage to foliage than does acid rain.

Nutrient Deficiency and Aluminum Toxicity

Acid rain damage, as opposed to damage from other forms of deposition, occurs mainly below ground. Magnesium and calcium are also plant nutrients. Where these cations are displaced by hydrogen, they enter water and are carried down into groundwater or away by rivers. If magnesium-hydrogen and calcium-hydrogen cation exchange takes place at a rate faster than that at which magnesium and calcium can be replaced by the weathering of the underlying soil parent material, what remains may be insufficient for the needs of plants, and trees may suffer a magnesium or calcium deficiency.

Cation exchange may also involve exchangeable aluminum. Aluminum is very abundant in rocks and especially in clays, but almost all of it is securely bound in the chemical compounds from which these minerals are made. Aluminum never occurs naturally as the pure metal, because it is so powerfully reactive. (Aluminum utensils in our homes are covered with a very thin layer of aluminum oxide that forms the instant aluminum is exposed to air.) In soils, however, there are some free aluminum cations and these adhere to exchange sites. They are exchangeable and at a pH of 5.5 or below some are dislodged by overwhelmingly large numbers of hydrogen cations.

Liberated into the soil water, aluminum cations form groups in which an aluminum atom is surrounded by six molecules of water or hydroxyl radicals. At a pH of about 5.0, one of the water molecules will lose a hydrogen ($H_2O \rightarrow OH + H$). This increases the acidity, exacerbating any adverse effect already arising from the low pH.

One of those effects is a slowing in the rate at which organic matter decomposes (page 84). Since decomposition is the mechanism by which nutrients are recycled, this can lead to nutrient depletion.

Aluminum cations can also enter root hairs. They are absorbed in the same way as calcium and magnesium and can take their place, blocking further uptake of calcium and magnesium. This leads to a nutrient deficiency in the plant, and, in addition, aluminum can interfere with the transport of water through the plant, which can increase its susceptibility to drought.

Water-borne aluminum is also poisonous to fish. The permeability of gill membranes is regulated by calcium cations, which can be displaced by aluminum cations at a pH of 5.0–5.5. At the same time, aluminum causes the release of mucus, which clogs the gills. Older fish are more susceptible to aluminum poisoning than young ones, but the effect in lakes can be serious. It is made worse by the fact that the lower the pH of water the less phytoplankton (small, mainly single-celled, aquatic plants that float near the surface) it contains and the phytoplankton forms the base of the aquatic food chain. Acidified lakes become very clear. They look clean, and so they are, but this is because they support relatively few living organisms.

Drought, Pests, and Disease

It was in the early 1980s, when the amount of damage was increasing, apparently rapidly, that there were fears of what became known in Germany as *neuartige Waldschaden*, "new forms of forest damage." Pollution is not the only cause. Trees may suffer from drought, an entirely natural phenomenon, but trees are large, complex plants that respond slowly. Symptoms may not appear until a few years after the rains have returned. The forest damage observed in Europe around 1980, for example, followed a severe drought that affected all of western Europe in 1976. Beech (*Fagus sylvatica*) has shallow roots and is especially susceptible to drought. In 1985, Friends of the Earth surveyed beech trees in Britain and discovered their leaves were changing color and falling some weeks earlier than usual. This was more probably due to stress induced by drought than to pollution, and the phenomenon was not repeated in subsequent years.

Trees may also be attacked by infestations of pests or disease organisms, and there were some outbreaks during the period of the worst damage. Studies of German soils in the 1980s found viruses and viruslike particles in soils and water from forest sites, as well as in the needles of spruces, pines, and firs showing signs of ill-health; the studies did not suggest that viral infection was the primary cause of the observed damage.

Finally, these causes are likely to interact. Just as you or I will be more susceptible to infectious disease if we are severely malnourished or dehydrated, so trees suffering a nutrient deficiency will be more vulnerable to frost, drought, pest attacks, and disease, and a tree weakened by drought, pest, or disease may be killed by a con-

---

Opposite: Sickly Norway spruce forest due to the effects of acid rain, Poland (David Woodfall/ENP Images)

centration of acid it would otherwise have survived.

During the 1980s "acid rain" became a hotly debated and controversial topic, and this is why. Unraveling just what was harming forests turned out to be very difficult.

Defining Damage

The Scandinavian worries, starting in the 1960s, centered on the acidification of lakes. It was in Germany that forest trees were the main cause for concern and Norway or common spruce (*Picea abies*) was the species identified as the first victim of *neuartige Waldschaden*. It is the most widely grown tree, making up about 40 percent of the German forests, and commercially it is the most important.

Damage was defined in terms of the proportion of its needles a tree had lost; at first Norway spruce was believed injured if it had lost more than 10 percent of its needles. On this basis, one-third of all spruce trees were classed as damaged. Further studies showed the diagnosis was incorrect. All coniferous trees shed needles, and the number they are without at any one time varies from one individual to another. Some perfectly healthy trees lose more than 10 percent of their needles.

Today, foresters accept an international scheme for classifying damage. Up to 10 percent needle loss indicates no damage (class 0), 11–25 percent, slight damage (class 1), 26–60 percent, moderate damage (class 2), 61–98 percent severe damage (class 3), and with more than 99 percent loss the tree is dead (class 4). Applied to all tree species, this classification reduced the scale of damage from more than half to less than 20 percent of the total forest area.

Different Damage, Different Causes

There are several visible signs of ill health, now often called "decline," and these vary from one species to another. In Norway spruce, five different kinds of damage are known, with different causes. At high elevations in the mountains of central Germany, and also in Austria, France, Belgium, and the Netherlands, there is a yellowing and then dropping of needles exposed directly to sunlight. This is due to magnesium deficiency and may lead to the death of the tree if there is also injury from another cause, such as frost, drought, insect infestation, or disease. Where Norway spruce grows alongside other species, such as silver fir (*Abies alba*), Douglas fir (*Pseudotsuga menziesii*), Scotch pine (*Pinus sylvestris*), and beech (*Fagus sylvatica*), they can also be affected.

PERCENTAGE OF TREES DAMAGED IN GERMAN FORESTS, BY SPECIES AND DAMAGE CLASS

Damage class	Spruce	Pine	Fir	Beech	Oak	Others	Total
0	45.9	46.0	17.1	39.9	39.3	65.8	46.3
1	32.4	39.5	22.5	41.2	41.2	24.5	34.8
2	20.1	13.1	49.1	17.5	18.7	8.5	17.3
3 and 4	1.6	1.4	11.4	1.4	0.8	1.2	1.6

At middle elevations in the German mountains, mainly on soils poor in nutrients about 1,300–2,000 feet (400–600 m) above sea level, there is thinning of the tree crowns, sometimes accompanied by yellowing of the needles. This is associated with fairly high sulfur dioxide concentrations and wet deposition of hydrogen cations, and nutrient deficiency, especially of calcium and magnesium, but in some places also of phosphorus and potassium.

In southern Germany, needles were seen to turn orange-yellow in September, and then red and finally brown. The brown needles may remain on the tree for some months, but most fall around the end of October, causing a marked thinning of the crown. In the absence of other stresses, it rarely leads to the death of trees. This damage is due to infection by various fungal species.

There has been yellowing of needles and thinning of crowns at elevations above about 3,300 feet (1,000 m) on shallow, calcareous (calcium-rich) soils in parts of the Alps where the underlying rock is limestone. This has been observed in Austria, Switzerland, Italy, and Germany: it is linked to nutrient deficiencies, especially of potassium.

Crown thinning has been observed in coastal areas. In 1983, aerial surveys found that one-third of the Norway spruces more than 60 years old in German coastal forests showed signs of damage in classes 2 to 4 and tree growth was very slow. Similar damage occurred in Belgium and the Netherlands. The cause is uncertain.

The table above shows the extent of damage to German forests reported in 1986 by the *Bundesministerium für Ernährung, Landwirtschaft, und Forsten* (Federal Ministry for Nutrition, Agriculture, and Forestry).

European forests have also experienced needle yellowing, needle death, crown thinning, and other injury to silver fir (*Abies alba*). Beech (*Fagus sylvatica*) has shown signs of damage, due to a variety of causes. Insect infestations and fungal infections have caused some damage, there has been an excessive supply of nitrogen associated with deficiencies of other nutrients, and soil acidification has been found in affected areas.

In Britain, routine monitoring of the health of trees was initiated in 1984 and gradually expanded in subsequent years. It now covers Sitka spruce (*Picea sitchensis*), Norway spruce (*P. abies*), Scotch pine (*Pinus sylvestris*), oak (*Quercus* species), and beech (*Fagus sylvatica*). At each of 310 sites, 24 trees are studied in detail, 7,440 trees in all. An additional, smaller, monitoring program, required by European Union legislation, examines about 1,800 trees at 75 sites. Once data from different countries are adjusted to ensure that they are all applying the same standards, British forests emerge as little different from those elsewhere in Europe. There is no conclusive evidence, however, of a clear relationship between patterns of air pollution and the health of trees. In fact, trees in areas of high air pollution appear healthier than those growing in clean air: probably this is because the climate in the polluted regions of England favors trees with dense crowns. Evidence does suggest, however, damage to lakes due to acidification in areas underlain by igneous rocks.

North America

Particular pollution episodes have affected forests in the western United States. Ponderosa pines (*Pinus ponderosa*), and Jeffrey pines (*P. jeffreyi*), growing in mixed conifer forests in Southern California, were found in the 1970s to have been suffering from ozone damage since the 1950s. In descending order of susceptibility, white fir (*Abies concolor*), California black oak (*Quercus kellogii*), incense cedar (*Libocedrus decurrens*), and sugar pine (*P. lambertiana*) were also affected.

In general, however, forest damage due to acid rain in North America is primarily a phenomenon of the eastern side of the continent, where it has been observed over a large area. South of the Great Lakes, a line drawn from the western tip of Lake Superior to the Gulf coast just west of New Orleans, marks a boundary to the east of which the average pH of rainfall is below 5.0. The acidity of precipitation increases to a maximum, averaging pH 4.4, in the northeastern states and southeastern Canada and the distribution of acidity closely matches the deposition of sulfate.

Spruce and Fir in the Appalachians

Since 1983, a sharp deterioration seems to have been occurring in the health of spruce and fir stands along the crest of the Appalachian mountain chain from eastern Canada to North Carolina. This has been monitored closely on Mount Mitchell, in the Black Mountain range of the southern Appalachians, where it seems especially severe.

The deterioration was rapid. A study of an admittedly very small sample, of 272 red spruce (*Picea rubens*) and 213 Fraser fir (*Abies fraseri*) between 25 and 100 years old in 16 plots in the Black Mountains found the trees to be reasonably healthy in 1984. Spruce were the healthier of the two species, with 79 percent of the trees having lost less than 10 percent of their needles (class 1), and 19 percent less than 50 percent (class 2). Of the firs, 60 percent were in class 1, 15 percent in class 2, and 25 percent had lost up to 99 percent of their needles (class 3), although there were no dead trees in the sample stands. By 1986, however, 9 percent of red spruce and 16 percent of the firs had died and by the spring of 1987, 41 percent of the spruce and 49 percent of the firs were dead.

Several causes probably contributed. Starting around 1935, the balsam wooly adelgid, a serious insect pest similar to an aphid (page 109), has been ravaging fir trees throughout the southern Appalachians. Adelgid damage is believed to account for the relatively poorer health of fir trees in the Black Mountain study. Damage inflicted by the pests weakened trees, increasing the damage caused by a prolonged summer drought in 1986, followed by heavy rime icing in December of the same year. (Rime is a white covering of ice caused when supercooled water droplets freeze on contact with a solid surface.) Acid precipitation is likely to have exacerbated the situation. Montane forests (growing on mountainsides below the tree line) are more exposed than those at lower elevations, because cloud droplets are significantly more acid than rain or snow falling from the clouds. Mountain forests are exposed to mists with a pH of 3.0 to 4.0 for between 30 and 80 days each year in the northern Appalachians and for 200 to 280 days in the southern Appalachians.

Red Spruce in the Adirondacks and Appalachians

Red spruce has also declined during the 1980s at elevations above 3,000 feet (900 m) in the northern Appalachians and Adirondacks. Balsam fir is the dominant species above about 3,300 feet (1,000 m) and sugar maple (*Acer saccharum*) below 2,300 feet (700 meters), red spruce being a minor species between about 2,600 and 3,300 feet (800–1,000 m) and rare above about 4,000 feet (1,200 m). These forests support a number of species, so changes in the abundance of red spruce might pass unnoticed were it not being monitored. Between 1982 and 1987, red spruce above 3,000 feet (900 m) were dying at a rate of about 4 percent each year, compared with a rate of 0.5 percent at lower elevations. After 1987 it seemed probable that the remaining severely damaged trees (class 3) would die, but the healthy trees (classes 1 and 2) were showing no sign of deterioration.

Trees growing at high altitudes are subject to more climatic stress than those at lower elevation. Spruces also suffered from pests and fungal attacks, although at high altitudes these are less severe. It is possible that air pollution contributed to the decline in red spruce, although this remains unproven.

Effect of Emissions Limits for Gases and Particles

By the late 1980s, acid rain damage appeared to have stabilized. Governments had set limits to industrial emissions of sulfur dioxide and nitrogen oxides, and the atmospheric levels of these pollutants were starting to fall. In 1996, German monitoring of 5,000 sites found 60 percent of trees showing some signs of damage and the European Union published a survey showing damage to 20 percent of trees at monitored sites. The most widespread damage was in central Europe, although there is no conclusive evidence that this damage is due to airborne acid.

There are now fears that acid rain problems may reappear as a direct consequence of pollution controls. Sulfur emissions have fallen dramatically over Europe and eastern North America, but so have dust emissions. Dust particles can be harmful to people with respiratory illnesses, and they cause haze, which reduces visibility, so there would seem to be no good reason not to prevent their release where that is possible. Not all fine particles are chemically inert, however. Some behave like base cations, buffering cloud water and thereby exerting a neutralizing effect on acid droplets. In Chilean forests, southern beech (*Nothofagus* species) obtain almost all their calcium from atmospheric particles.

At the Hubbard Brook Experimental Forest, in New Hampshire, the concentration of atmospheric base cations has fallen 49 percent since 1965. In the forests of Sjoangen, in southern Sweden, there has been a 74 percent drop since 1971. Similar reductions have occurred over most of Europe and North America and some scientists believe the extent of the loss of atmospheric base cations is large enough to have offset between 54 percent and 68 percent of the reduction in atmospheric sulfur in Sweden and up to 100 percent of the sulfur reduction at some places in eastern North America.

Recovery

When acid deposition ceases, soil and water recovery may be slow. Acidification involves the loss of base cations and once they are gone it may take a long time for them to be replaced. Until this happens, the pH will remain low. At Hubbard Brook, for example, a report published in 1996 showed that the acidity of surface waters had not declined, despite the fall in acid emissions, because of the loss of base cations from soil through which the water drained.

Acid precipitation has contributed to the decline of forests in Europe and North America, but is not the only cause. Over the last 200 years there have been five forest declines in different parts of Europe and there have been 13 in North America during this century, with airborne pollutants being implicated in six. It is very misleading, therefore, to attribute all damage to forest trees to acid rain. Pests and diseases have also caused harm, as have episodes of severe weather.

Emissions of sulfur and nitrogen oxides have fallen in response to the implementation of pollution controls. Provided the resulting improvement is not offset by the reduction in atmospheric base cations, we may hope that in time most acidified soils and waters will recover and tree damage from this cause will cease.

Climatic Effect of Forest Clearance

At those times of year when the ground is bare, a spell of dry weather can reduce a finely textured soil to the consistency of a powder you can trickle through your fingers. In this condition, a spell of windy weather can blow tons of it away in a dust storm that clogs ditches, reduces visibility, and darkens the sky. In the worst cases, the wind carries away expensive fertilizer and seed along with the soil. This is not a new problem. At one time such storms happened fairly often in parts of eastern England, Denmark, Norway, and on the wide plains of Russia, as well as in the southern part of the Great Plains of North America, which is where so many farms failed tragically in the Dust Bowl years of the 1930s.

The Dust Bowl region has always had a climate subject to periodic episodes of severe drought and it was drought that caused the damage of the 1930s. Only a drastic change in farming methods could make that land reliably cultivable. Elsewhere, in less arid climates, there is no mystery about how such dust storms can be prevented. European farmers found a solution as long ago as the 18th century. They planted trees, as lines or small, isolated clumps, in strategically chosen places. The trees absorb much of the energy of the wind, sheltering the land downwind of them. Today it is standard farming practice in all temperate regions to plant shelter belts of trees. In some places, shelter trees have a powerful effect on the landscape. In the Rhône valley, in southern France, cypress trees are used for this purpose and contribute much to the appearance of the countryside, as do the tall Lombardy poplars planted to provide shelter in the Netherlands.

Shelter belts alter the climate on their downwind side over a distance proportional to the height of the trees, and the effect can be increased by planting two or more belts parallel to one another some hundreds of yards apart.

If planting trees can reduce the speed of the wind, it is reasonable to suppose that removing groups of trees will also affect climate. As the original forests of temperate Europe and North America were cleared, mainly to provide land for cultivation, locally the climate must have changed: a change in wind speed will have been only one of the ways in which it did so.

Wind

Walk into a forest on a day when the wind in the open is blowing at, say, 20 miles per hour (32 km/h) and by the time you are 100 feet (30 m) from the edge, depending on the composition and density of the forest, the wind speed will have dropped to between 12–16 miles per hour (19–26 km/h). If you move 400 feet (120 m) from the edge, regardless of the composition of the forest, the wind speed will be reduced to about 1.2 mph (2 km/h). Near the edge of the forest, the effect is the same throughout the year if the trees there are conifers, but if they are broad-leaved deciduous species they will reduce wind speed more in summer than in winter. This is because their leaves absorb a great deal of the wind energy. Inside a broad-leaved deciduous forest in Tennessee, for example, wind speed in January was 12 percent of that in adjacent open country and in August, when the trees were in full leaf, it was only 2 percent.

Remove the forest, and the climate becomes windier, not only over the area that was formerly covered by trees, but also in a belt about a half-mile (1 km) wide surrounding it. It is not only inside the forest that wind speed is reduced, but on the downwind side as well, where the forest provides shelter.

Most open, level land is windy. In East Anglia, the "bulge" in eastern England north of the River Thames, there is usually a wind. The region is flat, low-lying, and exposed directly to winds off the North Sea. At one time much of the land was forested and the remainder was swamp; in those days the climate inland would have been less windy. There is a similar story to be told in many other parts of the temperate latitudes.

Dust and Fog

Once the forest is gone, fog, which rolls gently forward on a light wind, travels farther. It happens because a forest is like a filter. Trees and shrubs trap water droplets, which adhere to leaves and bark, so the air leaving the forest on the downwind side is drier than the air entering it. This is especially important near coasts, where sea fogs may penetrate much farther inland than they did before the forest was cleared.

The air also becomes dustier because some solid particles are trapped by forests in the same way. Others fall, because the amount of solid material that can be transported through the air depends on the amount of energy the wind possesses. Friction, as the wind flows into and around trees and over the uneven ground surface, absorbs much of its energy. That is why the wind speed decreases inside forests, and the capacity of the wind to transport material is reduced. Particles fall to the ground or onto plant surfaces, from where rain soon washes them to the ground. There they remain, because the wind speed inside the forest is never high enough to raise them again.

Clear-cut temperate rain forest, Prince of Wales Island, Alaska (Gerry Ellis / ENP Images)

Frost and Wind Chill

Wind also affects the temperature in several ways. Regardless of the air temperature, you will feel colder outdoors on a windy day than on a still day, because the wind carries away the thin layer of air surrounding and warmed by your body. Your body expends its own warmth warming this air and the result is that the wind can actually reduce your body temperature. This is called wind chill, and at low air temperatures it can be dangerous. Fell the trees and you may need to dress more warmly in winter.

You may have noticed on the TV weather forecasts that sometimes, usually in spring or fall, the forecaster predicts that although the temperature overnight will fall close to freezing, frost is unlikely because of the wind. Given that the same forecast may also have warned of wind chill, the absence of frost may seem paradoxical, but it is not.

Ground frosts decrease when forests are cleared and wind speeds increase. During the day, the ground and plants close to it are warmed by the sun. They also radiate the heat they receive, but while they receive more energy than they radiate away, they grow warmer. In the evening, the balance shifts and radiation from the surface exceeds the energy received from the sun, and plants and the ground surface cool. This chills the layer of air in contact with them. If this air is still and moist, its water vapor condenses onto cold surfaces as dew or, if the surfaces are cold enough, as ice crystals. If the air is moving, however, the layer at ground level is constantly mixing with air above and there is no opportunity for the layer of still air to form and be chilled, so frost and dew are much less common.

This effect is not so beneficial as it may seem. Dew forms when water vapor condenses onto surfaces out of humid air. Condensation releases about 17,000 calories of latent heat for every ounce of water that condenses (2.5 million Jkg^{-1}) and the energy released is absorbed by the surface onto which the water condenses, warming it

(page 24). Frost, formed by the sublimation of water vapor directly into ice, releases even more warmth: 19,000 calories per ounce (2.83 million Jkg⁻¹). Wind has no effect whatever on the rate at which plants and the ground radiate away their heat at night, but by preventing the formation of dew and frost it allows the ground surface temperature to fall further than it would in still air. The ground inside a forest freezes later and to a shallower depth than ground outside. Clearing the forest reduces the formation of dew and frost, but in winter the ground freezes earlier and harder.

Reflection and Absorption of Solar Energy

Removing the forest produces a still more dramatic change in the amount of solar energy that reaches the ground surface and is absorbed by it. When electromagnetic radiation, such as radiant heat and visible light, strikes a surface, some of the radiation is reflected and some is absorbed. The proportion reflected varies from one type of surface to another and is measured as the "albedo" of the surface (page 21), expressed as a percentage of the total.

A coniferous forest, dark in color because of the dark green of its needles, has an albedo between about 8 percent and 14 percent, meaning that between 86 percent and 92 percent of the solar energy falling on it is absorbed. A broad-leaved deciduous forest, with generally somewhat paler leaves and, of course, no leaves at all in winter, is more reflective. It has an albedo between 12 percent and 18 percent, so it absorbs between 82 percent and 88 percent of the energy it receives. The energy is absorbed by the tree foliage, so it is the leaves that experience any warming effect, and it is used to drive photosynthesis (page 72).

Energy that is absorbed by the forest canopy cannot reach the floor, but this does not mean the floor is in almost total darkness, or that no warmth reaches it from above. If no more than 8 percent of the warmth of the sunshine reached the floor of a forest where 92 percent was absorbed in the canopy, it is unlikely the forest could survive at all, because the ground at its base would be permanently frozen. Absorption and penetration vary according to the wavelength of the radiation: a relatively high proportion of the absorbed radiation is at short wavelengths. More ultraviolet radiation and blue light is absorbed than red light and heat.

In addition, solar radiation reaches the surface most intensely from the direction of the sun only when the sky is cloudless. Clouds scatter incoming radiation, so it reaches the surface from all angles. It casts no sharp shadows, because objects are illuminated evenly on all sides. In the forest, a proportion of the radiation, arriving almost horizontally, avoids absorption by foliage. Light intensity on the forest floor is greater on cloudy than on sunny days. This may seem paradoxical, but on a sunny day brightly lit patches of ground are surrounded by very deep shadow, whereas on cloudy days the entire area is illuminated by diffuse light.

Some types of forest allow more radiation to penetrate than others. In a forest dominated by birch and beech, for example, about 50 percent of the incoming radiation may reach the floor in summer and 75 percent in winter. Pine forests allow between 20 percent and 40 percent of the incoming radiation to reach the floor and the much denser fir and spruce forests between 10 percent and 25 percent.

One consequence is that inside the forest there are fewer hours of daylight. This means there is a shorter time for the ground to warm during the day than there is outside the forest. The shading of the ground also reduces the extent of warming. Daytime air and ground temperatures are lower, so there is less radiative cooling at night, and the diurnal range of temperature is smaller inside than outside the forest.

In temperate latitudes, not all the heat absorbed by the ground during the day in summer is radiated away on summer nights, because the nights are short and before the balance can be restored the Sun has risen. By the end of summer, the ground just below the surface is warmer than it was in spring and its completes its cooling during the fall. Just as the diurnal temperature range is lower inside a forest than it is outside, so is the annual temperature range. In open country the ground reaches a higher temperature by day and over the summer than it does inside a forest.

Clear the forest and this complicated pattern of radiation, reflection, and absorption vanishes. The albedo of the surface changes. If the forest has been replaced by fields growing wheat, their albedo is between about 18 percent and 25 percent—much higher than that of a forest—so less energy is absorbed at ground level. If the crop is corn or potatoes, on the other hand, the albedo will be between 3 percent and 15 percent. Between crops, when the ground is bare, the albedo is between 5 percent and 25 percent depending on the color of the soil. It is only when the ground is bare, of course, that it absorbs all the unreflected energy. At other times most of the energy is absorbed by crops.

Although the albedo becomes highly variable once the forest has gone, the surface where energy is being reflected or absorbed is at a much lower level. More light and warmth reaches the ground and its temperature rises higher during the day and the summer, falling again at night and in the fall.

Evaporation and Humidity

The warmer the ground, the more readily water will evaporate from it. This is an immediate and obvious consequence that you can see for yourself. Except in very dry weather, scrape away the dead leaves or needles lying on the surface and the ground inside a forest is usually wetter than the ground outside. It lies in deeper shade and is cooler, so water is slower to evaporate from it. In a pine forest in Arizona, evaporation from the ground in summer is about 70 percent of that on open ground outside the forest.

That is only part of the effect forest clearance has on atmospheric humidity. All plants take water from the ground, transport it upward, and lose it by transpiration through their leaf stomata (page 28), but the rate of which trees do so varies from one species to another, depending on the efficiency with which they conserve moisture. Pines transpire much less water than fir trees, for example, and trees transpire much less water in winter than in summer, because leaf temperature is lower and, therefore, so is the rate of evaporation from open stomata. Transpiration ceases in winter in deciduous trees, of course. In a Northern Hemisphere mixed deciduous forest of birch, beech, and maple, the relative humidity in early June might be about 1 percent higher inside the forest than outside, but by the middle of July the difference might have increased to about 5 percent and in some forests it can reach about 11 percent.

Trees also intercept falling rain, a proportion of which evaporates from leaf and bark surfaces without ever reaching the ground. Together, evapotranspiration and the evaporation of intercepted rain can vaporize a considerable amount of water. In the Harz Mountains of Germany, it has been calculated that Norway spruce (*Picea abies*) forests return to the atmosphere annually about 13.4 inches (340 mm) of precipitation by evapotranspiration and about 9.5 inches (240 mm) by the evaporation of intercepted rain, a total of about 23 inches (580 mm).

Changes in Precipitation

This affects the hydrological cycle by an amount that varies according to whether the ground is level or sloping and the direction sloping ground faces. For a European oak forest, of all the precipitation falling through a year, an average of 13 percent is intercepted by the canopy and evaporates, 30.5 percent is transpired by trees, 12.25 percent is evapotranspired by ground vegetation, 16.75 percent runs off ground vegetation, 8.75 percent runs off through the soil, and 18.75 percent penetrates the ground and joins the groundwater.

It might seem, therefore, that if the trees were cleared from the Harz Mountains the annual precipitation there would increase by about 23 inches (580 mm) a year, or that removing an oak forest would mean that 43.5 percent of precipitation returned to the air from trees would reach the ground. Unfortunately, it is not so straightforward.

Transpiration only involves water that enters plants through their roots. It is called soil water, and some tree species obtain it from deep below the surface. A proportion of the moisture in the air above forests has been placed there by the trees themselves. Water evaporates because it is warmed. It absorbs the latent heat of evaporation from the surface from which it vaporizes. This cools the surface, and is the principal mechanism by which plants avoid overheating to an extent that inhibits photosynthesis. Water vapor transpired by trees enters warm air and rises, on warm days in rapid thermal upcurrents. As the air rises it cools, and if it is moist enough the water vapor will start to condense. It is not uncommon for

clouds to form above forests. To some extent, therefore, the forest itself generates the precipitation that falls on it.

A forest can also force approaching air to rise, in much the same way as a mountain does, though on a smaller scale. If the air is already unstable (page 38), and especially if the forest is on a hillside where the air has already started to rise, the additional forcing can further destabilize the air and cause clouds of the cumulus type to form. In stable air, stratified clouds may develop. Both cloud types can produce rain or snow, either as showers or lighter but more prolonged precipitation.

Remove the trees, therefore, and the air will be drier above the ground where the forest once stood. But this does not necessarily mean precipitation will decrease in an area from which the forest has been cleared. Much depends on the scale of clearance, because air moves horizontally, transporting its water vapor and clouds, and may travel some distance before those clouds start to produce rain or snow. It does suggest that clearing forest from a large area is likely to reduce the average annual precipitation over that area and in regions adjacent to it.

Reducing the amount of water returned to the air by evaporation from tree surfaces means a higher proportion of the precipitation will reach the ground. Even if the overall amount of precipitation is smaller, the actual amount reaching the ground may not be. At the same time, reducing the amount of water being transpired may allow water to accumulate in the ground. The most probable overall effect is that on well-drained land, clearing a forest will make the ground drier, but on poorly drained land it will become wetter.

Clearing temperate forests has no measurable effect on the climate of the world as a whole, but it can have a substantial local and regional effect. The climate is likely to become windier and the air dustier. Sea fogs may penetrate farther inland. There is likely to be an increase in the difference between maximum and minimum temperatures, daily and seasonally. Where the ground freezes in winter, it will do so earlier and to a greater depth than it did formerly. Precipitation is likely to decrease and, as the climate becomes drier, in places this may increase the risk of dust storms.

Forests and the Greenhouse Effect

Sunshine warms the ground and the surface of the oceans. Warmed, these surfaces radiate heat. Over the course of a year, the amount of heat the surface of Earth radiates into space is equal to the amount it receives from the Sun. If this were not so, Earth would grow steadily warmer or cooler.

Although incoming and outgoing radiation balance, some of the warmth is retained. There is a store, like a kind of blanket, that keeps us warmer than we would be without it.

Incoming radiation spans a wide wave band, from ultraviolet at the shortwave end to infrared and heat at the longwave end. It is most intense in the wave band of visible light, between 0.39 micrometers (μm) at the violet end of the spectrum and 0.74 μm at the red end (1 μm = 10^{-6} m). About 9 percent of the radiation we receive from the Sun is in the ultraviolet wavelengths, down to about 0.30 μm, about 45 percent is visible light, and 46 percent is infrared and heat, at wavelengths of more than 0.74 μm. Earth radiates from about 4.0 μm to 100.0 μm, with a peak intensity at about 10.0 μm.

The Radiation Trap

The atmosphere is transparent to visible light. Shortwave ultraviolet radiation is absorbed in the stratosphere by oxygen and ozone, and some infrared and heat radiation is absorbed by water vapor and carbon dioxide, but almost all of the solar radiation that is not reflected by clouds reaches the surface. The surface, however, radiates at very much longer wavelengths, to which the atmosphere is partially opaque. Water vapor absorbs radiation at about 1.0–4.0 μm, 6.0–9.0 μm, and 25.0–60.0 μm. Carbon dioxide absorbs at about 5.0 μm and 19.0–20.0 μm. Ozone, methane, and various other gases also absorb radiation, each at different wavelengths. There is a "window," at about 10.0 μm, where radiation is not absorbed and heat from below can escape directly into space, but most radiation at wavelengths outside the window is trapped.

This complicates the radiation balance. Incoming radiation passes through the atmosphere and is absorbed by the surface of land and water. Outgoing radiation is absorbed in the atmosphere. This warms the air, which then reradiates its heat in all directions, some of it to the sides and some downward to warm the air and surface still further. Wherever the radiation is absorbed it is reradiated, so radiation is moving in all directions. The overall effect is to trap heat near the surface. The energy balance is preserved, because only the half of Earth facing the Sun receives incoming radiation (it arrives only by day), but outgoing radiation leaves constantly from the whole of the surface (by night as well as by day).

The amount of solar radiation reaching the top of the atmosphere is called the solar constant, and it has been measured at about 44 calories per square foot per minute (1,380 watts per sq m). The amount reaching the surface and the amount reradiated from the surface can be calculated and,

Steelworks, Port Auiles, Asturias, Spain (David Woodfall/ENP Images)

from that, so can the surface temperature. These calculations indicate that the average temperature at the surface of Earth should be 0.4°F (-18°C). In fact it is 59°F (15°C). This difference, of 58.6°F (33°C), is due to the absorption of outgoing radiation by atmospheric water vapor, carbon dioxide, and certain other gases. It is called the "greenhouse effect," because the inside of a greenhouse is warmed by the Sun and the warmed air cannot escape. Were it not for the greenhouse effect, life on Earth would be exceedingly difficult.

Greenhouse Gases

Around the middle of the last century, as manufacturing industries expanded throughout Europe and North America and cities grew to accommodate the factories and their workers, coal production started to rise. It was the most widely used fuel, joined during this century by oil and natural gas. All of these fuels are based on carbon. Their energy is released through the oxidation of their carbon to carbon dioxide, and the carbon dioxide is released into the air. Before the great industrial expansion, the atmospheric concentration of carbon dioxide was about 280 parts per million (ppm). It is now about 350 ppm, an increase of 25 percent, and the concentration is still rising. Carbon dioxide is a very minor constituent of the atmosphere, amounting to only 0.35 percent of the total, but because it absorbs radiation at infrared wavelengths, there are fears that a continuing increase in its concentration will lead to a general climatic warming. This is called an "enhanced greenhouse effect" and carbon dioxide is known as a "greenhouse gas." In this context, the amount in the atmosphere is usually reported as tonnes of carbon (1 tonne = 1.1 ton).

Carbon dioxide is not the only greenhouse gas. Methane (CH_4), nitrous oxide (N_2O), ozone (O_3), and chlorofluorocarbon compounds (CFCs) are also greenhouse gases. These are much less abundant than carbon dioxide, however, so for convenience their climatic effect is counted as a multiple of that of carbon dioxide and called the "global warming potential" (GWP) for that gas. Methane has a GWP of 11, meaning it causes 11 times more warming than carbon dioxide, and nitrous oxide has a GWP of 270.

Emissions of carbon dioxide from the burning of coal, oil, and gas continue to increase. Between 1990 and 1996 they rose by 8.7 percent in the United States, 37 percent in the Middle East, Asia, and the Pacific regions, and 0.8 percent in the European Union. This is not the only source of emissions. In the Tropics, the clearing of forests to provide farmland is accompanied by the burning of surface vegetation, and the agriculture practiced is of the slash-and-burn type, where fire is used to clear sites in preparation for sowing. This releases more carbon dioxide than is absorbed by the growing crop plants.

Global Warming

Eventually, from all these sources, the atmospheric concentration will reach the equivalent of a doubling of carbon dioxide (to about 700 ppm), possibly by about the end of the 21st century. This would exert a warming influence, but one partly offset by emissions of sulfate and dust particles. These tend to reflect sunlight and they also act as cloud condensation nuclei (page 25), increasing the formation of clouds. Recent warming has resulted mainly from increased nighttime cloudiness in winter, due to increased humidity with an abundance of condensation nuclei. Low-level clouds reflect and absorb longwave radiation, which reduces the rate at which the surface cools at night, but the clouds also shade and cool the surface by day.

Allowing for the effect of particles, scientists calculate that a doubling of the concentration of carbon dioxide would cause the average global temperature to rise between 1.8°F (1°C) and 6.3°F (3.5°C), with the most likely increase about 2.7–3.6°F (1.5–2°C). There would be a small rise in sea levels, due mainly to the expansion of seawater as it warmed, but no major melting of the polar icecaps. Indeed, these might thicken due to the increased precipitation predicted in these latitudes, in which case the sea level rise would be proportionally smaller, because of the larger amount of water held as ice.

So far, there is no clear evidence of such warming. Average temperatures have risen since about 1850 by about .97°F (.54°C), but this has not been a steady increase. Most of it occurred before 1940, and there was then a period of cooling until the early 1980s, when the warming resumed. These changes are within the limits of natural climatic variation; satellite measurements show the rise to be very small—0.02°F (0.01°C) per year. A similar warming was recorded in several places in Europe during several decades in the first half of the 16th century. It was followed by a sharp cooling that lasted until about 1850 and was called the Little Ice Age.

Estimating the Consequences

Should the average temperature rise, the consequences are very difficult to predict. It is not necessarily the case that we will enjoy the weather we have now, only it will always be that much warmer, although this might happen. The predicted warming will produce temperatures in Europe only a little higher than those of medieval times, between about 800 and 1300 C.E. Then, average summer temperatures in Britain appear to have been 1.3–1.8°F (0.7–1.0°C) higher than they are today and in central Europe 1.8–2.5°F (1.0–1.4°C) higher. Fields were made and cultivated at higher elevations and in higher latitudes, with cereals, probably barley, being grown in Norway at 69.5° N, and vineyards prospered as far north as the English Midlands.

A rise in temperature means more water will evaporate. This has a cooling effect, due to the latent heat of vaporization absorbed from the surroundings. As the water vapor is carried aloft, it will be cooled and condense. This will release latent heat, warming the surrounding air. The water droplets will form clouds. If these are at a low or medium height they will reflect incoming radiation, cooling the surface below them. If they form very high, on the other hand, the ice crystals from which they are made will absorb longwave radiation, warming the air.

Plants will respond to an increase in the carbon dioxide concentration partly by growing faster, but also by opening their stomata for shorter periods. This will also reduce the rate at which they lose water by transpiration, so they will use water more efficiently.

It may happen that, in effect, the climatic belts of the world will be shifted towards the poles. Scientists anticipate that such warming as occurs will be most marked in high latitudes, that equatorial temperatures will change little, or not at all, and that temperatures will rise more over land than over the oceans. Precipitation will increase in high latitudes and in the monsoon regions, and in winter in middle latitudes. In some parts of continental interiors, soils will become drier in summer.

This suggests a slight expansion of the humid tropical belt into what are now desert regions, including the Sahel zone, and an expansion into a higher latitude of the tropical and subtropical arid belt. Southern Europe could become desert, or at least semi-arid, and the area with a Mediterranean climate could extend much farther north.

Migrating Forests

In this case, the area in the Northern Hemisphere covered by temperate forests would shift northward. The North American and European boreal forest and Russian taiga would occupy most of what is now tundra and, because there is no land farther north into which the tundra could migrate, its extent would be much reduced. Mixed and broad-leaved deciduous forests would expand into Canada, Scandinavia, and Siberia, and sclerophyllous forest might appear in Europe, perhaps as far north as Paris, and in North America away from coasts to around the Great Lakes. The southern continents barely extend into latitudes where the climate supports temperate forest, so this type of forest might disappear from the Southern Hemisphere.

In the centuries following the end of the last ice age, plants steadily migrated northward. A few years ago many biologists were expressing the fear that this type of migration cannot be repeated, partly because the warming being anticipated will be much more rapid than that which occurred then. Probably this fear is misplaced. The amount of anticipated warming has been scaled down a little in recent years, and there is evidence that at times the postglacial warming was very rapid indeed. There is a much more serious risk, however, that migrating plants will find their way blocked. Unless we are prepared to allow our farmlands to be colonized by wild plants migrating northward, the cultivated fields of Europe and North America will present a formidable obstacle. Farmers tend to remove plants that compete with their crops, and migrating species, including trees, are likely to be treated as "weeds." Ordinarily, a climatic warming would be unlikely to cause the extinction of any plant or animal species, but with migration routes blocked this becomes a risk.

Ocean Heat Transport

Increasingly, scientists are suggesting a very different kind of development. Warnings of the effects of a general warming have been based mainly on calculations of the way the atmosphere would respond, and they are at best approximate. They include many assumptions about the location and types of cloud that would form and have to be adjusted to make them correspond to the climatic conditions actually observed. More important, until recently they took little account of what would happen to ocean currents.

Oceans transport heat from low to high latitudes, as warm ocean currents. The warm water of these currents warms the air crossing them, and this has a major effect on climates. The most important of these ocean systems is the one operating in the Atlantic, sometimes called the Atlantic conveyor.

When seawater freezes, the salt is removed, so the ice is made of fresh water but the adjacent sea water becomes saltier. This increases its density. At the same time, the water is at just above freezing temperature, and water is at its densest at 39°F (4°C). Because of this, in the north near the edge of the sea ice, there is water denser than the adjacent water. The dense water sinks to the ocean floor and flows slowly south, as the North Atlantic Deep Water (NADW), all the way to Antarctica. Its place is taken by warmer water flowing northward at the surface, then cooling, becoming saltier, and sinking in its turn.

The warm water flows from the equator, through the Caribbean, along the southeast coast of the United States, then westward across the ocean as the Gulf Stream. The Gulf Stream turns south in the latitude of Portugal and Spain, returning to the equator, but a branch breaks away, as the North Atlantic Drift (or Current). This heads northeast, past the coast of Britain and to Norway.

The effect can be seen in temperatures. At St. John's, Newfoundland, at 47°34' N, the average summer temperature, between May and September, is 76.6°F (24.8°C). In Plymouth, England, at 50°21' N, it is 84.6°F (29.2°C). The difference in winter temperatures, between October and April, is even more marked. The average for St. John's is 14°F (-10.0°C) and for Plymouth 61.0°F (16.1°C). Due to the North Atlantic Drift, Plymouth has a significantly warmer climate, despite being 192 miles (308 km) further north than St. John's.

Destabilizing the Atlantic Conveyor

A warming of the atmosphere will increase evaporation. More clouds will form and there will be more precipitation. Much of this will fall over the oceans, because of the large area they cover, and river flows will increase. More freshwater will reach the ocean surface than reaches it today and, because freshwater is less dense than saltwater, it will float on the surface. Freshwater freezes at a higher temperature than saltwater, but with less effect on the density of adjacent water, because no salt is removed. Scientists calculate that a large increase in the amount of freshwater at the surface of the North Atlantic might alter the circulation of currents. NADW formation would weaken and the North Atlantic Drift would cease to flow, a weaker Gulf Stream turning south in the latitude of southern Europe. Were this to happen, west European climates would cool dramatically.

Plymouth might find itself with a climate similar to that of Newfoundland, but it could be much worse. Another consequence of increased precipitation would be a growth of ice sheets in Greenland and northeastern Canada, which would chill air flowing across them. Some scientific studies suggest this could trigger the rapid onset of an ice age. Far from temperate forests extending their range northward, climatic change of this kind implies that the tundra would extend into lower latitudes and the forests would retreat towards the equator.

The circulation of water in the Atlantic has not changed during about the last 10,000 years, so we are tempted to think of it as very stable. Scientists now believe this period of stability is unusual, that the circulation has been much less stable in the past, and that it might be destabilized rather easily. The danger arises not from the amount of carbon dioxide in the atmosphere, but the rate at which it accumulates. The present current regime would survive a slow accumulation and slow increase in precipitation, but a rapid change would disrupt it.

Temperate Forests and the Missing Carbon

This makes it important to discover what happens to the carbon dioxide we release into the air. Not all of it accumulates. Plants use some, growing somewhat faster when more carbon dioxide is available for photosynthesis. Some dissolves in the oceans. Add together the amount added each year to the atmosphere and the amount entering plants and dissolving in the oceans and compare this total with the amount emitted annually, and some carbon remains unaccounted for. There is between 1.1 billion to 2.2 billion tons (1 to 2 billion t) of this "missing carbon," or 20 percent of the amount of carbon emitted each year.

By the mid 1990s some of it had been found. Between 8 percent and 10 percent of the overall total is stored in European forests. In the world as a whole, each year about 770,000 tons (700,000 t) of carbon is stored away in temperate forests. Only about one-third of the carbon is stored in trees, shrubs, herbs, and other organisms living above the ground surface. The remainder is in the soil itself, and especially in peat soils, which are widespread in temperate latitudes. The fact that the carbon is hidden from view explains why it remained unnoticed for so long. When the volume of living and decomposing matter in the broad-leaved and coniferous forests was calculated, two-thirds of the total was missed—this explains at least part of the missing 20 percent.

Temperate forests are expanding, so the amount of carbon they store is increasing, and using timber and wood products also helps store carbon. Wooden furniture and buildings, and books made from wood pulp, last for a long time. The carbon they contain sits for many years in our homes and on our shelves.

Monterey pine (*Pinus radiata*) is grown for timber in New Zealand, where a study by scientists at the New Zealand Forest Research Institute has found that by the time its trees have grown to full size, each crop of trees, replanted after the previous crop has been removed, stores 50 tons of carbon for every acre of plantation (112 t per ha). If about 40,470 acres (100,000 ha) of forest were to be planted in New Zealand each year from 2008 to 2026, enough carbon would be stored to more than compensate for the amount released by burning fossil fuels in New Zealand during that period.

Growing trees for fuel also helps. Burning wood releases carbon dioxide, of course, but this is carbon dioxide that would soon have returned to the atmosphere in any case, when the trees died and decomposed. It is part of the current carbon cycle and adds no extra carbon dioxide to the air. As a fuel, wood is a substitute for coal, oil, and gas. These "fossil" fuels are themselves carbon stores. Their carbon was removed from the atmosphere millions of years ago, when they began to form, so burning them returns that carbon to the atmosphere, adding to the present concentration of carbon dioxide.

Tree planting helps, and in the United States some electricity utilities have been planting forests, to offset part of the carbon dioxide they release by generating power from burning fossil fuels. At Klamath Falls, Oregon, for example, the Klamath Cogeneration Project plans to reforest 405 acres (1,000 ha) of grassland and scrub to offset some of the carbon dioxide emitted from its gas-fired generating plant.

Helpful though it is, tree planting is not an alternative to reducing emissions of greenhouse gases. Eventually, trees will be growing on all the available land and the forests will be able to expand no further. That day is fairly distant, however, and until then increased afforestation, improved forest management, and encouraging the use of durable forest products could go a long way toward limiting the atmospheric accumulation of greenhouse gases.

In December 1997 representatives of the 160 nations that signed the United Nations Framework Convention on Climate Change met in Kyoto, Japan, for what the U.N. called a "Conference of the Parties." Their purpose was to agree on targets and timetables for the reduction of emissions of the so-called greenhouse gasses, and especially of carbon dioxide. Not all the participating nations accepted the proposals, and there is considerable doubt over whether the suggested targets can be met.

If the targets are met, it is much less certain that they will have very much effect. Estimates of the size of the threat of global warming have been scaled down, so reducing gaseous emissions may make little difference. Regardless of any risk of global warming, however, it is clearly sensible to minimize any interference we may be causing to the chemical composition of the atmosphere.

Schoolchildren planting trees, West Midlands, U.K. (David Woodfall/ENP Images)

Forest Clearance and Soil Erosion

Forests make the soil on which they stand. Thick tree roots run through the ground, some of them penetrating to a considerable depth, and the roots of trees, shrubs, and herbs form an intricate network of fibers a little way below the ground surface. When roots die, they leave tunnels through the soil, ventilating it and facilitating the movement of animals and the growth of more roots. Falling trees overturn the soil and decomposing leaves, branches, and other plant material form a deep layer in which complex organic compounds are converted into plant nutrients, with molecules small enough to enter the root hairs of living plants.

Clear the forest, and at once the soil begins to change. This may be intentional: the plan may be, and historically usually has been, to convert forest into farmland, by making space for cultivation and at the same time exploiting the accumulated fertility of the forest soil. Trees are felled and removed, an operation that may involve dragging them some distance across the ground, and the land is plowed and harrowed in preparation for sowing.

Clear-cutting may be the method of tree harvesting, with no intention of changing the use of the land. Once the crop has been removed the land will be prepared for more trees.

Waterlogging and Erosion

Usually all will be well, and farming or a second tree crop will succeed, but there are dangers. In temperate regions, where most of the low-lying, level ground was converted to agriculture long ago, natural and plantation forests are often located on hillsides or level ground at high elevations, places where the rainfall is often heavy. In these conditions, ground that is left bare may erode. Soil may simply wash away down the slope. On fine-textured, usually peaty soils, and soils that are strongly compacted in the subsoil, or B horizons (page 11), there is also a risk of waterlogging.

Logging destruction,
Siuslaw National Forest, Oregon
(Gerry Ellis/ENP Images)

Trees move large volumes of water from the ground and release it into the air by transpiration. Fell a stand of Norway spruce, transpiring the equivalent of 13 inches (330 mm) of rain a year (page 28), and that is the amount of water which is no longer being removed from the ground. Fine texture or subsurface compaction inhibit the horizontal and vertical movement of water. If water enters the soil faster than it can be removed, the water table may rise. Before long it may be high enough to harm the following tree crop by producing cold, wet, airless soil conditions at a depth tree roots seek to penetrate.

Surplus water can be removed by installing land drains about 66 feet (20 m) apart, on peat soils with a shallow slope, and to 164 feet (50 m) apart, on coarser soil with a steeper slope. Care must be taken to ensure the drainage system does not allow water to collect in natural hollows. Where the subsoil is strongly compacted, deep plowing before the first crop is planted will break up the compacted layer, improving the movement of water and also the root penetration.

Improving the drainage will prevent waterlogging, but it does not reduce the risk of erosion, the actual loss of soil. Vulnerability to erosion varies widely, but it can be predicted. There is a universal soil-loss equation that allows soil scientists to take account of all the factors affecting erosion, such as the intensity of rainfall, soil type, angle of slope, and the distance from the top to the bottom of the slope. The equation is very complicated to use, but it gives a value, in tons per acre for the amount of soil likely to be lost by erosion each year. Wind erosion is rarely a problem on forest soils in temperate regions, which usually receive a high rainfall distributed evenly through the year, so they are unlikely to dry out sufficiently to be blown.

Impacting Raindrops

Not all the rain falling onto the canopy of a forest reaches the ground and most or all of the rain that does will have had its fall broken by leaves or branches. Breaking the fall of the raindrops slows them, so it seems obvious that they strike the forest floor with less energy than the raindrops that fall on open ground. In fact, they strike the ground harder.

The drops form in a different way. Even in the middle of summer, in temperate latitudes almost all raindrops are snowflakes that have drifted gently down to a level, in their cloud or beneath it, where the temperature is several degrees above freezing. The snowflakes melt and if the resulting drops of water are too heavy to be carried aloft by air currents, they fall to the ground. This is not what happens to water that has been intercepted on its way to the ground. As the rain runs off leaves and branches, tiny rivulets merge and the drops that fall are rather bigger than ordinary raindrops. They fall, not because they are too heavy to be carried aloft, but because they are flowing down a gradient and reach a point where they are no longer moving over a supporting surface.

Once they fall, like any falling bodies, they accelerate. If they drip from a height of about 33 feet (10 m) they will accelerate for long enough to reach their terminal velocity, which is the speed at which the gravitational force, accelerating them, and air friction, slowing them, balance one another. When a falling body reaches its terminal velocity, that is the speed at which it continues to fall all the way to the ground and the larger a drop of water is, the higher its terminal velocity. A drop of water about 0.08 inch (2 mm) in diameter falls at about 18 miles per hour (8 m per second). A drop more than about 0.2 inch (5.5 mm) in diameter is unstable and will quickly break into two or more smaller drops, but a drop of that size has a terminal velocity of about 20 miles per hour (9 meters per second). Allowing for the amount of rain that reaches the forest floor not as drops but as small streams flowing down tree trunks, and the amount that evaporates before reaching the floor, in forests of some tree species the total energy of drops striking the ground is greater inside the forest than it is outside, on open ground. The rain does not impact on bare soil, of course, but on vegetation close to ground level and, below that, on the surface litter, a layer mainly of leaves or needles.

Splash Erosion

On bare ground, however, the situation is very different. Raindrops striking the soil knock particles free from the lumps to which they were attached. Very heavy rain can splash soil particles 2 feet (60 cm) into the air. This is called "splash erosion," and it liberates very small particles that can be washed and beaten by further raindrops into the small pores and crevices in the soil surface. In extreme cases this can destroy the structure of the soil by filling all its pores with fine particles. Even without removing soil, this greatly reduces the ability of the soil to sustain plants. Strictly speaking it is not erosion, since no soil is lost, but the process is called "puddle erosion," because it is most likely to occur beneath large puddles.

Splash erosion partly seals the soil beneath an impermeable cap, reducing the amount of water that is able to drain vertically downward and increasing the amount flowing across the surface. The fine particles not held in crevices are then carried over the surface by the flowing water, and eventually are removed from the area. If the subsoil is compacted and has not been broken by plowing, in time erosion may remove the overlying material and expose the surface of the compacted layer. As it does so, the topsoil becomes progressively thinner and less able to support deep-rooting plants. Once the compacted layer is exposed, it will be almost impossible for roots to penetrate.

Years ago, this kind of surface flow was called "sheet" erosion, suggesting an even flow over the surface, like a very wide, very shallow river. This image is misleading. In the first place, it is the splashing of raindrops that has by far the biggest effect. The kinetic energy of falling rain is more than 200 times greater than that of water running off the soil surface. Kinetic energy is the energy of motion, related to the mass and speed of the moving body, and the more energy available, the greater the number of particles that can be transported.

It is easy to see why this is so. Kinetic energy (KE) is calculated by $KE = 1/2mV^2$, where m is the mass and V the velocity. Suppose a mass of rainwater W is falling at 9 meters per second, and $KE = 1/2 \times W \times 9 \times 9 = 81W/2 = 40.5W$. If one-third of the water runs off at, say, 1 meter per second (a realistic value), then the mass of runoff water is W/3 and $KE = 1/2 \times W/3 \times 1 \times 1 = W/6$; comparing the two values for KE, as 40.5W divided by W/6, shows falling rain to have 243 times more kinetic energy than runoff water.

Using real amounts of rainfall and measured values for rainfall intensity, calculations of kinetic energy can be used to determine the erosive power of rain and the results plotted on a map, with lines joining places of equal erosivity. These show, not surprisingly, that the regions of the United States most vulnerable to splash erosion are inland from the Gulf and Atlantic coasts, from about San Antonio, Texas, to Jacksonville, Florida, the area that most often experiences rainstorms of tropical intensity.

Rills, Gullies, and Mass Wasting

In the second place, water does not flow across the surface as a smooth sheet. Bare soil is not smooth like a parking lot. There are small depressions where it gather, then overflows, cutting small channels as it does so. Some of these channels grow larger, with side channels feeding into them, and they may become established as rills. At this stage they are small enough to be removed easily by ordinary cultivation methods. Left untreated on bare ground, however, rills may grow deeper and wider, large ones capturing the flow from small ones, until they become gullies. Land crossed by gullies looks severely damaged, but appearances can be deceptive. In semiarid and desert climates, where rain falls rarely but as intense downpours, gullies are known as wadis or arroyos, between downpours appearing as dried riverbeds. In these climates it is not practicable to cultivate the land, so it has no value for agriculture or forestry and, therefore, any erosion it suffers causes no harm. Similarly, where there are gullies in temperate latitudes, in most cases they have been allowed to develop because the land is of too little value for it to be worth the high cost of removing them.

This is not to say gullies are unimportant, only that they often do little economic harm to the land on which they occur. They do indicate soil erosion, and this can be serious away from the eroded land.

Gullies form when there is a large increase in the volume of water draining across a sloping surface at times of very heavy rain. Usually, the surface runoff finds its way to the small streams and rivers you can see tumbling down the sides of many steep hills. Sometimes these streams carry very little water, at other times their channels are full, but at all times that is where the water drains and the route by which it is removed. The system fails when the amount of water greatly exceeds the capacity of the stream channels. Water overflows, and new channels form that develop into gullies. After that, water has a network of channels through which to flow.

Soil often erodes by the removal of fine particles, but there are more dramatic alternatives on the steep slopes that are often exposed when forests are cleared. Water flowing below the surface can detach the overlying material. Destabilized, this then begins to move down the slope, sliding on the layer of mud at its base. The result is a landslide. If the ground is wet enough, the slide may be of mud, as a mudflow, and if the lubricating mud layer is very close to the surface, the flow may occur as an avalanche of surface debris. Less spectacularly, on land left bare for any length of time, soil, lubricated from beneath, may creep down the slope a little at a time, but as a mass. Geologists describe all these forms of erosion as "mass wasting." Creep is not a dangerous form of mass wasting the way landslides, avalanches, and mudflows are, but it is a more serious form of soil loss. With each rainstorm, the topsoil shifts a short distance, then stops when the ground dries, only to move again with the next rain. Left unchecked, creep erosion can strip away an entire hillside down to bare rock.

Changing Land Use

There are many ways to increase the flow of surface water inadvertently. Most changes of land use will do so under certain circumstances, and one change very likely to do so is the clearance of forest. Over the cleared area interception and transpiration cease, so a large proportion of the falling rain reaches the surface and a smaller proportion is removed from the ground. The surface has been laid bare.

Fire can also increase erosion, because that, too, exposes the ground. Over a 10-year period in Oklahoma, for example, during which the amount of rainfall was identical on two forest sites, one protected from fire and the other burned, 10 times more soil was lost by erosion from the burned site than from the protected one. Results from a similar comparison in North Carolina were still more dramatic. In nine years there, the burned site lost over 150 times more soil than the protected site.

There have been measurements of the rate of erosion before and after the clearance of forest on steep slopes with sandy soil in England. These show there was no erosion where the hillside was forested. Grass afforded less protection, and on grass slopes about 2.4 tonnes of soil was lost from each hectare every year (1 ton per acre per year). On bare soil, erosion carried away about 17.7 tonnes per hectare per year (8 tons per acre per year).

Forest roads are a major cause of soil erosion. In plantations that will remain forested permanently, roads are often built in much the same way as public roads, and surfaced. But surfacing is expensive, and since the roads carry only light traffic until the tree crop is harvested, many forest roads are little more than dirt tracks, made as cheaply as possible. They are often on steep slopes in regions of high rainfall, and at harvest time are used by very heavy vehicles. Unless they are well maintained, with drains across them at intervals and plants encouraged to grow on them, dirt roads on steep gradients turn into gullies, and their erosion can continue for years after the harvest operations that caused the initial damage.

Sedimentation

Eroded soil is washed downhill and much of it eventually enters rivers. After a few days of heavy rain, rivers are usually brown with the load of soil they are carrying. Brown water is also contaminated water, because in addition to soil particles it carries organic matter that alters the chemical composition of the river. The waters flow rapidly, driven by pressure from the increased volume draining into them upstream, and their energy allows them to transport large quantities of soil particles. Precisely how much depends on the volume of water and its rate of flow and on the size of soil particles.

When the river flow slows, the water has less energy to carry soil particles, and they begin to settle, the heaviest first. Rivers slow, and often become wider, when they cross a shallower gradient such as a plain. They also slow where they flow into the sea and where they enter a reservoir held behind a dam. After each storm the rivers carry more soil, and the soil is deposited downstream, at the coast, or in a reservoir. Layers of sediment form and grow thicker.

Where a slow-moving river crosses a plain, the increasing depth of sediment on its bed reduces the depth of water. The channel becomes shallower. This increases the risk of flooding, because the river is now less able to carry the volume of water released by storms, or the melting of snow near its source. Navigation is also restricted as the river depth decreases.

In harbors the problem may be even more serious. As the river meets the sea, and its flow is opposed by the movement of sea currents, it can lose energy rapidly. At the same time, chemical reactions between saltwater and the fine particles carried by the freshwater cause the particles to adhere to one another (the technical term is "flocculate") and sink. This is how mudbanks form, and eddies can carry the sinking sediment into harbors that then have to be dredged to maintain a sufficient depth of water.

Dams are constructed to hold back rivers while reservoirs fill and then to regulate river flow farther downstream. They halt river flow, so an inflowing river loses all its energy and deposits its entire load of soil particles on the bed of the reservoir. This progressively reduces the amount of freshwater that can be stored and shortens the life of the dam.

Minimizing Erosion

Erosion is caused by the splashing of raindrops on bare ground, often with the sealing of the surface by fine particles, followed by the flow of water carrying soil down the slope. To prevent it, foresters minimize the area of ground laid bare by harvesting. Then they seek to prevent water flowing across the surface. Trenches cut at right angles to the direction of slope often help. The trenches themselves are level, because it is not intended that water should flow along them. They capture water and retain it long enough for it to soak into the ground.

As soon after harvesting as is practicable, the ground is prepared for the next tree crop. Preparation nowadays often involves using machines to break up the surface around the place where a new tree is to be planted. The operation is called "scarification" and it chops up and scatters the remains of small branches and foliage (called "brash") from the previously harvested crop. Scarification leaves an uneven surface through which water penetrates more easily than through an unbroken surface. Except on very well drained soils, the young tree is planted on a mound made by excavating soil from a hollow. This also breaks up the surface, aiding the vertical penetration of water and helping prevent surface flow down the slope.

Erosion is a natural phenomenon, resulting from the same weathering processes that release the small mineral particles which form the basis of soil. Such geological erosion is unavoidable and acceptable, because soil forms at about the same rate as erosion removes it. Accelerated erosion removes soil faster than it can be replaced and this is unacceptable. Forest clearance is one of the two principal causes of soil erosion, the other being agriculture, and in both cases better land management can minimize it.

Warm-Temperate and Mediterranean-Type Forests

*Western red cedar temperate rain forest,
Pacific Coast, North America
(Gerry Ellis/ENP Images)*

Rain forest is not confined to the Tropics. It may also develop in higher latitudes where temperatures are mild and the rainfall is abundant. Possibly the largest temperate rain forest is in the United States, extending for about 12 miles (19 km) along the valleys of the rivers Bogachiel, Hoh, Queets, and Quinalt in the Olympic National Park, in the state of Washington. The park was established in 1938, to protect the Olympic Mountains, and in 1953 the boundaries were extended to include an 50-mile (80-km) stretch of coastline. The Olympic Mountains, and the park, lie on the Olympic Peninsula, to the west of Seattle and bordered to the north by Vancouver Island, Canada, across the Juan de Fuca Strait. The whole park occupies an area of about 897,000 acres (363,000 ha).

This coast is washed by a branch of the Kuroshio Current. Part of the North Pacific gyre (page 000), the Kuroshio Current begins where the North Equatorial Current, flowing from east to west, meets the Asian coast and turns north. It passes along the coast of the Japanese island of Honshu, then turns east, flowing directly across the Pacific in about latitude 45° N. Warm water from one arm of the Kuroshio Current flows parallel to the coast of Washington and British Columbia. Air above the current is warmed, but the adjacent sea and air are cool, and the rate of condensation is high. In summer, sea fogs are frequent in the Olympic Peninsula and the annual rainfall on west-facing slopes exceeds 140 inches (3,550 mm).

Such conditions encourage the growth of mosses, lichens, and club mosses, and the trees are festooned with epiphytes. Every acre of the forest is said to contain around 6,000 pounds (2,700 kg) of these plants (14,800 pounds [6,700 kg] per hectare). The principal tree species are Sitka spruce (*Picea sitchensis*), western hemlock (*Tsuga heterophylla*), and groups of bigleaf maple (*Acer macrophyllum*). Curiously, considering the climate, this forest is maintained naturally by fire. Spells of dry weather are quite common in summer and occasionally lightning ignites flammable material on the valley sides. The shapes of the valleys can funnel air, fanning the flames, so the fire spreads to the valley bottom. Red alder (*Alnus rubra*) grows among the ashes, followed by spruce and then hemlock. It is from spruces and western hemlocks taken from this forest that modern British conifer plantations were developed.

Part of the Olympic Forest was clear-cut in the early years of this century. Second-growth forest developed, matured, and was then logged, the area being replanted with Douglas fir (*Pseudotsuga menziesii*), although some of the old-growth forest remains. Elsewhere, the original forest survives, with spruces, some 300 or more years old, up to 280 feet (85 m) tall. Where old trees fall, they decay slowly and young seedlings grow in rows along the decaying trunks. Because of the thickness of these mighty stems, the seedlings are several feet above ground level and they develop long stilt roots that remain after the old trunks beneath them have disappeared. Other trees have buttress roots reaching to 13 feet (4 m) or more up the trunks. Because in many places the forest is fairly open, the ground vegetation is lush. The forest is rich in animal life. There are several species of deer, black bears, cougars, and about 140 species of birds. Grazing by large numbers of Roosevelt elk (a local variety of the wapiti, *Cervus canadensis*) control the regeneration of trees in some of the valleys.

Rain forests also occur further south in California, dominated by the Sierra redwoods (*Sequoiadendron giganteum*) of the Yosemite National Park. Elsewhere, they are commoner near the eastern coasts of continents.

Southern-Hemisphere Temperate Rain Forests

In Australia, the coastal belt of Victoria and New South Wales supports temperate rain forests dominated by various species of southern beeches (*Nothofagus*) and coachwood (*Ceratopetalum*). They merge further north in Queensland with bunya bunya (*Araucaria bidwillii*) and kauri pines (*Agathis* species). Still farther north, the temperate rain forest merges almost imperceptibly with tropical rain forest.

The natural vegetation over much of New Zealand is also temperate rain forest, dominated by *Nothofagus*, red pines (*Dacrydium* species), and podocarps (*Podocarpus* species), with kauri pines in North Island. Maori people once built their war canoes from kauri pines. The brown kiwi (*Apteryx australis*), the emblem of New Zealand, forages for berries, worms, and insects on the floor of the New Zealand rain forest and the tui (*Prosthemdera novaeseelandiae*) hunts in the canopy.

There are much smaller areas of rain forest in South Africa, along the coast and in the Drakensburg Mountains. In South America, the Valdivian rain forest, west of the Andes in Chile, is famous for the Chile pine or monkey puzzle tree (*Araucaria araucana*) and Patagonian cypress (*Fitzroya cupressoides*).

Kyushu, the southernmost island of Japan, and sheltered parts of Honshu, to its north, also support temperate rain forest as the natural climax vegetation. This forest is similar in composition to the rain forest of southern China. Both are dominated by a variety of oaks (*Quercus* species) and beeches (*Fagus* species), with some coniferous trees. A mild, wet climate favors rice-growing as well as rain forest and much of this part of eastern Asia is forest no longer, but cropland.

Himalayas and Caucasus

At elevations of around 4,000 feet (1,200 m) in the Himalayas, temperate rain forests occur in tropical latitudes. In Nepal, for example, these forests include large stands of bamboos up to 50 feet (15 m) tall. In Nepal, as elsewhere in Asia, forests of all kinds have been seriously depleted to provide fuel (page 154) as well as land for farming. Clearance has led to soil erosion and now steps are being taken to protect such natural forest as remains and to increase the forest area.

A temperate rain forest that has been protected since 1924 occupies part of the Caucasus Biosphere Nature Reserve in Russia. The reserve covers 1,017 square miles (2,635 sq km) and the rain forest is on the western side, which receives the highest rainfall in Russia, of about 197 inches (5,000 mm) a year. The rain forest is dominated by rhododendron, laurel, holly, and oak.

Mediterranean Forest, Maquis, Chaparral, and Mallee Scrub

Around the Mediterranean, the original forest, mostly dominated by holm oak (*Quercus ilex*) and Aleppo pine (*Pinus halepensis*), has disappeared almost completely. Cleared in classical times to provide farmland, its soils subsequently eroded and now support the scrub vegetation known as maquis or, when more open, garrigue.

Maquis is a type of chaparral, the best known example being in southern California, on the western side of the Sierra Nevada. There the composition varies according to the aridity, but in many parts of the mixed chaparral having intermediate rainfall, the dominant plants are evergreen oaks, such as California scrub oak (*Quercus dumosa*), and tall shrubs such as California lilac (*Ceanothus* species) and chamise (*Adenostoma fasciculatum*). Chaparral also occurs in Arizona, where the dominant tree is shrub live oak (*Quercus turbinella*).

There is a somewhat similar, Mediterranean-type vegetation in Cape Province, South Africa, known as fynbos. It differs from maquis and chaparral in having very few trees, although otherwise it is rich in plant species. In Chile, the matorral is another variety of chaparral.

In southern and western Australia the climate produces plant communities, known as mallee scrub, dominated by *Eucalyptus* species, silk oaks (*Grevillea* species), *Banksia*, and *Protea* small trees or shrubs, all broad-leaved evergreens, as well as small trees belonging to the family Epacridaceae, most adapted to dry conditions and many with

very thick trunks. This family includes the Southern-Hemisphere equivalents of the heather family (Ericaceae) of the Northern Hemisphere. In places, silver wattle (*Acacia dealbata*), a tree up to 100 feet (30 m) tall and known to florists as "mimosa," occurs as an understory species, growing where fire has removed competition.

Marginal Forests at Risk

Where sclerophyll forest and plant communities of the chaparral type occur near coasts, they are at risk. The climate that produces this vegetation, of hot, dry summers and mild, wet winters, is very attractive. Understandably, people who are able to do so choose to live there, but in clearing space for the homes, roads, and services they need the natural vegetation is likely to be destroyed. This risk, and the comparative rarity of the vegetation type, are now recognized in most countries. The American chaparral is protected, but nowhere is protection perfect and forests have never fared well in any competition over land use.

Mild temperatures and abundant rainfall mean temperate rain forests, like their tropical counterparts, tend to produce giant trees. These are of great value for timber, and there is a clear commercial pressure to exploit them. The forests are ecologically fragile, however, and even where their appearance is restored by secondary growth some of the species they support may be lost. Obviously, even more are lost when such forests are replaced by plantations. The risk to them is recognized and many are now protected. Those of North America are contained within the boundaries of national parks, and the integrity of those in Australia and New Zealand is closely guarded by conservationists.

Temperate rain forests and sclerophyllous forests occupy a much smaller area than the commoner broad-leaved deciduous and boreal forests. They have always inhabited the vulnerable margins of our forests. Rain forests are found in foggy, wet places where people are not eager to build homes, but they produce giant trees that are attractive to logging companies. Sclerophyllous forest produces some useful timber and many more useful herbs, including lavender, rosemary, thymes, myrrh (*Cistus creticus*), and many others that are now cultivated. Its attraction arises not so much from its plants, however, as from its climate, and where this coincides with spectacular scenery the pressure to develop the area for housing and/or tourism may be hard to resist. What remains of marginal forests such as these is in special need of protection.

Deciduous Forests

Broad-leaved deciduous forests develop naturally where moderate rainfall is distributed fairly evenly through the year, winters are not too long, and summers are warm. This is the kind of climate found at low elevations throughout the temperate regions.

The climate that suits these forests so well also attracts farmers, with the fertile soils that form beneath the forests as an added bonus. In Britain and many other parts of Europe, for example, farmland made more than 2,000 years ago by clearing the natural forest (page 144) is as productive today as it has ever been. So far as anyone can tell, with good farming methods these soils can remain in cultivation forever.

Not surprisingly, therefore, of all the types of forest in the world it is the broad-leaved deciduous forests of the Northern Hemisphere that have suffered most from the ax and saw. For the most part, these are the forests that have been felled to provide the land that feeds and clothes us.

Despite the need for cultivable land, however, quite large tracts survived. There were several reasons. Forests themselves were an important source of food, such as game, and of sport in the procurement of it. Hunting was an amusement reserved for the rich and powerful and it was they who protected areas of forest. Timber and small wood were also needed and in the days before plantation forestry based on conifers, broad-leaved forests were the only source in regions where this was the natural climax vegetation. So some forests survive and today, in the world as a whole, broad-leaved deciduous and mixed broad-leaved and coniferous forests occupy about 2.8 million square miles (7.2 million sq km). This is not all ancient or old-growth forest: the total includes secondary growth and broad-leaved plantations. Nevertheless, the area is substantial. It is about two-thirds the area of the forests of the humid Tropics.

North American Old-Growth Forest

North American old-growth forests survived as patches separated by fields, areas farmers never needed for crops, and in remote places that farming families never reached. These forests are found mainly in the mountains of the east, from the Adirondacks down to the southern Appalachians, and on the floodplains farther south. With so vast an area available, settlers could afford to pick and choose, and farmers preferred the areas with the best climate. Mesophytic forests, typical of moderate climates, were the ones most likely to be cleared for farming. These were the forests dominated by oak, hickory, sugar maple, tulip tree, and beech, as well as chestnut until this was destroyed by disease (page 108).

Forests also provided lumber and fuel. Many areas, not destined to become farmland, were cleared for their timber, pitch, and resin and then abandoned, the land being required for no other use. Forest returned to these areas, as secondary growth.

Comparisons between the histories of North American and European forests can be misleading. There is a temptation to assume that only Europeans were involved in both cases, that the people who had created the agricultural landscapes of Europe crossed the Atlantic and reproduced the process by clearing the previously untouched American forest. This is not so: Native Americans had made major modifications over the thousands of years they occupied the land before the settlers began to arrive.

They lived in villages, owning land as tribes rather than as individuals, and grew plant crops by a type of slash-and-burn cultivation. Around the village they cleared the forest, burned it, and grew their crops on the exposed land. They also used fire to make paths through the forest, to drive game, and to keep away dangerous animals and those that damaged their crops. They used the forest as a source of fuel, gradually cutting it back, farther and farther from the village, until, after a number of years, the entire village moved to a new location. The old site was abandoned and no new trees were planted. Forest clearance encouraged the growth of grass, herbs, and tree seedlings on which herbivores such as deer grazed and browsed. Herbivore populations increased and strongly affected the regeneration of the forest.

In some places, therefore, what appears to be old-growth forest may be secondary growth, but no record has survived of the original clearance. This pre-settlement treatment is not confined to the east, of course, but extended to all forests. There are oakwoods in California that are known to have been burned and converted into fields long before the arrival of Europeans.

If this casts doubt on the status of North American old-growth forest, there is no question about the condition of secondary growth. It has been expanding rapidly throughout this century. Second-growth forest now covers between 65 percent and 85 percent of upland New England, for example, and ecologists participating in the Harvard Long Term Ecological Research program report that today in many ways the landscape of New England appears more natural than at any time since the 18th century.

Białowieża Forest

Fragments of the original primeval forest also survive in Europe. Some were hunting forests, protected by their status for long enough to survive the expansion of agriculture. Others are on land of a quality too poor to be farmed economically.

Probably the largest single forest is the one covering about 502 square miles (1,300 sq km) in Poland and Belarus and known by its Polish name of Białowieża. It was a hunting forest until about 200 years ago, but since then it has had other uses, not to mention disturbance from the warring armies that have passed its way. Cattle have been grazed in it, leaf litter removed for horticultural use, and parts may have been cleared and cultivated. It suffered a major fire early in the last century, and from 1895 to 1915 the deer population was deliberately increased to such a level that in places the forest came close to disappearing, then the deer were removed and the last herd of European bison with them. Both animals have now returned. The forest itself is divided into numbered square blocks by a grid of wide, straight paths, called rides.

The history of the forest is complex, as is its ecology, but there is no doubt of its value. At least in places, it is a remnant of the types of lowland forest that were once widespread in Europe from France to Russia. The most valuable area, of 18.32 square miles (47.47 sq km) lying at the center, has been fully protected since 1921 as the Białowieża National Park. This area contains broad-leaved deciduous forest dominated by oak, lime, and hornbeam on higher ground, alder and ash near the rivers, and ash and elm elsewhere, with spruce and pine on the very wet or acid soils. In all, the forest contains about 3,000 species of plants, some of them rare, and 8,500 of animals. The animals include wolf (*Canis lupus*), red deer (*Cervus elephas*), wild boar (*Sus scrofa*), beaver (*Castor fiber*), lynx (*Felis lynx*), and the last herd of European bison or wisent (*Bison bonasus*) living freely (rather than in zoos and parks). They were reintroduced in 1929.

In 1991, the governments of Poland and Belarus agreed on plans to establish the forest as a Biosphere Reserve, under the auspices of the U.N. Educational, Scientific, and Cultural Organization

(UNESCO). In August 1996, however, the Polish government merely doubled the size of the National Park. Outside this securely protected area, most of the forest is used for recreation and some for logging, although a moratorium on logging was declared in 1995. Conservationists are campaigning to extend national park status to the entire forest.

Old-growth white ash tree,
Monroe State Park, Maine
(Gary Braasch/ENP Images)

European Primeval Forest

Hunting forests survived in many parts of central and eastern Europe, but in these areas the conversion of forests to farms was slow. Prior to medieval times, settlements grew along river valleys, where land was cleared for cultivation and the remaining forests were managed to provide timber, small wood, and fuel. Once developed, this pattern of land use changed little for centuries. It left many areas in the mountains remote and, for a long time, unoccupied.

Major changes in land use began early in the 19th century and accelerated as roads and railroads improved communications and European economies industrialized. Factories were built where there was access to the raw materials they needed, and the forests provided fuel.

Clearances accelerated and natural forest was being logged regularly in Ukraine in the early 1930s and as late as the 1980s on the border between Croatia and Slovenia. It might have been worse, but the establishment of forest reserves helped to check the process. Landowners were the first to appreciate the value of their forests, and it was they who began to create reserves. The very first reserve to protect virgin forest was established in 1838 at Zofin, Czech Republic, and others followed.

Today, patches of natural forest survive and are protected throughout Europe. Most are to be found in the southeast, in Austria, Slovenia, Croatia, Bosnia-Hercegovina, and especially in the Czech Republic and Slovakia. There are some in Spain and France. The nearest to Britain is the La Tillaie reserve in the Fontainebleu Forest, near Paris.

No more than about 6 percent of the total area of the broad-leaved deciduous forests of the world is protected by having been formally designated a national park, wilderness area, or allotted to one of the other internationally recognized conservation categories. Conservationists are campaigning to extend protection more widely, especially to old-growth and primeval forests. Such designation seldom confers absolute security, but it does acknowledge the importance attributed to an area. It may be, however, that the value of forests, and especially of natural forest, is now widely appreciated and guarded by the vigilance of those who live in and near them. That is the most reliable protection of all.

Boreal Forests

Canada occupies a total area of 3.85 million square miles (9.97 million sq km), of which 3.56 million square miles (9.22 million sq km) is land and the remainder freshwater. Forests cover 1.75 million square miles (4.53 million sq km). The Canadian forest is the third largest in the world, after those of Eurasia (page 120) and the South American Tropics, and it accounts for one-tenth of the entire forested area of the world.

Most of the Canadian forest is boreal, comprising a broad belt extending from the Atlantic to the Alaskan border and from northern Newfoundland, Quebec, and the Yukon at about 60° N to the Great Lakes, with a tongue stretching southward along the eastern slopes of the Rockies. Along its northern edge, the forest becomes more open, merging with the tundra, and with grasslands in northern Manitoba, Saskatchewan, and Alberta, with the prairie farms to the south.

Boreal forests grow in a cool, wet climate, where summers are short and winters long. Boreas, from which the word "boreal" is derived, was the Greek god of the north wind. It is not a climate suitable for farming and so the Canadian forest has never been cleared to any large extent to provide farmland. Nonetheless, the forest is of immense economic importance. Forestry, and industries associated with it, provide around 900,000 jobs, about 7 percent of all employment, and are the main support of nearly 350 communities. Forest products account for about 17 percent of Canada's total exports. Obviously, the forest is managed. About 247.1 million acres (100 million ha), amounting to 22 percent of the forest area, produces timber commercially and about 2.471 million acres (1 million ha) is harvested each year.

Composition and Control

The composition of the boreal forest is less diverse than that of forests in lower latitudes. In eastern Canada, the only trees over large areas are black spruce (*Picea mariana*), white spruce (*P. glauca*), and balsam fir (*Abies balsamea*). In central Canada there are jack pine (*Pinus banksiana*), lodgepole pine (*P. contorta*), and tamarack (*Larix laricina*), and in the west Sitka spruce (*Picea sitchensis*). To the south, these merge with some broadleaved species, including paper birch (*Betula papyrifera*), balsam poplar (*Populus balsamifera*), and quaking aspen (*P. tremuloides*). This may make the forest seem monotonous, but these are only the dominant species. In all, the Canadian forest contains 131 species of trees and about 3,000 other species of plants, not to mention 200 species of mammals, almost 550 of birds, and almost 90 of reptiles and amphibians, as well as around 100,000 invertebrate species.

Management of this forest is controversial, partly because of its vast size. The 10 provincial governments are responsible for the administration of about 80 percent of the overall forest, about 10 percent is administered by the federal government, and about 10 percent is owned privately. Usually, the provincial authorities license private companies to harvest timber on the land they control. This authorization specifies the harvesting methods that may be employed and includes a requirement for reforestation.

Boreal forest, Yukon, Alaska
(Gerry Ellis/ENP)

Old-Growth Forest

Of the area producing timber, conservationists classify about 71 percent, or 175 million acres (71 million ha) as old-growth forest that should not be altered. This area includes stands of Sitka spruce in British Columbia that are known to be 500 years old, and areas of pine forest in central Canada that are about 140 years old. These, and similar areas, are clearly old-growth forest, but the status of some of the forest included in the conservationist estimate is more controversial. Even within old-growth forest, companies are permitted to remove certain old, very large trees that are close to dying and liable to become highly flammable, or prone to pest infestation or diseases that could harm the trees around them. Old-growth forest contains trees of great age, but this fact alone may be insufficient reason for preserving them in a country where the forest is so vast, and so much of it has never been exploited. Old trees are large and this makes them valuable. Harvesting them yields profits that can be invested in the management of protected areas of greater scientific or historical importance.

Patches of forest that exemplify particular forest types or are of special ecological interest are being identified and protected. These include old-growth forest, of course, but also secondary-growth forest that supports a wide range of species or is important for some other reason. Varying levels of protection are provided by a hierarchy of designations, including natural areas, ecological reserves, wilderness areas, wildlife parks, provincial parks, and national parks. There are more than 3,000 protected areas, and when it is completed, the network of 34 national parks will represent all 39 of the natural types of plant and animal communities found in the country. Within the forests, by the early 1990s conservation areas covered 12.5 million acres (31 million ha), and the federal government was committed to expanding it.

Clear-Cutting

Conservationists throughout North America are especially worried about the effects of clear-cutting, the harvesting method in which all the trees are removed from a tract of land, leaving it bare. There is no doubt this is a visually intrusive technique. The bare ground, often incongruously rectangular with sharply defined edges set amid intact forest, can be seen from far away and it is ugly. As the years pass, of course, new growth restores the appearance, but there are other concerns. Clear-cutting destroys habitat and although this returns, the recreated habitat may be inferior

to the one that was lost. It is also possible that some patches of the clear-cut area may remain bare. During the time the ground is bare, erosion might damage it (page 178) and harm fish in nearby rivers. It can also cause distress to local people who live by hunting.

The dangers are recognized and clear-cutting is only one of the harvest techniques that are used, but sometimes it can replicate the natural events experienced in a forest, where at intervals storms and fires destroy all the trees in particular areas. Where many of the trees are very old, or all of much the same age, clear-cutting may be the best way to open up the forest, allowing light to penetrate and young saplings to grow. Clear-cutting policy is under review in Canada, however, and henceforth it is likely to be used with greater sensitivity, for example by reducing the size of cut-over areas. Already, companies that clear-cut areas of public forest are required to replant it.

Regeneration and Replanting

Eventually, plantations and the natural regeneration of secondary-growth forests should supply most timber and forest products, but until these mature, maybe 50 years from the time they were planted, logging of the natural, primary forest will continue. Each year about 1 billion young trees are planted. This is roughly double the number felled each year, so the Canadian forest is expanding.

Natural regeneration is the preferred method, and this is what is encouraged on more than half the harvested area. The reason is partly ecological and partly commercial. Regeneration restocks the area with the trees that thrive best in it and, because it is a natural process, the resulting forest closely approximates that which is best adapted to the site. Trees that are well adapted to their site are likely to grow more vigorously and be healthier than introduced species, so they will yield a more valuable crop more quickly. Not all areas regenerate easily, however, so some planting is necessary. Replanting is used on less than half the harvested land, and the seedlings used are chosen to maximize the genetic diversity.

Scandinavian Forest

Across the Atlantic, the boreal forest continues in Scandinavia. The forest covers about 45,930 square miles (119,000 sq km) in Norway, 99,000 square miles (256,500 sq km) in Sweden, and 77,586 square miles (201,000 sq km) in Finland, making a total approaching 225,000 square

miles (576,500 sq km). Of the total land area, boreal forest occupies about 66 percent in Finland, 57 percent in Sweden, and 23 percent in Norway.

Ownership is more complex than in Canada—it is shared between private individuals and families, forestry companies, communities, and the state. In Norway, about 79 percent of the forest is owned by private individuals, in Sweden about 50 percent, and in Finland rather more than 60 percent. There are about 125,000 privately owned productive forests in Norway, and in Finland nearly 440,000 private forests of 1 hectare (0.4 acre) or more in area.

This division of ownership complicates management, and there have been worries that old-growth forest was being lost and replaced by monoculture plantations. Along the Finnish border with Karelia (Russia), for example, old-growth forest has been clear-cut in patches up to 1,235 acres (500 ha) in area. These are densely forested countries, however, with long traditions of living in, with, and from the forest. One Finnish family in five owns a forest, even if it is only a small one. Livestock are grazed in them and game hunted, and for centuries roundwood, timber, and tar have been important exports. The ecological value of certain types of forest has been recognized only recently.

It is recognized now, and the Scandinavian countries are protecting their forests. In Finland there are 53 conservation areas, amounting to 3,000 acres (1,200 ha), protecting particular types of forest and an additional 52,000 acres (21,000 ha) of old-growth forest is protected. This is in addition to the forest that is protected by virtue of lying within the boundaries of the 29 national parks, 19 nature reserves, and 12 wilderness areas, with a combined area of 9,114 square miles (23,600 sq km). The large national parks and wilderness areas—each occupying more than 1,295 square miles (500 sq km)—are concentrated in the north of the country near the border with Karelia, where most of the area is protected, imposing a limit to the area of old-growth forest that can be clear-cut.

The overall area of Scandinavian boreal forest is maintained by replanting, a practice the Norwegian government has been subsidizing since 1863.

There is no possibility of the boreal forest disappearing and it is very unlikely that its area will diminish in the foreseeable future. Indeed, the trend is for the area to increase. Its composition may change, if natural forest is replaced by plantation, but the consequences of such a change are now widely appreciated. Not only would the ecological value of the forests be diminished, but in the accessible areas, so would their commercial value for tourism and recreation.

The Taiga

Across northern Eurasia, from Finland to the Pacific and from the Arctic Circle south to about latitude 52° N, the latitude of Irkutsk and the southern tip of Lake Baikal, there stretches the taiga. It is a vast ocean of trees, more open in the north, where it merges gradually into tundra, and in the south, where it gives way to the steppe grasslands.

In all, forests cover nearly 36 percent of the land area of the Commonwealth of Independent States (C.I.S.), and the taiga accounts for almost all of this. Of all the timber in the C.I.S.—around 3 trillion cubic feet (about 84 billion cubic meters)—80 percent is from coniferous trees.

The taiga is the second largest forest in the world: only the tropical forest of South America is slightly bigger. It covers about 3 million square miles (7.7 million sq km), almost all of it in Russia. Larch (*Larix* species) occupies about 1.03 million square miles (2.65 million sq km), Siberian stone pine (*Pinus sibirica*) 154,400 square miles (400,000 sq km), other pine species 444,000 square miles (1.15 million sq km), and spruces (*Picea* species) 297,000 square miles (770,000 sq km).

Wildlife

As you would expect in so vast an area with so sparse a human population, the taiga supports much wildlife, although the range of species is limited by the harsh winters and the lack of variety among habitats. The Siberian spruce grouse (*Falcipennis falcipennis*) is one of several species that are found nowhere else. One of Europe's rarest mammals, the Russian desman (*Desmana moschata*) occurs in the taiga, although it is also found elsewhere in eastern Europe. It is a member of the mole family (Talpidae) that has abandoned the subterranean life and taken to the water, acquiring a waterproof coat, a flattened tail it uses as a rudder and for swimming, and webbed feet it uses as paddles. It is fully protected in the C.I.S. The wisent or European bison (*Bison bonasus*) became extinct in 1925, but has been reintroduced.

There are eight or nine subspecies of wolf (*Canis lupus*), an animal still thriving in the taiga, but now extinct in most parts of Europe. The wolverine (*Gulo gulo*), a member of the weasel family strong enough to kill a reindeer, is found in the North American and Scandinavian boreal forest as well as the taiga. In Russia it is hunted for its fur, as are the Siberian weasel or kolinsky (*Mustela sibirica*) and sable (*Martes zibellina*).

Moose (*Alces alces*), known in Europe as the elk, feed on water plants in the swampy parts of the forest and by rivers and streams and on grass and young shoots in forest clearings. They are abundant in some areas and their numbers are controlled by hunting, as they are in North America.

Conservation and Forest Reserves

In the days of the USSR, what were then Soviet forests were the property of the state and their management was centrally controlled. They were exploited, of course, and throughout history they have been of great economic importance.

The need to conserve the forests has long been recognized. In 1888 conservation laws were enacted with the aim of protecting all forests (page 151) and more recently especially valuable areas have been designated as forest nature reserves: there are 38 of these. In addition, many of the 50 mountain nature reserves contain coniferous forest.

A herd of bison and the Russian desman live in the Prioksko-Terrasny Biosphere Nature Reserve, a mixed-forest reserve of 19 square miles (49 sq km) not far from Moscow. There are also Russian desmans in the Oka Reserve, a little to its east, and the reserve contains 800 species of flowering plants and 230 species of birds. Since 1956, the Oka Reserve contains the site of the central ornithological station for the C.I.S. Established in 1935, the reserve covers 88 square miles (229 sq km) of which 75 square miles (194 sq km) are taiga.

About 745 miles (1,200 km) northeast of Moscow, the Pechoro-Ilyich Reserve, created in 1930 on the River Pechora in the western foothills of the Ural Mountains, is much bigger. Its total area is 2,785 square miles (7,213 sq km) of which 2,412 square miles (6,246 sq km) is taiga, with 204 species of birds and 43 of mammals. Taiga comprises about 90 percent of the Pinezh Reserve, about 466 miles (750 km) northwest of the Pechoro-Ilyich Reserve, in the Archangelsk region. It was created in 1975 and has an area of 159 square miles (412 sq km). In the mountains bordering Mongolia, in the south of central Siberia to the southeast of Novosibirsk, the Sayano-Shushen Reserve, established in 1976, has an area of 1,504 square miles (3,896 sq km), almost 60 percent of which is taiga forest. The Baikal State Nature Reserve, established in 1979 on the shores of Lake Baikal, includes 453 square miles (1,172 sq km) of taiga, the Sokhondo Reserve, east of Irkutsk near the Mongolian border, protects 815 square miles (2,110 sq km), and

the Stolby Reserve, by the Yenisei River to the east of Tomsk, contains 175 square miles (454 sq km) of forest.

Logging Increasing

The areas are large, but conservationists are concerned at the extent and rate of uncontrolled logging that has been taking place in recent years, mainly in European Russia, to the west of the Urals. Following the constitutional changes by which the old USSR became the C.I.S., the forests remained in state ownership, but responsibility for their management shifted. Under the New Forestry Act of 1993, forests are managed jointly by the federal and regional authorities, but there is confusion about where boundaries between the jurisdictions of the two levels of authority should be drawn. There are also internal paradoxes, such as the fact that the federal ministry responsible for forest conservation not only issues licenses for logging, but also is financed by revenues from logging. Conservationists believe local officials have sold licenses permitting logging inside some forest reserves. There are also fears that Russian organized crime has interests in the timber industry.

Logging, often by clear-cutting, is performed by partnerships between Russian and foreign companies. Not all the cut-over areas have been replanted, although if left alone most will regenerate naturally, which is a better technique than replanting (page 187).

Karelian Taiga

Increased logging has earned the country foreign currency, which it badly needs, but it has done so by allowing bribed officials to sell timber at low prices. This is what nearly happened in Karelia, near the Finnish border. Enso, a major Finnish timber company, had been prepared to start felling, licensed by the Republic of Karelia, but in October 1996 the company was persuaded to declare a moratorium. With warm support from regional conservation organizations that had pressed for it, Enso, the Ministry of Environment of Finland, and the Karelian government announced that they would establish a working group to prepare a conservation plan for the ecologically most valuable areas of Karelian forest. These would include areas of old-growth forest adjacent to those in northern Finland.

As well as defining areas in need of protection from all forestry activities, the working group would devise improved forestry practices for the commercially managed forests. This would lead to the international certification of Karelian forests by the Forest Stewardship Council (FSC), an organization representing the international forestry and timber industries and conservation bodies. With FSC certification, companies and individuals purchasing Karelian timber or products made from it would know it came from well-managed forests.

The arrangement was ideal, but less than a year later it was in trouble. Enso was abiding by the agreement, but it looked as though requests that other companies respect it were being ignored. Members of the Finnish Forest Industries Federation are required to observe certain standards of practice, which include observation of the Karelian agreement, but not all Finnish

Boreal vegetation, north slope Alaska Ranges (Gerry Ellis/ENP Images)

companies belong to the federation. One of the smaller—and in the view of conservationists less scrupulous—companies obtained a logging permit from the Karelian authorities to clear 5,000 acres (2,024 ha) in an area conservationists were seeking to have designated as the Kalevala National Park. There was no forest reserve in that part of Karelia, so the arrangement was perfectly lawful. Near Lake Onega, northeast of St. Petersburg, the Kivach Nature Reserve protects 41 square miles (105 sq km) of the Karelian taiga, but this is the only area with formal protection.

Although it was alleged that Karelian timber was being sold at far below the proper price, the authorities were in a difficult position. Iron-ore mining and the metallurgical industry has provided income and employment since the reign of Peter the Great in the 17th century. The name of the capital, Petrozavodsk, means "Peter's factory." Despite this, the forest is Karelia's principal natural resource and forestry its most important industry. The authorities claimed the economy could not survive without the sale of some tim-

ber from old-growth forests. Environmental groups publicized the issue, but the fate of the Karelian old-growth forest remains uncertain.

Long-Term Risks

Much of the taiga is remote and inaccessible. Harvesting its timber is impracticable without roads or railroads to transport the logs, so there is a check to the rate at which logging can expand. Nor is the taiga subject to the pressures causing deforestation in the tropical lowlands: there is no urgent demand for agricultural land to draw migrants in the wake of the logging companies, clearing more forest to either side of the forestry roads. Russia is not short of farmland and in any case the taiga cannot be farmed for climatic reasons.

The risk is not that the taiga will diminish in size significantly, but that its most ecologically valuable areas may be damaged or even cleared. This would reverse some of the achievements made by conservationists over many decades.

The Need for Conservation

In July 1997, Tray Biasiolli and Jason Halbert were arrested in the George Washington National Forest, near Roanoke, Virginia. Members of the Shenandoah Ecosystems Defense Group, based in Charlottesville, they had fastened themselves to buried pipes on a forest road and remained there for 12 hours blocking the road, as what Biasiolli described as "human speed bumps." Their purpose was to draw attention to and protest against the cutting of timber from 187 acres (76 ha) of the forest near Covington, following the rejection by a federal court of a lawsuit challenging the legality of the logging.

This was just one of countless protests against logging. In Britain, the most dramatic environmental protests of the mid-1990s concerned road building and the building of a new runway at Manchester Airport. These protests involved much more than obstructing roads. Protestors dug and occupied networks of tunnels, sealed behind several steel doors, handcuffing themselves to heavy blocks of half-buried concrete. They built tree houses and aerial walkways linking them. Their opposition was to the building of the runway and of roads in general, but also to the felling of trees this involved.

Everywhere, people strongly oppose the clearance of forests. In the Republic of Karelia (page 188) it was environmental groups opposed to clear-cutting that protested against the timber company which ignored the agreement to halt logging in the old-growth forest. In California, in February 1997, the state authorities sought to prevent a lumber company felling 3,000 acres (1,200 ha) of old-growth redwoods in the Head-waters Forest by buying that area as part of the 7,500-acre (3,035-ha) tract of the Humboldt Forest in which it lies. The idea was to pay the company $380 million in cash or public property, but it outraged conservation groups. They demanded protection for the entire 60,000 acres (24,300 ha) of the Headwaters Forest.

Earth Summit + 5

This local and regional insistence on preserving the integrity of particular forests and parts of forests is mirrored at international level by attempts to regulate the activities of logging companies. The U.N. Conference on Environment and Development, or "Earth Summit," held in Rio de Janeiro in 1992, failed to agree on a plan to protect forests, but the desirability of doing so was not in doubt.

Forest protection was debated at a special session of the U.N. General Assembly held in New York on June 26, 1997, and known as the "Earth Summit + 5," but little progress was made. The European Union, supported by the governments of Canada and Malaysia and some environmental groups, tried to push through a legally binding convention that would limit logging throughout the world. This was opposed by other environmental groups and governments with strong forestry interests, including those of the United States, Brazil, and India. They argued that the convention likely to be accepted would be a weak compromise that did more harm than good. An alternative idea, devised by the World Wide Fund for Nature (WWF) and supported by the World Bank and 20 countries, was to protect areas equal to a tenth of each of the types of forest in the world with a network of reserves that would be in place by the year 2000.

So far, none of these schemes has attracted sufficient support to be implemented, but the search will continue until some workable program has been devised. The main threat is to tropical forests, but a different threat to temperate forests is also acknowledged. These are unlikely to disappear, but they are being converted from natural and old-growth forest to plantation forest.

Tree Farms

This troubles conservationists, which is why they are not impressed by demonstrations of an increase in the total number of trees or area of forest achieved by commercial afforestation. In 1996, for example, plans by Senator Larry Craig, who chairs the Senate Energy and Natural Resources subcommittee on forests, to rewrite the National Forest Management Act were attacked by environmentalists, who feared the change would allow natural forests to be converted into plantations. The change would have restricted the ability of appeals and lawsuits to prevent logging and would have reduced the environmental reviews and consultation with the Fish and Wildlife Service and National Marine Fisheries Service needed before logging is authorized. This, Craig maintained, would bring more order into the Forest Service.

Although plantation forestry may be inferior to the gentle management of natural forest from the point of view of conservation, it has real environmental advantages. Temperate forests are now recognized as a huge "sponge," absorbing carbon dioxide (page 176) and plantations are likely to be the best way to maximize carbon dioxide absorption. Not all tree species, and the soils they produce, are equally efficacious, so there could be advantages in growing the essentially monocultural stands conservationists find objectionable.

Plantations do contain wildlife, of course, and proper management can improve the quality of the habitats they provide. In Britain the expansion of conifer plantations has allowed the wild

Demonstration against old-growth logging in Opal Creek, Oregon (Gerry Ellis/ENP Images)

cat (*Felis sylvestris*), which had become extremely rare, to increase its range into regions from which it had long been excluded.

Conservationists seek to protect natural habitats for the species they support, and it is natural forests that provide the widest variety of habitats. Once adequate safeguards are in place, habitats can even be improved. In the 1920s, the last wolves disappeared from Yellowstone National Park and in 1995 and 1996 a total of 31 gray wolves were reintroduced from Canada. Some lived singly, but the others formed nine packs and by 1997, the wolves were well established and their numbers were increasing. Large predators, such as wolves, help regulate the populations of prey species. They complete the ecosystem, which improves the habitat. It has been suggested that wolves be reintroduced in remote parts of the Highlands of Scotland, although there is strong opposition from farmers and many local people. The reintroduction of European bison into Polish and Russian forests is also a form of habitat enrichment.

Habitat Conservation Plans

Wolves and bison need large areas of forest and freedom from disturbance. Without these they cannot survive. They are not unique, of course, merely familiar examples of a general principle. Every plant and animal species has needs that must be supplied if it is to survive. This fact leads to the concept of the habitat conservation plan (HCP), devised in the United States and based on recommendations from a team of scientists working for a number of agencies, including the U.S. Fish and Wildlife Service and the National Marine Fisheries Service. Its proponents hope the implementation of HCPs will allow commercial logging and the conservation of endangered species to prosper side by side.

An HCP starts by identifying within a large area those small areas that provide the habitats essential for the well-being of certain species. These species are chosen because they are rare or endangered and it is their habitat areas that are protected. Those areas form a network throughout the larger area, but their total area is relatively small. Species do not live in isolation, of course, and the HCP concept includes the reasonable assumption that if the habitat of an endangered species is protected many other species will also benefit. The protection afforded to designated areas is intended to last a long time. It cannot be permanent, because no one can tell what future

generations will wish to decide and there are real dangers that "permanent" protection will seem vague and will erode over the years, leading to no protection at all. Instead, the period of each plan is specified.

Stands of old-growth forest, caves, cliff faces, abandoned and overgrown quarries, and the banks and strips to either side of streams are among the areas of local habitat that might be left untouched. Outside the protected habitats there would be no special constraints on commercial forestry. It would not even be an offense to injure or kill a member of one of the endangered species being protected, provided this was an inadvertent consequence of forestry operations and did not increase the likelihood that the species would become extinct.

This permission is similar to one allowed in Britain, under the Wildlife and Countryside Act, but outside an HCP it is not allowed under the equivalent United States legislation, the Endangered Species Act. In Britain, it is not an offense to injure or kill a member of an endangered species if this was the accidental consequence of a lawful activity. The Endangered Species Act makes no such allowance. Killing, harming, or harassing a member of a species classed as endangered, or modifying the habitat to its disadvantage is permitted only with special authorization from the Fish and Wildlife Service.

By the end of 1996, several HCPs had been launched in various parts of the United States and four large timber companies in the northwest had entered into HCP agreements. On January 30, 1997, Kathleen A. McGinty, chair of the White House Council on Environmental Quality, Bruce Babbitt, Secretary of the Interior, and Jennifer Belcher, Commissioner of Public Lands for the state of Washington announced in Seattle the largest program to date on forested land. Covering 1.6 million acres (650,000 ha) and lasting between 70 and 100 years, depending on the particular areas protected, the HCP aimed to protect more than 285 species across the state. It used as its emblem the northern spotted owl (*Strix occidentalis*), an endangered species found in the old-growth forests of the northwest over which foresters and conservationists had been arguing bitterly for years. This was one bird species the HCP would protect. Another was the marbled murrelet (*Brachyramphus marmoratus*), a member of the auk family (Alcidae) that feeds at sea but flies inland to breed in forests and mountains.

The plan was controversial. Some foresters feared the timber-harvesting target included in the HCP would be difficult to achieve because of

Spotted owl, Northwest coast, North America (Gerry Ellis/ENP Images)

the number of areas declared off-limits. Meanwhile some ecologists questioned whether the program would provide the protection it promised. Most ecologists and environmentalists did agree, however, that it was a move in the right direction.

For years, concerns over the condition and future of forests centered on the forests of the humid Tropics. It is only relatively recently that the importance of temperate forests has come to be fully recognized. Many of the plants and animals native to the temperate regions occur in or near the edges of forests. Only forest, and especially old-growth forest, may provide the habitats they need to survive. In addition, temperate forests absorb and store carbon in amounts that are significant in terms of the global climate. The desirability of retaining the natural forests that still exist and increasing the overall area of forest is not disputed. Today, the arguments revolve around the best ways this may be achieved.

Sustainable Forest Management

Everyone now accepts that if forests are to be managed, the most important aim of that management should be "sustainability." This is a concept introduced some years ago, perhaps first in the *World Conservation Strategy: Living Resource Conservation for Sustainable Development,* a document published in 1980 by the International Union for Conservation of Nature and Natural Resources (IUCN), in collaboration with the World Wide Fund for Nature (WWF), United Nations Environment Program (UNEP), the Food and Agriculture Organization of the U.N. (FAO), and the U.N. Educational, Scientific and Cultural Organization (UNESCO). The *World Conservation Strategy* was based on the assumption that the human population would continue to increase in size and that a consequence of this would be a reduction in the share of global resources available to each person. This reduction was compounded by the loss or degradation of a range of natural resources, including forests. The document was presented to governments and although it seemed to produce little effect, its idea of sustainability took hold.

In 1987 the concept was defined in *Our Common Future,* the report of the World Commission on Environment and Development, chaired by then prime minister of Norway Gro Harlem Brundtland. "Sustainable development," the report stated, "is development that meets the needs of the present without compromising the ability of future generations to meet their own needs." The commission spent several years studying the issues, then tried to compress an overview of the entire subject into a single book. Not surprisingly, its recommendations did not go into detail. In the case of forests, it suggested policies should begin with "an analysis of the capacity of forests and the land under them to perform various functions." Following proper analysis, some forests might be cleared for arable or livestock farming, some managed for increased timber production, and some left intact to protect the way water drains through the land, to conserve living species, or to provide recreational amenities. Whatever plan is implemented, the commission urged it be made in collaboration with local people.

At one level, the sustainable management of a temperate forest would define the forest as a area of land producing timber and other forest products and aim to ensure that it continued to do so indefinitely. Our descendants could continue for as long as they chose to obtain from the area the same materials we do. This management aim is hardly original. In Europe it has been applied since medieval times (page 145). Nowadays, throughout the temperate regions, forest plantations provide a regular harvest of products grown by methods that safeguard the capacity of the site to sustain a desired level of production. Forestry differs from farming only in the much longer time needed for each crop to mature. It aims to be sustainable indefinitely.

Sustaining Biodiversity

There is another level, however, where "sustainability" has a rather different meaning, because it accepts a different definition of a forest. This describes a forest not simply as a large stand of trees, but as a community of living organisms, the integrity of the whole being dependent on the diversity of its component species. According to this view, the sustainability of a forest, or any other type of ecosystem, is directly related to its biodiversity: the more species there are, the more stable the system will be. It follows, therefore, that the species diversity of forests should be preserved for the good of the forests themselves. Conservationists place such emphasis on protecting all the species living in a forest, or anywhere else, partly for this utilitarian reason: we need forests, forests need a great diversity of species, therefore we need a great diversity of species. This is not the only conservationist reason, of course. There is also an ethical one, according to which we have no right to deprive members of another species of the resources they need to survive, and an aesthetic one, according to which the diversity of species is delightful to us and we should not deny ourselves or our descendants enjoyment of it.

Whether biodiversity is linked to ecological stability is uncertain. It sounds as though it ought to be true, but so far ecologists have found little convincing evidence that it is true. Boreal forests cover vast areas with stands containing very few species, yet are no less stable than the much more diverse tropical forests. Stability seems to depend on the characteristics of the species comprising an ecosystem rather than their variety.

Conservation v. Forestry

Conserving biodiversity as a means of achieving sustainability often leads to conflict between conservationists and foresters. Holding the condition of the primeval forest prior to the arrival of humans as an ideal, and regarding humans as standing outside nature and opposed to its interests, conservationists are inherently suspicious of human intervention. Many would prefer people to leave the forests strictly alone, a view that conflicts with their wish to popularize forests and encourage people to visit them. Foresters, in contrast, grow and harvest trees and consider it desirable to manage forests in ways that promote tree growth and health.

Plantations resolve the conflict, at least in principle. There, foresters can plant, tend, and harvest tree crops. Forest plantations need not consist wholly of a limited number of species exotic to the area. In Britain, conservationists criticized the Forestry Commission for planting large upland tracts with introduced conifers, but it was compelled to do so in order to fulfill the function for which it was established. It was required to create a national forest to provide a strategic reserve of timber. Once that objective had been achieved, the "coniferization" policy was relaxed. As conifer stands mature and are cleared, mixtures of species are being planted. The transformation of British forests is slow, because the growth and maturation of trees takes decades, but as the years pass changes in the composition of the state forests will become increasingly evident.

It matters, of course, that plantations do not expand at the expense of natural forest. In Britain, where most of the original forest was lost many centuries ago, there is sufficient room for plantations outside ancient forests, but in other countries this is not always so. In North America, Scandinavia, and the C.I.S., exploiting natural forest and replacing some of it with plantation forest is unavoidable, because the natural forest is so vast.

Need for Compromise

Provided the more extreme environmentalist attitudes do not pervade the entire conservation movement, compromise is possible. In April 1997, Patrick Moore, one of the founders of Greenpeace, showed members of a Congressional panel studying problems relating to forestry pictures of forestry management, including ones of clear-cut logging, to show that commercial forestry is not necessarily environmentally disruptive. Moore, a Canadian working for the Forest Alliance of British Columbia, an organization backed by the forestry industry, said responsible logging could increase biodiversity and reduce the risk of catastrophic fires. His view was rejected by others—most especially by representatives of the Sierra Club, which opposes all commercial logging in national forests—but it allowed the possibility of communication between conservationists and foresters that might moderate harmful effects that result from commercial forestry.

In Britain, forests on public land are now managed as recreational amenities as well as sources of timber and so far as possible the wildlife value of forest habitat is enhanced. This has made the Forestry Commission much more popular with conservationists than it once was. Some areas are now managed primarily for conservation, and visitors are informed of the species present in the forest.

Similar efforts to accommodate conservation needs are being made by other countries. Canadian forests are encouraged to regenerate naturally wherever possible and where replanting of cut-over areas is necessary, it is designed to mimic the distribution patterns of species in the surrounding forest. This is a conservation measure that is supported by sound economic arguments (page 187) and a planned tree genetics center will underpin both the selection of trees for replanting and the establishment of a network of ecological forest reserves. In Finland, the Ministry of the Environment is identifying and mapping the location of old-growth forest. Already those areas on public land that deserve protection have been identified and attention has turned to areas on private land. In Norway and Sweden, commercial forestry now takes account of conservation needs.

Subsidized Forests

The reason for the apparently sudden interest in conservation is not entirely altruistic. Some years ago, it became evident in Britain that the rate of economic return from commercial forestry was lower than that expected from most investments. This is also true of national forests in the United States: the annual report of the Council of Economic Advisers published in February 1997 identified $234 million in subsidies paid by the Forest Service in the fiscal year ending September 30, 1995. The subsidy, hidden in the accounts published by the Forest Service, covered part of the costs of road construction and the 25 percent share of its revenue from timber sales it is required to pass on to states. Such discoveries suggest that the part of the forestry industry accountable to the public needs a justification for its existence beyond the production and marketing of timber. The provision of recreational facilities may not be enough. The White House report showed this cost to be about $170 million a year more than it earns in the fees the Forest Service charges. Conserving species and protecting biodiversity is a task beyond economic challenge. It benefits everyone, but in ways that cannot be tallied in financial terms.

There is no difficulty in managing forest lands in ways that will allow them to continue permanently to yield satisfactory amounts of timber. Commercial forestry in temperate regions is sustainable and has been so for centuries. Indeed, it is expanding. The debate over sustainability turns now on the extent to which the integrity of ancient and old-growth forests can be protected. At present, these are being exploited. So far as they are concerned, clear-cut logging is not sustainable. Forests may continue to occupy the sites, but old-growth forests will not.

Traditional Management

The well-wooded and humid hills are turned into ridges of dry rock, which encumbers the low grounds and chokes the watercourses with its debris. . . . There are parts of Asia Minor, of Northern Africa, of Greece, and even of Alpine Europe, where the operation of causes set in action by man has brought the face of the earth to a desolation almost as complete as that of the moon. . . .

Should we fail to manage forests in a sustainable fashion, more is at stake than a shortage of timber some time in the future. George Perkins Marsh (1801–82) saw this clearly more than a century ago. The passage quoted here is taken from his book *Man and Nature,* published in 1864, and it was meant as a warning to Americans. It attracted a great deal of attention and led to the establishment of federal forest reserves in the United States and a range of conservation measures in other countries.

Marsh was a remarkable man. A lawyer, diplomat, and politician, who spoke 20 languages, he was U.S. ambassador to Italy from 1862 until his death. It was there, among impoverished communities scratching a living from the eroded lands around the shores of the Mediterranean, that he saw the consequences of forest clearance, and there that he wrote his impassioned plea for greater care in the management of the natural environment. "Man has too long forgotten that the earth was given to him for usufruct [the right to enjoy and use, but not to waste or destroy] alone," he wrote, "not for consumption, still less for profligate waste."

Americans were on the move in the middle of the last century, settling ever farther west. Railroads were improving communications and new towns were springing up across the continent, towns in which many of the buildings were made from wood. Wood was also needed for railroad ties, telegraph poles, wagons, and, of course, for fuel to drive the locomotives and furnaces as well as to heat homes and cook food. That wood was

taken from the seemingly endless forests. Marsh was not the only person to recognize that the forests were not really endless and were being plundered. His book expressed in words a concern felt by many, which is why it struck so clear a chord.

Sustainability

Reserves, like those established in response to Marsh's book, protect forests from exploitation, at least in principle, but protection is not management in an economic sense. Economic management permits the forest to supply products and, therefore, to sustain industries, but in a controlled way.

This does not necessarily imply planting replacements for trees that are felled. In boreal forests and the taiga, the preferred method nowadays is to encourage natural regeneration (page 187) and plant only where this is impracticable. A stand of just one species of coniferous trees may be harvested by clear-cutting, but in mixed and broad-leaved forests it may be just certain trees that are commercially valuable. Perhaps, therefore, the best way to manage the forest is to remove the more valuable trees and leave the rest.

Techniques for sustainable forest management are now being tested in the Tropics; they are controversial and the arguments may be relevant to temperate forests. On one side are those arguing for sustainability. By this they mean the most valuable trees in an area should be cut, seedlings of commercially desirable species planted to replace them, and the seedlings protected while they grow by weeding and the prevention of damage by animals. In this way gaps made in the forest by harvesting favored species will be filled, and the forest will remain productive indefinitely.

Those who disagree maintain that the technique does not work very well. In removing trees and protecting the replacement seedlings, so

much ground has to be cleared that the forest is seriously damaged. What is more, the method is difficult, and in remote areas often impossible, to police. There is no way to guarantee that quotas for particular species are observed. This type of forest management is a good deal less sustainable than its supporters suppose. The alternative, they suggest, is to allow forestry companies to take as many as they wish of the valuable tree species. Once those have gone the economic value of that area of forest will plummet. The area can then be purchased cheaply by a government agency or voluntary group and made into a protected reserve.

Both sides agree that forests should yield a harvest of timber, but they disagree over definitions of sustainability. The conventional approach to sustainability is concerned with yield, but this would allow natural forest to be converted to a plantation, provided the timber yield from the plantation is sustainable. A sustainable yield does not mean the forest as a complex community is sustained.

Combining Forestry with Other Land Uses

A third style of management would integrate forestry with other land uses. One version of this is now widespread in temperate regions, where managed forests and plantations also provide recreational and educational facilities for the general public. Another version is also common in Europe, where livestock are often raised in very open forests. Many of these parklike woodlands were planted deliberately by landscape designers to produce a kind of arcadian effect (page 196).

In parts of Germany a system of management was once practiced that seems to have had no equivalent elsewhere. An area of forest would be clear-cut, and once all the useful timber had been removed, the remaining vegetation would be burned. Then a crop of rye would be grown in the ashes between the stumps of the felled trees. By the time the cereal was ready to harvest tree seedlings would be appearing naturally and these would be left to grow.

In Britain, the consequences of uncontrolled deforestation became evident many centuries ago. Vast areas of the original forest were cleared during the Roman occupation (page 143). By medieval times most of the countryside in lowland England consisted of islands of forest in an ocean of farmed fields.

The woodland itself was classified according to its use. Those areas producing mainly small wood were distinguished from those producing timber. Most forests were owned privately, but with local people having the right to use them for specified purposes. "Wasteland" was land owned and used by the community, rather than by a landowner.

Whether the ownership was private or communal, the trees were protected. Fences, or more substantial boundaries made from a ditch and bank, kept out livestock that might trample or eat seedlings or damage bark. Beneath the rough, outer bark of a tree, there lies a very thin layer, the cork cambium, and beneath that the phloem through which nutrients are transported around the plant. This is renewed from the vascular cambium, an underlying layer usually one cell thick. Together, these layers comprise the outer and inner bark. Should the inner bark be damaged, the tree will be left with a wound through which infection can enter and which will leave a scar when it heals. Cutting through the inner bark all the way round the tree is called "ring barking" or "girdling," and it kills the tree, because it severs the channels transporting essential nutrients. Animals that might nibble or gnaw through the bark must be excluded from well-managed forest.

Occasionally, animals were allowed to graze in parts of a forest during a stage in its cycle of growth when they were unlikely to cause much harm. Such grazing was known as agistment and it was more commonly used in park woodland than in close-canopy forest, as was pannage, allowing pigs to forage for acorns, beech mast, and fallen fruit. People were sometimes granted the right of herbage, entitling them to cut and remove grass and other herbs. Bracken was gathered for use as bedding for people as well as livestock. Bast, the inner part of the bark (phloem) from lime trees, was used as a source of fiber. Small branches, and sometimes even leaves, were also used. Bark itself was used in tanning and certain types of galls were used to make ink. Once a tree had been felled, nothing was wasted.

Coppicing

Although ringbarking a tree will certainly kill it, felling it may not. Ringbarking makes it impossible for nutrients to reach those parts of the tree above the injury, but a felled tree has no parts above the injury and in many species, although not all, new growth will sprout from the stump, called a "stool." Cutting a tree close to the ground in order to allow the stool to sprout is called "coppicing," and it was discovered in prehistoric times. The remains of coppiced trees have been found in peat, in Somerset, England, and dated as 6,000 years old. By the time of the Norman conquest, in 1066, coppicing was being practiced widely in Britain.

Coppicing does not produce a new, single trunk, of course, because a tree trunk grows outwards and the center is composed of dead wood. Instead, the new growth occurs around the edges of the cut stool as a circle of thin shoots.

Coppice growth is rapid. Often within about five years, depending on the species, it produces a dense clump of poles. These are harvested, cutting down to the original stool, and some years later there is a fresh crop of poles to be cut. The traditional rotation varied in length from about four to about 30 years, with an average interval of about 12 to 15 years between cuts. A stool will go on producing coppice poles for many years. Indeed, coppicing seems to increase the longevity of most trees.

Uses for Underwood

Obviously, this does not produce timber, only thin poles, known as "underwood," but this is what was needed. Small wood was used to make furniture, tool handles, and other articles of everyday use (page 158), but such items were durable. Society at that time was not founded on the principle of consuming goods, by frequently replacing them and throwing away the old ones. Items were handed down from one generation to the next until they were so worn as to be useless. As a result, the demand for wood for these uses was modest. Builders exerted a bigger demand for small wood. They needed laths to make ceilings and walls they would then cover with mud or plaster, the "wattle" in the type of construction known as "wattle-and-daub" that was widely used. "Wattle-and-daub" sounds flimsy and reminiscent of mud huts; done well, however, it lasts a very long time. There are houses built this way that are still standing, and occupied, up to five centuries after they were made.

There was a much more vigorous demand for fencing. Metal wire was far too costly to be used to confine or exclude livestock. Instead, hedges made from growing plants, most commonly hawthorn (*Crataegus monogyna*), were used for permanent enclosures. Gaps in hedges were sealed by driving rows of stakes firmly into the ground and weaving thin, flexible rods between them. The stakes and rods were coppice products. Hurdles were used as temporary fences to corral animals and make the most efficient use of pasture by controlling their grazing. These consisted of flexible rods woven horizontally between vertical poles and made as sections that could be joined as necessary. Finally, wood was the most widely used fuel, either directly or as charcoal, and small wood makes the best fire.

The Spread of Coppicing

As a management system in Britain, coppicing spread farther and farther north, eventually into the Highlands of Scotland, as demand for iron and steel grew in the early decades of the industrial revolution. The ironmasters, who owned the foundries, contracted with landowners for a regular, reliable supply of the charcoal they needed, and it was only by coppicing that sufficient charcoal could be produced.

It mattered little which tree species were used for coppicing. Most types of wood could be used as fuel and to make charcoal, and thin poles are usually flexible regardless of the tree from which they are taken. Hazel (*Corylus avellana*) was popular, especially for making hurdles and fences, sweet chestnut (*Castanea sativa*) was also good for fencing, willow (*Salix* species) was used for basket-making, and oak (*Quercus* species), alder (*Alnus* species), ash (*Fraxinus excelsior*), field maple (*Acer campestre*), hornbeam (*Carpinus betulus*), and several other species were also coppiced.

By the time it reached its peak, in the late 18th century, coppicing was by far the commonest system of forest management. It was being practiced over most of lowland Britain and most broad-leaved tree species were being treated in this way. Coniferous trees die when they are felled, so they cannot be coppiced. In any case, Scotch pine (*Pinus sylvestris*) is the only conifer native to Britain.

Coppicing developed as a method for managing natural forest, and this is how it remained until the last century. From about 1800, landowners began to "improve" their coppiced forests by clear-cutting and then replanting with the species they preferred. Progressively, remaining natural forests were replaced by areas of coppiced chestnut and hazel in the south and east and oak in the north and west.

Park Woodland

Nowadays, a park is a place for recreation. It is where families walk on weekends, where people exercise their dogs, where children play. The park is a green space in an urban area, a patch of simulated countryside surrounded by streets and buildings, usually with well-made paths, flower beds, toilets, and notices to tell you what you may and may not do.

Alternatively, in some European countries a park is a large, formal garden where the careful control of nature is flaunted. Here, the visitor may delight in natural things, but they are highly ordered. Lawns have sharply defined edges, flowers grow in weed-free beds, and trees grow where they will guide the eye toward splendid vistas or into secluded corners where there are scenes to surprise and delight. Such gardens celebrate our mastery of the environment, reflecting the order imposed on nature by the straight furrow lines of a plowed field. A well-cultivated countryside provides reassurance that, for this year, there will be no famine; the ordering of nature reminds us we are safe.

Town parks of these kinds are not new: they have existed at least since the 17th century. The less formal type of park, with more open space, more trees, and fewer flower beds, incorporates three earlier traditions.

In-Fields and Out-Fields

Early North European farmers employed an in-field and out-field system of cultivation. The in-fields were small, irregular in shape, and formed an approximate circle around the dwellings and farmyard. They were cultivated all the time. Beyond them there lay a circle of larger fields that were cultivated in a rotation, periodically being left fallow. These were the out-fields. They were enclosed by walls or hedges, and each was called a "park." So a "park" was an out-field, simply an enclosed area of land. This use still survives in some place and field names.

Later, in an extension of this meaning of the word, wealthy landowners attached the name "park" to the uncultivated land a little way from their houses. The park was managed, but increasingly its value was aesthetic rather than commercial. It was where the wealthy could ride, or rest in the shade of a tree, and this meant the ground had to be fairly open, with the trees scattered.

Deer Parks

Meanwhile, "park" had a different meaning, as an area of enclosed land in which animals were kept.

The animals most often found there were fallow deer (*Dama dama*), sometimes known as park deer. Originally a native of southern Europe and Asia Minor, the fallow deer was probably introduced to Britain in medieval times, perhaps by the Normans, and kept for hunting in parks and royal forests. The deer were a source of food, at least for the rich, and raising them was a type of land use, rather like the ranching of cattle. Other animals shared the parks with them. In various places there were wild pigs (*Sus scrofa*), red deer (wapiti, *Cervus elaphus*), and white cattle, sometimes called "park cattle."

Hunting forests were not securely enclosed, but parks were. Fallow deer are good at escaping, and keeping them captive was costly. The park had to be surrounded by a wall too high for the deer to jump or climb, a tall, dense hedge, or by a strong fence made from chestnut stakes, called a "pale" (hence our expression "beyond the pale," meaning "in the outer wilderness"). To this day, a park is an enclosed place, even if the deer are long vanished.

In time, the deer altered the landscape. Deer eat young tree seedlings, grass grows on ground unshaded by trees, so unless they are controlled in time the deer will convert forest to pasture. One way to deal with the problem is to allow much of the park to develop as pasture, while retaining the bigger, stronger trees as small groups or isolated individuals.

Pollarding

These trees could be protected, and their lifespan increased, by pollarding, a management technique that is still applied to trees lining city streets. Pollarding involves cutting the tree about 6.5 feet (2 m) above ground level. What remains of the trunk is called a "bolling." At first a bolling is no more than a stump, but soon thin poles sprout from around its edge. When they grow to a suitable size these can be cut and used (page 158). Pollarding differs from coppicing only in the height at which the tree is cut. Like coppicing, it increases the lifespan of the tree. Its advantage in a park is that the young shoots are well out of reach of deer, and deer cannot harm the tough lower trunk. Trees and deer can live together.

Not all the trees were pollarded. Some were allowed to continue growing, just as some in coppice woodland, but usually to a larger size. These big trees supplied timber.

Some landowners practiced a form of management with deer but without pollarding. This involved dividing the land into areas, some

retained as closed forest and others either open woodland or grassland. When trees were felled, deer would be excluded from that area until replacement trees had grown too big to be harmed by them. The more open areas provided grazing and space in which the deer could be hunted.

Hunting is all very well as an amusement for the wealthy, but over the centuries improvements in livestock husbandry made it a relatively inefficient way of procuring meat. A landowner might well conclude that the sensible way to manage the park was to remove the deer and other half-wild animals. Then, depending on its quality, the land could be brought into cultivation or developed as coppice. Parks might well have disappeared, but a third force was at work.

Trees for Shelter and Shade

In winter trees provide shelter from the wind, and from wind-driven rain and snow, and in summer they provide shade. To farmers and estate owners with homes in exposed locations these were important attributes. Houses were drafty at the best of times, and English rain can "fall" in horizontal sheets, while in summer it was thought pleasant to sit outdoors shaded from the full intensity of the sunlight. So trees were preserved or planted to provide shelter and shade around houses and also around churches.

It was not only landowners who planted them. By the 17th century trees had been planted around cottages and in villages, where they served an additional purpose: people dried their washing on them. Londoners also grew them. A visitor noted in 1748 that trees had been planted in the garden of almost every house and square, and that trees lined both sides of the roads outside the city center.

As trees came to be appreciated for their utility, their beauty was also recognized. Seventeenth-century writers bemoaned the absence of groves on bare hillsides and there was stiff opposition when attempts were made to sell off patches of woodland so the land could be converted to agricultural use. People had learned to love trees; a visually attractive countryside was held to be one where trees, as individuals or small groves, were scattered among the pastures and cultivated fields. This produced a much richer landscape, full of detail to catch and hold the eye, yet a landscape that was clearly under human control. It was a benign landscape, that fed and sheltered its human inhabitants, and its trees were tamed. These were not the trees of the dark, dangerous, primeval forest (page 146).

Landscape Architecture

The concept of an attractive landscape having been defined, by the 18th century wealthy landowners were paying to have existing landscapes modified so they conformed more closely to the ideal. A tradition began of what came to be known as landscape architecture. Lancelot ("Capability") Brown

Fall foliage, Zion National Park, Utah (Gerry Ellis/ENP Images)

(1716–83) is the most famous name associated with this movement. Thousands upon thousands of ash, oak, elm, and beech were planted under his direction, most of them in small groves. Critics thought these "clumps" unnatural, as indeed they are, but many of them remain to this day.

By then, tree-planting had become fashionable and a recognized way to improve an estate. Not all landowners could afford to embark on large-scale landscaping, but they could plant trees, and they did. The result was a major expansion of the area of what was, in effect, park woodland. It looked

informal, cattle and sheep grazed among the trees, and some of these parks even contained fallow deer, but now for ornament rather than food.

By a long and devious route, what had once been close-canopy forest over much of Europe was replaced by open woodland intermingled with farms and pasture. Cultivated fields are the most important component of this landscape in the lowlands, but in scattered groves, on field boundaries, and on pastureland surrounded on all side by grass, a significant proportion of our trees is now to be seen.

Plantation Forestry

Most of the forests we see around us today are plantations, and as different from natural forest as an arable farm is from the original prairie. Walk through a plantation and you see trees growing in rows, all much the same height. Watch forest workers (for which you will need permission, because forest operations can be dangerous) and you will see them planting, spraying, and harvesting. It looks simple. It is not.

A plantation does not just happen as the result of some workers going out to plant trees. It must be planned, and the planning begins with collecting information. The first step, therefore, is to identify clearly the boundaries of the plantation site, its altitude, the location of any roads, railroads, ponds, rivers, streams, or overhead power lines that cross it, the gradient of its hillsides and which direction they face, the soils, and the existing vegetation cover. Work begins, therefore, with a good map, aerial photographs (preferably stereoscopic ones), measuring, and a lot of walking.

With these important features clearly marked, the next step is to divide the site into compartments and draw their boundaries on the map. Those are the fairly large areas bounded by forest roads, rivers, or other natural features. They will vary in size, most being up to about 50 acres (20 ha), and they are permanent. Within each of them there will be several individual stands of trees, in subcompartments with boundaries that may change over the years as circumstances require.

Wind and Fire

This initial survey will also involve learning as much as possible about the local climate. Average summer and winter temperatures, and the amount and seasonal distribution of precipitation obviously affect all growing plants, but in the case of trees so does the wind. It is important to identify those parts of the site where trees will be exposed to winds strong enough to blow them down. Often, cotton flags are the tools used to measure the wind strength. Leave a flag flapping in the wind, and little by little it will tear at its outer edge until it is very tattered. How long it takes to reach this sorry state depends on the strength of the wind, so the rate at which cotton flags become tattered is a good indication of places where trees may be blown down or "windthrown." When the places at risk of windthrow have been identified, the shape of the forest edge can be modified to reduce the likely damage.

As the details are drawn on the map, safety features must also be included. Should part of the forest catch fire, if at all possible the fire must be contained, so it cannot spread to adjacent blocks. Firebreaks are strips of ground separating blocks. They must be at least 33 feet (10 meters) wide and contain nothing that will burn readily. Forest roads and rides, which are paths wide enough for horse riders, give little protection against fire. Some tree species, such as larches, are difficult to ignite and do not burn well. Surrounding a subcompartment with a belt of these trees can help slow the spread of fire.

Predicting the Yield

Armed with the results of the survey, it is possible to decide which tree species are likely to be most suitable for the conditions. Once that is decided, it is possible to estimate how many trees the site will support, the eventual annual sustainable yield of timber and small wood, and how soon that yield will be obtained. This is obviously important. Managers must know the size of the financial investment needed to secure a particular yield, and the rate of return they may expect on that investment. They must also know how many workers and what machinery they will need and when. If the first harvest of full-grown trees will not take place for 60 years, there is no point in buying heavy harvesting machines just to have them sit idle for more than half a century, quietly rusting and growing obsolete.

Future yield will depend on the species grown, and it is estimated from the "yield class." As a stand of trees grows, each year the total volume of useful wood increases. This increase includes the volume of dead trees and trees removed from a stand by thinning. The increase, measured in cubic meters of timber per hectare of land, is known as the mean annual increment (MAI). At first it increases rapidly as young trees grow to their full size, but beyond a certain age the rate of increase declines, so plotted on a graph it appears as a curve. The peak of the curve, where MAI reaches a maximum, gives the yield class for that particular stand. This is an abstract number equal to the maximum MAI that stand can achieve. A stand of some coniferous trees, for example, may attain a peak MAI of 30 cubic meters per hectare (429 cubic feet per acre), giving that stand a yield class of 30. Many broad-leaved trees have very much lower yield classes, some as low as 4.

So far not a single tree has been planted, so there is nothing to measure. In a general way, yield classes are known for each tree species, so they can be looked up in published tables. Once a stand is growing it can be calculated by a kind of rule of thumb from the age of the stand and the height of its trees. This is possible because the age and height of a tree is closely related to the volume of timber it will produce. If you know the age of a stand of a given species, all you need measure is the average height of the trees. A stand of Sitka spruce 50 years old and with trees 30 feet (9 m) tall, for example, has a yield class of about 17 (which is not very good for Sitka).

All the same, this is an estimate, known as a general yield class (GYC). When the plantation has been established long enough for there to be actual production figures from particular parts of it, these will make it possible to calculate the yield class much more precisely, as a local yield class (LYC).

Conservation and Recreation

Plantation forestry is a commercial operation, an industry that grows trees in order to sell timber and wood. At one time that might have been thought a sufficient objective, but nowadays other factors must also be considered. A temperate forest is not merely a large number of trees. It is a community of plants and animals (page 204) and account must be taken of their needs. Forests serve an important conservation role and must be planned with this in mind.

Conservation requirements may have a very high priority on sites of particular value. Elsewhere it may be enough to keep forest trees away from the banks of streams, so these can be colonized naturally, and to manage roadsides and open spaces sensitively, to maximize their quality as habitat. Wildlife will fare best in a forest composed of tree species natural to the area, so most modern plantations include stands of native species even where the important timber species are exotic. This is especially important in Britain, where Scotch pine (*Pinus sylvestris*) is the only

*Opposite: Douglas-fir tree farm,
50–60 years old, Western Cascades
(Gerry Ellis/ENP Images)*

native conifer and plantations are dominated by imported species. Conifers occupy about 3.2 million acres (1.3 million ha) in Britain, of which Scotch pine accounts for about 0.59 million acres (0.24 million ha), and native broad-leaved trees occupy only about 1.38 million acres (0.56 million ha). For years, British conservationists were opposed to afforestation, not because they disliked forests as such, but because plantations consisted of just a few species of imported conifers. That situation is now changing. As plantations complete the first cycle of their rotation, more broad-leaved species are being included in the replanting and in new plantations they are grown from the beginning.

Forests near large population centers are also public amenities. People demand to be allowed to visit them, to walk, ride bikes or horses, picnic, and generally enjoy themselves in an informal atmosphere. Again, at one time such free public access was thought to be incompatible with the needs of forestry, but the public won. At least in publicly owned forests, whose managers are accountable to elected politicians, people are now welcomed and basic facilities, such as toilets, maps, and information about the trees and wildlife, are provided. As with conservation, recreational requirements must be allowed for in the initial planning. Most of the time, forest blocks take care of themselves and tree-growing can be combined with recreational uses of the land.

Preparing the Site

So far, people living nearby have seen very little sign of activity on the land they have been told is due to become forest. A few individuals have been seen walking around. There were some surveyors, with their striped poles, measuring tapes, and theodolites. One day a helicopter seemed to spend rather a long time flying back and forth, probably taking photographs, but that is about all. They might conclude the scheme had been abandoned, or at least postponed. In fact, the activity has been intense, but almost all of it has taken place indoors.

The surveys complete, it is time to prepare the site. That is when the neighbors will see some action, and may not like what they see. Wet ground may have to be drained, because trees will not grow well, or in some cases not at all, where the water table is higher than the depth to which their roots extend. Installing drains means that large, plowlike machines will cut deep gashes across the land, clearing away the existing vegetation as they go and leaving the area looking as though tanks have fought a battle across it. Some roads may have to be realigned, which means destroying the existing road and making another.

These operations will prepare the whole site, but only a part of the site will be planted in the first year. The eventual aim is to produce an annual yield, which means that once the rotation is established, each year a certain number of trees must be ready to harvest. Unless a change in policy calls for it to be removed, an established plantation becomes a permanent feature of the landscape. Each year some of its subcompartments will be clear-cut, but these are usually quite small compared with the size of the plantation as a whole, and a few years later, with a new crop of trees, they merge once more with the surrounding blocks. The species chosen may change from one rotation to the next. Little by little this will alter the appearance of the forest, but it will still be a plantation.

Cultivation

It follows, therefore, that the first trees to be cut must also be the first to be planted. The site will be planted a few areas at a time and it will be several years before the whole of it is forested. At first, therefore, only some blocks need to be made ready for planting.

Preparation means cultivation. A large machine, either a scarifier or a disk trencher depending on the soil type, breaks up the ground surface. Then another machine, often an excavator, scoops up topsoil to make mounds into which the young trees will be planted. It is now standard practice to plant trees on mounds. Despite the large machines, the aim is to cause the least disturbance possible and the ground is prepared only in those patches where the trees will be located.

On some sites, the mounds and areas about 3.3 feet (1 m) in diameter around them are sprayed with herbicide once cultivation is completed. This kills weeds as they are germinating and suppresses them for long enough to allow the trees to become established. Once the trees are too tall to be shaded, further weed control is unnecessary.

Tree Nurseries and Orchards

Now, at long last, planting can begin. It may be feasible to sow tree seeds into the prepared mounds, but in most cases, and especially on a new site, it is not seeds that are planted, but tree seedlings. These are produced by tree nurseries, which are run as part of the forestry operation. It is there that young trees are grown from seed, and a major part of the task is selecting the best seed for the purpose.

Trees are individuals, just as animals are. Even within a species no two individuals are completely identical. The differences distinguishing them may not be visible, but for all that they may be very important, because they result from the ways trees adapt over many generations to a particular site. They look the same, but one tree may be better suited than the other to the soils or climate at the new plantation, or more resistant to the local pests and diseases. The only way to find out is to keep meticulous records of trees and the places from which they were originally taken, and then of the source of the seeds.

Seeds taken from trees chosen for their desirable qualities are germinated, to test that they germinate well, then grown in orchards. Pollination is carefully controlled, so the parents of each seedling are known. Especially suitable trees are often cloned, by taking cuttings from them or, increasingly nowadays, by growing them from tissue samples, a technique called micropropagation. Cloning produces a stand of trees that are genetically identical to one another. They provide seed of a quality that is known thoroughly and can be guaranteed. A great deal of forestry research takes place in the seed nurseries and orchards.

Planting and Protection

Depending on the species, the seedlings delivered for planting will have spent one or two years in seedbeds and a similar length of time in an orchard. They are 8–16 inches (20–40 cm) tall, with well developed roots, and they will be planted 6.5–10 feet (2–3 m) apart.

The young trees will need protection. If the subcompartment adjoins farmland, livestock might enter and damage the trees. It is the responsibility of the farmer to prevent his stock from straying, but if the field has no stockproof fence, the forest may have to have one. It may also need one to keep out wild deer. Alternatively, trees can be protected by enclosing them in cylinders of wire or plastic mesh. This method is very widely used, because not only does the guard protect the tree from animals, it also shelters it, stimulating it to grow, and makes it very easy to distinguish small trees from weeds. Where herbicides are used to kill weeds, the guard also protects the trees from accidentally being sprayed.

Beating Up and Thinning

Inevitably, some young trees will die within the first couple of years. If the loss leaves unacceptably large gaps, these will have to be filled, but by now the surviving trees will be much bigger than the seedlings ordinarily supplied by the nursery. The replacements will have a better chance of competing for light and nutrients if they are about the same age as the rest of the stand or if they belong to a different, faster-growing species. Replacing trees lost in this way is called "beating up."

After a few more years, unwanted woody undergrowth is cleared away and some branches may be pruned from the trees to improve the quality of timber they will produce. Unless people need to move freely among the trees, foresters no longer remove the lower branches. This operation, called brashing, involves removing all the branches below a height of about 6.5 feet (2 m), but it is time-consuming and therefore costly.

Thinning is also time-consuming, but it contributes to its own cost. The aim is to remove the thinner, weaker trees to make more room for the stronger ones, which will then grow thicker trunks. This makes the strong trees more valuable, but the thinnings can also be sold as small wood or for fuel (page 158 and 154).

Harvesting

Finally, harvest time will come. This is the most dangerous operation. Trees are felled and their

Pacific yew tree nursery
Pacific Coast, North America
(Michael Durham/ENP Images)

branches removed using chain saws. Fallen trees must then be removed from the site and loaded onto vehicles. Workers engaged in harvesting must be highly trained in the use and maintenance of their equipment. They must also know how to work safely and how to deal with emergencies. Under no circumstances must an untrained person be allowed to use a chain saw.

Forwarders, which are machines that lift whole trees and load them on trailers, or skidders, which lift one end of a tree and drag it, are big, and very expensive; there are several varieties of each, and they are not necessarily alternatives to one another. Conditions at the site determine which machine to use and sometimes it is necessary to use cranes. Because of the high cost of machinery and the skilled workforce needed, harvesting is often undertaken by specialist contractors.

Like all forestry tasks, harvesting is planned carefully and performed methodically. First the routes, called "racks," along which timber will be extracted must be identified and marked. The block to be cleared is divided into sections, the trees in each section are felled by one or two workers, and the felling is planned so that workers are always separated by a distance not less than twice the height of the tallest tree. The first few trees to be cut all fall in the same direction, then

the remainder are cut so they fall at right angles, across the first trees. This makes it much easier to remove their branches (called "snedding") and then lift them.

Broad-leaved trees are especially difficult. If they fall awkwardly or their branches are removed clumsily, the wood may split. If that happens the tree may be ruined. They are also dangerous: there may be dead branches that fall when the tree starts to move, not only from the tree being felled but also from adjacent trees. When the tree is on the ground it may roll, and branches may spring back suddenly.

The logs are driven away to the sawmill, the chain saws and heavy machinery leave the area, and the subcompartment is left abandoned and bare. It is time to think about preparing the ground for the next crop. On an established site, where a subcompartment has been cleared and is to be restocked, natural regeneration may be the preferred method (page 187). Mature trees surrounding the cleared block will supply the necessary seeds and over several generations the trees will adapt to the site conditions. Where regeneration is not practicable, or where a different species is to be grown, seed or seedlings will be needed and mounds made to receive them. The rotation is complete and the cycle begins again.

Pest Control

Elms were once an important feature of English lowland landscapes, but in the 1960s Dutch elm disease killed more than 80 percent of them (page 108). The disease was caused by a fungus, but the fungus was spread by bark beetles. Trees, like other plants, are susceptible to insect attack, and it can be serious, occasionally even devastating.

Trees are large and offer a variety of habitats, so it is not surprising to discover they harbor many species of insects. There are opportunities for insect larvae and adults that feed on leaves, including the needles of conifers, either munching their way around the edges or through the inside, which is the method favored by leaf miners. There is nourishment for those that feed on the materials they find in the crevices of the bark, and those that feed on wood beneath the bark. There are insects that feed on flowers and fruits, seed-eaters, those that live below ground and eat roots, and many others. More than 170 insect species can be found on pine trees, about 90 on spruces, and there are even more on broad-leaved trees.

The great majority of these insects do no harm to the tree. Even those that feed on its leaves or bark do not eat enough to cause any real damage. The insect population includes predators as well as herbivores; to some extent, the insect population regulates itself, keeping levels too low to cause serious harm. If the numbers of one species start to increase, so do those of the predators that feed on it. Many of these are insects, but birds and bats also eat insects, and they are voracious. All the bats that live in temperate regions feed exclusively on insects. There are also other arthropods with an appetite for insects. On a morning when dew makes spider webs clearly visible, you will see them festooning every shrub and the spaces between shrubs, presenting a total screen you would think no insect could evade, and below that screen, on the ground, there are more spiders, ones that chase their prey rather than trapping it, as well as centipedes and other carnivores. Small mammals will also eat any insects they come across in the course of their general foraging. Nor is the curbing of insect numbers a job only for predators. Insects suffer from parasites, just like all animals, as well as from diseases caused by viruses.

Age and Health

Self-regulation by the insect population and all the other insectivores is very effective, but it is not the whole story. Time also plays a part. A seedling, standing barely taller than the herbs around it, harbors few insects and most of those are just alighting to rest, drink, or feed before moving on. They do not live on the young tree. As the seedling grows into a sapling, some resident insects will establish themselves, and more will join them as the years pass. Trees do not start life with a full complement of insects: they acquire them gradually. For this reason, there are fewer species of insects among stands of young trees than there are among stands of mature trees. Young trees are also better able to resist insect attacks than are old trees, because they are healthier and more vigorous.

Healthy trees are less vulnerable to pest attack than unhealthy trees. An unhealthy tree will have dead and rotting branches or twigs, open wounds where branches have been torn away or bark stripped, or cracks and fissures providing access to the xylem and phloem, pathways through which water, nutrients, and infections are transported to all parts of the plant (page 63). Insects find ample food among this dead or damaged tissue and they either carry fungal spores with them, or make it easier for fungal spores to enter.

Old-Growth Forest

Beyond this, however, the comparison with ourselves does not hold. An elderly person can be perfectly sound in wind and limb and certainly free from open wounds and dead and decaying arms and legs. This is not the case with a tree. An old tree will have dead and decaying tissue and the scars of old wounds. These do little or no harm in themselves. Explore any old-growth broad-leaved forest and you will find hollow trees, in which so much of the center of the trunk has rotted away that what remains is barely sufficient to prevent the tree from falling. Around it, on the ground, you may find old, dead branches it has shed. No animal could possibly survive for long in such an apparently poor condition, yet the tree produces leaves each spring and may well continue to do so for another century or more, provided it does not succumb to a major infection or insect infestation. The tree is alive, but barely so. It is old and sick, and once infected, disease can spread from it to its neighbors and from there throughout a large area of the forest.

Old-growth forests contain old and sick trees growing alongside young and healthy ones and so these are the forests most likely to suffer from major pest attacks and outbreaks of disease.

Monoculture and Plantation Forest

Many people suppose that monoculture, the growing of one or a very few species of plants year after year over a large area, encourages pest infestations. This is because herbivorous insects tend to specialize in particular plants, so a large monocultural stand of those plants represents a vast food supply to the specialists, and their numbers are almost certain to increase. Eventually, so the argument goes, such a large number of specialist insects will be feeding that they will do real harm to the plants. Where these specialists find their preferred plants scattered among other species they cannot eat, not only is there less food for them overall, it is also more difficult for them to migrate from one plant to another.

This is partly true for agricultural and horticultural crops, although the dynamics of insect populations is fairly complex and monocultural agricultural and horticultural systems can be ecologically stable. It is not at all true for forests. Monocultural plantation forests are far less susceptible to pest damage and diseases than more diverse natural forests, possibly because plantation trees are felled before they bear wounds that could be infected, and the plantations themselves have not been in existence long enough for the full complement of insects and fungi to have accumulated.

The Cost of Pests and Disease

When a forest suffers a serious infestation the effects can be catastrophic. There are moths and sawflies with larvae capable of defoliating and killing entire trees and large areas of forest. Bark beetles excavate tunnels and galleries beneath bark, greatly reducing the value of the timber and introducing fungal infections, such as Dutch elm disease. Bark beetles, loopers, bud moths (with larvae known as budworms), and various weevils can, and sometimes do, destroy entire forests.

Countries that rely heavily for their timber on logging in old-growth forests cannot afford to accept the level of damage pests and diseases are capable of inflicting. Every year, for example, Canada loses the equivalent of almost two-thirds of its timber harvest to insect pests and fungal diseases, simply because most Canadian forests are mature or older than mature. In the United States insects and fungal disease destroy several times more trees than are lost by fire. It is reasonable to suppose that similar losses occur in the European boreal forest and the taiga.

An obvious consequence is that achieving a target yield of timber involves clearing a substantially larger area of forest than would be needed if the pest and disease losses were smaller. Logging causes inevitable damage to wildlife, so an obvious way to reduce its adverse environmental effect is to reduce outbreaks of pests and diseases.

Weed control may also be necessary. Natural regeneration or planting will repopulate an area of old-growth forest that has been clear-cut, but the natural process may be slowed by competition from other plants, growing rapidly where they suddenly find themselves exposed to full sunlight. Some of these are likely to be trees, useless as sources of timber but able to grow faster than the more desirable species.

Control of weeds may involve cultivating an area that is to be planted. This kills weeds that have emerged and allows planted seedlings to establish themselves. Cultivation cannot be used in areas regenerating naturally, because it would destroy tree seedlings, so it may be necessary to use an herbicide that is toxic to the most vigorous weeds but harmless to the trees. Unfortunately, herbicides are not very specific in the plants they affect, so unless the crop plant has a natural immunity to the herbicide, weed control must take place before the crop appears (page 200). Genes for herbicide resistance have been inserted into some agricultural field crops and in years to come commercially valuable plantation trees may also carry them, but, of course, existing mature trees in old-growth forests cannot benefit from them.

Defining Pests and Weeds

Although species of herbivorous insects can experience sudden vast increases in their populations, so they kill all the trees of certain species over a large area simply by feeding on them, and although the seedlings that will replace the lost trees may be choked by competing plants, "pests" and "weeds" are never found in natural forests. Such destruction is entirely natural, unavoidable, and not at all serious. All types of forest experience it, including temperate forests, and in time they recover. The idea that a natural forest stands eternally, or even for a mere thousand years, in just the condition it is in on the day you visit it is quite wrong. It changes constantly and sometimes the change is dramatic, but temporarily so. Chestnut blight and Dutch elm disease were devastating, so natural recovery from them might take centuries, but meanwhile other tree species would occupy the vacated sites. The forest would survive, although its composition would change.

"Pests" and "weeds" can be defined economically, but ecologically the terms have no meaning. There are no pests or weeds in the natural forest as long as it remains unexploited. They exist only in those forests from which we need to obtain timber and they exist then because they reduce the value of the forests.

Insecticides

Once a pest infestation is causing widespread damage in a mature forest, probably it can be dealt with only by spraying an insecticide and, because the damage is occurring in the crowns, spraying has to be by aircraft. Aerial spraying is an expensive last resort and must be done with great care to ensure the insecticide reaches its target without drifting outside the affected area. Quite apart from the cost, it always carries some risk of harm to other species, although there is much less risk from modern insecticides than from those used in the past.

Control by Bacteria

No one supposes insecticides are popular, and alternatives are constantly being sought, but nowadays at least the chemicals sprayed in forests are fairly safe. Organophosphate compounds are often used. They do not persist in the environment, breaking down into harmless compounds, and are only mildly poisonous to wildlife, but are very toxic to the insects against which they are used. There are also a few biological insecticides, the best known of which is based on *Bacillus thuringiensis*, a species of bacteria. A dusting powder containing *B. thuringiensis* is a very safe and effective insecticide, used widely in Canadian forests.

Control by Management

Modern pest control begins with detailed knowledge of the life cycle of the pest. This reveals the stages at which a species is most likely to be vulnerable and sometimes suggests a simple preventive method that involves no spraying at all. The fungus *Cronartium ribicola* (or *flaccidum*), for example, causes a serious disease called white pine blister on the branches of several pines, including white or Weymouth pine (*Pinus strobus*). It often attacks trees that have been damaged by a stem-feeding insect, *Pineus strobi,* although the insect causes little harm in itself. The fungus spends part of its life cycle on currant and gooseberry bushes (*Ribes* species), so if these are never grown anywhere near pine trees, the disease is prevented.

Scotch pine (*P. sylvestris*) suffers from a similar blister disease caused by the fungus *Coleosporium senecionis*. In this case the secondary hosts are groundsels (*Senecio* species), so efficient weeding prevents fungal infection.

Biological Control

Females of many species of flying insects use chemical attractants, called pheromones, to attract males for mating. These, too, can form the basis for a biological method of pest control. If the pheromone to which a pest species responds can be identified and synthesized, it can be used to attract males into traps where they can be killed. Males can also be separated from colonies of pest insects bred for the purpose, sterilized, and then released to mate unproductively with females that will mate only once.

With some species, pest numbers can also be held in check by encouraging their natural predators. The great spruce bark beetle (*Dendroctonus micans*) causes serious damage to all species of spruce (*Picea*), but there is another beetle, *Rhizophagus grandis,* that feeds on *D. micans*. It is being bred for release into spruce forests as a biological control agent.

Plantation forests suffer fewer pest attacks and outbreaks of disease than do mature and old-growth forests, so it makes good sense to obtain timber and other forest products from plantations. This would allow the old-growth forests to be conserved, responding in their own way to the insects and fungi they harbor, while at the same time reducing the need for pest control. In years to come this is what will happen, but it cannot happen quickly. At least half a century must pass before a new forest plantation starts yielding useful amounts of timber and some time after that the old problems may return. When permanent plantations are widespread and have been established for a century or more, it is possible that they may start to suffer pest and disease problems at levels similar to those of mature natural forests.

Forest nurseries are treated differently from the plantations themselves. Nurseries are much more like horticultural enterprises, or fruit orchards. As far as possible seedlings are kept free of pests and parasites to ensure they carry no infection into a plantation.

Pesticides will continue to be used for some years to come, but the scale of their use should not be exaggerated. Forests are sprayed much less than farms. Of all the chemical pesticides used in Canada, only 2 percent are sprayed over forests, and this proportion, which is probably typical of most temperate regions, is unlikely to increase.

Modern Forestry

"Forestry" is the commercial production of timber, small wood, and other materials from a forest, either by logging or by raising trees for the purpose. "Silviculture" is the care of every aspect of the forest, not only its trees, and regardless of whether or not any part of the forest is being exploited commercially. Clearly, the two are different. For many years forestry was the primary concern of the owners of forested land in the temperate regions of the world. Today, although many forests remain commercial enterprises, the emphasis is moving strongly in the direction of silviculture.

Attitudes change over the years. For a long time the shift is gradual and passes unnoticed by people not directly involved. Then, apparently all of a sudden, the new ideas are everywhere and it is as though this is what everyone thought and believed all along. Usually, and certainly in the case of the transition from forestry to silviculture, several factors drive the process of change.

Forestry was born out of the realization that, first, we have always needed wood, we use it in countless ways, and there is no reason to suppose a time will ever come when we can do without it. Second, we obtain our wood by felling trees. Third, if we continue to fell trees as and when we need wood and that is all we do, then a time is bound to come when the forests have been cleared from the land. This need not be so. Plant trees to replace those that are felled or assist cleared areas of forest to regenerate naturally and establish plantations to satisfy as much as possible of the demand, and there will always be wood.

Conservation measures aimed at ensuring a continuing supply of forest products were introduced in Europe in the Middle Ages (page 145). The application of resource management to forests is not a novel idea, although plantation forests are a much more recent invention. So far, however, the purpose is economic. Resource management is an economic activity, and the trees themselves are being evaluated by the type, quality, and volume of wood they represent.

When it came to implementing this type of management, difficulties arose. Forests occupy land and in many cases that land can be put to more profitable use. Farms are more profitable than forests, so forests tended to be squeezed onto land that was unsuitable for agriculture, mainly at high levels on exposed hillsides. Trees are plants, however, with physical requirements not much different from those of other plants. Conditions that were harsh for farm crops were also harsh for trees. It proved possible to grow trees in the hills, of course, but the enterprise was never highly profitable. In fact, the return on the capital invested was usually rather lower than the return offered by most investments. A sensible economist with no interest in fancy ideas about resources would have handed the better land over to farmers and abandoned upland afforestation schemes, investing the money in sounder industrial undertakings.

Wildlife Conservation

Some other reason was needed for supporting the forests. Happily, one was already available. It was supplied by the naturalists, comprising in Europe and North America literally millions of members of the societies, associations, clubs, and groups devoted to the study and protection of plants and animals. They enjoyed traveling into the countryside to observe wildlife and often found commercial forests closed to them and clearly being managed only for monetary profit. Naturally, they complained, long and loud, and eventually they were heard. When a new reason was needed, they provided one. Forests were seen to exist for wildlife conservation as well as commercial production. From there it was but a short step to recognizing the amenity value of forests and opening them to the public for recreational use.

Management styles were modified, and most forest workers themselves welcomed the change. They live and work in the forests, after all, and it is not surprising they are familiar with and care about the plants and animals that share the land with them. Some animals have to be excluded or otherwise controlled, because they damage trees, but in general forestry and conservation can function side by side. Silviculture is possible.

A few elementary changes can make a disproportionately big difference. Widening rides—the wide paths suitable for horse riding—then leaving the edges to develop as long strips of habitat for wild plants has a major effect. It can be done when subcompartments are thinned. If thinning is done early and vigorously, sunlight will penetrate to patches on the forest floor long enough for many plants to establish themselves securely before the canopy closes and shades them. Nesting boxes for bats and certain bird species, strategically placed on trees, provide accommodation that may not be available in the trees themselves.

Naturalists used to point out that conifer plantations provide poorer wildlife habitat than broad-leaved stands. This is usually true, but the difference can be narrowed. Pine and larch have fairly open canopies, and other species, including spruces, can be thinned so they allow light to penetrate. With good light penetration, by the time these trees mature the wildlife around them is as diverse as that in many broad-leaved areas.

Apart from general modifications in management style, conservation of forest wildlife now begins at the initial planning stage. Among all the other information obtained from site surveys, forest planners must identify sites of particular importance for wildlife, as well as sites of geological, archaeological, or other interests. Marked on the site maps, wildlife areas will be managed differently from the rest of the forest, perhaps with different mixtures of tree species growing to different ages. Operations near places that are important for other reasons will take care not to damage or in some cases obscure valuable features.

The Silvicultural Forest

Silviculture creates a rather different forest. Plantations no longer consist of endless straight rows of trees all of the same species and the same size, standing above the deep shade of a silent, bare floor. There is more light, more variety of tree species to provide visual interest, and a great deal more flowers, birds, mammals, butterflies, and other wildlife.

Obviously, it is the forests within reach of population centers that attract visitors for whom facilities must be provided. Where there are few accessible forests, there are often plans to plant new ones. In Britain, which has a smaller forest area than many countries, such plans are well advanced. The new forests will be very extensive and will contain only native species. They will not really be simulations of the original, primeval forest, and even less of the medieval forest. Rather, they will be forests of our time, existing for the enjoyment of people and for the benefit of wild plants and animals. They will be managed, of course, but the management will be silvicultural.

Elsewhere, in the more remote places, forests see few visitors. Recreational facilities are not needed in them, but they, too, are being affected by the change in management style, and those who work in them are as aware as anyone else of the desirability of conserving habitats. Wildlife conservation is at least as important there. Indeed, it may be more so, because the absence of people means less disturbance to natural habitats; forests in remote regions often occupy a larger area than those closer to the cities, so they can accommodate animals that need large ranges in which to seek food.

Forests and Cultural Heritage

Throughout the temperate regions of the world, forests are now regarded as having great cultural importance. This arises from their role as communities of plants and animals. These are not just any plants and animals, but the ones that feature in our folk and fairy tales and our myths and leg-

Logged clear-cutting, Pacific Coast, North America (Gerry Ellis/ENP Images)

ends. "Forestry is deeply engrained in the culture and fabric of Finnish society," says a brochure published by the Finnish Forest Industries Federation. "Forests and their benefits . . . are part of Canada's heritage and culture," says a similar Canadian brochure, and Canada is described as "a forest nation."

Obviously, the change is not yet complete. There are still regions in which temperate forests, especially coniferous forests, are being cleared and not replaced (page 188), but overall the area is increasing. A study by the European Forest Institute has found that between 1950 and 1990 the growing stock of forest trees in Europe increased by nearly 43 percent, and it is possible to increase the sustainable timber yield by nearly 40 percent.

Schemes involving permanent clearances arouse such strong opposition among local people that sometimes they can be halted or modified. In October 1997, plans to clear-cut 530

acres (214 ha) of old-growth cedar forest in Kootenai County, Idaho, led to a deal in which the U.S. Forest Service traded 2,305 acres (933 ha) of mainly prime timberland to save it. The logging company paid $2 million for the cedar forest and the land it was given in exchange was worth $8.7 million. That the public was willing to pay more than $6 million to save the cedars indicates the value people attach to their forests.

A large proportion of the European forest was cleared centuries ago, and more recently major inroads were made into the North American forest. Europeans and Americans saw there was a risk of losing all of their forests. Britain actually paid for its loss, in the form of the high cost of importing almost all its timber. The lesson was learned, and the losses began to be reversed. Provided we remember the lesson and continue to plant more trees than we fell, the temperate forests will expand and prosper.

Appendix A

PROPORTION OF LAND AREA FORESTED IN SELECTED COUNTRIES

Country	Percent of land area
Finland	76
Japan	67
Sweden	64
C.I.S.	42
Portugal	40
Canada	38
Spain	31
Germany	30*
U.S.A.	29
France	27
Norway	27
Italy	23
Belgium/Luxembourg	21
Greece	20
Denmark	12
UK	10
Netherlands	9
Ireland	5

Figures were compiled prior to the reunification of Germany and refer to the former West Germany only.

Source: Forestry Facts and Figures 1988/9, published by the Forestry Commission, Edinburgh.

Appendix B

AREA OF NORTHERN HEMISPHERE TEMPERATE FOREST

	Coniferous (million acres)	Coniferous (million ha)	Broad-leaved (million acres)	Broad-leaved (million ha)
N. America	663.7	268.6	170.2	420.6
W. Europe	162.8	65.9	32.3	79.8
Russia & E. Europe	801.1	324.2	131.8	325.7
TOTAL	**1,627.6**	**658.7**	**334.3**	**826.1**

Source: Sten Nilsson, Forest Resources Project, International Institute for Applied Systems Analysis, 1997.

Appendix C

AREA OF PROTECTED FOREST WORLDWIDE, BY TYPE

	Total biome (1,000 sq mi)	Total biome (1,000 sq km)	Currently protected (1,000 sq mi)	Currently protected (1,000 sq km)
subtropical/temperate rain forest	1,516	3,928	141	366
sclerophyll	1,450	3,757	68	177
temperate broad-leaved	4,342	11,249	138	357
temperate coniferous	6,572	17,026	188	487

Source: Sten Nilsson, Forest Resources Project, International Institute for Applied Systems Analysis, 1997.

Appendix D

ROUNDWOOD PRODUCTION 1993

	Fuelwood & charcoal (million ft³)	Fuelwood & charcoal (million m³)	Coniferous (million ft³)	Coniferous (million m³)	Broad-leaved (million ft³)	Broad-leaved (million m³)
World total	66,238.0	1,875.9	32,813.6	929.3	18,675.5	528.9
N. & C. America	5,533.1	156.7	16,196.7	458.7	4,519.7	128.0
Oceania	310.7	8.8	833.3	23.6	496.6	13.3
Europe	1,797.3	50.9	6,754.8	191.3	2,185.7	61.9
C.I.S.	1,818.5	51.5	3,372.1	95.5	1,299.4	36.8

Source: Sten Nilsson, Forest Resources Project, International Institute for Applied Systems Analysis, 1997.

Appendix D (cont'd.)

ESTIMATED AVAILABILITY OF INDUSTRIAL ROUNDWOOD IN 1993, 2010, AND 2020 (IN MILLION CUBIC FEET AND MILLION CUBIC METERS UNDER BARK)

1993	Coniferous (cubic feet)	Coniferous (cubic meters)	Broad-leaved (cubic feet)	Broad-leaved (cubic meters)
Canada	5,836.7	165.3	278.9	7.9
U.S.A.	10,091.6	285.8	4,120.7	116.7
Oceania	833.3	23.6	469.6	13.3
Japan	63.8	18.9	240.1	6.8
C.I.S.	3,043.7	86.2	1,119.3	31.7
W. Europe	2,757.7	78.1	1,264.1	35.8
Asia	423.7	12.0	4,703.3	133.2
Nordic region	3,001.4	85.0	339.0	9.6
TOTAL	**33,187.9**	**939.9**	**19,067.4**	**540.0**

2010	Coniferous (cubic feet)	Coniferous (cubic meters)	Broad-leaved (cubic feet)	Broad-leaved (cubic meters)
Canada	4,484–5,579	127–158	1,342–1,766	38–50
U.S.A.	8,651–10,205	245–289	4,131–4,943	117–140
Oceania	1,165–1,448	33–41	600–636	17–18
Japan	706–1,942	20–55	282–318	8–9
C.I.S.	4,590–6,850	130–194	1,059–2,472	30–70
W. Europe	3,037–3,813	86–108	1,377–1,977	39–56
Asia	494–565	14–16	2,295–4,378	65–124
Nordic region	3,143–3,813	89–108	388–494	11–14
TOTAL	**33,545–42,690**	**950–1,209**	**19,244–26,306**	**545–745**

2020	Coniferous (cubic feet)	Coniferous (cubic meters)	Broad-leaved (cubic feet)	Broad-leaved (cubic meters)
Canada	4,767–5,720	135–162	1,483–1,942	42–55
U.S.A.	9,357–11,193	265–317	4,414–5,473	125–155
Oceania	1,871–2,048	53–58	671–741	19–21
Japan	777–1,942	22–55	318–353	9–10
C.I.S.	6,179–8,298	175–235	1,059–2,824	30–80
W. Europe	3,213–3,990	91–113	1,448–2,048	41–58
Asia	565–671	16–19	2,295–4,555	65–129
Nordic region	3,143–4,096	89–116	424–530	12–15
TOTAL	**38,099–46,856**	**1,079–1,327**	**586–801**	**20,692–28,283**

Source: Sten Nilsson, Forest Resources Project, International Institute for Applied Systems Analysis, 1997.

Appendix E

UNITS AND CONVERSIONS

Board foot (bd. ft)

The volume of a piece of timber 1 inch (2.54 cm) thick, 12 inches (30.5 cm) wide, and 12 inches (30.5 cm) long.

12 bd. ft = 1 cubic foot   424 bd. ft = 1 cubic meter   1,980 bd. ft = 1 standard

Cord

A stack of wood, usually of material of small diameter, that is 8 ft 4 in (2.54 m) long and 4 ft 3 in (1.27 m) high (but with local variations). A cord measures about 128 cubic feet (3.6 cubic meters) and contains 75–100 cubic feet (2–2.8 cubic meters) of wood (the remainder is air space).

1 short cord = 1/2 cord.   1 standard = 1,980 bd. ft

Appendix E (cont'd.)

SI UNITS

SI stands for the Système Internationale d'Unités, the units used throughout the world by scientists. Some of the SI units are also in everyday use in many countries.

SI Unit	US (UK) Unit
Length	
1 millimeter (mm)	0.0394 inch
1 centimeter (cm)	0.3937 inch
2.54 cm	1 inch
30.48 cm	1 foot
1 meter (m)	1.0936 yard
0.914 m	1 yard
1 kilometer (km)	0.6214 mile
1.6093 km	1 mile
Area	
1 sq cm	0.155 sq inch
6.4516 sq cm	1 sq inch
9.29 sq cm	1 sq foot
1 sq m	1.196 sq yard
0.8361 sq m	1 sq yard
1 hectare (ha)	2.471 acres
0.4047 ha	1 acre
1 sq km	0.3861 sq mile
2.59 sq km	1 sq mile
Volume	
1 liter (l)	1.7597 pint
0.5683 l	1 pint
3.7854 l	1 gallon (US)
4.546 l	1 gallon (UK)
1 cubic cm	0.061 cubic inch
16.3871 cubic cm	1 cubic inch
1 cubic m	35.3147 cubic feet
0.0283 cubic m	1 cubic foot
0.7646 cubic m	1 cubic yard
Mass	
1 gramme (g)	0.0353 ounce (avoirdupois)
28.3495 g	1 ounce
1 kilogram (kg)	2.2046 pounds
0.4536 kg	1 pound
1 tonne (£)	0.9842 (UK)
1 tonne	1.1023 ton (US)
.09072 t	1 ton (US)
1.016 t	1 ton (UK)
Pressure	
1 bar	0.145 pounds per sq inch
0.0689 bar	1 pound per sq inch
0.0339 bar	1 inch of mercury
1 bar = 1,000 millibar (mb)	

Temperature

To convert °F to °C: $(°F - 32) \times 5/9$

To convert °C to °F: $(°C \times 9/5) + 32$

Web Sites

There is a virtual library dealing exclusively with forestry and covering both temperate and tropical forests. It lists downloadable files, magazines, scientific and technical journals, and many sources of further information.

http://www.metla.fi/info/vlib/Forestry.html

The European Forest Institute provides a large amount of information, with links to many (not all) of its 80-plus members. These are located in many European countries (with links to Russia and Poland, but not to all eastern European countries) as well as the U.S., Canada, and Australia. A very useful, informative site.

http://www.efi.joensuu.fi/

The Temperate Forest Foundation, based on Oregon, provides educational information, mainly about North American forests, forestry, and forest wildlife, with pages to help teachers. It also carries links to many other relevant web sites, which makes it especially useful.

http://www.forestinfo.org

The World Wide Fund for Nature, Canada, web site dealing with endangered species and conservation is especially concerned with conservation in temperate forests, which occupy nearly half of Canada.

http://www.wwfcanada.org.facts/tempfor.html

The World Wide Fund for Nature has its own project to conserve forests of all kinds. Its web site describes its work with forests, including temperate forests, and provides a large amount of useful and interesting information. It also allows you to ask questions and to join WWF. Start at the background page and use the links to travel further.

http://www.panda.org/tda/forest/new/background.html

The Forest Engineering and Research Institute of Canada (FERIC) is a commercial organization engaged in research and development of all aspects of forestry, obviously forestry of the kind practiced in Canada. Its web site carries a great deal of interesting and useful information about forestry, and FERIC has a catalog of publications which you can search by topic and from which you can order. All the text is available in both English and French.

http://www.feric.ca/

The Georgia Forestry Commission publishes its own pages. There you can find lists of trees to plant in your neighborhood, details of the work of the commission, and links to many other sites. This is a very useful place to visit.

http://www.state.ga.us/GFC/index.htm

Nebraska University Forestry Department publishes details of forestry in the state.

http://ffw1.unl.edu/FFW_docs/FFW_Home.html

Norway also has a large forest area. This is described, along with many other aspects of the Norwegian environment, on its State of the Environment pages. These load quickly and contain much useful information.

http://www.grida.no/soeno95/

The World Conservation Union (or, to give it its full title, the International Union for Conservation, Nature and Natural Resources) is the body that compiles and publishes the Red Data and Green Data lists of endangered species. It is also concerned about the loss of natural habitat, including forests. The web site links you to up-to-date information about forests in many countries. Not all countries are included, but the list is being increased.

http://www.iucn.org/themes/ssc/index.html

The Whyfiles, designed for schools, are a useful source of information about the science behind stories in the news. You cannot be certain to find information about forests, but if forests have been in the news, for example because of forest fires, the issues will be explained.

http://whyfiles.news.wisc.edu

Books

Allaby, Michael. *Basics of Environmental Science.* London: Routledge, 1996.
A general introduction to all branches of the environmental sciences, written mainly for students who may be thinking of taking courses in one of the relevant disciplines, or students taking nonscientific courses who may need some background environmental understanding. It assumes no previous knowledge, so it is simply written and easy to read.

———. *Elements: Earth.* New York: Facts On File, 1993.
One of a series of four Elements books, this one provides simple explanations for soil formation, plant growth, and the relationship of both to climate.

Emiliani, Cesare. *Planet Earth: Cosmology, Geology, and the Evolution of Life and the Environment.* Cambridge: Cambridge University Press, 1992 (reprinted with corrections 1995).

An immense amount of information packed into a single volume by a very distinguished geologist. It is simply and clearly written, places developments in their historical context, which is helpful, and provides an invaluable reference that will fill in the background to other, more specialized books.

Foth, H. D. *Fundamentals of Soil Science,* 8th ed. New York: John Wiley & Sons, 1991.
A thorough description of the way soils form, how one differs from another, how soils are classified, and how they are related to different types of vegetation. Although intended for more advanced students, the book is so well written and its ideas so clearly explained that everyone will be able to find useful information in it.

Gaston, Kevin J., ed. *Biodiversity: A Biology of Numbers and Difference.* Oxford: Blackwell Science, 1996.
A series of essays by scientists working in the field of biodiversity that explain what the concept means, how biodiversity is measured, and how its rate of loss may be reduced. The writing is fairly technical, but suitable for anyone with some knowledge of ecology.

Havins, Peter J. *The Forests of England.* London: Robert Hale & Co., 1976.
As its title suggests, a historical account of English forests that also describes forest industries and the ways of life associated with them.

Hibberd, B. G. *Forestry Practice,* 11th ed. Forestry Commission Handbook 6, Stationery Office, London: Stationery Office, 1991.
A textbook of forestry issued by the agency responsible for British state-owned forests. The book covers every aspect of seed germination, planting, management, and harvesting, and includes pest and weed control, the protection of wildlife, and the management of forests to provide public recreation.

Hinde, Thomas. *Forests of Britain.* London: Victor Gollancz, 1985.
A straightforward account of British forests, with many anecdotes, legends, and historical stories. The book recounts the history and stories associated with famous forests, including Arden and Sherwood.

Knystautas, Algirdas. *The Natural History of the USSR.* London: Century Hutchinson, 1987.
Written before the collapse of the Soviet Union, this book, illustrated with maps and many color photographs, provides a broad description of the scenery, plants, and animals of this vast region. Dr. Knystautas is a Lithuanian naturalist and conservationist who worked in the Department of Forestry of the Lithuanian Agricultural Academy from 1979 to 1983.

MacKenzie, James J. and Mohamed T. El-Ashry, eds. *Air Pollution's Toll on Forests and Crops.* New Haven: Yale University Press, 1989.
This is a fairly technical book for more advanced students, describing in some detail the situation in Central Europe and the United States.

Moore, David M. *Green Planet: The Story of Plant Life on Earth.* Cambridge: Cambridge University Press, 1982.
Professor Moore is a very distinguished botanist and for this book he recruited a team of scientists. The result is a comprehensive description of vegetation throughout the world. The book is well illustrated, easy to read and understand, and describes methods used to study plants and plant communities as well as the vegetation patterns themselves.

Peterken, George F. *Natural Woodland: Ecology and Conservation in Northern Temperate Regions.* Cambridge: Cambridge University Press, 1996.
A highly authoritative description of the forests of North America and Europe, including their ecology and conservation. The text is advanced, but easy to read and difficult concepts are explained clearly.

Rackham, Oliver. *Trees and Woodland in the British Landscape,* 2nd ed. London: J.M. Dent & Sons, 1993.
First published in 1976 and now updated, this short book tells the story of British forests since the end of the last ice age, together with details of individual tree species. Scholarly and authoritative it has deservedly become a classic.

Tanner, Heather and Robin. *Woodland Plants.* London: Impact Books, 1987.
This book describes 69 herbs that grow in temperate broad-leaved forests, but the descriptions are not botanical. Instead, the origin of the common name of each plant is given, together with its traditional uses and folklore connected with it, accompanied by a black-and-white illustration. The book, and the herbs it describes, are Old World, but the many literary references to them gives them a universal appeal.

Tivy, Joy. *Biogeography: A Study of Plants in the Ecosphere,* 3rd ed. New York: John Wiley & Sons, 1993.
A classic textbook for university students that first appeared more than 25 years ago. It packs a huge amount of information into a single volume, which makes the text somewhat condensed and rather technical, but its coverage is very wide.

Westbrook, Peter. *Life as a Geological Force: Dynamics of the Earth.* New York: W.W. Norton and Co., 1992.
A story told in simple, straightforward language by a leading Dutch scientist, this book explains the biogeochemical cycles and the way rocks form, weather, and return to the sea. It also comments on the Gaia hypothesis.

World Commission on Environment and Development. *Our Common Future.* Oxford: Oxford University Press, 1987.
The final report of the commission set up in 1983 by the General Assembly of the United Nations and chaired by Gro Harlem Brundtland, then Prime Minister of Norway. This is the report that examines critical environmental and developmental problems and propose means to solve them. In doing this it made the first serious attempt to define "sustainable development."

There are several books describing the Gaia hypothesis. Some of the more useful ones are:

Allaby, Michael. *A Guide to Gaia: A Survey of the New Science of Our Living Earth.* New York: E.P. Dutton, 1990.

Lawrence, E. Joseph. *Gaia: The Growth of an Idea.* New York: St Martin's Press, 1990.

Lovelock, James. *The Ages of Gaia.* Oxford: Oxford University Press, 1988.

———. *Gaia: A New Look at Life on Earth.* Oxford: Oxford University Press, 1979.